Probability, Statistics & Symmetry

Probability, Statistics & Symmetry

Guest Editors

Diego I. Gallardo
Marcelo Bourguignon

MDPI

Basel • Beijing • Wuhan • Barcelona • Belgrade • Novi Sad • Cluj • Manchester

Guest Editors
Diego I. Gallardo
Department of Statistics
Universidad del Bío-Bío
Concepción
Chile

Marcelo Bourguignon
Statistics Department
Federal University of Rio
Grande do Norte
Natal
Brazil

Editorial Office
MDPI AG
Grosspeteranlage 5
4052 Basel, Switzerland

This is a reprint of the Special Issue, published open access by the journal *Mathematics* (ISSN 2227-7390), freely accessible at: https://www.mdpi.com/journal/mathematics/special_issues/XZ9G21QXL8.

For citation purposes, cite each article independently as indicated on the article page online and as indicated below:

Lastname, A.A.; Lastname, B.B. Article Title. *Journal Name* **Year**, *Volume Number*, Page Range.

ISBN 978-3-7258-7953-3 (Hbk)
ISBN 978-3-7258-7954-0 (PDF)
https://doi.org/10.3390/books978-3-7258-7954-0

Contents

About the Editors

Diego I. Gallardo

Diego I. Gallardo is an Associate Professor in the Department of Statistics, University of Bío-Bío, Chile. He received his Ph.D. degree in Statistics from the University of São Paulo in 2014, and his B.S. degree in Statistics and Computation in 2009 from the University of Santiago, Chile. He was Executive Editor of the *Chilean Journal of Statistics* and the maintainer of the following packages in R: skewMLRM, tpn, extrafrail, MCPModBC, PScr and RBE3.

Marcelo Bourguignon

Marcelo Bourguignon is an Associate Professor at the Federal University of Rio Grande do Norte, located in Natal (Brazil). His studies are related to fatigue life models, regression analysis and count time series analysis. He won the "2017 ISI Jan Tinbergen Award" (ISI). He has published over 130 papers.

mathematics

MDPI

Editorial

Preface to the Special Issue "Probability, Statistics & Symmetry"

Diego I. Gallardo [1,*] and Marcelo Bourguignon [2]

1 Departamento de Estadística, Facultad de Ciencias, Universidad del Bío-Bío, Concepción 4081112, Chile
2 Statistics Department, Federal University of Rio Grande do Norte, Natal 59078-970, RN, Brazil; marcelo.bourguignon@ufrn.br
* Correspondence: dgallardo@ubiobio.cl

This Special Issue of *Mathematics* is devoted to new survival analysis, regression, time series, and entropy analysis-based models and their applications. In the call for papers, a wide range of topics was covered, including distribution theory, regression models, survival analysis, inference for stochastic processes, machine learning, and time series analysis. Following a rigorous refereeing process, the Special Issue includes 13 articles, which were selected from a total of 32 submissions (with an acceptance rate of 40.6%). A summary of the main contributions of the selected papers in the Special Issue is provided below.

Contribution 1 presents an alternative to the log-skew-normal distribution by transforming the modified skew-normal model, yielding a more flexible distribution (with wider ranges for asymmetry and kurtosis). The model's performance is illustrated using data on air pollutant concentrations in New York.

Contribution 2 considers a general class of bivariate proportional hazard distributions based on the family of asymmetric proportional hazard distributions and the bivariate Pareto copula. Furthermore, the authors particularize this general bivariate distribution to the case where the univariate normal distribution is considered so that the bivariate proportional hazard normal distribution is obtained.

Contribution 3 proposes a new multivariate extension for the log-Birnbaum–Saunders distribution. The authors also discuss how to introduce covariates in the model and perform residual analysis. Parameter estimation is discussed using the method of moments and maximum likelihood.

Contribution 4, titled "COVID-19 Active Case Forecasts in Latin American Countries Using Score-Driven Models," applies score-driven time series models to forecast active COVID-19 cases in several Latin American countries. The study demonstrates the model's effectiveness in capturing pandemic dynamics using real-world data.

In contribution 5, a slash-type model in survival analysis with cure rate is introduced for the first time in the literature. The model was illustrated using patients who underwent bone marrow transplantation.

Contribution 6 introduces a new method for reconstructing a gross domestic product (GDP) series, which is particularly relevant given the lack of official methods that are available for such reconstruction in Chile.

In Contribution 7, a new bimodal extension with positive support is introduced based on elliptical distributions. The model, which has three parameters, is highly flexible, yielding a kurtosis coefficient that can be particularly high, depending only on one parameter.

Contribution 8 introduces the "New Better than Renewal Used in the Laplace Transform in Increasing Convex Order" (NBRULC) class of distributions and defines a hypothesis test to decide between the exponential distribution and a distribution in the NBRULC class.

 https://doi.org/10.3390/math14071167

Contribution 9 introduces a new model with positive support that can assume both unimodal and bimodal, as well as symmetric and asymmetric, shapes. The model includes, as particular cases, the log-normal and log-skew-normal distributions.

Contribution 10 introduces a new interesting bivariate model with unit Weibull marginal distributions. The model has many interesting properties, including closed-form expressions for many related functions and for some statistics.

The contribution 11 presents the K-record values in an extended Farlie–Gumbel–Morgenstern family of distributions. The authors also discuss nonparametric estimation of certain entropy-related measures.

Contribution 12 revisits the Weibull distribution and its various parameterizations, proposing two new parameterizations. The authors discuss the biunivocal relationship among the different parameterizations when only the intercept term is included in the regression for the shape parameter. This paper was distinguished as a Highly Cited Paper by Web of Science in the period October–November 2024.

In Contribution 13, a new bivariate power Lindley distribution is introduced. The model is characterized by both conditions following a power Lindley distribution. The authors discuss estimation using the method of moments and maximum likelihood based on the pseudo-log-likelihood function.

It is our pleasure to thank all authors for submitting their recent works, all reviewers for their timely and insightful reports, and the staff of the Editorial Office for their support in preparing this Special Issue. We hope that the readers of this Special Issue will be exposed to stimulating ideas that will inspire new research in this interesting field of great practical importance.

Conflicts of Interest: The authors declare no conflicts of interest.

List of Contributions

1. Arrué, J.; Arellano-Valle, R.B.; Venegas, O.; Bolfarine, H.; Gómez, H.W. An Alternative to the Log-Skew-Normal Distribution: Properties, Inference, and an Application to Air Pollutant Concentrations. *Mathematics* **2022**, *10*, 4336. https://doi.org/10.3390/math10224336.
2. Martínez-Flórez, G.; Barrera-Causil, C.; Lemonte, A.J. Power Families of Bivariate Proportional Hazard Models. *Mathematics* **2022**, *10*, 4410. https://doi.org/10.3390/math10234410.
3. Martínez-Flórez, G.; Vergara-Cardozo, S.; Tovar-Falón, R.; Rodriguez-Quevedo, L. The Multivariate Skewed Log-Birnbaum–Saunders Distribution and Its Associated Regression Model. *Mathematics* **2023**, *11*, 1095. https://doi.org/10.3390/math11051095.
4. Contreras-Espinoza, S.; Novoa-Muñoz, F.; Blazsek, S.; Vidal, P.; Caamaño-Carrillo, C. COVID-19 Active Case Forecasts in Latin American Countries Using Score-Driven Models. *Mathematics* **2023**, *11*, 136. https://doi.org/10.3390/math11010136.
5. Gallardo, D.I.; Gómez, Y.M.; Gómez, H.J.; Gallardo-Nelson, M.J.; Bourguignon, M. The Slash Half-Normal Distribution Applied to a Cure Rate Model with Application to Bone Marrow Transplantation. *Mathematics* **2023**, *11*, 518. https://doi.org/10.3390/math11030518.
6. Caamaño-Carrillo, C.; Contreras-Espinoza, S.; Nicolis, O. Reconstructing the Quarterly Series of the Chilean Gross Domestic Product Using a State Space Approach. *Mathematics* **2023**, *11*, 1827. https://doi.org/10.3390/math11081827.
7. Tovar-Falón, R.; Martínez-Flórez, G.; Ceña-Tapia, I. Some Extensions of the Asymmetric Exponentiated Bimodal Normal Model for Modeling Data with Positive Support. *Mathematics* **2023**, *11*, 1563. https://doi.org/10.3390/math11071563.
8. Etman, W.B.H.; Eliwa, M.S.; Alqifari, H.N.; El-Morshedy, M.; Al-Essa, L.A.; EL-Sagheer, R.M. The NBRULC Reliability Class: Mathematical Theory and Goodness-of-Fit Testing with Applications to Asymmetric Censored and Uncensored Data. *Mathematics* **2023**, *11*, 2805. https://doi.org/10.3390/math11132805.

9. Martínez-Flórez, G.; Tovar-Falón, R.; Bolfarine, H. The Log-Bimodal Asymmetric Generalized Gaussian Model with Application to Positive Data. *Mathematics* **2023**, *11*, 3587. https://doi.org/10.3390/math11163587.
10. Tovar-Falón, R.; Martínez-Flórez, G.; Páez-Martínez, L. Bivariate Unit-Weibull Distribution: Properties and Inference. *Mathematics* **2023**, *11*, 3760. https://doi.org/10.3390/math11173760.
11. Abd Elgawad, M.A.; Barakat, H.M.; Alawady, M.A.; Abd El-Rahman, D.A.; Husseiny, I.A.; Hashem, A.F.; Alotaibi, N. Extropy and Some of Its More Recent Related Measures for Concomitants of K-Record Values in an Extended FGM Family. *Mathematics* **2023**, *11*, 4934. https://doi.org/10.3390/math11244934.
12. Gómez, Y.M.; Gallardo, D.I.; Marchant, C.; Sánchez, L.; Bourguignon, M. An In-Depth Review of the Weibull Model with a Focus on Various Parameterizations. *Mathematics* **2024**, *12*, 56. https://doi.org/10.3390/math12010056.
13. Martínez-Flórez, G.; Arnold, B.C.; Gómez, H.W. A Bivariate Power Lindley Survival Distribution. *Mathematics* **2024**, *12*, 3334. https://doi.org/10.3390/math12213334.

https://doi.org/10.3390/math14071167

mathematics

MDPI

Article

An Alternative to the Log-Skew-Normal Distribution: Properties, Inference, and an Application to Air Pollutant Concentrations

Jaime Arrué [1], Reinaldo Boris Arellano-Valle [2], Osvaldo Venegas [3,*], Heleno Bolfarine [4] and Héctor W. Gómez [1]

1 Departamento de Matemáticas, Facultad de Ciencias Básicas, Universidad de Antofagasta, Antofagasta 1240000, Chile
2 Departamento de Estadística, Facultad de Matemáticas, Pontificia Universidad Católica de Chile, Santiago 7820436, Chile
3 Departamento de Ciencias Matemáticas y Físicas, Facultad de Ingeniería, Universidad Católica de Temuco, Temuco 4780000, Chile
4 Departamento de Estatítica, IME, Universidade de São Paulo, São Paulo 05508-090, Brazil
* Correspondence: ovenegas@uct.cl; Tel.: +54-45-220-5351

Abstract: In this study, we consider an alternative to the log-skew-normal distribution. It is called the modified log-skew-normal distribution and introduces greater flexibility in the skewness and kurtosis parameters. We first study several of the main probabilistic properties of the new distribution, such as the computation of its moments and the non-existence of the moment-generating function. Parameter estimation by the maximum likelihood approach is also studied. This approach presents an overestimation problem in the shape parameter, which in some cases, can even be infinite. However, as we demonstrate, this problem is solved by adapting bias reduction using Firth's approach. We also show that the modified log-skew-normal model likewise inherits the non-singularity of the Fisher information matrix of the untransformed model, when the shape parameter is null. Finally, we apply the modified log-skew-normal model to a real example related to pollution data.

Keywords: log-normal distribution; non-singular information matrix; modified likelihood; modified score; bias prevention

MSC: 62E15; 62E20

1. Introduction

The log-normal distribution is commonly used to model the behavior of data with positive asymmetry, in which most of the observations are concentrated near the minimum value. Some applications of the log-normal model are in species abundance patterns, environmental concentrations, stock prices, the distribution of the molecular weights of polymers, the production of copper nano-particles, etc.

The log-normal (LN) distribution arises from the transformation $Y = e^X$, where $X \sim N(\mu, \sigma^2)$ is the normal distribution with mean μ and variance σ^2 and has the density given by

$$f_Y(y) = \frac{1}{\sigma y}\phi\left(\frac{\log y - \mu}{\sigma}\right), \quad y > 0, \tag{1}$$

where $\phi(\cdot)$ is the standard normal density. The notation $Y \sim LN(\mu, \sigma^2)$ is typically used for the log-normal distribution with parameters $\mu \in \mathbb{R}$ and $\sigma^2 > 0$. More simply, we can say that a random variable $Y \sim LN(\mu, \sigma^2)$ if and only if $\log Y \sim N(\mu, \sigma^2)$. As noted by Jones and Arnold [1], this distribution is both log-symmetric about its mean/median

$E(Y) = e^{\mu}$ and R-symmetric about its mode $\delta = e^{\mu+\sigma^2}$, a condition called double symmetry. As defined by Mudholkar and Wang [2], in density terms, a non-negative random variable Y is said to be R-symmetric about δ if $f_Y(\delta y) = f_Y(\delta/y)$ for some $\delta > 0$ and all $y > 0$, which is equivalent to $\delta Y \overset{d}{=} \delta/Y$, where "$\overset{d}{=}$" means equal in distribution. When f_Y is unimodal, then δ is the (unique) mode of Y, which is less than the mean of Y. Thus, R-symmetric distributions are always positively skewed. Despite these good properties, there are data that are not adequately modeled by the log-normal distribution, since they have symmetry and kurtosis indices that are outside their natural range. A model that presents this characteristic is the log-skew-normal (LSN) distribution, introduced and studied by Azzalini et al. [3]. It is a version with positive support of the skew-normal (SN) distribution, defined as follows: for a skew-normal random variable $Z \sim SN(\lambda)$, where $\lambda \in \mathbb{R}$ is the skewness parameter, we say that the random variable $Y = e^Z$ follows a log-skew-normal distribution with skewness parameter λ, denoted by $Y \sim LSN(\lambda)$, if its probability density function (pdf) is given by

$$f_Y(y;\lambda) = \frac{2}{y}\phi(\log(y))\Phi(\lambda\log(y)), \quad y > 0,$$

where $\Phi(\cdot)$ denotes the cumulative distribution function (cdf) of the standard $\mathrm{N}(0,1)$.

Applications of this model to real datasets are reported in Azzalini et al. [3], Marchenko and Genton [4], and Bolfarine et al. [5], where a bimodal version of the model was used to fit a real (bimodal) dataset. Chai and Bailey [6] extended the SN model to a situation of continuous datasets with a discrete component at zero. On the other hand, the modified skew-normal (MSN) distribution is a particular case of the generalized skew-normal (GSN) distribution introduced by Arellano-Valle et al. [7], for $\lambda_2 = 1$. Later, Arellano-Valle et al. [8] investigated the Fisher information matrix (FIM) for the location-scale version of the GSN model. Thus, the MSN model is a fair competitor to the SN model since for both control asymmetry with a single scalar parameter, say $\lambda \in \mathbb{R}$, such that, if $\lambda = 0$, then the ordinary normal model results. Moreover, one advantage of the MSN model over the SN model in location-scale situations is that its FIM is nonsingular at $\lambda = 0$, which is not the case with the SN model (see Arellano-Valle et al. [8] and Arrué et al. [9]). The present paper focuses on investigating the possibility of developing a more flexible distribution for positive data, such that the regularity conditions for inference in large samples remain valid when a maximum likelihood approach is used. We considered it natural to use the log version of the MSN for this situation, calling it the modified log-skew-normal(MLSN) model.

This paper is organized as follows. Section 2 presents some probabilistic properties of the MSN model. It includes the derivation of the first few moments of the distribution and the moment-generating function. Plots and ranges for the asymmetry and kurtosis coefficients are reported. The score functions are derived, and the observed information matrix is presented. Section 3 is devoted to the definition of the new distribution, termed the MLSN distribution. The survival and the associated risk functions are derived. A general expression for the moments is obtained, and the non-existence of the moment-generating function is proven. Parameter estimation is conducted by the maximum likelihood (ML) approach. Observed and expected (Fisher) information matrices are derived. It is shown that the FIM for a location-scale extension of the model is non-singular so that large sample properties of the ML estimators (MLE) are satisfied. In Section 4, we present a brief introduction to Firth's approach (see Firth [10]) for bias reduction and some tables related to a small-scale simulation study, illustrating the amount of bias reduction in the asymmetry parameter. Finally, in Section 5, a real data illustration is presented indicating that the new model outperforms its most direct competitors. The closing section summarizes the main contributions of the paper.

2. Preliminaries

We say that a random variable Z follows a standard MSN distribution with parameter λ, denoted $Z \sim MSN(\lambda)$, if its pdf is given by

$$f_Z(z;\lambda) = 2\phi(z)\Phi(\lambda u(z)), \quad z \in \mathbb{R}, \tag{2}$$

where $u(z) = z/\sqrt{1+z^2}$ and $\lambda \in \mathbb{R}$. If $\lambda = 0$, then the MSN pdf in (2) reduces to the pdf of the standard normal distribution. Non-null values of the parameter λ directly affect the model's asymmetry so that, in the limit, as $\lambda \to \infty$, the MSN model becomes the half-normal (HN) distribution. All that is required to obtain the location-scale version of the model is to make the transformation $X = \mu + \sigma Z$, where $\mu \in \mathbb{R}$ and $\sigma > 0$ are the location and scale parameters, respectively. We use the notation $X \sim MSN(\mu, \sigma, \lambda)$. As shown in Arellano-Valle et al. [8] the FIM for the location-scale version is nonsingular at $\lambda = 0$. Thus, the ordinary properties of the MLE (consistency and asymptotic normality) remain valid for the MSN model.

Figure 1 shows plots of the pdf for the standard MSN model for several values of λ. The subtle difference between the MSN and SN densities for the same parameter value can be observed, say for the case $\lambda = 1$ (dotted line and segmented line).

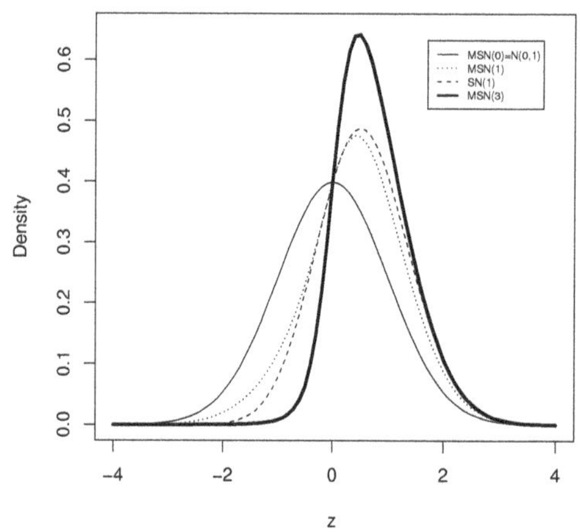

Figure 1. Plots of the MSN(λ) model for different values of λ: MSN(0) (solid line), MSN(1) (dotted line), SN(1) (dashed line), and MSN(3) (thick solid line) models.

The following properties follow from Arellano-Valle et al. [7].

2.1. Properties

Let $Z \sim MSN(\lambda)$; then:

1. $Z \sim \mathrm{MSN}(\lambda) \Rightarrow -Z \sim \mathrm{MSN}(-\lambda)$;
2. If $Z \sim \mathrm{MSN}(\lambda)$, then $|Z| \sim \mathrm{HN}(0,1)$;
3. If $Z|S = s \sim \mathrm{SN}(s)$ and $S \sim \mathrm{N}(\lambda, 1)$, then $Z \sim \mathrm{MSN}(\lambda)$;
4. $\mathrm{MSN}(0) \overset{d}{=} \mathrm{N}(0,1)$, and $\mathrm{MSN}(\lambda) \overset{d}{=} \mathrm{MGSN}(\lambda, 1) \overset{d}{=} \mathrm{GSN}(\lambda, 1)$.

According to Property 3, the MSN distribution can be represented as a mixture of the asymmetry parameter between the skew-normal and standard normal distributions. For the location-scale extension, that is $X = \mu + \sigma Z$, so that $X \sim \mathrm{MSN}(\mu, \sigma, \lambda)$, with pdf

$$f_X(x;\mu,\sigma,\lambda) = \frac{2}{\sigma}\phi\left(\frac{x-\mu}{\sigma}\right)\Phi\left(\lambda u\left(\frac{x-\mu}{\sigma}\right)\right). \tag{3}$$

2.2. Moments of the MSN Model

According to Property 3, the moments of the MSN distribution can be obtained by using the fact that it is a mixture between the SN and the $N(0,1)$ so that we can write $E(Z^k) = E(E(Z^k|S))$, where $E(Z^k|S)$, $k = 0, 1, ...,$ are the moments for the SN model with asymmetry parameter s. Thus, for even values of k, the moments of the SN(s) distribution are constant, coinciding with the moments for the MSN distribution. For the odd moments, making use of the stochastic representation for the skew-normal distribution in Henze [11], we can write

$$
\begin{aligned}
E(Z^{2k+1}) &= E(E(Z^{2k+1}|S)) \\
&= E\left(\frac{b(2k+1)!}{2^k}\sum_{v=0}^{k}\frac{v!2^{2v}}{(2v+1)!(k-v)!}\frac{S^{2v+1}}{(1+S^2)^{(2k+1)/2}}\right) \\
&= \frac{b(2k+1)!}{2^k}\sum_{v=0}^{k}\frac{v!2^{2v}}{(2v+1)!(k-v)!}E\left(\frac{S^{2v+1}}{(1+S^2)^{(2k+1)/2}}\right),
\end{aligned}
$$

where $k = 0, 1, 2, ..., b = \sqrt{\frac{2}{\pi}}$. Considering

$$
\psi_{k,v} = \psi_{k,v}(\lambda) = E\left(\frac{S^{2v+1}}{(1+S^2)^{(2k+1)/2}}\right) = \int_{-\infty}^{\infty}\frac{s^{2v+1}}{(1+s^2)^{(2k+1)/2}}\phi(s-\lambda)ds
$$

and $\psi_k = \psi_{k,k}$, we have that

$$
E(Z^{2k+1}) = \frac{b(2k+1)!}{2^k}\sum_{v=0}^{k}\frac{v!2^{2v}}{(2v+1)!(k-v)!}\psi_{k,v}. \tag{4}
$$

Therefore, the first four moments of the standard MSN distribution are given by

$$
E(Z) = b\psi_0, \quad E(Z^2) = 1, \quad E(Z^3) = b(3\psi_0 - \psi_1) \quad \text{and} \quad E(Z^4) = 3.
$$

The odd moments can also be obtained from Arellano-Valle et al. [7]:

$$
E(Z^{2k+1}) = 2c_k - 2^k k! b,
$$

for $k = 0, 1, 2, ...$ where $c_k := c_k(\lambda) = \int_0^{\infty} x^k \phi(\sqrt{x})\Phi(\lambda u(\sqrt{x}))dx$.

2.3. Moment-Generating Function

As mentioned previously, if $Z|S = s \sim SN(s)$ and $S \sim N(\lambda, 1)$, then $Z \sim MSN(\lambda)$, so that we can write

$$
M_Z(t) = E(E(e^{Zt}|S)) = E(M_{Z|S}(t)) = 2e^{t^2/2}E\left(\Phi\left(\frac{S}{\sqrt{1+S^2}}t\right)\right). \tag{5}
$$

Therefore, all the moments for the random variable Z are defined as follows:

$$
E(Z^n) = \left.\frac{\partial^n M_Z(t)}{\partial^n t}\right|_{t=0} = E\left(\left.\frac{\partial^n M_{Z|S}(t)}{\partial^n t}\right|_{t=0}\right).
$$

2.4. Observed Information Matrix for MSN Model

Consider a random sample $x_1, x_2, .., x_n$ from the MSN(θ) distribution, with $\theta = (\mu, \sigma, \lambda)$, so that the corresponding log-likelihood function is given by

$$
l(\theta) = \frac{n}{2}\log\left(\frac{2}{\pi}\right) - n\log(\sigma) - \frac{1}{2}\sum_{i=1}^{n} z_i^2 + \sum_{i=1}^{n}\log(\Phi(\lambda u(z_i))),
$$

where $z_i = (x_i - \mu)/\sigma$, $u(x) = x/\sqrt{1+x^2}$, $\mu \in \mathbb{R}$, $\sigma > 0$, $\lambda \in \mathbb{R}$, and $x \in \mathbb{R}$. The entries of the observed information matrix for the MSN model have the same structure as the corresponding moments for the MLSN model considered in Section 4.3, with the appropriate transformation.

3. The Modified Log-Skew-Normal Distribution

If $Z \sim \text{MSN}(\lambda)$, then we have that $Y = e^Z$ is distributed according to the standard MLSNdistribution with parameter λ, denoted by $Y \sim \text{MLSN}(\lambda)$, if its pdf is given by

$$f_Y(y;\lambda) = \frac{2}{y}\phi(\log(y))\Phi(\lambda u(\log(y))),$$

where $u(x) = x/\sqrt{1+x^2}$, $y \in \mathbb{R}^+$, and $\lambda \in \mathbb{R}$.

Figure 2 depicts plots of the pdf for the MLSN(λ) model for several values of λ. If $\lambda = 0$, then it coincides with the log-normal distribution (solid line), illustrating the fact that the MLSN model is an extension of the LN model. Concerning the location-scale situation, that is $Y \sim \text{MLSN}(\mu, \sigma, \lambda)$, where $\mu \in \mathbb{R}$, $\sigma > 0$, and $\lambda \in \mathbb{R}$, its density is given by

$$f_Y(y;\mu,\sigma,\lambda) = \frac{2}{y\sigma}\phi(z)\Phi(\lambda u(z)), \tag{6}$$

where $z = (\log(y) - \mu)/\sigma$, $u(x) = x/\sqrt{1+x^2}$, and $y \in \mathbb{R}^+$. In a survival analysis scenario, it is important to study the following functions: the survival function $S(t) = 1 - F(t)$ and the risk function $r(t) = f(t)/S(t)$, which for the model under study can be shown to be given by

$$S(t) = 1 - \int_0^t \frac{2}{w}\phi(\log(w))\Phi(\lambda u(\log(w)))dw$$

and

$$r(t) = \frac{\frac{2}{t}\phi(\log(t))\Phi(\lambda u(\log(t)))}{1 - \int_0^t \frac{2}{w}\phi(\log(w))\Phi(\lambda u(\log(w)))dw}.$$

Clearly, using L'Hopital´s rule, it follows that $r(t) \to 0$ as $t \to \infty$, as can also be appreciated graphically.

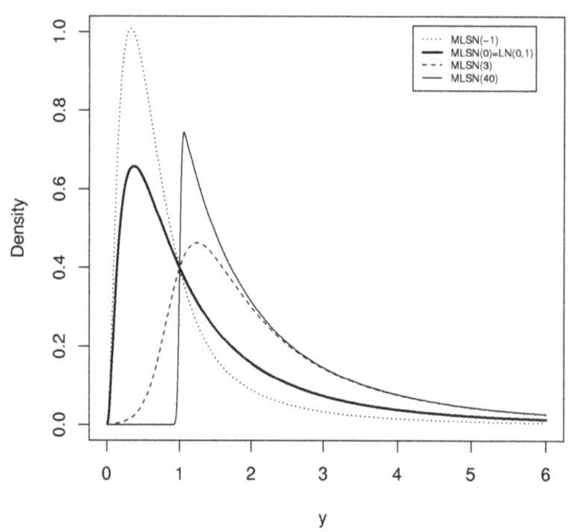

Figure 2. Plots of the MLSN(λ) model for different values of λ.

Figure 3 illustrates the behavior of the risk function $r(t)$ for some values of λ. The maximum values of the risk function for each λ decrease for $\lambda \in (-\infty, 1.4484)$ and increase otherwise. Moreover, $\lambda = -\infty$, $r(t)$ tends to a strictly increasing function defined in the interval $(0,1]$, otherwise being zero. On the other hand, $\lambda = \infty$, $r(t)$ is a strictly increasing function defined in the interval $[1,\infty)$, coinciding with the risk function of the log-normal model in this interval and taking the value zero in the interval $(0,1)$.

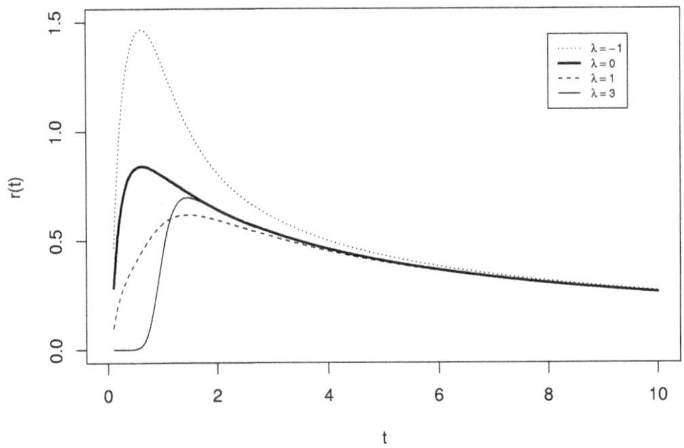

Figure 3. Plots of the risk function of the MLSN model for different values of λ.

3.1. Moments for the MLSN Model

The r-th moment is given by

$$\mu_r = 2e^{r^2/2}E\left(\Phi\left(\frac{S}{\sqrt{1+S^2}}r\right)\right),$$

for $r = 0,1,2.....$ and $S \sim N(\lambda,1)$. This expression is obtained directly from the moment-generating function of the MSN model, given in (5), since it is valid for all $t > 0$, particularly for $t = r$. Alternatively, the moments can be obtained from

$$\mu_r = E(Y^r) = \int_0^\infty y^r \frac{2}{y}\phi(\log(y))\Phi(\lambda u(\log(y)))dy.$$

3.1.1. Non-Existence of the Moment-Generating Function for the MLSN Distribution

Proposition 1. *For all $\lambda \in \mathbb{R}$, variable $Y \sim MLSN(\lambda)$ has no moment-generating function.*

Proof. Part of the proof parallels that of Lin and Stoyanov [12] for a similar proof. Thus, for each $t > 0$,

$$E(e^{tY}) = \int_0^\infty h_\lambda(y)dy,$$

where

$$h_\lambda(y) = \frac{e^{ty}}{y}\phi(\log(y))\Phi(\lambda u(\log(y))) > 0, \quad \forall y > 0,$$

so that, for

$$\lambda \geq 0, \quad \lim_{y\to\infty} \Phi(\lambda u(\log(y))) \geq \frac{1}{2}$$

and

$$\lambda < 0, \quad \lim_{y \to \infty} \Phi(\lambda u(\log(y))) \geq \Phi(\lambda),$$

in both cases, $h_\lambda(y) \to \infty$ as $y \to \infty$. Therefore, given $t > 0$, $E(e^{tY}) = \infty$, for any λ. □

3.1.2. Skewness and Kurtosis Coefficients

To obtain expressions for the kurtosis and skewness coefficients, we have to compute the central moments using the following relationships:

$$\mu_2' = \mu_2 - \mu_1^2, \quad \mu_3' = \mu_3 - 3\mu_1\mu_2 + 2\mu_1^3 \quad \text{and} \quad \mu_4' = \mu_4 - 4\mu_1\mu_3 + 6\mu_1^2\mu_2 - 3\mu_1^4.$$

This allows us to compute the variance, standard deviation (SD), coefficient of variation (CV), asymmetry (γ_1), and kurtosis (γ_2) coefficients, respectively, given by:

$$\mu_2' = Var(Y), \quad CV(Y) = \frac{SD(Y)}{\mu_2}, \quad \gamma_1 = \frac{\mu_3'}{(\mu_2')^{3/2}} \quad \text{and} \quad \gamma_2 = \frac{\mu_4'}{(\mu_2')^2}.$$

Table 1 reveals that the variation ranges for the variance and CV are relatively short, while the variation range for the asymmetry and kurtosis coefficients are relatively long if compared with the ordinary LSN model.

Table 1. Range of values for statistics corresponding to variance, CV, skewness, and kurtosis.

Statistics	Variance	CV	γ_1	γ_2
Minimum	0.062	0.477	0.110	1.952
Maximum	6.986	1.395	10.985	524.351

Figure 4 shows the behavior of the variance, CV, skewness, and kurtosis as a function of the lambda parameter. It can be observed that the minimum values correspond to the asymptotes of the left tail. On the other hand, for small values of λ, say $\lambda > 4$, the plots of the right tail stabilize around the horizontal asymptotes with values of 6.74, 0.936, 5.83, and 97.93, respectively, for the corresponding indices.

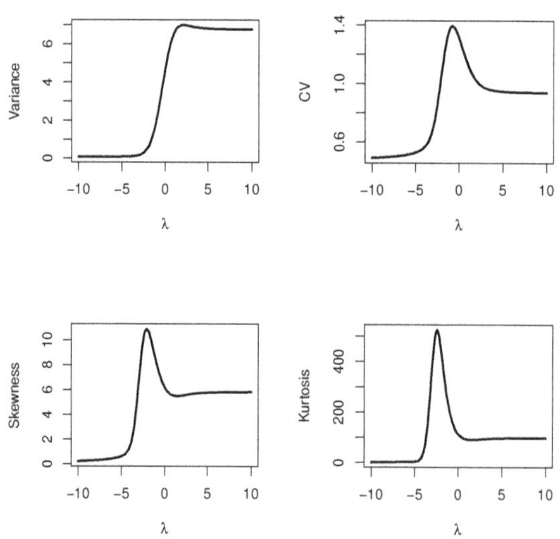

Figure 4. Plots of the variance, CV, skewness, and kurtosis.

3.2. MLE for the MLSN Model

Given a random sample $y_1, y_2, .., y_n$ from a random variable $Y \sim MLSN(\theta)$, with $\theta = (\mu, \sigma, \lambda)$, so that the corresponding log-likelihood is given by

$$l(\theta) = \frac{n}{2}\log\left(\frac{2}{\pi}\right) - n\log(\sigma) - \sum_{i=1}^{n}\log(y_i) - \frac{1}{2}\sum_{i=1}^{n} z_i^2 + \sum_{i=1}^{n}\log(\Phi(\lambda u(z_i))), \tag{7}$$

where $z_i = (\log(y_i) - \mu)/\sigma$, $u(x) = x/\sqrt{1+x^2}$, $\mu \in \mathbb{R}$, $\sigma > 0$, $\lambda \in \mathbb{R}$, and $y \in \mathbb{R}^+$. Using the following notation:

$$\rho_{nmi} = \frac{z_i^n}{(1+z_i^2)^{m/2}}\zeta(\lambda u(z_i)), \quad \eta_{nmi} = \frac{z_i^n}{(1+z_i^2)^m}\zeta^2(\lambda u(z_i)), \quad \overline{\eta}_{nm} = \frac{1}{n}\sum_{i=1}^{n}\rho_{nmi} \quad \text{and} \quad \zeta(x) = \frac{\phi(x)}{\Phi(x)},$$

we have that the associated scoring vector is given by

$$S_\mu = \frac{n}{\sigma}(\overline{z} - \lambda\overline{\rho}_{03}), \quad S_\sigma = \frac{n}{\sigma}\left(-1 + \overline{z^2} - \lambda\overline{\rho}_{13}\right) \quad \text{and} \quad S_\lambda = n\overline{\rho}_{11}.$$

Equating the scoring functions to zero, it follows that the likelihood equations are given as

$$\overline{z} = \lambda\overline{\rho}_{03}, \quad \overline{z^2} - 1 = \lambda\overline{\rho}_{13} \quad \text{and} \quad \overline{\rho}_{11} = 0.$$

Solving this system of equations, which require numerical procedures, leads to the MLE for μ, σ, and λ.

4. Bias Prevention of the MLE

4.1. Abstract for Firth's Approach

One problem with the ML approach is that the likelihood function can be unbounded for the parameter λ. In the standard case (just λ unknown), the MLE of λ is infinite given that all observations are positive. In the location-scale situation, the same happens because all observations are greater than μ, the location parameter. Therefore, the MLE overestimates parameter λ, which is always of concern in a statistical analysis. The percentage of overestimation of the shape parameter λ depends on the sample size n and on the true parameter value. It is of interest to reduce the amount of bias in a statistical problem. One approach considered previously in the literature was proposed by Firth [10] and had previously been used by Sartori [13] for the skew-normal and skew-t (ST) distributions. The reduced bias estimator is of order $O(n^{-2})$ (see also Cox and Snell [14]). To arrive at the reducedbias estimator, the following notation is used: Let $l(\theta)$ be the log-likelihood function for a parametric regular family of distributions, and denote by $U(\theta) = l'(\theta)$ the score function, $j(\theta) = -l''(\theta)$ the second derivative of the log-likelihood function, and l' its first derivative. We also consider the expectation of those functions that are of order $O(n)$. Therefore, we have

$$i(\theta) = E_\theta\{j(\theta)\}, \quad \nu_{\theta,\theta,\theta}(\theta) = E_\theta\{l'(\theta)^3\}, \quad \nu_{\theta,\theta\theta}(\theta) = E_\theta\{l'(\theta)l''(\theta)\}.$$

Briefly speaking, Firth's approach consists of modifying the score function keeping the score unchanged, that is

$$U_M(\theta) = U(\theta) + M(\theta), \tag{8}$$

where $M(\theta)$ is $O(1)$ as $n \to \infty$. The solution to the modified likelihood equation $U_M(\theta) = 0$ produces the modified MLE, say $\widehat{\theta}_M$ with bias of order $O(n^{-2})$. The modification factor $M(\theta)$ is given by

$$M(\theta) = -i(\theta)b(\theta) = \frac{1}{2}i(\theta)^{-1}(\nu_{\theta,\theta,\theta} + \nu_{\theta,\theta\theta}). \tag{9}$$

From the modified score function, the modified quasi-log-likelihood function is defined as

$$l_M(\theta) = \int_c^{\theta} U_M(t)dt = l(\theta) - l(c) + \int_c^{\theta} M(t)dt,$$

where c is an arbitrary constant. This penalized log-likelihood function has a penalty of order $O(1)$. It is also possible to define a modified log-likelihood ratio statistic:

$$W_M(\theta) = 2\{l_M(\widehat{\theta}_M) - l_M(\theta)\},$$

which is asymptotically distributed as a χ_1^2 distribution, which can be used for testing hypotheses about θ, as well as for confidence interval construction.

4.2. Simulation Study

Below, we present a simulation study based on 5000 iterations for $\mu = 0$, $\sigma = 1$, $\lambda = 5, 10$, and several sample sizes. Table 2 shows the bias for the modified and ordinary MLE, the empirical coverage of the confidence intervals based on $W_M^P(\lambda)$, and the percentage of cases in which the un-modified MLE for λ is finite. It can be observed that the MLEs $\widehat{\mu}$ and $\widehat{\sigma}$ present satisfactory behavior concerning bias, and they seem to be unaffected by the sometimes erratic behavior of estimator $\widehat{\lambda}$, so that Firth's method is only applied for the parameter λ.

Table 2. Results are based on 5000 samples simulated from the MSN$(0, 1, \lambda)$ model.

λ	n	$\widehat{\mu}(sd)$	$\widehat{\sigma}(sd)$	$\widehat{\lambda}^{\,a}(sd)$	$\widehat{\lambda}_M(sd)$	$W_M^P(\lambda)IC$	$\%(\widehat{\lambda} < \infty)$
5	50	−0.00351	0.99853	7.00103	4.35954	96.16	86.48
		(0.10073)	(0.12670)	(4.63146)	(1.18831)		
	100	−0.00208	0.99873	6.44116	4.80315	94.18	97.84
		(0.07114)	(0.08973)	(2.91069)	(0.93203)		
	200	0.00038	0.99838	5.53622	4.89744	94.04	99.98
		(0.05080)	(0.06355)	(1.43447)	(0.42190)		
10	50	0.01599	0.98026	11.36052	6.56160	87.98	66.00
		(0.07556)	(0.11462)	(9.14682)	(2.39887)		
	100	0.00359	0.99319	13.52624	8.71761	92.08	87.74
		(0.04890)	(0.08054)	(8.63025)	(2.92047)		
	200	0.00095	0.99748	12.95004	9.54944	93.38	98.42
		(0.03409)	(0.05698)	(6.00251)	(1.74399)		

$\widehat{\mu}$, $\widehat{\sigma}$, $\widehat{\lambda}$, and $\widehat{\lambda}_M$ are the estimates of the true values of the parameters, and *sd* denotes the respective standard deviations; the empirical coverage of the 0.95 confidence interval is based on $W_M^P(\lambda)$ and the empirical (theoretical) percentage for the situation that $\widehat{\lambda}$ exists. [a] Computed as $\widehat{\lambda} < \infty$.

The notation $W_M^P(\lambda) = 2\{l_M^P(\widehat{\lambda}_M) - l_M^P(\lambda)\}$ defines the likelihood ratio statistic based on the profile log-likelihood function $l^P(\lambda) = l(\widehat{\mu}(\lambda), \widehat{\sigma}(\lambda), \lambda)$, where $\widehat{\mu}$ and $\widehat{\sigma}$ are the MLEs for μ and σ, respectively, for a fixed value of λ.

4.3. Observed Information Matrix for the MLSN Model

The entries for the observed information matrix of the MLSN distribution, corresponding to the log-likelihood given in (7), are $J_{\theta_i\theta_j} = -\frac{\partial^2 l(\theta)}{\partial\theta_i\partial\theta_j}$, for $i, j = 1, 2, 3$ (see Appendix A):

$$J_{\mu\mu} = -\frac{n}{\sigma^2}\left(1 + 3\lambda\overline{\rho}_{15} + \lambda^3\overline{\rho}_{17} + \lambda^2\overline{\eta}_{03}\right), \qquad J_{\mu\sigma} = \frac{n}{\sigma^2}\left(-2\overline{z} + \lambda\overline{\rho}_{05} - 2\lambda\overline{\rho}_{25} - \widehat{\lambda^3}\overline{\rho}_{27} - \lambda^2\overline{\eta}_{13}\right),$$

$$J_{\mu\lambda} = -\frac{n}{\sigma}\left(\overline{\rho}_{03} - \lambda^2\overline{\rho}_{25} - \lambda\overline{\eta}_{12}\right), \qquad J_{\sigma\sigma} = \frac{n}{\sigma^2}\left(1 - 3\overline{z^2} + \lambda\overline{\rho}_{13} + \lambda\overline{\rho}_{15} - 2\lambda\overline{\rho}_{35} - \lambda^3\overline{\rho}_{37} - \lambda^2\overline{\eta}_{23}\right),$$

$$J_{\sigma\lambda} = \frac{n}{\sigma}\left(-\overline{\rho}_{13} + \lambda^2\overline{\rho}_{35} + \lambda\overline{\eta}_{22}\right), \qquad J_{\lambda\lambda} = -n(\lambda\overline{\rho}_{33} + \overline{\eta}_{21}).$$

4.4. Fisher Information

For a random sample $y_1, y_2, .., y_n$ from the MLSN(θ) distribution, with $\theta = (\mu, \sigma, \lambda)$, the FIM associated with (7) is given by the following entries (see Appendix A):

$$I_{\mu\mu} = \frac{1}{\sigma^2}\left(1 + \lambda^2 \eta_{03}\right), \quad I_{\sigma\mu} = -\frac{1}{\sigma^2}\left(-2E(z) + \lambda\rho_{05} - 2\lambda\rho_{25} - \lambda^3\rho_{27} - \lambda^2\eta_{13}\right),$$

$$I_{\mu\lambda} = \frac{1}{\sigma}\left(\rho_{03} - \lambda^2\rho_{25} - \lambda\eta_{12}\right), \quad I_{\sigma\sigma} = \frac{1}{\sigma^2}\left(2 + \lambda^2\eta_{23}\right), \quad I_{\lambda\sigma} = -\frac{\lambda}{\sigma}\eta_{22}, \quad I_{\lambda\lambda} = \eta_{21},$$

where

$$\rho_{nm} = E\left(\frac{z^n}{(1+z^2)^{m/2}}\zeta\right), \quad \rho_{nm} = 0 \quad if \quad n = \text{odd number}$$

$$\eta_{nm} = E\left(\frac{z^n}{(1+z^2)^m}\zeta^2\right), \quad \text{with } \zeta := \zeta(\lambda u(z)) = \frac{\phi(\lambda u(z))}{\Phi(\lambda u(z))}.$$

For the case $\lambda = 0$, we have that

$$\text{FIM} = \begin{pmatrix} \frac{1}{\sigma^2} & 0 & \frac{d_1}{\sigma} \\ 0 & \frac{2}{\sigma^2} & 0 \\ \frac{d_1}{\sigma} & 0 & d_2 \end{pmatrix},$$

where $d_1 = 2(2/\pi)^{1/2}\int_0^\infty \frac{\phi(x)}{(1+x^2)^{3/2}}dx$ and $d_2 = \frac{2}{\pi}(1 - (2\pi)^{1/2}e^{1/2}\Phi(-1))$ have to be computed numerically. It is clearly seen that the above FIM is non-singular at $\lambda = 0$.

5. An Application

The dataset analyzed in this section was previously studied in Nadarajah [15] and Leiva et al. [16]. It consists of daily measurements of ozone concentration (in $ppb = ppm \times 1000$) in New York city between May and September 1973. The data were supposed to be independent, without the presence of tendencies or cyclical components (see Gokhale and Khare [17]). Table 3 presents the summary statistics, in particular the asymmetry and kurtosis coefficients, which are represented by the sample quantities (b_1) and (b_2), respectively.

Table 3. Descriptive statistics of ozone concentration level measurement data.

Data	n	Mean	sd	b_1	b_2
Ozone	116	42.129	32.987	1.209	4.112

Table 4 shows the MLE for the three parameters for the MLSN, LN, and LSN distributions, respectively, where values in parentheses correspond to standard errors. Note also from the table that the AIC for the LSN model is slightly smaller than that for the MLSN model; it is our opinion that the latter model should be preferred because the LSN model has a singular covariance matrix, and so, the likelihood ratio statistics for testing $H_0 : \lambda = 0$ is not distributed according to a central chi-squared distribution in large samples. On the other hand, under the MLSN model, for which the FIM is non-singular, we have that the hypothesis $H_0 : \lambda = 0$ is rejected at the 5% level, using the likelihood ratio statistics; this is given by

$$\Lambda = \frac{L_{LN(\hat{\mu},\hat{\sigma})}}{L_{MLSN(\hat{\mu},\hat{\sigma},\hat{\lambda})}}.$$

Replacing the MLE from Table 4, we have that $-2log\Lambda = -2(-543.883 + 542.105) = 9.516$, greater than the critical value $\chi_1^2 = 3.84$. Furthermore, from the table, a large sample 95% confidence interval for λ based on the MLSN model does not contain $\lambda = 0$.

Table 4. MLEs for the MLSN, LN, and LSN models.

MLEs	MLSN	LN	LSN
$\widehat{\mu}$	4.532 (0.105)	3.418 (0.080)	4.372 (0.234)
$\widehat{\sigma}$	1.411 (0.121)	0.861 (0.056)	1.285 (0.193)
$\widehat{\lambda}$	−4.095 (1.057)	-	−2.411 (1.396)
log-likelihood	−542.105	−543.883	−541.655
AIC	1090.211	1091.766	1089.31

Figure 5 presents the data histogram with the corresponding fitted fdp for the MLSN$(\widehat{\mu},\widehat{\sigma},\widehat{\lambda})$ (solid line) and LN$(\widehat{\mu},\widehat{\sigma},\widehat{\lambda})$ distributions (dotted line) and the fit cdf for the MLSN and LN models, jointly with the empirical cdf. It can be shown from the figure that the MLSN model seems to provide a (graphically) satisfactory fit.

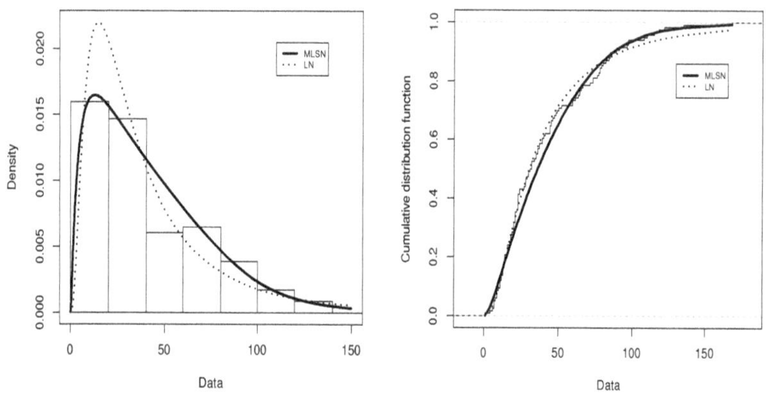

Figure 5. Left panel: Kernel density plot of the ozone concentration level data fit by the LN and MLSN distributions. **Right panel**: Empirical cdf of the LN (dotted line) and MLSN (solid line) models, whose parameters are estimated by the ML method for ozone concentration level data.

Graphical corroboration of the better fit of the MLSN model than the LN model is also illustrated with the QQ-plots in Figure 6.

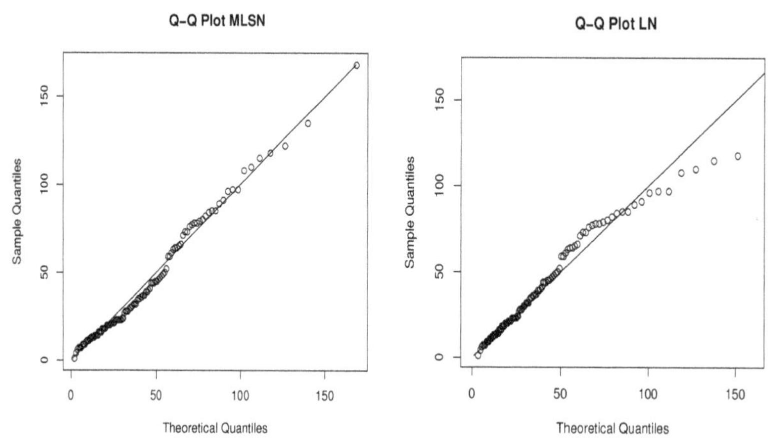

Figure 6. Left panel: QQ-plot for the MLSN model. **Right panel**: QQ-plot for the LN model.

Table 5 presents the MLEs $\hat{\mu}$, $\hat{\sigma}$, and $\hat{\lambda}$ and the modified $\hat{\lambda}_M$ with the corresponding standard errors (in parentheses), obtained by using the estimated FIM for the MLSN model, bearing in mind that the asymptotic distribution of $\hat{\theta}$ is $N_3(\theta, I(\theta)^{-1}/n)$, where $\theta = (\mu, \sigma, \lambda)$ or $\theta = (\mu, \sigma, \lambda_M)$. The table indicates that the modified MLE $\hat{\lambda}_M$ is greater than the ordinary MLE $\hat{\lambda}$ and is expected to have smaller bias.

Table 5. MLEs of the μ, σ, λ, and λ_M parameters.

$\hat{\mu}$	$\hat{\sigma}$	$\hat{\lambda}$	$\hat{\lambda}_M$	$l(\hat{\mu}, \hat{\sigma}, \hat{\lambda})$	$l(\hat{\mu}, \hat{\sigma}, \hat{\lambda}_M)$
4.532(0.105)	1.411(0.121)	−4.095(1.057)	−	−542.105	
4.532(0.123)	1.411(0.130)	−	−3.342(0.791)	−	−542.663

Table 6 presents confidence intervals for $\hat{\lambda}$ and $\hat{\lambda}_M$ for several confidence coefficients. Comparing the lengths of the intervals for the two estimators, there is strong evidence that the modified estimator $\hat{\lambda}_M$ presents shorter intervals.

Table 6. Confidence intervals for the estimated values of $\hat{\lambda}$ and $\hat{\lambda}_M$.

MLE	95%	98%	99%
$\hat{\lambda}$	(−5.834, −2.356)	(−6.266, −1.924)	(−6.554, −1.636)
$\hat{\lambda}_M$	(−4.644, −2.040)	(−4.968, −1.716)	(−5.183, −1.500)

6. Concluding Remarks

This paper focused on a transformation of the MSN model (Arellano-Valle et al. [8]), which led to a more flexible distribution (wider ranges for asymmetry and kurtosis). This model, which we call the MLSN distribution, is suitable for positive data, its main competitors being the LN and LSN distributions. One interesting aspect of the new model is that its FIM is non-singular so that the large sample theory for the MLE remains valid. This is not the case with the LSN model, for which the FIM is singular in the location-scale version. Thus, in particular for testing $H_0 : LN$ against $H_0 : MLSN$, under the MLSN model, the likelihood ratio statistics in large samples are distributed as in the chi-squared distribution. Large sample confidence intervals could also be constructed and used for testing the hypothesis $H_0 : \lambda = 0$, where λ is the skewness parameter. Rejection of H_0 indicates that the MLSN model should be preferred. It is also noticed with the simulation study that the MLE of λ can overestimate λ (which could be infinite for some samples). Thus, the bias-reducing approach of Firth [10] was used to derive a less-biased estimator. Estimations for the location and scale parameters remain stable, however, and do not need to be corrected. An application to a real dataset revealed that the new model can be a valuable alternative for modeling positive data.

Author Contributions: Conceptualization, J.A., R.B.A.-V., and H.W.G.; methodology, R.A.-V., H.B., and H.W.G.; software, J.A. and O.V.; validation, R.B.A.-V., H.B., and H.W.G.; formal analysis, R.A.-V. and H.W.G.; investigation, J.A., O.V., and H.W.G.; writing—original draft preparation, J.A. and R.B.A.-V.; writing—review and editing, J.A. and O.V.; funding acquisition, H.W.G. and O.V. All authors have read and agreed to the published version of the manuscript.

Funding: The research of Jaime Arrué and Héctor W. Gómez was supported by SEMILLERO UA-2022 (Chile).

Institutional Review Board Statement: Not applicable.

Informed Consent Statement: Not applicable.

Data Availability Statement: The dataset is available in [15,16].

Conflicts of Interest: The authors declare no conflict of interest.

Appendix A

Considering the notation:

$$\theta = (\mu, \sigma), \quad z = \frac{x-\mu}{\sigma}, \quad u(x) = \frac{x}{\sqrt{1+x^2}}, \quad \zeta = \zeta(\lambda u(z)) = \frac{\phi(\lambda u(z))}{\Phi(\lambda u(z))},$$

and the following derivatives:

$$\frac{\partial z}{\partial \mu} = -\frac{1}{\sigma}, \qquad \frac{\partial z}{\partial \sigma} = -\frac{z}{\sigma}, \qquad \frac{\partial u(z)}{\partial \theta} = \frac{1}{(1+z^2)^{3/2}}\frac{\partial z}{\partial \theta},$$

$$\begin{aligned}
\frac{\partial \zeta}{\partial \theta} &= \left(-\frac{\lambda^2 z}{(1+z^2)^2}\zeta - \frac{\lambda}{(1+z^2)^{3/2}}\zeta^2\right)\frac{\partial z}{\partial \theta}, \\
\frac{\partial}{\partial \theta}\left(\frac{z}{(1+z^2)^{3/2}}\right) &= \frac{1-2z^2}{(1+z^2)^{5/2}}\frac{\partial z}{\partial \theta}, \\
\frac{\partial \zeta}{\partial \lambda} &= -\frac{\lambda z^2}{(1+z^2)}\zeta - \frac{z}{(1+z^2)^{1/2}}\zeta^2,
\end{aligned}$$

we have that the score functions score for μ, σ, and λ for the MSN(λ) model are given by

$$S_\mu = \frac{1}{\sigma}\left(z - \frac{\lambda}{(1+z^2)^{3/2}}\zeta\right), \quad S_\sigma = \frac{1}{\sigma}\left(-1 + z^2 - \frac{\lambda z}{(1+z^2)^{3/2}}\zeta\right), \quad S_\lambda = \frac{z}{(1+z^2)^{1/2}}\zeta,$$

so that the entries of the FIM are given by:

$$\begin{aligned}
I_{\mu\mu} &= -E(S_{\mu\mu}) = -\frac{1}{\sigma^2}E\left(-1 - \frac{3\lambda z}{(1+z^2)^{5/2}}\zeta - \frac{\lambda^3 z}{(1+z^2)^{7/2}}\zeta - \frac{\lambda^2}{(1+z^2)^3}\zeta^2\right) \\
&= \frac{1}{\sigma^2}\left(1 + \lambda^2 \eta_{03}\right), \\
I_{\mu\sigma} &= -E(S_{\sigma\mu}) = -\frac{1}{\sigma^2}E\left(-2z + \frac{\lambda(1-2z^2)}{(1+z^2)^{5/2}}\zeta - \frac{\lambda^3 z^2}{(1+z^2)^{7/2}}\zeta - \frac{\lambda^2 z}{(1+z^2)^3}\zeta^2\right) \\
&= -\frac{1}{\sigma^2}\left(-2E(z) + \lambda\rho_{05} - 2\lambda\rho_{25} - \lambda^3\rho_{27} - \lambda^2\eta_{13}\right), \\
I_{\mu\lambda} &= -E(S_{\mu\lambda}) = -\frac{1}{\sigma}E\left(-\frac{1}{(1+z^2)^{3/2}}\left\{\zeta - \frac{\lambda^2 z^2}{(1+z^2)}\zeta - \frac{\lambda z}{(1+z^2)^{1/2}}\zeta^2\right\}\right) \\
&= \frac{1}{\sigma}\left(\rho_{03} - \lambda^2\rho_{25} - \lambda\eta_{12}\right), \\
I_{\sigma\sigma} &= -E(S_{\sigma\sigma}) \\
&= -\frac{1}{\sigma^2}E\left(1 - 3z^2 + \frac{\lambda z}{(1+z^2)^{3/2}}\zeta + \frac{\lambda(z-2z^3)}{(1+z^2)^{5/2}}\zeta - \frac{\lambda^3 z^3}{(1+z^2)^{7/2}}\zeta - \frac{\lambda^2 z^2}{(1+z^2)^3}\zeta^2\right) \\
&= \frac{1}{\sigma^2}\left(2 + \lambda^2\eta_{23}\right), \\
I_{\sigma\lambda} &= -E(S_{\lambda\sigma}) = -\frac{1}{\sigma}E\left(-\frac{z}{(1+z^2)^{3/2}}\zeta + \frac{\lambda^2 z^3}{(1+z^2)^{5/2}}\zeta + \frac{\lambda z^2}{(1+z^2)^2}\zeta^2\right) \\
&= -\frac{\lambda}{\sigma}\eta_{22}, \\
I_{\lambda\lambda} &= -E(S_{\lambda\lambda}) = -E\left(-\frac{\lambda z^3}{(1+z^2)^{3/2}}\zeta - \frac{z^2}{1+z^2}\zeta^2\right) \\
&= \eta_{21}.
\end{aligned}$$

References

1. Jones, M.C.; Arnold, B.C. Distributions that are both log-symmetric and R-symmetric. *Electron. J. Stat.* **2008**, *2*, 1300–1308. [CrossRef]
2. Mudholkar, G.S.; Wang, H. IG-symmetry and R-symmetry: interrelations and applications to the inverse Gaussian theory. *J. Stat. Plan. Inference* **2007**, *137*, 3655–3671. [CrossRef]
3. Azzalini, A.; Cappello, D.; Kotz, S. Log-skew-normal and log-skew-t distributions as models for family income data. *J. Income Distrib.* **2003**, *11*, 12–20. [CrossRef]
4. Marchenko, Y.V.; Genton, M.G. Multivariate log-skew-elliptical distributions with applications to precipitation data. *Environmetrics* **2010**, *21*, 318–340. [CrossRef]
5. Bolfarine, H.; Gómez, H.W.; Rivas, L. The log-bimodal-skew-normal model. A geochemical application. *J. Chemom.* **2011**, *25*, 329–332. [CrossRef]
6. Chai, H.; Bailey, K. Use of log-normal distribution in analysis of continuous data with a discrete component at zero. *Stat. Med.* **2008**, *27*, 3643–3655. [CrossRef] [PubMed]
7. Arellano-Valle, R.B.; Gómez, H.W.; Quintana, F.A. A new class of skew-normal distributions. *Commun. Stat.-Theory Methods* **2004**, *33*, 1465–1480. [CrossRef]
8. Arellano-Valle, R.B.; Gómez, H.W.; Salinas, H.S. A note on the Fisher information matrix for the skew-generalized-normal model. *SORT* **2013**, *37*, 19–28.
9. Arrué, J.; Arellano-Valle, R.B.; Gómez, H.W. Bias reduction of maximum likelihood estimates for a modified skew normal distribution. *J. Stat. Comput. Simul.* **2016**, *86*, 2967–2984. [CrossRef]
10. Firth, D. Bias reduction of maximum likelihood estimates. *Biometrika* **1993**, *80*, 27–38; Amended in *Biometrika* **1995**, *82*, 667. [CrossRef]
11. Henze, N. A probabilistic representation of the skew-normal distribution. *Scand. J. Stat.* **1986**, *13*, 271–275.
12. Lin, G.D.; Stoyanov, J. The logarithmic skew-normal distributions are moment-indeterminate. *J. Appl. Prob.* **2009**, *46*, 909–916. [CrossRef]
13. Sartori, N. Bias prevention of maximum likelihood estimates for scalar skew normal and skew t distributions. *J. Stat. Plan. Inference* **2006**, *136*, 4259–4275. [CrossRef]
14. Cox, D.R.; Snell, E.J. A general definition of residuals. *J. R. Stat. Soc. Ser. B* **1968**, *30*, 248–275. [CrossRef]
15. Nadarajah, S. A truncated inverted beta distribution with application to air pollution data. *Stoch. Environ. Res. Risk Assess.* **2008**, *22*, 285–289. [CrossRef]
16. Leiva, V.; Vilca-Labra, F.; Balakrishnan, N.; Sanhueza, A. A Skewed Sinh-Normal Distribution and its Properties and Application to Air Pollution. *Commun. Stat.-Theory Methods* **2010**, *39*, 426–443. [CrossRef]
17. Gokhale, S.; Khare, M. Statistical behavior of carbon monoxide from vehicular exhausts in urban environments. *Environ. Model. Softw.* **2007**, *22*, 526–535. [CrossRef]

mathematics

MDPI

Article

Power Families of Bivariate Proportional Hazard Models

Guillermo Martínez-Flórez [1,†], Carlos Barrera-Causil [2,*,†] and Artur J. Lemonte [3,†]

1 Departamento de Matemáticas y Estadística, Facultad de Ciencias Básicas, Universidad de Córdoba, Montería 230002, Colombia
2 Grupo de Investigación Davinci, Facultad de Ciencias Exactas y Aplicadas, Instituto Tecnológico Metropolitano, Medellín 050034, Colombia
3 Departamento de Estatística, Universidade Federal do Rio Grande do Norte, Natal 59077-000, RN, Brazil
* Correspondence: carlosbarrera@itm.edu.co
† These authors contributed equally to this work.

Abstract: In this paper, we propose a general class of bivariate proportional hazard distributions, which is based on the family of asymmetric proportional hazard distributions and the bivariate Pareto copula. Distributional properties of the bivariate proportional hazard distribution are derived. We specialize the bivariate proportional hazard family of distributions to the normal case, and so we introduce the bivariate proportional hazard normal distribution. Parameter estimation by the maximum likelihood method of the bivariate proportional hazard normal distribution is then discussed. Finally, an application of the new bivariate distribution to real data is considered for illustrative purposes.

Keywords: asymmetric distribution; bivariate distribution; copula; two-stage estimation

MSC: 60E05

1. Introduction

The proportional hazard distribution was presented as an extension of the distribution of the minimum of a random sample replacing $n \in \mathbb{Z}$ with $b > 0$ in a random variable Z with probability density function (PDF) f, and cumulative distribution function (CDF) F. So, this distribution could be considered as a distribution of fractional order statistics ([1]). Here, we start defining the proportional hazard (PHF) distribution, which was studied by [2]; see also [3] where inference under progressively type II right-censored sampling for the PHF distribution is considered. Let F be a continuous CDF with PDF $f = dF$, and hazard function $h = f/(1-F)$. We say that Z has a PHF distribution associated with F and f, if its PDF is of the form

$$\varphi_F(z) = \beta f(z)\{1 - F(z)\}^{\beta-1}, \quad z \in \mathbb{R}, \tag{1}$$

where $\beta > 0$ is the shape parameter. We use the notation $Z \sim \text{PHF}(\beta)$ to refer to this distribution. The CDF of the PHF distribution is given by

$$\mathbb{F}(z) = 1 - \{1 - F(z)\}^{\beta}, \quad z \in \mathbb{R}. \tag{2}$$

The hazard function of this model is $h_F(z) = \beta f(z)/\{1 - F(z)\}$; that is, the proportional hazard function of the PDF f. From Equation (2), we can use the inversion method for generating a random variable with PHF distribution; that is, if $U \sim \mathcal{U}(0,1)$, i.e., a uniform distribution on the interval $(0,1)$, then the random variable $X = \mu + \sigma F^{-1}(1 - (1-U)^{1/\beta})$ is distributed according to the PHF distribution with parameter vector $\boldsymbol{\theta} = (\mu, \sigma, \beta)'$, where $F^{-1}(\cdot)$ denotes the inverse of $F(\cdot)$. The distributional properties of the PHF distribution, as well as inferential procedures and information matrix for the model parameters are studied by [2].

The location-scale extension of model (1) is obtained using the linear transformation $X = \mu + \sigma Z$, where $\mu \in \mathbb{R}$ is a location parameter, $\sigma > 0$ is a scale parameter, and $Z \sim \text{PHF}(\beta)$. The PDF of the random variable X is given by

$$\varphi(x) = \frac{\beta}{\sigma} f\left(\frac{x-\mu}{\sigma}\right)\left(1 - F\left(\frac{x-\mu}{\sigma}\right)\right)^{\beta-1}, \quad x \in \mathbb{R}. \tag{3}$$

If a random variable X follows the model (3), it is denoted by $X \sim \text{PHF}(\mu, \sigma, \beta)$. If $f = \phi$ and $F = \Phi$, where ϕ and Φ detone the PDF and CDF of a standard normal distribution, we write $X \sim \text{PHN}(\mu, \sigma, \beta)$, and so we obtain the proportional hazard normal (PHN) distribution. Note that $\text{PHN}(\mu, \sigma, \beta = 1) \equiv \mathcal{N}(\mu, \sigma)$, and so the normal distribution is a special case of the PHN distribution. Hence, it is more flexible than the normal model in terms of skewness and kurtosis, due to the inclusion of the shape parameter β. We have that the Kumaraswamy-G (KwG) distribution, proposed by [4], is defined by the PDF

$$\varphi_G(z) = abg(z)G^{a-1}(z)\{1 - G^a(z)\}^{b-1}, \quad z \in \mathbb{R}, \tag{4}$$

where G is an arbitrary continuous CDF, and $g = dG$. Also, $a > 0$ and $b > 0$ are additional shape parameters to that of G. If Z is a random variable with PDF (4), we write $Z \sim \text{KwG}(a, b)$. It is worth stressing that when $a = 1$, we obtain the $\text{PHF}(b)$ distribution, i.e., $\text{KwG}(a = 1, b) \equiv \text{PHF}(b)$, and so this kind of distribution arises as a possible solution when we have asymmetric data.

The construction of multivariate distributions from copula theory can be carried out using the Sklar's theorem. The way to obtain a multivariate distribution from the Sklar's theorem is as follows: Let $X_1, \ldots, X_p$ be p random variables with continuous CDFs $F_{X_1}(x_1), \ldots, F_{X_p}(x_p)$, respectively. Then, according to Sklar's theorem, $F_{X_1,\ldots,X_p}(x_1, \ldots, x_p)$ has a unique copula representation:

$$F_{X_1,\ldots,X_p}(x_1, \ldots, x_p) = C(F_{X_1}(x_1), \ldots, F_{X_p}(x_p)).$$

Moreover, it is well known that many dependence properties of a multivariate distribution depend only on the corresponding copula. Therefore, many dependence properties of a multivariate distribution can be obtained by studying the corresponding copula. By using Clayton copula, Ref [5] proposed a bivariate extension of the power-normal distribution. Specifically, a bivariate random variable (X_1, X_2) has a bivariate power-normal distribution, denoted by $\text{BPN}(\delta, \beta_1, \beta_2)$, if for $\beta_1 > 0$ and $\beta_2 > 0$, (X_1, X_2) has the following joint CDF

$$F_{X_1,X_2}(x_1, x_2) = (\{\Phi(x_1)\}^{-\beta_1/\delta} + \{\Phi(x_2)\}^{-\beta_2/\delta} - 1)^{-\delta}, \quad (x_1, x_2) \in \mathbb{R}^2,$$

where $\delta > 0$ is the parameter that controls the dependence in the Clayton copula. The Clayton copula is usually attributed to [6], but it has also been studied by [7]. For $(u, v) \in [0, 1] \times [0, 1]$, it is defined as

$$C_\delta(u, v) = (u^{-1/\delta} + v^{-1/\delta} - 1)^{-\delta}, \quad \delta > 0.$$

The first systematic study of this model was conducted by [8], who interpreted the parameter δ as a measure of the dependence between u and v. Therefore, the independence between the variables is obtained when δ tends to zero. Obviously there are other forms of constructing multivariate distributions, and so new multitariate distributions have been proposed in the statistical literature. To mention a few, but not limited to, we refer the reader to the works by [9–12], among others.

It is worth emphasizing that the univariate PHF family of distributions has received significant attention over the last years in the statistical literature, mainly due to its flexibility in considering different models in its construction given by f and F; see expression (1). On the other hand, multivariate extensions of this univariate family of distributions has been little explored. This paper fills this gap and provides a bivariate extension of this univariate distribution. The bivariate PHF distribution is quite simple and, hence, may be widely applied in analyzing bivariate real data in practice. Additionally, distributional properties of the bivariate PHF distribution are investigated in details. An important claim to introduce the bivariate PHF distribution relies on the fact that the practitioners will have new bivariate model to use in bivariate settings. Additionally, the formulae related with the new bivariate model are manageable and with the use of modern computer resources and its numerical capabilities, the bivariate PHF distribution may prove to be an useful addition to the arsenal of applied statisticians. We hope that the bivariate distribution introduced in this paper may serve as an alternative bivariate model to some well-known bivariate model available in the statistical literature. We also hope that the bivariate PHF distribution may work better (at least in terms of model fitting) than some bivariate distributions available in the literature in certain practical situations, although it cannot always be guaranteed. Here, the bivariate PHF family of distributions we introduce is obtained from a multivariate distribution which was constructed from Pareto copula (descried in the next section) coupled with PHF marginals. It is worth stressing that many types of copulas are available o construct multivariate distributions, namely: Clayton copula, Frank copula, Joe copula, and Gumbel copula, among others. Perhaps, the most common copula is the Clayton copula. In this paper, instead, we shall consider the Pareto copula to introduce the new bivariate model due to its simplicity and interesting properties (descried in the next section). In addition, the Pareto copula yields a simple form of the likelihood function, so it makes the estimation of the model parameters easy to deal with. In short, it is evident that few works about bivariate generalizations of the PHF distribution have been published in the statistical literature and, hence, a new, simple and tractable bivariate PHF extension of the univariate PHF distribution through Pareto copula is welcome.

The paper is organized as follows. Section 2 presents the Pareto copula and discusses with details the structural properties derived from it. The bivariate proportional hazard distribution is proposed in Section 3. Distributional properties of this bivariate family of distributions are also derived in this section. In Section 4, we study the bivariate PHN distribution, where the univariate normal distribution is taken into account. Location-scale extension, as well as parameter estimation for the bivariate PHN distribution are also discussed in this section. An empirical appliction of the bivariate PHN distribution that considers real data is provided in Section 5 for illustrative purposes. Finally, Section 6 concludes the paper.

2. Pareto Copula

The Pareto distribution, or Pareto type I distribution, has been extensively used in economic literature and in reliability theory. Its CDF is given by

$$G_X(x) = 1 - \left(\frac{x}{\sigma}\right)^{-\alpha}, \quad x > 0,$$

where $\sigma > 0$ and $\alpha > 0$. Another type of Pareto distribution is the Pareto type II distribution, whose CDF takes the form

$$F_X(x) = 1 - \left(1 + \frac{x}{\sigma}\right)^{-\alpha}, \quad x > 0.$$

Its survival function is given by

$$S_X(x) = \left(1 + \frac{x}{\sigma}\right)^{-\alpha}, \quad x > 0.$$

The bivariate Pareto distribution of the random vector $X = (X_1, X_2)$ has joint CDF in the form

$$F_{X_1,X_2}(x_1, x_2) = F_{X_1}(x_1) + F_{X_2}(x_2) - 1 + [\{S_{X_1}(x_1)\}^{-1/\alpha} + \{S_{X_2}(x_2)\}^{-1/\alpha} - 1]^{-\alpha},$$

where $(x_1, x_2) \in \mathbb{R}^2_+$. Then, using the Sklar's theorem for continuous marginal distributions, the bivariate Pareto copula is given by

$$C(u_1, u_2) = F_{X_1,X_2}(F_{X_1}^{-1}(u_1), F_{X_2}^{-1}(u_2)) = u_1 + u_2 - 1 + [(1-u_1)^{-1/\alpha} + (1-u_2)^{-1/\alpha} - 1]^{-\alpha}.$$

Next, we shall consider some properties of the bivariate Pareto copula:

1. The joint PDF of the Pareto copula is

$$c(u_1, u_2) = \frac{\partial^2 C(u_1, u_2)}{\partial u_1 \partial u_2} = \frac{\alpha+1}{\alpha} \frac{[(1-u_1)(1-u_2)]^{-\frac{\alpha+1}{\alpha}}}{[(1-u_1)^{-1/\alpha} + (1-u_2)^{-1/\alpha} - 1]^{\alpha+2}}.$$

2. The joint survival function of the Pareto copula is

$$S(u_1, u_2) = P(U_1 \geq u_1, U_2 \geq u_2) = [(1-u_1)^{-1/\alpha} + (1-u_2)^{-1/\alpha} - 1]^{-\alpha}.$$

3. For all $u_2 \in [0, 1]$, the bivariate Pareto copula is a concave function on u_1 for fixed u_2. This result follows from

$$\frac{\partial^2 C(u_1, u_2)}{\partial u_1^2} = \frac{\alpha+1}{\alpha} \frac{(1-u_1)^{-\frac{2\alpha+1}{\alpha}}}{[(1-u_1)^{-1/\alpha} + (1-u_2)^{-1/\alpha} - 1]^{\alpha+2}} \geq 0.$$

4. The bivariate dependency measures for continuous variables, usually used in copulas, are Kendall's tau correlation coefficient (τ), Spearman's rho (ρ_s), and the medial correlation coefficient. The first two coefficients are invariant to increasing transformations. The Kendall's tau measures the difference between the probability of two concordant random pairs and the probability of two discordant random pairs. For a continuous bivariate distribution function F, τ is defined by

$$\tau = 4 \int F dF - 1.$$

Spearman's rho correlation coefficient measures the correlation between the two CDFs, $F_{X_1}(x_1)$ and $F_{X_2}(x_2)$. Then, given that F_{X_1} and F_{X_2} are continuous uniform random variables on $(0, 1)$ with mean and variance $1/2$ and $1/12$, respectively, it can be shown that

$$\rho_s = 12 \int_0^1 \int_0^1 C(u_1, u_2) du_1 du_2 - 3.$$

If M_{X_1} and M_{X_2} denote the medians of X_1 and X_2, respectively, the medial correlation coefficient of X_1 and X_2, say $M_{X_1X_2}$, is given by (see [13])

$$M_{X_1X_2} = 4C\left(\frac{1}{2}, \frac{1}{2}\right).$$

For the bivariate Pareto copula, we have that

$$\begin{aligned}\tau &= -\frac{2\alpha}{2\alpha+1},\\ \rho_s &= 12\int_{-1}^{0}\int_{-1}^{0}\left[u_1^{-1/\alpha}+u_2^{-1/\alpha}-1\right]^{-\alpha}du_1du_2-3, \qquad (5)\\ M_{X_1X_2} &= 4\left(2^{(\alpha+1)/\alpha}-1\right)^{-\alpha}.\end{aligned}$$

5. A non-negative function b is totally positive of order 2 (TP_2) if for all $x_1 < x_2$ and $y_1 < y_2$, with $x, y \in \mathbb{R}$, if is verified that

$$b(x_1, y_1)b(x_2, y_2) \geq b(x_2, y_1)b(x_1, y_2).$$

This is a condition of positive dependence when it is performed on the PDF, and means that two pairs with components matching high-low and low-low are more likely than two pairs with high-low and low-high components. For all $u_1, u_2 \in [0, 1]$, the bivariate Pareto copula is a non-negative function of order 2 (or TP_2).

6. The bivariate tail dependence concept is related to the amount of dependency on the tail of the bivariate distribution, in the upper or lower quadrant. The λ symbol is used to determine a tail dependence parameter. If a bivariate copula C, with survival copula $\bar{C}$, is such that

$$\lambda_U = \lim_{u\to 1}\frac{\bar{C}(u,u)}{1-u}$$

exists, then C has an upper tail dependence if $\lambda_U \in (0, 1]$ and has no upper tail dependence if $\lambda_U = 0$. It can be shown that

$$\lambda_U = \lim_{v\to 1}\frac{1-2v+C(v,v)}{1-v},$$

where v refers to the component u_2. Similarly, if a bivariate copula C is such that

$$\lambda_L = \lim_{u\to 0}\frac{C(u,u)}{u}$$

exists, then C has lower tail dependence if $\lambda_L \in (0, 1]$ and has no lower tail dependence if $\lambda_L = 0$. The reasoning behind these definitions is that

$$\lambda_U = \lim_{u\to 1}\Pr[U_1 > u \mid U_1 > u], \quad \lambda_L = \lim_{u\to 0}\Pr[U_1 \leq u \mid U_1 \leq u].$$

For the bivariate Pareto copula, we have that $\lambda_u = \infty$ and $\lambda_L = 0$. Then, the Pareto copula has a lower tail dependence. That is, for a value u arbitrarily close to zero, there is a positive probability that one of the variables u_1 or u_2 takes values smaller than u, given that the other is smaller than u.

3. Bivariate Proportional Hazard Distribution

In what follows, the joint CDF of (X_1, X_2), $F_{X_1,X_2}(x_1, x_2)$, is constructed from the bivariate Pareto copula, with marginal distributions $X_1 \sim \text{PHF}(\alpha_1)$ and $X_2 \sim \text{PHF}(\alpha_2)$, where $\alpha_1 > 0$ and $\alpha_2 > 0$. Then, from the Sklar's theorem, the joint CDF of (X_1, X_2) is given by

$$F_{X_1,X_2}(x_1, x_2) = C(F_{X_1}(x_1), F_{X_2}(x_2)).$$

We have the following definition.

Definition 1. *A bivariate random vector* (X_1, X_2) *has a bivariate proportional hazard distribution, if its joint CDF is given by*

$$\begin{aligned} F_{X_1,X_2}(x_1,x_2) &= 1-(1-F_{X_1}(x_1))^{\alpha_1}-(1-F_{X_2}(x_2))^{\alpha_2} \\ &\quad + [(1-F_{X_1}(x_1))^{-\frac{\alpha_1}{\alpha}}+(1-F_{X_2}(x_2))^{-\frac{\alpha_2}{\alpha}}-1]^{-\alpha}, \end{aligned}$$

where $(x_1, x_2) \in \mathbb{R}^2$, $\alpha_1 > 0$, $\alpha_2 > 0$ *and* $\alpha > 0$.

Remark 1. *We denote the bivariate proportional hazard distribution in Definition 1 by* $(X_1, X_2) \sim \text{BPHF}(\alpha_1, \alpha_2, \alpha)$.

Remark 2. *Let* $(X_1, X_2) \sim \text{BPHF}(\alpha_1, \alpha_2, \alpha)$. *Then, the joint PDF of* (X_1, X_2) *has the form*

$$f_{X_1,X_2}(x_1,x_2) = \frac{(\alpha+1)\alpha_1\alpha_2}{\alpha}\frac{f_{X_1}(x_1)[1-F_{X_1}(x_1)]^{-\frac{\alpha_1}{\alpha}-1}f_{X_2}(x_2)[1-F_{X_2}(x_2)]^{-\frac{\alpha_2}{\alpha}-1}}{[(1-F_{X_1}(x_1))^{-\frac{\alpha_1}{\alpha}}+(1-F_{X_2}(x_2))^{-\frac{\alpha_2}{\alpha}}-1]^{\alpha+2}}.$$

We have the following propositions.

Proposition 1. *Let* $(X_1, X_2) \sim \text{BPHF}(\alpha_1, \alpha_2, \alpha)$. *We have that*

(i) $X_j \sim \text{PHF}(\alpha_j)$, *for* $j = 1, 2$.

(ii) The CDF of X_1, *given* $X_2 = x_2$, *is*

$$F_{X_1|X_2}(x_1 \mid X_2 = x_2) = \frac{[1-F_{X_2}(x_2)]^{-\alpha_2(\frac{\alpha+1}{\alpha})}}{[(1-F_{X_1}(x_1))^{-\frac{\alpha_1}{\alpha}}+(1-F_{X_2}(x_2))^{-\frac{\alpha_2}{\alpha}}-1]^{\alpha+1}}.$$

(iii) The PDF of X_1, *given* $X_2 = x_2$, *is*

$$f_{X_1|X_2}(x_1 \mid X_2 = x_2) = \frac{(\alpha+1)\alpha_1}{\alpha}\frac{f_{X_1}(x_1)[1-F_{X_1}(x_1)]^{-\frac{\alpha_1}{\alpha}-1}[1-F_{X_2}(x_2)]^{-\alpha_2(\frac{\alpha-1}{\alpha})}}{[(1-F_{X_1}(x_1))^{-\frac{\alpha_1}{\alpha}}+(1-F_{X_2}(x_2))^{-\frac{\alpha_2}{\alpha}}-1]^{\alpha+2}}. \quad (6)$$

(iv) The joint survival function of (X_1, X_2) *is*

$$\begin{aligned} S_{X_1,X_2}(x_1,x_2) &= P(X_1 \geq x_1, X_2 \geq x_2) \\ &= F_{X_1}(x_1)+F_{X_2}(x_2)-1+C(1-F_{X_1}(x_1),1-F_{X_2}(x_2)) \\ &= [(1-F_{X_1}(x_1))^{-\frac{\alpha_1}{\alpha}}+(1-F_{X_2}(x_2))^{-\frac{\alpha_2}{\alpha}}-1]^{-\alpha}. \end{aligned}$$

Proposition 2. *Let* $(X_1, X_2) \sim \text{BPHF}(\alpha_1, \alpha_2, \alpha)$. *We have that* X_1 *is stochastically decreasing in* X_2, *and vice versa, for any value of* α_1, α_2, *and* α.

Proof. Since Pareto copula is a concave function on u_1 for fixed u_2, the result holds. □

The bivariate hazard rate of X_1 and X_2 was defined by [14] and it is given by

$$h(x_1,x_2) = \left(-\frac{\partial}{\partial x_1}, -\frac{\partial}{\partial x_2}\right)\log[\Pr(X_1 > x_1, X_2 > x_2)] = (h_1(x_1,x_2), h_2(x_1,x_2)).$$

Proposition 3. *Let* $(X_1, X_2) \sim \text{BPHF}(\alpha_1, \alpha_2, \alpha)$. *We have that*

(i) For fixed x_2, $h_1(x_1, x_2)$ *is an increasing function of* x_1.

(ii) For fixed x_1, $h_2(x_1, x_2)$ *is an increasing function of* x_2.

Proof. This result can be verified as follows. Let $u_1 = (1 - F_{X_1}(x_1))^{-\frac{\alpha_1}{\alpha}}$ and $k_2 = (1 - F_{X_2}(x_2))^{-\frac{\alpha_2}{\alpha}} - 1$. It can be shown that

$$\frac{\partial h_1(x_1,x_2)}{\partial x_1} = \frac{\partial Q_1(x_1,x_2)}{\partial u_1}\frac{\partial u_1}{\partial x_1} < 0,$$

where $Q_1(x_1,x_2) = -\partial \log(u_1+k)^{-\alpha}/\partial u_1$ and, hence, the result follows. □

Proposition 4. *Let* $(X_1, X_2) \sim \mathrm{BPHF}(\alpha_1, \alpha_2, \alpha)$. *We have that the Kendall's tau correlation coefficient, Spearman's rho and the medial correlation coefficient, are given by the expressions provided in* (5).

Proof. Kendall's tau and Spearman's rho correlation coefficients are invariant to increasing transformations, and so the resut follows. Note that is enough to take the transformation $u_1 = 1-(1-F_{X_1}(x_1))^{-\alpha_1}$, and $u_2 = 1-(1-F_{X_2}(x_2))^{-\alpha_2}$, which leads to the PDF Pareto copula. Since the medial coefficient is defined directly from the Pareto copula, the result is obtained directly. □

Remark 3. *The upper and lower limits for* ρ_s *are*

$$-\frac{4\alpha(\alpha+1)-1/2}{(2\alpha+1)^2} \le \rho_s \le \frac{-2\alpha+1/2}{2\alpha+1}.$$

Proof. Since the Pareto copula has a lower tail dependence, the result holds. □

Proposition 5. *The bivariate distribution* $\mathrm{BPHF}(\alpha_1, \alpha_2, \alpha)$ *has a lower tail dependence.*

4. Bivariate Proportional Hazard Normal Distribution

When $F_{X_1} = F_{X_2} = \Phi$, i.e., the standard normal CDF, we obtain the bivariate PHN distribution, denoted by $\mathrm{BPHN}(\alpha_1,\alpha_2,\alpha)$. The joint PDF of $(X_1, X_2) \sim \mathrm{BPHN}(\alpha_1,\alpha_2,\alpha)$ is given by

$$f_{X_1,X_2}(x_1,x_2) = \frac{(\alpha+1)\alpha_1\alpha_2}{\alpha}\frac{\phi(x_1)[1-\Phi(x_1)]^{-\frac{\alpha_1}{\alpha}-1}\phi(x_2)[1-\Phi(x_2)]^{-\frac{\alpha_2}{\alpha}-1}}{[(1-\Phi(x_1))^{-\frac{\alpha_1}{\alpha}} + (1-\Phi(x_2))^{-\frac{\alpha_2}{\alpha}} - 1]^{\alpha+2}},$$

where $(x_1,x_2) \in \mathbb{R}^2$, $\alpha_1 > 0$, $\alpha_2 > 0$ and $\alpha > 0$. The joint CDF takes the form

$$\begin{aligned} F_{X_1,X_2}(x_1,x_2) &= 1 - (1-\Phi(x_1))^{\alpha_1} - (1-\Phi(x_2))^{\alpha_2} \\ &+ [(1-\Phi(x_1))^{-\frac{\alpha_1}{\alpha}} + (1-\Phi(x_2))^{-\frac{\alpha_2}{\alpha}} - 1]^{-\alpha}. \end{aligned}$$

The marginal distributions of $(X_1, X_2) \sim \mathrm{BPHN}(\alpha_1,\alpha_2,\alpha)$ are $X_j \sim \mathrm{PHN}(\alpha_j)$ for $j = 1,2$. The PDF of X_1, given $X_2 = x_2$, is given by

$$f(X_1 \mid X_2 = x_2) = \frac{(\alpha+1)\alpha_1}{\alpha}\frac{\phi(x_1)[1-\Phi(x_1)]^{-\frac{\alpha_1}{\alpha}-1}[1-\Phi(x_2)]^{-\alpha_2(\frac{\alpha-1}{\alpha})}}{[(1-\Phi(x_1))^{-\frac{\alpha_1}{\alpha}} + (1-\Phi(x_2))^{-\frac{\alpha_2}{\alpha}} - 1]^{\alpha+2}},$$

and the CDF of X_1, given $X_2 = x_2$, is

$$F(X_1 \mid X_2 = x_2) = \frac{[1-\Phi(x_2)]^{-\alpha_2(\frac{\alpha+1}{\alpha})}}{[(1-\Phi(x_1))^{-\frac{\alpha_1}{\alpha}} + (1-\Phi(x_2))^{-\frac{\alpha_2}{\alpha}} - 1]^{\alpha+1}}.$$

The joint survival function of $(X_1, X_2) \sim \mathrm{BPHN}(\alpha_1,\alpha_2,\alpha)$ has the form

$$S_{X_1,X_2}(x_1,x_2) = [(1-\Phi(x_1))^{-\frac{\alpha_1}{\alpha}} + (1-\Phi(x_1))^{-\frac{\alpha_2}{\alpha}} - 1]^{-\alpha}.$$

4.1. Location-Scale Extension

The family of BPHN distributions with location-scale parameters is defined as the joint distribution of $X_1 = \mu_1 + \sigma_1 Z_1$ and $X_2 = \mu_2 + \sigma_2 Z_2$, where $Z_j \sim \text{PHN}(\alpha_j)$, $\mu_j \in \mathbb{R}$ and $\sigma_j > 0$ for $j = 1, 2$. The corresponding joint PDF is given by

$$f_{X_1,X_2}(x_1, x_2) = \frac{(\alpha+1)\alpha_1\alpha_2}{\sigma_1\sigma_2\alpha} \frac{\phi(z_1)[1-\Phi(z_1)]^{-\frac{\alpha_1}{\alpha}-1}\phi(z_2)[1-\Phi(z_2)]^{-\frac{\alpha_2}{\alpha}-1}}{[(1-\Phi(z_1))^{-\frac{\alpha_1}{\alpha}} + (1-\Phi(z_2))^{-\frac{\alpha_2}{\alpha}} - 1]^{\alpha+2}},$$

where μ_j is the location parameter, σ_j is the scale parameter, and

$$z_j = \frac{x_j - \mu_j}{\sigma_j}, \quad j = 1, 2.$$

We use the notation $\text{BPHN}(\mu_1, \sigma_1, \alpha_1, \mu_2, \sigma_2, \alpha_2, \alpha)$ to denote this location-scale extension. Figures 1 and 2 display contour plots of the BPHN distribution for some parameter values.

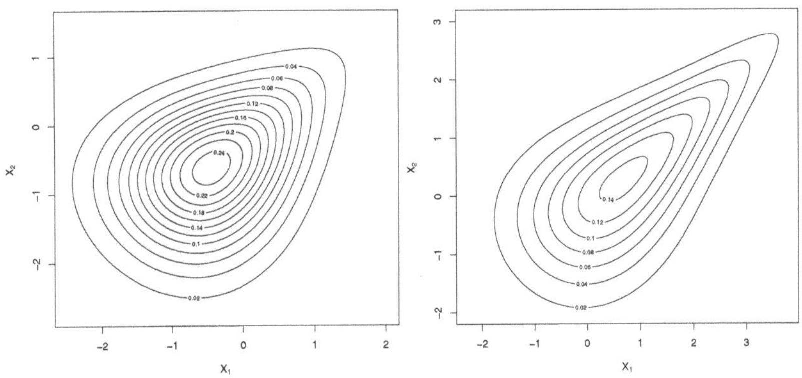

(a) (b)

Figure 1. Contour plots: (**a**) BPHN(0,1,1.75,0,1,2.25,2), and (**b**) BPHN(0,1,0.5,0,1,0.75,0.75).

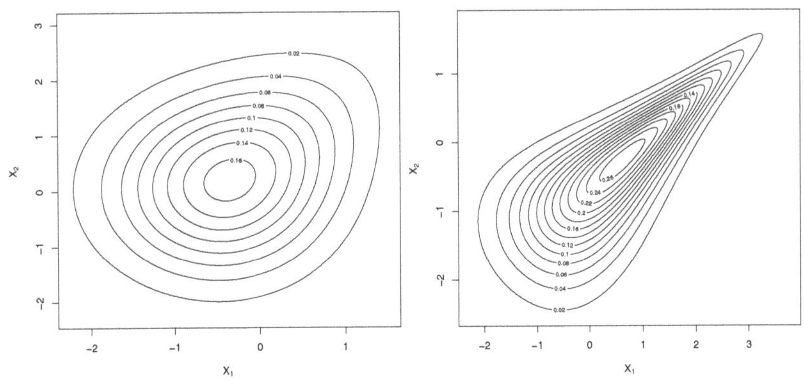

(a) (b)

Figure 2. Contour plots: (**a**) BPHN(0,1,1.5,0,1,0.75,3.5), and (**b**) BPHN(0,1,0.75,0,1,2,0.5).

4.2. Parameter Estimation

In what follows, we consider the issue of estimating the parameters of the BPHN distribution. Given the dependency structure induced by Pareto copula, we use the maximum likelihood (ML) method, and the two-stage method (see [15]) to estimate the parameter vector $\boldsymbol{\theta} = (\mu_1, \sigma_1, \alpha_1, \mu_2, \sigma_2, \alpha_2, \alpha)'$. Initially, as in [5], we perform the following reparameterizations: $\alpha_1 = \alpha\gamma_1$, and $\alpha_2 = \alpha\gamma_2$, so that the interest is focused on the parameter vector $\boldsymbol{\theta}_1 = (\mu_1, \sigma_1, \gamma_1, \mu_2, \sigma_2, \gamma_2, \alpha)'$. Thus, for a sample of size n from the BPHN$(\mu_1, \sigma_1, \gamma_1, \mu_2, \sigma_2, \gamma_2, \alpha)$ distribution, say $(x_{11}, x_{12}), \ldots, (x_{n1}, x_{n2})$, the log-likelihood function is given by

$$\begin{aligned}
\ell(\boldsymbol{\theta}_1) = {} & n\left[\log(\alpha+1) + \log(\alpha) + \sum_{j=1}^{2}\log(\gamma_j) - \sum_{j=1}^{2}\log(\sigma_j)\right] \\
& + \sum_{i=1}^{n}\log(\phi(z_{i1})) + \sum_{i=1}^{n}\log(\phi(z_{i2})) \\
& - \gamma_1\sum_{i=1}^{n}\log[1-\Phi(z_{i1})] - \gamma_2\sum_{i=1}^{n}\log[1-\Phi(z_{i2})] \\
& - (\alpha+2)\sum_{i=1}^{n}\log[(1-\Phi(z_{i1}))^{-\gamma_1} + (1-\Phi(z_{i2}))^{-\gamma_2} - 1],
\end{aligned}$$

where

$$z_{ij} = \frac{x_{ij}-\mu_j}{\sigma_j}, \quad j = 1,2, \quad i = 1,2,\ldots,n.$$

The ML estimate $\widehat{\boldsymbol{\theta}}_1 = (\widehat{\mu}_1, \widehat{\sigma}_1, \widehat{\gamma}_1, \widehat{\mu}_2, \widehat{\sigma}_2, \widehat{\gamma}_2, \widehat{\alpha})'$ of $\boldsymbol{\theta}_1 = (\mu_1, \sigma_1, \gamma_1, \mu_2, \sigma_2, \gamma_2, \alpha)'$ can be obtained from the direct maximization of the log-likelihood function $\ell(\boldsymbol{\theta}_1)$ with respect to the model parameters. Using the R programming language, specifically applying the `optim` function, the maximization of the log-likelihood function can be performed. Also, using the invariance property of the ML estimator, we can easily obtain the ML estimates $\widehat{\alpha}_1$ and $\widehat{\alpha}_2$ of α_1 and α_2, respectively.

The score functions are

$$\begin{aligned}
\frac{\partial\ell(\boldsymbol{\theta}_1)}{\partial\mu_j} = {} & \frac{1}{\sigma_j}\sum_{i=1}^{n} z_{ij} - \frac{\gamma_j}{\sigma_j}\sum_{i=1}^{n}\frac{\phi(z_{ij})}{1-\Phi(z_{ij})} \\
& + \frac{(\alpha+2)\gamma_j}{\sigma_j}\sum_{i=1}^{n}\frac{\phi(z_{ij})(1-\Phi(z_{ij}))^{-\gamma_j-1}}{(1-\Phi(z_{i1}))^{-\gamma_1} + (1-\Phi(z_{i2}))^{-\gamma_2} - 1},
\end{aligned}$$

$$\begin{aligned}
\frac{\partial\ell(\boldsymbol{\theta}_1)}{\partial\sigma_j} = {} & -\frac{n}{\sigma_j} + \frac{1}{\sigma_j}\sum_{i=1}^{n} z_{ij}^2 - \frac{\gamma_j}{\sigma_j}\sum_{i=1}^{n}\frac{z_{ij}\phi(z_{ij})}{1-\Phi(z_{ij})} \\
& + \frac{(\alpha+2)\gamma_j}{\sigma_j}\sum_{i=1}^{n}\frac{z_{ij}\phi(z_{ij})(1-\Phi(z_{ij}))^{-\gamma_j-1}}{(1-\Phi(z_{i1}))^{-\gamma_1} + (1-\Phi(z_{i2}))^{-\gamma_2} - 1},
\end{aligned}$$

$$\begin{aligned}
\frac{\partial\ell(\boldsymbol{\theta}_1)}{\partial\gamma_j} = {} & \frac{n}{\gamma_j} - \sum_{i=1}^{n}\log(1-\Phi(z_{ij})) \\
& + (\alpha+2)\sum_{i=1}^{n}\frac{(1-\Phi(z_{ij}))^{-\gamma_j}\log(1-\Phi(z_{ij}))}{(1-\Phi(z_{i1}))^{-\gamma_1} + (1-\Phi(z_{i2}))^{-\gamma_2} - 1},
\end{aligned}$$

$$\frac{\partial\ell(\boldsymbol{\theta}_1)}{\partial\alpha} = \frac{n}{\alpha+1} + \frac{n}{\alpha} - \sum_{i=1}^{n}\log[(1-\Phi(z_{i1}))^{-\gamma_1} + (1-\Phi(z_{i2}))^{-\gamma_2} - 1],$$

where $j = 1,2$. The ML estimate $\widehat{\boldsymbol{\theta}}_1 = (\widehat{\mu}_1, \widehat{\sigma}_1, \widehat{\gamma}_1, \widehat{\mu}_2, \widehat{\sigma}_2, \widehat{\gamma}_2, \widehat{\alpha})'$ can also be obtained by solving simultaneously the nonlinear system of equations

$$\begin{cases} \dfrac{\partial \ell(\boldsymbol{\theta}_1)}{\partial \mu_j} = 0, \\ \dfrac{\partial \ell(\boldsymbol{\theta}_1)}{\partial \sigma_j} = 0, \\ \dfrac{\partial \ell(\boldsymbol{\theta}_1)}{\partial \gamma_j} = 0, \\ \dfrac{\partial \ell(\boldsymbol{\theta}_1)}{\partial \alpha} = 0. \end{cases}$$

Numerical approaches are required for solving the above nonlinear system of equations, which requires the specification of initial values. To obtain initial values for the model parameters to be used in the iterative process, we can use the two-stage estimation procedure proposed by [15], since this procedure was defined for multivariate copula-based models. The first stage considers ML estimation from univariate marginals, while the second stage considers ML estimation of the dependence parameter with the other parameters held fixed from the first stage:

First stage. Considering that $X_j \sim \text{PHN}(\mu_j, \sigma_j, \alpha_j)$ for $j = 1,2$. We have that the ML estimaties of μ_j, σ_j and α_j are obtained from the solutions of the nonlinear equations

$$\begin{cases} \dfrac{n}{\alpha_j} + \sum\limits_{i=1}^{n} \log(1 - \Phi(z_{ij})) = 0, \\ \sum\limits_{i=1}^{n} z_{ij} + (\alpha_j - 1) \sum\limits_{i=1}^{n} W_{ij} = 0, \\ \sum\limits_{i=1}^{n} z_{ij}^2 + (\alpha + 1) \sum\limits_{i=1}^{n} z_{ij} W_{ij} = n, \end{cases}$$

where

$$W_{ij} = \frac{\phi(z_{ij})}{1 - \Phi(z_{ij})}, \quad j = 1,2, \quad i = 1,2,\ldots,n.$$

The solution of the previous system of equations for each j allows us to obtain the ML estimates $\widetilde{\mu}_j$, $\widetilde{\sigma}_j$ and $\widetilde{\alpha}_j$ of μ_j, σ_j and α_j, respectively, for $j = 1,2$.

Second stage. In this stage, we estimate the parameter α by replacing the unknown parameters with the ML estimates from the previous stage and then maximize the resulting log-likelihood function; that is, we need to maximize the function

$$L(\alpha) = \sum_{i=1} \log[C_\alpha((1 - \Phi(z_{i1}))^{-\hat{\alpha}_1}, (1 - \Phi(z_{i2}))^{-\hat{\alpha}_2}],$$

where

$$\log[C_\alpha(u,v)] = \log\left(\frac{\alpha+1}{\alpha}\right) - \left(1 + \frac{1}{\alpha}\right) \log((1-u)(1-v)) \\ - (\alpha+2) \log[(1-u)^{-\frac{1}{\alpha}} + (1-v)^{-\frac{1}{\alpha}} - 1],$$

so that we have the score function

$$\frac{\partial L(\alpha)}{\partial \alpha} = -\frac{1}{\alpha(\alpha+1)} + \frac{1}{\alpha^2} \log[(1-u)(1-v)] \\ - \log[(1-u)^{-\frac{1}{\alpha}} + (1-v)^{-\frac{1}{\alpha}} - 1].$$

The solution of the resulting equation $\partial L(\alpha)/\partial\alpha = 0$ lead us to the estimate $\widetilde{\alpha}$ of α.

We can also consider another alternative to obtain initial values for the model parameters by using the method proposed by [16], where we initially normalize each variable to obtain a model that depends only on α_1, α_2 and α; that is, we have the log-likelihood function

$$\begin{aligned}\ell(\gamma_1,\gamma_2,\alpha) &= \alpha n \log(\alpha(\alpha+1)\gamma_1\gamma_2) - \sum_{i=1}^{n}\sum_{j=1}^{2}\gamma_j \log(1-\Phi(z_{ij})) \\ &\quad - (\alpha+2)\sum_{i=1}^{n}\log((1-\Phi(z_{i1}))^{-\gamma_1} + (1-\Phi(z_{i2}))^{-\gamma_2} - 1).\end{aligned}$$

After doing

$$\frac{\partial \ell(\gamma_1,\gamma_2,\alpha)}{\partial \alpha} = 0,$$

we obtain

$$\widetilde{\alpha}(\gamma_1,\gamma_2) = \frac{(2-A)+\sqrt{4+A^2}}{2A},$$

where

$$A := A(\gamma_1,\gamma_2) = \frac{1}{n}\sum_{i=1}^{n}\log((1-\Phi(z_{i1}))^{-\gamma_1} + (1-\Phi(z_{i2}))^{-\gamma_2} - 1).$$

Thus, the new profiled log-likelihood function $\ell_p(\widetilde{\alpha}(\gamma_1,\gamma_2),\gamma_1,\gamma_2)$ is reached. After obtaining the estimates $\widetilde{\gamma}_1$ and $\widetilde{\gamma}_2$ of γ_1 and γ_2, respectively, we then obtain an estimate for α as $\widetilde{\alpha}(\widetilde{\gamma}_1,\widetilde{\gamma}_2)$. We can take as initial values for μ_1 and μ_2 the sample means, and for σ_1 and σ_2 the sample standard deviations, or we can replace $\widetilde{\gamma}_1$, $\widetilde{\gamma}_2$ and $\widetilde{\alpha}$ in the original log-likelihood to obtain the initial values for μ_1, μ_2, σ_1 and σ_2.

When n is large, we have that $\widehat{\boldsymbol{\theta}}_1 \overset{a}{\sim} \mathcal{N}_7(\boldsymbol{\theta}_1, \boldsymbol{J}(\boldsymbol{\theta}_1)^{-1})$, where "$\overset{a}{\sim}$" means approximately distributed, $\boldsymbol{J}(\boldsymbol{\theta}_1) = -E(\boldsymbol{H}(\boldsymbol{\theta}_1))$ is the expected Fisher information matrix for $\boldsymbol{\theta}_1$, and $\boldsymbol{H}(\boldsymbol{\theta}_1) = \partial^2\ell(\boldsymbol{\theta}_1)/\partial\boldsymbol{\theta}_1\partial\boldsymbol{\theta}_1'$ is the Hessian matrix, whose elements are provided in the Appendix A. Using the transformation method, we have that $\widehat{\boldsymbol{\theta}} \overset{a}{\sim} \mathcal{N}_7(\boldsymbol{\theta}, \boldsymbol{K}(\boldsymbol{\theta})^{-1})$, where $\boldsymbol{K}(\boldsymbol{\theta}) = \boldsymbol{D}'\boldsymbol{J}(\boldsymbol{\theta}_1)\boldsymbol{D}$ with $\boldsymbol{K}(\boldsymbol{\theta})^{-1}$ denoting its inverse, and

$$\boldsymbol{D} = \begin{pmatrix} 1 & 0 & 0 & 0 & 0 & 0 & 0 \\ 0 & 1 & 0 & 0 & 0 & 0 & 0 \\ 0 & 0 & \alpha & 0 & 0 & 0 & \dfrac{\alpha_1}{\alpha} \\ 0 & 0 & 0 & 1 & 0 & 0 & 0 \\ 0 & 0 & 0 & 0 & 1 & 0 & 0 \\ 0 & 0 & 0 & 0 & 0 & \alpha & \dfrac{\alpha_2}{\alpha} \\ 0 & 0 & -\dfrac{\alpha}{\alpha_1} & 0 & 0 & -\dfrac{\alpha}{\alpha_2} & 1 \end{pmatrix}.$$

The elements of $\boldsymbol{J}(\boldsymbol{\theta}_1)$ are obtained in terms of numerical integration. On the other hand, the observed Fisher information matrix given by $-\boldsymbol{H}(\widehat{\boldsymbol{\theta}}_1)$ can also be used for computing asymptotic standard errors for the ML estimates of the model parameters (see Appendix A). After computing $-\boldsymbol{H}(\widehat{\boldsymbol{\theta}}_1)$, we obtain the observed Fisher information matrix under $\boldsymbol{\theta}$-parametrization as $-\widehat{\boldsymbol{D}}'\boldsymbol{H}(\widehat{\boldsymbol{\theta}}_1)\widehat{\boldsymbol{D}}$, where $\widehat{\boldsymbol{D}} := \boldsymbol{D}(\widehat{\alpha}_1,\widehat{\alpha}_2,\widehat{\alpha})$. It is worth emphisizing that the observed information matrix can be computed numerically from standard maximization routines, which now provide the observed information matrix as part of their output. For example, one can use the R functions `optim` or `nlm` to compute the observed Fisher information matrix numerically.

4.3. Monte Carlo Simulation

In the following, we consider Monte Carlo simulation experiments to evaluate the performance of the ML estimation procedure discussed in the previous section to estimate the BPHN distribution parameters. It is worth emphasizing that is rather easy to generate random variates from the BPHN distribution. We consider the following steps to generate (X_1, X_2) from BPHN$(\mu_1, \sigma_1, \alpha_1, \mu_2, \sigma_2, \alpha_2, \alpha)$ distribution:

Step 1. Generate two independent random variates $U_1 \sim \mathcal{U}(0,1)$ and $U_2 \sim \mathcal{U}(0,1)$, where $\mathcal{U}(0,1)$ means a uniform distribution on $(0,1)$.

Step 2. Compute

$$X_2 = \mu_2 + \sigma_2 \Phi^{-1}(1 - (1 - U_2)^{1/\alpha_2}),$$

where $\Phi^{-1}(\cdot)$ is the standard normal quantile function.

Step 3. Define $B_1 = [1 - \Phi(X_2)]^{-\alpha_2(\alpha+1)/\alpha}$ and $B_2 = [1 - \Phi(X_2)]^{-\alpha_2/\alpha} - 1$. Let $B_3 = [(B_1/U_1)^{1/(\alpha+1)} - B_2]^{-\alpha/\alpha_1}$. For each value of X_2, compute

$$X_1 = \mu_1 + \sigma_1 \Phi^{-1}(1 - B_3).$$

Then, $(X_1, X_2) \sim$ BPHN$(\mu_1, \sigma_1, \alpha_1, \mu_2, \sigma_2, \alpha_2, \alpha)$.

The Monte Carlo experiments were performed using the R programming language, and we consider 10,000 Monte Carlo replications. The performance of the ML procedure to estimate the BPHN distribution parameters was evaluated on the basis of the following quantities for each sample size: the empirical mean, and the empirical standard deviation, which are computed from 10,000 replications. The sample sizes we consider are $n = 90$ and 150. Without loss of generality, we consider $\mu_1 = 1.5$, $\sigma_1 = \sigma_2 = 1.0$, $\alpha_1 = 0.5$, $\mu_2 = -0.5$, $\alpha_2 = 1.2$, and $\alpha = 0.2, 0.4, 0.6, 0.8, 1.0, 1.2$ and 1.5. The emprical mean is listed in Table 1, while the empirical standard deviation is listed in Table 2. In general, from Table 1, note that the ML estimates of μ_1, σ_1, α_1, μ_2, σ_2 and α_2 are close to their respective true values, while the parameter that controls the dependence in the Pareto copula, α, is overestimated, mainly as this parameter increases. As expected, the standard deviation of the ML estimates of all parameters decreases as the sample size increases (see Table 2). In short, the Monte Carlo simulation experiments reveal that the ML method can be used effectively to estimate the BPHN parameters.

Table 1. Parameter estimates; empirical mean.

n	α	μ_1	σ_1	α_1	μ_2	σ_2	α_2	α
90	0.2	1.024	0.876	0.495	−0.378	1.034	1.539	0.321
	0.4	1.192	0.903	0.566	−0.403	1.008	1.371	0.632
	0.6	1.364	0.950	0.665	−0.483	0.986	1.271	0.941
	0.8	1.376	0.948	0.632	−0.555	0.965	1.176	1.256
	0.8	1.419	0.959	0.651	−0.576	0.959	1.178	1.553
	1.0	1.406	0.953	0.619	−0.591	0.956	1.145	1.821
	1.5	1.426	0.962	0.613	−0.612	0.949	1.121	2.303
150	0.2	0.990	0.864	0.471	−0.339	1.053	1.599	0.318
	0.4	1.172	0.898	0.540	−0.395	1.016	1.362	0.625
	0.6	1.319	0.936	0.608	−0.487	0.991	1.248	0.931
	0.8	1.391	0.955	0.635	−0.550	0.974	1.167	1.224
	1.0	1.427	0.963	0.643	−0.543	0.978	1.182	1.523
	1.2	1.430	0.963	0.628	−0.552	0.976	1.178	1.805
	1.5	1.458	0.972	0.627	−0.601	0.960	1.125	2.192

Table 2. Parameter estimates; empirical standard deviation.

n	α	μ_1	σ_1	α_1	μ_2	σ_2	α_2	α
90	0.2	0.251	0.117	0.158	0.195	0.081	0.326	0.037
	0.4	0.370	0.152	0.259	0.273	0.102	0.416	0.089
	0.6	0.460	0.175	0.389	0.314	0.117	0.452	0.153
	0.8	0.426	0.169	0.319	0.315	0.117	0.412	0.248
	1.0	0.480	0.178	0.372	0.387	0.137	0.533	0.348
	1.2	0.470	0.180	0.329	0.368	0.135	0.465	0.387
	1.5	0.463	0.181	0.326	0.364	0.124	0.483	0.620
150	0.2	0.236	0.103	0.147	0.193	0.072	0.326	0.028
	0.4	0.289	0.120	0.202	0.207	0.075	0.312	0.065
	0.6	0.348	0.137	0.255	0.263	0.094	0.359	0.113
	0.8	0.384	0.149	0.295	0.283	0.100	0.359	0.165
	1.0	0.420	0.156	0.317	0.293	0.101	0.378	0.223
	1.2	0.431	0.164	0.311	0.316	0.109	0.411	0.290
	1.5	0.432	0.161	0.311	0.352	0.119	0.428	0.368

5. Real Data Application

Next, we consider an application of the BPHN distribution to real data for illustrative purposes. The data set contains two different measures of stiffness of each of the 30 boards. The considered stiffness measures are the Shock (X_1) and Vibration (X_2) of each of the 30 boards. The data were reported by [17]. The first measurement involves sending a shock wave down the board, and the second measurement is determined while vibrating the board. All numerical computations provided in this were done by using the R program.

We assume that $(X_{1i}, X_{2i}) \sim \text{BPHN}(\mu_1, \sigma_1, \alpha_1, \mu_2, \sigma_2, \alpha_2, \alpha)$ for $i = 1, 2, \ldots, 30$. To estimate the BPHN model parameters, we initially estimate the marginal PDFs corresponding to each variable. We thus obtain the following estimates: $\widetilde{\mu}_1 = 1554.82$, $\widetilde{\sigma}_1 = 176.34$, $\widetilde{\alpha}_1 = 0.18$, $\widetilde{\mu}_2 = 1393.59$, $\widetilde{\sigma}_2 = 173.79$, and $\widetilde{\alpha}_2 = 0.17$. Figure 3a,b display the QQ-plots for the estimated marginal distributions. Note the goodness-of-fit of each estimated marginal distribution to the real data, which means that the BPHN distribution may be a good choice for modeling these data. Now, using the above estimates in the copula function, we obtain an estimate for the parameter α, that is, $\widetilde{\alpha} = 0.35$. Finally, taking the above estimates as initial values for the iterative process, we obtain the following ML estimates (standard errors in parentheses): $\widehat{\mu}_1 = 1529.91(184.47)$, $\widehat{\sigma}_1 = 277.53(48.13)$, $\widehat{\alpha}_1 = 0.28(0.17)$, $\widehat{\mu}_2 = 1428.44(87.82)$, $\widehat{\sigma}_2 = 184.49(33.33)$, $\widehat{\alpha}_2 = 0.16(0.05)$, and $\widehat{\alpha} = 0.27(0.12)$. Visual inspection of the contour plot in Figure 3c confirms a satisfactory fit of the BPHN distribution to the data.

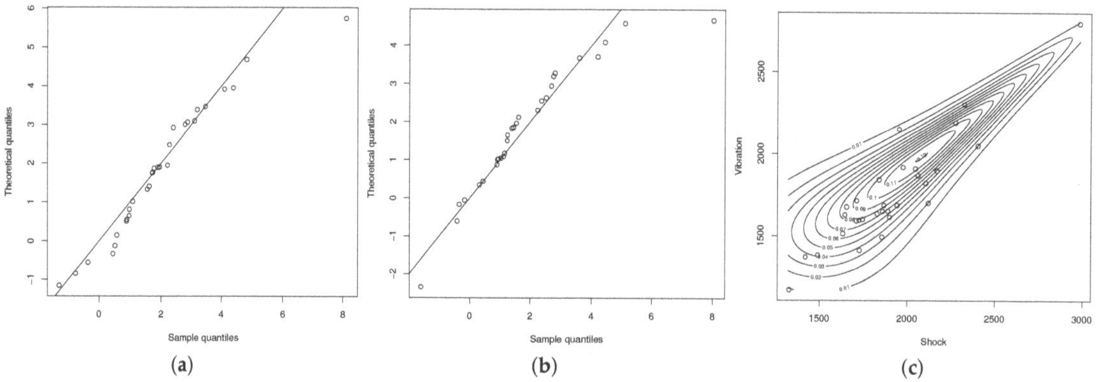

Figure 3. QQ-plots and contour plot: (**a**) Shock, (**b**) Vibration, and (**c**) contour plot of the BPHN distribution.

Next, for the sake of comparison, we also consider the following bivariate distributions to fit the current real data: the bivariate skew-normal conditional (BVSNC) distribution introduced by [9], denoted by BVSNC$(\xi_1, \eta_1, \xi_2, \eta_2, \lambda)$, and the bivariate Birnbaum-Saunders (BVBS) distribution studied by [10], denoted by BVBS$(\alpha_1, \beta_1, \alpha_2, \beta_2, \lambda)$. The ML estimates (standard errors in parentheses) of the BVSNC parameters are $\widehat{\xi}_1 = 1927.51(26.65)$, $\widehat{\xi}_2 = 1745.35(30.38)$, $\widehat{\eta}_1 = 320.31(41.40)$, $\widehat{\eta}_2 = 313.23(40.43)$ and $\widehat{\lambda} = 10.88(5.01)$, whereas the ML estimates (standard errors in parentheses) of the BVBS parameters are $\widehat{\alpha}_1 = 0.1621(0.0210)$, $\widehat{\alpha}_2 = 0.1701(0.0219)$, $\widehat{\beta}_1 = 1917.22(22.26)$, $\widehat{\beta}_2 = 1734.76(29.32)$ and $\widehat{\lambda} = 10.29(4.86)$. To compare the bivariate distributions, we make use of the Akaike information criterion (AIC), and Bayesian information criterion (BIC). The smaller the values of AIC and BIC, the better the fitted distribution to the real data. Table 3 lists the AIC and BIC values for all bivariate distributions, which leads to the conclusion that the BPHN distribution is better than the other bivariate distributions to model the current bivariate real data.

Table 3. AIC and BIC values.

Measure	BVSNC	BVBS	BPHN
AIC	842.99	835.82	828.27
BIC	850.00	842.83	838.08

6. Concluding Remarks

The univariate proportional hazard distribution has found several applications in the literature and has many attractive properties. However, the extension of the univariate proportional hazard distribution in a multivariate setting has been so neglected in the statistical literature. In this paper, based on the Pareto copula, we have introduced a simple and tractable bivariate proportional hazard family of distributions that may be very useful to deal with bivariate data in practice. We also derive several distribution properties for this bivariate family of distributions. In addition, we particularize this general bivariate distribution to the case where the univariate normal distribution is considered, so that the bivariate proportional hazard normal distribution is obtained. The estimation of the bivariate proportional hazard normal model parameters is approached by the maximum likelihood method, and the observed and expected Fisher information matrixes are derived. Finally, an application to real data set is presented to illustrate the bivariate proportional hazard normal distribution in practice.

Author Contributions: Conceptualization, G.M.-F., A.J.L. and C.B.-C.; data curation, G.M.-F., A.J.L. and C.B.-C.; formal analysis, G.M.-F., A.J.L. and C.B.-C.; funding acquisition, C.B.-C.; investigation, G.M.-F. and A.J.L. and C.B.-C.; methodology, G.M.-F., A.J.L. and C.B.-C.; project administration, G.M.-F., A.J.L. and C.B.-C.; resources, G.M.-F., A.J.L. and C.B.-C.; supervision, G.M.-F., A.J.L. and C.B.-C.; visualization, C.B.-C.; writing—original draft, G.M.-F. and A.J.L. and C.B.-C.; writing—review and editing, A.J.L. and C.B.-C. All authors have read and agreed to the published version of the manuscript.

Funding: This research was funded by the Instituto Tecnológico Metropolitano (ITM).

Data Availability Statement: Not applicable.

Acknowledgments: G.M.-F. acknowledges the support given by Universidad de Córdoba, Montería, Colombia. A.J.L. acknowledges the financial support of the Brazilian agency *Conselho Nacional de Desenvolvimento Científico e Tecnológico* (CNPq grant 304776/2019–0). C.B.-C. extends their sincere gratitude to the Instituto Tecnológico Metropolitano (ITM). The authors would like to thank the anonymous reviewers for their insightful comments and suggestions.

Conflicts of Interest: The authors declare no conflict of interest.

Appendix A. Observed Fisher Information Matrix

In the following, we calculate the elements of the Hessian matrix $\boldsymbol{H}(\boldsymbol{\theta}_1)$ and their respective expected values. For $j = 1, 2$ and $i = 1, 2, \ldots, n$, let

$$f_{ij} = \frac{\gamma_j}{\sigma_j}\phi(z_{ij})(1 - \Phi(z_{ij}))^{-\gamma_j - 1}, \quad W_{ij} = \frac{\phi(z_{ij})}{1 - \Phi(z_{ij})},$$

$$DN_i = (1 - \Phi(z_{i1}))^{-\gamma_1} + (1 - \Phi(z_{i2}))^{-\gamma_2} - 1,$$
$$H_{ij} = (1 - \Phi(z_{ij}))^{-\gamma_j} \log((1 - \Phi(z_{ij}))).$$

We have the following derivatives ($j' = 1, 2$):

$$\frac{\partial^2 \ell(\boldsymbol{\theta}_1)}{\partial \alpha^2} = -\frac{n}{(\alpha+1)^2} - \frac{n}{\alpha^2}, \quad \frac{\partial^2 \ell(\boldsymbol{\theta}_1)}{\partial \alpha \partial \gamma_j} = \sum_{i=1}^{n} \frac{H_{ij}}{DN_i},$$

$$\frac{\partial^2 \ell(\boldsymbol{\theta}_1)}{\partial \alpha \partial \mu_j} = \sum_{i=1}^{n} \frac{f_{ij}}{DN_i}, \quad \frac{\partial^2 \ell(\boldsymbol{\theta}_1)}{\partial \alpha \partial \sigma_j} = \sum_{i=1}^{n} \frac{z_{ij} f_{ij}}{DN_i},$$

$$\frac{\partial^2 \ell(\boldsymbol{\theta}_1)}{\partial \gamma_j^2} = -\frac{n}{\gamma_j^2} + (\alpha+2) \sum_{i=1}^{n} [H_{ij} - \log(1 - \Phi(z_{ij}))] \frac{H_{ij}}{DN_i},$$

$$\frac{\partial^2 \ell(\boldsymbol{\theta}_1)}{\partial \gamma_1 \partial \gamma_2} = (\alpha+2) \sum_{i=1}^{n} \prod_{j=1}^{2} \frac{H_{ij}}{DN_i^2},$$

$$\begin{aligned}\frac{\partial^2 \ell(\boldsymbol{\theta}_1)}{\partial \mu_j \partial \gamma_j} &= -\frac{1}{\sigma_j} \sum_{i=1}^{n} W_{ij} \\ &\quad - (\alpha+2) \sum_{i=1}^{n} \frac{f_{ij}}{DN_i} \left[\log(1 - \Phi(z_{ij})) - \frac{H_{ij}}{DN_i} - \frac{1}{\gamma_j} \right],\end{aligned}$$

$$\begin{aligned}\frac{\partial^2 \ell(\boldsymbol{\theta}_1)}{\partial \sigma_j \partial \gamma_j} &= -\frac{1}{\sigma_j} \sum_{i=1}^{n} z_{ij} W_{ij} \\ &\quad - (\alpha+2) \sum_{i=1}^{n} \frac{z_{ij} f_{ij}}{DN_i} \left[\log(1 - \Phi(z_{ij})) - \frac{H_{ij}}{DN_i} - \frac{1}{\gamma_j} \right],\end{aligned}$$

$$\frac{\partial^2 \ell(\boldsymbol{\theta}_1)}{\partial \mu_{j'} \partial \mu_j} = -(\alpha+2) \sum_{i=1}^{n} \frac{f_{ij} f_{ij'}}{DN_i^2}, \quad j \neq j',$$

$$\frac{\partial^2 \ell(\boldsymbol{\theta}_1)}{\partial \mu_{j'} \partial \gamma_j} = -(\alpha+2) \sum_{i=1}^{n} \frac{H_{ij} f_{ij'}}{DN_i^2}, \quad j \neq j',$$

$$\frac{\partial^2 \ell(\boldsymbol{\theta}_1)}{\partial \sigma_{j'} \partial \gamma_j} = -(\alpha+2) \sum_{i=1}^{n} \frac{z_{ij'} H_{ij} f_{ij'}}{DN_i^2}, \quad j \neq j',$$

$$\begin{aligned}\frac{\partial^2 \ell(\boldsymbol{\theta}_1)}{\partial \mu_j^2} &= -\frac{n}{\sigma_j^2} - \frac{\gamma_j}{\sigma_j^2} \sum_{i=1}^{n} [z_{ij} W_{ij} + W_{ij}^2] \\ &\quad + \frac{\alpha+2}{\sigma_j} \sum_{i=1}^{n} \frac{f_{ij}}{DN_i} \left[z_{ij} - (\gamma_j + 1) W_{ij} + \frac{\sigma_j}{\gamma_j} \frac{f_{ij}}{DN_i} \right],\end{aligned}$$

$$\frac{\partial^2 \ell(\boldsymbol{\theta}_1)}{\partial \mu_j \partial \sigma_{j'}} = -(\alpha+2) \sum_{i=1}^{n} \frac{z_{ij'} f_{ij} f_{ij'}}{DN_i^2}, \quad j \neq j',$$

$$\frac{\partial^2\ell(\boldsymbol{\theta}_1)}{\partial\mu_j\partial\sigma_j} = -\frac{2}{\sigma_j^2}\sum_{i=1}^{n} z_{ij} + \frac{\alpha+2}{\sigma_j}\sum_{i=1}^{n}\frac{f_{ij}}{DN_i}\left[z_{ij}^2 - 1 - (\gamma_j+1)z_{ij}W_{ij} + \frac{\sigma_j z_{ij} f_{ij}}{DN_i}\right] - \frac{\gamma_j}{\sigma_j}\sum_{i=1}^{n}[(z_{ij}^2 - z_{ij}W_{ij} - 1)W_{ij}],$$

$$\frac{\partial^2\ell(\boldsymbol{\theta}_1)}{\partial\sigma_j\partial\sigma_{j'}} = -(\alpha+2)\sum_{i=1}^{n}\frac{z_{ij}z_{ij'}f_{ij}f_{ij'}}{DN_i^2}, \quad j \neq j',$$

$$\frac{\partial^2\ell(\boldsymbol{\theta}_1)}{\partial\sigma_j^2} = \frac{n}{\sigma_j} - \frac{3}{\sigma_j^2}\sum_{i=1}^{n} z_{ij}^2 + \frac{\alpha+2}{\sigma_j}\sum_{i=1}^{n}\frac{z_{ij}f_{ij}}{DN_i}\left[z_{ij}^2 - 2 - \frac{(\gamma_j+1)}{\gamma_j}f_{ij} + \frac{z_{ij}f_{ij}}{DN_i}\right] - \frac{\gamma_j}{\sigma_j}\sum_{i=1}^{n}[(z_{ij}^2 + z_{ij}W_{ij} - 1)z_{ij}W_{ij}].$$

Let

$$a_{kj} = E\left[z^k\left(\frac{\phi(z)}{1-\Phi(z)}\right)^j\right],$$

and $g(u) = \Phi^{-1}(1 - u^{1/\gamma_j})$, where $\Phi^{-1}(\cdot)$ is the quantile function of the standard normal distribution. We have the expected values:

$$E\left(\frac{\partial^2\ell(\boldsymbol{\theta}_1)}{\partial\gamma_j^2}\right) = -\frac{n}{\gamma_j^2}\left[1 + \frac{2(\alpha+1)}{(\alpha+3)\alpha^2}\right],$$

$$E\left(\frac{\partial^2\ell(\boldsymbol{\theta}_1)}{\partial\alpha\partial\gamma_j}\right) = -\frac{n(\alpha+1)}{\alpha\gamma_j},$$

$$E\left(\frac{\partial^2\ell(\boldsymbol{\theta}_1)}{\partial\gamma_j\partial\gamma_{j'}}\right) = -n\alpha(\alpha+1)(\alpha+2)\int_1^{\infty}\int_1^{0}\frac{uv\log(u)\log(v)}{(u+v-1)^{\alpha+4}}dudv, \quad j \neq j',$$

$$E\left(\frac{\partial^2\ell(\boldsymbol{\theta}_1)}{\partial\alpha^2}\right) = \frac{n}{\alpha^2} + \frac{n}{(1+\alpha)^2},$$

$$E\left(\frac{\partial^2\ell(\boldsymbol{\theta}_1)}{\partial\alpha\partial\mu_j}\right) = -\frac{n\alpha(\alpha+1)\gamma_j}{\sigma_j(\alpha+2)}\int_1^{\infty}\phi(g(u))u^{\frac{1}{\gamma_j}-\alpha-1}du,$$

$$E\left(\frac{\partial^2\ell(\boldsymbol{\theta}_1)}{\partial\alpha\partial\sigma_j}\right) = -\frac{n\alpha(\alpha+1)\gamma_j}{\sigma_j(\alpha+2)}\int_1^{\infty}g(u)\phi(g(u))u^{\frac{1}{\gamma_j}-\alpha-1}du,$$

$$E\left(\frac{\partial^2\ell(\boldsymbol{\theta}_1)}{\partial\mu_j\partial\gamma_j}\right) = -\frac{na_{01}}{\sigma_j} + \frac{n\alpha(\alpha+1)}{\sigma_j}\int_1^{\infty}\phi(g(u))\log(u)u^{\frac{1}{\gamma_j}-\alpha-1}du + \frac{n}{\sigma_j(\alpha+3)}\int_1^{\infty}\phi(g(u))\log(u)u^{\frac{1}{\gamma_j}-\alpha-1}du,$$

$$E\left(\frac{\partial^2\ell(\boldsymbol{\theta}_1)}{\partial\sigma_j\partial\gamma_j}\right) = -\frac{na_{11}}{\sigma_j} + \frac{n\alpha(\alpha+1)}{\sigma_j}\int_1^{\infty}g(u)\phi(g(u))\log(u)u^{\frac{1}{\gamma_j}-\alpha-1}du,$$

$$E\left(\frac{\partial^2\ell(\boldsymbol{\theta}_1)}{\partial\mu_{j'}\partial\gamma_j}\right)=-\frac{n(\alpha+2)(\alpha+1)}{\sigma_j}\int_1^\infty\int_1^\infty\frac{u\phi(g(u))\log(u)v^{\frac{1}{\gamma_j}+1}}{(u+v-1)^{\alpha+4}}dudv,$$

$$E\left(\frac{\partial^2\ell(\boldsymbol{\theta}_1)}{\partial\sigma_{j'}\partial\gamma_j}\right)=-\frac{n\alpha(\alpha+1)(\alpha+2)}{\sigma_{j'}}\times$$
$$\int_1^\infty\int_1^\infty\frac{ug(u)\phi(g(u))\log(u)v^{\frac{1}{\gamma_j}+1}}{(u+v-1)^{\alpha+4}}dudv,\quad j\neq j',$$

$$E\left(\frac{\partial^2\ell(\boldsymbol{\theta}_1)}{\partial\mu_j\partial\mu_{j'}}\right)=-\frac{n\alpha(\alpha+1)(\alpha+2)\gamma_j\gamma_{j'}}{\sqrt{2\pi}\sigma_j\sigma_{j'}}\times$$
$$\int_1^\infty\int_1^\infty\frac{\phi(g(u)+g(v))u^{\frac{1}{\gamma_j}+1}}{(u+v-1)^{\alpha+4}}dudv,\quad j\neq j',$$

$$E\left(\frac{\partial^2\ell(\boldsymbol{\theta}_1)}{\partial\mu_j\partial\sigma_{j'}}\right)=-\frac{n\alpha(\alpha+1)(\alpha+2)\gamma_j\gamma_{j'}}{\sqrt{2\pi}\sigma_j\sigma_{j'}}\times$$
$$\int_1^\infty\int_1^\infty\frac{g(v)\phi(g(u)+g(v))u^{\frac{1}{\gamma_j}+1}v^{\frac{1}{\gamma_j}+1}}{(u+v-1)^{\alpha+2}}dudv,\quad j\neq j',$$

$$E\left(\frac{\partial^2\ell(\boldsymbol{\theta}_1)}{\partial\sigma_j\partial\sigma_{j'}}\right)=-\frac{n\alpha(\alpha+1)(\alpha+2)\gamma_j\gamma_{j'}}{\sigma_j\sigma_{j'}}\times$$
$$\int_1^\infty\int_1^\infty\frac{g(u)g(v)\phi(g(u)+g(v))u^{\frac{1}{\gamma_j}+1}v^{\frac{1}{\gamma_j}+1}}{(u+v-1)^{\alpha+4}}dudv,\quad j\neq j',$$

$$E\left(\frac{\partial^2\ell(\boldsymbol{\theta}_1)}{\partial\mu_j^2}\right)=-\frac{n}{\sigma_j^2}-\frac{n\gamma_j[a_{11}+a_{02}]}{\sigma_j^2}+\frac{n\alpha(\alpha+2)(\alpha+1)}{\sigma_j}\times$$
$$\int_1^\infty\int_1^\infty\frac{\phi(g(u))}{(u+v-1)^{\alpha+3}}\left[g(u)-(\gamma_j+1)\phi(g(u))u^{\frac{1}{\gamma_j}}\right.$$
$$\left.+\frac{\phi(g(u))u^{1+\frac{1}{\gamma_j}}}{(u+v-1)}\right]dudv,$$

$$
\begin{aligned}
E\left(\frac{\partial^2 \ell(\boldsymbol{\theta}_1)}{\partial \sigma_j^2}\right) = & \frac{n}{\sigma_j^2} - \frac{3na_{20}}{\sigma_j^2} - \frac{n\gamma_j}{\sigma_j^2}[a_{21} - a_{11} + a_{22}] \\
& - \frac{\alpha(\alpha+1)(\alpha+2)\gamma_j}{\sigma_j^2} \int_1^\infty \int_1^\infty \frac{g(u)\phi(g(u))u^{\frac{1}{\gamma_j}+1}}{(u+v-1)^{\alpha+3}} dudv \\
& + \frac{n\alpha(\alpha+1)(\alpha+2)}{\sigma_j} \times \\
& \int_1^\infty \int_1^\infty \left[\frac{\sqrt{2\pi}\gamma_j}{\sigma_j^2} \frac{\phi(g(u))u^{\frac{1}{\gamma_j}+1}}{(u+v-1)^{\alpha+3}} [-1 + (g(u))^2 + (\gamma_j+1)\sqrt{2\pi}\phi(g(u))] \right. \\
& \left. + \frac{\gamma_j^2 (g(u))^2 \phi(g(u)) u^{\frac{2}{\gamma_j}+2}}{\sqrt{2\pi}\sigma_j^2 (u+v-1)^2} \right] dudv.
\end{aligned}
$$

References

1. Durrans, S.R. Distributions of fractional order statistics in hydrology. *Water Resour. Res.* **1992**, *28*, 1649–1655. [CrossRef]
2. Martínez-Flórez, G.; Moreno-Arenas, G.; Vergara-Cardoso, S. Properties and Inference for Proportional Hazard Models. *Colomb. J. Stat.* **2013**, *36*, 95–114.
3. Wang, B.; Yu, K.; Jones, M. Inference under progressively type II right-censored sampling for certain lifetime distributions. *Technometrics* **2010**, *52*, 453–460. [CrossRef]
4. Cordeiro, G.M.; de Castro, M. A new family of generalized distributions. *J. Stat. Comput. Simul.* **2011**, *81*, 883–898. [CrossRef]
5. Kundu, D.; Gupta, R. Power normal distribution. *Statistics* **2013**, *47*, 110–125. [CrossRef]
6. Clayton, D.G. A model for association in bivariate life tables and its application in epidemiological studies of familial tendency in chronic disease incidence. *Biometrika* **1978**, *65*, 141–152. [CrossRef]
7. Kimeldorf, G.; Sampson, A.R. Uniform representations of bivariate distributions. *Commun. Stat. Theory Methods* **1975**, *4*, 617–627. [CrossRef]
8. Cook, R.D.; Johnson, M.E. A family of distributions for modelling non-elliptically symmetric multivariate data. *J. R. Stat. Soc. B* **1981**, *43*, 210–218. [CrossRef]
9. Arnold, B.C.; Castilho, E.; Sarabia, J.M. Conditionally specified multivariate skewed distributions. *Sankhya A* **2002**, *64*, 206–226.
10. Lemonte, A.J.; Martínez-Flórez, G.; Moreno-Arenas, G. Multivariate Birnbaum–Saunders distribution: Properties and associated inference. *J. Stat. Comput. Simul.* **2015**, *85*, 374–392. [CrossRef]
11. Martínez-Flórez, G.; Lemonte, A.J.; Salinas, H.S. Multivariate skew-power-normal distributions: Properties and associated inference. *Symmetry* **2019**, *11*, 1509. [CrossRef]
12. Zhang, L.; Xu, A.; An, L.; Li, M. Bayesian inference of system reliability for multicomponent stress-strength model under Marshall-Olkin Weibull distribution. *Systems* **2022**, *10*, 196. [CrossRef]
13. Nelsen, R.B. *An Introduction to Copulas*; Springer: New York, NY, USA, 2006.
14. Marshall, A.W. Some comments on the hazard gradient. *Stoch. Process. Their Appl.* **1975**, *3*, 293–300. [CrossRef]
15. Joe, H. Asymptotic efficiency of two-stage estimation method for copula-based models. *J. Multivar. Anal.* **2005**, *94*, 401–419. [CrossRef]
16. Gupta, D.; Gupta, R.C. Analyzing skewed data by power normal model. *Test* **2008**, *17*, 197–210. [CrossRef]
17. Johnson, R.A.; Wichern, D.W. *Applied Multivariate Statistical Analysis*; Pearson Prentice Hall: Upper Saddle River, NJ, USA, 2007.

mathematics

MDPI

Article

COVID-19 Active Case Forecasts in Latin American Countries Using Score-Driven Models

Sergio Contreras-Espinoza [1,*], Francisco Novoa-Muñoz [1], Szabolcs Blazsek [2], Pedro Vidal [1] and Christian Caamaño-Carrillo [1]

1 Departamento de Estadística, Facultad de Ciencias, Universidad del Bío-Bío, Concepción 4081112, Chile
2 Escuela de Negocios, Universidad Francisco Marroquín, Guatemala City 01011, Guatemala
* Correspondence: scontre@ubiobio.cl; Tel.: +56-9-75873480

Abstract: With the aim of mitigating the damage caused by the coronavirus disease 2019 (COVID-19) pandemic, it is important to use models that allow forecasting possible new infections accurately in order to face the pandemic in specific sociocultural contexts in the best possible way. Our first contribution is empirical. We use an extensive COVID-19 dataset from nine Latin American countries for the period of 1 April 2020 to 31 December 2021. Our second and third contributions are methodological. We extend relevant (i) state-space models with score-driven dynamics and (ii) nonlinear state-space models with unobserved components, respectively. We use weekly seasonal effects, in addition to the local-level and trend filters of the literature, for (i) and (ii), and the negative binomial distribution for (ii). We find that the statistical and forecasting performances of the novel score-driven specifications are superior to those of the nonlinear state-space models with unobserved components model, providing a potential valid alternative to forecasting the number of possible new COVID-19 infections.

Keywords: COVID-19; score-driven models; unobserved components; negative binomial distribution

MSC: 37M10; 46N30

1. Introduction

In the work of Barrado [1], the author presents that the sanitary (health) crisis produced by the coronavirus disease 2019 (COVID-19) pandemic generated by the Sars-CoV-2 (severe acute respiratory syndrome coronavirus 2) is not the first zoonotic disease (i.e., rabies in the seventeenth century; 1918 influenza pandemic; pandemic of AIDS/HIV—acquired immune deficiency syndrome/human immunodeficiency virus—infection of 1981 to date) and, unfortunately, it will not be the last that humanity will face. Diseases, in fact, have been powerful levers of historical change; they have the ability to change a society.

The plagues in Egypt (1570 to 1440 BC, before Christ) caused notable changes in the way of life of the population, since they affected the characteristics of social relations [2]. The Black Death, a pandemic that ravaged Europe between 1347 and 1351, gave rise to an epidemic reaching all the European continent geographically, causing the death of about one-third of its population [3] and changing its socioeconomic structure. The encounter between Europeans and Native Americans (1770s to 1850) caused epidemics that devastated the native society, being one of the main causes of the destruction of their culture [4]. In all three examples, for both political structures and individuals involved, the changes were dramatic and left multiple victims, but new opportunities were also opened up.

During the emergence of the modern states, statistics began to be used to know precisely the forces of the state, starting with the birth, mortality, and disease records. In this way, the health statistics kept an accurate record of the cases of illness and death of the population emerged. Those records made possible the study of epidemic phenomena by using modern scientific tools [5]. The work of [6] presents models to predict the evolution of the COVID-19 pandemic and the impact of the measures for its control. The work of [7] also presents that there are many models developed to understand the dynamics of the COVID-19 disease. However, the different sociocultural contexts of different countries make it necessary to specifically adjust those models to each scenario [7]. The first contribution of our paper is empirical. To the best of our knowledge, our paper provides the most complete analysis on COVID-19 forecasting for Latin American countries in the literature. We study the forecasting performances of new time series models in the sociocultural contexts of nine Latin American countries for the period of April 2020 to December 2021. In Table A1 of Appendix A, we cite several works from the literature on COVID-19 forecasting.

In the present paper, we use two classes of time series models for COVID-19 forecasting. For the first class of time series models, we use score-driven models which are introduced in the works of [8,9]. In those papers, score-driven models are named generalized autoregressive score (GAS) and dynamic conditional score (DCS) models, respectively. Score-driven models are observation-driven state-space models [10], in which the dynamic parameters are observable and updated by past observations. For reviews on score-driven models, we refer to [11,12]. For the statistical inference of score-driven models, we refer to the works of [11,13–19]. From the literature, the most relevant works for us are [20,21], in which one of the models for the log of new COVID-19 cases is a score-driven model for the negative binomial distribution using score-driven local-level and trend components. The second contribution of our paper, in relation to score-driven models, is methodological. We extend the works of [20,21] by adding a weekly seasonal component for new COVID-19 cases. In addition, we also refer to relevant works in which score-driven seasonal components are used for macroeconomic data: [22–26].

For the second class of time series models, we use space-state models with unobserved components [11,27–30], which are also called structural models [30]. The most relevant papers for us are [20,21], in which one of the models for the log of new COVID-19 cases is a Gaussian linear state-space model with unobserved components of local level and trend. The third contribution of our paper, in relation to state-space models with unobserved components, is methodological. We extend the state-space model with unobserved components of [20,21] at two points: (i) We add a weekly seasonal component for new COVID-19 cases that we observe at the daily frequency. (ii) We assume that the data-generating process (DGP) for the state-space model with unobserved components is the negative binomial distribution, and we use the estimation method of [31]. The use of the negative binomial distribution is motivated by the works of [20,21] due to robustness to possible small numbers of new COVID-19 cases in the data series.

By using the new state-space model with unobserved components for the negative binomial distribution, we separately model the trend, seasonality, and seasonal components of new COVID-19 cases, and we study the out-of-sample forecasting accuracy for COVID-19 cases using alternative forecasting horizons. Our estimation results indicate that the COVID-19 forecasting performances of the score-driven models are superior to those of the state-space models with unobserved components.

In the remainder of this paper, Section 2 presents the statistical models, Section 3 presents the results, and Section 4 concludes.

2. Materials and Methods

We use COVID-19 data from Latin American countries for which data are available to us, and we discuss in detail the results for Chile. The first cases of the COVID-19 pandemic in Chile were confirmed on 3 March 2020, when a 33-year-old man from the commune of San Javier (Maule Region) and a passenger of a flight from Singapore were hospitalized in the Regional Hospital of Talca [32]. From these first proven cases, the epidemic outbreak spread to sixteen regions of the country. By April 2020, Chile was the country that performed the most PCR (polymerase chain reaction) tests per million inhabitants in Latin America.

The data of the present paper are from the COVID-19 Data Repository of the Center for Systems Science and Engineering (CSSE) at Johns Hopkins University [33] for the period of 1 April 2020 to 31 December 2021 of nine Latin American Countries for which daily data were available in the study period. For the data under study, various specifications of state-space models with unobserved components and score-driven models are estimated, and in-sample model fits are compared.

Out-of-sample forecasts of COVID-19 cases are also performed for the alternative forecasting windows of 7, 14, and 28 days. By evaluating the alternative state-space models, we find that the in-sample statistical and out-of-sample forecasting performances of a score-driven model with dynamic local-level, trend, and seasonal components are superior to those of the nonlinear state-space model with unobserved components. The novel score-driven model may be used to decide on alternative actions, such as quarantines and vaccination processes, to control the current COVID-19 or other future pandemics.

Next, we present the score-driven model of location, trend, and seasonality for the negative binomial distribution. Then, we review the corresponding nonlinear state-space model for the same probability distribution.

2.1. Score-Driven Models

In the score-driven models of new COVID-19 cases of the present paper, the score-driven parameter f_t and the constant parameters of the vector Θ influence the conditional density of the dependent variable $y_t \sim p_y(y_t|y_1,\ldots,y_{t-1},f_t,\Theta)$, where y_t denotes the number of new COVID-19 cases in period t. Similar to the work of [20], we assume that the DGP for new COVID-19 cases is the negative binomial distribution. Hence, the conditional density of y_t is defined in Equation (1) next,

$$p(y_t|y_1,\ldots,y_{t-1},f_t,\Theta) = \frac{\Gamma(v+y_t)}{y_t!\Gamma(v)} f_t^{y_t}(v+f_t)^{-y_t}(1+f_t/v)^{-v}, \tag{1}$$

where $\Gamma(x)$ is the gamma function, $n! = (1 \times 2 \times \cdots \times n)$ denotes factorial, v is the shape parameter, the conditional mean of new COVID-19 cases is $\mathrm{E}(y_t|y_1,...,y_{t-1}) = f_t$, the conditional variance of new COVID-19 cases is $\mathrm{Var}(y_t|y_1,...,y_{t-1}) = f_t + (f_t^2)/v$, and the dynamics of $\ln f_t$ are driven as formulated in Equations (2)–(7) follows:

$$\ln f_t = \delta_t + s_t \tag{2}$$
$$\delta_t = \delta_{t-1} + \beta_{t-1} + \kappa_1 u_{t-1} \tag{3}$$
$$\beta_t = \beta_{t-1} + \kappa_2 u_{t-1} \tag{4}$$
$$s_t = D_t \gamma_t \tag{5}$$
$$D_t = (D_{\mathrm{Monday},t},\ldots,D_{\mathrm{Sunday},t}) \tag{6}$$
$$\gamma_t = \gamma_{t-1} + \kappa_t u_{t-1} \tag{7}$$

where δ_t (1×1) is the local level component, β_t (1×1) is the trend component, and s_t (1×1) is the seasonality component. The score-driven model can be extended by adding strictly exogenous variables to Equation (2) ([11], p. 56), which influence the new cases of COVID-19. Moreover, γ_t is a (7×1) vector of seasonality filter, where its elements are of the form of Equation (8):

$$\gamma_t = (\gamma_{\mathrm{Monday},t},\ldots,\gamma_{\mathrm{Sunday},t})^\top, \tag{8}$$

where κ_t is a (7×1) vector, where each element of κ_t is parameterized as in Equation (9):

$$\kappa_{j,t} = \begin{cases} \kappa_j, & \text{if } D_{j,t} = 1; \\ -\frac{\kappa_j}{7-1}, & \text{if } D_{j,t} = 0. \end{cases} \tag{9}$$

where $j \in \{$Monday, Tuesday, ..., Sunday$\}$. Hence, parameters κ_j where $j \in \{$Monday, Tuesday, ..., Sunday$\}$ are time-invariant parameters which are jointly estimated with the rest of the parameters. Finally, the conditional score of the log-likelihood with respect to f_t (i.e., score function) is given by Equation (10):

$$\frac{\partial \ln p(y_t|y_1,\ldots,y_{t-1},f_t,\Theta)}{\partial f_t} = \frac{v(y_t - f_t)}{f_t(v+f_t)}. \tag{10}$$

In the literature on score-driven models (e.g., [11,13]), in many cases, the conditional score is scaled by the inverse information matrix. Hence, following the work of [20], the scaled score function updating term in Equations (3), (4) and (7) is given by $u_t = y_t/f_t - 1$, which is the score function divided by the information quantity.

We consider alternative specifications of the general score-driven model of this section; the specification presented in this section is denoted by SD 1 (score-driven 1). An alternative specification assumes that all seasonality parameters are identical, i.e., $\kappa_j = \kappa$ for all j, which we denote by SD 2 (score-driven 2). Moreover, another alternative specification assumes that only local-level and trend components are included in the model, i.e., $s_t = 0$ for $t = 1,\ldots,T$. We denote the latter specification by SD WS (score-driven, without seasonality), which coincides with the score-driven models of [20,21].

2.2. State-Space Model

We use the exponential family state-space model and apply it to the negative binomial distribution, as seen in the work of [31]. We use the same conditional density for y_t as for the score-driven model; see Equation (1). The estimation method uses a Gaussian model which approximates the negative binomial model. Then, the estimation is performed by using the Kalman filter procedure. The log-mean of y_t is formulated by Equations (11)–(17):

$$\ln f_t = \delta_t + s_t \tag{11}$$
$$\delta_t = \delta_{t-1} + \beta_{t-1} + \epsilon_{\delta,t} \tag{12}$$
$$\beta_t = \beta_{t-1} + \epsilon_{\beta,t} \tag{13}$$
$$s_t = D_t \gamma_t \tag{14}$$
$$D_t = (D_{\text{Monday},t},\ldots,D_{\text{Sunday},t}) \tag{15}$$
$$\gamma_t = \gamma_{t-1} + \epsilon_{\gamma,t} \tag{16}$$
$$\epsilon_{\gamma,t} = (\epsilon_{\text{Monday},\gamma,t},\ldots,\epsilon_{\text{Sunday},\gamma,t})' \tag{17}$$

where δ_t (1×1) is the local level component, β_t (1×1) is the tend component, s_t (1×1) is the seasonality component, and γ_t (7×1) is the seasonality filter of time-varying parameters. We assume that $\epsilon_{\delta,t} \sim N(0,\sigma_\delta^2)$ and $\epsilon_{\beta,t} \sim N(0,\sigma_\beta^2)$. Moreover, we also assume that $\epsilon_{\gamma,t}$ has a seven-dimensional multivariate normal distribution where the mean is a zero vector and the variance is specified as follows: $\text{Var}(\epsilon_{\gamma,t}) = \sigma_\gamma^2(I_7 - (1/7)i_7 i_7')$ where I_7 is the identity matrix and i_7 is a (7×1) vector of ones. This specification of the covariance matrix ensures that the sum of each column of that matrix is zero, i.e., the sum of the seasonality filters is zero in each period. The nonlinear state-space model with unobserved components for the negative binomial distribution of this section is denoted SS (state-space).

2.3. Parameter Estimation and Statistical Performance

All models are estimated by using the maximum likelihood (ML) method, in which the following log-likelihood (LL) function is maximized with respect to the parameter vector Θ as is defined in (18):

$$\hat{\Theta} = \text{argmax}_\Theta \text{LL}(y_1,\ldots,y_T,\Theta) = \text{argmax}_\Theta \sum_{t=1}^{T} \ln p(y_t|y_1,\ldots,y_{t-1},f_t,\Theta). \tag{18}$$

For the estimation of the nonlinear state-space model, we refer to the work of [31]. For the estimation of the score-driven model, we refer to the works of [11,13,14].

The statistical performances of different models are compared by using the following likelihood-based model performance metrics defined as Equations (19)–(21):

$$\text{AIC} = 2K - 2\hat{\text{LL}} \tag{19}$$

$$\text{AICc} = \text{AIC} + \frac{2K^2 + 2K}{T - K - 1} \tag{20}$$

$$\text{BIC} = K\ln(T) - 2\hat{\text{LL}} \tag{21}$$

where $\hat{\text{LL}}$ is the maximum value of the log-likelihood, K is the number of time-invariant parameters, and T denotes the sample size. Moreover, AIC denotes Akaike information criterion, AICc is a corrected AIC which is robust to small sample size, and BIC denotes Bayesian information criterion. The use of these model selection metrics for score-driven models is motivated by the work of [11] (p. 56).

3. Results

To evaluate the in-sample and out-of-sample performances of the models, a time series of new daily infections of COVID-19 in nine Latin American countries, for the period of 1 April 2020 to 31 December 2021, with a total of $T = 640$ observations, is considered [33]. Table 1 presents summary statistics of the data and the p-values of the Jarque–Bera (JB) [34] and augmented Dickey–Fuller (ADF) tests [35]. For the JB test, the null hypothesis of normal distribution is rejected for all countries at the 1% level of significance. This supports the use of the negative binomial distribution for the score-driven model. For the ADF test, the null hypothesis of unit root process cannot be rejected for any of the countries, which supports the use of the unit root specifications for δ_t in Equations (3) and (12).

Table 1. Descriptive statistics, JB test, and ADF test for new COVID-19 cases.

	Mean	SDev	Minimum	Maximum	Skewness	Kurtosis	JB p-Value	ADF p-Value
Argentina	8833.3656	8478.1008	0.0000	50,506.0000	1.5262	5.6897	0.0000	0.8786
Brazil	10,490.3422	9139.8157	0.0000	63,523.0000	1.6401	6.6768	0.0000	0.5559
Chile	2820.9703	2168.6074	265.0000	13,990.0000	1.2857	4.6445	0.0000	0.7233
Colombia	8057.0844	7314.7682	67.0000	33,594.0000	1.2759	4.2166	0.0000	0.6428
Cuba	1509.0906	2618.5288	0.0000	9907.0000	1.9932	5.5462	0.0000	0.8492
Guatemala	981.7516	1090.4835	0.0000	5826.0000	2.0654	7.0469	0.0000	0.9058
Jamaica	146.6938	190.1864	0.0000	1430.0000	2.2203	8.8093	0.0000	0.4927
Panama	765.6219	723.4916	0.0000	5186.0000	2.4510	10.8399	0.0000	0.5985
Uruguay	645.6234	1072.7704	0.0000	7289.0000	2.2389	8.0831	0.0000	0.8074

For the full sample period, parameter estimates for SD 1, SD2, SD WS, and SS are reported in Tables A2–A10 of Appendix B for all countries. To evaluate the predictive capacity, first, the sample was divided into two equal parts, each of 320 observations. The last 7, 14, and 28 observations were removed from the initial half of the data, which were predicted using the fitted model for the remaining data, and measures were calculated to evaluate the predictive capacity of the models considered. Then, the next observation was included, having now a total of 321 observations. Again, the last 7, 14, and 21 final observations were removed, the prediction of these was made and measurements of the quality of the prediction quality were calculated. The procedure described above was repeated until the total set of available observations was considered.

In Figure 1 (graph of the analyzed time series of Chile), it is possible to see five periods of significant increase in the number of new cases of infection with COVID-19.

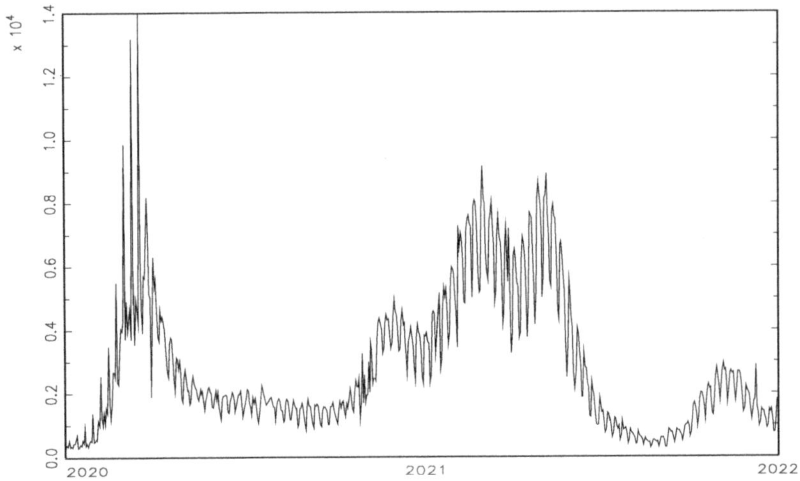

Figure 1. New cases of infection with COVID-19 in Chile (1 April 2020 to 31 December 2021).

The quality of predictions is compared by using the following mean absolute percentage error (MAPE), mean absolute error (MAE), and mean square error (MSE) loss functions presented in Equations (22)–(24).

$$\text{MAPE} = \frac{1}{T}\sum_{t=1}^{T}\frac{|y_t - y_{f,t}|}{y_t} \tag{22}$$

$$\text{MAE} = \frac{1}{T}\sum_{t=1}^{T}|y_t - y_{f,t}| \tag{23}$$

$$\text{MSE} = \frac{1}{T}\sum_{t=1}^{T}(y_t - y_{f,t})^2 \tag{24}$$

The precision of the forecasts is studied for models SD 1, SD 2, SD WS, and SS.

Table 2 shows the mean values of AIC, AICc, BIC, MSE, MAE, and MAPE of different models for the estimation window of the countries used in the present study by excluding the last seven observations, which are used to evaluate the predictive capacity of the models in question. Table 3 also presents the same results when the last 14 observations were excluded from the sample. Table 4 presents similar result for the estimation window by excluding the last 28 observations which are used to evaluate the predictive capacity of the models in question.

According to the tables, in which the best values have been highlighted in bold, the SD 1 or SD 2 model has a superior performance according to all in-sample model performance metrics and out-of-sample loss functions. Furthermore, when the prediction horizon increases, the prediction quality values decrease, and in the particular case of Chile, the values of MAPE is 12.4% for the forecast by the next seven days, 16.2% by 14 days and 26.8% by 28 days. The other countries present similar conducts.

Figure 2 shows the 28-day ahead forecasts for SD 1. The filtered estimate of f_t and the 28-day out-of-sample ahead forecast $y_{f,t}$ are presented. The thick red line indicates the forecasting period for this example. The figures for the other econometric models of this paper are similar and are available from the authors upon request. When comparing Figures 1 and 2, it can be seen that the prediction is close to the real value and the fit follows the behavior of the data.

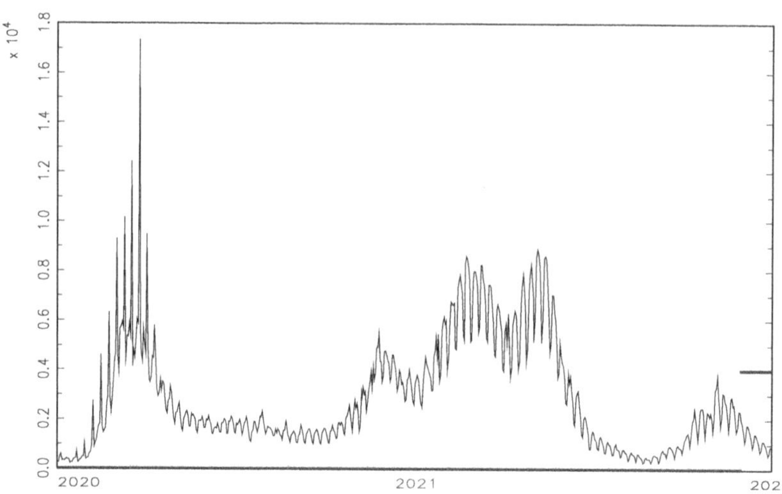

Figure 2. Filtered estimates and forecasts of new cases of infection with COVID-19 in Chile (1 April 2020 to 31 December 2021). *Note:* The thick red line indicates the forecasting period for this example.

Table 2. AIC, AICc, BIC, and loss functions (forecasting window: last 7 days).

Country	Model	AIC	AICc	BIC	MSE	MAE	MAPE
Argentina	SD 1	**8296.3733**	**8297.9455**	**8370.9011**	**2301.2016**	**1946.0298**	**18.8640**
	SD 2	8377.7886	8378.4967	8427.4559	2316.1415	1974.9102	19.0833
	SD WS	8535.3791	8535.5133	8556.0693	34,343,289.6112	3551.2989	40.0326
	SS	8498.8841	8499.3802	8540.2884	13,108,686.9670	2017.2896	22.0692
Brazil	SD 1	8768.5371	8770.1093	8843.0649	**2274.6951**	**1911.7838**	**19.9625**
	SD 2	8767.4572	8768.1673	8817.0885	2602.3998	2228.8968	22.7865
	SD WS	**8534.4407**	**8534.5821**	**8554.8778**	42,251,093.3462	4151.6625	49.4397
	SS	8998.2551	8998.7500	9039.6803	16,851,638.8005	2361.7759	25.4773
Chile	SD 1	**7001.2412**	**7002.8134**	**7075.7690**	415.3421	339.2591	12.4051
	SD 2	7049.7117	7050.4198	7099.3798	**405.6187**	**336.4485**	**12.2171**
	SD WS	7492.7113	7492.8451	7513.4124	749,400.2033	622.5042	22.9498
	SS	7097.0747	7097.5709	7138.4791	348,105.9045	414.0706	16.4325
Colombia	SD 1	7775.4984	7776.2069	7825.1567	1499.3427	1306.5852	14.8406
	SD 2	**7748.3902**	**7749.9624**	**7822.9179**	**1467.6770**	**1292.4946**	**14.4201**
	SD WS	7854.5344	7854.6684	7875.2237	6,187,717.7639	1472.9147	16.4635
	SS	7833.7131	7834.2092	7875.1174	5,658,909.4517	1473.1866	17.9121
Cuba	SD 1	5194.5309	5196.1031	5269.0587	**523.5462**	**464.6705**	19.5876
	SD 2	5233.4356	5234.1439	5283.0955	699.1034	637.0687	21.9416
	SD WS	**5192.3540**	**5192.4877**	**5213.0588**	1,546,392.2398	563.7378	**18.7016**
	SS	5032.0991	5032.5952	5073.5034	641,855.0899	454.5395	21.3560
Guatemala	SD 1	6293.7668	6294.4892	**6343.1756**	374.9546	288.7362	**26.0893**
	SD 2	**6270.1159**	**6271.7105**	6344.3708	**368.5360**	**282.5509**	27.0558
	SD WS	6461.8271	6461.9663	6482.3146	1,062,506.0989	754.4205	95.6340
	SS	6588.5849	6589.0859	6629.8826	1,266,745.7849	635.2117	52.7323

Table 2. *Cont.*

Country	Model	AIC	AICc	BIC	MSE	MAE	MAPE
Jamaica	SD 1	**4658.5020**	**4660.0741**	4733.0297	**97.2971**	81.5668	**38.4807**
	SD 2	4704.6173	4705.3228	4754.3235	105.9428	89.4866	40.5211
	SD WS	4705.8447	4705.9785	**4726.5435**	18,850.7210	**80.7728**	42.7940
	SS	4837.9013	4838.4036	4879.1967	107,479.4776	171.1706	75.7571
Panama	SD 1	**6569.8656**	**6571.4378**	6644.3934	**134.0009**	**108.6573**	**21.8896**
	SD 2	6571.3742	6572.0812	**6621.0594**	136.3494	110.4343	22.2704
	SD WS	6850.5974	6850.7311	6871.2995	42,451.3021	139.0089	28.3498
	SS	6222.0811	6222.6217	6262.5795	28,495.6600	111.9751	22.9152
Uruguay	SD 1	4884.0880	4884.7952	4933.7672	329.8169	271.7384	24.2383
	SD 2	4784.3311	4785.9033	**4858.8589**	**320.9517**	**261.6523**	**23.6438**
	SD WS	4842.6633	4842.7969	4863.3720	335,154.0779	292.6989	28.2122
	SS	**4737.7469**	**4738.2430**	4779.1512	298,958.1937	279.8100	26.9180

Table 3. AIC, AICc, BIC, and loss functions (forecasting window: last 14 days).

Country	Model	AIC	AICc	BIC	MSE	MAE	MAPE
Argentina	SD 1	**8175.2700**	**8176.8691**	**8249.5185**	**3197.9468**	**2639.5945**	**24.1452**
	SD 2	8271.6612	8272.3811	8321.1430	3371.1225	2809.3709	25.2801
	SD WS	8406.7033	8406.8398	8427.3150	49,140,353.3414	4196.7107	45.3911
	SS	8379.6315	8380.1359	8420.8807	18,184,571.1667	2578.3910	30.0359
Brazil	SD 1	8647.7178	8649.3169	8721.9664	**2894.9226**	**2384.5114**	**25.6791**
	SD 2	**8637.4367**	**8638.1589**	**8686.8794**	3065.6126	2554.0550	27.6030
	SD WS	8838.0213	8838.1575	8858.6376	30,982,304.8005	3506.3766	43.2434
	SS	8876.8100	8877.3134	8918.0787	26,819,716.2958	3169.0974	36.5192
Chile	SD 1	**6900.4569**	**6902.0560**	**6974.7054**	**569.6145**	**462.6948**	**16.1672**
	SD 2	6947.1479	6947.8681	6996.6269	570.1986	467.3224	16.1924
	SD WS	7382.4926	7382.6286	7403.1159	1,067,731.3998	735.1098	26.8141
	SS	6994.4527	6994.9572	7035.7019	691,370.5675	583.3890	24.0062
Colombia	SD 1	**7636.0628**	**7637.6619**	7710.3113	2041.0238	1760.6786	19.5618
	SD 2	7644.9216	7645.6422	**7694.3920**	**2020.2438**	**1731.1616**	**19.1392**
	SD WS	7739.3255	7739.4618	7759.9365	10,868,589.6806	1987.7646	21.5616
	SS	7719.2850	7719.7895	7760.5342	11,493,721.1180	2106.8066	26.9954
Cuba	SD 1	5087.1428	5088.7419	5161.3913	**685.2727**	**601.0140**	**24.4800**
	SD 2	5155.6897	5156.4089	5205.1788	961.0687	857.5462	27.9208
	SD WS	5086.2412	5086.3770	5106.8676	2,245,995.6206	723.6386	23.9827
	SS	**4933.7971**	**4934.3016**	**4975.0463**	1,476,321.3263	707.0039	37.1587
Guatemala	SD 1	6274.8259	6276.4240	6349.0671	**432.2001**	**322.0076**	**33.8236**
	SD 2	6344.1386	6344.8575	6393.6230	439.7635	333.0616	35.3578
	SD WS	**6231.7189**	**6231.8619**	**6252.0626**	1,238,553.6801	831.8914	93.8069
	SS	6396.6383	6397.1523	6437.6775	2,093,344.2267	826.1275	64.7631
Jamaica	SD 1	**4577.2449**	**4578.8440**	**4651.4934**	**127.0198**	**106.1333**	**45.8103**
	SD 2	4627.4318	4628.1483	4676.9655	136.2133	114.0903	47.4340
	SD WS	4634.5638	4634.6997	4655.1884	29,838.2604	101.3054	49.0764
	SS	5202.6202	5203.0954	5244.4736	138,632.3748	187.4398	76.6255

Table 3. *Cont.*

Country	Model	AIC	AICc	BIC	MSE	MAE	MAPE
Panama	SD 1	6470.3736	6471.9727	6544.6222	**150.5995**	**119.7430**	**25.3388**
	SD 2	6471.8290	6472.5479	6521.3280	153.2067	121.4780	25.5953
	SD WS	6703.3882	6703.5243	6724.0094	45,059.8159	148.5483	30.9317
	SS	**5994.4678**	**5995.0285**	**6034.6011**	49,498.3959	149.1045	29.7651
Uruguay	SD 1	4739.2554	4740.8554	4813.4939	**392.8616**	**322.5024**	**28.8932**
	SD 2	4843.9065	4844.6268	4893.3837	409.2816	334.2830	31.5082
	SD WS	4806.4207	4806.5566	4827.0487	426,375.0069	351.6242	33.1181
	SS	**4649.3840**	**4649.8886**	**4690.6331**	494,822.8223	369.7121	37.6505

Table 4. AIC, AICc, BIC, and loss functions (forecasting window: last 28 days).

Country	Model	AIC	AICc	BIC	MSE	MAE	MAPE
Argentina	SD 1	**7933.59216**	**7935.2480**	**8007.2728**	**5189.7655**	4219.0258	**36.2552**
	SD 2	8046.926927	8047.6706	8096.0505	5367.0909	4366.9248	38.2809
	SD WS	8136.394036	8136.5355	8156.8363	82,370,566.8139	5322.1663	54.2638
	SS	8088.467599	8088.9933	8129.3335	32,170,702.1469	**3753.4018**	44.5420
Brazil	SD 1	8396.9131	8398.5706	8470.5747	**4007.0473**	**3318.6124**	**37.0109**
	SD 2	**8384.3370**	**8385.0852**	**8433.3866**	4134.1578	3442.6450	38.8869
	SD WS	8534.4407	8534.5821	8554.8778	42,251,093.3462	4151.6625	49.4397
	SS	8536.3283	8536.8557	8577.1623	75,839,238.9418	5397.3759	55.1246
Chile	SD 1	**6758.694984**	**6760.3524**	**6832.3550**	**996.1884**	**805.6067**	**26.8196**
	SD 2	6760.079588	6760.8265	6809.1586	1012.6425	820.0937	27.3999
	SD WS	7130.248944	7130.3902	7150.6921	2,689,008.2871	1070.7300	37.1054
	SS	6788.432479	6788.9545	6829.3637	1,681,886.1884	908.0762	40.4911
Colombia	SD 1	**7409.855313**	**7411.5113**	**7483.5314**	3857.9707	3264.2294	36.3053
	SD 2	7429.951682	7430.6957	7479.0645	**3636.0051**	**3041.9816**	**33.2373**
	SD WS	7507.145544	7507.2866	7527.5960	31,129,971.4861	3367.9660	36.2210
	SS	7477.488416	7478.0112	7518.4103	28,223,384.5131	3245.6306	41.7716
Cuba	SD 1	4850.0780	4851.7383	4923.7095	**1008.8684**	**861.4322**	**35.6252**
	SD 2	4942.4274	4943.1732	4991.5171	1236.3509	1068.8652	40.0612
	SD WS	4849.2351	4849.3760	4869.6902	4,131,481.9817	968.8769	36.2243
	SS	**4244.8179**	**4245.3741**	**4285.0725**	3,133,873.0682	1062.5131	39.7491
Guatemala	SD 1	6034.6615	6036.3211	6108.2611	604.4476	463.1176	44.4914
	SD 2	6058.5938	6059.3445	6107.5678	**592.5558**	**454.5504**	**39.5764**
	SD WS	**6013.4898**	**6013.6373**	**6033.6838**	1,449,870.5471	912.3629	92.5962
	SS	8798.9832	8799.3545	8843.0131	134,451.6239	232.2018	97.9899
Jamaica	SD 1	**4345.2526**	**4346.9332**	**4418.6825**	146.7090	119.2289	57.5685
	SD 2	4451.0057	4451.7509	4500.1125	**143.1995**	114.7898	53.4278
	SD WS	4531.9877	4532.1268	4552.5144	35,160.6978	**105.0457**	**51.1179**
	SS	6034.1902	6034.5985	6077.3523	65,056.8814	130.9791	91.3099
Panama	SD 1	6273.7113	6275.3673	6347.3874	**192.1973**	**151.0401**	**30.7112**
	SD 2	6274.8232	6275.5673	6323.9407	194.7002	153.1452	31.1234
	SD WS	6403.5157	6403.6567	6423.9690	60,999.7748	175.9676	35.3154
	SS	**5635.3098**	**5635.9036**	**5674.8490**	105,743.2413	210.5126	41.5893

Table 4. *Cont.*

Country	Model	AIC	AICc	BIC	MSE	MAE	MAPE
Uruguay	SD 1	4509.681247	4511.3419	4583.3386	528.6854	426.8793	**38.0930**
	SD 2	4635.014697	4635.7589	4684.1502	**512.4454**	**415.3082**	38.3145
	SD WS	4568.527711	4568.6686	4588.9937	777,495.0436	454.9869	41.2574
	SS	**4464.8041**	**4465.3277**	**4505.7387**	734,336.1219	430.1770	39.5965

4. Conclusions

In this paper, we apply new score-driven and state-space models for the negative binomial distribution for new cases of infection with COVID-19 to a specific dataset of nine Latin American countries. We use daily data for the period of 1 April 2020 to 31 December 2021 and control for weekly seasonal effects in new cases of infection with COVID-19. We use the same econometric specifications for these countries, because they have similar geographical and social structures.

The in-sample model fits and out-of-sample forecasting performances of alternative models for predicting the number of new COVID-19 infections are compared. Assuming that data are generated by the negative binomial distribution, the predictive accuracies of (i) different specifications of score-driven models and (ii) a nonlinear state-space model with unobserved components are analyzed. We extend the relevant literature on score-driven models by considering a weekly seasonality component for the daily COVID-19 observations for both (i) and (ii) and the use of the negative binomial distribution for (ii).

We find that the score-driven model provides the most accurate forecast of COVID-19 cases. This has the potential to motivate the future use of score-driven models for forecasting daily cases during pandemics. The novel statistical models of the present work may be used by authorities to decide on alternative actions, such as quarantines and vaccination processes, to control the current COVID-19 or other future pandemics.

Our results are robust as we find that the forecasting performance of the score-driven model is superior to that of the nonlinear state-space model with unobserved components for all countries. For the sociocultural context of Latin American countries, the score-driven models for forecasting new cases of infection with COVID-19 seem to work well. A scientific implication of our paper is the potential future use of the new score-driven models for forecasting new COVID-19 cases for other countries.

The limitations of our paper include the use of the negative binomial distribution and the specific dataset for nine Latin American countries for which data are available for us. Future work may consider other score-driven discrete probability distributions as alternatives to the score-driven negative binomial distribution. Moreover, future work may use a more complete dataset that includes further Latin American countries.

Author Contributions: Conceptualization, S.C.-E. and F.N.-M.; methodology, S.C.-E., S.B. and F.N.-M.; software, P.V. and F.N.-M.; validation, C.C.-C. and S.B.; data creation, C.C.-C. and P.V.; writing—original draft preparation, S.C.-E. and P.V.; writing—review and editing, S.B., C.C.-C. and F.N.-M. All authors have read and agreed to the published version of the manuscript.

Funding: Contreras-Espinoza's research was fully supported by Proyecto Regular DIUBB 190908244 3/R of the Universidad del Bío-Bío. Novoa-Muñoz's research was fully supported by project 2220529 IF/R and Fondo de Apoyo a la Participación a Eventos Internacionales (FAPEI) at Universidad del Bío-Bío, Chile. Blazsek gratefully acknowledges research funding from Universidad Francisco Marroquín. Caamaño-Carrillo's research was funded by FONDECYT (Chile) grant No. 11220066 and by Proyecto Regular DIUBB 2120538 IF/R de la Universidad del Bío-Bío.

Institutional Review Board Statement: Not applicable.

Informed Consent Statement: Not applicable.

Data Availability Statement: The COVID-19 data set was taken from the COVID-19 Data Repository of the Center for Systems Science and Engineering (CSSE) at Johns Hopkins University.

Conflicts of Interest: The authors declare no conflict of interest.

Abbreviations

ANFIS	Adaptive neuro-fuzzy inference system
AIC	Akaike information criterion
AICc	Corrected Akaike information criterion
AIDS	Acquired immune deficiency syndrome
ADF	Augmented Dickey–Fuller
ARIMA	Autoregressive integrated moving average
AI	Artificial intelligence
SARIMA	Seasonal ARIMA
BC	Before Christ
BIC	Bayesian information criterion
COVID-19	Coronavirus disease 2019
CSSE	Center for Systems Science and Engineering
DCS	Dynamic conditional score
DGP	Data generating process
DL	Deep learning
GAS	Generalized autoregressive score
HIV	Human immunodeficiency virus
JB	Jarque–Bera
LL	Log-likelihood
LSTM	Long short-term memory
MAPE	Mean Absolute Percentage Error
MAE	Mean Absolute Error
MSE	Mean Square Error
PCR	Polymerase chain reaction
Sars-CoV-2	Severe acute respiratory syndrome coronavirus 2
SDev	Standard deviation
SD 1	Score-driven 1
SD 2	Score-driven 2
SD WS	Score-driven, without seasonality
SS	State space
SEIR	Susceptible, exposed, infected, and recovered
SIR	Susceptible, infected, recovered
SIRD	SIR deceased

Appendix A

Table A1. COVID-19 forecasting models from the literature.

Forecasting Model	Citation
Adaptive neuro-fuzzy inference system (ANFIS)	[36]
Artificial intelligence (AI)	[37]
Autoregressive integrated moving average (ARIMA) model	[38–42]
Ecological Niche models	[43]
Flower pollination algorithm	[36]
Genetic programming	[41,42,44–46]
Hybrid approaches that include ARIMA and wavelet model	[40,41]
Iteration method	[47]
Logistic growth model	[48–50]
Long short-term memory (LSTM) network	[51]
Machine learning	[52]
Models based on growth curves	[20]
Moving average (MA) model	[53]
Neural network	[42,54]

Table A1. *Cont.*

Forecasting Model	Citation
Phenomenological model	[55]
Polynomial neural network	[56]
Predictive models based on the Gompertz curves	[57]
Prophet algorithm	[58]
Random forest	[52]
Regression methods	[52,59–61]
Regression tree algorithm	[40]
SARIMA (seasonal ARIMA) model	[62]
Support vector Kuhn–Tucker	[63]
Support vector machine	[52,56,63]
Susceptible, exposed, infected, and recovered (SEIR)	[64,65]
Susceptible, infected, recovered (SIR) model	[66,67]
Susceptible, infected, recovered, and deceased (SIRD)	[68,69]
SutteARIMA method	[70]

Appendix B

Table A2. Parameter estimates for Argentina.

	SD 1	SD 2	SD WS	SS
κ_1	0.4810 *** (0.0250)	0.4245 *** (0.0422)	0.6822 *** (0.0738)	NA
κ_2	0.0563 *** (0.0111)	0.0387 *** (0.0093)	0.0178 (0.0111)	NA
κ_{Monday}	0.0530 *** (0.0166)	0.1499 *** (0.0301)	NA	NA
κ_{Tuesday}	0.2202 *** (0.0141)	NA	NA	NA
$\kappa_{\text{Wednesday}}$	0.0191 (0.0268)	NA	NA	NA
κ_{Thursday}	0.4169 *** (0.0861)	NA	NA	NA
κ_{Friday}	0.0000 (0.0165)	NA	NA	NA
κ_{Saturday}	0.3287 * (0.1779)	NA	NA	NA
κ_{Sunday}	0.1711 *** (0.0455)	NA	NA	NA
υ	13.6133 *** (0.8289)	12.9432 *** (0.7937)	6.6132 *** (0.3795)	NA
σ^2_δ	NA	NA	NA	0.0092 *** (0.0002)
σ^2_β	NA	NA	NA	0.0049 *** (0.0004)
σ^2_γ	NA	NA	NA	0.0003 (0.0005)

Notes: Standard deviations are in parentheses. *** and * is parameter significance at the 1% and 10% levels, respectively. For SD 2, $\kappa_j = \kappa_{\text{Monday},t}$ for j = Tuesday, …, Sunday.

Table A3. Parameter estimates for Brazil.

	SD 1	SD 2	SD WS	SS
κ_1	0.6955 *** (0.0445)	0.6792 *** (0.0488)	0.7908 *** (0.0462)	NA
κ_2	0.0155 ** (0.0070)	0.0142 (0.0088)	0.0000 (0.0008)	NA
κ_{Monday}	0.0000 (0.0307)	0.0598 *** (0.0109)	NA	NA
κ_{Tuesday}	0.0248 (0.0185)	NA	NA	NA
$\kappa_{\text{Wednesday}}$	0.0000 (0.0223)	NA	NA	NA
κ_{Thursday}	0.0000 (0.0246)	NA	NA	NA
κ_{Friday}	0.0000 (0.0227)	NA	NA	NA
κ_{Saturday}	0.1071 ** (0.0525)	NA	NA	NA
κ_{Sunday}	0.1815 *** (0.0492)	NA	NA	NA
υ	13.8207 *** (0.7742)	13.2981 *** (0.7523)	7.3978 *** (0.4104)	NA
σ^2_δ	NA	NA	NA	0.0205 *** (0.0002)
σ^2_β	NA	NA	NA	0.0143 *** (0.0002)
σ^2_γ	NA	NA	NA	0.0001 (0.0006)

Notes: Standard deviations are in parentheses. *** and ** is parameter significance at the 1% and 5% levels, respectively. For SD 2, $\kappa_j = \kappa_{\text{Monday},t}$ for j = Tuesday, …, Sunday.

Table A4. Parameter estimates for Chile.

	SD 1	SD 2	SD WS	SS
κ_1	0.3536 *** (0.0312)	0.3265 *** (0.0290)	0.1373 *** (0.0166)	NA
κ_2	0.0508 *** (0.0062)	0.0480 *** (0.0058)	0.0381 *** (0.0037)	NA
κ_{Monday}	0.2165 *** (0.0763)	0.2599 *** (0.0298)	NA	NA
κ_{Tuesday}	0.2138 *** (0.0689)	NA	NA	NA
$\kappa_{\text{Wednesday}}$	0.1546 *** (0.0478)	NA	NA	NA
κ_{Thursday}	0.0000 (0.0190)	NA	NA	NA
κ_{Friday}	0.0097 (0.0162)	NA	NA	NA
κ_{Saturday}	0.5496 *** (0.0784)	NA	NA	NA
κ_{Sunday}	0.3805 *** (0.0984)	NA	NA	NA
v	39.9089 *** (2.2882)	37.1677 *** (0.0171)	13.1141 *** (0.0218)	NA
σ^2_ξ	NA	NA	NA	0.0046 *** (0.0002)
σ^2_β	NA	NA	NA	0.0013 * (0.0006)
σ^2_γ	NA	NA	NA	0.0002 (0.0005)

Notes: Standard deviations are in parentheses. *** and * is parameter significance at the 1% and 10% levels, respectively. For SD 2, $\kappa_j = \kappa_{\text{Monday},t}$ for $j = \text{Tuesday}, \ldots, \text{Sunday}$.

Table A5. Parameter estimates for Colombia.

	SD 1	SD 2	SD WS	SS
κ_1	0.6284 *** (0.0450)	0.5723 *** (0.0449)	0.7356 *** (0.0455)	NA
κ_2	0.0356 *** (0.0073)	0.0512 *** (0.0094)	0.0000 *** (0.0004)	NA
κ_{Monday}	0.1836 *** (0.0534)	0.0000 (0.0287)	NA	NA
κ_{Tuesday}	0.0000 (0.0147)	NA	NA	NA
$\kappa_{\text{Wednesday}}$	0.0000 (0.0185)	NA	NA	NA
κ_{Thursday}	0.1300 *** (0.0385)	NA	NA	NA
κ_{Friday}	0.0000 (0.0177)	NA	NA	NA
κ_{Saturday}	0.0264 * (0.0152)	NA	NA	NA
κ_{Sunday}	0.1600 *** (0.0417)	NA	NA	NA
v	42.4229 *** (0.0263)	42.5514 *** (2.4817)	33.0859 *** (1.9223)	NA
σ^2_ξ	NA	NA	NA	0.0006 *** (0.0002)
σ^2_β	NA	NA	NA	0.0005 * (0.0003)
σ^2_γ	NA	NA	NA	0.0000 (0.0211)

Notes: Standard deviations are in parentheses. *** and * is parameter significance at the 1% and 10% levels, respectively. For SD 2, $\kappa_j = \kappa_{\text{Monday},t}$ for $j = \text{Tuesday}, \ldots, \text{Sunday}$.

Table A6. Parameter estimates for Cuba.

	SD 1	SD 2	SD WS	SS
κ_1	0.4972 *** (0.0373)	0.5128 *** (0.0391)	0.4451 *** (0.0450)	NA
κ_2	0.0074 *** (0.0024)	0.0094 *** (0.0036)	0.0131 * (0.0071)	NA
κ_{Monday}	0.0000 (0.0142)	0.0180 (0.0110)	NA	NA
κ_{Tuesday}	0.0192 * (0.0116)	NA	NA	NA
$\kappa_{\text{Wednesday}}$	0.0000 (0.0170)	NA	NA	NA
κ_{Thursday}	0.0000 (0.0143)	NA	NA	NA
κ_{Friday}	0.0116 (0.0171)	NA	NA	NA
κ_{Saturday}	0.0000 (0.0222)	NA	NA	NA
κ_{Sunday}	0.0757 *** (0.0272)	NA	NA	NA
v	17.7669 *** (1.3024)	18.6270 *** (1.4951)	18.7317 *** (1.5171)	NA
σ^2_ξ	NA	NA	NA	0.0162 *** (0.0002)
σ^2_β	NA	NA	NA	0.0087 *** (0.0004)
σ^2_γ	NA	NA	NA	0.0001 (0.0020)

Notes: Standard deviations are in parentheses. *** and * is parameter significance at the 1% and 10% levels, respectively. For SD 2, $\kappa_j = \kappa_{\text{Monday},t}$ for $j = \text{Tuesday}, \ldots, \text{Sunday}$.

Table A7. Parameter estimates for Guatemala.

	SD 1	SD 2	SD WS	SS
κ_1	0.2173 *** (0.0257)	0.2454 *** (0.0262)	0.1447 *** (0.0265)	NA
κ_2	0.0075 ** (0.0031)	0.0000 (0.0215)	0.0028 ** (0.0012)	NA
κ_{Monday}	0.2426 *** (0.0480)	0.1443 *** (0.0215)	NA	NA
κ_{Tuesday}	0.1587 *** (0.0615)	NA	NA	NA
$\kappa_{\text{Wednesday}}$	0.0907 ** (0.0421)	NA	NA	NA
κ_{Thursday}	0.0358 (0.0452)	NA	NA	NA
κ_{Friday}	0.0440 (0.0295)	NA	NA	NA
κ_{Saturday}	0.0000 (0.0176)	NA	NA	NA
κ_{Sunday}	0.1493 ** (0.0585)	NA	NA	NA
v	5.4384 *** (0.3232)	5.2768 *** (0.3325)	2.0380 *** (0.1097)	NA
σ^2_δ	NA	NA	NA	0.1427 *** (0.0002)
σ^2_β	NA	NA	NA	0.09732 *** (0.0009)
σ^2_γ	NA	NA	NA	0.0035 *** (0.0005)

Notes: Standard deviations are in parentheses. *** and ** is parameter significance at the 1% and 5% levels, respectively. For SD 2, $\kappa_j = \kappa_{\text{Monday},t}$ for $j = \text{Tuesday}, \ldots, \text{Sunday}$.

Table A8. Parameter estimates for Jamaica.

	SD 1	SD 2	SD WS	SS
κ_1	0.1906 *** (0.0218)	0.1860 *** (0.0238)	0.1901 *** (0.0247)	NA
κ_2	0.0186 *** (0.0032)	0.0178 *** (0.0030)	0.0177 *** (0.0030)	NA
κ_{Monday}	0.0000 (0.0146)	0.0000 (0.0118)	NA	NA
κ_{Tuesday}	0.0692 * (0.0400)	NA	NA	NA
$\kappa_{\text{Wednesday}}$	0.0000 (0.0293)	NA	NA	NA
κ_{Thursday}	0.0000 (0.0137)	NA	NA	NA
κ_{Friday}	0.0000 (0.0216)	NA	NA	NA
κ_{Saturday}	0.0493 (0.0303)	NA	NA	NA
κ_{Sunday}	0.0000 (0.0207)	NA	NA	NA
v	2.4836 *** (0.1558)	2.4600 *** (0.1557)	2.3768 *** (0.1501)	NA
σ^2_δ	NA	NA	NA	0.1025 *** (0.0005)
σ^2_β	NA	NA	NA	0.0284 *** (0.0001)
σ^2_γ	NA	NA	NA	0.0506 *** (0.0006)

Notes: Standard deviations are in parentheses. *** and * is parameter significance at the 1% and 10% levels, respectively. For SD 2, $\kappa_j = \kappa_{\text{Monday},t}$ for $j = \text{Tuesday}, \ldots, \text{Sunday}$.

Table A9. Parameter estimates for Panama.

	SD 1	SD 2	SD WS	SS
κ_1	0.1515 *** (0.0281)	0.1523 *** (0.0284)	0.1354 *** (0.0273)	NA
κ_2	0.0186 *** (0.0048)	0.0185 *** (0.0048)	0.0171 *** (0.0040)	NA
κ_{Monday}	0.0746 * (0.0451)	0.0453 *** (0.0165)	NA	NA
κ_{Tuesday}	0.0486 (0.0410)	NA	NA	NA
$\kappa_{\text{Wednesday}}$	0.0403 (0.0377)	NA	NA	NA
κ_{Thursday}	0.0000 (0.0107)	NA	NA	NA
κ_{Friday}	0.0000 (0.0145)	NA	NA	NA
κ_{Saturday}	0.0000 (0.0081)	NA	NA	NA
κ_{Sunday}	0.0853 (0.0648)	NA	NA	NA
v	2.9190 *** (0.1732)	2.8883 *** (0.1730)	2.6564 *** (0.1569)	NA
σ^2_δ	NA	NA	NA	0.0150 *** (0.0003)
σ^2_β	NA	NA	NA	0.0089 *** (0.0005)
σ^2_γ	NA	NA	NA	0.4780 *** (0.0001)

Notes: Standard deviations are in parentheses. *** and * is parameter significance at the 1% and 10% levels, respectively. For SD 2, $\kappa_j = \kappa_{\text{Monday},t}$ for $j = \text{Tuesday}, \ldots, \text{Sunday}$.

Table A10. Parameter estimates for Uruguay.

	SD 1	SD 2	SD WS	SS
κ_1	0.3761 *** (0.0224)	0.3810 *** (0.0219)	0.3202 *** (0.0217)	NA
κ_2	0.0106 *** (0.0020)	0.0110 *** (0.0027)	0.0136 *** (0.0032)	NA
κ_{Monday}	0.0000 (0.0240)	0.0537 *** (0.0115)	NA	NA
κ_{Tuesday}	0.0519 * (0.0302)	NA	NA	NA
$\kappa_{\text{Wednesday}}$	0.0000 (0.0183)	NA	NA	NA
κ_{Thursday}	0.0350 (0.0225)	NA	NA	NA
κ_{Friday}	0.0499 *** (0.0147)	NA	NA	NA
κ_{Saturday}	0.0000 (0.0161)	NA	NA	NA
κ_{Sunday}	0.1108 *** (0.0220)	NA	NA	NA
v	13.8626 *** (1.0409)	12.7228 *** (0.9896)	9.6245 *** (0.0136)	NA
σ^2_δ	NA	NA	NA	0.0186 *** (0.0002)
σ^2_β	NA	NA	NA	0.0949 *** (0.0004)
σ^2_γ	NA	NA	NA	0.0002 (0.0008)

Notes: Standard deviations are in parentheses. *** and * is parameter significance at the 1% and 10% levels, respectively. For SD 2, $\kappa_j = \kappa_{\text{Monday},t}$ for $j = \text{Tuesday}, \ldots, \text{Sunday}$.

References

1. Barrado, D. Vivimos un Punto de Inflexión: La Generación 2020 y la Nueva Sociedad. 2020. Available online: https://telos.fundaciontelefonica.com/punto-de-inflexion-la-generacion-2020-y-la-nueva-sociedad/ (accessed on 1 December 2022).
2. Norrie, P. *A History of Disease in Ancient Times: More Lethal than War*; Springer Nature: Berlin/Heidelberg, Germany, 2016.
3. Zietz, B.P.; Dunkelberg, H. The History of the Plague and the Research on the Causative Agent Versinia Pestis. *Int. J. Hyg. Envir. Heal.* **2004**, *207*, 165–178. [CrossRef] [PubMed]
4. Guerra, F. Origen de las Epidemias en la Conquista de América. *Quinto Centen.* **1998**, *14*, 43–51.
5. López, S.; Garrido, F.; Hernández, M. Desarrollo Histórico de la Epidemiología: Su Formación Como Disciplina Científica. *Salud Pública de México* **2000**, *42*, 133–143. [CrossRef]
6. González, B.; Tomaino, L.; Serra, L.; Barber, Rodríguez, P. -Mireles, S. COVID-19: Pandemia de Modelos Matemáticos. 2020. Avaliable online: https://theconversation.com/covid-19-pandemia-de-modelos-matematicos-136212 (accessed on 1 December 2022).
7. Grillo-Ardila, E.K.; Santaella-Tenorio, J.; Guerrero, R.; Bravo, L.E. Mathematical Model and COVID-19. *Colomb. Méd.* **2020**, *51*, 1–9.
8. Creal, D.; Koopman, S.J.; Lucas, A. A General Framework for Observation Driven Time-Varying Parameter Models. Tinbergen Institute Discussion Paper 08-108/4. 2008. Available online: https://papers.tinbergen.nl/08108.pdf (accessed on 1 December 2022).
9. Harvey, A.C.; Chakravarty, T. Beta−t−EGARCH. *Cambridge Working Paper in Economics, CWPE 0840*. 2008. Available online: https://www.econ.cam.ac.uk/research-files/repec/cam/pdf/cwpe0840.pdf (accessed on 1 December 2022).
10. Cox, D.R. Statistical Analysis of Time Series: Some Recent Developments. *Scand. J. Stat.* **1981**, *8*, 93–115.
11. Harvey, A. *Dynamic Models for Volatility and Heavy Tails: With Applications to Financial and Economic Time Series (Econometric Society Monographs)*; Cambridge University Press: Cambridge, UK, 2013.
12. Blazsek, S.; Licht, A. Dynamic Conditional Score Models: A Review of Their Applications. *Appl. Econ.* **2020**, *52*, 1181–1199. [CrossRef]
13. Creal, D.; Koopman, S.J.; Lucas, A. Generalized Autoregressive Score Models with Applications. *J. Appl. Econom.* **2013**, *28*, 777–795. [CrossRef]
14. Blasques, F.; Koopman, S.J.; Lasak, K.; Lucas, A. In-Sample Confidence Bands and Out-of-Sample Forecast Bands for Time-Varying Parameters in Observation-Driven Models. *Int. J. Forecast.* **2016**, *32*, 875–887. [CrossRef]
15. Blasques, F.; van Brummelen, J.; Koopman, S.J.; Lucas, A. Maximum Likelihood Estimation for Score-Driven Models. *J. Econom.* **2022**, *227*, 325–346. [CrossRef]
16. Harvey, A.; Luati, A. Filtering With Heavy Tails. *J. Am. Stat. Assoc.* **2014**, *109*, 1112–1122 [CrossRef]
17. Creal, D.; Koopman, S.J.; Lucas, A. A Dynamic Multivariate Heavy-Tailed Model for Time-Varying Volatilities and Correlations. *J. Bus. Econ. Stat.* **2011**, *29*, 552–563 [CrossRef]
18. Caivano, M.; Harvey, A. Time-Series Models with an EGB2 Conditional Distribution. *J. Time Ser. Anal.* **2014**, *35*, 558–571 [CrossRef]
19. Contreras, S.; Caamaño-Carrillo, C.; Contreras-Reyes, J. Generalized Autoregressive Score Models Based on Sinh-Arcsinh Distributions for Time Series Analysis. *J. Comput. Appl. Math.* 2022. *in press*.
20. Harvey, A.C.; Kattuman, P. Time Series Models Based on Growth Curves with Applications to Forecasting Coronavirus. In *Harvard Data Science Review, Special Issue 1−COVID-19*; MIT Press: Cambridge, MA, USA, 2020; pp. 1–39.
21. Harvey, A.; Lit, R. Coronavirus and the Score-Driven Negative Binomial Distribution. Time Series Lab—Article Series. 2020. Available online: https://www.timeserieslab.com/articles/negbin.pdf (accessed on 1 December 2022).
22. Ayala, A.; Blazsek, S.; Licht, A. Score-Driven Stochastic Seasonality of the Russian Rouble: An Application Case Study for the Period of 1999 to 2020. *Empir. Econ.* **2022**, *62*, 2179–-2203. [CrossRef]
23. Blazsek, S.; Escribano, A.; Licht, A. Multivariate Markov-Switching Score-Driven Models: An Application to the Global Crude Oil Market. *Stud. Nonlinear Dyn. E* **2022**, *26*, 313–335. [CrossRef]

24. Ayala, A.; Blazsek, S. Score-Driven Models of Stochastic Seasonality in Location and Scale: An Application Case Study of the Indian Rupee to USD Exchange Rate. *Appl. Econ.* **2019**, *51*, 4083–4103. [CrossRef]
25. Ayala, A.; Blazsek, S. Score-Driven Currency Exchange Rate Seasonality as Applied to the Guatemalan Quetzal/US Dollar. *SERIEs* **2019**, *10*, 65–92. [CrossRef]
26. Caivano, M.; Harvey, A.; Luati, A. Robust Time Series Models with Trend and Seasonal Components. *SERIEs* **2016**, *7*, 99–120. [CrossRef]
27. Harvey, A.C. *Forecasting, Structural Time Series Models and the Kalman Filter*; Cambridge University Press: Cambridge, UK, 1990.
28. Harvey, A.C.; Shephard, N. Structural Time Series Models. In *Handbook of Statistics*; Econometrics; Maddala, G.S., Rao, C.R., Vinod, H.D., Eds.; Elsevier: Amsterdam, The Netherlands, 1993; Volume 11; pp. 261–302.
29. Commandeur, J.J.; Koopman, S.J. *An Introduction to State Space Time Series Analysis*; Oxford University Press: Oxford, UK, 2007.
30. Durbin, J.; Koopman, S.J. In *Time Series Analysis by State Space Methods*; Oxford University Press: Oxford, UK, 2012.
31. Helske, J.; Helske, M.J.; Suggests, M.A. CRAN Package KFAS. 2021. Available online: https://cran.r-project.org/web/packages/KFAS/index.html (accessed on 1 December 2022).
32. Gavilán, A. Tecnóloga Médica Que Verificó Muestra de Coronavirus en Chile. Available online: https://www.biobiochile.cl/noticias/nacional/region-del-maule/2020/03/03/angelica-gavilan-tecnologa-que-verifico-muestra-de-coronavirus-en-chile-no-lo-podia-creer.shtml (accessed on 1 December 2022).
33. COVID-19 Data Repository by the Center for Systems Science and Engineering (CSSE) at Johns Hopkins University. Available online: https://coronavirus.jhu.edu/map.html (accessed on 1 December 2022).
34. Jarque, C.M.; Bera, A.K. Efficient Tests for Normality, Homoscedasticity and Serial Independence of Regression Residuals. *Econ. Lett.* **1980**, *6*, 255–259. [CrossRef]
35. Dickey, D.A.; Fuller, W.A. Distribution of the Estimators for Autoregressive Time Series with a Unit Root. *J. Am. Stat. Assoc.* **1979**, *74*, 427–431.
36. Al-qaness, M.A.A.; Ewees, A.A.; Fan, H.; Abd El Aziz, M. Optimization Method for Forecasting Confirmed Cases of COVID-19 in China. *J. Clin. Med.* **2020**, *9*, 674. [CrossRef]
37. Naudé, W. Artificial Intelligence against COVID-19: An Early Review. IZA Discussion Paper No. 13110. 2020. Available online: https://ssrn.com/abstract=3568314 (accessed on 1 December 2022).
38. Dehesh, T.; Mardani-Fard, H.A.; Dehesh, P. Forecasting of COVID-19 Confirmed Cases in Different Countries with ARIMA Models. *MedRxiv*. 2020. Available online: https://www.medrxiv.org/content/10.1101/2020.03.13.20035345v1 (accessed on 1 December 2022).
39. Chintalapudi, N.; Battineni, G.; Amenta, F. COVID-19 Virus Outbreak Forecasting of Registered and Recovered Cases after Sixty Day Lockdown in Italy: A Data Driven Model Approach. *J. Microbiol. Immunol. Infect.* **2020**, *53*, 396–403. [CrossRef]
40. Chakraborty, T.; Ghosh, I. Real-Time Forecasts and Risk Assessment of Novel Coronavirus (COVID-19) Cases: A Data-Driven Analysis. *Chaos Solitons Fractals* **2020**, *135*, 109850. [CrossRef]
41. Singh, S.; Singh Parmar, K.; Kumar, J.; Singh Makkhan, S.J. Development of New Hybrid Model of Discrete Wavelet Decomposition and Autoregressive Integrated Moving Average (ARIMA) Models in Application to One Month Forecast the Casualties Cases of COVID-19. *Chaos Solitons Fractals* **2020**, *135*, 109866. [CrossRef] [PubMed]
42. Moftakhar, L.; Seif, M.; Safe, M.S. Exponentially Increasing Trend of Infected Patients with COVID-19 in Iran: A Comparison of Neural Network and ARIMA Forecasting Models. *Iran. J. Public Health* **2020**, *49*, 92–100. [CrossRef]
43. Ren, H.; Zhao, L.; Zhang, A.; Song, L.; Liao, Y.; Lu, W.; Cui, C. Early Forecasting of the Potential Risk Zones of COVID-19 in China's Megacities. *Sci. Total Environ.* **2020**, *729*, 138995. [CrossRef] [PubMed]
44. Salgotra, R.; Gandomi, M.; Gandomi, A.H. Time Series Analysis and Forecast of the COVID-19 Pandemic in India Using Genetic Programming. *Chaos Solitons Fractals* **2020**, *138*, 109945. [CrossRef] [PubMed]
45. Salgotra, R.; Gandomi, M.; Gandomi, A.H. Evolutionary Modelling of the COVID-19 Pandemic in Fifteen Most Affected Countries. *Chaos Solitons Fractals* **2020**, *140*, 110118. [CrossRef]
46. Salgotra, R.; Gandomi, A.H. Time Series Analysis of the COVID-19 Pandemic in Australia Using Genetic Programming. *Data Sci. COVID-19* **2021**, 399–411. [CrossRef]
47. Perc, M.; Gorisek Miksic, N.; Slavinec, M.; Stozer, A. Forecasting COVID-19. *Front. Phys.* **2020**, *8*, 127. 2020.00127. [CrossRef]
48. Chen, D.G.; Chen, X.G.; Chen, J.K. Reconstructing and Forecasting the COVID-19 Epidemic in the United States Using a 5-Parameter Logistic Growth Model. *Glob. Health Res. Policy* **2020**, *5*, 7. [CrossRef]
49. Li, Q.; Feng, W.; Quan, Y.H. Trend and Forecasting of the COVID-19 Outbreak in China. *J. Infect.* **2020**, *80*, 472–474. [CrossRef] [PubMed]
50. Qeadan, F.; Honda, T.; Gren, L.H.; Dailey-Provost, J.; Benson, L.S.; VanDerslice, J.A.; Porucznik, C.A.; Waters, A.B.; Lacey, S.; Shoaf, K. Naive Forecast for COVID-19 in Utah Based on the South Korea and Italy Models – The Fluctuation between Two Extremes. *Int. J. Environ. Res. Public Health* **2020**, *17*, 2750. [CrossRef] [PubMed]
51. Reddy Chimmula, V.K.; Zhang, L. Time Series Forecasting of COVID-19 Transmission in Canada Using LSTM Networks. *Chaos Solitons Fractals* **2020**, *135*, 109864. [CrossRef]
52. Dal Molin Ribeiro, M.H.; Gomes da Silva, R.; CoccoMariani, V.; dos SantosCoelho, L. Short-Term Forecasting COVID-19 Cumulative Confirmed Cases: Perspectives for Brazil. *Chaos Solitons Fractals* **2020**, *135*, 109853. [CrossRef] [PubMed]

53. Chaudhry, R.M.; Hanif, A.; Chaudhary, M.; Minhas, S.; Mirza, K.; Ashraf, T.; Gilani, S.A.; Kashif, M. Coronavirus Disease 2019 (COVID-19): Forecast of an Emerging Urgency in Pakistan. *Cureus* **2020**, *12*, 15. [CrossRef] [PubMed]
54. Tamang, S.K.; Singh, P.D.; Datta, B. Forecasting of Covid-19 Cases Based on Prediction Using Artificial Neural Network Curve Fitting Technique. *Glob. J. Environ. Sci. Manag.* **2020**, *6*, 53–64.
55. Roos, K.; Lee, Y.; Luo, R.; Kirpich, A.; Rothenberg, R.; Hyman, J.M.; Yan, P.; Chowell, G. Real-Time Forecasts of the COVID-19 Epidemic in China from February 5th to February 24th, 2020. *Infect. Dis. Model.* **2020**, *5*, 256–263. [CrossRef]
56. Fong, S.; Li, G.; Dey, N.; Crespo, R.G.; Herrera-Viedma, E. Finding an Accurate Early Forecasting Model from Small Dataset: A Case of 2019-nCoV Novel Coronavirus Outbreak. *Int. J. Interact. Multimed. Artif. Intell.* **2020**, *6*, 132–140. [CrossRef]
57. Sánchez-Villegas, P.; Daponte-Codina, A. Modelos Predictivos de la Epidemia de COVID-19 en España con Curvas de Gompertz. *Gac. Sanit.* **2020**. [CrossRef]
58. Abdulmajeed, K.; Adeleke, M.; Popoola, L.J.D. Online Forecasting of Covid-19 Cases in Nigeria Using Limited Data. *Data Brief* **2020**, *30*, 105683. [CrossRef]
59. Ji, D.; Zhang, D.; Xu, J.; Chen, Z.; Yang, T.; Zhao, P.; Chen, G.; Cheng, G.; Wang, Y.; Bi, J.; Tan, L.; Lau, G.; Qin, E. Prediction for Progression Risk in Patients with COVID-19 Pneumonia: The CALL Score. *Clin. Infect. Dis.* **2020**, *71*, 1393–1399. [CrossRef]
60. Sujath, R.; Chatterjee, J.M.; Hassanien, A.E. A Machine Learning Forecasting Model for COVID-19 Pandemic in India. *Stoch. Environ. Res. Risk Assess.* **2020**, *34*, 959–972. [CrossRef] [PubMed]
61. Gallardo, D.I.; Bourguignon, M.; Gómez, Y.M.; Caamaño-Carrillo, C.; Venegas, O. Parametric Quantile Regression Models for Fitting Double Bounded Response with Application to COVID-19 Mortality Rate Data. *Mathematics* **2022**, *10*, 2249. [CrossRef]
62. Yadav, S.; Yadav, P.K. The Peak of COVID-19 in India. *medRxiv*. **2020**. [CrossRef]
63. Parbat, D.; Chakraborty, M. A Python Based Support Vector Regression Model for Prediction of COVID19 Cases in India. *Chaos Solitons Fractals* **2020**, *138*, 109942. [CrossRef] [PubMed]
64. Zhao, C.; Tepekule, B.; Criscuolo, N.G.; Wendel Garcia, P.D.; Hilty, M.P.; Risc-Icu Consortium Investigators In Switzerland; Fumeaux, T.; Van Boeckel, T. icumonitoring.ch: a Platform for Short-Term Forecasting of Intensive Care Unit Occupancy During the COVID-19 Epidemic in Switzerland. *Swiss. Med. Wkly.* **2020**, *150*, w20524.
65. Reno, C.; Lenzi, J.; Navarra, A.; Barelli, E.; Gori, D.; Lanza, A.; Valentini, R.; Tang, B.; Fantini, M.P. Forecasting COVID-19-Associated Hospitalizations under Different Levels of Social Distancing in Lombardy and Emilia-Romagna, Northern Italy: Results from an Extended SEIR Compartmental Model. *J. Clin. Med.* **2020**, *9*, 11. [CrossRef]
66. Putra, S.; Khozin Mutamar, Z. Estimation of Parameters in the SIR Epidemic Model Using Particle Swarm Optimization. *Am. J. Math. Comput. Model.* **2019**, *4*, 83–93. [CrossRef]
67. Dil, S.; Dil, N.; Maken, Z.H. COVID-19 Trends and Forecast in the Eastern Mediterranean Region with a Particular Focus on Pakistan. *Cureus* **2020**, *12*, e8582. [CrossRef]
68. Fanelli, D.; Piazza, F. Analysis and Forecast of COVID-19 Spreading in China, Italy and France. *Chaos Solitons Fractals* **2020**, *134*, 109761. [CrossRef]
69. Anastassopoulou, C.; Russo, L; Tsakris, A.; Siettos, C. Data-Based Analysis, Modelling and Forecasting of the COVID-19 Outbreak. *PLoS ONE* **2020**, *15*, e0230405. [CrossRef] [PubMed]
70. Ahmar, A.S.; del Val, E.B. SutteARIMA: Short-Term Forecasting Method, a Case–COVID-19 and Stock Market in Spain. *Sci. Total Environ.* **2020**, *729*, 138883. [CrossRef] [PubMed]

mathematics

MDPI

Article

The Slash Half-Normal Distribution Applied to a Cure Rate Model with Application to Bone Marrow Transplantation

Diego I. Gallardo [1,*], Yolanda M. Gómez [1,2], Héctor J. Gómez [3], María José Gallardo-Nelson [2] and Marcelo Bourguignon [4]

[1] Mathematics Department, Faculty of Engineering, University of Atacama, Copiapó 1530000, Chile
[2] Medicine Department, Faculty of Medicine, University of Atacama, Copiapó 1530000, Chile
[3] Department of Mathematical and Physical Sciences, Faculty of Engineering, Catholic University of Temuco, Temuco 4780000, Chile
[4] Statistics Department, Federal University of Rio Grande do Norte, Natal 59078-970, Brazil
* Correspondence: diego.gallardo@uda.cl; Tel.: +56-52-2255565

Abstract: This paper proposes, for the first time, the use of an asymmetric positive and heavy-tailed distribution in a cure rate model context. In particular, it introduces a cure-rate survival model by assuming that the time-to-event of interest follows a slash half-normal distribution and that the number of competing causes of the event of interest follows a power series distribution, which defines six new cure rate models. Several properties of the model are derived and an alternative expression for the cumulative distribution function of the model is presented, which is very useful for the computational implementation of the model. A procedure based on the expectation–maximization algorithm is proposed for the parameter estimation. Two simulation studies are performed to assess some properties of the estimators, showing the good performance of the proposed estimators in finite samples. Finally, an application to a bone marrow transplant data set is presented.

Keywords: half-normal distribution; kurtosis; power series; blood and marrow transplantation

MSC: 62F10; 62N02

1. Introduction and Motivation

Survival models that incorporate a proportion of cured subjects are becoming increasingly popular in the analysis of data from clinical trials and other studies, mainly due to advances in medicine. In a cure rate model context, specifically using a competitive risk model framework, it is assumed that the event of interest is produced due to $M \in \mathbb{N}_0$ carcinogenic cells (a latent variable), each of them with an associated survival function $S(\cdot;\boldsymbol{\lambda})$, where $\boldsymbol{\lambda}$ is a vector of unknown parameters from a distribution defined on the positive line, and $M = 0$ represents the cure individuals. Different models are assumed for the number of cells (M) and the survival function $S(\cdot;\boldsymbol{\lambda})$. Specifically for the latter, we can mention Weibull, log-normal, generalized gamma, Birnbaum–Saunders distributions, among others. In particular, we focus on the proposed extension in Olmos et al. [1]. This model (parsimonious, since it only has two parameters) is called a slash half-normal (SHN) distribution. This distribution with a heavy tail has not yet been used in a cure rate model context. The objective of the proposed model is to increase the kurtosis with respect to its half-normal basal distribution, being more useful for modeling data sets that may have heavy tails. A version of the SHN reparameterized in terms of the mean with covariates was presented in Gómez et al. [2].

On the other hand, bone marrow transplantation is an important treatment for more than 50 fatal diseases such as leukemia, lymphoma, solid organ neoplasia, autoimmune diseases, among others. Bone marrow transplantation has unique biological characteristics and associated problems that markedly differ from solid organ transplantation, such as kidney, liver, or heart (Hardy et al. [3]). The problems are associated with the fact that immunocompetent cells can reject each other, which can cause graft rejection and generate graft-versus-host disease (GVHD). Furthermore, successful engraftment requires a strict match with the major histocompatibility complex (MHC) class II antigen of the donor and the recipient. Added to this is that patients must receive prior treatment with cytotoxic and myeloablative agents to avoid graft rejection (Chinen and Buckley [4], Simpson and Dazzi [5]). For these reasons, bone marrow transplantation is associated with considerable morbidity and mortality.

From a biological point of view, it makes sense to assume a heavy-tailed distribution when following patients over a period of time and following patient survival to assess transplant efficacy. These models can describe in detail the progression of the disease and allow us to make predictions for future clinical trials.

The motivation to introduce the SHN distribution in a cure rate model is given by a real data set application from the European Society for Blood and Marrow Transplantation (EBMT). The EBMT is a nonprofit medical, educational and scientific organization founded more than forty years ago, focused in the field of hematopoietic stem cell transplantation. The EBMT has more than 5000 members from 85 countries. This organization is focused on innovation, research and the advancement in the field of hematopoietic stem cell transplantation. The EBMT hosts a unique patient registry providing a pool of data to researchers all over the world to perform studies and assess new improvements in the field (EBTM [6]). Acute myeloid leukemia (AML) in children is rare in comparison with acute lymphoid leukemia and has overall survival of almost 75% at five years. Patients with high-risk characteristics need to achieve remission and undergo bone marrow transplantation with an overall survival of 70% (de Rooij et al. [7]). Post-transplant relapse is common and involves almost 80% of treated AML, of which 75% occur in the first year after transplantation (Sander et al. [8]).

The data were presented in Fiocco et al. [9] and are available in the `mstate` R package [10], labeled as ebmt4. The data set includes 2279 patients transplanted between 1985 and 1998. We considered the time in years from transplantation to relapse as the response variable, which had 84% of censored times. Figure 1 shows the Kaplan–Meier (KM) estimator for this data set and the histogram for the failure times.

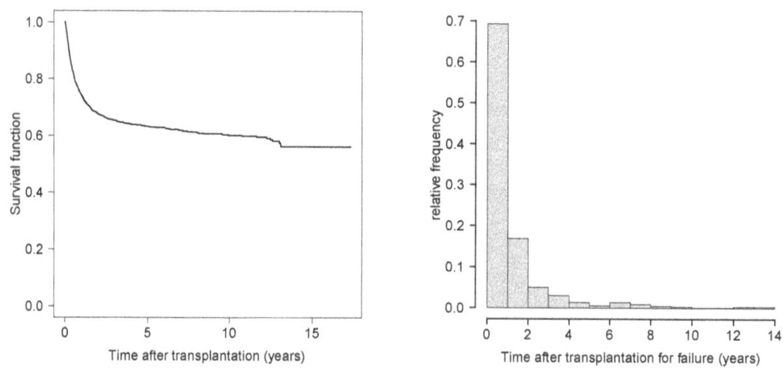

Figure 1. Kaplan–Meier estimator for the ebmt4 data set (**left panel**) and histogram for the failure times (**right panel**).

Note that there is a plateau in the KM estimator, suggesting the presence of cure individuals for this problem. In addition, the histogram of failure times suggest a heavy-tailed distribution for the noncured individuals. Some descriptive statistics for such failure times are mean = 1.14, median = 0.52, standard deviation = 1.84 and kurtosis = 18.71. The high kurtosis for these data, again, suggests the use of a heavy-tailed model for this problem.

Allogeneic stem cell transplantation (allo-HSCT) is a therapeutic approach used for a wide array of malignant and nonmalignant hematologic disorders. Its effectiveness is related to mortality and morbidity. Several complications can occur, including hemorrhages, infections, GVHD and endothelial-damage-related toxicities. There are new immunological and genetic therapies to avoid these complications and reduce mortality (See Horio et al. [11], Radujkovic et al. [12] and Tsai et al. [13]). Other immunodeficiency diseases such as ataxia-telangiectasia can be treated by bone marrow transplantation as mentioned in Sabino Pinho de Oliveira et al. [14]. Further studies with an increased cohort of patients and a longer period of follow-ups are required to validate and monitor the associated risks of transplantation. For this reason, it is important to use a heavy-tailed distribution such as the SHN distribution to study the survival in this type of bone marrow transplant and therapies. We emphasize that, up to this moment, this distribution has not been used in a cure rate model context. In this context, we define the power series–SHN (PS–SHN) class of univariate cure rate models obtained by compounding the SHN and power series distributions. The proposed model defines six new cure rate models as special cases.

The contents in this paper are organized in the following manner. In Section 2, we introduce the SHN distribution and derive some of its distributional properties. In Section 3, we introduce a general cure rate model. In Section 4, we describe a parameter estimation by the maximum likelihood method using the expectation–maximization (EM) algorithm. In Section 5, we present two simulation studies, where the first one is related to assessing the performance of the maximum likelihood estimation (MLE) using the EM algorithm and the second one is the misspecification for the time-to-event for the concurrent causes. In Section 6, we present a real data set on bone marrow transplantation. Finally, some conclusions are included in Section 7.

2. The SHN Distribution

The SHN distribution [1] with parameters $\sigma > 0$ and $\alpha > 0$ (denoted by SHN(σ, α)) is a model with positive support. Its probability density function (pdf) is given by

$$f_{SHN}(t; \boldsymbol{\lambda}) = \alpha\sqrt{\frac{2^{\alpha}}{\pi}}\sigma^{\alpha} t^{-(\alpha+1)}\gamma\left(\frac{t^2}{2\sigma^2}, \frac{\alpha+1}{2}\right), \quad t > 0, \tag{1}$$

where $\lambda = (\alpha, \sigma)$ and $\gamma(x, a) = \int_0^x u^{a-1}e^{-u}du$ is the lower incomplete gamma function. The cumulative distribution function (cdf) of the SHN model is given by

$$F_{SHN}(t; \boldsymbol{\lambda}) = \int_0^t f_{SHN}(w; \boldsymbol{\lambda})dw = \alpha\sqrt{\frac{2^{\alpha}}{\pi}}\sigma^{\alpha}\int_0^t w^{-(\alpha+1)}\gamma\left(\frac{w^2}{2\sigma^2}, \frac{\alpha+1}{2}\right)dw.$$

In the next Proposition, we present an alternative expression for the cdf.

Proposition 1. *The cdf of the SHN distribution is given by*

$$F_{SHN}(t; \boldsymbol{\lambda}) = 2\Phi\left(\frac{t}{\sigma}\right) - 1 - \sqrt{\frac{2^{\alpha}}{\pi}}\left(\frac{\sigma}{t}\right)^{\alpha}\Gamma\left(\frac{\alpha+1}{2}\right)G\left(\frac{w^2}{2\sigma^2}, \frac{\alpha+1}{2}\right), \quad t > 0,$$

where $\Phi(\cdot)$ denotes the cdf of the standard normal model and $G(\cdot, a)$ is the cdf of the gamma model with shape and rate parameters equal to a and 1, respectively.

Proof. By definition

$$F_{SHN}(t; \boldsymbol{\lambda}) = \alpha\sqrt{\frac{2^{\alpha}}{\pi}}\sigma^{\alpha}\int_0^t w^{-(\alpha+1)}\Gamma\left(\frac{\alpha+1}{2}\right)G\left(\frac{w^2}{2\sigma^2}, \frac{\alpha+1}{2}\right)dw.$$

Using techniques of integration by parts, we have that

$$u = G\left(\frac{w^2}{2\sigma^2}, \frac{\alpha+1}{2}\right) \Rightarrow du = \frac{w}{\sigma^2} g\left(\frac{w^2}{2\sigma^2}, \frac{\alpha+1}{2}\right) dw = \frac{w}{\sigma^2 \Gamma\left(\frac{\alpha+1}{2}\right)} \left(\frac{w^2}{2\sigma^2}\right)^{\frac{\alpha+1}{2}-1} \exp\left\{-\frac{w^2}{2\sigma^2}\right\} dw$$

$$dv = w^{-(\alpha+1)} \Rightarrow v = -\frac{w^{-\alpha}}{\alpha},$$

where $g(\cdot,\cdot)$ denotes the density function of the gamma distribution. Therefore,

$$\begin{aligned} F_{SHN}(t;\boldsymbol{\lambda}) &= \alpha\sqrt{\frac{2^\alpha}{\pi}} \sigma^\alpha \Gamma\left(\frac{\alpha+1}{2}\right) \\ &\times \left[-G\left(\frac{t^2}{2\sigma^2}, \frac{\alpha+1}{2}\right)\frac{t^{-\alpha}}{\alpha} + \frac{1}{\Gamma\left(\frac{\alpha+1}{2}\right)\alpha\sigma^\alpha}\sqrt{\frac{\pi}{2^\alpha}} \int_0^t \frac{1}{\sqrt{2\pi}\sigma} \exp\left\{-\frac{w^2}{2\sigma^2}\right\} dw\right]. \end{aligned}$$

and the result follows after identifying the pdf for the normal distribution within the integral. □

Corollary 1. *The survival function for the SHN model is given by*

$$S_{SHN}(t;\boldsymbol{\lambda}) = 2\Phi\left(-\frac{t}{\sigma}\right) + \sqrt{\frac{2^\alpha}{\pi}} \left(\frac{\sigma}{t}\right)^\alpha \Gamma\left(\frac{\alpha+1}{2}\right) G\left(\frac{t^2}{2\sigma^2}, \frac{\alpha+1}{2}\right), \quad t > 0. \tag{2}$$

Note that Corollary 1 provides an alternative way to program the survival function, especially from a computational point of view, because many software tools include the cdf of the standard normal and gamma models and the lower incomplete gamma function.

The SHN distribution has a convenient stochastic representation. If $X \sim HN(\sigma)$ and $Y \sim U(0,1)$ are independent (i.e., the half-normal and uniform distributions, respectively), then

$$T = \frac{X}{Y^{1/\alpha}} \sim SHN(\sigma, \alpha). \tag{3}$$

The mean, variance, asymmetry ($\sqrt{\beta_1}$) and kurtosis (β_2) coefficients from this distribution are

- $\mathbb{E}(T) = \sqrt{\frac{2}{\pi}} \frac{\alpha\sigma}{\alpha-1}, \quad \alpha > 1.$
- $\mathrm{Var}(T) = \frac{\alpha\sigma^2[(\pi-2)\alpha(\alpha-2)+\pi]}{\pi(\alpha-1)^2(\alpha-2)}, \quad \alpha > 2.$
- $\sqrt{\beta_1} = \frac{\pi\sqrt{2(\alpha-2)}\left[\frac{4}{\pi}\alpha^2(\alpha-2)(\alpha-3)-(\alpha-1)^2(\alpha-4)(\alpha+1)\right]}{\sqrt{\alpha}(\alpha-3)[\alpha(\pi-2)(\alpha-2)+\pi]^{3/2}}, \quad \alpha > 3.$
- $\beta_2 = \frac{3\alpha(\alpha-2)^2(\alpha-3)\left[\pi^2(\alpha-1)^4-4\alpha^3(\alpha-4)\right]-4\pi\alpha^2(\alpha-1)^2(\alpha-2)(\alpha-4)(\alpha^2-3\alpha+8)}{\alpha^2(\alpha-3)(\alpha-4)[\alpha(\pi-2)(\alpha-2)+\pi]^2}, \quad \alpha > 4.$

Note that σ is a scale parameter and α is related mainly with the kurtosis of the model. In fact, as discussed in Olmos et al. [1], low values for α allow us to accommodate distributions with greater kurtosis coefficients. On the other hand, when $\alpha \to \infty$, the HN distribution is recovered. Besides being a parsimonious model, an interesting property from the SHN distribution is that its tails are heavier than common distributions with positive support, as we enunciate in the following proposition.

Proposition 2. *Suppose a distribution with positive support satisfying the following conditions:*

(A1) Its density function can be written in the form $f(t;\boldsymbol{\lambda}) = Ct^a \exp\{-g(t;\boldsymbol{\lambda})\}, \quad t > 0$, *where C does not depend on t,* $a \in \mathbb{R}$ *and* $g(t;\boldsymbol{\lambda}) \geq 0, \forall t > 0$.

(A2) $\lim_{t\to\infty} t^{a'} \exp\{-g(t;\boldsymbol{\lambda})\} = 0, \quad \forall a' > a+1.$

Then, the SHN model has heavier tails than such a distribution.

Proof. To show that the SHN model has heavier tails than a model with a density function given as in assumption A1, it is enough to prove that

$$\lim_{t\to+\infty} \frac{f(t;\boldsymbol{\lambda})}{f_{SHN}(t;\sigma,\alpha)} = 0.$$

Therefore,

$$\begin{aligned}\lim_{t\to+\infty} \frac{f(t;\boldsymbol{\lambda})}{f_{SHN}(t;\sigma,\alpha)} &= \lim_{t\to+\infty} \frac{Ct^a \exp\{-g(t;\boldsymbol{\lambda})\}}{\alpha\sigma^\alpha\sqrt{\frac{2^\alpha}{\pi}}t^{-(\alpha+1)}\gamma\left(\frac{t^2}{2\sigma^2},\frac{\alpha+1}{2}\right)} \\ &= \frac{C}{\alpha\sigma^\alpha\sqrt{\frac{2^\alpha}{\pi}}} \lim_{t\to+\infty} \frac{t^{a+\alpha+1}\exp\{-g(t;\boldsymbol{\lambda})\}}{\gamma\left(\frac{t^2}{2\sigma^2},\frac{\alpha+1}{2}\right)}.\end{aligned}$$

As $\lim_{t\to+\infty}\gamma(t,c') = \Gamma(c'), \forall c' > 0, \alpha > 0$, by assumption A2 and by the continuity of the limit, we have the result. □

Corollary 2. *If X_1 and X_2 are two random variables with density functions satisfying conditions A1 and A2 in Proposition 2 and $Y = pX_1 + (1-p)X_2$, $p \in (0,1)$, then the SHN model also has heavier tails than the distribution related to Y.*

Remark 1. *Common distributions used in a cure rate model context satisfy the conditions A1 and A2 in Proposition 2. For instance:*

(a) If $C = \alpha/\sigma^\alpha$, $a = \alpha - 1$ and $g(t;\boldsymbol{\lambda}) = (t/\sigma)^\alpha$, the Weibull model is recovered (Chen et al. [15], Rodrigues et al. [16], Pal and Balakrishnan [17]).

(b) If $C = [\Gamma(\alpha)\sigma^\alpha]^{-1}$, $a = \alpha - 1$ and $g(t;\boldsymbol{\lambda}) = t/\sigma$, the gamma distribution is recovered (Balakrishnan and Pal [18], Wiangnak and Pal. [19], Ortega et al. [20]).

(c) If $C = [\sigma\sqrt{2\pi}]^{-1}$, $a = -1$ and $g(t;\boldsymbol{\lambda}) = (\log t - \alpha)^2/(2\sigma^2)$, we obtain the log-normal model (Balakrishnan and Pal [21], Gallardo et al. [22]).

(d) If $C = \sqrt{\sigma/(2\pi)}\exp(\sigma/\alpha)$, $a = -3/2$ and $g(t;\boldsymbol{\lambda}) = (\sigma/2)\left[t/\alpha^2 + 1/t\right]$, the inverse Gaussian model is recovered. We denote it as $IG(\alpha,\sigma)$.

(e) If $C = \sqrt{\sigma/(2\pi)}\exp(\sigma\alpha)$, $a = -1/2$ and $g(t;\boldsymbol{\lambda}) = (\sigma/2)\left[t/\alpha^2 + 1/t\right]$, the density function of the reciprocal of an inverse Gaussian random variable is recovered. Up to this moment, this model has not been used in a cure rate model context. We denote it as $RIG(\alpha,\sigma)$.

(f) If $C = [B(\alpha,\sigma)]^{-1}$, $a = \alpha - 1$ and $g(t;\boldsymbol{\lambda}) = (\alpha+\sigma)\log(1+t)$, the density of the beta prime distribution is recovered (Leao et al. [23]).

Remark 2. *The Birnbaum–Saunders (BS, Birnbaum and Saunders [24,25]) model with density function given by*

$$f(t;\alpha,\sigma) = \frac{1}{\sqrt{2\pi}}\exp\left(-\frac{1}{2\alpha^2}\left[\frac{t}{\sigma} + \frac{\sigma}{t} - 2\right]\right)\frac{(t+\sigma)}{2\alpha\sqrt{\sigma t^3}}, \quad t > 0,$$

can be written as a mixture between $IG(\beta,\beta/\alpha^2)$ and $RIG(\beta,1/(\beta\alpha^2))$ with equal probabilities (see Desmond [26] for details). Therefore, by Corollary 2, the SHN distribution has heavier tails than the BS distribution.

In the next Section, we discuss the use of the SHN model in the presence of long-term survivors.

3. A General Cure Rate Model and the SHN Distribution

To exemplify the use of the SHN distribution in a cure rate model context, we consider a general class of models based on a competitive risk scheme. The reader is referred to Chen et al. [15] for more details. Let M be a random variable denoting the initial number of carcinogenic cells of an individual. Several models have been considered for this scheme, among others, Bernoulli [27], Poisson [15] and negative binomial [16].

Let W_a, $a = 1,\ldots,M$ be the random variable representing the time at which the ath concurrent cause produces the event of interest. For instance, in a cancer context, W_a

represents the progressive time for the ath tumor cell. As shown in the Appendix A, a general class of model is produced when it is assumed that M follows a power series distribution (PS, Cancho et al. [28]). As is common in this context, it is also assumed that, conditional on M, the W_a's are independent identically distributed with a common cumulative distribution function $F(\cdot;\boldsymbol{\lambda})$ and survival function $S(\cdot;\boldsymbol{\lambda}) = 1 - F(\cdot;\boldsymbol{\lambda})$, where $\boldsymbol{\lambda}$ is a vector of unknown parameters. Moreover, it is assumed that the sequence $W_1, W_2, \ldots,$ is independent of M. Assuming that only one concurrent cause can produce the of interest, the observable time of the occurrence of the event of interest is given by

$$T = \begin{cases} +\infty & \text{, if } M = 0, \\ \min(W_1, \ldots, W_M) & \text{, if } M > 0. \end{cases}$$

Under this setting, the population survival function is given by

$$S_{pop}(t;\theta,\boldsymbol{\lambda}) = \frac{A(\theta S(t;\boldsymbol{\lambda}))}{A(\theta)}, \tag{4}$$

where $A(\cdot)$ is related to the PS distribution. Details about the function $A(\cdot)$ for different particular models are presented in Appendix A. From Equation (4), it is immediate that the cure rate of the model is given by $q_0 = a_0/A(\theta)$ and the survival function for the susceptible individuals is

$$S_{sus}(t;\theta,\boldsymbol{\lambda}) = \frac{a_0 - A(\theta S(t;\boldsymbol{\lambda}))}{a_0 - A(\theta)}. \tag{5}$$

For heterogeneous populations, we consider a set of covariates of dimension $r+1$ for the ith individual, say $\mathbf{x}_i = (1, x_{i1}, x_{i2}, \ldots, x_{ir})^\top$ (i.e., considering the intercept term), related to the cure rate term of the model. For the Poisson, binomial and COM-Poisson, such covariates can be introduced as

$$\theta_i = \exp\left(\mathbf{x}_i^\top \boldsymbol{\beta}\right), \quad i = 1, \ldots, n, \tag{6}$$

where n is the sample size and $\boldsymbol{\beta} = (\beta_0, \beta_1, \ldots, \beta_r)$ is the vector of unknown regression coefficients. For the rest of the discrete models, the covariates can be included as

$$\theta_i = \frac{\exp(\mathbf{x}_i^\top \boldsymbol{\beta})}{1 + \exp(\mathbf{x}_i^\top \boldsymbol{\beta})}, \quad i = 1, \ldots, n. \tag{7}$$

In the literature, many models have been considered for $S(\cdot;\boldsymbol{\lambda})$. As discussed in Remark 1, Weibull, gamma and log-normal models are common alternatives, to name a few. However, we remark that, up to this moment, no distribution with heavy tails has been used in this context and in particular, the SHN distribution has not been considered to model the survival function for the concurrent causes. Henceforth, we refer this model as PS–SHN. It is interesting to explore the use of the SHN distribution in a cure rate model context because it is usual that most failures occur until a certain time and from that moment mainly censoring times are observed. However, in diseases, from a certain time, it is considered that the patient is "cured". In practice, and especially in clinical trials with large sample sizes, it may occur that failure times are observed in unusual times, higher than expected.

4. Estimation

In order to estimate the model parameters, we utilize the maximum likelihood (ML) method. Let us consider the situation when the time-to-event is not completely observed and is subject to right-censoring. Let c_i denote the censoring time for the ith individual. We observe $y_i = \min(t_i, c_i)$ and $\delta_i = \mathbb{I}(t_i \leq c_i)$, where $\delta_i = 1$ if t_i is a time-to-event and $\delta_i = 0$

if right-censored, $i = 1, \ldots, n$. From n observed vectors $(y_1, \delta_1, \boldsymbol{x}_1^\top), \ldots, (y_n, \delta_n, \boldsymbol{x}_n^\top)$, the corresponding likelihood function, under noninformative censoring, can be expressed as

$$\begin{aligned}\ell(\boldsymbol{\psi}) &= \sum_{i=1}^{n} \Big\{ \delta_i \log[f_{pop}(y_i; \theta_i, \boldsymbol{\lambda})] + (1-\delta_i) \log[S_{pop}(y_i; \theta_i, \boldsymbol{\lambda})] \Big\} \\ &= \sum_{i=1}^{n} \Big\{ (1-\delta_i) \log[A(\theta_i S_{SHN}(y_i; \boldsymbol{\lambda}))] - \log[A(\theta_i)] \\ &\quad + \delta_i \Big(\log(\theta_i) + \log[f_{SHN}(y_i; \boldsymbol{\lambda})] + \log[A'(\theta_i S_{SHN}(y_i; \boldsymbol{\lambda}))] \Big) \Big\}, \end{aligned} \tag{8}$$

where $\boldsymbol{\psi} = (\boldsymbol{\beta}^\top, \boldsymbol{\lambda}^\top)^\top$, and $f_{SHN}(\cdot;\cdot)$ and $S_{SHN}(\cdot;\cdot)$ are defined in (1) and (2). Details for the construction of Equation (8) can be seen in Cancho et al. [28] and Gallardo et al. [29].

The MLE of $\boldsymbol{\psi}$, denoted by $\widehat{\boldsymbol{\psi}}$, can be obtained by maximizing Equation (8) in relation to $\boldsymbol{\psi}$. However, this procedure can be computationally expensive and it would not necessarily provide a global maximum, especially when the dimension of $\boldsymbol{\beta}$ is high. To facilitate the obtainment of the MLE for $\boldsymbol{\psi}$, we can use the EM algorithm developed in Gallardo et al. [29] for this class of models. The kth iteration of such procedure consists of the following steps:

- E-step: For $i = 1, \ldots, n$, compute

$$\widetilde{M}_i^{(k)} = (1-\delta_i)\mathbb{E}\Big(M_i; \theta_i^{(k-1)} S_i^{(k-1)}\Big) + \delta_i \frac{\mathbb{E}\Big(M_i^2; \theta_i^{(k-1)} S_i^{(k-1)}\Big)}{\mathbb{E}\Big(M_i; \theta_i^{(k-1)} S_i^{(k-1)}\Big)},$$

  where $\mathbb{E}(M_i; \mu_i)$ and $\mathbb{E}(M_i^2; \mu_i)$ denote the two first moments of the PS distribution with parameter μ_i given by

$$\mathbb{E}(M_i; \mu_i) = \mu_i \frac{\partial \log A(\mu_i)}{\partial \mu_i} \quad \text{and} \quad \mathbb{E}\Big(M_i^2; \mu_i\Big) = \mu_i \frac{\partial \mathbb{E}(M_i; \mu_i)}{\partial \mu_i} + \mathbb{E}^2(M_i; \mu_i).$$

- M1-step: Given $\boldsymbol{M}^{(k)} = (\widetilde{M}_1^{(k)}, \ldots, \widetilde{M}_n^{(k)})$, find $\boldsymbol{\beta}$ that maximizes $Q_1(\boldsymbol{\beta} \mid \psi^{(k)})$ in relation to $\boldsymbol{\beta}^{(k)}$, where

$$Q_1(\boldsymbol{\beta} \mid \psi^{(k)}) = \sum_{i=1}^{n} \Big\{ \widetilde{M}_i^{(k)} \log(\theta_i) - \log[A(\theta_i)] \Big\}.$$

- M2-step: Given $\boldsymbol{M}^{(k)}$, find $\boldsymbol{\lambda}^{(k)}$ that maximizes $Q_2(\boldsymbol{\lambda} \mid \psi^{(k)})$ in relation to $\boldsymbol{\lambda}$, where

$$\begin{aligned} Q_2(\boldsymbol{\lambda} \mid \psi^{(k)}) = \sum_{i=1}^{n} \Bigg\{ & (\widetilde{M}_i^{(k)} - \delta_i) \log \Bigg[2\Phi\Big(-\frac{y_i}{\sigma}\Big) \\ & + \sqrt{\frac{2^\alpha}{\pi}} \Big(\frac{\sigma}{y_i}\Big)^\alpha \Gamma\Big(\frac{\alpha+1}{2}\Big) G\Big(\frac{y_i^2}{2\sigma^2}, \frac{\alpha+1}{2}\Big) \Bigg] \\ & + \delta_i \Bigg[\log(\alpha) + \frac{\alpha}{2}\log(2) + \alpha \log(\sigma) - (\alpha+1)\log(y_i) \\ & + \log\Bigg[\gamma\Big(\frac{y_i^2}{2\sigma^2}, \frac{\alpha+1}{2}\Big) \Bigg] \Bigg] \Bigg\}. \end{aligned}$$

The E-, M1- and M2-steps are repeatedly alternated until a suitable convergence rule is satisfied, e.g., the difference in successive values of the estimates is less than a prespecified tolerance. Note that this procedure requires two independent maximization procedures in relation to $\boldsymbol{\beta}$ and $\boldsymbol{\lambda}$ of dimensions $r+1$ and 2, respectively, instead of a unique maximization procedure in relation to $\boldsymbol{\psi}$, which has a dimension $(r+3)$. Standard errors for $\widehat{\boldsymbol{\psi}}$ can be computed based on the Hessian matrix, i.e., $\mathbf{H}(\widehat{\boldsymbol{\psi}}) = \partial^2\ell(\boldsymbol{\psi})/\partial\boldsymbol{\psi}^\top\partial\boldsymbol{\psi}\big|_{\boldsymbol{\psi}=\boldsymbol{\psi}^\top}$. This matrix can be estimated numerically using, for instance, the package pracma [30] of R [31]. As the estimators obtained via the EM algorithm are MLE, they satisfy the asymptotic distribution

$$\sqrt{n}(\widehat{\boldsymbol{\psi}} - \boldsymbol{\psi}) \xrightarrow{\mathcal{D}} N\Big(\mathbf{0}, \big[\mathbf{H}(\widehat{\boldsymbol{\psi}})\big]^{-1}\Big), \quad \text{as } n \to +\infty, \tag{9}$$

where $\xrightarrow{\mathcal{D}}$ denotes convergence in distribution. This result allows us to compute an approximated confidence interval for the parameters. Moreover, based on the delta method (see Sen et al. [32] for details), we can also build a confidence interval for any scalar function of $\boldsymbol{\psi}$, say $g(\boldsymbol{\psi})$, using

$$\sqrt{n}[g(\widehat{\boldsymbol{\psi}}) - g(\boldsymbol{\psi})] \xrightarrow{\mathcal{D}} N\Big(\mathbf{0}, [\nabla g(\boldsymbol{\psi})]^\top \big[\mathbf{H}(\widehat{\boldsymbol{\psi}})\big]^{-1} \nabla g(\boldsymbol{\psi})\Big), \quad \text{as } n \to +\infty, \tag{10}$$

where $\nabla g(\boldsymbol{\psi}) = \partial g(\boldsymbol{\psi})/\partial\boldsymbol{\psi}$ denotes the gradient of $g(\boldsymbol{\psi})$. In particular, a very useful case is $g(\boldsymbol{\psi}) = a_0/A(\theta_i)$, i.e., the cure rate of the corresponding model. The described estimation procedure was incorporated in the package PScr [33] of R [31].

5. Simulation Studies

In this Section, we present two simulation studies. The first one is related to assessing the performance of the MLE using the EM algorithm discussed in Section 3. The second study is devoted to assessing the performance of the PS–SHN compared with the PS–Weibull model when data are drawn from the PS–Weibull model with some modified scheme. The software tool used for this study was R [31].

5.1. Assessing the Performance of MLE in a Finite Sample Size

In this subsection, we present a simulation study to evaluate the performance of the MLE estimators of the PS–SHN in a finite sample size. We considered three particular distributions belonging to the PS model for the number of concurrent causes: Poisson, logarithmic and geometric. We also considered three sample sizes: 100, 200 and 400. For each individual, we drew two covariates, say x_1 and x_2, where x_1 was drawn from the Bernoulli distribution with a success probability of 0.5 and x_2 from the standard normal model. For this reason, $\boldsymbol{\beta} = (\beta_0, \beta_1, \beta_2)$ had dimension three. For each particular distribution for the concurrent causes, we considered two scenarios, named high and low cure rates. For the high cure rate, we considered that for β_2 fixed at zero, the values of the two levels for x_1 for the cure rate were 0.7 and 0.45. With such information, the values of β_0 and β_1 could be determined from the equations

$$\exp(-\exp(\beta_0)) = 0.7 \qquad \text{and} \qquad \exp(-\exp(\beta_0 + \beta_1)) = 0.45$$

for the Poisson case and

$$\frac{1}{A\left(\frac{\exp(\beta_0)}{1+\exp(\beta_0)}\right)} = 0.7 \qquad \text{and} \qquad \frac{1}{A\left(\frac{\exp(\beta_0+\beta_1)}{1+\exp(\beta_0+\beta_1)}\right)} = 0.45,$$

for the logarithmic and geometric cases. A similar procedure could be applied for the low cure rate case, where we considered that, for β_2 fixed at zero, the values of the two levels for x_1 for the cure rate were 0.5 and 0.25. Summarizing, for the Poisson model, we had $\beta_0 = -1.031$, $\beta_1 = 0.806$ and $\beta_2 = 0$ for the high cure rate case and $\beta_0 = -0.367$, $\beta_1 = 0.693$ and $\beta_2 = 0$ for the lower cure rate case; for the logarithmic distribution we had $\beta_0 = 0.132$, $\beta_1 = 1.588$ and $\beta_2 = 0$ for the high cure rate case and $\beta_0 = 1.366$, $\beta_1 = 2.534$ and $\beta_2 = 0$ for the lower cure rate case; and for the geometric model, we had $\beta_0 = -0.847$, $\beta_1 = 1.048$ and $\beta_2 = 0$ for the high cure rate case and $\beta_0 = 0$, $\beta_1 = 1.099$ and $\beta_2 = 0$ for the lower cure rate case. Finally, we also considered two values for α, 0.75 and 2.5 and two values for σ, 1 and 3. The combinations of distributions for the concurrent causes, sample size, type of cure rate (high or low), α and σ produced 72 different scenarios. However, we only present the cases for the Poisson and geometric models, although conclusions are similar for the logarithmic distribution. For each, we considered 1000 replicates and computed the MLE based on the EM algorithm described in Section 3. Such results are summarized in Tables 1 and 2 through the average of the estimated bias (bias), the average of the estimated standard error (s.e.) based on the Hessian matrix numerically evaluated at $\boldsymbol{\psi} = \widehat{\boldsymbol{\psi}}$, the root of the estimated mean squared error (RMSE) and the 95% coverage probability (CP). As expected, the bias of the estimators was reduced and the terms s.e. and RMSE were closer when the sample size was increased, suggesting the asymptotic consistency of the estimators. Additionally, the terms CP were closer to the nominal values used for their construction when n increased.

Table 1. Simulation study to assess the performance of MLE in the Poisson–SHN model.

Cure Rate	σ	α	Parameter	$n=100$ bias	s.e.	RMSE	CP	$n=200$ bias	s.e.	RMSE	CP	$n=400$ bias	s.e.	RMSE	CP
High	1	0.75	$\widehat{\beta}_0$	0.023	0.370	0.255	0.978	0.012	0.248	0.200	0.974	0.010	0.177	0.147	0.965
			$\widehat{\beta}_1$	−0.019	0.335	0.302	0.961	−0.006	0.234	0.210	0.953	−0.001	0.164	0.145	0.952
			$\widehat{\beta}_2$	0.005	0.165	0.144	0.963	0.003	0.116	0.104	0.958	−0.002	0.081	0.074	0.949
			$\widehat{\alpha}$	0.294	0.979	0.751	0.975	0.172	0.600	0.505	0.960	0.055	0.376	0.335	0.951
			$\widehat{\sigma}$	0.082	0.452	0.372	0.965	0.052	0.321	0.276	0.955	0.015	0.227	0.206	0.952
		2.5	$\widehat{\beta}_0$	0.002	0.208	0.180	0.962	0.002	0.145	0.124	0.959	0.001	0.102	0.089	0.956
			$\widehat{\beta}_1$	−0.014	0.316	0.281	0.959	−0.013	0.221	0.192	0.958	−0.008	0.155	0.140	0.953
			$\widehat{\beta}_2$	−0.011	0.155	0.140	0.942	−0.005	0.109	0.103	0.943	−0.003	0.077	0.071	0.951
			$\widehat{\alpha}$	0.287	1.637	1.416	0.929	0.140	1.342	1.091	0.937	0.127	0.995	0.854	0.946
			$\widehat{\sigma}$	−0.039	0.302	0.229	0.933	−0.011	0.211	0.171	0.941	−0.010	0.146	0.131	0.943
	3	0.75	$\widehat{\beta}_0$	−0.140	0.922	0.307	0.962	−0.125	0.738	0.250	0.952	−0.101	0.614	0.212	0.950
			$\widehat{\beta}_1$	0.013	0.371	0.327	0.960	0.009	0.258	0.226	0.954	0.003	0.181	0.170	0.953
			$\widehat{\beta}_2$	0.006	0.183	0.164	0.948	0.002	0.127	0.111	0.948	0.000	0.089	0.080	0.950
			$\widehat{\alpha}$	0.687	1.658	1.304	0.972	0.657	1.389	1.269	0.961	0.584	1.193	1.169	0.955
			$\widehat{\sigma}$	−0.269	1.073	0.846	0.957	−0.088	0.892	0.719	0.956	−0.040	0.652	0.602	0.953
		2.5	$\widehat{\beta}_0$	0.100	0.505	0.263	0.969	0.085	0.339	0.201	0.963	0.078	0.223	0.160	0.958
			$\widehat{\beta}_1$	−0.011	0.325	0.295	0.958	−0.009	0.226	0.201	0.952	−0.008	0.159	0.144	0.951
			$\widehat{\beta}_2$	0.005	0.161	0.151	0.939	0.005	0.112	0.097	0.942	0.003	0.078	0.068	0.949
			$\widehat{\alpha}$	−0.791	1.976	1.583	0.938	−0.549	1.797	1.496	0.941	−0.409	1.490	1.442	0.949
			$\widehat{\sigma}$	−0.641	1.428	0.893	0.919	−0.409	1.237	0.691	0.928	−0.319	0.939	0.592	0.930
Low	1	0.75	$\widehat{\beta}_0$	0.013	0.441	0.296	0.977	0.009	0.285	0.226	0.960	0.005	0.206	0.172	0.954
			$\widehat{\beta}_1$	−0.015	0.413	0.369	0.960	−0.013	0.289	0.270	0.952	−0.001	0.202	0.181	0.951
			$\widehat{\beta}_2$	0.013	0.198	0.180	0.951	0.008	0.138	0.125	0.950	0.003	0.096	0.088	0.950
			$\widehat{\alpha}$	0.293	1.127	0.747	0.972	0.262	0.778	0.632	0.965	0.094	0.459	0.391	0.959
			$\widehat{\sigma}$	0.084	0.531	0.385	0.944	0.063	0.392	0.324	0.947	0.037	0.272	0.243	0.949
		2.5	$\widehat{\beta}_0$	0.004	0.238	0.210	0.961	0.002	0.163	0.144	0.953	0.001	0.114	0.104	0.951
			$\widehat{\beta}_1$	−0.010	0.384	0.329	0.965	−0.009	0.270	0.239	0.957	−0.004	0.189	0.178	0.953
			$\widehat{\beta}_2$	0.012	0.185	0.166	0.960	0.008	0.129	0.118	0.959	0.004	0.091	0.081	0.951
			$\widehat{\alpha}$	0.175	1.975	1.271	0.924	0.134	1.722	1.144	0.938	0.087	1.198	0.968	0.944
			$\widehat{\sigma}$	−0.057	0.353	0.258	0.912	−0.016	0.244	0.190	0.940	−0.002	0.170	0.146	0.943
	3	0.75	$\widehat{\beta}_0$	−0.151	0.999	0.346	0.941	−0.139	0.805	0.282	0.948	−0.105	0.679	0.227	0.950
			$\widehat{\beta}_1$	−0.012	0.464	0.402	0.969	−0.010	0.323	0.279	0.962	−0.007	0.225	0.202	0.958
			$\widehat{\beta}_2$	0.012	0.221	0.206	0.943	0.010	0.153	0.140	0.946	0.004	0.107	0.098	0.950
			$\widehat{\alpha}$	0.526	1.660	1.336	0.971	0.371	1.378	1.251	0.965	0.294	1.276	1.154	0.959
			$\widehat{\sigma}$	−0.467	1.285	0.938	0.929	−0.176	2.077	0.719	0.936	−0.025	1.785	0.619	0.940
		2.5	$\widehat{\beta}_0$	0.107	0.586	0.295	0.973	0.093	0.405	0.225	0.962	0.086	0.261	0.177	0.959
			$\widehat{\beta}_1$	0.013	0.398	0.365	0.955	0.008	0.276	0.239	0.954	0.000	0.194	0.179	0.951
			$\widehat{\beta}_2$	−0.017	0.192	0.173	0.965	−0.002	0.133	0.119	0.961	0.000	0.093	0.081	0.959
			$\widehat{\alpha}$	−0.912	4.181	1.545	0.934	−0.682	3.910	1.489	0.936	−0.493	3.601	1.462	0.942
			$\widehat{\sigma}$	−0.743	1.490	0.969	0.961	−0.526	1.287	0.764	0.960	−0.379	1.038	0.647	0.958

Table 2. Simulation study to assess the performance of MLE in the geometric–SHN model.

Cure Rate	σ	α	Estimator	$n = 100$ bias	s.e.	MSE	CP	$n = 200$ bias	s.e.	MSE	CP	$n = 400$ bias	s.e.	MSE	CP
High	1	0.75	$\widehat{\beta}_0$	0.025	0.556	0.391	0.970	0.008	0.374	0.278	0.983	0.006	0.259	0.219	0.966
			$\widehat{\beta}_1$	0.023	0.469	0.424	0.955	0.021	0.328	0.289	0.956	0.001	0.230	0.204	0.955
			$\widehat{\beta}_2$	0.004	0.234	0.213	0.954	0.003	0.162	0.150	0.942	0.001	0.114	0.106	0.936
			$\widehat{\alpha}$	0.284	1.203	0.741	0.996	0.218	0.796	0.627	0.982	0.109	0.495	0.431	0.961
			$\widehat{\sigma}$	0.078	0.546	0.379	0.949	0.070	0.394	0.342	0.950	0.033	0.280	0.251	0.948
		2.5	$\widehat{\beta}_0$	−0.014	0.353	0.302	0.959	−0.003	0.241	0.218	0.947	0.003	0.168	0.152	0.949
			$\widehat{\beta}_1$	0.016	0.453	0.403	0.959	0.012	0.315	0.294	0.956	0.008	0.221	0.199	0.941
			$\widehat{\beta}_2$	0.006	0.225	0.200	0.959	0.004	0.156	0.143	0.944	0.002	0.109	0.100	0.943
			$\widehat{\alpha}$	0.242	1.871	1.434	0.854	0.163	1.752	1.270	0.910	0.081	1.332	1.018	0.946
			$\widehat{\sigma}$	−0.078	0.375	0.272	0.911	−0.017	0.266	0.206	0.944	−0.014	0.184	0.153	0.964
	3	0.75	$\widehat{\beta}_0$	−0.153	0.609	0.417	0.989	−0.135	0.488	0.329	0.960	−0.111	0.323	0.262	0.964
			$\widehat{\beta}_1$	−0.012	0.510	0.448	0.959	−0.003	0.353	0.310	0.961	−0.001	0.247	0.225	0.946
			$\widehat{\beta}_2$	−0.006	0.253	0.226	0.948	−0.004	0.174	0.155	0.959	−0.003	0.121	0.105	0.961
			$\widehat{\alpha}$	0.534	1.577	1.389	1.000	0.381	1.402	1.313	1.000	0.194	1.356	1.309	1.000
			$\widehat{\sigma}$	−0.490	1.302	0.974	0.910	−0.197	1.153	0.747	0.972	−0.029	0.825	0.638	0.987
		2.5	$\widehat{\beta}_0$	0.121	0.505	0.385	0.989	0.095	0.380	0.289	0.990	0.083	0.232	0.215	0.985
			$\widehat{\beta}_1$	−0.005	0.460	0.427	0.961	−0.003	0.321	0.279	0.961	−0.002	0.225	0.199	0.957
			$\widehat{\beta}_2$	0.012	0.228	0.196	0.960	0.002	0.159	0.137	0.955	−0.001	0.111	0.099	0.949
			$\widehat{\alpha}$	−0.921	2.029	1.755	0.841	−0.709	1.903	1.570	0.835	−0.569	1.661	1.535	0.819
			$\widehat{\sigma}$	−0.788	1.333	1.004	0.851	−0.555	1.052	0.825	0.886	−0.407	0.899	0.672	0.914
Low	1	0.75	$\widehat{\beta}_0$	0.008	0.477	0.344	0.981	0.003	0.338	0.254	0.969	0.001	0.226	0.194	0.971
			$\widehat{\beta}_1$	0.004	0.422	0.384	0.954	0.003	0.294	0.256	0.957	0.003	0.207	0.189	0.951
			$\widehat{\beta}_2$	−0.011	0.212	0.197	0.940	−0.006	0.147	0.133	0.953	−0.003	0.103	0.095	0.948
			$\widehat{\alpha}$	0.280	1.043	0.702	0.998	0.190	0.693	0.583	0.981	0.097	0.441	0.387	0.957
			$\widehat{\sigma}$	0.071	0.480	0.349	0.960	0.059	0.352	0.300	0.960	0.037	0.251	0.217	0.952
		2.5	$\widehat{\beta}_0$	0.012	0.309	0.274	0.954	0.010	0.213	0.186	0.956	0.004	0.149	0.136	0.953
			$\widehat{\beta}_1$	0.010	0.409	0.360	0.957	0.007	0.286	0.247	0.964	0.003	0.201	0.180	0.942
			$\widehat{\beta}_2$	−0.007	0.206	0.190	0.961	−0.005	0.143	0.125	0.957	−0.002	0.100	0.084	0.962
			$\widehat{\alpha}$	0.353	1.622	1.301	0.868	0.274	1.438	1.258	0.932	0.269	1.025	0.968	0.939
			$\widehat{\sigma}$	−0.078	0.340	0.260	0.900	−0.040	0.244	0.184	0.956	−0.015	0.167	0.144	0.952
	3	0.75	$\widehat{\beta}_0$	−0.155	0.524	0.379	0.970	−0.128	0.415	0.284	0.973	−0.109	0.266	0.240	0.961
			$\widehat{\beta}_1$	0.009	0.448	0.399	0.963	0.005	0.311	0.271	0.962	0.003	0.219	0.187	0.956
			$\widehat{\beta}_2$	−0.016	0.223	0.196	0.965	−0.006	0.155	0.136	0.959	−0.003	0.109	0.099	0.950
			$\widehat{\alpha}$	0.605	1.893	1.506	1.000	0.481	1.501	1.388	1.000	0.276	1.372	1.292	1.000
			$\widehat{\sigma}$	−0.340	1.372	0.894	0.929	−0.089	1.116	0.703	0.966	−0.053	0.773	0.612	0.993
		2.5	$\widehat{\beta}_0$	0.090	0.607	0.347	0.987	0.074	0.439	0.268	0.990	0.051	0.282	0.201	0.982
			$\widehat{\beta}_1$	0.011	0.415	0.378	0.954	0.005	0.289	0.270	0.946	0.001	0.203	0.180	0.949
			$\widehat{\beta}_2$	−0.005	0.208	0.187	0.952	−0.001	0.145	0.135	0.937	−0.001	0.101	0.094	0.944
			$\widehat{\alpha}$	−0.865	1.780	1.612	0.852	−0.630	1.708	1.517	0.837	−0.449	1.629	1.462	0.838
			$\widehat{\sigma}$	−0.695	1.283	0.927	0.887	−0.492	1.097	0.762	0.905	−0.341	0.732	0.605	0.924

5.2. *Misspecification for the Time-to-Event for the Concurrent Causes*

In this subsection, we assessed the performance of the MLE for the Poisson–SHN and geometric–SHN models when data were drawn from an artificial model with heavy tails based on the Weibull distribution.

The generation of the data was very similar to that in the last subsection, considering the following changes:

- The times related to the concurrent causes were drawn from the Weibull model with mean $\mathbb{E}(W) = \mu$ and variance 1. We considered three values for μ: 2.5, 5.0 and 7.5. For the parameterization considered in part a) from Remark 1, this corresponded to $\alpha = 2.70$ and $\sigma = 7.90$, $\alpha = 5.80$ and $\sigma = 29.16$ and $\alpha = 8.97$ and $\sigma = 62.75$, respectively.

- A determined number of failure times (2% of the sample size, i.e., two observations for $n = 100$, four observations for $n = 200$ and eight observations for $n = 400$), were imputed as $\max\left(t^{fail}\right) + U\sigma_t^{fail}$, where $\max\left(t^{fail}\right)$ and σ_t^{fail} denote the maximum and the standard error of the failure times and $U \sim U(1,2)$. This scheme artificially simulated a distribution for the time-to-event of the concurrent causes with a heavier tail than the Weibull distribution, but not corresponding to the SHN.

The main goal of this study was to compare the coefficients related to the cure (i.e., the components of the vector $\boldsymbol{\beta}$) obtained with the Poisson–SHN and Poisson–Weibull models (when the true model for M is the Poisson distribution) and geometric–SHN and geometric–Weibull models (when the true model is the geometric distribution). All the considered combinations of $\mathbb{E}(W)$, sample size, type of cure (high/low) and model for M (Poisson/geometric), totalizing 36 cases. Each was replicated 1000 times. Table 3 summarizes the bias and RMSE for each combination. Note that, in all the considered cases, the bias and RMSE were lower (or at least the same) for the models considering the SHN rather than the Weibull model. Such differences in favor of the SHN were minimized when the sample size was increased.

Table 3. Misspecification simulation study for Poisson–SHN and geometric–SHN models.

			$n = 100$				$n = 200$				$n = 400$			
							Poisson Case							
			bias		RMSE		bias		RMSE		bias		RMSE	
Cure Rate	$\mathbb{E}(W)$	**Estimator**	**SHN**	**Weibull**	**SHN**	**Weibull**	**SHN**	**Weibull**	**SHN**	**Weibull**	**SHN**	**Weibull**	**SHN**	**Weibull**
High	2.5	$\widehat{\beta}_0$	0.059	0.089	0.394	0.431	0.053	0.084	0.248	0.309	0.051	0.073	0.168	0.221
		$\widehat{\beta}_1$	−0.018	−0.066	0.356	0.430	−0.006	−0.049	0.248	0.316	−0.003	−0.048	0.175	0.227
		$\widehat{\beta}_2$	−0.002	−0.003	0.176	0.255	−0.002	−0.003	0.122	0.187	−0.001	−0.002	0.086	0.131
	5.0	$\widehat{\beta}_0$	−0.109	−0.159	0.344	0.347	−0.077	−0.126	0.225	0.239	−0.058	−0.123	0.134	0.169
		$\widehat{\beta}_1$	−0.014	−0.020	0.402	0.773	−0.007	−0.018	0.280	0.601	−0.005	−0.017	0.197	0.451
		$\widehat{\beta}_2$	−0.005	−0.006	0.197	0.288	−0.003	−0.004	0.138	0.209	0.000	0.000	0.097	0.146
	7.5	$\widehat{\beta}_0$	−0.307	−0.359	0.246	0.297	−0.276	−0.355	0.201	0.210	−0.251	−0.322	0.107	0.159
		$\widehat{\beta}_1$	−0.017	−0.025	0.443	0.933	−0.012	−0.015	0.311	0.773	−0.011	−0.013	0.219	0.650
		$\widehat{\beta}_2$	0.011	0.012	0.218	0.317	−0.003	−0.003	0.152	0.230	0.001	0.001	0.107	0.160
Low	2.5	$\widehat{\beta}_0$	0.087	0.097	0.287	0.314	0.070	0.079	0.181	0.211	0.058	0.063	0.139	0.144
		$\widehat{\beta}_1$	−0.014	−0.069	0.437	0.448	−0.012	−0.061	0.306	0.334	−0.007	−0.052	0.215	0.228
		$\widehat{\beta}_2$	−0.001	0.000	0.207	0.297	0.000	0.000	0.146	0.215	−0.001	−0.001	0.102	0.155
	5.0	$\widehat{\beta}_0$	−0.093	−0.100	0.234	0.255	−0.071	−0.092	0.165	0.176	−0.052	−0.078	0.110	0.121
		$\widehat{\beta}_1$	−0.029	−0.048	0.489	0.809	−0.022	−0.025	0.344	0.656	−0.008	−0.012	0.244	0.487
		$\widehat{\beta}_2$	−0.003	−0.004	0.231	0.336	−0.001	−0.001	0.164	0.241	−0.001	−0.001	0.116	0.172
	7.5	$\widehat{\beta}_0$	−0.204	−0.285	0.197	0.217	−0.194	−0.282	0.133	0.155	−0.192	−0.279	0.102	0.111
		$\widehat{\beta}_1$	−0.012	−0.018	0.533	0.893	−0.003	−0.014	0.379	0.742	−0.002	−0.004	0.267	0.583
		$\widehat{\beta}_2$	−0.008	−0.008	0.252	0.372	−0.005	−0.006	0.179	0.265	−0.003	−0.003	0.127	0.187

Table 3. *Cont.*

			$n=100$				$n=200$				$n=400$			
							Geometric Case							
High	2.5	$\widehat{\beta}_0$	0.071	0.092	0.196	0.244	0.053	0.082	0.163	0.190	0.031	0.048	0.124	0.139
		$\widehat{\beta}_1$	−0.105	−0.127	0.209	0.281	−0.083	−0.094	0.153	0.218	−0.054	−0.056	0.148	0.164
		$\widehat{\beta}_2$	−0.003	−0.005	0.254	0.435	0.001	0.002	0.176	0.299	0.001	0.001	0.123	0.207
	5.0	$\widehat{\beta}_0$	−0.091	−0.129	0.135	0.154	−0.088	−0.119	0.098	0.103	−0.071	−0.106	0.042	0.071
		$\widehat{\beta}_1$	−0.089	−0.130	0.352	0.427	−0.080	−0.120	0.287	0.329	−0.057	−0.092	0.172	0.243
		$\widehat{\beta}_2$	0.001	0.000	0.274	0.478	−0.001	−0.001	0.192	0.330	0.001	0.001	0.135	0.229
	7.5	$\widehat{\beta}_0$	−0.288	−0.333	0.094	0.125	−0.251	−0.311	0.067	0.082	−0.242	−0.271	0.049	0.059
		$\widehat{\beta}_1$	−0.055	−0.099	0.493	0.512	−0.054	−0.096	0.314	0.389	−0.042	−0.053	0.290	0.301
		$\widehat{\beta}_2$	0.009	−0.010	0.293	0.524	0.005	−0.008	0.204	0.362	0.001	0.001	0.143	0.248
Low	2.5	$\widehat{\beta}_0$	−0.075	−0.109	0.245	0.298	−0.062	−0.081	0.219	0.234	−0.046	−0.069	0.147	0.165
		$\widehat{\beta}_1$	−0.094	−0.130	0.217	0.245	−0.074	−0.083	0.133	0.192	−0.050	−0.061	0.128	0.138
		$\widehat{\beta}_2$	0.012	0.016	0.235	0.397	0.011	0.012	0.163	0.270	0.002	0.003	0.114	0.187
	5.0	$\widehat{\beta}_0$	−0.224	−0.259	0.197	0.209	−0.216	−0.237	0.101	0.144	−0.153	−0.203	0.061	0.089
		$\widehat{\beta}_1$	−0.108	−0.126	0.303	0.385	−0.097	−0.106	0.251	0.283	−0.084	−0.099	0.146	0.207
		$\widehat{\beta}_2$	0.002	0.002	0.253	0.426	0.002	0.002	0.176	0.292	0.001	0.001	0.123	0.201
	7.5	$\widehat{\beta}_0$	−0.260	−0.459	0.116	0.150	−0.256	−0.424	0.096	0.106	−0.202	−0.392	0.042	0.073
		$\widehat{\beta}_1$	−0.050	−0.112	0.337	0.471	−0.049	−0.104	0.274	0.359	−0.035	−0.091	0.202	0.268
		$\widehat{\beta}_2$	−0.002	−0.004	0.269	0.456	−0.001	−0.002	0.187	0.315	−0.001	−0.001	0.131	0.216

6. Application to Bone Marrow Transplantation

In this section, we present a real data set application from the EBMT presented in the introduction section. Additionally, the prophylaxis covariate (dichotomous, 1730 patients with "no" and 549 patients with "yes") was available.

For the analysis, we considered some existent models in the literature, all of them belonging to the power-series cure rate model, such as the Poisson, logarithmic, negative binomial, Bernoulli, COM-Poisson and polylogarithm models. Additionally, we considered three commons models used for the concurrent causes such as the Weibull, gamma and BS models. Table 4 shows the Akaike information criterion (AIC) [34] and Bayesian information criterion (BIC) criteria [35] for those models in the ebmt4 data. Note that both criteria favored models where the SHN for concurrent causes was used.

Table 4. AIC and BIC criteria for some cure rate models in the literature based on a competing risk scheme for the ebmt4 data set.

Model for M	Weibull	Gamma	BS	SHN
Po	4650.0/4672.9	4683.0/4706.0	4580.8/4603.8	4537.9/4560.8
Lo	4628.7/4651.6	4639.6/4662.6	4628.1/4651.0	4547.3/4570.3
NB	4561.4/4590.1	4547.4/4576.1	4583.0/4611.7	4540.2/4568.8
Bern	4665.1/4688.0	4712.8/4735.8	4577.0/4599.9	4535.8/4558.8
COM-Po	4639.3/4667.9	4659.5/4688.1	4578.9/4607.6	4537.8/4566.5
PL	4612.1/4658.0	4615.9/4661.8	4585.1/4630.9	4545.3/4591.2

Table 5 shows the estimated parameters for the Bern/SHN cure rate model and its standard errors. Note that both parameters related to the cure were significant with 5% of significance. We also considered a residuals analysis in the selected model based on the Cox–Snell residuals [36,37] and the randomized quantile residuals [38]. The first residual was compared with its Nelson–Aalen estimator and the second with the quantile of the standard normal distribution. In both cases, if the model was correct, we expected to observe the identity function for the respective graphs. According to Figure 2, such residuals suggested that the choice model was correct. Finally, we also computed the Kaplan–Meier (K–M) estimator for patients with and without prophylaxis and the respective point estimation and 95% confidence interval for the survival function for each time. Such confidence interval was based on the delta method discussed in Equation (10). Figure 3 shows those results. Note the closeness of the estimation for the survival function and that provided by the K–M estimator. As expected, patients without prophylaxis had a lower survival function than patients with prophylaxis.

Table 5. Estimates and standard errors (s.e.) for the Bern/SHN cure rate model in the ebmt4 data set.

Parameter	β_0	β_1	α	σ
Estimate	−0.4912	−0.2224	0.3844	0.3120
s.e.	0.0907	0.1030	0.0753	0.0310

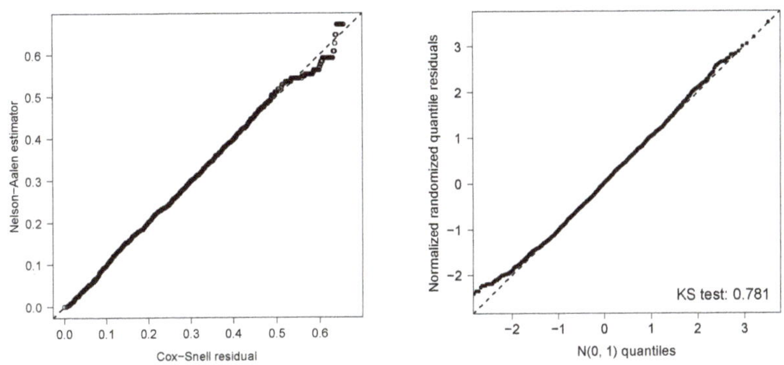

Figure 2. Cox–Snell residuals versus their Nelson–Aalen estimator (**left panel**) and the randomized quantile residuals versus the N(0,1) quantiles and its p-values for the Kolmogorov–Smirnov test (**right panel**).

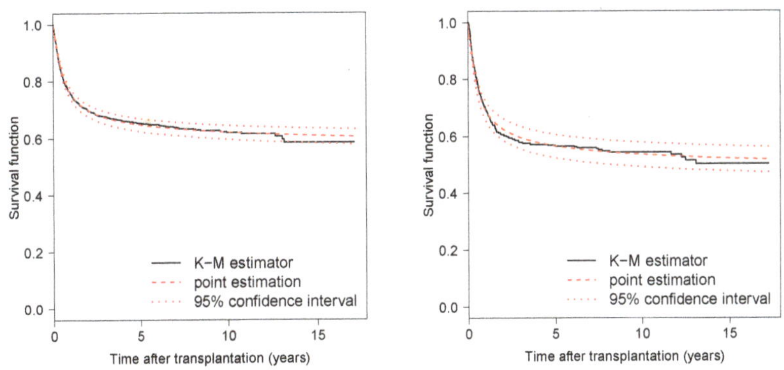

Figure 3. Kaplan–Meier (K–M) estimator for patients with and without prophylaxis and the respective point estimation and 95% confidence interval for the survival function for each time.

7. Conclusions

In this work, we introduced the PS–SHN cure rate model. We provided a mathematical treatment of the new distribution including an alternative expression for the cumulative distribution function. An EM algorithm to compute maximum likelihood estimation procedures in finite samples was discussed. Two simulation studies were performed to assess some properties of the estimators, showing the good performance of the proposed estimation procedure in finite samples. In the analysis of the bone marrow transplant data, the SHN cure rate model yielded a better fit when compared to other well-known models in the literature, according to the AIC and BIC criteria. We developed an R package to perform inference in the power-series cure rate models. As part of future research, we plan to explore other estimation methods for the proposed cure rate model, for instance, a Bayesian approach. A second line of a future research will be a bias-reduction methodology to estimate the parameters of the proposed regression model.

Author Contributions: Conceptualization, D.I.G. and Y.M.G.; formal analysis, Y.M.G. and H.J.G.; investigation, Y.M.G. and M.J.G.-N.; software, D.I.G. and M.B.; validation H.J.G., M.J.G.-N. and M.B.; writing—original draft preparation H.J.G.; writing—review and editing D.I.G., Y.M.G., M.J.G.-N. and M.B.; Supervision, D.I.G. and Y.M.G. All of the authors contributed significantly to this research article. All authors have read and agreed to the published version of the manuscript.

Funding: This research received no external funding.

Data Availability Statement: The data set used in Section 5 was duly referenced.

Conflicts of Interest: The authors declare no conflict of interest.

Appendix A. Parametrization Used for Some Discrete Models

The power series distribution has a probability mass function (p.m.f.) given by

$$P(M = m;\theta) = \frac{a_m\theta^m}{A(\theta)}, \qquad m = 0, 1, 2, \ldots,$$

where $A(\theta) = \sum_{m=0}^{\infty} a_m\theta^m$ and $\theta \in \mathbf{\Theta}$, with $\mathbf{\Theta}$ the parameter space for θ.

Table A1. Some particular cases of the power series distribution.

	Poisson	Negative Binomial	Binomial	Logarithmic	Polylogarithm	COM-Poisson
a_m	$(m!)^{-1}$	$\binom{m+q-1}{m}$	$\binom{q}{m}$	$(m+1)^{-1}$	$(m+1)^q$	$(m!)^{-q}$
$A(\theta)$	e^θ	$(1-\theta)^{-q}$	$(1+\theta)^q$	$-\frac{\log(1-\theta)}{\theta}$	$\frac{Li_q(\theta)}{\theta}$	$\frac{1}{Z(\theta,q)}$
$\mathbf{\Theta}$	$(0,\infty)$	$(0,1)$	$(0,\infty)$	$(0,1)$	$(0,1)$	$(0,\infty)$
Notation	Po(θ)	NB(q,θ)	Bin(q,θ)	Lo(θ)	PL(q,θ)	COM-Po(q,θ)

NOTE: *Li* denotes the polylogarithm defined as $Li_q(\theta) = \sum_{m=1}^{\infty} m^{-q}\theta^m$ and $Z(\theta,q) = \sum_{m=0}^{\infty}(m!)^{-q}\theta^m$. In the NB, Bin, PL and COM-Po distributions, q is considered known.

Observations:

- NB$(1,\theta)$ = Geo(θ), i.e., the geometric distribution.
- Bin$(1,\theta)$ = Bern(θ), i.e., the Bernoulli distribution.
- NB(q,θ) = Bin(q,θ), if $-q^{-1} \in \mathbb{N}$ and $0 < \theta/q < 1$.
- $\lim_{q\to\infty}$COM-Po(q,θ) = Bern$((1+\theta)^{-1})$.
- $\lim_{q\to 0}$COM-Po(q,θ) = Geo$(1-\theta)$, if $\theta < 1$.

References

1. Olmos, N.M.; Varela, H.; Gómez, H.W.; Bolfarine, H. An extension of the half-normal distribution. *Stat. Pap.* **2012**, *53*, 875–886. [CrossRef]
2. Gómez, Y.M.; Gallardo, D.I.; De Castro, M. A regression model for positive data based on the slash half-normal distribution. *Revstat* **2021**, *19*, 553–573.
3. Hardy, R.E.; Ikpeazu, E.V. Bone marrow transplantation: A review. *J. Natl. Med. Assoc.* **1989**, *81*, 518–523.
4. Chinen, J.; Buckley, R.H. Transplantation immunology: Solid organ and bone marrow. *J. Allergy Clin. Immunol.* **2010**, *125*, S324–S335. [CrossRef]

5. Simpson, E.; Dazzi, F. Bone Marrow Transplantation 1957–2019. *Front. Immunol.* **2019**, *10*, 1246. [CrossRef]
6. The European Society for Blood and Marrow Transplantation (s.f.). The EBMT. Available online: https://www.ebmt.org (accessed on 10 December 2022).
7. de Rooij, J.D.; Zwaan, C.M.; van den Heuvel-Eibrink, M. Pediatric AML: From Biology to Clinical Management. *J. Clin. Med.* **2015**, *4*, 127–149. [CrossRef]
8. Sander, A.; Zimmermann, M.; Dworzak, M.; Fleischhack, G.; von Neuhoff, C.; Reinhardt, D.; Kaspers, G.J.; Creutzig, U. Consequent and Intensified Relapse Therapy Improved Survival in Pediatric AML: Results of Relapse Treatment In 379 Patients of Three Consecutive Aml-Bfm Trials. *Leukemia* **2010**, *24*, 1422–1428. [CrossRef]
9. Fiocco, M.; Putter, H.; van Houwelingen, H.C. Reduced-rank proportional hazards regression and simulation-based prediction for multi-state models. *Stat. Med.* **2008**, *27*, 4340–4358. [CrossRef]
10. Putter, H.; de Wreede, L.; Fiocco, M. Mstate: Data Preparation, Estimation and Prediction in Multi-State Models. R package version 2016.0-2. 2016. Available online: https://CRAN.R-project.org/package=mstate (accessed on 10 December 2022).
11. Horio, T.; Morishita, E.; Mizuno, S.; Uchino, K.; Hanamura, I.; Espinoza, J.L.; Morishima, Y.; Kodera, Y.; Onizuka, M.; Kashiwase, K.; et al. Donor Heme Oxygenase-1 Promoter Gene Polymorphism Predicts Survival after Unrelated Bone Marrow Transplantation for High-Risk Patients. *Cancers* **2020**, *12*, 424. [CrossRef]
12. Radujkovic, A.; Kordelas, L.; Bogdanov, R.; Müller-Tidow, C.; Beelen, D.W.; Dreger, P.; Luft, T. Interleukin-18 and Hematopoietic Recovery after Allogeneic Stem Cell Transplantation. *Cancers* **2020**, *12*, 2789. [CrossRef]
13. Tsai, X.C.; Chen, T.T.; Gau, J.P.; Wang, P.N.; Liu, Y.C.; Lien, M.Y.; Li, C.C.; Yao, M.; Ko, B.S. Outcomes of Different Haploidentical Transplantation Strategies from the Taiwan Blood and Marrow Transplantation Registry. *Cancers* **2022**, *14*, 1097. [CrossRef]
14. Sabino Pinho de Oliveira, B.; Putti, S.; Naro, F.; Pellegrini, M. Bone Marrow Transplantation as Therapy for Ataxia-Telangiectasia: A Systematic Review. *Cancers* **2020**, *12*, 3207. [CrossRef]
15. Chen, M.H.; Ibrahim, J.G.; Sinha, D. A new Bayesian model for survival data with a surviving fraction. *J. Am. Stat. Assoc.* **1999**, *94*, 909–919. [CrossRef]
16. Rodrigues, J.; Cancho, V.G.; de Castro, M.A.; Louzada-Neto, F. On the unification of the long-term survival models. *Stat. Probab. Lett.* **2009**, *79*, 753–759. [CrossRef]
17. Pal, S.; Balakrishnan, N. Likelihood inference for COM-Poisson cure rate model with interval-censored data and Weibull lifetimes. *Stat. Methods Med. Res.* **2017**, *26*, 2093–2113. [CrossRef]
18. Balakrishnan, N.; Pal, S. Likelihood Inference for Flexible Cure Rate Models with Gamma Lifetimes. *Commun. Stat. Theory Methods* **2015**, *19*, 4007–4048. [CrossRef]
19. Wiangnak, P.; Pal, S. Gamma Lifetimes and Associated Inference for Interval Censored Cure Rate Model with COM-Poisson Competing Cause. *Commun. Stat. Theory Methods* **2018**, *47*, 1491–1509. [CrossRef]
20. Ortega, E.M.M.; Cordeiro, G.M.; Hashimoto, E.M.; Suzuki, A.K. Regression models generated by gamma random variables with long-term survivors. *Commun. Stat. Appl. Methods* **2017**, *24*, 43–65. [CrossRef]
21. Balakrishnan, N.; Pal, S. Lognormal lifetimes and likelihood-based inference for flexible cure rate models based on COM-Poisson family. *Comput. Stat. Data Anal.* **2013**, *67*, 41–67. [CrossRef]
22. Gallardo, D.I.; Bolfarine, H.; Pedroso-de-Lima, A.C. An EM algorithm for estimating the destructive weighted Poisson cure rate model. *J. Stat. Comput. Simul.* **2016**, *86*, 1497–1515. [CrossRef]
23. Leao, J.; Bourguignon, M.; Saulo, H.; Santos-Neto, M.; Calsavara, V. The Negative Binomial Beta Prime Regression Model with Cure Rate: Application with a Melanoma Dataset. *J. Stat. Theory Pract.* **2021**, *15*, 63. [CrossRef]
24. Birnbaum, Z.W.; Saunders, S.C. A new family of life distributions. *J. Appl. Probab.* **1969**, *6*, 319–327. [CrossRef]
25. Birnbaum, Z.W.; Saunders, S.C. Estimation for a family of life distributions with applications to fatigue. *J. Appl. Probab.* **1969**, *6*, 328–347. [CrossRef]
26. Desmond, A.F. On the relationship between two fatigue models. *IEEE Trans. Reliab.* **1986**, *35*, 167–169. [CrossRef]
27. Berkson, J.; Gage, R. Survival curve for cancer patients following treatment. *J. Am. Stat. Assoc.* **1952**, *47*, 501–515. [CrossRef]
28. Cancho, V.G.; Louzada, F.; Ortega, E.M. The power series cure rate model: An application to a cutaneous melanoma data. *Commun. Stat. Simul. Comput.* **2013**, *42*, 586–602. [CrossRef]
29. Gallardo, D.I.; Romeo, J.S.; Meyer, R. A simplified estimation procedure based on the EM algorithm for the power series cure rate model. *Commun. Stat. Simul. Comput.* **2017**, *46*, 6342–6359. [CrossRef]
30. Borchers, H.W. Pracma: Practical Numerical Math Functions. R Package Version 2.4.2. 2022. Available online: https://CRAN.R-project.org/package=pracma (accessed on 10 December 2022).
31. R Core Team. *R: A Language and Environment for Statistical Computing*; R Foundation for Statistical Computing: Vienna, Austria, 2022. Available online: https://www.R-project.org/ (accessed on 10 December 2022).
32. Sen, P.K.; Singer, J.M.; Pedroso-de-Lima, A.C. *From Finite Sample to Asymptotic Methods in Statistics*; Cambridge University Press: New York, NY, USA, 2010.
33. Gallardo, D. PScr: Estimation for the Power Series Cure Rate Model. R Package Version 1.0. 2022. Available online: https://CRAN.R-project.org/package=PScr (accessed on 10 December 2022).
34. Akaike, H. A new look at the statitstical model identification. *IEEE Trans. Autom. Control* **1974**, *19*, 716–723. [CrossRef]
35. Schwarz, G. Estimating the dimension of a model. *Ann. Stat.* **1978**, *6*, 461–464. [CrossRef]

36. Conlon, A.S.; Taylor, J.M.; Sargent, D.J. Multi-state models for colon cancer recurrence and death with a cured fraction. *Stat. Med.* **2014**, *33*, 1750–1766. [CrossRef]
37. Cox, D.R. A general definition of residuals. *J. R. Stat. Soc. Ser. B* **1968**, *30*, 248–275. [CrossRef]
38. Dunn, P.K.; Smyth, G.K. Randomized quantile residuals. *J. Comput. Graph. Stat.* **1996**, *5*, 236–244.

mathematics

MDPI

Article

The Multivariate Skewed Log-Birnbaum–Saunders Distribution and Its Associated Regression Model

Guillermo Martínez-Flórez [1,*,†], Sandra Vergara-Cardozo [2], Roger Tovar-Falón [1,*,†] and Luisa Rodriguez-Quevedo [2]

1 Departamento de Matemáticas y Estadística, Facultad de Ciencias Básicas, Universidad de Córdoba, Montería 230002, Colombia
2 Departamento de Estadística, Facultad de Ciencias, Universidad Nacional de Colombia, Bogotá 111321, Colombia
* Correspondence: guillermomartinez@correo.unicordoba.edu.co (G.M.-F.); rjtovar@correo.unicordoba.edu.co (R.T.-F.)
† These authors contributed equally to this work.

Abstract: In this article, a multivariate extension of the unit-sinh-normal (USHN) distribution is presented. The new distribution, which is obtained from the conditionally specified distributions methodology, is absolutely continuous, and its marginal distributions are univariate USHN. The properties of the multivariate USHN distribution are studied in detail, and statistical inference is carried out from a classical approach using the maximum likelihood method. The new multivariate USHN distribution is suitable for modeling bounded data, especially in the $(0,1)^p$ region. In addition, the proposed distribution is extended to the case of the regression model and, for the latter, the Fisher information matrix is derived. The numerical results of a small simulation study and two applications with real data sets allow us to conclude that the proposed distribution, as well as its extension to regression models, are potentially useful to analyze the data of proportions, rates, or indices when modeling them jointly considering different degrees of correlation that may exist in the study variables is of interest.

Keywords: multivariate log-Birnbaum–Saunders distribution; multivariate regression model; unit-sinh-normal distribution; bounded data

MSC: 60E05; 62H05

1. Introduction

Data whose response falls in the interval $(0,1)$ such as indices, proportions, or rates appear very frequently in different fields of knowledge, mainly the areas of social sciences, engineering, economic sciences, and medicine. Some practical examples of these types of data are the proportion of patients who die from a certain disease or virus (SARS-CoV-2, Diabetes, HIV or Cancer) in a country or city; the Human Development Index or the illiteracy rate in a region or country; the proportion of deaths due to exposure to smoking or other exposure factors; the mortality rate from traffic accidents in a city; the percentage of items that do not meet the minimum requirements in an assembly line; and the portion of income that a family spends on entertainment.

For the analysis of data such as those described above, statistical methodologies developed from distributions with support in the interval $(0,1)$ are required. In this sense, several probability distributions and regression models have been proposed; see Ferrari and Cribari-Neto [1], Kumaraswamy [2], Martínez-Flórez et al. [3,4], Kieschnick and Mccullough [5], Mazucheli et al. [6,7].

The univariate sinh-normal (SHN) distribution introduced by Rieck and Nedelman [8] has received special attention for modeling material-fatigue-related problems. The probability density function (pdf) of this distribution is given by:

$$\varphi(y) = \frac{2}{\sigma\alpha}\cosh\left(\frac{y-\gamma}{\sigma}\right)\phi\left(\frac{2}{\alpha}\sinh\left(\frac{y-\gamma}{\sigma}\right)\right), \quad y \in \mathbb{R}, \tag{1}$$

where $\alpha > 0$ and γ are shape and location parameters, respectively; $\sigma > 0$ is a scale parameter, and $\phi(\cdot)$ is the pdf of the normal distribution. The pdf in (1) can also be written as:

$$\varphi(y) = b'_y\phi(b_y) \tag{2}$$

where $b'_y = \frac{2}{\sigma\alpha}\cosh\left(\frac{y-\gamma}{\sigma}\right)$ is a derivative of $b_y = \frac{2}{\alpha}\sinh\left(\frac{y-\gamma}{\sigma}\right)$. The distribution function in (2) is denoted by $\text{SHN}(\alpha, \gamma, \sigma)$. Several extensions of the SHN distribution have been studied by numerous authors, for example, Martínez-Flórez et al. [9] proposed the extended generalized SHN distribution, which has great applicability in the fit of datasets presenting high skewness and bimodality simultaneously; Lemonte [10] introduced an extension named skewed log-Birnbaum–Saunders (log-BS) regression model which is based on the asymmetric SHN distribution proposed by Leiva et al. [11]. The log-BS regression model is suitable for fitting data with high degrees of skewness. On the other hand, Moreno et al. [12] proposed a generalization of the Birnbaum–Saunders (BS) distribution [13] that affords flexibility for fitting data with greater skewness and kurtosis compared with other distributions.

Multivariate extensions of the SHN distribution have also been considered, for instance, by Martínez-Flórez et al. [14], Díaz-García and Domínguez-Molina [15], Lemonte [16], Marchant et al. [17] and, recently, by Martínez-Flórez et al. [18], among others.

For modeling material fatigue data, the most widely known distribution is the BS whose pdf is given by:

$$f_T(t) = \phi(a_t)\frac{t^{-3/2}(t+\beta)}{2\alpha\sqrt{\beta}}, \quad t > 0, \tag{3}$$

where $a_t = \frac{1}{\alpha}\left(\sqrt{t/\beta} - \sqrt{\beta/t}\right)$, $\alpha > 0$ is a shape parameter, and $\beta > 0$ is a scale parameter and the median distribution. The distribution in (3) is denoted by $T \sim \text{BS}(\alpha, \beta)$. Rieck and Nedelman [8] showed that, if $Y \sim \text{SHN}(\alpha, \gamma, \sigma = 2)$, then $T = \exp(Y)$ follows a BS distribution with parameters α and $\beta = \exp(\gamma)$. From this last relationship between the BS and SHN distributions, the SHN regression model can be formulated as follows: if $\boldsymbol{x}_i = (x_{i1}, \ldots, x_{ip})^\top$ is a vector of covariates such that,

$$Y_i = \log(T_i) = \boldsymbol{x}_i^\top\boldsymbol{\theta}, \tag{4}$$

for $i = 1, \ldots, n$, and,

$$Y_i \sim \text{SHN}(\alpha, \boldsymbol{x}_i^\top\boldsymbol{\theta}, \sigma)$$

then, the model in (4) is known as the log-linear BS regression model. More details about this regression model can be found in Rieck and Nedelman [8].

The BS distribution has great applicability to analyze data in several areas of knowledge, such as biology, medicine, engineering, etc.; however, so far, no extension of the BS distribution has been proposed to study the modeling of rates and proportions, i.e., of a random variable in the unit interval $(0,1)$ from the BS model. In response to this special case, Mazucheli et al. [19] presented an extension of the BS distribution for fitting random variables in the unit interval $(0,1)$. The pdf of this model is given by:

$$f(x) = \frac{1}{2x\alpha\beta\sqrt{2\pi}}\left[\left(-\frac{\beta}{\log x}\right)^{1/2} + \left(-\frac{\beta}{\log x}\right)^{3/2}\right]\exp\left\{\frac{1}{2\alpha^2}\left[\frac{\log x}{\beta} + \frac{\beta}{\log x} + 2\right]\right\}, \tag{5}$$

where $x \in (0,1)$, $\alpha > 0$ is the shape parameter and $\beta > 0$ is a scale parameter. Based on the work of Mazucheli et al. [19], Martínez-Flórez et al. [3] studied the unit sinh-normal (USHN) distribution to deal with the problem of bounded observations on the interval $(0,1)$ which has a pdf given by:

$$\varphi(y) = \frac{1}{(1-y)\log(1-y)^{-1}}\frac{2}{\sigma\alpha}\cosh\left(\frac{\log(-\log(1-y))-\gamma}{\sigma}\right) \times \phi\left(\frac{2}{\alpha}\sinh\left(\frac{\log(-\log(1-y))-\gamma}{\sigma}\right)\right), \tag{6}$$

where $y \in (0,1)$, $\alpha > 0$ is a shape parameter, γ is a location parameter, and $\sigma > 0$ is a scale parameter. The natural extension to the case of the model which considers covariates is the USHN linear regression (USHNR) model. The USHNR model is defined by considering a set of p explanatory variables that are denoted by $\boldsymbol{x}_i = (x_{i1}, \ldots, x_{ip})^\top$ and, such that,

$$\log(-\log(1-Y_i)) = \boldsymbol{x}_i^\top \boldsymbol{\theta} + \varepsilon_i, \quad \text{for} \quad i = 1, \ldots, n \tag{7}$$

where $\boldsymbol{\theta} = (\theta_1, \ldots, \theta_p)^\top$ is a p dimensional vector of unknown parameters and $\varepsilon_i \sim \text{SHN}(\alpha, 0, \sigma)$. More details can be found in [3].

The main objective of this work is to introduce a new multivariate probability distribution capable of modeling data in the region $(0,1)^p$. The new distribution is obtained from the extension of the univariate skewed unit-sinh-normal distribution and to do so, we rely on the conditionally specified distributions methodology introduced by Arnold. In addition, from the new distribution, we propose the multivariate unit-sinh-normal skewed regression model, which allows modeling data in the region $(0,1)^p$ through linear predictors. The new proposals are useful for the analysis of data on proportions, rates, or indices that arise in different fields of knowledge, such as those described at the beginning of this section. The results of a simulation presented in this work also show that these methodologies are viable alternatives to those existing in the current statistical literature.

This paper is organized as follows. In Section 2, the multivariate skew-normal distribution is revised, and its main properties are commented on. In Section 3, the new multivariate skewed unit sinh-normal distribution is introduced. Some properties are also derived, and the value of the coefficient correlation for the bivariate case is presented for some selected values of the parameter distribution. Section 4 presents the extension of the USHN to the case of the multivariate regression model and its respective statistical inference. Finally, two applications with real data to illustrate the applicability of the proposed methodologies and a small simulation study are presented in Section 5.

2. Multivariate Skew-Normal Distribution

The multivariate skew-normal (SN) distribution was studied by Arnold et al. [20] by using the theory of conditionally specified distributions; see [21]. The construction of the multivariate SN distribution is as follows: for each $j = 1, 2, \ldots, p$, define the vector $\mathbf{Z}_{(j)}$ to be the $(p-1)$ dimensional random vector obtained from $\mathbf{Z}$ by deleting Z_j. In parallel, for a real vector $\boldsymbol{z} = (z_1, z_2, \ldots, z_p)^\top$, $\boldsymbol{z}_{(j)}$ is obtained by deleting the jth coordinate z_j of $\boldsymbol{z}$. Now, suppose that, for each $j = 1, 2, \ldots, p$, the conditional distribution of Z_j given $\mathbf{Z}_{(j)} = \boldsymbol{z}_{(j)}$ is a SN distribution with a parameter which is a function of $\boldsymbol{z}_{(j)}$. Thus, it is assumed for each j that

$$Z_j \mid \mathbf{Z}_{(j)} = \boldsymbol{z}_{(j)} \sim \text{SN}\left(\lambda \prod_{j' \neq j} z_{j'}\right).$$

The joint pdf of $\mathbf{Z} = (Z_1, Z_2, \ldots, Z_p)$ is given by

$$f_{\mathbf{Z}}(\boldsymbol{z}) = 2\left(\prod_{j=1}^{p} \phi(z_j)\right)\Phi\left(\lambda \prod_{j=1}^{p} z_j\right). \tag{8}$$

In the distribution (8), the marginal densities follow a standard normal distribution, that is, for $j = 1, 2, \ldots, p$, and

$$Z_j \sim \mathrm{N}(0,1),$$

the conditional distribution follows a SN distribution, (see Azzalini [22]) of parameter $\lambda \prod_{j' \neq j} z_{j'}$, with the pdf given by:

$$f(Z_j \mid \mathbf{Z}_{(j)} = \mathbf{z}_{(j)}) = 2\phi(z_j)\Phi\left(\lambda \prod_{j' \neq j} z_{j'}\right)$$

From this distribution, Lemonte et al. [23] presented the multivariate Birnbaum–Saunders distribution, whose joint pdf is given by:

$$f_{T_1,\ldots,T_p}(t_1,\ldots,t_p) = 2\prod_{j=1}^{p}\phi(a_{t_j})\Phi\left(\lambda\prod_{j=1}^{p}a_{t_j}\right)\prod_{j=1}^{p}\frac{t_j^{-3/2}(t_j+\eta_j)}{2\alpha_j\sqrt{\eta_j}}, \quad t_1,\ldots,t_p > 0, \tag{9}$$

where

$$a_{t_j}(\alpha_j,\eta_j) = a_{t_j} = \frac{1}{\alpha_j}\left(\sqrt{\frac{t_j}{\eta_j}} - \sqrt{\frac{\eta_j}{t_j}}\right), \tag{10}$$

for $j = 1, 2, \ldots, p$, with $\alpha_j > 0$ and $\eta_j > 0$ being the shape and scale parameters, respectively. The distribution (9) is denoted by $\mathrm{MVBS}(\boldsymbol{\alpha}, \boldsymbol{\eta}, \lambda)$.

Another extension based on the multivariate SN model of Arnold et al. [20] is the multivariate asymmetric SHN distribution, studied by Martínez-Flórez et al. [24], whose joint pdf is given by:

$$f_{Y_1,\ldots,Y_p}(y_1,\ldots,y_p) = 2\left(\prod_{j=1}^{p}b_j'\right)\left(\prod_{j=1}^{p}\phi(b_j)\right)\Phi\left(\lambda\prod_{j=1}^{p}b_j\right), \quad y_1,\ldots,y_p \in \mathbb{R}, \tag{11}$$

where $b_j = \frac{2}{\alpha_j}\sinh\left(\frac{Y_j-\gamma_j}{\sigma_j}\right)$, and $b_j' = \frac{2}{\alpha_j\sigma_j}\cosh\left(\frac{Y_j-\gamma_j}{\sigma_j}\right)$ for $j = 1, 2, \ldots, p$ is a derivative of b_j with respect to Y_j; $\alpha_j > 0$ and $\sigma_j > 0$ are shape and scale parameters, respectively, and $\gamma_j, \lambda \in \mathbb{R}$ are location and asymmetry parameters, respectively. The distribution in (11) is denoted by $\mathrm{MVSHN}(\boldsymbol{\alpha}, \boldsymbol{\gamma}, \boldsymbol{\sigma}, \lambda)$, with $\boldsymbol{\alpha} = (\alpha_1, \ldots, \alpha_p)^\top$, $\boldsymbol{\gamma} = (\gamma_1, \ldots, \gamma_p)^\top$ and $\boldsymbol{\sigma} = (\sigma_1, \ldots, \sigma_p)^\top$.

Although MVBS and MVSHN distributions, which are defined in $\mathbb{R}^{2p+1}$ and $\mathbb{R}^{3p+1}$, respectively, can be used to fit sets of random variables whose domain is the unit interval $(0,1)$, these are not appropriate given the support of these distributions and the support of a bounded random variable vector. In the statistical literature, there are few distributions studied to fit sets of variables in the unit interval, that is, whose domain of definition is $(0,1)^p$, which can be useful to fit rates and proportions. The interest for these type of distributions has been very little; we highlight the works of Cepeda et al. [25], Souza and Moura [26] and Lemonte and Moreno-Arenas [27], among others.

3. Multivariate Skewed Unit-Sinh-Normal Distribution

Following the idea of Arnold et al. [20], Lemonte et al. [23] and Martínez-Flórez et al. [24], in this section, a multivariate extension of the SHN distribution to fit vectors of rates and proportions is proposed, which is named multivariate skewed USHN distribution (MVSUSHN). The construction of the MVSUSHN is as follows: for $j = 1, 2, \ldots, p$, let

$$Y_j = 1 - \exp\left(-\exp\left(\gamma_j + \sigma_j \sinh^{-1}\left(\frac{\alpha_j Z_j}{2}\right)\right)\right),$$

where $Z_j \sim \mathrm{N}(0,1)$ for $j = 1,2,\ldots,p$. Then, the joint pdf of the vector with MVSUSHN distribution is given by,

$$f_{Y_1,\ldots,Y_p}(y_1,\ldots,y_p) = 2\left(\prod_{j=1}^{p} b'_j\right)\left(\prod_{j=1}^{p}\phi(b_j)\right)\Phi\left(\lambda\prod_{j=1}^{p} b_j\right), \quad y_1,\ldots,y_p \in (0,1), \tag{12}$$

where

$$b_j = \frac{2}{\alpha_j}\sinh\left(\frac{\log(-\log(1-y_j)) - \gamma_j}{\sigma_j}\right)$$

and

$$b'_j = \frac{2}{\alpha_j\sigma_j(1-y_j)(-\log(1-y_j))}\cosh\left(\frac{\log(-\log(1-y_j)) - \gamma_j}{\sigma_j}\right)$$

for $j = 1,2,\ldots,p$ is the derivative of b_j with respect to y_j; $\alpha_j > 0$ and $\sigma_j > 0$ are shape and scale parameters, and γ_j and $\lambda \in \mathbb{R}$ are location and asymmetry parameters, respectively. The MVSUSHN is denoted as MVSUSHN$(\boldsymbol{\alpha},\boldsymbol{\gamma},\boldsymbol{\sigma},\lambda)$, with $\boldsymbol{\alpha} = (\alpha_1,\ldots,\alpha_p)^\top$, $\boldsymbol{\gamma} = (\gamma_1,\ldots,\gamma_p)^\top$ and $\boldsymbol{\sigma} = (\sigma_1,\ldots,\sigma_p)^\top$. For $\lambda = 0$, the case of independence is obtained, that is, the product of the pdf of USHN random variables studied by Martínez-Flórez et al. [3]. It follows that the parameter λ is directly associated with the correlation parameter. The Figure 1 shows the contours of the bivariate skewed USHN (BVSUSHN) distribution for some selected values of the parameters, while the Figure 2 presents the shape of the density function for particular values of the parameter of the the BVSUSHN distribution.

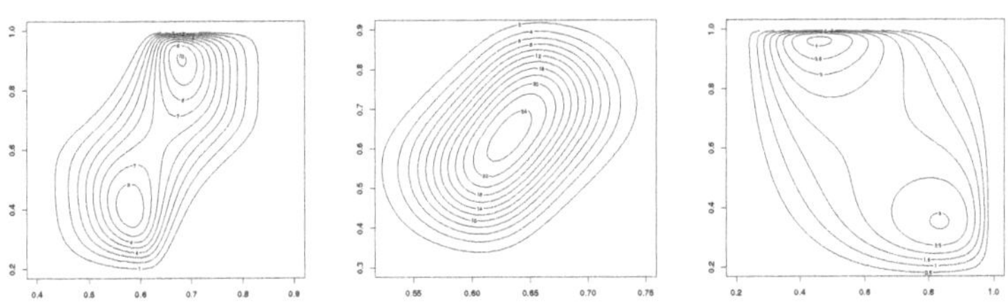

(**a**) (**b**) (**c**)

Figure 1. Graphs of contours for the BVSUSHN distribution for: (**a**) BVSUSHN$(0.5, 1.5, 0, 0, 1, 1, 1.5)$, (**b**) BVSUSHN$(0.25, 0.75, 0, 0, 1, 1, 0.75)$, and (**c**) BVSUSHN$(1.25, 1.75, 0, 0, 1, 1, -0.75)$.

The following theorem provides the marginal and conditional distributions of the MVSUSHN distribution.

Theorem 1. *If* $(Y_1, Y_2, \ldots, Y_n) \sim MVSUSHN(\boldsymbol{\alpha},\boldsymbol{\gamma},\boldsymbol{\sigma},\lambda)$ *then,*

1. $Y_j \sim USHN(\alpha_j, \gamma_j, \sigma_j)$ *for* $j = 1,2,\ldots,n$.
2. *The conditional pdf of* $Y_j \mid \mathbf{Y}_{(j)} = \mathbf{y}_{(j)}$ *is given by*

$$f_{Y_j|\mathbf{Y}_{(j)}}(y_j \mid \mathbf{Y}_{(j)} = \mathbf{y}_{(j)}) = 2b'_j\phi(b_j)\Phi\left(\lambda\prod_{j=1}^{n} b_j\right). \tag{13}$$

3. *The cumulative distribution function (cdf) of* $Y_j \mid \mathbf{Y}_{(j)} = \mathbf{y}_{(j)}$ *is given by*

$$P(Y_j \le y_j \mid \mathbf{Y}_{(j)} = \mathbf{y}_{(j)}) = \Phi(b_j) - 2T\left(b_j, \lambda\prod_{j' \neq j} b_{j'}\right), \tag{14}$$

where $T(\cdot)$ is the Owen function; see [28].

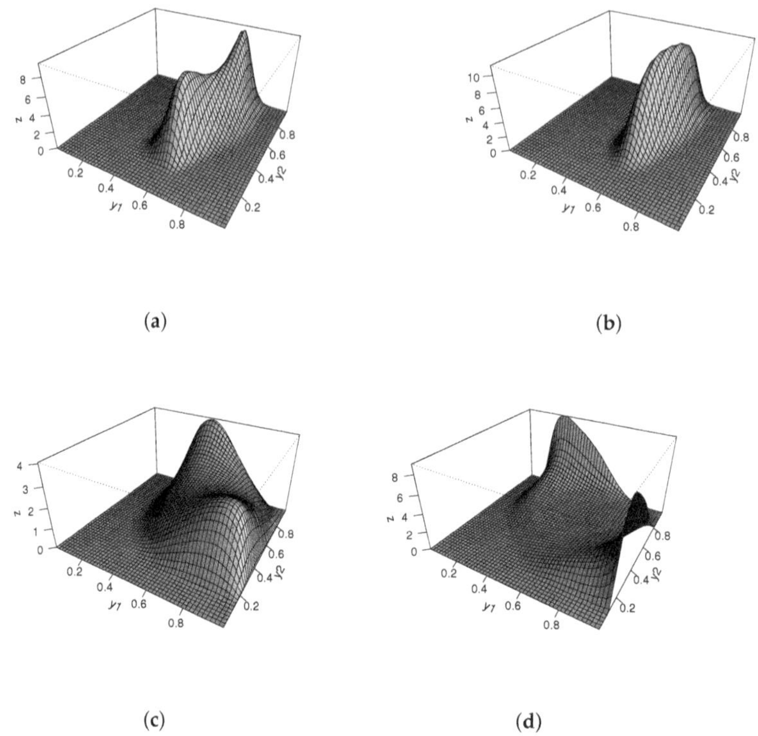

Figure 2. Graphs of density function of the BVSUSHN distribution for: (**a**) BVSUSHN$(0.5, 1.5, 0.0, 0.0, 1.0, 1.0, 1.5)$, (**b**) BVSUSHN$(0.25, 0.75, 0.0, 0.0, 1.5, 1.5, 0.75)$, (**c**) BVSUSHN$(1.25, 1.75, 0.0, 0.0, 1.0, 1.0, -0.75)$, and (**d**) BVSUSHN$(2.5, 2.5, 0.0, 0.0, 1.0, 1.0, -2.5)$.

Proof.

1. For $k = 1, 2, \ldots, p$ and applying the integral over all subindex k (given by j'), other than j, we obtain,

$$
\begin{aligned}
f_{Y_j}(y_j) &= \int_{(0,1)} \overset{j' \neq j}{\cdots} \int_{(0,1)} 2\left(\prod_{k=1}^{p} b'_{k'}\phi(b_k)\right)\Phi\left(\lambda \prod_{k=1}^{p} b_k\right)\prod_{j' \neq j} dy_{j'} \\
&= b'_j\phi(b_j)\int_{(0,1)} \overset{j' \neq j}{\cdots} \int_{(0,1)} 2\left(\prod_{j' \neq j} b'_{j'}\phi(b_{j'})\right)\Phi\left((\lambda b_j)\prod_{j' \neq j} b_{j'}\right)\prod_{j' \neq j} dy_{j'}.
\end{aligned}
$$

Now, using the transformation $Z_{j'} = \frac{2}{\alpha_{j'}}\sinh\left(\frac{\log(-\log(1-Y_{j'})) - \gamma_{j'}}{\sigma_{j'}}\right)$ for all $j' \neq j$

$$
\begin{aligned}
f_{Y_j}(y_j) &= b'_j\phi(b_j)\int_{\mathbb{R}} \overset{j' \neq j}{\cdots} \int_{\mathbb{R}} 2\left(\prod_{j \neq j'} \phi(z_{j'})\right)\Phi\left((\lambda z_j)\prod_{j' \neq j} z_{j'}\right)\prod_{j' \neq j} dz_{j'} \\
&= b'_j\phi(b_j)(1) \\
&= b'_j\phi(b_j).
\end{aligned}
$$

where the second last result follows from Arnold et al. [20].

2. Let

$$f_{Z_j|\mathbf{Z}_{(j)}}(Z_j \mid \mathbf{Z}_{(j)} = z_{(j)}) = 2\phi(z_j)\Phi\left(\left(\lambda \prod_{j'\neq j} z_{j'}\right) z_j\right),$$

then, with the transformation $Y_j = 1 - \exp\left(-\exp\left(\gamma_j + \sigma_j \sinh^{-1}\left(\frac{\alpha_j Z_j}{\sigma_j}\right)\right)\right)$, it is found that $Z_j = \frac{2}{\alpha_j}\sinh\left(\frac{\log(-\log(1-Y_j))-\gamma_j}{\sigma_j}\right) = b_j$ and $\frac{dZ_j}{dY_j} = b_j'$ and, by the Transformation Theorem, it follows:

$$f_{Y_j|\mathbf{Y}_{(j)}}(Y_j \mid \mathbf{Y}_{(j)} = y_{(j)}) = 2b_j'\phi(b_j)\Phi\left(\lambda \prod_{j=1}^{p} b_j\right).$$

3. It has that

$$P(Y_j \leq y_j \mid \mathbf{Y}_{(j)} = y_{(j)}) = \int_{-\infty}^{y_j} f_{Y_j}(t_j \mid \mathbf{Y}_{(j)} = y_{(j)}) dt_j$$

through the transformation $Z_j = \frac{2}{\alpha_j}\sinh\left(\frac{\log(-\log(1-T_j))-\gamma_j}{\sigma_j}\right) = b_j$, it follows that

$$\begin{aligned} P(Y_j \leq y_j \mid \mathbf{Y}_{(j)} = y_{(j)}) &= \int_{-\infty}^{b_j} 2\phi(z_j)\Phi\left(\left(\lambda \prod_{j'\neq j} b_{j'}\right) z_j\right) dz_j \\ &= \Phi(b_j) - 2T(b_j, \lambda \prod_{j'\neq j} b_{j'}) \end{aligned}$$

where the last equality follows the properties of the cdf of the SN distribution, which is widely known in the literature.

□

Martínez-Flórez et al. [3] showed that, when $\alpha \to 0$, the random variable

$$\frac{\log(-\log(1-Y)) - \gamma}{\alpha\sigma/2},$$

converges to a standard normal distribution. From here, if $\alpha_j \to 0$ with $j = 1, 2, \ldots, p$, then

$$\mathbf{Y} \sim \text{MVSN}(\boldsymbol{\gamma}, \boldsymbol{\sigma}, \lambda).$$

Furthermore, if $X_j = \log(-\log(1 - Y_j))$ for $j = 1, 2, \ldots, p$, then

$$\mathbf{X} \sim \text{MVSHN}(\boldsymbol{\alpha}, \boldsymbol{\gamma}, \boldsymbol{\sigma}, \lambda).$$

If $\mathbf{Y} \sim \text{MVSUSHN}(\boldsymbol{\alpha}, \boldsymbol{\gamma}, \boldsymbol{\sigma}, \lambda)$ then, $Z_j = \frac{2}{\alpha_j}\sinh\left(\frac{\log(-\log(1-Y_j))-\gamma_j}{\sigma_j}\right) \sim N(0,1)$, for all $j = 1, 2, \ldots, p$, then,

$$\mathbf{Z} = (Z_1, Z_2, \ldots, Z_p)^\top \sim \text{MVSN}(\mathbf{0}, \mathbf{I}, \lambda).$$

(see [3]). It can be seen that, if $\sigma_1 = \sigma_2 = \cdots = \sigma_q = 2$, the multivariate standard USHN distribution follows, which is denoted by $\text{MVSUSHN}(\boldsymbol{\alpha}, \boldsymbol{\gamma}, 2\mathbf{1}_q, \lambda)$. In this case, the marginals are standard USHN, and the variables $X_j = \log(-\log(1 - Y_j))$ for $j = 1, 2, \ldots, p$ follow the SHN distribution of Rieck and Nedelman [8].

In order to study the unimodal distribution, let $p = 2$, and suppose that $\alpha_1 = \alpha_2$, $\gamma_1 = \gamma_2 = 0$, and $\sigma_1 = \sigma_2 = 1$. By differentiating the logarithm of the conditional distributions and equaling to zero, it has

$$\frac{\partial \log f(y_2 \mid y_1)}{\partial y_2} = (1+\log(1-y_2)) + \frac{b_{y_2}}{b'_{y_2}} - b'_{y_2}b_{y_2} + \lambda b'_{y_2}b_{y_1}\frac{\phi(\lambda b_{y_1}b_{y_2})}{\Phi(\lambda b_{y_1}b_{y_2})},$$

$$\frac{\partial \log f(y_1 \mid y_2)}{\partial y_1} = (1+\log(1-y_1)) + \frac{b_{y_1}}{b'_{y_1}} - b'_{y_1}b_{y_1} + \lambda b'_{y_1}b_{y_2}\frac{\phi(\lambda b_{y_1}b_{y_2})}{\Phi(\lambda b_{y_1}b_{y_2})},$$

the following equations are obtained:

$$\frac{b_{y_2}}{b'_{y_2}} - b'_{y_2}b_{y_2} + \lambda b'_{y_2}b_{y_1}\frac{\phi(\lambda b_{y_1}b_{y_2})}{\Phi(\lambda b_{y_1}b_{y_2})} = -(1+\log(1-y_2)) \tag{15}$$

$$\frac{b_{y_1}}{b'_{y_1}} - b'_{y_1}b_{y_1} + \lambda b'_{y_1}b_{y_2}\frac{\phi(\lambda b_{y_1}b_{y_2})}{\Phi(\lambda b_{y_1}b_{y_2})} = -(1+\log(1-y_1)) \tag{16}$$

Multiplying the equation in (15) by $b_{y_2}b'^2_{y_1}$ and the equation in (16) by $b_{y_1}b'^2_{y_2}$, and subtracting these two results, it follows that

$$\begin{aligned} &b^2_{y_2}b'^2_{y_1} - b^2_{y_2}b'^2_{y_2}b'^2_{y_1} - b'^2_{y_2}b^2_{y_1} + b'^2_{y_2}b'^2_{y_1}b^2_{y_1} \\ &\quad = (1+\log(1-y_1))b'^2_{y_2}b'_{y_1}b_{y_1} - (1+\log(1-y_2))b_{y_2}b'_{y_2}b'^2_{y_1}. \end{aligned} \tag{17}$$

Note that by letting $y_2 = y_1$ and substituting in (17), it follows:

$$\begin{aligned} b^2_{y_1}b'^2_{y_1} - b^2_{y_1}b'^4_{y_1} - b'^2_{y_1}b^2_{y_1} + b'^4_{y_1}b^2_{y_1} &= (1+\log(1-y_1))b'^3_{y_1}b_{y_1} - (1+\log(1-y_1))b_{y_1}b'^3_{y_1} \\ 0 &= 0 \end{aligned}$$

Therefore, $y_1 = y_2$ is a trivial solution of the Equation (17). Then, by replacing $y_1 = y_2$ in (15), it has

$$b_{y_2}(1-b'_{y_2})\Phi(\lambda b_{y_2}) + (1+\log(1-y_2))b'_{y_2}\Phi(\lambda b_{y_2}) + \lambda b_{y_2}b'_{y_2}\phi(\lambda b_{y_2}) = 0$$

from which results the function

$$g(y_2;\lambda) = b_{y_2}(1-b'_{y_2})\Phi(\lambda b_{y_2}) + (1+\log(1-y_2))b'_{y_2}\Phi(\lambda b_{y_2}) + \lambda b_{y_2}b'_{y_2}\phi(\lambda b_{y_2}).$$

Then, by applying the transformation $Y_j = 1 - \exp(-\exp(\sigma_j \operatorname{arcsinh}(\alpha_j Z_j/2) + \gamma_j))$, the bivariate distribution with conditional SN distributions is obtained.

The bivariate distribution with conditional asymmetric USHN is a one-to-one transformation. The λ values for which the SBVUSHN distribution is unimodal are the same as for which the bivariate SN distribution is unimodal and, according to Arnold et al. [20], the bivariate SN distribution is unimodal for $\lambda \leq \sqrt{\pi/2}$. One can note that the equation $g(y_2;\lambda)$ is similar to the equation found by Arnold et al. [20] for the BVSN distribution. The modes of the BVSUSHN distribution can be obtained by solving the equation $g(y_2;\lambda) = 0$ and $Y_1 - Y_2 = 0$.

Moments and Correlation

The covariance for the random variables Y_j and $Y_{j'}$ is given by:

$$\operatorname{cov}(Y_j, Y_{j'};\lambda) = \mathbb{E}(Y_jY_{j'}) - \mathbb{E}(Y_j)\mathbb{E}(Y_{j'})$$

where the moment product $\mathbb{E}(Y_j Y_{j'})$ for two random variables is given by

$$\mathbb{E}(Y_j Y_{j'}) = 2\int_{(0,1)}\int_{(0,1)} y_j y_{j'} b'_{y_j} b'_{y_{j'}} \phi(b_{y_j})\phi(b_{y_{j'}})\Phi\left(\lambda b_{y_j} b_{y_{j'}}\right) dy_j dy_{j'}$$

and

$$\mathbb{E}(Y^r) = \sum_{j=0}^{r}\sum_{l=0}^{\infty}\binom{r}{j}\frac{(-1)^{j+l}(je^{\gamma})^l}{l!}\left[\frac{k_{a_1}(\alpha^{-2}) + k_{b_1}(\alpha^{-2})}{k_{1/2}(\alpha^{-2})}\right] \tag{18}$$

with $a = \frac{r\sigma+1}{2}$, $b = \frac{r\sigma-1}{2}$, and $k_\lambda(\cdot)$ being the third-order function of Bessel defined by

$$k_\lambda(v) = \frac{1}{2}\left(\frac{v}{2}\right)^{\lambda}\int_0^{\infty} u^{-\lambda-1} e^{-u-\frac{v^2}{4u}} du. \tag{19}$$

A proof of the result in (18) can be seen in the Appendix A. Using (18) the variances: $\text{var}(Y_i;\lambda) = \mathbb{E}(Y_i^2) - \mathbb{E}^2(Y_i)$ are obtained for $i = j, j'$; thus, the correlation coefficient is obtained from:

$$\text{cor}(Y_j, Y_{j'};\lambda) = \frac{\text{cov}(Y_j, Y_{j'};\lambda)}{\sqrt{\text{var}(Y_j;\lambda)\text{var}(Y_{j'};\lambda)}}.$$

To compute $\text{cor}(Y_j, Y_{j'};\lambda)$, it is necessary to use numerical methods to determine the simple moments and the product moments. It can be shown that for this distribution $\text{cov}(Y_j, Y_{j'};-\lambda) = -\text{cov}(Y_j, Y_{j'};\lambda)$, whereby $\text{cor}(Y_j, Y_{j'};-\lambda) = -\text{cor}(Y_j, Y_{j'};\lambda)$. To study the range of the correlation coefficient, $\text{cor}(Y_j, Y_{j'};\lambda)$ was evaluated for some parameter values. The values taken for the parameters: $\sigma_1 = \sigma_2 = 1$ and $\gamma_1 = \gamma_2 = 0$, α_1, α_2, and λ varying. The Table 1 shows the values for the parameters α_1, α_2, λ, and the values of $\text{cor}(Y_j, Y_{j'};\lambda)$ for a pair of variables Y_j and $Y_{j'}$. The values were obtained for the case of $\lambda > 0$ and the case of $\lambda < 0$ results for symmetry, given that $\text{cor}(Y_j, Y_{j'};-\lambda) = -\text{cor}(Y_j, Y_{j'};\lambda)$.

As can be seen, the case of independence occurs for $\lambda = 0$, i.e., $\text{cor}(Y_j, Y_{j'};0) = 0$, then according to the Table 1, for the values $|\text{cor}(Y_j, Y_{j'};\lambda)| \leq 0.9938$, which leads us to the conclusion that for this model $|\text{cor}(Y_j, Y_{j'};\lambda)| \leq 1.0$.

Table 1. Correlation coefficient for BVUSHN distribution.

λ	α_1/α_2	**0.085**	**0.5**	**0.75**	**1.5**	**2.25**	**3.0**	**5.0**	**7.5**	**10.0**
	0.095	0.5124	0.3401	0.3410	0.3410	0.3388	0.3347	0.3077	0.2846	0.2759
	0.45	0.3513	0.3160	0.3169	0.3173	0.3155	0.3117	0.2716	0.2239	0.1966
	0.75	0.3524	0.3171	0.3181	0.3183	0.3165	0.3126	0.2722	0.2243	0.1969
0.5	1.0	0.3528	0.3177	0.3186	0.3188	0.3168	0.3128	0.2722	0.2243	0.1969
	2.0	0.3507	0.3163	0.3171	0.3169	0.3148	0.3106	0.2697	0.2220	0.1949
	3.0	0.3456	0.3119	0.3126	0.3122	0.3099	0.3057	0.2650	0.2180	0.1915
	5.0	0.3261	0.2718	0.2722	0.2713	0.2690	0.2650	0.2318	0.1964	0.1775
	7.5	0.3170	0.2240	0.2243	0.2234	0.2213	0.2180	0.1964	0.1774	0.1693
	10.0	0.3188	0.1967	0.1969	0.1962	0.1943	0.1915	0.1775	0.1693	0.1684
	0.095	0.8258	0.5950	0.6003	0.6123	0.6177	0.6183	0.5809	0.5252	0.4904
	0.45	0.6192	0.5269	0.5321	0.5442	0.5504	0.5517	0.5070	0.4343	0.3845
	0.75	0.6260	0.5331	0.5383	0.5504	0.5565	0.5576	0.5120	0.4381	0.3877
	1.0	0.6311	0.5379	0.5431	0.5551	0.5611	0.5621	0.5156	0.4408	0.3900
1.5	2.0	0.6425	0.5497	0.5548	0.5662	0.5717	0.5722	0.5232	0.4460	0.3941
	3.0	0.6446	0.5527	0.5576	0.5685	0.5735	0.5736	0.5232	0.4451	0.3932
	5.0	0.6140	0.5079	0.5120	0.5207	0.5241	0.5232	0.4774	0.4096	0.3661
	7.5	0.5695	0.4349	0.4381	0.4444	0.4464	0.4451	0.4096	0.3610	0.3315
	10.0	0.5434	0.3850	0.3877	0.3930	0.3945	0.3932	0.3661	0.3315	0.3117

Table 1. *Cont.*

λ	α_1/α_2	0.085	0.5	0.75	1.5	2.25	3.0	5.0	7.5	10.0
	0.095	0.9317	0.6733	0.6812	0.7013	0.7131	0.7184	0.6878	0.6282	0.5857
	0.45	0.6975	0.5875	0.5945	0.6128	0.6242	0.6294	0.5900	0.5163	0.4623
	0.75	0.7073	0.5958	0.6030	0.6214	0.6327	0.6379	0.5976	0.5224	0.4677
	1.0	0.7154	0.6028	0.6099	0.6284	0.6397	0.6448	0.6036	0.5273	0.4718
2.5	2.0	0.7375	0.6222	0.6294	0.6478	0.6588	0.6635	0.6194	0.5396	0.4820
	3.0	0.7469	0.6307	0.6379	0.6559	0.6665	0.6708	0.6250	0.5432	0.4847
	5.0	0.7243	0.5912	0.5976	0.6132	0.6219	0.6250	0.5823	0.5092	0.4579
	7.5	0.6772	0.5172	0.5224	0.5348	0.5414	0.5432	0.5092	0.4534	0.4157
	10.0	0.6430	0.4632	0.4677	0.4781	0.4834	0.4847	0.4579	0.4157	0.3882
	0.095	0.9765	0.7038	0.7128	0.7374	0.7531	0.7616	0.7367	0.6801	0.6363
	0.45	0.7267	0.6135	0.6214	0.6428	0.6570	0.6645	0.6290	0.5567	0.5025
	0.75	0.7379	0.6227	0.6307	0.6523	0.6666	0.6742	0.6379	0.5642	0.5090
	1.0	0.7474	0.6307	0.6387	0.6605	0.6749	0.6824	0.6453	0.5705	0.5144
3.5	2.0	0.7755	0.6542	0.6624	0.6845	0.6988	0.7061	0.6662	0.5874	0.5288
	3.0	0.7895	0.6659	0.6742	0.6962	0.7102	0.7172	0.6755	0.5945	0.5345
	5.0	0.7730	0.6303	0.6379	0.6576	0.6698	0.6755	0.6367	0.5633	0.5098
	7.5	0.7297	0.5579	0.5642	0.5805	0.5902	0.5945	0.5633	0.5064	0.4656
	10.0	0.6951	0.5035	0.5090	0.5230	0.5311	0.5345	0.5098	0.4656	0.4348
	0.095	0.9938	0.7228	0.7324	0.7601	0.7790	0.7903	0.7707	0.7182	0.6763
	0.45	0.7446	0.6323	0.6405	0.6643	0.6808	0.6903	0.6583	0.5881	0.5346
	0.75	0.7563	0.6418	0.6502	0.6743	0.6910	0.7006	0.6681	0.5967	0.5421
	1.0	0.7669	0.6505	0.6590	0.6834	0.7002	0.7099	0.6767	0.6040	0.5486
5.0	2.0	0.7992	0.6772	0.6860	0.7110	0.7281	0.7377	0.7021	0.6254	0.5672
	3.0	0.8170	0.6917	0.7006	0.7258	0.7428	0.7523	0.7149	0.6358	0.5760
	5.0	0.8061	0.6597	0.6681	0.6913	0.7066	0.7149	0.6803	0.6084	0.5544
	7.5	0.7672	0.5894	0.5967	0.6164	0.6291	0.6358	0.6084	0.5521	0.5102
	10.0	0.7350	0.5357	0.5421	0.5594	0.5703	0.5760	0.5544	0.5102	0.4776

4. Multivariate Skewed USHN Regression Model

This section presents an extension of the USHN regression model for the case of multiple bounded response variables (rates and proportions). Suppose that we have q variables measuring rates or proportions in a sample of size n, i.e., for $i = 1, 2, \ldots, n$, we have the vector of dimension $q \times 1$

$$\boldsymbol{y}_i = (y_{i1}, y_{i2}, \ldots, y_{iq})^\top.$$

Assume also that there are p explanatory variables $X_1, X_2, \ldots, X_p$ where, for $i = 1, 2, \ldots, n$,

$$\boldsymbol{X}_i = (x_{i1}, x_{i2}, \ldots, x_{iq})^\top,$$

and there is a matrix $q \times p$ associated to the ith observed response $\boldsymbol{y}_i$ with

$$\boldsymbol{x}_{ij} = (x_{ij1}, x_{ij2}, \ldots, x_{ijp})^\top,$$

for $j = 1, 2 \ldots, q$, a p dimensional vector of values of the explanatory variables. For the vector of response variables, we use the operator vec$(\cdot)$, which transforms matrices into a column vector from the columns of the matrix. Therefore,

$$\boldsymbol{y} = \text{vec}(\boldsymbol{y}_1, \boldsymbol{y}_2, \ldots, \boldsymbol{y}_n).$$

Thus, the MVSUSHN regression model is given by

$$\boldsymbol{Z}_i = \boldsymbol{X}_i \boldsymbol{\beta} + \boldsymbol{\varepsilon}_i, \quad i = 1, 2, \ldots, n, \tag{20}$$

where $z_{ij} = \log(-\log(1-y_{ij})))$, being $\boldsymbol{\beta}$ is a vector of unknown parameters of dimension p, and the vectors $\boldsymbol{\varepsilon}_i$ for $i = 1,2,\ldots,n$ are vectors of independent and identically distributed random variables such that $\boldsymbol{\varepsilon}_i \sim \text{MVSHN}(\boldsymbol{\alpha}, \mathbf{0}_q, \boldsymbol{\Sigma}, \lambda)$ where $\boldsymbol{\Sigma} = \text{diag}(\sigma_1, \sigma_2, \ldots, \sigma_q)$, and $\mathbf{0}_q$, a vector of zeros of dimension q. It follows that, $\boldsymbol{z}_i \sim \text{SMVSHN}(\boldsymbol{\alpha}, \boldsymbol{X}_i\boldsymbol{\beta}, \boldsymbol{\Sigma}, \lambda)$.

From this result, we have by the theorem shown above that $y_{ij} \sim \text{USHN}(\alpha_j, \boldsymbol{x}_{ij}^\top \boldsymbol{\beta}_j, \sigma_j)$ for $j = 1,2,\ldots,q$ i.e., each marginal follows a USHN regression model. Thus, defining $\boldsymbol{X} = \text{diag}(\boldsymbol{X}_1, \boldsymbol{X}_2, \ldots, \boldsymbol{X}_q)$, where $\boldsymbol{X}_j$ for $j = 1,2,\cdots,q$ is a matrix of size $n \times p_j$ and $\boldsymbol{X}$ of dimension $nq \times (p_1 + p_2 + \ldots + p_q)$, then the MVSUSHN can be represented by

$$\boldsymbol{Z} = \boldsymbol{X}\boldsymbol{\beta} + \boldsymbol{\varepsilon}, \tag{21}$$

where $\boldsymbol{Z}_{ij} = \boldsymbol{X}_{ij}\boldsymbol{\beta}_j + \varepsilon_{ij}$, $i = 1,2,\ldots,n$, $j = 1,2,\ldots,q$ taking values $z_{ij} = \log(-\log(1-y_{ij})))$, with $\boldsymbol{\beta} = \text{vec}(\boldsymbol{\beta}_1, \boldsymbol{\beta}_2, \ldots, \boldsymbol{\beta}_q)$ with $\boldsymbol{\beta}_j$ a vector of dimension $p_j \times 1$, i.e., $\boldsymbol{\beta}$ is a vector of dimension $p \times 1$ being $p = p_1 + p_2 + \cdots + p_q$, $\boldsymbol{\varepsilon} = \text{vec}(\boldsymbol{\varepsilon}_1, \boldsymbol{\varepsilon}_2, \ldots, \boldsymbol{\varepsilon}_q)$ is an error vector with $\boldsymbol{\varepsilon}_j \sim \text{MVSHN}(\boldsymbol{\alpha}, \mathbf{0}_{nq}, \boldsymbol{\Sigma}, \lambda)$ where $\boldsymbol{\varepsilon}_j = (\varepsilon_{1j}, \varepsilon_{2j}, \ldots, \varepsilon_{nj})$ with $\varepsilon_{ij} \sim \text{SHN}(\alpha_j, 0, \sigma_j)$ it follows that $z_{ij} \sim \text{SHN}(\alpha_j, \boldsymbol{X}_{ij}\boldsymbol{\beta}_j, \sigma_j)$ for $j = 1,2,\ldots,q$.

Statistical Inference

For $i = 1,2,\ldots,n$ and $j = 1,2,\ldots,q$, define: $\boldsymbol{\delta}_1 = (\delta_{11}, \delta_{21}, \ldots, \delta_{n1})$, $\boldsymbol{\delta}_2 = (\delta_{12}, \delta_{22}, \ldots, \delta_{n2})$ and $\boldsymbol{\delta}_3 = (\delta_{13}, \delta_{23}, \ldots, \delta_{n3})$; with $\delta_{i1} = (\delta_{i11}, \delta_{i12}, \ldots, \delta_{i1q})$, $\delta_{i2} = (\delta_{i21}, \delta_{i22}, \ldots, \delta_{i2q})$ and $\delta_{i3} = (\delta_{i31}, \delta_{i32}, \ldots, \delta_{i3q})$ where

$$\delta_{i1j} = \frac{2}{\alpha_j\sigma_j(1-y_{ij})(-\log(1-y_{ij}))} \cosh\left(\frac{z_{ij} - \boldsymbol{x}_{ij}^\top \boldsymbol{\beta}}{\sigma_j}\right), \quad \delta_{i2j} = \frac{2}{\alpha_j} \sinh\left(\frac{z_{ij} - \boldsymbol{x}_{ij}^\top \boldsymbol{\beta}}{\sigma_j}\right)$$

and

$$\delta_{i3j} = \Phi\left(\lambda \prod_{j=1}^{p} \delta_{i2j}\right).$$

for $j = 1,2,\ldots,p$. The log-likelihood function for the parameter vector $\boldsymbol{\theta} = (\boldsymbol{\alpha}, \boldsymbol{\beta}, \boldsymbol{\Sigma}, \lambda)^\top$ is

$$\ell(\boldsymbol{\theta}) = \sum_{i=1}^{n} \ell_i(\boldsymbol{\theta}),$$

where

$$\begin{aligned}\ell_i(\boldsymbol{\theta}) = &-\frac{q}{2}\log(2\pi) + \sum_{i=1}^{q} \sigma_j + \sum_{i=1}^{q} \log(-(1-y_{ij})(\log(1-y_{ij}))) \\ &+ \sum_{i=1}^{q} \log(\delta_{i1j}) - \frac{1}{2}\sum_{i=1}^{q} \delta_{i2j}^2 + \log(\delta_{i3j}).\end{aligned}$$

To obtain the score function, denoted $U(\boldsymbol{\theta})$, we took the derivative of the log-likelihood function with respect to each of the parameters, so the elements of the score function are given by

$$U(\beta_{jk}) = \frac{1}{\sigma_j}\sum_{i=1}^{n} x_{ijk}\left(\delta_{i1j}\delta_{i2j} - \frac{\delta_{i2j}}{\delta_{i1j}}\right) + \frac{\lambda}{\sigma_j}\sum_{i=1}^{n} x_{ijk}\delta_{i1j}\omega_i\left(\prod_{j' \neq j} \delta_{i2j'}\right), \quad k = 1,\ldots,p_j, \tag{22}$$

$$U(\alpha_j) = -\frac{n}{\alpha_j} + \frac{1}{\alpha_j}\sum_{i=1}^{n} \delta_{i2j}^2 - \frac{\lambda}{\alpha_j}\sum_{i=1}^{n} \omega_i\left(\prod_{j=1}^{q} \delta_{i2j}\right), \tag{23}$$

$$U(\sigma_j) = -\frac{n}{\sigma_j} - \frac{1}{\sigma_j}\sum_{i=1}^{n} v_{ij}\tanh(v_{ij}) + \frac{1}{\sigma_j}\sum_{i=1}^{n} v_{ij}\delta_{i1j}\delta_{i2j} - \frac{\lambda}{\sigma_j}\sum_{i=1}^{n}\delta_{i1j}\omega_i\left(\prod_{j'\neq j}\delta_{i2j'}\right), \tag{24}$$

$$U(\lambda) = \sum_{i=1}^{n}\omega_i\left(\prod_{j=1}^{q}\delta_{i2j}\right), \tag{25}$$

where $v_{ij} = (\log(-\log(1-y_{ij}) - \boldsymbol{x}_{ij}^\top \boldsymbol{\beta}_j)/\sigma_j$, for $i = 1,\ldots,n$, and $j = 1,2,\ldots p$ and; $w_i = \phi\left(\lambda\prod_{j=1}^{q}\delta_{i2j}\right)/\Phi\left(\lambda\prod_{j=1}^{q}\delta_{i2j}\right)$.

The maximum likelihood estimator (MLE) for $\beta_{j1},\ldots,\beta_{jp_j},\alpha_j$ and σ_j are the solutions to the equations $U(\beta_{jk}) = 0$, $U(\alpha_j) = 0$ and $U(\sigma_j) = 0$ for $j = 1,2,\ldots,q,\quad k = 1,2,\ldots,p_j$, which require numerical procedures. To start the iterative process, the least squares estimates can be used for the $\boldsymbol{\beta}_j$, i.e., $\tilde{\boldsymbol{\beta}}_{j0} = (\boldsymbol{X}_j^\top \boldsymbol{X}_j)^{-1}\boldsymbol{X}_j z_j$, from where $\hat{\sigma}_{j0}^2 = \frac{1}{n-p_j}\sum_{i=1}^{n}(z_{ij} - \boldsymbol{x}_j^\top \tilde{\boldsymbol{\beta}}_{j0})^2$, while for the α_j, the initial values could be implemented $\hat{\alpha}_{j0} = \sqrt{\tilde{\alpha}_j}$, where $\tilde{\alpha}_j = \frac{4}{n}\sum_{i=1}^{n}\sinh\left(\frac{z_{ij}-\boldsymbol{x}_j^\top\tilde{\boldsymbol{\beta}}_{j0}}{\hat{\sigma}_{j0}}\right)$. With these initial values, and assuming them to be the true values of the parameters, a one-dimensional function for the parameter λ can be obtained, which can be estimated by some numerical method such as uniroot from R Development Core Team [29].

The elements of the observed information matrix that are calculated as minus the second derivative of the log-likelihood function with respect to the parameters, denoted by $I_{\theta_j\theta_k}$, are given by

$$I_{\theta_j\theta_k} = -\frac{\partial\ell(\boldsymbol{\theta})}{\partial\theta_j\partial\theta_k} \tag{26}$$

The explicit expressions of these elements are presented in the Appendix B. The elements of the Fisher information matrix (denoted $\kappa_{\theta_j\theta_k}$) are given by the expectation of the elements of the observed information matrix, that is $\kappa_{\theta_j\theta_k} = \mathbb{E}(I_{\theta_j\theta_k})$, these are calculated numerically, therefore, the information matrix is expressed by

$$\kappa_{\boldsymbol{\theta\theta}} = -\mathbb{E}\left[\frac{\partial\ell(\boldsymbol{\theta})}{\partial\theta_j\partial\theta_k}\right] = \begin{pmatrix} \kappa_{\boldsymbol{\alpha\alpha}} & \kappa_{\boldsymbol{\alpha\beta}} & \kappa_{\boldsymbol{\alpha\Sigma}} & \kappa_{\boldsymbol{\alpha}\lambda} \\ \kappa_{\boldsymbol{\alpha\beta}}^T & \kappa_{\boldsymbol{\beta\beta}} & \kappa_{\boldsymbol{\beta\Sigma}} & \kappa_{\boldsymbol{\beta}\lambda} \\ \kappa_{\boldsymbol{\alpha\Sigma}}^T & \kappa_{\boldsymbol{\beta\Sigma}}^T & \kappa_{\boldsymbol{\Sigma\Sigma}} & \kappa_{\boldsymbol{\Sigma}\lambda} \\ \kappa_{\boldsymbol{\alpha}\lambda}^T & \kappa_{\boldsymbol{\beta}\lambda}^T & \kappa_{\boldsymbol{\Sigma}\lambda}^T & \kappa_{\lambda\lambda} \end{pmatrix}$$

When $\lambda = 0$, the case of the independence of univariate USHN distribution is obtained; thus, it follows that: $\boldsymbol{\kappa}_{\boldsymbol{\beta\beta}} = \text{bloq.diag}(c(\alpha_1)\boldsymbol{x}_1^\top \boldsymbol{x}_1/4, c(\alpha_2)\boldsymbol{x}_2^\top \boldsymbol{x}_2/4,\ldots,c(\alpha_q)\boldsymbol{x}_q^\top \boldsymbol{x}_q/4)$, is a diagonal block matrix where $c(\alpha_j) = 1 + \frac{4}{\alpha_j^2} - \sqrt{2\pi/\alpha_j^2}\left(1 - \text{erf}[(2/\alpha_j^2)^{1/2}]\exp(2/\alpha_j^2)\right)$ and $\text{erf}(x)$ is the error function given by: $\text{erf}(x) = \frac{2}{\sqrt{\pi}}\int_0^x e^{-t^2}dt$, see Rieck and Nedelman [8]; $\boldsymbol{\kappa}_{\boldsymbol{\alpha\alpha}} = \text{diag}(2/\alpha_1^2, 2/\alpha_2^2,\cdots,2/\alpha_q^2)$, $\boldsymbol{\kappa}_{\boldsymbol{\Sigma\Sigma}} = \text{diag}(\kappa_{\sigma_1\sigma_1},\kappa_{\sigma_2\sigma_2},\cdots,\kappa_{\sigma_q\sigma_q})$, where $\kappa_{\sigma_j\sigma_j} = \frac{a_2(\alpha_j,\sigma_j)}{\sigma_j^2} + 2\frac{b(\alpha_j,\sigma_j)-d(\alpha_j,\sigma_j)}{\sigma_j^2}$ with $a_l(\alpha_j,\sigma_j) = \mathbb{E}\left(v_j^l\left[2\delta_{2j}^2 + \frac{4}{\alpha_j^2} - 1 + \frac{\delta_{2j}^2}{\delta_{2j}^2+4/\alpha_j^2}\right]\right)$, $b(\alpha_j,\sigma_j) = \mathbb{E}(v_j\delta_{1j}\delta_{2j})$ and $d(\alpha_j,\sigma_j) = \mathbb{E}\left(v_j\frac{\delta_{1j}}{\delta_{2j}}\right)$. Expectations in the above expressions must be calculated numerically, $\boldsymbol{\kappa}_{\boldsymbol{\alpha\beta}} = \mathbf{0}$ is a matrix of zeros, $\boldsymbol{\kappa}_{\boldsymbol{\alpha\Sigma}} = \text{diag}(\kappa_{\alpha_1\sigma_1},\kappa_{\alpha_2\sigma_2},\cdots,\kappa_{\alpha_q\sigma_q})$ with $\kappa_{\alpha_j\sigma_j} = \frac{2}{\alpha_j\sigma_j}b(\alpha_j,\sigma_j)$, $\boldsymbol{\kappa}_{\boldsymbol{\beta\Sigma}} = \text{diag}(\kappa_{\beta_1\sigma_1},\kappa_{\beta_2\sigma_2},\cdots,\kappa_{\beta_q\sigma_q})$ with $\kappa_{\beta_j\sigma_j} = \frac{a_1(\alpha_j,\sigma_j)}{2\sigma_j}\boldsymbol{x}_j$, $\boldsymbol{\kappa}_{\boldsymbol{\alpha}\lambda} = \mathbf{0}$ is a vector of size q, $\boldsymbol{\kappa}_{\boldsymbol{\beta}\lambda} = \mathbf{0}$ is a vector of size $p_1 + p_2 + \ldots + p_q$ $\boldsymbol{\kappa}_{\boldsymbol{\Sigma}\lambda} = \mathbf{0}$ is a vector of size q and $\boldsymbol{\kappa}_{\lambda\lambda} = \frac{2}{\pi}$.

The rows (or columns) of the matrix $\boldsymbol{\kappa}_{\boldsymbol{\theta\theta}}$ are linearly independent, so the determinant is different than zero; this guarantees the existence of the inverse of $\boldsymbol{\kappa}_{\boldsymbol{\theta\theta}}$. Hence, for large samples, the MLE $\hat{\boldsymbol{\theta}}$ of $\boldsymbol{\theta}$ is asymptotically normal, that is,

$$\hat{\boldsymbol{\theta}} \xrightarrow{D} N_{p+2q+1}(\boldsymbol{\theta}, \boldsymbol{\kappa}_{\boldsymbol{\theta\theta}}^{-1}),$$

resulting that the asymptotic variance of the MLE $\hat{\boldsymbol{\theta}}$ is the inverse of $I(\hat{\boldsymbol{\theta}})$. The approximation to the $N_{p+2q+1}(\boldsymbol{\theta}, \boldsymbol{\kappa}_{\boldsymbol{\theta\theta}}^{-1})$ can be used to construct confidence intervals for α_j, β_{jk_j}, σ_j y λ, these are given by $\hat{\alpha}_j \mp z_{1-\xi/2}\sqrt{\hat{\kappa}(\hat{\alpha})}$, $\hat{\beta}_{jk_j} \mp z_{1-\xi/2}\sqrt{\hat{\kappa}(\hat{\beta}_{jk_j})}$ and $\hat{\lambda} \mp z_{1-\xi/2}\sqrt{\hat{\kappa}(\hat{\lambda})}$, where $\hat{\kappa}(\cdot)$ is on the diagonal of the matrix $\boldsymbol{\kappa}_{\boldsymbol{\theta\theta}}^{-1}$ for each parameter and $z_{1-\xi/2}$ is the quantil $100(\delta/2)\%$ of the standard normal distribution.

The hypothesis of interest

$$H_0: \ \lambda = 0 \quad \text{versus} \quad \lambda \neq 0$$

can be tested by the statistic test (for large n)

$$-2[\hat{\ell}(\hat{\boldsymbol{\theta}}^*, \hat{\lambda}) - \hat{\ell}(\hat{\boldsymbol{\theta}}^*, 0)] \sim \chi_1^2$$

where $\boldsymbol{\theta}^*$ is the vector $\boldsymbol{\theta}$ without the parameter λ, and $\hat{\boldsymbol{\theta}}^*$ is the MLE of $\boldsymbol{\theta}$ restricted on H_0.

5. Numerical Results

In this section, the results of the simulation study and two applications to illustrate the applicability of the proposed models are presented.

5.1. Simulation Study

In order to study the behavior of the MLE of the parameter vector of the MVSUSHN regression model, a small Monte Carlo simulation study with covariates in the model was carried out. We considered $X_{1i} \sim N(0,1)$ and $X_{2i} \sim U(0,1)$ for $i = 1, 2, \ldots, n$. For $\lambda = 0$, the case of independence; the results for each model can be seen in the studies conducted by Martínez-Flórez et al. [3].

We used the bivariate MVSUSHN$((\alpha_1, \alpha_2), (\beta_{10}, \beta_{11}, \beta_{20}, \beta_{21}), (\sigma_1, \sigma_2), \lambda)$ regression model, and we took the values: $\alpha_1 = 1.5$, $\alpha_2 = 0.75$, $\beta_{10} = -0.75$, $\beta_{11} = 0.50$, $\beta_{20} = 0.50$, and $\beta_{21} = 1.5$ and $\sigma_1 = \sigma_2 = 2$, while $\lambda = 1.75$, 3.5, and 5.25. The sample size was $n = 40, 80, 120$, and 200, and the number of iterations was 5000. We studied the absolute value of the relative bias (RB), root of mean square error (RMSE), length of confidence interval (LCI), and coverage probability (CP). To generate the samples, we performed the following algorithm:

1. Generate a uniform random $U_1 \sim U(0,1)$ and a random number x_1 with distribution $N(0,1)$.
2. Generate $\varepsilon_1 = 2\,\text{arcsinh}(\alpha_1 \Phi^{-1}(U1)/2)$ with $\Phi^{-1}(\cdot)$ the inverse of the standard normal function.
3. Let $y_1 = 1 - \exp(-\exp(\beta_{10} + \beta_{11}x_1 + \varepsilon_1))$.
4. Compute $b = (2/\alpha_1)\sinh((\log(-\log(1 - y_1)) - (\beta_{10} + \beta_{11}x_1))/2)$.
5. Generate another uniform random number (independent of U_1) $U_2 \sim U(0,1)$ and x_2 also with distribution $U(0,1)$
6. Compute the error ε_2 such that $\varepsilon_2 = 2\,\text{arcsinh}(\alpha_2 \Phi_{SN}^{-1}(U_2, 0, 1, \lambda b1)/2)$, where $\Phi_{SN}^{-1}(\cdot, 0, 1, \cdot)$ is the inverse function of the standard skew-normal and $\text{arcsinh}(\cdot)$ is the inverse of the hyperbolic sine function.
7. Let $y_2 = 1 - \exp(-\exp(\beta_{20} + \beta_{21}x_2 + \varepsilon_2))$. This algorithm is generated n times, finally obtaining the USHN bivariate random sample.

The results of the simulations can be seen in the Table 2. In general, it can be seen that the RB, RSME, and LCI of the model parameters decrease as n increases; this decrease is slower for some parameters. It can also be seen that the CP increases as n increases.

Table 2. Relative bias, root of mean square error, length of confidence interval, and coverage probability for the MVSUSHN regression model.

		$\lambda = 1.75$				$\lambda = 3.50$				$\lambda = 5.25$			
n	θ_i	RB	RMSE	LCI	CP	RB	RMSE	LCI	CP	RB	RMSE	LCI	CP
40	α_1	0.2279	0.6529	4.3944	0.9992	0.1858	0.5632	4.2347	1.0000	0.1588	0.4897	4.1603	1.0000
	α_2	0.5797	0.3882	3.9557	1.0000	0.4186	0.2454	3.7913	1.0000	0.2729	0.1752	3.7730	1.0000
	β_{10}	0.1648	0.0446	0.6471	0.7258	0.1059	0.0301	0.5543	0.7723	0.0844	0.0226	0.5062	0.8373
	β_{11}	0.0631	0.0295	0.6283	0.9223	0.0414	0.0218	0.5472	0.9272	0.0314	0.0189	0.5046	0.9346
	β_{20}	0.0225	0.0313	0.6037	0.8949	0.0210	0.0228	0.5251	0.9103	0.0162	0.0166	0.4833	0.9279
	β_{21}	0.1725	0.1681	1.1539	0.6816	0.1047	0.0956	0.9631	0.7742	0.0838	0.0685	0.8842	0.7535
	σ_1	0.0546	0.4598	4.5055	0.8934	0.0308	0.4418	4.6131	0.9272	0.0284	0.3935	4.4996	0.9519
	σ_2	0.3359	0.6907	9.3760	0.7098	0.2693	1.0002	6.5228	0.8036	0.3444	1.5870	6.2103	0.9096
	λ	0.1705	0.7552	3.4734	0.8446	0.2084	4.6158	8.5285	0.7551	0.2087	6.2440	10.3860	0.7217
80	α_1	0.0422	0.1841	2.6664	1.0000	0.0424	0.1732	2.6472	1.0000	0.0396	0.1109	2.7276	1.0000
	α_2	0.1296	0.0798	2.6892	1.0000	0.2238	0.0657	2.8055	1.0000	0.2974	0.0727	2.7864	1.0000
	β_{10}	0.1580	0.0270	0.4598	0.8239	0.1048	0.0167	0.3987	0.8683	0.0784	0.0099	0.3591	0.8871
	β_{11}	0.0549	0.0141	0.4374	0.9282	0.0403	0.0091	0.3740	0.9424	0.0306	0.0079	0.3440	0.9392
	β_{20}	0.0173	0.0118	0.4293	0.9276	0.0152	0.0092	0.3683	0.9380	0.0051	0.0068	0.3269	0.9286
	β_{21}	0.1698	0.1033	0.7948	0.7658	0.1040	0.0541	0.6637	0.8320	0.0797	0.0336	0.5786	0.8199
	σ_1	0.0301	0.2265	3.0365	0.9973	0.0289	0.1868	2.9427	0.9993	0.0223	0.1192	2.7508	1.0000
	σ_2	0.1044	0.4867	7.9724	0.9606	0.2363	0.8463	5.8032	1.0000	0.2265	1.2797	5.8860	1.0000
	λ	0.1038	0.1931	1.8814	0.9043	0.1782	0.7432	4.0199	0.9170	0.1674	1.4969	6.6811	0.8465
120	α_1	0.0363	0.0903	2.2934	1.0000	0.0313	0.0793	2.1980	1.0000	0.0208	0.1048	2.0728	1.0000
	α_2	0.1172	0.0413	2.6855	1.0000	0.1760	0.0594	2.3182	1.0000	0.1853	0.0613	2.4098	1.0000
	β_{10}	0.1522	0.0196	0.3802	0.8248	0.1037	0.0112	0.3217	0.8755	0.0776	0.0090	0.2899	0.9029
	β_{11}	0.0537	0.0078	0.3533	0.9294	0.0375	0.0062	0.3008	0.9431	0.0306	0.0051	0.2762	0.9444
	β_{20}	0.0043	0.0092	0.3635	0.9408	0.0116	0.0056	0.2964	0.9448	0.0020	0.0052	0.2672	0.9410
	β_{21}	0.1675	0.0790	0.6467	0.8606	0.1042	0.0357	0.5260	0.8499	0.0794	0.0304	0.4765	0.8885
	σ_1	0.0103	0.0793	2.2790	1.0000	0.0034	0.0690	2.1409	1.0000	0.0104	0.1054	2.2788	1.0000
	σ_2	0.0599	0.4395	6.8628	1.0000	0.0990	0.5798	3.1258	1.0000	0.2055	0.5280	4.7802	1.0000
	λ	0.0909	0.1370	1.5647	0.9151	0.0893	0.5541	3.2542	0.9274	0.1199	1.3591	4.5893	0.9413
200	α_1	0.0055	0.0611	1.5785	1.0000	0.0073	0.0573	1.5689	1.0000	0.0012	0.0603	1.5590	1.0000
	α_2	0.1022	0.0350	1.7030	1.0000	0.0316	0.0316	1.8231	1.0000	0.1446	0.0280	1.9242	1.0000
	β_{10}	0.1299	0.0186	0.2872	0.8766	0.0905	0.0100	0.2490	0.8795	0.0656	0.0064	0.2220	0.9357
	β_{11}	0.0360	0.0055	0.2693	0.9552	0.0314	0.0037	0.2323	0.9481	0.0260	0.0029	0.2103	0.9487
	β_{20}	0.0014	0.0053	0.2691	0.9464	0.0051	0.0035	0.2280	0.9438	0.0011	0.0028	0.2041	0.9455
	β_{21}	0.1407	0.0701	0.4915	0.9187	0.0859	0.0344	0.4086	0.9020	0.0724	0.0239	0.3628	0.8919
	σ_1	0.0063	0.0605	1.6167	1.0000	0.0028	0.0645	1.6578	1.0000	0.0095	0.0673	1.6935	1.0000
	σ_2	0.0527	0.2503	5.3491	1.0000	0.0508	0.1961	2.2176	1.0000	0.0672	0.1795	2.5655	1.0000
	λ	0.0864	0.1210	1.0579	0.9497	0.0822	0.4112	2.1510	0.9580	0.0734	0.8740	3.2651	0.9598

5.2. Illustration 1

To show the relevance of the MVSUSHN distributio, a real data set from a study conducted by Freeman [30] on drunk driving legislation and traffic fatalities in 48 states in the United States of America (USA) during the period from 1980 to 2004 is considered. The database is available in the wooldridge library by Shea and Brown [31] of the software R Development Core Team [29] under the name of driving, and it contains information associated with current legislation, accident records, and some demographic characteristics. For this illustration, the unemployment rate variables (y_1) and the percent of the population aged 14 through 24 (y_2) were used. The bivariate beta (BVBeta) model of Cepeda et al. [25], the bivariate Johnson SB (BVJSB) model of Lemonte and Moreno-Arenas [27], and the

BVSUSHN model were fitted. The BVBeta distribution of Cepeda et al. [25] is based on the e Farlie–Gumbel–Morgentern copula; see Nelsen [32], and their joint pdf is given by

$$f_{X_1X_2}(x_1,x_2) = f_{X_1}(x_1)f_{X_2}(x_2)(1+\theta(1-2F_{X_1}(x_1))(1-2F_{X_2}(x_2)),$$

where $f_{X_j}(x_j)$ and $F_{X_j}(x_j)$ correspond, respectively, to the pdf and cdf of the beta distributions of parameters α_j and β_j for $j=1,2$ and $\theta \in (-1,1)$. To compare models, we used the Akaike information criterion (AIC) of [33] and the Bayesian information criterion (BIC) of [34], defined, respectively, by

$$AIC = -2\ell(\hat{\theta}) + 2p \quad \text{and} \quad BIC = -2\ell(\hat{\theta}) + n\log(n),$$

where p is the number of parameters and $\ell(\cdot)$ is the log-likelihood function evaluated at the MLEs of parameters. The best model is the one with the smallest AIC or BIC.

For fitting the bivariate model, we used the optim function of R Development Core Team [29]. The parameter estimates of these models, accompanied by their standard errors in parentheses, obtained using the maximum likelihood method, are given in the Table 3. According to the AIC and BIC criteria, the BVSUSHN model presents the best fit.

Table 3. MLE (SE) for BVBeta, BVSJB, and BVSUSHN models.

Parameters	BVSJB	BVBeta	BVSUSHN
α_1	0.1554 (0.0010)	57.0023 (2.2745)	1.5520 (0.1731)
α_2	0.0624 (0.0018)	312.5664 (12.5410)	−1.7849 (0.0035)
β_1	5.0188 (0.9010)	8.2716 (0.3220)	0.2001 (0.0163)
β_2	2.7763 (0.1020)	128.3064 (5.1770)	0.1729 (0.1590)
σ_1	1.7204 (0.6972)		−2.8302 (0.0097)
σ_2	8.0839 (0.2439)		4.0036 (3.6538)
λ	3.2156 (0.5746)	0.9995 (0.0001)	0.6239 (0.0547)
KS test (p-value)	$D_1 = 0.14\ (6\times10^{-10})$ $D_2 = 0.07\ (0.00234)$	$D_1 = 0.12\ (5\times10^{-8})$ $D_2 = 0.08\ (0.00234)$	$D_1 = 0.5725\ (0.8987)$ $D_2 = 0.5175\ (0.9518)$
AIC	−10,980.07	−12,446.15	−12,559.71
BIC	−10,944.44	−12,440.69	−12,524.08

The graphs in the Figure 3 show the contours of the fitted models. For the BVSUSHN distribution, we have that $X_j = \log(-\log(1-Y_j)) \sim \text{USHN}(\alpha_j,\gamma_j,\sigma_j)$ for $j=1,2$ and $(X_1,X_2) \sim \text{BVSUSHN}(\alpha_1,\alpha_2,\gamma_1,\gamma_2,\sigma_1,\sigma_2,\lambda)$, then it follows that

$$W_j = \frac{2}{\alpha_j}\sinh\left(\frac{X_j-\gamma_j}{\sigma_j}\right) \sim \text{N}(0,1), \quad j=1,2$$

and

$$(W_1,W_2) \sim \text{SBSN}(\mathbf{0}_2,\mathbf{I}_2,\lambda)$$

where $\mathbf{0}_2$ and $\mathbf{I}_2$ are a column vector of size 2 and an identity matrix of size 2×2, respectively. The statistic of the Kolmogorov–Smirnov (KS) goodness-of-fit test joint with the respective p-values for the marginal distributions for the BVSJB, BVBeta, and BVSUSHN distribution are presented in Table 3. From here, it can be see that the BVSUSHN distribution shows a good fit compared with the BVSJB and BVBeta models.

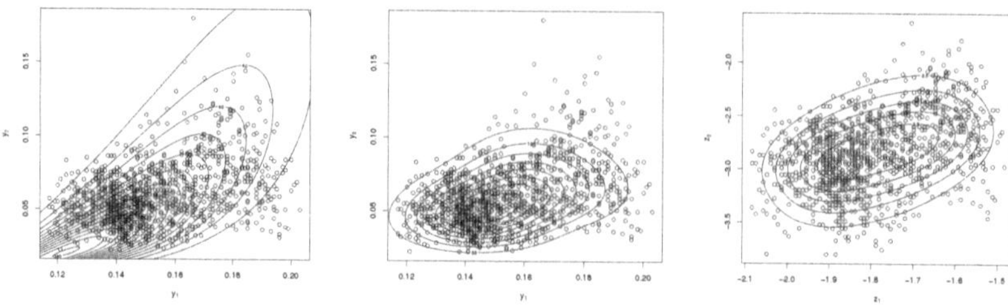

(a) (b) (c)

Figure 3. Contour plots for the fitted models. (**a**) VBJSB, (**b**) VBBeta, and (**c**) SMVUSHN.

5.3. Illustration 2

In the second illustration, the USHN bivariate regression model is fitted. The real data were taken from http://www.pe.undp.org (accessed on 31 August 2022), and they correspond to measurements made on 195 districts in Peru. In this illustration, the interest is to model the human development index (Y_1) and illiteracy rate (Y_2) as functions of the proportion of people with high poverty level (HPL) by using the MVSUSHN regression model. As far as poverty is concerned, poor are identified as those unable to obtain minimum required calorie per day to keep body and soul together. We have that $\log(-\log(1-Y_{1i})) = \beta_{10} + \beta_{11}HPL + \varepsilon_{1i}$ and $\log(-\log(1-Y_{2i})) = \beta_{20} + \beta_{21}HPL + \varepsilon_{2i}$ with $(\varepsilon_1, \epsilon_2) \sim \mathrm{BVSHN}((\alpha_1, \alpha_2), (0,0), \mathrm{diag}(\sigma_1, \sigma_2), \lambda)$.

The MLEs of the vector of model parameters, with standard errors in parenthesis are given by $\hat{\alpha}_1 = 0.3938(0.1539)$, $\hat{\beta}_{10} = -0.0269(0.0075)$, $\hat{\beta}_{11} = -0.5734(0.0277)$, $\hat{\sigma}_1 = 0.3765(0.1384)$, $\hat{\alpha}_2 = 0.1303(0.0654)$, $\hat{\beta}_{20} = -2.8999(0.0500)$, $\hat{\beta}_{21} = 3.5010(0.1832)$, $\hat{\sigma}_2 = 7.8736(3.9272)$, and $\hat{\lambda} = -3.1520(0.6167)$.

$$W_j = \frac{2}{\alpha_j}\sinh\left(\frac{\log(-\log(1-Y_{ji})) - \beta_{j0} - \beta_{j1}HPL}{\sigma_j}\right) \sim \mathrm{N}(0,1), \quad j = 1,2,$$

and

$$(W_1, W_2) \sim \mathrm{SBSN}(\mathbf{0}_2, \mathbf{I}_2, \lambda),$$

where $\mathbf{0}_2$ and $\mathbf{I}_2$ are a column vector of size 2 and an identity matrix of size 2×2. To study the model fit, we perform the Kolmogorov–Smirnov test for the bivariate vector $(\varepsilon_1, \varepsilon_2)$.

For the multivariate Kolmogorov–Smirnov test of goodness of fit proposed by Justel [35], special for the case of a bivariate distribution, which we denote by BKS (bivariate Kolmogorov–Smirnov), the statistic is given by

$$d_n = \sup_{(x_1,x_2)\in\mathbb{R}^2} \left|\mathcal{F}_n(x_1,x_2) - \mathcal{F}(x_1,x_2)\right|$$

where $\mathcal{F}_n$ is the empirical distribution function of the sample, and $\mathcal{F}$ is some specified distribution function. When the $\mathcal{F}$ distribution is unknown, the Kolmogorov–Smirnov statistic is defined by

$$d_n(\mathcal{F}) = \max\{D^1, D^2\},$$

where

$$D^1 = \sup_{(x_1,x_2)\in\mathbb{R}^2} \left|\mathcal{G}_n(y_1,y_2) - y_1 \times y_2\right|$$

by using the transformations $y_1 = \mathcal{F}_{X_1}(x_1)$, $y_2 = \mathcal{F}_{X_2|X_1}(x_2 \mid x_1)$, and

$$D^2 = \sup_{(x_1,x_2)\in\mathbb{R}^2} \left|\mathcal{G}_n(y_2,y_1) - y_2 \times y_1\right|$$

by using the transformations $y_2 = \mathcal{F}_{X_2}(x_2)$ and $y_1 = \mathcal{F}_{X_1|X_2}(x_1 \mid x_2)$, where $\mathcal{G}_n$ is the empirical distribution function of the sample. For the special case of the BVSUSHN model,

$$d_n(\text{BPSN}) = \max\{0.08622004, 0.0750111\} = 0.08622004,$$

which is less than 0.1265 (for $n = 200$), which is the critical value given by Justel [35] at level of 5%. Therefore, it is concluded that the MVSUSHN model fits the data set well.

We also performed univariate Kolmogorov–Smirnov goodness-of-fit tests for W_j with $j = 1, 2$ yielding the test statistics of $D_1 = 0.5282$ with $p-$ value $= 0.949$ and $D_2 = 0.5076$ with $p-$ value $= 0.9898$, indicating that the marginals show a good fit.

The Figure 4 shows the envelope plots for the marginal and contour distributions for the residuals of the fitted model. For the envelope plot, we used the martingale residual transformation, rMT_i, proposed by Barros et al. [36]. These residuals are defined by

$$rMT_i = \text{sgn}(rM_i)\sqrt{-2[rM_i + \alpha_i \log(\delta_i - rM_i)]}; \quad i = 1, 2, \ldots, n$$

where $rM_i = \delta_i + \log(S(e_i, \hat{\theta}))$ is the martingale residual proposed by Ortega et al. [37], where $\delta_i = 0, 1$ indicates whether the i-th observation is censored or not, respectively, $\text{sgn}(rM_i)$ denotes the sign of rM_i, and $S(e_i; \hat{\boldsymbol{\theta}})$ represents the survival function evaluated at e_i, where $\hat{\boldsymbol{\theta}}$ are the MLE for $\boldsymbol{\theta}$.

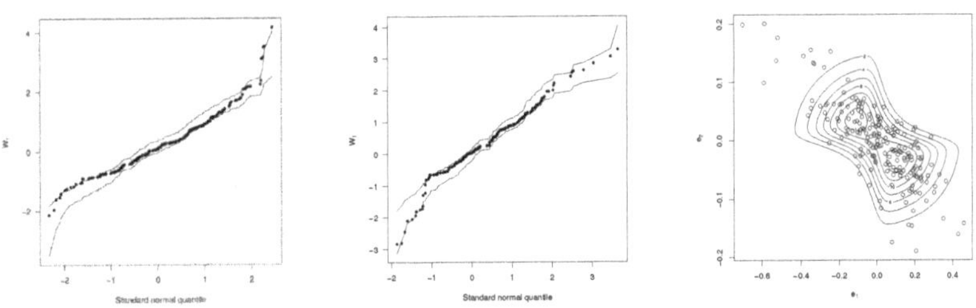

(a) **(b)** **(c)**

Figure 4. Envelope plots for the marginals and contour for the fitted model. (**a**) W_1, (**b**) W_2, and (**c**) MVSUSHN.

6. Concluding Remarks

Diverse distributions to deal with the problem of bounded data on the interval $(0, 1)$ were proposed, with great applicability in all fields of knowledge, especially in the social sciences, humanities, medicine, and engineering, among others. However, few proposals have been developed in the statistical literature to jointly model two or more variables, such as those described above, and especially that incorporate covariates to explain the variability of the variables of interest.

In this paper, a new multivariate distribution was introduced from the conditionally specified distributions methodology useful for modeling responses in the $(0, 1)^p$ region jointly. The new distribution, which is absolutely continuous, is called the skewed log-Birnbaum–Saunders distribution and is also extended to the case of regression models. For the multivariate distribution, the marginal densities and conditional distributions were presented, and the Fisher information matrix of the multivariate regression model was also presented. For the estimation of the parameters in the models, a classical approach was used together with the maximum likelihood method. A small Monte Carlo simulation study was carried out to study the benefits and limitations of the new methodologies, which allows us to conclude that the parameter estimators behave asymptotically well. Two applications with real data to illustrate the usefulness of the introduced methodologies showed great flexibility to model data in $(0,1)^p$ for the particular case $p = 2$, which makes them excellent alternatives to existing methodologies in the statistical literature.

Author Contributions: Conceptualization, G.M.-F., S.V.-C., and R.T.-F.; data curation, G.M.-F., S.V.-C., and R.T.-F; formal analysis, G.M.-F., S.V.-C., R.T.-F., and L.R.-Q.; funding acquisition, G.M.-F., and R.T.-F.; investigation, G.M.-F., S.V.-C., R.T.-F., and L.R.-Q.; resources, G.M.-F., and R.T.-F.; software, G.M.-F., and R.T.-F; supervision, G.M.-F., and R.T.-F.; validation, G.M.-F., S.V.-C, R.T.-F., and L.R.-Q.; visualization, G.M.-F., S.V.-C., R.T.-F., and L.R.-Q.; writing—original draft, G.M.-F., S.V.-C., and R.T.-F.; writing—review and editing, G.M.-F., S.V.-C., and R.T.-F. All authors have read and agreed to the published version of the manuscript.

Funding: The research of G. Martínez-Flórez and R. Tovar-Falón was supported by project: Resolución de Problemas de Situaciones Reales Usando Análisis Estadístico a través del Modelamiento Multidimensional de Tasas y Proporciones; Esquemas de Monitoreamiento para Datos Asimétricos no Normales y una Estrategia Didáctica para el Desarrollo del Pensamiento Lógico-Matemático. Universidad de Córdoba, Colombia, Acta de Compromiso Número FCB-05-19.

Institutional Review Board Statement: Not applicable.

Informed Consent Statement: Not applicable.

Data Availability Statement: Details about available data are given in Section 5.

Acknowledgments: G. Martínez-Flórez and R. Tovar-Falón acknowledge the support given by Universidad de Córdoba, Montería, Colombia. S. Vergara-Cardozo recognizes the support given by Universidad Nacional de Colombia, Sede Bogotá.

Conflicts of Interest: The authors declare no conflict of interest.

Appendix A. Expected Value of the LSHN Distribution

This Appendix presents the derivation of the expected value of a random variable with LSHN distribution, which is used to obtain the Equation (18).

Let $Z \sim \text{SHN}(\alpha, \gamma\sigma)$, then $X = \exp(Z) \sim \text{LSHN}(\alpha, \gamma\sigma)$, where LSHN denotes the pdf of a non-negative SHN distribution; see Martínez-Flórez et al. [3].

Thus, if $X \sim \text{LSHN}$, then $Z = -\log(X) \sim \text{SHN}$. Following Rieck and Nedelman [8], we have that

$$\begin{aligned} X = \exp(-Z) &\Longrightarrow X^r = \exp(-rZ) \\ &\Longrightarrow \mathbb{E}(X^r) = \mathbb{E}(e^{-rZ}) \\ &\Longrightarrow \mathbb{E}(X^r) = \sum_{k=0}^{\infty} \frac{(-r)^k}{k!} \mathbb{E}(Z^k) \\ &\Longrightarrow \mathbb{E}(X^r) = \sum_{k=0}^{\infty} \frac{(-r)^k}{k!} e^{kr} \frac{k_a(\alpha^{-2}) + k_b(\alpha^{-2})}{k_{1/2}(\alpha^{-2})} \end{aligned}$$

where $a = (r\sigma + 1)/2$, $b = (r\sigma - 1)/2$ and $k_\Lambda(\cdot)$ is the third-order function of Bessel.

Now, if $X \sim \text{LSHN}(\alpha, \gamma\sigma)$, then $Y = 1 - \exp(-X) \sim \text{USHN}(\alpha, \gamma, \sigma)$.

Hence,

$$\begin{aligned} \mathbb{E}(Y^n) &= \mathbb{E}[(1 - e^{-X})^n] \\ &= \sum_{j=0}^{n} \binom{n}{j} (-1)^j \mathbb{E}(e^{-jX}) \\ &= \sum_{j=0}^{n} \sum_{l=0}^{\infty} \binom{n}{j} \frac{(-1)^{j+1}(-je^{\gamma})^l}{l!} \frac{k_{a_1}(\alpha^{-2}) + k_{b1}(\alpha^{-2})}{k_{1/2}(\alpha^{-2})} \end{aligned}$$

The last term is obtained by using Taylor expansion for e^{-jX} for the jth moment of the LSHN(α, γ, σ).

Appendix B. Elements of the Observed Information for the SMVSHN Regression Model

This Appendix presents the elements of the observed information, which are calculated from Equation (26).

$$
\begin{aligned}
I_{\alpha_j\alpha_j} &= -\frac{n}{\alpha_j^2} + \frac{3}{\alpha_j^2}\sum_{i=1}^{n}\delta_{i2j}^2 \\
&\quad + \frac{\lambda}{\alpha_j^2}\sum_{i=1}^{n}\left(\prod_{j=1}^{q}\delta_{i2j}\right)\omega_i\left[-\frac{2}{\alpha_j} + \lambda\left(\prod_{j=1}^{q}\delta_{i2j}\right)\left(\lambda\left(\prod_{j=1}^{q}\delta_{i2j}\right) + \omega_i\right)\right],
\end{aligned}
$$

$$
I_{\alpha_j\alpha_{j'}} = \frac{\lambda}{\alpha_j\alpha_{j'}}\sum_{i=1}^{n}\left(\prod_{j=1}^{q}\delta_{i2j}\right)\omega_i\left[-1 + \lambda\left(\prod_{j=1}^{q}\delta_{i2j}\right)\left(\lambda\left(\prod_{j=1}^{q}\delta_{i2j}\right) + \omega_i\right)\right],
$$

$$
\begin{aligned}
I_{\alpha_j\beta_{jk}} &= \frac{2}{\alpha_j\sigma_j}\sum_{i=1}^{n}x_{ijk}\delta_{i1j}\delta_{i2j} \\
&\quad + \frac{\lambda}{\alpha_j\sigma_j}\sum_{i=1}^{n}x_{ijk}\delta_{i1j}\left(\prod_{j'\neq j}\delta_{i2j'}\right)\omega_i\left[-1 + \lambda\left(\prod_{j=1}^{q}\delta_{i2j}\right)\left(\lambda\delta_{i2j}\left(\prod_{j'\neq j}\delta_{i2j'}\right) + \omega_i\right)\right],
\end{aligned}
$$

$$
I_{\alpha_j\beta_{j'k}} = \frac{\lambda}{\alpha_j\sigma_{j'}}\sum_{i=1}^{n}x_{ij'k}\delta_{i1j'}\left(\prod_{j\neq j'}\delta_{i2j}\right)\omega_i\left[-1 + \lambda\left(\prod_{j=1}^{q}\delta_{i2j}\right)\left(\lambda\delta_{i2j'}\left(\prod_{j\neq j'}\delta_{i2j}\right) + \omega_i\right)\right],
$$

$$
\begin{aligned}
I_{\alpha_j\sigma_j} &= \frac{2}{\alpha_j\sigma_j}\sum_{i=1}^{n}v_{ij}\delta_{i1j}\delta_{i2j} \\
&\quad + \frac{\lambda}{\alpha_j\sigma_j}\sum_{i=1}^{n}v_{ij}\delta_{i1j}\left(\prod_{j'\neq j}\delta_{i2j'}\right)\omega_i\left[-1 + \lambda\left(\lambda\delta_{i2j}\left(\prod_{j'\neq j}\delta_{i2j'}\right) + \omega_i\right)\right],
\end{aligned}
$$

$$
I_{\alpha_j\sigma_{j'}} = \frac{\lambda}{\alpha_j\sigma_{j'}}\sum_{i=1}^{n}v_{ij'}\delta_{i1j'}\left(\prod_{j\neq j'}\delta_{i2j}\right)\omega_i\left[-1 + \lambda\left(\lambda\delta_{i2j'}\left(\prod_{j\neq j'}\delta_{i2j}\right) + \omega_i\right)\right],
$$

$$
I_{\alpha_j\lambda} = \frac{1}{\alpha_j}\sum_{i=1}^{n}\left(\prod_{j=1}^{q}\delta_{i2j}\right)\omega_i\left[1 - \lambda\left(\prod_{j=1}^{q}\delta_{i2j}\right)\left(\lambda\left(\prod_{j=1}^{q}\delta_{i2j}\right) + \omega_i\right)\right],
$$

$$
\begin{aligned}
I_{\beta_{jk}\beta_{jk'}} &= \frac{1}{\sigma_j^2}\sum_{i=1}^{n}x_{ijk}x_{ijk'}\left\{2\delta_{i2j}^2 + \frac{4}{\alpha_j^2} - 1 + \frac{\delta_{i2j}^2}{\delta_{i2j}^2 + 4/\alpha_j^2}\right\} \\
&\quad + \frac{\lambda}{\sigma_j^2}\sum_{i=1}^{n}x_{ijk}x_{ijk'}\left(\prod_{j'\neq j}\delta_{i2j'}\right)\omega_i\left[-\delta_{i2j'} + \lambda\delta_{i1j}^2\left(\prod_{j'\neq j}\delta_{i2j'}\right)\left(\lambda\delta_{i2j}\left(\prod_{j'\neq j}\delta_{i2j'}\right) + \omega_i\right)\right],
\end{aligned}
$$

$$
I_{\beta_{jk}\beta_{j'k'}} = \frac{\lambda}{\sigma_j\sigma_j^{'}}\sum_{i=1}^{n}x_{ijk}x_{ij'k'}\delta_{i1j}\delta_{i1j'}\omega_i\left[-\left(\prod_{l\neq j,j'}\delta_{i2l}\right) + \lambda\left(\prod_{j'\neq j}\delta_{i2j'}\right)\left(\prod_{j\neq j'}\delta_{i2j}\right)\left(\lambda\delta_{i2j'}\left(\prod_{j\neq j'}\delta_{i2j}\right) + \omega_i\right)\right]
$$

$$
\begin{aligned}
I_{\beta_{jk}\sigma_j} &= \frac{1}{2\sigma_j}\sum_{i=1}^{n} x_{ijk}v_{ij}\left[\delta_{i1j}^2+\delta_{i2j}^2-sech^2 v_{ij}\right]-\frac{\lambda}{\sigma_j^2}\sum_{i=1}^{n} x_{ijk}\omega_i(\delta_{i1j}+\delta_{i2j}v_{ij})\left(\prod_{j'\neq j}\delta_{i2j'}\right)\\
&+\frac{\lambda^2}{\sigma_j^2}\sum_{i=1}^{n} x_{ijk}v_{ij}\delta_{i2j}^2\omega_i\left(\prod_{j'\neq j}\delta_{i2j'}\right)^2\left(\lambda\delta_{i2j}\left(\prod_{j'\neq j}\delta_{i2j'}\right)+\omega_i\right)
\end{aligned}
$$

$$
I_{\beta_{jk}\sigma_{j'}} = \frac{\lambda}{\sigma_j\sigma_j'}\sum_{i=1}^{n} x_{ijk}v_{ij'}\delta_{i1j}\delta_{i1j'}\omega_i\left[-\left(\prod_{l\neq j,j'}\delta_{i2l}\right)+\lambda\left(\prod_{j'\neq j}\delta_{i2j'}\right)\left(\prod_{j\neq j'}\delta_{i2j}\right)\left(\lambda\delta_{i2j'}\left(\prod_{j\neq j'}\delta_{i2j}\right)+\omega_i\right)\right]
$$

$$
I_{\beta_{jk}\lambda} = \frac{1}{\sigma_j}\sum_{i=1}^{n} x_{ijk}\delta_{i1j}\left(\prod_{j'\neq j}\delta_{i2j'}\right)\omega_i\left[1-\lambda\left(\prod_{j=1}^{q}\delta_{i2j}\right)\left(\lambda\left(\prod_{j=1}^{q}\delta_{i2j}\right)+\omega_i\right)\right],
$$

$$
\begin{aligned}
I_{\sigma_j\sigma_j} &= \frac{2}{\sigma_j^2}\sum_{i=1}^{n} v_{ij}\left(\delta_{i1j}\delta_{i2j}-\frac{\delta_{i2j}}{\delta_{i1j}}\right)+\frac{1}{\sigma_j^2}\sum_{i=1}^{n} v_{ij}^2\left\{2\delta_{i2j}^2+\frac{4}{\alpha_j^2}-1+\frac{\delta_{i2j}^2}{\delta_{i2j}^2+4/\alpha_j^2}\right\}\\
&+\frac{\lambda}{\sigma_j^2}\sum_{i=1}^{n}\left(\prod_{j'\neq j}\delta_{i2j'}\right)\omega_i\left[-2v_{ij}\delta_{i1j}-v_{ij}^2\delta_{i2j}+\lambda v_{ij}^2\delta_{i1j}^2\left(\prod_{j'\neq j}\delta_{i2j'}\right)\left(\lambda\delta_{i2j}\left(\prod_{j'\neq j}\delta_{i2j'}\right)+\omega_i\right)\right]
\end{aligned}
$$

$$
I_{\sigma_j\sigma_{j'}} = \frac{\lambda}{\sigma_j\sigma_{j'}}\sum_{i=1}^{n} v_{ij}v_{ij'}\delta_{i1j}\delta_{i1j'}\omega_i\left[-\left(\prod_{l\neq j,j'}\delta_{i2l}\right)+\lambda\left(\prod_{j\neq j'}\delta_{i2j}\right)\left(\prod_{j'\neq j}\delta_{i2j'}\right)\left(\lambda\delta_{i2j'}\left(\prod_{j\neq j'}\delta_{i2j}\right)+\omega_i\right)\right]
$$

$$
I_{\sigma_j\lambda} = \frac{1}{\sigma_j}\sum_{i=1}^{n} v_{ij}\delta_{i1j}\left(\prod_{j'\neq j}\delta_{i2j'}\right)\omega_i\left[1-\lambda\left(\prod_{j=1}^{q}\delta_{i2j}\right)\left(\lambda\left(\prod_{j=1}^{q}\delta_{i2j}\right)+\omega_i\right)\right],
$$

$$
I_{\lambda\lambda} = \sum_{i=1}^{n}\left(\prod_{j=1}^{q}\delta_{i2j}\right)^2\omega_i\left(\lambda\left(\prod_{j=1}^{q}\delta_{i2j}\right)+\omega_i\right),
$$

References

1. Ferrari, S.; Cribari-Neto, F. Beta regression for modelling rates and proportions. *J. Appl. Stat.* **2004**, *31*, 799–815. [CrossRef]
2. Kumaraswamy, P. A generalized probability density function for double-bounded random processes. *J. Hydrol.* **1980**, *46*, 79–88. [CrossRef]
3. Martínez-Flórez, G.; Tovar-Falón, R. Regression Models Based on the Unit Sinh-Normal Distribution. *Mathematics* **2021**, *9*, 1231. [CrossRef]
4. Martínez-Flórez, G.; Azevedo-Farias, R.B.; Tovar-Falón, R. New Class of Unit-Power-Skew-Normal Distribution and Its Associated Regression Model for Bounded Responses. *Mathematics* **2022**, *10*, 3035. [CrossRef]
5. Kieschnick, R.; Mccullough, B.D. Regression analysis of variates observed on (0,1). *Stat. Model.* **2003**, *3*, 193–213. [CrossRef]
6. Mazucheli, J.; Menezes, A.F.B.; Ghitany, M.E. The unit-Weibull distribution and associated inference. *J. Appl. Probab. Stat.* **2018**, *13*, 1–22.
7. Menezes, A.F.B.; Mazucheli, J.; Dey, S. The unit-logistic distribution: Different methods of estimation. *Pesqui. Oper.* **2018**, *38*, 555–578. [CrossRef]
8. Rieck, J.R.; Nedelman, J.R. A log-linear model for the Birnbaum-Saunders distribution. *Technometrics* **1991**, *33*, 51–60.
9. Martínez-Flórez, G.; Elal-Olivero, D.; Barrera-Causil, C. Extended Generalized Sinh-Normal Distribution. *Mathematics* **2021** *9*, 2793. [CrossRef]

10. Lemonte, A.J. A log-Birnbaum-Saunders regression model with asymmetric errors. *J. Stat. Comput. Simul.* **2011**, *82*, 1775–1787. [CrossRef]
11. Leiva, V.; Vilca-Labra, F.; Balakrishnan, N.; Sanhueza, A. A skewed sinh-normal distribution and its properties and application to air pollution. *Commun. Stat. Theory Methods* **2010**, *39*, 426–443. [CrossRef]
12. Moreno-Arenas, G.; Martínez-Flórez, G.; Barrera-Causil, C. Proportional Hazard Birnbaum-Saunders Distribution with Application to the Survival Data Analysis. *Rev. Colomb. Estad.* **2016**, *39*, 129–147 [CrossRef]
13. Birnbaum, Z.W.; Saunders, S.C. A new family of life distributions. *J. Appl. Probab.* **1969**, *6*, 319–327. [CrossRef]
14. Martínez-Flórez, G.; Bolfarine, H.; Gómez, H.W. The Log-Linear Birnbaum-Saunders Power Model. *Methodol. Comput. Appl. Probab.* **2017**, *19*, 913–933. [CrossRef]
15. Díaz–García, J.A.; Domínguez–Molina, J.R. Some generalisations of Birnbaum–Saunders and sinh–normal distributions. *Int. Math. Forum* **2014**, *1*, 1709–1727.
16. Lemonte, A. A Multivariate Birnbaum-Saunders regression model. *J. Stat. Comput. Simul.* **2013**, *12*, 2244–2257. [CrossRef]
17. Marchant, C.; Leiva, V.; Cysneiros, F. A multivariate log-linear model for Birnbaum-Saunders distributions. *IEEE Trans. Reliab.* **2016**, *65*, 816–864. [CrossRef]
18. Martínez-Flórez, G.; Azevedo-Farias, R.B.; Tovar-Falón, R. An exponentiated multivariate extension for the Birnbaum-Saunders log-linear model. *Mathematics* **2022**, *10*, 1299. [CrossRef]
19. Mazucheli, J.; Menezes, A.; Dey, S. The unit-Birnbaum-Saunders distribution with applications. *Chil. J. Stat.* **2018**, *9*, 47–57.
20. Arnold, B.C.; Castillo, E.; Sarabia, J.M. Conditionally specified multivariate skewed distributions. *Sankhya A* **2002**, *64*, 206–226.
21. Arnold, B.C.; Castillo, E.; Sarabia, J.M. Conditionally specified distributions. In *Lecture Notes in Statistics*; Berger, J., Fienberg, J., Gani, J., Krickeberg, I., Singer, B., Eds.; Springer: New York, NY, USA, 1992; Volume 73.
22. Azzalini, A. A class of distributions which includes the normal ones. *Scand. J. Stat.* **1985**, *12*, 171–178.
23. Lemonte, A.J.; Martínez-Flórez, G.; Moreno-Arenas, G. Multivariate Birnbaum-Saunders distribution: Properties and associated inference. *J. Stat. Comput. Simul.* **2015**, *85*, 374–392. [CrossRef]
24. Martínez-Flórez, G.; Azevedo-Farias, R.; Moreno-Arenas, G. Multivariate log-Birnbaum-Saunders regression models. *Commun. Stat. Theory Methods* **2017**, *46*, 10166–10178. [CrossRef]
25. Cepeda-Cuervo, E.; Achcar, J.A.; Garrido-Lopera, L. Bivariate beta regression models: Joint modeling of the mean, dispersion and association parameters. *J. Appl. Stat.* **2014**, *41*, 677–687. [CrossRef]
26. Souza, D.F.; Moura, F.A.S. Multivariate Beta Regression with Application in Small Area Estimation. *J. Off. Stat.* **2016**, *32*, 747–768. [CrossRef]
27. Lemonte, A.J.; Moreno-Arenas, G. On a multivariate regression model for rates and proportions. *J. Appl. Stat.* **2019**, *46*, 1084–1106. [CrossRef]
28. Tables for computing bi-variate normal probabilities. *Ann. Math. Stat.* **1976**, *27*, 1075–1090.
29. R Development Core Team. *R: A Language and Environment for Statistical Computing*; R Foundation for Statistical Computing: Vienna, Austria, 2021. Available online: http://www.R-project.org (accessed on 31 August 2022).
30. Freeman, D.G. Drunk Driving Legislation and Traffic Fatalities: New Evidence on BAC 08 Laws. *Contemp. Econ. Policy* **2007**, *25*, 293–308. [CrossRef]
31. Shea, J.M.; Brown, K.J. Wooldridge: 115 Data Sets. In *Introductory Econometrics: A Modern Approach, 7e*; Wooldridge, J.M., Ed.; R package version 1.4-2; Cengage Learning: Boston, MA, USA, 2022.
32. Nelsen, R.B. *An Introduction to Copulas*; Springer Series in Statistics; Springer: New York, NY, USA, 2006; p. 272.
33. Akaike, H. A new look at statistical model identification. *IEEE Trans. Autom. Control.* **1974**, *AU-19*, 716–722. [CrossRef]
34. Schwarz, G. Estimating the dimension of a model. *Ann. Stat.* **1978**, *6*, 461–464. [CrossRef]
35. Justel, A.; Peña, D.; Zamar, Z. A multivariate Kolmogorov-Smirnov test of goodness of fit. *Stat. Probab. Lett.* **1997**, *35*, 251–259. [CrossRef]
36. Barros, M.; Galea, M.; Gonzalez, M.; Leiva, V. Influence diagnostics in the tobit censored response model. *Stat. Methods Appl.* **2010**, *19*, 379–397. [CrossRef]
37. Ortega, E.M.; Bolfarine, H.; Paula, G.A. Influence diagnostics in generalized log-gamma regression models. *Comput. Stat. Data Anal.* **2003**, *42*, 165–186. [CrossRef]

mathematics

MDPI

Article

Some Extensions of the Asymmetric Exponentiated Bimodal Normal Model for Modeling Data with Positive Support

Roger Tovar-Falón *,†, Guillermo Martínez-Flórez *,† and Isaías Ceña-Tapia

Departamento de Matemáticas y Estadística, Facultad de Ciencias Básicas, Universidad de Córdoba, Montería 230002, Colombia

* Correspondence: rjtovar@correo.unicordoba.edu.co (R.T.-F.); guillermomartinez@correo.unicordoba.edu.co (G.M.-F.)

† These authors contributed equally to this work.

Abstract: It is common in many fields of knowledge to assume that the data under study have a normal distribution, which often generates mistakes in the results, since this assumption does not always coincide with the characteristics of the observations under analysis. In some cases, the data may have degrees of skewness and/or kurtosis greater than what the normal model can capture, and in others, they may present two or more modes. In this work, two new families of skewed distributions are presented that fit bimodal data with positive support. The new families were obtained from the extension of the bimodal normal distribution to the alpha-power family class. The proposed distributions were studied for their main properties, such as their probability density function, cumulative distribution function, survival function, and hazard function. The parameter estimation process was performed from a classical perspective using the maximum likelihood method. The non-singularity of Fisher's information was demonstrated, which made it possible to find the stochastic convergence of the vector of the maximum likelihood estimators and, based on the latter, perform statistical inference via the likelihood ratio. The applicability of the proposed distributions was exemplified using real data sets.

Keywords: bimodal log-power-normal distribution; elliptical bimodal log-power-normal distribution; asymmetric data; positive data

MSC: 60E05

1. Introduction

The problem of considering alternative distributions to the normal one to fit asymmetric data that present bimodal or multimodal behavior has been addressed by different authors. Elal-Olivero et al. [1], for example, introduced a bimodal extension of the skew-normal (SN) distribution of Azzalini [2] for modeling skewed bimodal data. In addition, Elal-Olivero [3] studied the bimodal-normal (BN) model, which provides a methodology for analyzing variables with two modes as an extension of the normal distribution. On the other hand, Gómez et al. [4] proposed a class of flexible bimodal SN distributions. Kim [5] considered a type of symmetric bimodal SN distribution, whereas Arnold et al. [6] extended Kim's distribution to the situation of the asymmetric bimodal SN. Other works in this same direction were undertaken by Elal-Olivero et al. [7], who presented a class of distributions for data with positive support; Bolfarine et al. [8] studied a bimodal extension of the power-normal (PN) family of distribution, and Martínez-Flórez et al. [9] proposed a distribution that can be useful for fitting data with up to three modes.

Chakraborty et al. [10] proposed a multimodal skewed extension of the normal distribution based on the use of a trigonometric periodic skew function. The suitability of the proposed distribution was investigated by fitting data from real situations. Venegas et al. [11]

considered an extension of the normal new extension of the generalized skew-normal distribution by incorporating an additional parameter that gave the distribution the flexibility to fit data with unimodal and bimodal behaviors. Statistical inference was carried out using the maximum likelihood method and the EM algorithm. Gómez-Déniz et al. [12] proposed a distribution suitable for modeling bimodality in discrete data, and that can fit biased data both positively and negatively. A virtue of this model is that it is capable of representing overdispersion phenomena present in count data obtained through a Poisson distribution. Elal-Olivero et al. [13] developed an alternative to the bimodal skew-normal distribution based on the mixture of skew-normal distributions. For a new proposal, which is called the bimodal skew-normal distribution, the authors studied the stochastic representation and verified the uniqueness of the Fisher data. This proposal presented satisfactory results for modeling bimodal data. Martínez-Flórez et al. [14] proposed two new families of distributions that are capable of modeling unimodal, bimodal, and trimodal data. The proposed distributions extended the normal model to symmetric and asymmetric trimodal situations, and involved fewer parameters to estimate than the mixtures of normal distributions. To fit positive unimodal data with high or low degrees of skewness, the gamma, Weibull, exponential, Birnbaum [15], and Birnbaum and Saunders [16] distributions and the log-normal (LN) distribution are commonly known, which involve transforming the ordinary normal distribution and are commonly used to fit right-skewed data. When the skewness and kurtosis of the distribution are above or below what is expected for the log-normal distribution, it is necessary to have distributions that fit these deviations. On the other hand, for positive data with more than one mode, Bolfarine et al. [17] presented the log-skewed bimodal distribution as a logarithmic extension of the skewed bimodal normal distribution introduced by Elal-Olivero [3]; the distribution can then be seen as an alternative to the log-normal distribution that is typically used to fit positive data with only one mode.

It is important to highlight that the bimodal distributions based on the skew-normal distribution of Azzalini [2] present information matrix singularity problems for values of the skewness parameter close to zero, which puts them at a disadvantage compared to other existing models in the literature, such as those obtained from the power-normal distribution of Durrans [18] that has a non-singular information matrix, which makes it useful for studying the behavior of distributions derived from the generic structure of these distributions and of distributions with a bimodal or multimodal basis.

In this work, bimodal distributions to model positive data are introduced. The proposals, which are based on the normal-skewed bimodal distribution and the bimodal power-normal distribution introduced by Martínez-Flórez et al. [19], are extensions of alpha-power distributions. The main properties of the resulting distributions were studied, including the probability density function, for which the shape of the cumulative distribution function, its survival function, and the Hazard function was studied. In addition, if the moments existed, the moment-generating function, the expectation, the variance, and the asymmetry and kurtosis coefficients were studied, among others.

The rest of the article is organized as follows: Section 2 introduces the exponentiated bimodal log-normal distribution and presents its main properties. The location–scale extension is performed and the statistical inference process of the distribution is carried out using the maximum likelihood method. The Fisher information matrix, which is non-singular, is also presented. In Section 3, the exponentiated elliptical bimodal log-normal distribution is presented. For this new distribution, the probability density function and the cumulative distribution function are shown explicitly. Moments and their properties in general are also presented. Parameter estimation is performed using the maximum likelihood method. Finally, in Section 4, an illustration of the new distribution is presented using a real data set, where it can be appreciated that this new distribution is a viable alternative to other existing methodologies in the statistical literature.

2. Exponentiated Bimodal Log-Normal Distribution

In this section, the exponentiated bimodal log-normal distribution is introduced, which is an extension of the EBN model of Martínez-Flórez et al. [19] in the case of bimodal data with positive support.

Definition 1. *A random variable X is said to have an exponentiated bimodal log-normal distribution if its probability density function (pdf) is given by:*

$$f_{\text{EBLN}}(x;\alpha) = \alpha(\log^2 x)\frac{\phi(\log x)}{x}[\Phi(\log x) - (\log x)\phi(\log x)]^{\alpha-1}; \quad x \in \mathbb{R}^+, \tag{1}$$

where $\alpha \in \mathbb{R}^+$ and $\phi(\cdot)$ and $\Phi(\cdot)$ are the pdf and cumulative distribution function (cdf) of the standard normal distribution, respectively. We used the notation $X \sim EBLN(\alpha)$.

Figure 1 shows some forms of the EBLN density for some selected values of the parameter α. Note that for values of $\alpha \leq 1$ or $\alpha > 10$, the EBLN density is unimodal with a high degree to the right asymmetry, while for values of $1 < \alpha < 10$, the shape of the EBLN density is bimodal with positive skewness, so α is a parameter that controls the skewness of the distribution and, therefore, the EBLN distribution can be useful for fitting unimodal or bimodal positively skewed data.

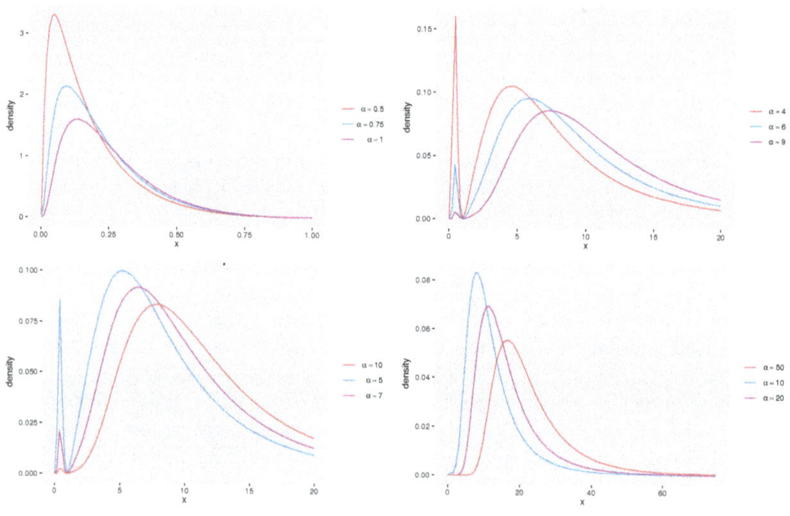

Figure 1. Probability density function of the EBLN distribution for some selected values of α.

Notice that, by letting:

$$u = \Phi(\log t) - (\log t)\phi(\log t) \Longrightarrow du = (\log^2 t)\frac{\phi(\log t)}{t}dt,$$

then:

$$\begin{aligned}\int \alpha(\log^2 t)\frac{\phi(\log t)}{t}[\Phi(\log t) - (\log t)\phi(\log t)]^{\alpha-1}dt &= \int \alpha u^{\alpha-1}du = u^{\alpha} \\ &= [\Phi(\log t) - (\log t)\phi(\log t)]^{\alpha}\end{aligned}$$

Therefore, it follows that the cdf of a continuous random variable EBLN is given by:

$$\mathcal{F}_{\text{EBLN}}(x;\alpha) = [\Phi(\log x) - (\log x)\phi(\log x)]^{\alpha}, \quad x \in \mathbb{R}^+. \tag{2}$$

Given the great flexibility of the EEBLN distribution for fitting data with positive support, it can be used to find, with greater precision, the probability that a subject will survive beyond a given period of time t. This function, which corresponds to the survival function of the EEBLN model, is given by:

$$\mathcal{S}_{\text{EBLN}}(t) = 1 - [\Phi(\log t) - (\log t)\phi(\log t)]^{\alpha}, \quad t > 0,$$

In the graphs of Figure 2, it can be seen that this is a decreasing monotonic function, with $\mathcal{S}_{\text{EBLN}}(0) = 1$ and tending to 0 as t tends to infinity.

Similarly, and supported by the flexibility of the EEBLN distribution in fitting non-negative data, this distribution can be used as a basis function to determine the failure rate of a system for data sets with positive support of the unimodal and bimodal types, or the probability of the survival of an object until the first failure occurs in the system, that is, the conditional probability of survival until failure occurs. This function, in the case of the EEBLN model, is represented by the hazard function of the distribution, which can be expressed in the form:

$$h_{\text{EBLN}}(t) = \frac{\alpha(\log^2 t)\phi(\log t)[\Phi(\log t) - (\log t)\phi(\log t)]^{\alpha-1}}{t\left[1 - [\Phi(\log t) - (\log t)\phi(\log t)]^{\alpha}\right]}; \quad t > 0,$$

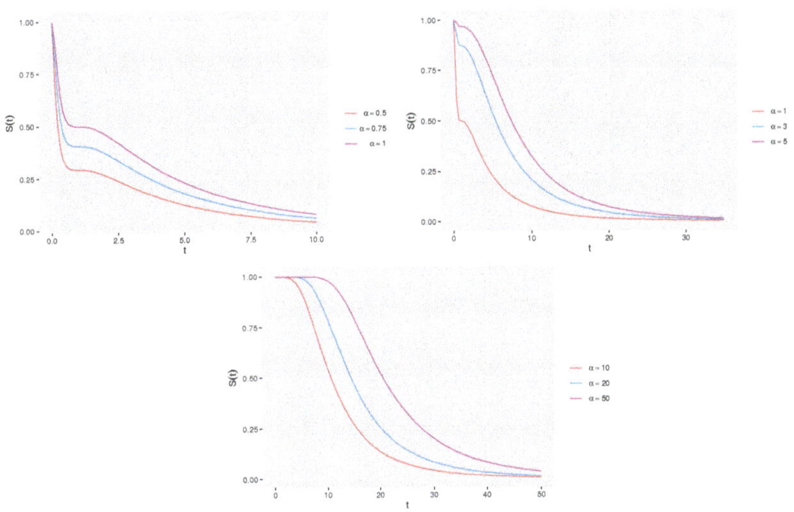

Figure 2. Survival function of the EBLN distribution for some selected values of α.

2.1. Properties

(i) The pdf (1) has, at most, two modes. Indeed:
Let $f(z) = \alpha(\log^2 z)\frac{\phi(\log z)}{z}[\Psi(\log z)]^{\alpha-1}$, where $\Psi(\log z) = [\Phi(\log z) - (\log z)\phi(\log z)]$. By letting $y = \log z$, then $z = e^{y}$, and therefore, $f(z)$ can be written as:

$$g(y) = \alpha y^2\phi(y)e^{-y}[\Psi(y)]^{\alpha-1} = \alpha y^2\phi(y+1)[\Psi(y)]^{\alpha-1}e^{1/2},$$

then:

$$\log g(y) = \log(\alpha) - \frac{1}{2}\log(2\pi) + \frac{1}{2} + 2\log(y) - \frac{1}{2}(y+1)^2 + (\alpha - 1)\log(\Psi(y))$$

then:

$$\begin{aligned}\frac{\partial \log g(y)}{\partial y} &= \frac{1}{y} - (y+1) + (\alpha-1)\frac{\Psi'(y)}{\Psi(y)}, \quad \text{where} \quad \Psi'(y) = y^2\phi(y),\\ &= \frac{-y^2 - y + 2}{y} + (\alpha-1)\frac{y^2\phi(y)}{\Psi(y)}\\ &= \frac{(\alpha-1)a(y)y^3 - y^2 - y + 2}{y} \quad \text{with} \quad a(y) = \frac{\phi(y)}{\Psi(y)}\end{aligned}$$

In addition,

$$\frac{\partial^2 \log g(y)}{\partial y^2} = -\frac{2}{y^2} - 1 + (\alpha-1)\left[\frac{\Psi''(y)}{\Psi(y)} - \left(\frac{\Psi'(y)}{\Psi(y)}\right)^2\right], \quad \text{where} \quad \Psi''(y) = -y(y^2-1)\phi(y),$$

If $\frac{\partial \log g(y)}{\partial y} = 0$, then:

$$(\alpha-1)a(y)y^3 - y^2 - y + 2 = 0 \tag{3}$$

Observe that, if $\alpha > 1$ and $a(y) > 0$, the polynomial in (3) is of the degree 3; therefore, it has at most three roots. In addition, it has two changes in sign; therefore, it has two positive real roots.
For $\alpha = 1$, it holds that $y^2 + y - 2 = 0$, which implies that $y = -2$ or $y = 1$, that is, $z = e^{-2}$ or $z = e$. In addition,

$$\frac{\partial^2 \log g(y)}{\partial y^2} = -\frac{2}{y^2} - 1 < 0$$

All the roots correspond to maximums, that is, the distribution is bimodal.
In general, notice that:

$$\frac{\partial^2 \log g(y)}{\partial y^2} = -\frac{y^2+2}{y^2} - (\alpha-1)\left[\frac{y(y^2-2)\phi(y)}{\Psi(y)} + \frac{y^2\phi^2(y)}{\Psi^2(y)}\right] = -\left[\frac{y^2+2}{y^2} + (\alpha-1)b(y)\right],$$

where $b(y) = \frac{y(y^2-2)\phi(y)}{\Psi(y)} + \frac{y^2\phi^2(y)}{\Psi^2(y)}$. Then, for all roots of (3) such that $b(y) > 0$ and $\alpha > 1$, there will be two maxima. The same is true for $b(y) < 0$ and $\alpha < 1$. Thus, it was concluded that there are, at most, two modes.

(*ii*) If $\alpha = 1$, it follows that there is a bimodal log-normal (BLN) distribution, with the pdf given by:

$$f_{\mathrm{BLN}}(x) = (\log^2 x)\frac{\phi(\log x)}{x}, \quad x \in \mathbb{R}^+, \tag{4}$$

and the cdf given by:

$$\mathcal{F}_{\mathrm{BLN}}(x;\alpha) = \Phi(\log x) - (\log x)\phi(\log x), \quad x \in \mathbb{R}^+. \tag{5}$$

2.2. Moments

The moments of the EBLN distribution do not have a closed analytic form and cannot be calculated explicitly; however, they can be calculated numerically. In general, the kth moment of a random variable X with an EBLN distribution can be obtained using the expression given by:

$$\mu_k = \mathbb{E}[X^k] = \alpha \int_0^\infty x^k (\log^2 x)\frac{\phi(\log x)}{x}[\Phi(\log x) - (\log x)\phi(\log x)]^{\alpha-1}dx \tag{6}$$

The expected value $\mathbb{E}(X)$, the variance $\mathbb{V}(X)$, and the skewness $\sqrt{\beta_1}$ and kurtosis β_2 coefficients of the EBLN distribution can be calculated by using (6) and (7):

$$\mathbb{E}[X] = \mu_1, \quad \mathbb{V}[X] = \mu_2', \quad \sqrt{\beta_1} = \frac{\mu_3'}{(\mu_2')^{3/2}} \quad \text{and} \quad \beta_2 = \frac{\mu_4'}{(\mu_2')^2}, \tag{7}$$

where:

$$\mu_2' = \mu_2 - \mu_1^2, \quad \mu_3' = \mu_3 - 3\mu_2\mu_1 + 2\mu_1^3, \quad \mu_4' = \mu_4 - 4\mu_3\mu_1 + 6\mu_2\mu_1^2 - 3\mu_1^4.$$

The ranges of values for the coefficients $\sqrt{\beta_1}$ and β_2 were calculated numerically for values of $0.01 < \alpha < 1000$, and we obtained:

$$2.855 < \sqrt{\beta_1} < 12.053 \quad \text{and} \quad \beta_2 > 22.540,$$

which shows that the EBLN distribution is capable of fitting data with a high degree of skewness and kurtosis.

2.3. Location–Scale Extension of the EBLN Distribution

The location–scale extension of the EBLN distribution follows from the transformation $\log Z = \xi + \eta X$, where X has an exponentiated bimodal normal distribution (EBN, see [19]), with $\xi \in \mathbb{R}$ and $\eta \in \mathbb{R}^+$. Its pdf is given by:

$$f_{\text{EBLN}}(z;\xi,\eta,\alpha) = \frac{\alpha}{\eta}x^2\frac{\phi(x)}{z}[\Phi(x) - x\phi(x)]^{\alpha-1}, \quad z > 0, \tag{8}$$

where $x = \frac{\log z - \xi}{\eta}$. The respective cdf is:

$$\mathcal{F}_{\text{EBLN}}(z;\xi,\eta,\alpha) = \left[\Phi\left(\frac{\log z - \xi}{\eta}\right) - \left(\frac{\log z - \xi}{\eta}\right)\phi\left(\frac{\log z - \xi}{\eta}\right)\right]^{\alpha}, \quad z > 0.$$

Note that, for $\alpha = 1$, the location–scale version of the BLN distribution was obtained, with the pdf and cdf given by:

$$f_{\text{BLN}}(z;\xi,\eta) = \frac{1}{\eta z}\left(\frac{\log z - \xi}{\eta}\right)^2\phi\left(\frac{\log z - \xi}{\eta}\right), \quad z > 0, \tag{9}$$

and

$$\mathcal{F}_{\text{BLN}}(z;\xi,\eta) = \Phi\left(\frac{\log z - \xi}{\eta}\right) - \left(\frac{\log z - \xi}{\eta}\right)\phi\left(\frac{\log z - \xi}{\eta}\right), \quad z > 0. \tag{10}$$

2.4. Moments and Moment-Generating Function for Location–Scale Case

The kth moment of a random variable Z with a distribution $\text{EBLN}(\xi,\eta,\alpha)$ is obtained from the following expression:

$$\mathbb{E}(Z^k) = \sum_{j=0}^{k}\binom{k}{j}\mu^j\sigma^{k-j}\mathbb{E}(Z^{k-j}), \quad \text{where} \quad Z \sim \text{EBLN}(\alpha).$$

Proposition 1. *If $X \sim EBLN(\xi,\eta,\alpha)$, then the moment-generating function (MGF) of X does not exist.*

Proof. Let us take $\alpha = \alpha_0$ as fixed, $\xi = 0$, and $\eta = 1$; then:

$$\begin{aligned} M_X(t) &= \int_0^\infty \frac{\alpha_0}{x} e^{tx} \left(\log^2 x\right) \phi(\log x) [\Phi(\log x) - (\log x)\phi(\log x)]^{\alpha_0 - 1} dx, \quad \alpha_0, x \in \mathbb{R}^+ \\ &= \int_0^\infty h(x, t; \alpha_0) g(x; \alpha_0) dx \qquad x \in \mathbb{R}^+, \end{aligned}$$

where $h(x, t; \alpha_0) = \frac{\alpha_0}{x} e^{tx} (\log^2 x) \phi(\log x)$ and $g(x; \alpha_0) = [\Phi(\log x) - \log x \phi(\log x)]^{\alpha_0 - 1}$ for all $x > 0$.

If $t > 0$ is fixed, then:

$$J(\alpha_0) = \int_0^\infty h(x, t; \alpha_0) g(x; \alpha_0) dx = \infty, \quad \text{for all} \quad \alpha_0 \in \mathbb{R}^+,$$

since $h(x, t; \alpha_0) \longrightarrow \infty$ when $x \longrightarrow \infty$. Thus, $g(x; \alpha_0) \longrightarrow 1$ when $x \longrightarrow \infty$ for all $\alpha_0 \in \mathbb{R}^+$. Consequently, $J(\alpha_0) \longrightarrow \infty$ when $x \longrightarrow \infty$. □

2.5. Parameter Estimation

Consider a random sample $\mathbf{Z} = (Z_1, Z_2, \ldots, Z_n)^\top$ of size n, such that $Z_i \sim \text{EBLN}(\xi, \eta, \alpha)$, for $i = 1, 2, \ldots, n$. The log-likelihood function for $\boldsymbol{\theta} = (\xi, \eta, \alpha)^\top$ is given by:

$$\begin{aligned} \ell(\boldsymbol{\theta}; \mathbf{Z}) = n \log \alpha - n \log \eta + 2 \sum_{i=1}^n \log x_i - \frac{1}{2} \sum_{i=1}^n x_i^2 - \sum_{i=1}^n \log z_i \\ + (\alpha - 1) \sum_{i=1}^n \log[\Phi(x_i) - x_i \phi(x_i)] - \frac{n}{2} \log 2\pi \end{aligned}$$

where $x_i = \frac{\log z_i - \xi}{\eta}$ for $i = 1, 2, \ldots, n$. After some calculations, the following elements of the score function are obtained:

$$\begin{aligned} \frac{\partial \ell}{\partial \xi} &= -\frac{1}{\eta} \left[\sum_{i=1}^n \frac{2}{x_i} - \sum_{i=1}^n x_i + (\alpha - 1) \sum_{i=1}^n \frac{x_i^2 \phi(x_i)}{\mathcal{F}_{\text{BLN}}(z_i)} \right] \\ \frac{\partial \ell}{\partial \eta} &= -\frac{1}{\eta} \left[3n - \sum_{i=1}^n x_i^2 + (\alpha - 1) \sum_{i=1}^n \frac{x_i^3 \phi(x_i)}{\mathcal{F}_{\text{BLN}}(z_i)} \right] \\ \frac{\partial \ell}{\partial \alpha} &= \frac{n}{\alpha} + \sum_{i=1}^n \log[\Phi(x_i) - x_i \phi(x_i)] \end{aligned}$$

where $\mathcal{F}_{\text{BLN}}(\cdot) = \mathcal{F}_{\text{BLN}}(\cdot; \xi, \eta)$ is the cdf of the BLN distribution given in (10), and $x_i = \frac{\log z_i - \xi}{\eta}$ for $i = 1, 2, \ldots, n$. Taking the second partial derivative to the log-likelihood function, the following elements of the observed information matrix are obtained:

$$\begin{aligned} j_{\xi\xi} &= \frac{1}{\eta^2} \left[\sum_{i=1}^n \frac{2}{x_i^2} + n + (\alpha - 1) \sum_{i=1}^n \frac{x_i \phi(x_i)}{\mathcal{F}_{\text{BLN}}^2(z_i)} \left[\left(x_i^2 - 2\right) \mathcal{F}_{\text{BLN}}(z_i) + x_i^3 \phi(x_i) \right] \right] \\ j_{\xi\eta} &= \frac{1}{\eta^2} \left[2 \sum_{i=1}^n x_i + (\alpha - 1) \sum_{i=1}^n \frac{x_i^2 \phi(x_i)}{\mathcal{F}_{\text{BLN}}^2(z_i)} \left[\left(x_i^2 - 3\right) \mathcal{F}_{\text{BLN}}(z_i) + x_i^3 \phi(x_i) \right] \right] \\ j_{\xi\alpha} &= \frac{1}{\eta} \sum_{i=1}^n \frac{x_i^2 \phi(x_i)}{\mathcal{F}_{\text{BLN}}(z_i)}, \quad j_{\eta\alpha} = \frac{1}{\eta} \sum_{i=1}^n \frac{x_i^3 \phi(x_i)}{\mathcal{F}_{\text{BLN}}(z_i)}, \quad j_{\alpha\alpha} = \frac{n}{\alpha^2} \\ j_{\eta\eta} &= \frac{1}{\eta^2} \left[-3n + 3 \sum_{i=1}^n x_i^2 + (\alpha - 1) \sum_{i=1}^n \frac{x_i^3 \phi(x_i)}{\mathcal{F}_{\text{BLN}}^2(z_i)} \left[\left(x_i^2 - 4\right) \mathcal{F}_{\text{BLN}}(z_i) + x_i^3 \phi(x_i) \right] \right] \end{aligned}$$

The elements of the Fisher information matrix $\mathbf{I}(\boldsymbol{\theta})$ are obtained by taking the expected value of the previous expressions, becoming:

$$\begin{aligned}
i_{\xi\xi} &= \frac{1}{\eta^2}\Big[\mathbb{E}(X^{-2}) + 1 + (\alpha-1)\mathbb{E}[a_1((X^2-2)+a_3)]\Big] \\
i_{\xi\eta} &= \frac{1}{\eta^2}\Big[2\mathbb{E}(X) + (\alpha-1)\mathbb{E}[a_2((X^2-3)+a_3)]\Big] \\
i_{\eta\eta} &= \frac{1}{\eta^2}\Big[3\mathbb{E}(X^2) - 3 + (\alpha-1)\mathbb{E}[a_3((X^2-4)+a_3)]\Big] \\
i_{\xi\alpha} &= \frac{a_2}{\eta} \quad j_{\eta\alpha} = \frac{a_3}{\eta} \quad i_{\alpha\alpha} = \frac{1}{\alpha^2}
\end{aligned}$$

where $a_j = \mathbb{E}\Big[\frac{X^j\phi(X)}{\mathcal{F}_{\mathrm{BLN}}(Z)}\Big]$ and $X = (\log Z - \xi)/\eta$. Taking $\alpha = 1$ and using numerical methods, the following information matrix is obtained:

$$\mathbf{I}(\boldsymbol{\theta}) = \begin{pmatrix} \frac{3}{\eta^2} & 0 & \frac{0.76}{\eta} \\ 0 & \frac{6}{\eta^2} & -\frac{1.01}{\eta} \\ \frac{0.76}{\eta} & -\frac{1.01}{\eta} & 1 \end{pmatrix} = \frac{1}{\eta^2}\begin{pmatrix} 3 & 0 & 0.76\eta \\ 0 & 6 & -1.01\eta \\ 0.76\eta & -1.01\eta & \eta^2 \end{pmatrix} \tag{11}$$

whose determinant is equal to:

$$\mid \mathbf{I}(\boldsymbol{\theta}) \mid = \frac{11.4741}{\eta^4} \neq 0$$

Note that:

$$\mid 3/\eta^2 \mid = 3/\eta^2 > 0, \quad \left|\begin{pmatrix} 3/\eta^2 & 0 \\ 0 & 6/\eta^2 \end{pmatrix}\right| = 18/\eta^2 > 0, \quad \text{and} \quad \mid \mathbf{I}(\boldsymbol{\theta}) \mid > 0$$

Then, $\mathbf{I}(\boldsymbol{\theta})$ is a positive definite matrix; hence, $\mathbf{I}(\boldsymbol{\theta})$ is non-singular, and therefore, the regularity conditions are satisfied (see Appendix A for more details). t follows that the variance–covariance matrix of the vector $\hat{\boldsymbol{\theta}}$ is given by $V(\hat{\boldsymbol{\theta}}) = \mathbf{I}^{-1}(\boldsymbol{\theta})$, and for a large sample size, it follows that:

$$\hat{\boldsymbol{\theta}} = (\hat{\xi}, \hat{\eta}, \hat{\alpha})^\top \xrightarrow{D} \mathrm{N}_3((\xi, \eta, \alpha)^\top, \mathbf{I}^{-1}(\boldsymbol{\theta})).$$

3. Exponentiated Elliptical Bimodal Log-Normal Distribution

In this section, a new bimodal distribution, called the exponentiated elliptical bimodal log-normal (EEBLN) distribution for positive data, is presented. This distribution is obtained from the exponentiated elliptical bimodal normal distribution that was also proposed by Martínez-Flórez et al. [19].

Definition 2. *A random variable X is said to have an exponentiated elliptical bimodal log-normal distribution if its pdf is given by:*

$$f_{\mathrm{EEBLN}}(x;\lambda,\alpha) = \alpha\left(\frac{1+\lambda\log^2 x}{1+\lambda}\right)\frac{\phi(\log x)}{x}\left[\Phi(\log x) - \frac{\lambda}{1+\lambda}(\log x)\phi(\log x)\right]^{\alpha-1}, \tag{12}$$

for $x \in \mathbb{R}^+$, where $\alpha \in \mathbb{R}^+$, $\lambda > 0$, and $\phi(\cdot)$ and $\Phi(\cdot)$ are the pdf and cumulative distribution function (cdf) of the standard normal distribution, respectively. We used the notation $X \sim EEBLN(\alpha)$.

Figure 3 presents some forms of the EEBLN distribution for selected values of the parameters α and γ. It can be seen from the figure that the EEBLN density can be useful for fitting unimodal or bimodal data.

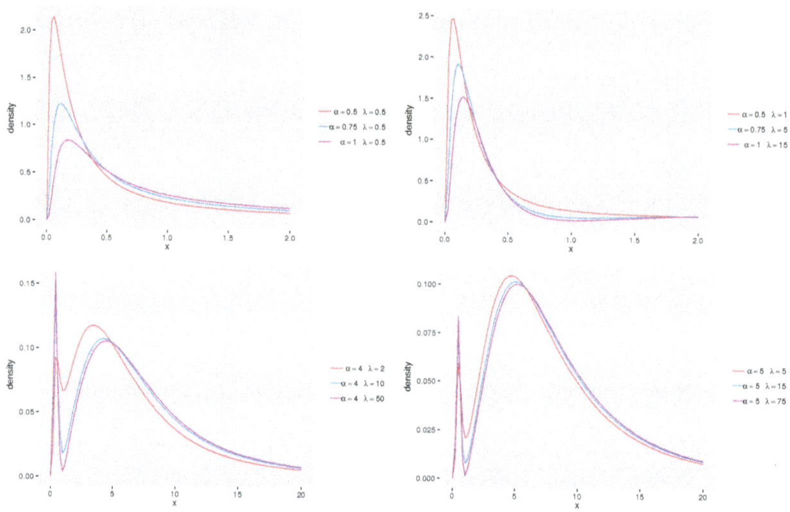

Figure 3. Probability density function of the EEBLN distribution for some selected values of α.

The cdf of a random variable with an EEBLN distribution is given by the expression:

$$\mathcal{F}_{\text{EEBLN}}(x;\lambda,\alpha)=\left[\Phi(\log x)-\frac{\lambda}{1+\lambda}(\log x)\phi(\log x)\right]^{\alpha},\quad x\in\mathbb{R}^{+}. \tag{13}$$

From (13), the survival and hazard functions of the EBLN distribution can be calculated as:

$$\mathcal{S}_{\text{EEBLN}}(t)=1-\left[\Phi(\log t)-\frac{\lambda}{1+\lambda}(\log t)\phi(\log t)\right]^{\alpha},\quad t>0,$$

and

$$h_{\text{EEBLN}}(t)=\frac{\alpha(1+\lambda\log^{2}t)\phi(\log t)\left[\Phi(\log t)-\frac{\lambda}{1+\lambda}(\log t)\phi(\log t)\right]^{\alpha-1}}{t(1+\lambda)\left[1-\left[\Phi(\log t)-\frac{\lambda}{1+\lambda}(\log t)\phi(\log t)\right]^{\alpha}\right]};\quad t>0,$$

respectively. The behavior of the survival function for $t>0$ values is presented in Figure 4, which is strictly non-decreasing and convergent.

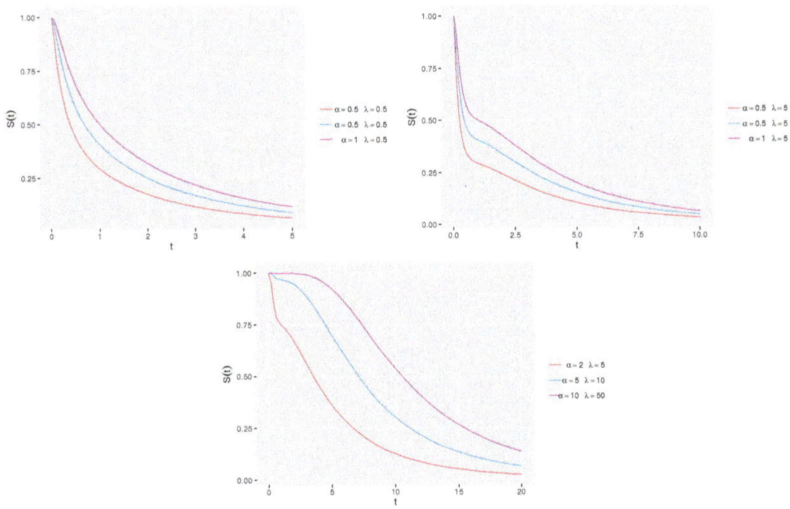

Figure 4. Survival function of the EEBLN distribution for some selected values of α.

3.1. Properties

(i) The pdf (12) has, at most, two modes. To demonstrate this, we took $\alpha = 1$ in (12) again, and derived it to obtain:

$$
\begin{aligned}
f'_{\text{EEBLN}}(x;\lambda,1) &= \frac{d}{dx}\left[\frac{1+\lambda\log^2 x}{1+\lambda}\frac{\phi(\log x)}{x}\right] \\
&= \frac{\phi(\log x)}{(1+\lambda)x^2}\Big[(2\lambda-1)\log x - \lambda\log^2 x - \lambda\log^3 x - 1\Big].
\end{aligned}
$$

By reasoning as in Elal-Olivero [3], it follows that $f'_{\text{EEBLN}}(x;\lambda,1)$ has a maximum of three zeros, so $f_{\text{EEBLN}}(x;\lambda,1)$ has a maximum of two modes.

(ii) If $\alpha = 1$, the elliptical bimodal log-normal (ELBLN) distribution is obtained with the pdf given by:

$$
f_{\text{ELBLN}}(x;\lambda) = \left(\frac{1+\lambda\log^2 x}{1+\lambda}\right)\frac{\phi(\log x)}{x}, \quad x > 0. \tag{14}
$$

1. If $\lambda = 0$, the pdf of the exponentiated log-normal or log-power-normal (LPN) distribution studied by Martínez-Flórez et al. [20] is:

$$
f_{\text{LPN}}(x;\alpha) = \frac{\alpha}{x}\phi(\log x)[\Phi(\log x)]^{\alpha-1}, \quad x > 0. \tag{15}
$$

2. If $\alpha = 1$ and $\lambda = 0$, the log-normal (LN) distribution is obtained.

3.2. Moments

Let X be a random variable with an EEBLN distribution. The expected value $\mathbb{E}(X)$, the variance $\mathbb{V}(X)$, and the skewness $\sqrt{\beta_1}$ and kurtosis β_2 coefficients of a random variable with an EEBLN distribution can be calculated by using (7) with:

$$
\mu_k = \mathbb{E}[X^k] = \alpha\int_0^\infty x^n\left(\frac{1+\lambda\log^2 x}{1+\lambda}\right)\frac{\phi(\log x)}{x}\left[\Phi(\log x) - \frac{\lambda}{1+\lambda}(\log x)\phi(\log x)\right]^{\alpha-1} dx,
$$

The ranges of values for the coefficients $\sqrt{\beta_1}$ and β_2 were calculated numerically for values of $0.01 < \alpha < 1000$, and we obtained:

$$1.823 < \sqrt{\beta_1} < 46.034 \quad \text{and} \quad \beta_2 > 22.645.$$

3.3. Location–Scale Extension of the EEBLN Distribution

The location–scale extension of the EEBLN distribution follows from the transformation $\log Z = \xi + \eta X$, where X has an exponentiated elliptical bimodal normal distribution (EEBN, see [19]) with $\xi \in \mathbb{R}$ and $\eta \in \mathbb{R}^+$. Its pdf is given by:

$$f_{\text{EEBLN}}(z;\xi,\eta,\lambda,\alpha) = \frac{\alpha}{\eta}\left(\frac{1+\lambda x^2}{1+\lambda}\right)\frac{\phi(x)}{z}\left[\Phi(x) - \frac{\lambda}{1+\lambda}x\phi(x)\right]^{\alpha-1}, \quad z > 0, \qquad (16)$$

where $x = \frac{\log z - \xi}{\eta}$. The respective cdf is:

$$\mathcal{F}_{\text{EEBLN}}(z;\xi,\eta,\lambda,\alpha) = \left[\Phi\left(\frac{\log z - \xi}{\eta}\right) - \frac{\lambda}{1+\lambda}\left(\frac{\log z - \xi}{\eta}\right)\phi\left(\frac{\log z - \xi}{\eta}\right)\right]^{\alpha}, \quad z > 0.$$

Note that for $\alpha = 1$, the location–scale version of the ELBLN distribution is obtained, with the cdf given by:

$$\mathcal{F}_{\text{ELBLN}}(z;\xi,\eta,\lambda) = \Phi\left(\frac{\log z - \xi}{\eta}\right) - \frac{\lambda}{1+\lambda}\left(\frac{\log z - \xi}{\eta}\right)\phi\left(\frac{\log z - \xi}{\eta}\right), \quad z > 0. \qquad (17)$$

3.4. Moments and Moment-Generating Function for Location–Scale Case

The kth moment of a random variable Z with a distribution of EEBLN(ξ,η,α) is obtained from the following expression:

$$\mathbb{E}(Z^k) = \sum_{j=0}^{k}\binom{k}{j}\mu^j\sigma^{k-j}\mathbb{E}(X^{k-j}), \quad \text{where} \quad X \sim \text{EEBLN}(\alpha).$$

Proposition 2. *If $X \sim$ EEBLN(α,ξ,η), then the moment-generating function (MGF) of X does not exist.*

Proof. This result is obtained by following a reasoning similar to that of the EBLN distribution. □

3.5. Parameter Estimation

We considered a random sample $\mathbf{Z} = (Z_1, Z_2, \ldots, Z_n)^\top$ of size n, such that $Z_i \sim$ EEBLN$(\xi,\eta,\lambda,\alpha)$, for $i = 1,2,\ldots,n$. The log-likelihood function for $\boldsymbol{\theta} = (\xi,\eta,\lambda,\alpha)^\top$ is given by:

$$\begin{aligned}\ell(\boldsymbol{\theta};\mathbf{Z}) = {} & n\log\alpha - n\log\eta - n\log(1+\lambda) + \sum_{i=1}^{n}\log(1+\lambda x_i^2) - \frac{1}{2}\sum_{i=1}^{n}x_i^2 - \sum_{i=1}^{n}\log z_i \\ & + (\alpha-1)\sum_{i=1}^{n}\log\left[\Phi(x_i) - \frac{\lambda}{1+\lambda}x_i\phi(x_i)\right] - \frac{n}{2}\log(2\pi)\end{aligned}$$

where $x_i = \frac{\log z_i - \xi}{\eta}$ for $i = 1,2,\ldots,n$. After some calculations, the following elements of the score function are obtained:

$$\frac{\partial \ell}{\partial \xi} = -\frac{1}{\eta}\left[\sum_{i=1}^{n}\frac{2\lambda x_i}{1+\lambda x_i^2} - \sum_{i=1}^{n} x_i + \frac{\alpha-1}{1+\lambda}\sum_{i=1}^{n}\frac{(1+\lambda x_i^2)\phi(x_i)}{\mathcal{F}_{\text{ELBLN}}(z_i)}\right]$$

$$\frac{\partial \ell}{\partial \eta} = -\frac{1}{\eta}\left[n + \sum_{i=1}^{n}\frac{2\lambda x_i^2}{1+\lambda x_i^2} - \sum_{i=1}^{n} x_i^2 + \frac{\alpha-1}{1+\lambda}\sum_{i=1}^{n}\frac{x_i(1+\lambda x_i^2)\phi(x_i)}{\mathcal{F}_{\text{ELBLN}}(z_i)}\right]$$

$$\frac{\partial \ell}{\partial \lambda} = \sum_{i=1}^{n}\frac{x_i^2}{1+\lambda x_i^2} - \frac{n}{1+\lambda} - \frac{\alpha-1}{(1+\lambda)^2}\sum_{i=1}^{n}\frac{x_i\phi(x_i)}{\mathcal{F}_{\text{ELBLN}}(z_i)}$$

$$\frac{\partial \ell}{\partial \alpha} = \frac{n}{\alpha} + \sum_{i=1}^{n}\log\left[\Phi(x_i) - \frac{\lambda}{1+\lambda}x_i\phi(x_i)\right]$$

where $\mathcal{F}_{\text{ELBLN}}(\cdot) = \mathcal{F}_{\text{ELBLN}}(\cdot;\xi,\eta,\lambda)$ is the cdf of the ELBLN distribution given in (17), and $x_i = \frac{\log z_i - \xi}{\eta}$ for $i = 1,2,\ldots,n$.

The maximum likelihood estimates are obtained as the solution of this system of equations that results from setting the score functions equal to zero, $\frac{\partial \ell}{\partial \xi} = 0$, $\frac{\partial \ell}{\partial \eta} = 0$, $\frac{\partial \ell}{\partial \lambda} = 0$, and $\frac{\partial \ell}{\partial \alpha} = 0$, which do not have a closed expression and must be solved via numerical methods such as the Newton–Raphson or quasi-Newton methods.

Taking the second partial derivative to the log-likelihood function, the following elements of the observed information matrix are obtained:

$$\begin{aligned} j_{\xi\xi} = {} & \frac{1}{\eta^2}\left[n - 2\lambda\sum_{i=1}^{n}\frac{1}{(1+\lambda x_i^2)^2} + 2\lambda^2\sum_{i=1}^{n}\frac{x_i^2}{(1+\lambda x_i^2)^2}\right] \\ & + \frac{\alpha-1}{\eta^2(1+\lambda)^2}\sum_{i=1}^{n}\frac{(1+\lambda)x_i\phi(x_i)\left[(1-2\lambda)+\lambda x_i^2\right]\mathcal{F}_{\text{ELBLN}}(z_i) + (1+\lambda x_i^2)^2\phi^2(x_i)}{\mathcal{F}^2_{\text{ELBLN}}(z_i)}, \end{aligned}$$

$$\begin{aligned} j_{\xi\eta} = {} & \frac{1}{\eta^2}\left[-2\lambda\sum_{i=1}^{n}\frac{x_i}{(1+\lambda x_i^2)^2} + 2\lambda^2\sum_{i=1}^{n}\frac{x_i^3}{(1+\lambda x_i^2)^2} + \sum_{i=1}^{n} x_i\right] \\ & + \frac{\alpha-1}{\eta^2(1+\lambda)^2}\sum_{i=1}^{n}\frac{(1+\lambda)x_i^2\phi(x_i)\left[(1-2\lambda)+\lambda x_i^2\right]\mathcal{F}_{\text{ELBLN}}(z_i) + x_i(1+\lambda x_i^2)\phi^2(x_i)}{\mathcal{F}^2_{\text{ELBLN}}(z_i)}, \end{aligned}$$

$$\begin{aligned} j_{\eta\eta} = {} & \frac{1}{\eta^2}\left[-n - 2\lambda\sum_{i=1}^{n}\frac{x_i^2(3+\lambda x_i^2)}{(1+\lambda x_i^2)^2} + 3\sum_{i=1}^{n} x_i^2\right] \\ & + \frac{\alpha-1}{\eta^2(1+\lambda)^2}\sum_{i=1}^{n}\frac{(1+\lambda)x_i\phi(x_i)\left[-2+(1-4\lambda)x_i^2+\lambda x_i^4\right]\mathcal{F}_{\text{ELBLN}}(z_i) + x_i^2(1+\lambda x_i^2)^2\phi^2(x_i)}{\mathcal{F}^2_{\text{ELBLN}}(z_i)}, \end{aligned}$$

$$\begin{aligned} j_{\xi\lambda} = {} & \frac{2}{\eta}\sum_{i=1}^{n}\frac{x_i}{(1+\lambda x_i^2)^2} \\ & + \frac{\alpha-1}{\eta(1+\lambda)^3}\sum_{i=1}^{n} x_i\frac{(1+\lambda)(x_i^2-1)\phi(x_i)\mathcal{F}_{\text{ELBLN}}(z_i) + x_i(1+\lambda x_i^2)\phi^2(x_i)}{\mathcal{F}^2_{\text{ELBLN}}(z_i)}, \end{aligned}$$

$$j_{\eta\lambda} = \frac{2}{\eta}\sum_{i=1}^{n}\frac{x_i^2(1-\lambda x_i+\lambda x_i^2)}{(1+\lambda x_i^2)^2} + \frac{\alpha-1}{\eta(1+\lambda)^3}\sum_{i=1}^{n}\frac{(1+\lambda)(x_i^2-1)\phi(x_i)\mathcal{F}_{\mathrm{ELBLN}}(z_i)+x_i(1+\lambda x_i^2)\phi^2(x_i)}{\mathcal{F}^2_{\mathrm{ELBLN}}(z_i)},$$

$$j_{\xi\alpha} = \frac{1}{\eta(1+\lambda)}\sum_{i=1}^{n}\frac{(1+\lambda x_i^2)\phi(x_i)}{\mathcal{F}_{\mathrm{ELBLN}}(z_i)}, \qquad j_{\eta\alpha} = \frac{1}{\eta(1+\lambda)}\sum_{i=1}^{n}\frac{x_i(1+\lambda x_i^2)\phi(x_i)}{\mathcal{F}_{\mathrm{ELBLN}}(z_i)},$$

$$j_{\lambda\alpha} = \frac{1}{(1+\lambda)^2}\sum_{i=1}^{n}\frac{x_i\phi(x_i)}{\mathcal{F}_{\mathrm{ELBLN}}(z_i)}, \qquad j_{\alpha\alpha} = \frac{n}{\alpha^2}.$$

The elements of the expected information matrix $i_{\theta_k\theta_{k'}}$ are obtained by calculating the expected value of the elements of the observed information matrix. Due to the shape of these elements, they cannot be found explicitly, so numerical methods must be used to find the respective expected values. By setting $i_{\theta_k\theta_{k'}} = \mathbb{E}(j_{\theta_k\theta_{k'}})$, the expected information matrix is $\mathbf{I}(\boldsymbol{\theta}) = (i_{\theta_k\theta_{k'}})$, where $\theta_k, \theta_{k'} \in \boldsymbol{\theta} = (\xi, \eta, \lambda, \alpha)^\top$. Since the observed information matrix converges asymptotically to the expected information matrix, for $\lambda \neq 0$ and large sample sizes, we have:

$$(\hat{\xi}, \hat{\eta}, \hat{\lambda}, \hat{\alpha})^\top \xrightarrow{D} \mathrm{N}_4((\xi, \eta, \lambda, \alpha)^\top, \mathbf{I}^{-1}(\boldsymbol{\theta})).$$

4. Application of the EEBLN Distribution

This section contains an illustration with real data from the studied bimodal distributions, which are compared with other existing methodologies.

The data set used in this illustration contains 85 observations regarding the nickel content in soil samples that were analyzed by the Mining Department of the Universidad de Atacama in Chile. The aim is to show the EEBLN distribution as an alternative to modeling unimodal and/or bimodal data. Table 1 contains the main descriptive statistics of the application data. Note that the data have a high degree of kurtosis and a high degree of positive asymmetry; therefore, the EBLN and EEBLN models can be considered viable to fit this data set.

Table 1. Main descriptive statistics for nickel concentration data.

n	$\bar{x}$	$\tilde{x}$	S^2	S	$\sqrt{b_1}$	b_2
85	21.59	17	274.673	16.573	2.392	8.325

To compare the proposed distributions (EBLN and EEBLN), the flexible Birnbaum–Saunders (FBS), skewed Birnbaum–Saunders (SBS), log-normal (LN), and log-power-normal (LPN) distributions were also fitted. The fits were made using the maxLik function of the R Development Core Team [21], obtaining the maximum likelihood estimates (MLE) with their respective standard errors in parentheses, which are obtained numerically as the square root of the diagonal elements of the matrix $\boldsymbol{J}^{-1}(\boldsymbol{\theta})$, where:

$$\boldsymbol{J}^{-1}(\boldsymbol{\theta}) = (j_{\theta_k\theta_l})$$

with $j_{\theta_k\theta_l} = -\frac{\partial^2\ell(\boldsymbol{\theta})}{\partial\theta_k\partial\theta_l}$ and $\theta_k, \theta_l \in \boldsymbol{\theta} = (\xi, \eta, \lambda, \alpha)$. The results are presented in Table 2 for each of the six distributions considered. To compare the distributions in question, the AIC criteria in [22], the corrected AIC (AICC) in [23], and the Bayesian information criterion (BIC) in [24] were used. The criteria were defined by:

$$AIC = -2\ell(\hat{\theta}) + 2p, \quad AICC = -2\ell(\hat{\theta}) + \frac{2n(p+1)}{n-p-2} \quad \text{and} \quad BIC = -2\ell(\hat{\theta}) + n\log(n),$$

where p is the number of parameters and $\ell(\cdot)$ is the log-likelihood function evaluated at the MLEs of the parameters. The best model is the one with the smallest AIC, AICC, or BIC.

Table 2. Maximum likelihood estimates (standard errors) of the fitted distributions.

Parameter	EBLN	EEBLN	FBS	SBS	LN	LPN
ξ	1.846 (0.021)	1.634 (0.170)	–	–	2.828 (0.078)	3.460 (0.454)
η	0.645 (0.027)	0.759 (0.064)	–	–	0.726 (0.055)	0.490 (0.180)
α	2.973 (0.345)	3.795 (0.709)	0.870 (0.104)	1.073 (0.201)	–	0.311(0.314)
λ	–	2.585 (1.630)	1.405 (0.341)	1.252 (0.590)	–	–
β	–	–	5.072 (0.763)	8.841 (1.998)	–	–
δ	–	–	−1.520 (0.282)	–	–	–
AIC	691.417	666.401	671.859	675.280	671.610	672.284
AICC	691.713	666.901	672.359	675.576	671.756	672.580
BIC	698.745	676.172	681.630	678.165	676.495	679.611

To test the significance of the bimodality parameter λ in the data set, we considered the hypothesis system as follows:

$$H_0 : \lambda = 0 \quad \text{versus} \quad H_1 : \lambda \neq 0,$$

which compares the fit of the LPN and EEBLN distributions to the set of data. We used the likelihood ratio (LR) statistic (see Lehmann and Romano [25]), which is given by:

$$\Lambda = \frac{\mathcal{L}_{\text{LPN}}(\hat{\xi}, \hat{\eta}, \hat{\alpha})}{\mathcal{L}_{\text{EEBLN}}(\hat{\xi}, \hat{\eta}, \hat{\lambda}, \hat{\alpha})}$$

where $\mathcal{L}_{\text{LPN}}(\hat{\xi}, \hat{\eta}, \hat{\alpha})$ and $\mathcal{L}_{\text{EEBLN}}(\hat{\xi}, \hat{\eta}, \hat{\lambda}, \hat{\alpha})$ are the likelihood functions associated with the log-power-normal and exponentiated elliptical bimodal log-normal distributions, respectively, evaluated in the maximum likelihood estimators. After evaluating, we found that $-2\log\Lambda = -2(\log(\mathcal{L}_{\text{LPN}}(\hat{\xi}, \hat{\eta}, \hat{\alpha})) - \log(\mathcal{L}_{\text{EEBLN}}(\hat{\xi}, \hat{\eta}, \hat{\lambda}, \hat{\alpha}))) = -2(-333.142 + 329.2007) = 7.8826$, with a $p-\text{value} = 0.00499 < 0.05$; therefore, the null hypothesis $H_0 : \lambda = 0$ was rejected, and the parameter λ was statistically significant to fit the nickel concentration data. Based on this hypothesis test, and the goodness-of-fit criteria AIC, AICC, and BIC (the smallest values among the considered models), it can be concluded that the EEBLN distribution has a better fit than the LPN distribution to the nickel concentration data.

Similarly, the hypothesis of EEBLN versus LN was tested through the hypothesis system:

$$H_0 : (\lambda, \alpha) = (0, 1) \quad \text{versus} \quad H_1 : (\lambda, \alpha) \neq (0, 1),$$

with the likelihood ratio statistic:

$$\Lambda = \frac{\mathcal{L}_{\text{LN}}(\hat{\xi}, \hat{\eta})}{\mathcal{L}_{\text{EEBLN}}(\hat{\xi}, \hat{\eta}, \hat{\lambda}, \hat{\alpha})}.$$

where $\mathcal{L}_{\text{LN}}(\hat{\xi}, \hat{\eta})$ is the likelihood function associated with the log-normal distribution. The sample data led to $-2\log\Lambda = -2(-333.8053 + 329.2007) = 9.2092$ with a p-value = 0.000 < 0.05. Then, the null hypothesis was rejected. A similar reasoning based on the results of the hypothesis test and the AIC, AICC, and BIC comparison criteria allows us to conclude that both the parameters λ and α are statistically significant to fit the nickel concentration data, that is, the EEBLN distribution also has a better fit than the LN distribution to the nickel concentration data. Due to all of the above, the EEBLN distribution captures the high degree of asymmetry and kurtosis, in addition to the bimodality present in the data set.

Figure 5 shows the fitted density functions and the empirical distribution function for the variable concentration of nickel, which reveals that the fit of the EEBLN model is quite good.

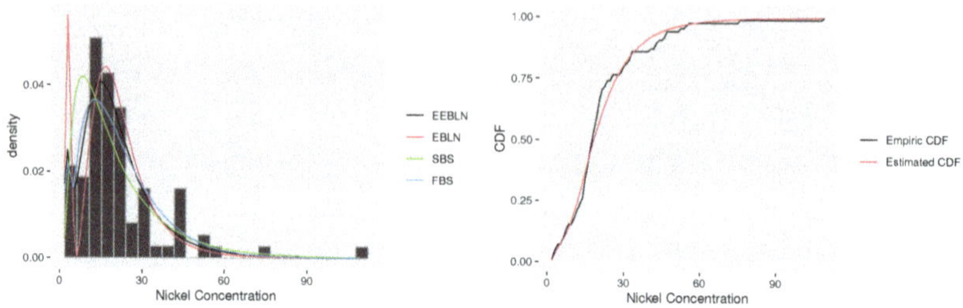

Figure 5. (**Left**) Fits of the EEBLN, EBLN, SBS, and FBS distributions for the nickel data. (**Right**) Empirical and estimated cdf of the EEBLN distribution.

In addition, we performed the Anderson–Darling (AD) goodness-of-fit test for the nickel concentration data. This test measures how well data follow a particular distribution (Anderson and Darling [26], Anderson and Darling [27]); the better the fit, the lower the AD statistic, and analogously if the p-value of the test is lower. At the specified level of significance (usually 0.05 or 0.10), it is concluded that the data do not follow the specified distribution. Therefore, the larger the p-value, the better the fit of the distribution to the data.

The hypotheses to be tested are:

Hypothesis 1 (H1). *The data follows distribution $\mathcal{F}$.*

versus

Hypothesis 2 (H2). *The data does not follow $\mathcal{F}$ distribution.*

with the test statistic:

$$AD = n \int_{-\infty}^{\infty} [\mathcal{F}_n(\cdot) - \mathcal{F}(\cdot)]^2 \psi(\mathcal{F}(\cdot)) d\mathcal{F}(\cdot),$$

where $\psi(\mathcal{F}(\cdot))$ is a distribution function chosen for testing.

Using the ad.test function from the goftest library of the R Development Core Team [21], we obtained the value of the AD statistic, as well as its corresponding p-value, from the nickel concentration data, yielding the results in Table 3.

Table 3. Anderson–Darling (AD) statistics for the EEBLN, EBLN, LPN, LN, FBS, and SBS distributions.

Distribution	AD	p-Value
EBLPN	0.694	0.563
BLPN	1.409	0.199
LPN	1.150	0.287
LN	1.284	0.237
FBS	2.060	0.085
SBS	22.317	0.000

It is clear that the EEBLN distribution presented a lower AD statistic as well as a higher p-value; therefore, it fit the nickel concentration data better compared to the other distributions considered.

5. Concluding Remarks

In this work, two new, absolutely continuous probability distributions were presented to model positive bimodal data with high or low degrees of skewness and kurtosis. The new proposals, which are called the exponentiated bimodal log-normal (EBLN) and the exponentiated elliptical bimodal log-normal (EEBLN), were obtained from the extension of the bimodal-normal distribution and the alpha-power family. For the introduced distributions, their main properties were studied as a function of probability density, cumulative distribution, survival, and hazard. Parameter estimates were made using the maximum likelihood method. It is highlighted that the expected information matrices for both distributions were non-singular.

In addition, an application was made with nickel concentration data in soil samples and the results were compared with different existing models in the literature. The results indicate that the EBLN and EEBLN distributions showed a good fit to the aforementioned data, being the best fit for the EBLPN distribution, which demonstrates the great applicability of the proposals in the analysis of real data from different areas of knowledge.

Future work contemplates extending the proposed distributions to situations where the data under analysis present censorship and regression models. Another field of interest is to carry out the inference of these types of distributions from a Bayesian perspective.

Author Contributions: Conceptualization, R.T.-F., G.M.-F. and I.C.-T.; Methodology, R.T.-F., G.M.-F. and I.C.-T.; Software, R.T.-F., G.M.-F. and I.C.-T.; Validation, R.T.-F. and G.M.-F.; Formal analysis, R.T.-F., G.M.-F. and I.C.-T.; Investigation, R.T.-F., G.M.-F. and I.C.-T.; Resources, R.T.-F.; Data curation, R.T.-F., G.M.-F. and I.C.-T.; Writing—original draft, R.T.-F. and G.M.-F.; Writing—review & editing, R.T.-F. and G.M.-F.; Supervision, R.T.-F. and G.M.-F.; Project administration, R.T.-F.; Funding acquisition, R.T.-F. All authors have read and agreed to the published version of the manuscript.

Funding: The research of R. Tovar-Falón, G. Martinez-Flórez and I. Ceña-Tapia was supported by Fondo de Investigación de la Vicerrectoría de Investigación, Universidad de Córdoba, Colombia.

Data Availability Statement: Details about available data are given in Section 4.

Acknowledgments: R. Tovar-Falón, G. Martinez-Flórez and I. Ceña-Tapia acknowledge the support given by Universidad de Córdoba, Montería, Colombia.

Conflicts of Interest: The authors declare no conflict of interest.

Appendix A. Regularity Conditions

Appendix A.1. Regularity Conditions for EBLN Distribution

Consider the density function (8), which is given by:

$$f(z;\xi,\eta,\alpha)=\frac{\alpha}{\eta z}\left(\frac{\log z-\xi}{\eta}\right)^2\phi\left(\frac{\log z-\xi}{\eta}\right)\left[\Phi\left(\frac{\log z-\xi}{\eta}\right)-\left(\frac{\log z-\xi}{\eta}\right)\phi\left(\frac{\log z-\xi}{\eta}\right)\right]^{\alpha-1},\quad z>0, \tag{A1}$$

For simplicity, we used the notation $f(z;\xi,\eta,\alpha)=f(z)$. Note that $f(z)$ can be written as:

$$g(x)=\frac{\alpha}{\eta}x^2\phi(x+\eta)[\Psi(x)]^{\alpha-1}e^{-\xi+\frac{1}{2}\eta^2} \tag{A2}$$

where $\Psi(x)=\Phi(x)-x\phi(x)$ and $x=\frac{\log z-\xi}{\eta}$.

By applying l'Hôpital, we have that:

$$\lim_{x\to\infty}x^2\phi(x+\eta)=\lim_{x\to-\infty}x^2\phi(x+\eta)=0,$$

We also know that $0 \leq \Psi(x) \leq 1$. Then, $g(x)$ is bounded. In addition, $x^2\phi(x)$ is continuous just like $\Psi(x) = \Phi(x) - x\phi(x)$. Then, $g(x)$ is continuous and bounded and exists for all $x \in \mathbb{R}$, that is, $\forall x > 0$.

Note that, for $h(x) = x^2\phi(x+\eta)$, $h'(x)$, $h''(x)$, and $h'''(x)$ exist and are continuous just like $\Psi'(x)$, $\Psi''(x)$, and $\Psi'''(x)$, as shown by:

$$\frac{\partial g}{\partial \theta_j} = \frac{\partial g}{\partial y}\frac{\partial y}{\partial \theta_j}$$

Then, it also holds that:

$$\frac{\partial^2 h}{\partial \theta_j \theta_{j'}}, \quad \frac{\partial^3 h}{\partial \theta_j \theta_{j'} \theta_k}, \quad \frac{\partial^3 \Psi}{\partial \theta_j \theta_{j'} \theta_k} \quad \text{and} \quad \frac{\partial^3 \Psi}{\partial \theta_j \theta_{j'} \theta_k}$$

exist and are continuous.

Following the same reasoning of Martínez-Flórez et al. [14], it can be shown that for $0 \leq \Phi(x) \leq 1$, we have that:

$$|\log \Psi(x)| \leq \max\{|\log \Psi(z_0)|, |\log \Psi(z_1)|\}$$

with z_0 and z_1 such as:

$$\log \Psi(z_0) < \log \Psi(z) < \log \Psi(z_1).$$

In the same way, it follows that $|\phi(x)| \leq \frac{1}{\sqrt{2\pi}}$, $|\phi'(x)| \leq \frac{e^{-1/2}}{\eta\sqrt{2\pi}}$, $-\frac{1}{\sqrt{2\pi}} < \phi''(x) < 0$, and $|\phi'''(x)| \leq \frac{1}{\eta^2\sqrt{2\pi}}(\sqrt{3}+1)\sqrt{2+\sqrt{3}}e^{-1/(2+\sqrt{3})}$.

Based on this result and on the first four moments of the random variable X, it is also possible to demonstrate, by applying l'Hôpital, that:

$$\log \Psi(x)[\Psi(x)]^{\alpha-1} = \frac{\alpha-1}{\alpha}\Psi(x)g(x) < +\infty$$

Using all the previous results, it can be shown that:

$$\frac{\partial g}{\partial \theta_j} \quad \text{and} \quad \frac{\partial^2 g}{\partial \theta_j \theta_k}$$

are bounded. In the same way, we can prove that:

$$\frac{\partial \log g}{\partial \theta_j}, \quad \frac{\partial^2 \log g}{\partial \theta_j \theta_k} \quad \text{and} \quad \frac{\partial^3 \log g}{\partial \theta_i \theta_j \theta_k}$$

are bounded. Since the information matrix is non-singular, its rows or columns are linearly independent, which guarantees that $|I(\boldsymbol{\theta})| < +\infty$. According to Lehmann and Casella [28], it was concluded that the regularity conditions were satisfied. Therefore, the maximum likelihood estimator $\hat{\boldsymbol{\theta}}$ is consistent, and asymptotically, we have that:

$$\hat{\boldsymbol{\theta}} \longrightarrow \mathrm{N}_3(\boldsymbol{\theta}, I^{-1}(\boldsymbol{\theta}))$$

Appendix A.2. Regularity Conditions for EEBLN Distribution

We considered the pdf (16), given by:

$$f_{\mathrm{EEBLN}}(z;\xi,\eta,\lambda,\alpha) = \frac{\alpha}{\eta}\left(\frac{1+\lambda x^2}{1+\lambda}\right)\frac{\phi(x)}{z}\left[\Phi(x) - \frac{\lambda}{1+\lambda}x\phi(x)\right]^{\alpha-1}, \quad z > 0, \tag{A3}$$

where $x = \frac{\log z - \xi}{\eta}$. Note that:

$$f_{\text{EEBLN}}(z;\xi,\eta,\lambda,\alpha) = g(x) = k(\xi,\eta,\alpha)M(x)\phi(x+\eta)[\Psi(x)]^{\alpha-1}, \quad \text{(A4)}$$

with $= k(\xi,\eta,\alpha) = (\alpha e^{-\xi+\frac{1}{2}\eta^2})/\eta$, $M(x) = \frac{1+\lambda x^2}{1+\lambda}$, and $\Psi(x) = \left[\Phi(x) - \frac{\lambda}{1+\lambda}x\phi(x)\right]^{\alpha}$.

It can be seen that $M(x) \geq 0$ is continuous and differentiable. Then, by l'Hôpital, we have that:

$$\lim_{x\to\infty} M(x)\phi(x+\eta) = \lim_{x\to\infty} M(x)\phi(x+\eta) = 0,$$

and, since $0 \leq \Phi(x) - \frac{\lambda}{1+\lambda}x\phi(x) \leq 1$ is continuous and exists everywhere $\mathbb{R}$, it follows that:

$$f(x) = \frac{\alpha}{\eta}\frac{1+\lambda x^2}{1+\lambda}\frac{\phi(x)}{z}\left[\Phi(x) - \frac{\lambda}{1+\lambda}x\phi(x)\right]^{\alpha-1}$$

is continuous and exists everywhere $\mathbb{R}$. Inasmuch as $\Psi(x) = \Phi(x) - \frac{\lambda}{1+\lambda}x\phi(x)$ is such that $0 \leq \Phi(x) \leq 1$, then $\log(\Phi(x)) \leq 0$ almost always exists. Likewise, it is easy to show that the first three derivatives of $M(x)$, $\phi(x)$, and $\Phi(x)$ with regards to z, ξ, η, λ, and α are continuous and exist almost always. The same happens for the second and third mixed derivatives of $M(x)$, $\phi(x)$, and $\Phi(x)$ with regards to θ_j, $\theta_{j'}$, θ_j, $\theta_{j''}$, and $\theta_{j''}$, where j, j', and j'' are in the range of ξ, η, λ, and α.

Again, following Martínez-Flórez et al. [14], we have that, for each x, it is always possible to find x_0 and x_1 such that:

$$|\log(\Psi(x))| \leq \max\{|\log(\Psi(x_0))|, |\log(\Psi(x_1))|\}$$

Note that $0 \leq \Psi(x) \leq 1$; then, it follows that $E_\theta[M(x)\phi(x+\eta)(\Psi(x))^{\alpha-1}] < \infty$, $E_\theta[M'(x)\phi(x+\eta)(\Psi(x))^{\alpha-1}] \leq E_\theta[M'(x)\phi(x+\eta)] < \infty$, $E_\theta[M''(x)\phi(x+\eta)(\Psi(x))^{\alpha-1}] < \infty$, and $\frac{2\alpha}{1+\alpha}E_\theta[\phi(x+\eta)] < \infty$, given that $|\phi(x+\eta)| < \frac{1}{\sqrt{2\pi}}$, $|\phi'(x+\eta)| < \frac{1}{\eta\sqrt{2\pi}}e^{-1/2}$, $-\frac{1}{\sqrt{2\pi}} \leq \phi''(x+\eta) \leq 0$, and $|\phi'''(x+\eta)| \leq \frac{1}{\eta^2\sqrt{2\pi}}(\sqrt{3}+1)\sqrt{2+\sqrt{3}}e^{-1/2(2+\sqrt{3})}$. In addition, notice that $M'''(x) = 0$. Likewise, by l'Hôpital:

$$\lim_{x\to-\infty} \log(\Psi(x))[\Psi(x)]^{\alpha-1} < \infty$$

With these results, it can be shown that $\frac{\partial f}{\partial\theta_j}$, $\frac{\partial^2 f}{\partial\theta_j\partial\theta_{j'}}$ are bounded; these same results follow for $\frac{\partial \log f}{\partial\theta_j}$, $\frac{\partial^2 \log f}{\partial\theta_j\partial\theta_{j'}}$, and $\frac{\partial^3 \log f}{\partial\theta_j\partial\theta_{j'}\partial\theta_{j''}}$. For $\alpha = 1$ and $\lambda > 0$, it can be shown that the rows or columns of the information matrix are linearly independent, from which it follows that the information matrix is non-singular, that is, $|\mathbf{I}(\boldsymbol{\theta})| < \infty$ and $V(\hat{\boldsymbol{\theta}}) = \mathbf{I}^{-1}(\boldsymbol{\theta})$. Under these regularity conditions, the MLE are consistent and such that:

$$\sqrt{n}(\hat{\boldsymbol{\theta}} - \boldsymbol{\theta}) \sim \mathrm{N}_4(\boldsymbol{\theta}, \mathbf{I}^{-1}(\boldsymbol{\theta})).$$

References

1. Elal-Olivero, D.; Gómez, H.W.; Quintana, F.A. Bayesian modeling using a class of bimodal skew-elliptical distributions. *J. Stat. Plan. Inference* **2009**, *139*, 1484–1492. [CrossRef]
2. Azzalini, A. A class of distributions which includes the normal ones. *Scand. J. Stat.* **1985**, *12*, 171–178.
3. Elal-Olivero, D. Alpha-skew-normal distribution. *Proyecciones J. Math.* **2010**, *29*, 224–240. [CrossRef]
4. Gómez, H.W.; Olivero, D.E.; Salinas, H.S.; Bolfarine, H. Bimodal extension based on the skew-normal distribution with application to pollen data. *Environmetrics* **2011**, *22*, 50–62. [CrossRef]
5. Kim, H.J. On a class of two-piece skew-normal distribution. *Statistics* **2005**, *39*, 537–553. [CrossRef]
6. Arnold, B.C.; Gómez, H.W.; Salinas, H.S. On multiple constraint skewed models. *Scand. J. Stat.* **2009**, *43*, 279–293. [CrossRef]
7. Elal-Olivero, D.; Olivares-Pacheco, J.F.; Gómez, H.W.; Bolfarine, H. A new class of non negative distributions generated by symmetric distributions. *Commun. Stat.-Theory Methods* **2009**, *38*, 993–1008. [CrossRef]

8. Bolfarine, H.; Martínez-Flórez, G.; Salinas, H.S. Bimodal symmetric-asymmetric power-normal families. *Commun. Stat.-Theory Methods* **2018**, *47*, 259–276. [CrossRef]
9. Martínez-Flórez, G.; Tovar-Falón, R.; Jiménez-Narváez, M. Likelihood-Based Inference for the Asymmetric Beta-Skew Alpha-Power Distribution. *Symmetry* **2020**, *12*, 613. [CrossRef]
10. Chakraborty, S.; Partha Jyoti Hazarika, P.J.; Ali, M.M. A multimodal skewed extension of normal distribution: Its properties and applications. *Statistics* **2015**, *4*, 859–877. [CrossRef]
11. Venegas, O.; Salinas, H.S.; Gallardo, D.I.; Bolfarine, H.; Gómez, H.W. Bimodality based on the generalized skew-normal distribution. *J. Stat. Comput. Simul.* **2018**, *88*, 156–181. [CrossRef]
12. Gómez-Déniz, E.; Pérez-Rodríguez, J.V.; Reyes, J.; Gómez, H.W. A Bimodal Discrete Shifted Poisson Distribution. A Case Study of Tourists' Length of Stay. *Symmetry* **2020**, *12*, 442. [CrossRef]
13. Elal-Olivero, D.; Olivares-Pacheco, J.F.; Venegas, O.; Bolfarine, H.; Gómez, H.W. On properties of the bimodal skew-normal distribution and an application. *Mathematics* **2020**, *8*, 703. [CrossRef]
14. Martínez-Flórez, G.; Tovar-Falón, R.; Elal-Olivero, D. Some new flexible classes of normal distribution for fitting multimodal data. *Statistics* **2022**, *1*, 182–205. [CrossRef]
15. Birnbaum, Z.W. Effect of linear truncation on a multinormal population. *Ann. Math. Stat.* **1950**, *21*, 272–279. [CrossRef]
16. Birnbaum, Z.; Saunders, S.C. A new family of life distributions. *J. Appl. Probab.* **1969**, *6*, 319–327. [CrossRef]
17. Bolfarine, H.; Gómez, H.W.; Rivas, L.I. The log-bimodal-skew-normal model. a geochemical application. *J. Chemom.* **2011**, *25*, 329–332. [CrossRef]
18. Durrans, S.R. Distributions of fractional order statistics in hydrology. *Water Resour. Res.* **1992**, *28*, 1649–1655. [CrossRef]
19. Martínez-Flórez, G.; Pacheco-López, M.; Tovar-Falón, R. Likelihood-based inference for the asymmetric exponentiated bimodal normal model. *Rev. Colomb. EstadíStica* **2022**, *45*, 301–326. [CrossRef]
20. Martínez-Flórez, G.; Bolfarine, H.; Gómez, H.W. The log-power-normal distribution with application to air pollution. *Environmetrics* **2014**, *25*, 44–56. [CrossRef]
21. R Development Core Team. *R: A Language and Environment for Statistical Computing;* R Foundation for Statistical Computing: Vienna, Austria, 2021. Available online: http://www.R-project.org (accessed on 31 March 2022).
22. Akaike, H. A new look at statistical model identification. *IEEE Trans. Autom. Control.* **1974**, *AU-19*, 716–722. [CrossRef]
23. Cavanaugh, J.E. Unifying the derivations for the Akaike and corrected Akaike information criteria. *Stat. Probab. Lett.* **1997**, *33*, 201–208. [CrossRef]
24. Schwarz, G. Estimating the dimension of a model. *Ann. Stat.* **1978** *6*, 461–464. [CrossRef]
25. Lehmann, E.L.; Romano, J.P. *Testing Statistical Hypotheses*, 4th ed.; Springer: New York, NY, USA, 2022.
26. Anderson, T.W.; Darling, D.A. Asymptotic theory of certain "Goodness of Fit" criteria based on stochastic processes. *Ann. Math. Stat.* **1952** *23*, 193–212. [CrossRef]
27. Anderson, T.W.; Darling, D.A. A test of goodness of fit. *J. Am. Stat. Assoc.* **1954**, *49*, 765–769. [CrossRef]
28. Lehmann, E.; Casella, G. *Theory of Point Estimation*, 2nd ed.; Springer: New York, NY, USA, 1998.

mathematics

Article

Reconstructing the Quarterly Series of the Chilean Gross Domestic Product Using a State Space Approach

Christian Caamaño-Carrillo [1,*,†], Sergio Contreras-Espinoza [1,†] and Orietta Nicolis [2,†]

1 Departament of Statistics, Faculty of Science, Universidad del Bío-Bío, Concepción 4081112, Chile; scontre@ubiobio.cl
2 Faculty of Engineering, Universidad Andres Bello, Viña del Mar 2520000, Chile; orietta.nicolis@unab.cl
* Correspondence: chcaaman@ubiobio.cl
† These authors contributed equally to this work.

Abstract: In this work, we use a cointegration state space approach to estimate the quarterly series of the Chilean Gross Domestic Product (GDP) in the period 1965–2009. First, the equation of Engle–Granger is estimated using the data of the yearly GPD and some related variables, such as the price of copper, the exports of goods and services, and the mining production index. The estimated coefficients of this regression are then used to obtain a first estimation of the quarterly GDP series with measurement errors. A state space model is then applied to improve the preliminary estimation of the GDP with the main purpose of eliminating the maximum error of measurement such that the sum of the three-month values coincide swith the yearly GDP. The results are then compared with the traditional disaggregation methods. The resulting quarterly GDP series reflects the major events of the historical Chilean economy.

Keywords: benchmarking; Engle–Granger equation; Kalman filter; state space models; GDP

MSC: 37M10; 62P20

1. Introduction

An important limitation in describing the Chilean economy is the unavailability of a sufficient number of observations for estimating a reliable econometric model. Among the economic variables, the gross domestic product (GDP) is one of the most important indexes for describing the country's economy. It constitutes the broadest measure of the country's economy, containing a wide range of constitutive factors representing different areas of economic activity. It can be defined as the total value of products and services produced by a nation in a specific period of time, usually a year or a quarter. The frequency with which GDP is calculated is of particular interest since the low number of data (for example, yearly) could cause serious problems in terms of the quality of quantitative analysis. However, for this variable, in Chile, there is no quarterly information before 1986 (only annual information is available), and there is not a formally recognized procedure for reconstructing it. The Benchmarking or disaggregation methods allow disaggregating or interpolating a low frequency to a higher frequency time series, while the sum remains consistent with the low-frequency series. The most used disaggregation methods in the literature for estimating the GDP of different countries have been proposed by [1–6]. In summary, a two-step procedure can be used to describe all these methods. First, a preliminary high-frequency series is evaluated by using indicators with the same frequency. Second, the differences between the preliminary low-frequency series and the observed series are distributed among the high-frequency series. The resulting estimated high-frequency series is obtained by the sum of the preliminary high-frequency series and distributed annual residuals. While the methods of Denton [4] and Denton–Cholette [3] attempt to preserve the movements by using a single indicator as their preliminary series (which is not necessarily correlated with the low-frequency series), Chow–Lin [2], Fernandez [5], and Litterman [6] performed a Generalized Least Squares Regression (GLS) of the low-frequency series on the high-frequency one for evaluating the preliminary series, which is obtained by the fitted values of the GLS regression. In the second step, the distribution matrix of all temporal disaggregation methods (except for the Denton–Cholette method) is a function of the variance-covariance matrix, as shown in Table 2 of [7]. While Denton proposed to minimize the squared absolute or relative deviations from a (differenced) indicator series, Denton–Cholette introduced a modification of Denton's original method, which removes spurious transient movement at the beginning of the resulting series ([7,8]). Instead, Chow–Lin [2] assumed that the high-frequency residuals follow a stationary autoregressive process of order 1, AR(1), while Fernandez [5] and Litterman [6] suppose that the quarterly residuals follow a nonstationary process where the residual term is an AR(1). In particular, Fernandez´s method is a special case of Litterman where the autoregression parameter is equal to zero, and the high-frequency residuals follow a random walk process. Several methods have been proposed for estimating the autoregressive parameter (denoted by ρ) of the residuals in the Chow–Lin and Litterman methods. Chow and Lin (1971) proposed an iterative procedure that infers the parameter from the observed autocorrelation of the low-frequency residuals. Bournay and Laroque [9] suggested the maximization of the likelihood of the GLS regression, and Barbone et al. [10] proposed the minimization of the weighted residual sum of squares (RSS). Two variants of minimization of the residual sum of squares of the Chow–Lin method have been proposed: one of these was originally implemented in the software Ecotrim introduced by Barcellan et al. [1], which used the correlation matrix instead of the variance-covariance matrix, and the other one in Matlab, by Quilis [11], which multiplied the correlation matrix by a factor of $1/(1-\rho^2)$. All the above methods are now implemented in the `tempdisagg` R package [7]. Further, some works compare the above-mentioned methods using some traditional accuracy prediction metrics, such as Root Mean Squared Error (RMSE), Absolute Mean Difference (MAD), and Theil's inequality coefficient (see, for example, [12–14]). In particular, Ajao et al. [14] compared the results of disaggregating techniques (Denton, Denton–Cholette, Chow–Lin, and Fernandez, and Litterman) for studying the Annual Gross Domestic Product (GDP) for Nigeria in the period 1981–2012 using quarterly export and import as the indicator variables. Some of these methods are also compared by Islaqm [12] for disaggregating the yearly export of Bangladesh to quarterly export in the period 2004–2012. In [13], different methods were used to disaggregate the annual series for personal consumption using the quarterly disposable income as an indicator.

Extensions to a dynamic framework have been considered by Guay and Maurin [15–17]. In particular, [16] extended the Chow–Lin procedure to flexible dynamic setting taking into account seasonality or calendar effects. Reference [15] presented a temporal disaggregation technique concerning the extension from static to dynamic autoregressive distributed lag regressions in a state-space framework with application to the Italian quarterly accounts. In [17], a state space approach is proposed for the temporal disaggregation problem by considering dynamic regression models with a particular concentration on the exact initialization of the different models. A set of annual series and the corresponding quarterly indicators, available by the Italian National Statistical Institute, Istat, are considered for real case studies. A different approach based on a two-step procedure (cointegration and state space regression) has been proposed by [18] for estimating the Brazilian GDP quarterly series in the period between 1960 and 1996. A different type of two-step procedure based on regression and Benchmarking has been proposed by [19] for the temporal disaggregation of quarterly GDP, and a novel sparse temporal-disaggregation procedure with an application to the UK gross domestic product data has been introduced by [20].

GPD is important because it represents an image of how a country's finances are doing and which areas are growing or shrinking. The growth of the PIB, which compares one quarter or one year with another, provides a reference to know if the economic situation is improving or worsening. PIB may be affected by many factors, such as public spending, trade, foreign investment, and productivity, and is a good financial indicator. When the PIB of a country grows, it means that its economy is prosperous. Companies are more profitable, they hire more people, and the investors will want to invest in the companies of the country. On the contrary, when the gross domestic product of a nation decreases, it means that its economy is experiencing a slowdown. The economic slowdown translates into less hiring of personnel, thus increases the unemployment rate. In addition, the profits of many companies decrease, so the distribution of dividends and the prices of their shares can also fall. The availability of official information produced by the state covers from 1940 to the present. The systematic construction of national accounts begins in CORFO (1957), which represents series prior to 1940–1954. This is followed by the accounts prepared by the Planning Office (ODEPLAN), which basically cover the decade of the nineteen-sixties. Finally, to this day, it is the Central Bank of Chile that is in charge of this task. The Central Bank of Chile has calculated the national accounts using 1977, 1986, 1996, and 2003 as base years [21]).

The main objective of this work is to propose a methodology for the estimation of Chilean quarterly GDP from 1965 to 2009. The procedure consists of an initial estimate of the quarterly GDP, which is obtained through the static Engle–Granger equation (see [22,23]) or cointegration analysis using the annual GDP data and variables related to GDP. The estimated coefficients of this regression are used to construct a quarterly equation between GDP and related variables by interpolating the estimated coefficients with the quarterly data of the aforementioned variables. This equation produces a first estimate of the quarterly GDP, called dirty GDP, due to the presence of errors. The second stage is to improve the estimates by minimizing the measurement errors and considering that the estimated measurements should be consistent with the annual GDP calculated by the Central Bank of Chile; that is, the sum of the quarterly estimates should be equal to the total annual GDP. The process of harmonization of quarterly and annual estimates is known, in the literature, as Benchmarking, and in this paper, it is addressed using the state space approach (see [24,25]). Important economical Chilean variables, such as the monetary aggregate, the price of copper, the terms of trade, the exports of goods and services and the mining production index, are used in the model to improve the estimation of the quarterly data. The application of the proposed method for reconstructing the quarterly Chilean GDP series constitutes a new contribution, which could be helpful to better understand the history of the Chilean economy additionally to the possibility of applying econometric models for predicting its future behavior. In summary, the main contributions of this work can be described as follows.

- Our proposal allows the introduction of a new method that is comparable with other methods used in other countries. Nowadays, there is no official method in Chile for reconstructing high-frequency series from low-frequency data.
- The proposed method allows the reconstruction of the GDP series in a critical historical period of Chile and better interpretation of the behavior of the economy of this country. In the new version of the paper, we have included a historical note of the period under study.
- Different from the traditional methods that are used for forward interpolation, the proposed method allows the reconstruction of high-frequency time series backward, which is very important for interpreting the economical situation of Chile. Further, this method could be applied to interprete economic variables of other countries in the world.
- From the methodological point of view, the state space approach for Benchmarking allows the elimination of measurement errors and assumptions such that the sum of the three-month values coincides with the yearly GDP.

The article is organized as follows: Section 2 briefly analyzes the methods used for the estimation of the quarterly GDP; Section 3 shows the results obtained by the estimated models. Finally, a discussion and conclusions are presented in Sections 4 and 5, respectively.

2. Materials and Methods

2.1. Engle–Granger Cointegration Analysis

Cointegration analysis is a frequently used technique in the study of time series. The concept of cointegration was introduced by Granger and subsequently studied in depth in [22,23]. This technique emerges as a procedure that allows the discrimination between real relationships and spurious relationships between variables. A spurious regression arises when we try to relate two variables when there is no type of cause-effect relationship through regression, and it is erroneously concluded, after regression, that such a relationship exists. According to what is stated in [26], one of the characteristics of spurious relations consists of having a very high coefficient of determination and a Durbin–Watson statistic close to zero.

From an econometric point of view, two or more time series with integration order $I(1)$ are cointegrated if there exists a linear combination of those series that has a lower order of integration, that is, $I(0)$. From an economic point of view, cointegration can be seen as a long-term equilibrium relationship between variables, such that these variables can deviate from the equilibrium situation in the short term, but with time, they will return to equilibrium. Another definition from the economic point of view says that two or more series are cointegrated if they move together over time and the differences between them are stable, i.e., stationary, even when each series is not stationary. The differences (or error term) in the cointegration equation are interpreted as the imbalance error for each particular point in time.

2.2. Benchmarking Method

According to [27], the concept of Benchmarking can be seen as a special form of signal extraction, which occurs when two (or more) data sources are available for the same target variable, which have different temporal frequencies, for example, monthly vs. annual, monthly vs. quarterly, annual vs. quarterly, etc. Generally, the two data sources do not correspond; for example, the quarterly sums of the measurements of a variable are not equal to the corresponding annual measure. Moreover, one of the data sources is more accurate than the other: the least frequent it is usually the more accurate since it is normally originated by censuses, which are hypothetically assumed free of sampling errors. The most reliable source is considered a Benchmark (comparative framework).

More specifically, Benchmarking is the process of trying to fit the most frequent series to the Benchmark. This is performed by decomposing the series into its structural elements: trend, seasonality, cycle, irregularities, and measurement errors, where the sum of these elements excludes the error.

According to [18], there are two main methods for applying Benchmarking to a time series: a purely numerical approach and a statistical method. The numerical approach covers the family of methods based on the minimization of a squared sum proposed by [4], and the statistical method, in turn, may be based on ARIMA processes such as those described by [28], the state space models proposed by [27], or the models that use a group of regressions, such as [29].

2.3. Methodological Procedure

2.3.1. First Stage: Analysis of Cointegration and Obtaining Dirty GDP

An initial estimate of the quarterly GDP is obtained through the static Engle–Granger equation or cointegration analysis using the data of annual GDP and variables related to GDP. Then, the estimated coefficients of the cointegrated model are used to interpolate the quarterly data, thus obtaining what is known as dirty GDP. The related variables to be used are: the monetary aggregate, the price of copper, the terms of trade, the exports of goods and services, and the mining production index. All these variables are available on the web page of the Central Bank of Chile (https://www.bcentral.cl (accessed on 14 October 2022)) on an annual and quarterly basis. Specifically, the calculation of dirty quarterly GDP is based on the estimation of a regression of GDP against the aforementioned series, with annual frequency expressed in base 1986 indices in order to obtain long-term coefficients that relate to the variables. After having estimated the cointegration vector by Ordinary Least Squares (OLS), we form a linear combination using the quarterly frequency series in order to obtain the interpolated series of the quarterly GDP. The estimated quarterly series are linked and compared to the series of the Central Bank of Chile, producing the dirty GDP series, which is refined in the second half of the procedure.

Prior to 1986, GDP data were only available on the annual frequency, which explains why the estimate was made on this frequency. It is of great importance that the estimated dirty GDP series incorporate the components present in the original series of GDP obtained by the Central Bank of Chile after 1986 and respect the annual information between 1965 and 2009 of the original series of GDP.

Therefore, dirty GDP is the first approximation of the quarterly GDP that recovers the lack of data prior to 1986 and that has a seasonal pattern thereafter that is identical to the series of the Central Bank of Chile.

2.3.2. Second Stage: State Space Models by Benchmarking and Obtaining Clean GDP

The state space approach provides a unified methodology for studying a wide variety of problems in time series. For example, by means of this approach, it is possible to model the behavior of the different components of a series separately and immediately combine these sub-models by obtaining a single model for the series of interest. In this context, the state space models are called Structural Models (see, for example, [24,25]). The state space models are formed by two types of variables: the non-observable variables of the state, which determine the movement of the system in time, and the observations of the series.

In general situations, the Gaussian general model of state space is defined by:

$$\begin{aligned} y_t &= Z_t\alpha_t + \epsilon_t,\ \epsilon_t \sim N(0, H_t), \\ \alpha_{t+1} &= T_t\alpha_t + R_t\eta_t,\ \eta_t \sim N(0, Q_t),\ t = 1, \ldots, n, \\ \text{with} &\quad \alpha_1 \sim N(a_1, P_1) \end{aligned} \tag{1}$$

where y_t is a $p \times 1$ vector of observations; α_t is an unobserved vector of dimension $m \times 1$ called state vector; and the terms of independent perturbations, ϵ_t and η_t are serially independent assumptions independent of each other at all times.

Matrices Z_t, T_t, R_t, H_t, and Q_t, with the appropriate dimensions, are constants, and they are called arrays of the system, assumed as known. In practice, some or all of these matrices depend on a vector of unknown hyperparameters ψ, whose estimation is described, for example, in [24,25]. It is assumed that R_t is a subset of columns of I_m, where I_m is the identity matrix of order m; R_t is called the selection matrix, which chooses the lines in the state equation that have non-null perturbations. The estimation of model (1) is performed by the Kalman filter in combination with maximum likelihood. The Kalman filter is a recursive algorithm that allows the updating of the knowledge of the system every time a new observation arrives and allows the calculation of the optimal estimator of the state vector based on the available information up to time t. It can be obtained through the application of existing results in the multivariate regression theory with Gaussian perturbations (see [24,25]). Some applications using the Kalman filter can be found in [30,31]. State space models by Benchmarking have been studied to some extent by [27]. One of these state space formulations was successively revised by [24].

This work presents a probabilistic version equivalent to the model of [27] as described in [18]. By denoting y_t the dirty quarterly GDP (theoretically with measurement errors) and x_t the quarterly GDP of the Central Bank of Chile (theoretically free of measurement errors). The state vector, according to the formulation of [27] is given by:

$$\alpha_t = [\mu_t, \ldots, \mu_{t-3}, \gamma_t, \ldots, \gamma_{t-3}, \epsilon_t, \ldots, \epsilon_{t-3}, u_t]'$$

where μ_t is the local level, γ_t is the stochastic seasonal component, ϵ_t is the irregular component, and u_t is the measurement error associated with dirty GDP, which assumes a stationary model $AR(1)$ with unit variance.

The matrix Z_t is defined as

$$Z_t = \begin{bmatrix} 1 & 0 & 0 & 0 & 1 & 0 & 0 & 0 & 1 & 0 & 0 & 0 & 1 \end{bmatrix}$$

if t is not a multiple of four, and

$$Z_t = \begin{bmatrix} 1 & 0 & 0 & 0 & 1 & 0 & 0 & 0 & 1 & 0 & 0 & 0 & 1 \\ 1 & 1 & 1 & 1 & 1 & 1 & 1 & 1 & 1 & 1 & 1 & 1 & 1 \end{bmatrix}$$

if t is a multiple of four.

On the other hand, matrix H_t is null for every t. The other matrixes associated to the state vector are invariant in time. Note that, given the formulation of the state space, the coherence between clean GDP (defined as $y_t^* = y_t - u_t$) and annual GDP, the Central Bank of Chile always occurs in multiples of four periods.

3. Results

3.1. The Dirty GDP

The results of the initial estimate of the quarterly GDP, obtained through the static Engle–Granger equation and associated with the first stage of the methodology, are reported in Table 1. The series of GDP of the Central Bank of Chile expressed in the index with an annual frequency with base 1986 corresponds to the dependent variable. The independent variables correspond to a linear trend term (TT), the logarithm of the monetary aggregate (L(AM)), the price of copper (PC), the logarithm of the terms of trade (L(TIR)), the logarithm of exports of goods and services (L(EBS)), and the mining production index (IPM). The adjusted coefficient of determination R^2 and the Durbin–Watson statistic is also reported. Note that the inclusion of the term trend component in the cointegrating regression is theoretically justified by [32,33]. Further, an example is given by [34].

Table 1. Results of the Engle–Granger procedure between annual GDP and variables related to GDP.

Variable	Coef.	Std. Error	t-Stat.	Prob.
TT	0.0335	0.0028	11.797	0.00
L(AM)	−0.0829	0.0083	−9.9362	0.00
PC	0.0790	0.0137	5.7490	0.00
L(TIR)	−0.3395	0.0539	−6.2986	0.00
L(EBS)	0.5950	0.0612	9,7139	0.00
IPM	0.2397	0.0568	4.2145	0.00
R−squared	0.9942	Mean dep. var		1.54
Ad. R−squared	0.9935	S.D. dep. var		0.88
S.E. of reg.	0.0712	AIC		−2.32
Sum sq. resid	0.1960	BIC		−2.08
Log Lik.	58.228	DW		1.76

In the estimation of the cointegrating regression in Table 1, we did not consider the intercept since it resulted in a non-significant preliminary analysis.

It is clearly observed in Table 1 that all the coefficients are significant, and the signs are those expected for the related variables. We estimate a relationship between annual GDP and variables that explain its behavior. We choose the model that best estimates GDP, eliminating non-significant coefficients. On the other hand, there is a high coefficient of determination that indicates the good fit of the model, in addition to a Durbin–Watson statistic (DW), which indicates independence in the residues, making it possible to ensure that there is no spurious regression.

In Table 2, trend, drift, and none denote the augmented Dickey–Fuller tests applied to regression with intercept and trend, intercept, and no deterministic parameters, respectively. The critical values are −3.50, −2.93, and −1.95, respectively. For series without differences, the unit root null hypothesis cannot be rejected at conventional significance levels in any case. However, the unit root null can be rejected at the 0.05 level for the first differences. Since the series given in the study are integrated in order one, the Engle–Granger two-stage estimation method can be applied.

Table 2. Augmented Dickey–Fuller test (ADF) for time series.

	Without Differences			First Difference		
	Trend	**Drift**	**None**	**Trend**	**Drift**	**None**
PIB	−1.597	1.084	2.330	−4.027	−3.399	−2567
LN(AM)	−1.154	−2.484	2.543	−7.322	−6.337	−2.477
PC	−3.261	−2.730	−0.750	−4.313	−4.215	−4.260
Ln(TIR)	−2.543	−2.290	1.524	−4.764	−4.824	−4.863
Ln(EBS)	−2.338	−0.208	−0.674	−5.555	−4.085	−5.475
IPM	−1.047	1.090	0.715	−4.834	−5.049	−4.006

In Table 3 we present the unit root test of Dickey–Fuller increased for the residues of the model, we reject the null hypothesis of non-cointegration and conclude that the residues are cointegrated of order $I(0)$. We perform the ADF method trying to find out if the trend or intercept are also statistically significant. Each of these coefficients has a significance level of 5%.

Table 3. Augmented Dickey–Fuller test (ADF) for residuals.

		Residuals	
	Trend	**Intercept**	**None**
Critical values	−5.76	−5.83	−5.91
test-statistic	−6.4789	−6.895	−7.018

By using the estimated coefficients of Table 1 for interpolating the quarterly series, we obtain an estimate of the GDP. This series should be related to the series of quarterly GDP of the Central Bank of Chile from 1986, and it is considered a first approximation of the Chilean quarterly GDP, called dirty GDP. Figure 1 shows the dirty GDP series.

Clearly, the estimated dirty GDP incorporates the components present in the quarterly series of Chilean GDP after 1986 as well as the cyclical dynamics of that period. It also respects the annual information between 1965 and 2009 of the original series of GDP.

3.2. Estimation of the Clean GDP

It is preceded to estimate the clean GDP by the model of state space by Benchmarking. To avoid the heteroscedasticity problem, a dirty GDP transformation is performed assuming that the variance of the error is proportional to the square of the export of goods and services (EBS), thus successfully capturing the inconsistency of the variance.

Using the programming language Ox, clean GDP estimation is performed using the STAMP package of [35] and the SsfPack package of [36] that uses the approximation BFGS method for the maximization process.

Table 4 and Figure 2 show the statistical summary of the estimated variances and the components referring to the estimation of the state space by the Benchmarking model for the normalized dirty GDP series, in addition to the verification of model assumptions.

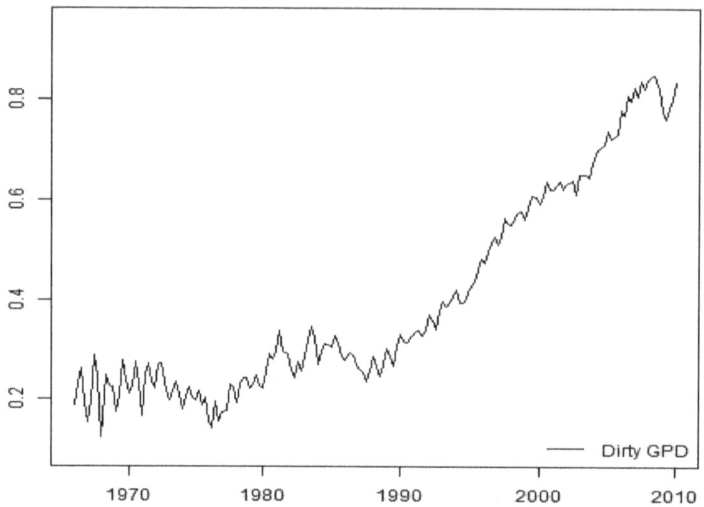

Figure 1. Quarterly dirty GDP.

Table 4. Information about the estimated model of state space by Benchmarking.

Log-Likelihood	288.559
Level Variance σ_{ε}^{2}	0.00053860
Seasonality variance σ_{w}^{2}	0.00011113
Irregularity variance σ_{ϵ}^{e}	0.0075303
Measurement Error Variance σ_{u}^{2}	0.00047772
MSE	0.0097188
Pseudo R^2	0.966332
AIC	−0.532673

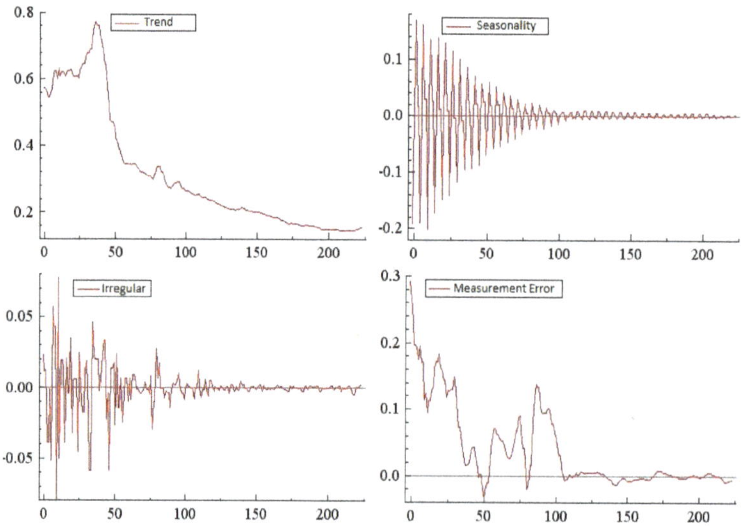

Figure 2. Estimations of the components of the model.

Changes are confirmed over time in Figure 2, indicating movements of both growth and decrease for certain periods of time (see trend). On the other hand, it can be seen that the peaks relative to the quarters do not remain constant over time (see seasonality).

3.3. Standardized Residuals Analysis

In order to test the independence of the residuals of the proposed model, some graphical and specification tests have been implemented. In particular, we considered the QQ-plot, the autocorrelation function total (ACF) and partial (PACF), the spectral density and the histogram for the graphical tests, and the Durbin–Watson, Ljung–Box and Jarque–Bera for the specification ones.

Figure 3 shows the graphical analysis of the standardized residuals. From the autocorrelation functions (ACF and PACF), we can conclude that the residuals are independent, and from the histogram and QQ-plot, we can observe a slight asymmetry in the distribution. Table 5 confirms the latter results with more formal statistical tests.

Table 5. Diagnostic test of standardized residuals: Ljung–Box Test; Jarque–Bera Test; Dickey–Fuller Test; and F Test of Heteroscedasticity.

Ljung–Box Test	5.982 (0.201)
Jarque–Bera Test	154.325 (2.2×10^{-16})
Dickey–Fuller Test	−7.232 (0.01)
F Test of Heteroscedasticity	0.584

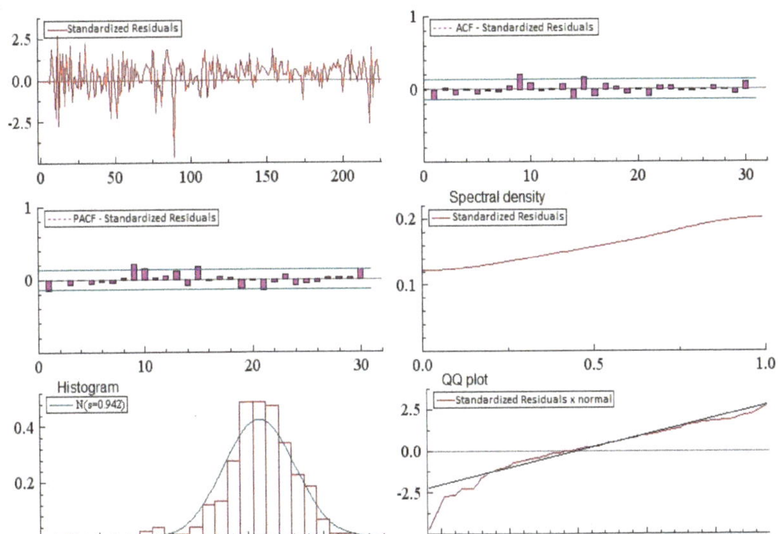

Figure 3. Standardized residuals analysis: standardized residuals (**upper left**); ACF (**upper right**); PACF (**middle left**); spectral density (**middle right**); histogram with the normal distribution overlapped (**bottom left**); and the QQ-plot respect the normal distribution (**bottom right**).

When observing the statistical tests, it can be concluded that the assumptions of homoscedasticity, independence, and stationarity of the residuals in the estimated model are met. As expected, the Jarque–Bera Test rejects the null hypothesis of normality.

3.4. The Clean GDP

Finally, in order to obtain the estimated clean GDP, we multiplied the estimation of the model of state space by Benchmarking with the macroeconomic variables that standardized the dirty GDP.

In Figure 4, a comparison of the clean GDP with the dirty GDP and quarterly GDP (calculated by the Central Bank of Chile after 1986) is shown.

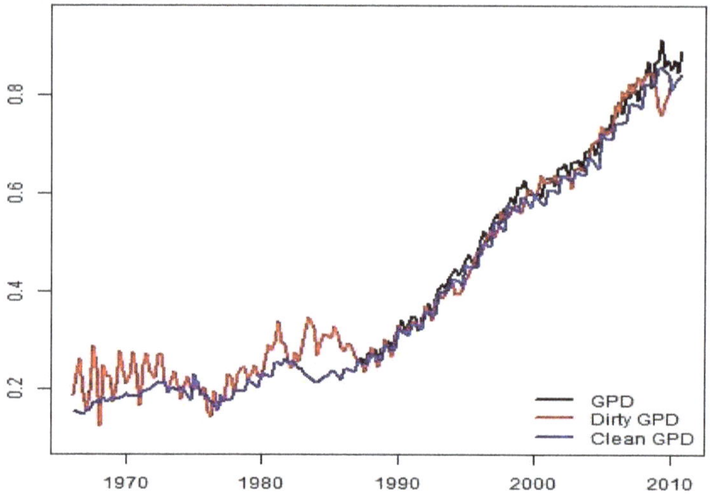

Figure 4. Real, dirty, and clean GDP.

From Figure 4, it is clearly observed that dirty quarterly GDP presents an overestimation in the period 1981–1986 that does not represent the annual GDP characteristic calculated by the Central Bank of Chile. This allows the proposed procedure to correct the quarterly operation and the measurement error by harmonizing the annual and quarterly GDP estimates. Thus, clean GDP incorporates the seasonal component in the quarterly series and respects the annual information of the series submitted by the Central Bank of Chile.

We think that the clean GDP represented in Figure 4 reflects the real history of the Chilean economy, characterized by different types of economic models (from socialist to liberalism). The socialist government antecedent to the Chilean coup (from 1970 to 1973) was characterized by a growing political polarization in society and a severe economic crisis reaching an inflation rate of around 600% and a reduction in GDP. At the same time, a drop in the price of copper in the international market affected the Chilean economy even more, given that copper exports constituted 80% of the total GDP. The economic crisis lasted until 1985, the year in which economic recovery recommenced thanks to some measures of economic policy (focused on economic liberalism), consisting of the reduction in spending in the public sector, privatization of banks and companies, and a devaluation of the national currency against the dollar with a consequent increase in exports. However, these measures initially resulted in greater inequality in the population increasing, and the economical situation improved significantly after the dictatorship that ended in 1990. This increase is clearly represented by the real and clean GDP in Figure 4. The level of exports and the price of copper played important roles in the Chilean economy, thus justifying the use of these covariates in the proposed model.

In Table 6, we compare the proposed method based on the two-step cointegration and space-time approach (Cointegration-SS) with those of the traditional disaggregation techniques using the R package `tempdisagg` [7]. In particular, we considered the Denton methods Denton [4] and Denton-Cholette [3]), and the generalized least squares (GLS) methods using different approaches for the parameter estimation: the maximum likelihood estimation for the Chow–Lin [2] and Litterman [6] methods, denoted by `Chow-lin-maxlog` and `litterman-maxlog`, respectively; the ecotrim [1] and the Quilis [11] proposals for the minimization of the residual sum of squares (RSS) for the Chow–Lin method, denoted by `Chow-lin-minrss-ecotrim` and `Chow-lin-minrss-quilis` respectively; the parameter estimation considering ρ fixed for Chow–Lin and Litterman methods, denoted by `Chow-lin-fixed` and `Litterman-fixed`, respectively; the minimization of RSS for the Litterman [6] method, denoted by `Chow-lin-minrss` and `litterman-maxlog`; and `Fernandez` approach [5]. The above methods are normally considered for comparison in the literature (see, for example, [12–14]) and utilized in the official statistics by some European countries [37].

Table 6. Goodness of fit indexes for the quarterly series from 1986 onward for different disaggregation methods.

Methods	MAPE	MAE	RMSE	BIAS	MSE
Cointegration-SS	0.03747975	0.02135661	0.02636679	0.02051961	0.0006952078
`Denton`	0.03821658	0.02147973	0.02541873	0.02080548	0.000646112
`Denton-Cholette`	0.03821658	0.02147973	0.02541873	0.02080548	0.000646112
`Chow-lin-maxlog`	0.03821645	0.02147971	0.02542294	0.02080548	0.0006463258
`Chow-lin-minrss-ecotrim`	0.0382112	0.02147881	0.0255776	0.02080548	0.0006542134
`Chow-lin-minrss-quilis`	0.03821645	0.02147881	0.02542294	0.02080548	0.0006463258
`Chow-lin-fixed`	0.03838849	0.02188879	0.02837915	0.02080548	0.0008053761
`Litterman-maxlog`	0.03826077	0.02149939	0.02549879	0.02080548	0.0006501883
`Litterman-minrss`	0.03826106	0.02149959	0.02553363	0.02080548	0.0006519662
`Litterman-fixed`	0.03824738	0.02149317	0.02544667	0.02080548	0.0006475331
`Fernandez`	0.03821658	0.02147973	0.02541873	0.02080548	0.000646112

Table 6 shows that the performance is very similar for the different methods. However, the results for the proposed Cointegration-SS method are slightly better than all other disaggregation techniques in terms of MAPE, MAE, and BIAS.

Figure 5 compares the real PIB with the predictions obtained by the Cointegration-SS and the Denton–Cholette methods. Although both methods slightly underestimate the true behavior of PIB (especially in the last years), the Cointegration-SS method seems to follow the real variation in the economy differently from the Denton–Cholette method, which shows smoother behavior.

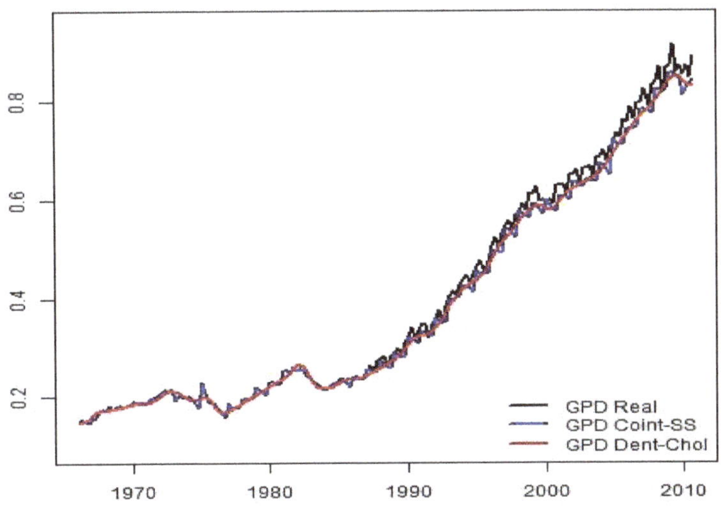

Figure 5. Real PIB and PIB predictions using the Cointegration-SS and the Denton–Cholette methods.

4. Discussion

The importance of reconstructing the quarterly GDP series for periods before 1986 arises from the need to cover a longer period in empirical studies of the history of the Chilean economy and the need to use a sufficient number of data that allow a reliable estimation of econometric models.

The results have shown a fairly satisfactory performance of the proposed model using the diagnosis of residuals and the comparative study with other methods. The cleaning of the estimated GDP with state space models by Benchmarking corrected the measurement error with respect to dirty GDP. Therefore, the resulting estimate is consistent with the annual GDP and provides an attractive estimation method. With reference to the historical context, the estimated clean GDP reflected the important events of the Chilean economy.

Some of the limitations of our proposal could inherit structures that are potentially embedded in the set of other components of the state vector, given by the first-order serial correlation coefficient of the estimated measurement error close to one. In other words, the estimated model without heteroskedasticity treatment yields practically the same clean GDP series without finding differences with the dirty GDP. However, the state space models by Benchmarking applied to the dirty GDP series, through the use of the Kalman filter, have proven to be robust to this type of violation of the basic assumptions. Secondly, there could be a systematic overestimation of the dirty GDP compared to the clean GDP, given the measurement errors of the dirty GDP. However, the clean GDP estimated with Benchmarking corrects, to the maximum, measurements error found in the dirty GDP.

Indeed, the data series may contain autocorrelation and other human-made patterns. Therefore, our proposal allows us to consider covariates that could influence the behavior of GDP and, in the second stage, to eliminate measurement errors and violation of assumptions, such as heteroskedasticity. Specifically, the state space models by Benchmarking try to adjust the series with the highest frequency by decomposing the series into its structural elements of trend, seasonality, cycle, irregularities, and measurement errors, where the sum of these elements excludes the error with the main purpose of eliminating the maximum error of measurement such that the sum of the three-month values coincides with the yearly GDP. Consequently, they are consistent with the annual GDP of Chile and, therefore, provide estimates with an additional attractive factor when compared with other proposed methodologies given in Table 6.

Finally, in this work, we could not compare our results with those of other works since, nowadays, there are no applications of disaggregating methods to the Chilean GDP. We think that this could be a benchmark work for the validation of new methods in the future.

5. Conclusions

In this work, we propose a methodology for estimating the quarterly Chilean GDP in the period 1965–2009 by incorporating Chilean economical variables. The results are then compared with the traditional disaggregation methods. Two important contributions are presented in this work: (i) the proposal of a method for reconstructing the quarterly Chilean GDP using important economic variables that can help to interpret the behavior of the Chilean economy. (ii) The use of a state space approach by Benchmarking that eliminates measurement errors and violation of assumptions, such that the sum of the quarterly series coincides with the yearly series.

Further, the proposed methodology could be applied for the estimation of other important indicators of the Chilean economy, such as the unemployment rate, for which quarterly data are available on the Chilean Central Bank web page, but it presents some discontinuities.

However, some further developments could be considered in future works, such as the extension of the model to a multivariate framework, which could provide greater accuracy and reliability to the quarterly GDP, additionally the use of the proposed model for predicting future values of the quarterly GDP. Further, an estimate of the Chilean quarterly GPD could also be made using Benchmarking models for other mentioned methods, involving models based on ARIMA processes [28] and models that use a group of regressions, such as [29].

Author Contributions: Conceptualization, C.C.-C. and S.C.-E.; methodology, C.C.-C. and S.C.-E.; validation, C.C.-C., O.N. and S.C.-E.; formal analysis, O.N. and S.C.-E.; investigation, C.C.-C. and O.N.; resources, C.C.-C.; data curation, O.N.; writing—original draft preparation, C.C.-C., O.N. and S.C.-E.; writing—review and editing, C.C.-C., O.N. and S.C.-E.; visualization, O.N.; supervision, S.C.-E.; project administration, C.C.-C.; funding acquisition, O.N. All authors have read and agreed to the published version of the manuscript.

Funding: Caamaño-Carrillo's research was funded by FONDECYT (Chile) grant No. 11220066 and by Proyecto Regular DIUBB 2120538 IF/R de la Universidad del Bío-Bío. Contreras's research was fully supported by Proyecto Regular DIUBB 190908244 3/R of the Universidad del Bío-Bío.

Data Availability Statement: All the dataset are available on the web page of the Central Bank of Chile (https://www.bcentral.cl).

Conflicts of Interest: The authors declare no conflict of interest.

Abbreviations

The following abbreviations are used in this manuscript:

GPD	Chilean Gross Domestic Product
OLS	Ordinary Least Squares
TT	Trend Term
L(AM)	Logarithm of f the Monetary Aggregate
PC	Price of Copper
L(TIR)	Logarithm of the Terms of Trade
L(EBS)	Logarithm of Exports of Goods and Services
MPI	Mining Production Index

References

1. Barcellan, R.; Di Fonzo, T.; Raffaele, D.; Staplehurst, V.; Buono, D. Ecotrim: A Program for Temporal Disaggregation of Time Series, 2003. Version 1.01. Available online: https://circabc.europa.eu/w/browse/c6049bc0-c633-4cab-9811-b476ffe08370 (accessed on 29 October 2022).
2. Chow, G.C.; Lin, A.-L. Best linear unbiased interpolation, distribution, and extrapolation of time series by related series. *Rev. Econ. Stat.* **1971**, *53*, 372–375. [CrossRef]
3. Dagum, E.B.; Cholette, P.A. *Benchmarking, Temporal Distribution, and Reconciliation Methods for Time Series*; Lecture Notes in Statistics; Springer: New York, NY, USA, 2006.
4. Denton, F.T. Adjustment of monthly or quarterly series to annual totals: An approach based on quadratic minimization. *J. Am. Stat. Assoc.* **1971**, *66*, 99–102. [CrossRef]
5. Fernández, R.B. A methodological note on the estimation of time series. *Rev. Econ. Stat.* **1981**, *63*, 471–476. [CrossRef]
6. Litterman, R.B. A random walk, Markov model for the distribution of time series. *J. Bus. Econ. Stat.* **1983**, *1*, 169–173.
7. Sax, C.; Steiner, P. tempdisagg: Methods for Temporal Disaggregation and Interpolation of Time Series. 2013. R package version 0.22. Available online: http://CRAN.R-project.org/package=tempdisagg (accessed on 25 September 2022).
8. Brent, G.; Stuckey, A.; Davidson, T. Reducing forward-series errors for benchmarked Quarterly National Accounts. EURONA—Eurostat review on National Accounts and Macroeconomic Indicators. 2015, 49. Available online: https://ec.europa.eu/eurostat/cros/system/files/eurona2-2015-art2.pdf (accessed on 23 October 2022).
9. Bournay J.; Laroque, J. Réflexions sur la méthode d'éla boration des comptes trimestriels. *Ann. L'INSÉÉ* **1979**, *36*, 3–30.
10. Barbone, L.; Bodo, G.; Visco, I. Costi e profitti nell'industria in senso stretto: Un'analisi su serie trimestrali, 1970–1980. *Bolletino Della Banca D'Italia* **1981**, *36*, 465–510.
11. Quilis, E.M. MATLAB Temporal Disaggregation and Interpolation Library. 2009. Available online: www.mathworks.com/matlabcentral/fileexchange/24438 (accessed on 23 September 2022).
12. Islaqm, M.R. Comparison of Temporal Disaggregation Techniques in the Case of Export of Bangladesh. *Int. J. Appl. Res. Stud.* **2013**, *2*, 214–218.
13. Santos Silva, J.M.C.; Cardoso, F.N. The Chow-Lin method using dynamic models. *Econ. Model.* **2001**, *18*, 269–280. [CrossRef]
14. Ajao, I.O.; Ayoola, F.J.; Iyaniwura, J.O. Temporal Disaggregation Methods in Flow Variables of Economic Data: Comparison Study. *Int. J. Stat. Probab.* **2015**, *15*, 36–46. [CrossRef]
15. Bisio, L.; Moauro, F. Temporal disaggregation by dynamic regressions: Recent developments in Italian quarterly national accounts. *Stat. Neerl.* **2018**, *72*, 471–494. [CrossRef]

16. Guay, A.; Maurin, A. Disaggregation methods based on MIDAS regression. *Econ. Model.* **2015**, *50*, 123–129. [CrossRef]
17. Proietti, T. Temporal disaggregation by state space methods: Dynamic regression methods revisited. *Econom. J.* **2006**, *9*, 357–372. [CrossRef]
18. Cerqueira, L.; Pizzinga, A.; Fernandes, C. Methodological Procedure for Estimating Brazilian Quarterly GDP Series. *Int. Adv. Econ. Res.* **2008**, *15*, 102–114. [CrossRef]
19. Wójcik, S. Temporal Disaggregation of Time Series with Regularization Term. *Barom. Reg. Anal. Prognozy* **2019**, *14*, 173–178. [CrossRef]
20. Mosley, L.; Eckley, I.; Gibberd, A. Sparse Temporal Disaggregation. *arXiv* **2021**, arXiv:2108.05783.
21. Luders, R.; Días, J.; Wagner, G. *La República en Cifras: Historical Statistics*; Ediciones UC, JSTOR , 2016, pp. 60–61. Available online: https://www.jstor.org/stable/j.ctt1h9cvqj (accessed on 11 November 2022).
22. Engle, R.F.; Granger, C. Co-integration and error correction: Representation, estimation, and Testing. *Econometrica* **1987**, *55*, 251–276. [CrossRef]
23. Engle, R.F.; Granger, C. *Long-Run Economic Relationships: Readings in Cointegration*; Oxford University Press: Oxford, UK, 1991.
24. Durbin, J.; Koopman, S.J. *Time Series Analysis by State Space Methods*, 2nd ed.; Oxford University Press: Oxford, UK, 2012.
25. Harvey, A.C. *Forecasting, Structural Time Series and The Kalman Filter*; Cambridge University Press: Cambridge, UK, 1990.
26. Granger, C.; Newbold, P. Spurius Regressions in Econometrics. *J. Econom.* **1974**, *2*, 111–120. [CrossRef]
27. Durbin, J.; Quenneville, B. *Benchmarking State Space Models*; Oxford University Press: Oxford, UK, 1997.
28. Hillmer, S.C.; Trabelsi, A. Benchmarking of economic time series. *J. Am. Stat. Assoc.* **1987**, *82*, 1064–1071. [CrossRef]
29. Cholette, P.A.; Dagum, E.B. Benchmarking time series with autocorrelated survey errors. *Int. Stat. Rev.* **1994**, *62*, 365–377. [CrossRef]
30. Alanis, A.Y. Electricity Prices Forecasting using Artificial Neural Networks. *IEEE Lat. Am. Trans.* **2018**, *16*, 105–111. [CrossRef]
31. Antoniou, C.; Ben-Akiva, M.; Koutsopoulos, H.N. Nonlinear Kalman Filtering Algorithms for On-Line Calibration of Dynamic Traffic Assignment Models. *IEEE Trans. Intell. Transp. Syst.* **2007**, *8*, 661–670. [CrossRef]
32. Bhaskara, B.R. *Cointegration for the Applied Economist*, 2nd ed.; Palgrave Macmillan: London, UK, 2007.
33. Perron, P.; Campbell, J.Y. A note on Johansen's cointegration procedure when trends are present. *Empir. Econ.* **1993**, *18*, 777–789. [CrossRef]
34. Karki, D. Stock Market Responses to Macroeconomic Dynamics: Testing for Long-Run Equilibrium in Nepal. *Pravaha* **2018**, *24*, 64. [CrossRef]
35. Koopman, S.J.; Harvey, A.C.; Doornik, J.A.; Shephard, N. *STAMP 6.0 Structural Time Series Analyser, Modeller and Predictor*; Timberlake Consultants Ltd.: London, UK, 2000.
36. Koopman, S.J.; Shephard, N.; Doornik, J.A. Statistical Algorithms for Models, in State Space Using SsfPack 2.2. *Econom. J.* **1999**, *2*, 113–166. [CrossRef]
37. Eurostat. European Statistical System (ESS) Guidelines on Temporal Disaggregation, Benchmarking and Reconciliation. 2018. Available online: https://ec.europa.eu/eurostat/web/products-manuals-and-guidelines/-/KS-06-18-355 (accessed on 28 November 2022).

mathematics

MDPI

Article

The NBRULC Reliability Class: Mathematical Theory and Goodness-of-Fit Testing with Applications to Asymmetric Censored and Uncensored Data

Walid B. H. Etman [1], Mohamed S. Eliwa [2,3], Hana N. Alqifari [2], Mahmoud El-Morshedy [4,5,*], Laila A. Al-Essa [6] and Rashad M. EL-Sagheer [7,8]

1 Faculty of Computer and Artificial Intelligence, Modern University for Technology and Information, Cairo 12613, Egypt
2 Department of Statistics and Operation Research, College of Science, Qassim University, Buraydah 51482, Saudi Arabia
3 Department of Statistics and Computer Science, Faculty of Science, Mansoura University, Mansoura 35516, Egypt
4 Department of Mathematics, College of Science and Humanities in Al-Kharj, Prince Sattam Bin Abdulaziz University, Al-Kharj 11942, Saudi Arabia
5 Department of Mathematics, Faculty of Science, Mansoura University, Mansoura 35516, Egypt
6 Department of Mathematical Sciences, College of Science, Princess Nourah bint Abdulrahman University, P.O. Box 84428, Riyadh 11671, Saudi Arabia
7 Mathematics Department, Faculty of Science, Al-Azhar University, Cairo 11884, Egypt
8 High Institute of Computer and Management Information System, First Statement, New Cairo 11865, Egypt
* Correspondence: mah_elmorshedy@mans.edu.eg or m.elmorshedy@psau.edu.sa

Abstract: The majority of approaches proposed in the past few decades to solve life test problems have differed markedly from those used for closely related, yet broader, issues. Due to the complexity of data that are generated each day in many practical domains, as a result of the development of scales for rating the success or failure of reliability, a new domain of reliability has been created. This domain is referred to as life classes, where specific probability distributions are presented. In this study, it is shown that the use of the quality-of-fit technique to solve problems involving life testing makes sense, and produces simpler processes that are roughly equivalent or superior to those used in traditional procedures. They may also behave better in limited samples. This work investigates a novel quality-of-fit test statistic; it is based on an exponential transform and is compared to the best renewal used Laplace test in increasing convex ordering (NBRULC). Evidence for approach normality is provided. The calculated variables include powers, Pitman asymptotic effectiveness, and critical points. Methods on how to handle censored data were also studied. Our experiments have real-world applications in the fields of medicine and engineering.

Keywords: NBRULC reliability class; goodness-of-fit approach; aging; life testing; right censored data; computer simulation; comparative study; COVID-19; statistics and numerical data

MSC: 62C07; 62G99; 62N01; 62N02; 62N05

1. Introduction

Reliability can be compared to quality over time. Since workmanship and manufacturing are quality factors, a product would be deemed as low quality if it malfunctions or breaks right after purchase. Poor reliability, on the other hand, is when product components fail before one anticipates them to. Therefore, there is a distinction between quality and reliability that has to do with time, more precisely, the product's lifetime. Reliability is officially defined as the capacity of a thing to carry out an essential task under predetermined circumstances for a predetermined amount of time. The likelihood of an item performing a necessary function under specified conditions for a specific amount of time is another definition that addresses the probabilistic nature of assessing reliability. As a result, reliability is a measure of technical uncertainty, and estimating reliability requires the application of statistics, specifically the probability theory. Testing completed items or components under settings that mimic real-world use until failure occurs is the typical method for gauging system reliability. Although it may seem that having more data would increase one's trust in the reliability level, this practice is frequently costly and time-consuming. Therefore, it is particularly important to consider the lifespan of products before all test units experience a malfunction. Aging concepts explain how a part or a system can experience improvements or deterioration as it ages. According to the aging characteristics, many types of life distributions are categorized or characterized in the literature. The exponential distribution almost always falls into one of these classifications, which is a significant feature in such classifications. Any reliability analysis must take stochastic aging into account, and numerous test statistics have been established in the literature, comparing exponential growth to various aging options. Our objective is to provide an overview of these advancements. Researchers in statistics and reliability analysis have looked at testing exponentiality problems using different age classes of life distributions from a variety of angles; for more information, see Bryson and Siddiqui [1], Bhattacharyya et al. [2], Barlow and Proschan [3], Klefsjo [4], Khan et al. [5], Kumazawa [6], Mahmoud et al. [7,8], Majumder and Mitra [9], Bhattacharyya et al. [10], Navarro [11], Abu-Youssef et al. [12], Ghosh and Mitra [13], Navarro and Pellerey [14], El-Morshedy et al. [15], EL-Sagheer et al. [16] Gadallah et al. [17], Mansour [18], Ghosh and Mitra [19], Majumder and Mitra [20], Lai and Xie [21], Etman et al. [22], Ghosh and Majumder [23], Bakr and Al-Babtain [24], and Ghosh and Mitra [25] and Alqifar et al. [26]. The goodness-of-fit test indicates whether the data in one's sample correspond to the data one would anticipate seeing in the actual population. More specifically, it is used to determine if sample data from a population with a normal distribution or a Weibull distribution fit the distribution. Numerous researchers have created tests for exponentiality against particular types of life distributions using the goodness-of-fit approach. To provide examples, Mahmoud and Abdul Alim [27], Kayid et al. [28], Bera et al. [29], Mahmoud et al. [30], Abu-Youssef et al. [31], Bakr et al. [32], Abu-Youssef and El-Toony [33], Abu-Youssef and Gerges [34], and Etman et al. [35]. We created a brand-new class of life distribution models to account for the efficacy and power of the test utilized in this study. The goal of creating a systematic method for studying events and processes occurring in the world was driven by the essential requirements of modern science and technology. It follows that the need for such an approach in the investigation of technological products and system reliability is quite natural. There are real-life instances where system components gradually degrade over time, eventually reaching the end of the manufacturer's warranty period; they then need to be renewed through the replacement of spare parts. In this case, renewal is intended to enhance the system's functionality, but it cannot surpass the superior state it had at age t. For example, after several hours of flight, the aviation administration may wish to replace a portion of an airplane engine. The airlines contend that this replacement is, at best, unneeded, and may potentially be detrimental to the aircraft. Airlines will examine if an aviation engine, after hours of renewal, is as good as a new engine by using operational data to support their claims.

The structure of this essay can be summarized as follows: The NBRU, NBRUL, and NBRULC classes of life distributions are defined in the remaining portions of this section. In Section 2, a goodness-of-fit test based on an exponentiality test is discussed regarding the NBRULC class. For several popular alternatives, the Pitman asymptotic is presented in Section 3. Section 4 includes simulations of the key areas, power estimates for the Monte Carlo null distribution, and a suggested test for right-censored data. Section 5 tabulates a few crucial numbers and deals with right-censored data. Finally, we discuss a few examples to show the utility of the statistical test in Section 6.

Preliminary:

A random variable X is said to be

(i) *'New better than renewal used'*, denoted by $X \in NBRU$, if

$$\overline{W}_F(x+t) \le \overline{F}(x)\overline{W}_F(t); \quad x,t, \ge 0.$$

(ii) *'New better (worse) than renewal used' in the Laplace transform order*, denoted by $X \in NBRUL$, if

$$\int_0^\infty e^{-sx}\overline{W}_F(x+t)dx \le \overline{W}_F(t)\int_0^\infty e^{-sx}\overline{F}(x)dx; \quad x,t,s \ge 0,$$

or

$$\int_0^\infty \int_{x+t}^\infty e^{-sx}\overline{F}(u)dudx \le \int_0^\infty \int_t^\infty e^{-sx}\overline{F}(x)\overline{F}(u)dudx,$$

where $\overline{W}_F(x+t) = \frac{1}{\mu}\int_{x+t}^\infty \overline{F}(u)du$.

(iii) *'New better than renewal used' in the Laplace transform in increasing convex order*, denoted by $X \in NBRULC$, if

$$\int_0^\infty \int_t^\infty e^{-sx}\overline{W}_F(x+u)dxdu \le (\ge) \int_0^\infty \int_t^\infty e^{-sx}\overline{F}(x)\overline{W}_F(u)dxdu; \quad x,t,s \ge 0,$$

or

$$\int_0^\infty \int_{x+t}^\infty e^{-sx}\overline{W}_F(u)dxdu \le (\ge) \int_0^\infty \int_t^\infty e^{-sx}\overline{F}(x)\overline{W}_F(u)dxdu,$$

this could be rewritten as

$$\int_0^\infty e^{-sx}\Gamma(x+t)dx \le \int_0^\infty e^{-sx}\overline{F}(x)\Gamma(t)dx,$$

where $\Gamma(x+t) = \int_{x+t}^\infty \overline{W}_F(u)du$. It is clear that

- $IFR \subset IFRA \subset NBU \subset NBUE \subset NBRU \subset NBRUL \subset NBRULC$.
- $IFR \subset IFRA \subset NBU \subset NBRU \subset NBRUL \subset NBRULC$.
- $IFR \subset IFRA \subset NBU \subset NBUE \subset HNBUE$.

2. Testing against NBRULC Alternatives

We discuss the potential that $H_0 : F$ is exponential in this section as opposed to the related hypothesis $H_1 : F$, which states that it is not exponential but NBRULC. Using the subsequent theorem is necessary for creating our test statistic.

Theorem 1. *Let X be an NBRULC random variable with distribution function F, then*

$$\zeta(s) - 1 \ge \mu[s^2 - s] + \mu_{(2)}\zeta(s)[\frac{1}{2}s^2 - \frac{1}{2}s^3] + (s^3 - s^2)[\mu\zeta(s) + \zeta(1)\zeta(s) - \zeta(s)] + s^2\zeta(1) - s^2, \tag{1}$$

for $s \ge 0$ and $s \ne 1$, where

$$\zeta(s) = Ee^{-sX} = \int_0^\infty e^{-sx}dF(x).$$

Proof. Since F is NBRULC, then

$$\int_0^\infty e^{-sx}\Gamma(x+t)dx \le \int_0^\infty e^{-sx}\overline{F}(x)\Gamma(t)dx; \quad x,t \ge 0.$$

Consider the following integral

$$\int_0^\infty \int_0^\infty e^{-t}e^{-sx}\Gamma(x+t)dxdt \le \int_0^\infty e^{-t}\Gamma(t)\int_0^\infty e^{-sx}\overline{F}(x)dxdt. \tag{2}$$

Setting

$$I_1 = \int_0^\infty \int_0^\infty e^{-t} e^{-sx} \Gamma(x+t) dx dt,$$

hence

$$\begin{aligned} I_1 &= \int_0^\infty \int_v^\infty e^{-v} e^{-s(u-v)} \Gamma(u) du dv \\ &= \int_0^\infty \int_0^v e^{-u} e^{-s(v-u)} \Gamma(v) du dv \\ &= \frac{1}{1-s} [\int_0^\infty e^{-sv} \Gamma(v) dv - \int_0^\infty e^{-v} \Gamma(v) dv]; s \neq 1. \end{aligned}$$

Note that,

$$\begin{aligned} \int_0^\infty e^{-sv} \Gamma(v) dv &= \frac{1}{2} E \int_0^\infty e^{-sv} [V-v]^2 I(V > v) dv \\ &= \frac{1}{2} E \int_0^V e^{-sv} [V^2 - 2vV + v^2] dv \\ &= \frac{\mu_{(2)}}{2s} - \frac{\mu}{s^2} - \frac{1}{s^3} \zeta(s) + \frac{1}{s^3}. \end{aligned}$$

Therefore,

$$I_1 = \frac{1}{1-s} \{ \frac{\mu_{(2)}}{2s} - \frac{\mu}{s^2} - \frac{1}{s^3} \zeta(s) + \frac{1}{s^3} - \frac{\mu_{(2)}}{2} + \mu + \zeta(1) - 1 \}. \tag{3}$$

Setting

$$\begin{aligned} I_2 &= \int_0^\infty e^{-t} \Gamma(t) \int_0^\infty e^{-sx} \overline{F}(x) dx dt \\ &= E \int_0^\infty e^{-t} \Gamma(t) \int_0^\infty e^{-sx} I(X > x) dx dt. \\ &= E \int_0^\infty e^{-t} \Gamma(t) \int_0^X e^{-sx} dx dt = \frac{1}{s} (1 - \zeta(s)) \int_0^\infty e^{-t} \Gamma(t) dt. \end{aligned}$$

Therefore,

$$I_2 = (\frac{1}{s} - \frac{1}{s} \zeta(s)) (\frac{\mu_{(2)}}{2} - \mu - \zeta(1) + 1). \tag{4}$$

Substituting (3) and (4) into (2), we have

$$\zeta(s) - 1 \geq \mu[s^2 - s] + \mu_{(2)} \zeta(s) [\frac{1}{2} s^2 - \frac{1}{2} s^3] + (s^3 - s^2) [\mu \zeta(s) + \zeta(1) \zeta(s) - \zeta(s)] + s^2 \zeta(1) - s^2.$$

Thus, the proof is complete. Let us put forward the starting point from exponentiality as follows

$$\begin{aligned} \delta(s) = & [\tfrac{1}{2} s^3 - \tfrac{1}{2} s^2] \mu_{(2)} \zeta(s) + [s^2 - s^3] \zeta(1) \zeta(s) + [s^2 - s^3] \mu \zeta(s) \\ & + [s^3 - s^2 + 1] \zeta(s) + [s - s^2] \mu - s^2 \zeta(1) + s^2 - 1. \end{aligned} \tag{5}$$

Be aware that while $\delta(s) = 0$ for H_0, $\delta(s) > 0$ for H_1. The empirical estimate of $\delta(s)$, given $X_1, X_2, ..., X_n$ as a sample at random from distribution F, can be found as

$$\begin{aligned} \hat{\delta}(s) = & \frac{1}{n^2} \sum_{i=1}^n \sum_{j=1}^n \{ [\frac{1}{2} s^3 - \frac{1}{2} s^2] X_i^2 e^{-sX_j} + [s^2 - s^3] e^{-X_i} e^{-sX_j} + [s^2 - s^3] X_i e^{-sX_j} \\ & + [s^3 - s^2 + 1] e^{-sX_i} + [s - s^2] X_i - s^2 e^{-X_i} + s^2 - 1 \}. \end{aligned}$$

Let $\Delta(s) = \frac{\delta(s)}{\mu^3}$, which is approximated by the formula $\hat{\Delta}(s) = \frac{\hat{\delta}(s)}{\overline{X}^3}$, $\overline{X}$ is the sample mean to make the test invariant. Then,

$$\hat{\Delta}(s) = \frac{1}{n^2\overline{X}^3}\sum_{i=1}^{n}\sum_{j=1}^{n}\{[\tfrac{1}{2}s^3-\tfrac{1}{2}s^2]X_i^2e^{-sX_j}+[s^2-s^3]e^{-X_i}e^{-sX_j}+[s^2-s^3]X_ie^{-sX_j} \\ +[s^3-s^2+1]e^{-sX_i}+[s-s^2]X_i-s^2e^{-X_i}+s^2-1\}. \tag{6}$$

It should be noted that $\hat{\Delta}(s)$ is an impartial estimator of $\delta(s)$. Set

$$\phi(X_i,X_j) = [\tfrac{1}{2}s^3-\tfrac{1}{2}s^2]X_i^2e^{-sX_j}+[s^2-s^3]e^{-X_i}e^{-sX_j}+[s^2-s^3]X_ie^{-sX_j} \\ +[s^3-s^2+1]e^{-sX_i}+[s-s^2]X_i-s^2e^{-X_i}+s^2-1, \tag{7}$$

and define the symmetric kernel

$$\psi_s(X_i,X_j)=\frac{1}{2!}\sum\phi_s(X_i,X_j),$$

where the total of all configurations of X_i, X_j. Then, $\hat{\Delta}(s)$ in (6) is comparable to the U_n-statistic, given by

$$U_n=\frac{1}{\binom{n}{2}}\sum_{i<j}^{n}\psi_s(X_i,X_j). \tag{8}$$

The following theorem can be used to prove that $\hat{\Delta}(s)$ is asymptotically normal. □

Theorem 2.

(a) *As $n\to\infty$, $\sqrt{n}(\hat{\Delta}(s)-\Delta(s))$ is asymptotically normal, having a mean of 0 and variance $\sigma^2(s)$, where $\sigma^2(s)$ is determined by*

$$\sigma^2(s) = Var\{[\tfrac{1}{2}s^3-\tfrac{1}{2}s^2]X^2\zeta(s)+[s^2-s^3]e^{-X}\zeta(s)+[s^2-s^3]X\zeta(s) \\ +[s^3-s^2+1]e^{-sX}+[s-s^2]X-s^2e^{-X}+[\tfrac{1}{2}s^3-\tfrac{1}{2}s^2]\mu_{(2)}e^{-sX} \\ +[s^2-s^3]e^{-sX}\zeta(1)+[s^2-s^3]\mu e^{-sX}+[s^3-s^2+1]\zeta(s) \\ +[s-s^2]\mu-s^2\zeta(1)+2s^2-2\}. \tag{9}$$

(b) *Under H_0, the variance $\sigma_0^2(s)$ is*

$$\sigma_0^2(s)=\frac{s^6(-1+s)^2(8+3s)(7+s)}{12(1+s)^3(1+2s)(2+s)}. \tag{10}$$

Proof. We may determine the mean and variance using the conventional U-statistics theory, see Lee [36], and by conducting the following calculations

$$\sigma^2=Var\{\eta(X)\},$$

where

$$\eta(X)=\eta_1(X)+\eta_2(X),$$

$$\eta_1(X) = E(\phi(X_1,X_2)\mid X_1)=[\frac{1}{2}s^3-\frac{1}{2}s^2]X^2\int_0^\infty e^{-sx}dF(x)+[s^2-s^3]e^{-X}\int_0^\infty e^{-sx}dF(x) \\ +[s^2-s^3]X\int_0^\infty e^{-sx}dF(x)+[s^3-s^2+1]e^{-sX}+[s-s^2]X-s^2e^{-X}+s^2-1,$$

and

$$\eta_2(X) = E(\phi(X_1,X_2)\mid X_2)=[\frac{1}{2}s^3-\frac{1}{2}s^2]e^{-sX}\int_0^\infty x^2dF(x)+[s^2-s^3]e^{-sX}\int_0^\infty e^{-x}dF(x) \\ +[s^2-s^3]e^{-sX}\int_0^\infty xdF(x)+[s^3-s^2+1]\int_0^\infty e^{-sx}dF(x)+[s-s^2]\int_0^\infty xdF(x) \\ -s^2\int_0^\infty e^{-x}dF(x)+s^2-1.$$

Therefore,

$$\begin{aligned}\eta(X) &= [\frac{1}{2}s^3 - \frac{1}{2}s^2]X^2 \int_0^\infty e^{-sx}dF(x) + [s^2 - s^3]e^{-X} \int_0^\infty e^{-sx}dF(x) \\ &+[s^2 - s^3]X \int_0^\infty e^{-sx}dF(x) + [s^3 - s^2 + 1]e^{-sX} + [s - s^2]X - s^2e^{-X} \\ &+[\frac{1}{2}s^3 - \frac{1}{2}s^2]e^{-sX} \int_0^\infty x^2dF(x) + [s^2 - s^3]e^{-sX} \int_0^\infty e^{-x}dF(x) \\ &+[s^2 - s^3]e^{-sX} \int_0^\infty xdF(x) + [s^3 - s^2 + 1] \int_0^\infty e^{-sx}dF(x) \\ &+[s - s^2] \int_0^\infty xdF(x) - s^2 \int_0^\infty e^{-x}dF(x) + 2s^2 - 2.\end{aligned}$$

Upon using (7), we have

$$\begin{aligned}\sigma_0^2(s) &= Var\{[\frac{s^3 - s^2 + 2}{2}]e^{-sX} - [\frac{2s^3}{s+1}]e^{-X} + [\frac{s^3 - s^2}{2(s+1)}]X^2 \\ &+[\frac{s^2 - 2s^3 + s}{s+1}]X + [\frac{3s^3 + s^2 - 2s - 2}{2(s+1)}]\}.\end{aligned}$$

From (9) and after some computations, (10) can be reported. □

3. Pitman's Asymptotic Efficiency of $\hat{\Delta}(s)$

Pitman's asymptotic efficiency is a term used to compare the effectiveness of two statistical tests based on the sizes of their sample populations. It is referred to as the percentage of the minimum sample sizes that must be used for each test to obtain a specific degree of significance and power, at which point, the alternative hypothesis begins to approach the null hypothesis. A test with a greater Pitman's efficiency needs fewer observations than a test with a lower efficiency to obtain the same accuracy. A comparison of several tests for mean, variance, or proportion equality between two populations, for instance, can be made using the asymptotic Pitman efficiency. Based on the bare minimum sample size necessary, the Pitman efficiency can assist the method in selecting the optimal test for a specific problem. The following are some possible restrictions or presumptions of the asymptotic Pitman efficiency: Its asymptotic foundation makes it susceptible to becoming unreliable for samples of small or medium sizes. The rate of convergence of the test statistics' finite distributions is influenced by the selection of alternative hypotheses and the level of significance; this rate of convergence also has an impact. Other factors, such as robustness, simplicity, or interpretability, which could influence the test selection, are not taken into consideration. It is conceivable that this does not accurately reflect how tests for other or higher levels are performed. Additionally, it does not account for the cost of errors or the loss function. In this section, we evaluate the effectiveness of Pitman's asymptotic efficiency (PAE) method for the linear failure rate (LFR), Weibull, and Makeham distributions, using the probability models listed below.

(i) The Weibull distribution: $\overline{F}_1(x) = e^{-x^\theta}$; $x \geq 0,\ \theta \geq 1$.

(ii) The LFR distribution: $\overline{F}_2(x) = e^{-x-\frac{\theta}{2}x^2}$; $x \geq 0,\ \theta \geq 0$.

(iii) The Makeham distribution: $\overline{F}_3(x) = e^{-x-\theta(x+e^{-x}-1)}$; $x \geq 0,\ \theta \geq 0$.

Be mindful that for $\theta = 0$, $\overline{F}_1(u)$ and $\overline{F}_3(u)$ minimize exponential distributions, whereas for $\theta = 1$, $\overline{F}_2(u)$ does the same. The PAE can be reported as

$$PAE(\Delta(s)) = \frac{1}{\sigma_0(s)} \left| \frac{d}{d\theta}\delta_\theta(s) \right|_{\theta \to \theta_0}, \tag{11}$$

where

$$\begin{aligned}\delta_\theta(s) &= [\frac{1}{2}s^3 - \frac{1}{2}s^2]\mu_{(2\theta)}\zeta_\theta(s) + [s^2 - s^3]\zeta_\theta(1)\zeta_\theta(s) + [s^2 - s^3]\mu_\theta\zeta_\theta(s) \\ &\quad +[s^3 - s^2 + 1]\zeta_\theta(s) + [s - s^2]\mu_\theta - s^2\zeta_\theta(1) + s^2 - 1,\end{aligned}$$

$$\zeta_\theta(s) = \int_0^\infty e^{-sx}dF_\theta(x), \mu_{(2\theta)} = 2\int_0^\infty x\overline{F}_\theta(x)dx, \mu_\theta = \int_0^\infty \overline{F}_\theta(x)dx.$$

Hence,

$$\begin{aligned}\frac{d}{d\theta}\delta_\theta(s) &= [\frac{1}{2}s^3 - \frac{1}{2}s^2][\mu_{(2\theta)}\zeta'_\theta(s) + \mu'_{(2\theta)}\zeta_\theta(s)] + [s^2 - s^3][\zeta_\theta(1)\zeta'_\theta(s) + \zeta'_\theta(1)\zeta_\theta(s)] \\ &\quad +[s^2 - s^3][\mu_\theta\zeta'_\theta(s) + \mu'_\theta\zeta_\theta(s)] + [s^3 - s^2 + 1]\zeta'_\theta(s) + [s - s^2]\mu'_\theta - s^2\zeta'_\theta(1),\end{aligned}$$

where

$$\mu'_\theta = \int_0^\infty \overline{F}'_\theta(x)dx, \mu'_{(2\theta)} = 2\int_0^\infty x\overline{F}'_\theta(x)dx, \zeta'_\theta(s) = -\int_0^\infty e^{-sx}d\overline{F}'_\theta(x).$$

Using the PAE definition in (11), we have

$$PAE(\delta) = \frac{1}{\sigma_0}\left|\begin{array}{l}[\frac{1}{2}s^3 - \frac{1}{2}s^2][\mu_{(2\theta)}\zeta'_\theta(s) + \mu'_{(2\theta)}\zeta_\theta(s)] + [s^2 - s^3][\zeta_\theta(1)\zeta'_\theta(s) + \zeta'_\theta(1)\zeta_\theta(s)] \\ +[s^2 - s^3][\mu_\theta\zeta'_\theta(s) + \mu'_\theta\zeta_\theta(s)] + [s^3 - s^2 + 1]\zeta'_\theta(s) + [s - s^2]\mu'_\theta - s^2\zeta'_\theta(1)\end{array}\right|_{\theta\to\theta_0}.$$

For a few different values of s, Table 1 compares our test $\hat{\Delta}(s)$ to those of Mugdadi and Ahmad [37] ($\delta_{(3)}$), Kango [38] (K^*), and Abdel-Aziz [39] ($\hat{\Delta}_{RN}$).

Table 1 demonstrates that statistic $\hat{\Delta}(s)$ is more effective than statistics $\delta_{(3)}$, K^* and $\hat{\Delta}_{RN}$ for the three alternative families.

Table 1. Some competitive tests are contrasted with the PAE test.

Distribution	$\delta_{(3)}$	K^*	$\hat{\Delta}_{RN}$	Our Test $\hat{\Delta}(s)$		
				$s = 0.09$	$s = 0.9$	$s = 2$
Weibull	0.170	0.132	0.223	0.597	0.851	1.023
LFR	0.408	0.433	0.535	0.851	0.974	0.996
Makeham	0.039	0.144	0.184	0.148	0.213	0.249

4. The Monte Carlo Method

The Monte Carlo simulation makes use of random sampling to predict the potential outcomes of an unknown event. It was developed in World War II by Stanislaw Ulam and John von Neumann. Using an expected range of values rather than using predetermined input values, a Monte Carlo simulation forecasts a succession of outcomes. It creates random samples using a probability distribution and then computes the outcomes for each sample. This procedure is repeated numerous times to produce a distribution of potential conclusions that may be statistically examined. The steps below can be used to evaluate the likelihood of an event occurring using a Monte Carlo simulation: choose the random variables that will affect the occurrence whose likelihood one wants to calculate.; identify each random variable's probability distribution and create random samples using it; analyze the event for each sample and determine its frequency; to calculate the percentage, divide the total number of samples by the number of iterations, and then multiply the result by 100; repeat this method numerous times, then determine the mean and standard deviations of the percentages. One will receive an assessment of the event likelihood and the level of uncertainty surrounding it as a result.

4.1. Critical Points

A critical value (C.V) in statistics refers to a specific point in a distribution of a test statistic; it is conducted to determine whether the null hypothesis may be rejected. This group is referred to as the rejection region or the critical zone. One critical value typically exists for one-sided tests, while two critical values often exist for two-sided tests. The statistical literature does not provide a clear consensus on whether the critical value or probability value method is preferable. Depending on the circumstance and preference, each has benefits and drawbacks. Using 10,000 samples, n = 5(5)100, this part mimics the crucial points of the null Monte Carlo distribution. For 90%, 95%, and 99%, the upper percentile of $\hat{\Delta}$ (0.09) was identified. As seen in Table 2 and Figure 1, the critical values rose with higher confidence levels and fell with higher sample sizes.

Table 2. The statistic's critical values of $\hat{\Delta}(0.09)$.

n	90%	95%	99%
5	0.0001268	0.0001343	0.0001457
10	0.0001041	0.0001100	0.0001194
15	0.0000951	0.0001003	0.0001085
20	0.0000906	0.0000955	0.0001034
25	0.0000868	0.0000916	0.0000994
30	0.0000839	0.0000887	0.0000952
35	0.0000817	0.0000865	0.0000942
40	0.0000795	0.0000843	0.0000916
45	0.0000775	0.0000822	0.0000890
50	0.0000763	0.0000810	0.0000887
55	0.0000745	0.0000799	0.0000868
60	0.0000734	0.0000785	0.0000861
65	0.0000713	0.0000769	0.0000848
70	0.0000706	0.0000765	0.0000839
75	0.0000693	0.0000748	0.0000824
80	0.0000685	0.0000738	0.0000818
85	0.0000667	0.0000725	0.0000802
90	0.0000662	0.0000722	0.0000805
95	0.0000655	0.0000711	0.0000793
100	0.0000647	0.0000703	0.0000781

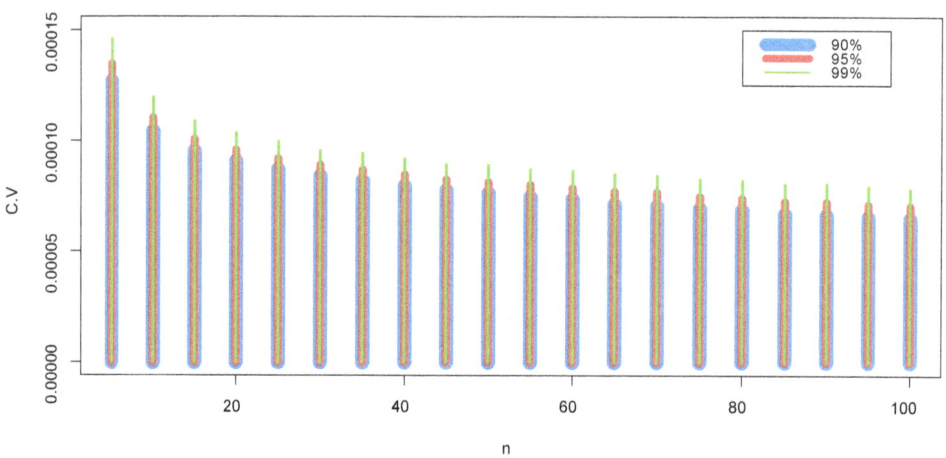

Figure 1. Relationship between the sample size, the level of confidence, and the critical values.

4.2. The Power Estimates of the Test

The calculations used to establish the minimal sample size for a study are referred to as power estimates in statistics. The probability that the null hypothesis will be correctly rejected, assuming it is true, is known as strength. It is based on four basic factors: power, significance level, sample size, and the number of observations or research participants. The proposed test's potency was evaluated at the $(1-\alpha)\%$ confidence level, $\alpha = 0.05$, using the 10,000 samples provided in Table 3 as a basis. Assume that θ has proper values for the Weibull distribution (WD), and gamma distribution (GD) at $n = 10, 20$, and 30, respectively. Table 3 demonstrates that the $\Delta_n(0.09)$ test we employed has adequate power for all other alternatives.

Table 3. Estimates of the power of $\Delta_n(0.09)$.

n	θ	Weibull	Gamma
10	2	0.9650	0.5671
	3	0.9997	0.8950
	4	1.0000	0.9568
20	2	0.9931	0.7116
	3	1.0000	0.9320
	4	1.0000	0.9847
30	2	0.9994	0.7498
	3	1.0000	0.9560
	4	1.0000	0.9922

5. Testing for Censored Data

It is recommended to use a test statistic to contrast H_0 and H_1 with data that have been randomly right-censored. In a life-testing model or a clinical study where patients may be lost (censored) before the completion of a trial, such censored data are frequently the only types of information that are accessible. This hypothetical experiment can be formalized as follows. Assume that n items are checked, with $X_1, X_2, \ldots, X_n$ representing the actual lifespan of each item. We allow $X_1, X_2, \ldots, X_n$ to be independently and identically distributed (i.i.d.) under the assumption of a continuous life distribution, F. Assume that $Y_1, Y_2, \ldots, Y_n$ are (i.i.d.) according to a continuous life distribution, G. Additionally, assume that X and Y are independent variables. The pairs are visible in the randomly right-censored model $(Z_j, \delta_j), j = 1, \ldots, n$, where $Z_j = \min(X_j, Y_j)$ and

$$\delta_j = \begin{cases} 1, & \text{if} \quad Z_j = X_j \text{ (j-th observation is uncensored)} \\ 0, & \text{if} \quad Z_j = Y_j \text{ (j-th observation is censored).} \end{cases} \tag{1}$$

Let $Z_{(0)} = 0 < Z_{(1)} < Z_{(2)} < \cdots < Z_{(n)}$ denote the ordered Z and $\delta_{(j)}$ is δ_j corresponding to $Z_{(j)}$. The product limit estimator was suggested by Kaplan and Meier [40] using the censored data (Z_j, δ_j), $j = 1, \ldots, n$.

$$\overline{F}_n(X) = \prod_{[j:Z(j) \le X]} \{(n-j)/(n-j+1)\}^{\delta_{(j)}}; \; X \in [0, Z_{(n)}].$$

We now propose the following test statistic to compare $H_0 : \hat{\phi}_c = 0$ to $H_1 : \hat{\phi}_c > 0$, using the randomized right censored data

$$\begin{aligned} \hat{\phi}_c \;=\; & [\frac{1}{2}s^3 - \frac{1}{2}s^2]\mu_{(2)}\zeta(s) + [s^2 - s^3]\zeta(1)\zeta(s) + [s^2 - s^3]\mu\zeta(s) \\ & + [s^3 - s^2 + 1]\zeta(s) + [s - s^2]\mu - s^2\zeta(1) + s^2 - 1, \end{aligned}$$

where $\zeta(s) = \int_0^\infty e^{-sx} dF_n(x)$. It is possible to rewrite $\hat{\phi}_c$ for computational purposes.

$$\begin{aligned}\hat{\phi}_c &= [\frac{1}{2}s^3 - \frac{1}{2}s^2]\Phi\eta + [s^2 - s^3]\tau\eta + [s^2 - s^3]\Omega\eta \\ &+[s^3 - s^2 + 1]\eta + [s - s^2]\Omega - s^2\tau + s^2 - 1,\end{aligned}$$

where

$$\begin{aligned}\Omega &= \sum_{k=1}^{n}[\prod_{m=1}^{k-1} C_m^{\delta(m)}\left(Z_{(k)} - Z_{(k-1)}\right)], \\ \Phi &= 2\sum_{i=1}^{n}[\prod_{v=1}^{i-1} Z_{(i)} C_v^{\delta(v)}\left(Z_{(i)} - Z_{(i-1)}\right)], \\ \eta &= \sum_{j=1}^{n} e^{-sZ_{(j)}}[\prod_{p=1}^{j-2} C_p^{\delta(p)} - \prod_{p=1}^{j-1} C_p^{\delta(p)}], \\ \tau &= \sum_{j=1}^{n} e^{-Z_{(j)}}[\prod_{p=1}^{j-2} C_p^{\delta(p)} - \prod_{p=1}^{j-1} C_p^{\delta(p)}],\end{aligned}$$

and

$$dF_n(Z_j) = \overline{F}_n(Z_{j-1}) - \overline{F}_n(Z_j), c_k = [n-k][n-k+1]^{-1}.$$

The test invariance is achieved by letting

$$\hat{\Delta}_c = \frac{\hat{\phi}_c}{\overline{Z}^3}, \text{ where } \overline{Z} = \sum_{i=1}^{n} \frac{Z_{(i)}}{n}. \quad (12)$$

In Table 4 and Figure 2, the crucial percentages of the $\hat{\Delta}_c$ tests for the samples taken $n = 10(10)100$ are displayed. The null Monte Carlo distribution's crucial values were found using the common exponential distribution, using the Mathematica 12 program at $s = 0.9$, and with 10,000 replications. The critical values increased as the confidence level increased and decreased as sample numbers increased, respectively, as shown in Figure 2 and Table 4.

Table 4. The superior percentages of $\hat{\Delta}_c$ with 10,000 replications at $s = 0.9$.

n	90%	95%	99%
10	0.0018839	0.0069971	0.0171796
20	0.0018178	0.0066184	0.0158503
30	0.0017509	0.0061387	0.0137694
40	0.0016926	0.0059580	0.0133870
50	0.0015313	0.0057832	0.0123716
60	0.0014402	0.0055886	0.0119811
70	0.0012656	0.0052264	0.0112588
80	0.0012082	0.0045355	0.0101906
90	0.0011823	0.0044339	0.0098655
100	0.0010760	0.0040471	0.0090138

Estimates of the Test Power $\Delta_c(s)$

At a significance level of $\alpha = 0.05$, we assessed the test power using the occasion parameter values of θ based on 10,000 samples, at $n = 10, 20$ and 30 for the gamma, LFR, and Weibull distributions. Table 5 exemplifies how the power estimations for this test $\Delta_c(0.9)$ for all other options were suitable.

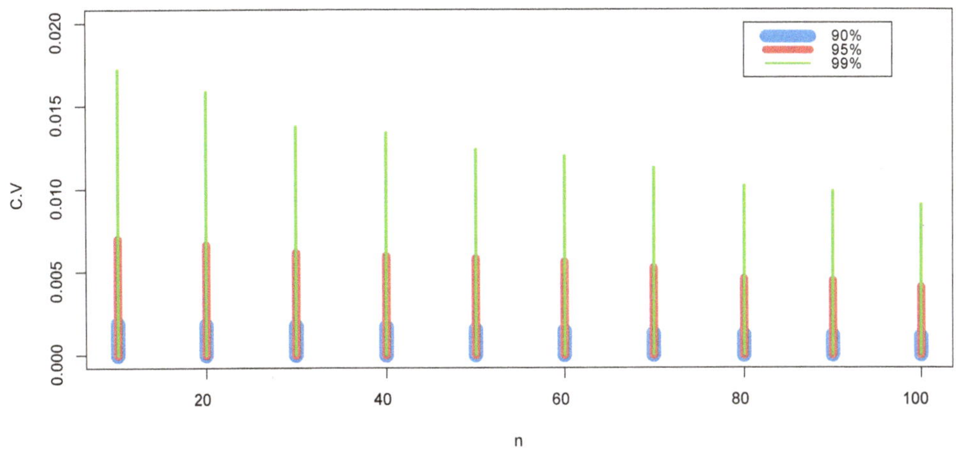

Figure 2. Relationship between the sample size, the level of confidence, and the critical values.

Table 5. Estimates of the power of $\Delta_c(0.9)$.

n	θ	Weibull	LFR	Gamma
10	2	0.6162	0.4496	0.3541
	3	0.6219	0.4843	0.3954
	4	0.6222	0.5035	0.4173
20	2	0.8289	0.6308	0.4049
	3	0.8328	0.6792	0.4647
	4	0.8351	0.7203	0.5278
30	2	0.9148	0.7376	0.5497
	3	0.9193	0.7994	0.6949
	4	0.9193	0.8224	0.8167

6. Censored and Uncensored Observations in Applications to Real Data

Data that are controlled (censored) exist, suggesting that some details are omitted or are not comprehensive. Data that have not been filtered are completely known, indicating that they contain all pertinent information. Controlled data can be difficult to analyze statistically since they call for unique approaches and presumptions to deal with missing or insufficient data. Data that are unsupervised (uncensored) do not suffer from these problems, making them easier to analyze. In this Section, the data sets have been discussed and analyzed based on a significance level $\alpha = 0.05$.

6.1. Non-Censored Data

6.1.1. Dataset I: Methylmercury Poisoning

The listed times of death within the week were recorded (using single dosage levels) in a Florida State University experiment to study the effects of methylmercury poisoning on the life spans of fish (see Kochar [41]).

6.000	6.143	7.286	8.714	9.429
9.857	10.143	11.571	11.714	11.714

The data representation plots are presented in Figure 3; it was found that there are no extreme observations and the nucleation intensity is asymmetric (left-bimodal-skewed). It was discovered that the critical value, which can be found in Table 2, is exceeded by $\hat{\Delta} = 0.0001122$. We then accept H_1, which says that the data collection has $NBRULC$ properties rather than exponential growth.

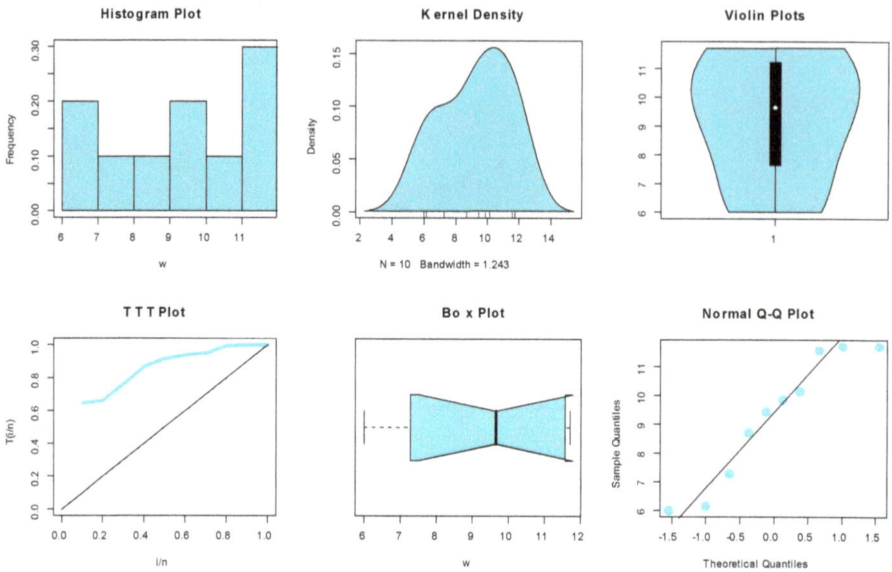

Figure 3. Non-parametric plots for dataset I.

6.1.2. Dataset II: Endurance of Ball Bearings

Pavur et al. [42] took into consideration the information below. The findings of a life test investigation on 23 ball bearings are shown in the following, indicating the number of revolutions (in ten million) until failure.

1.788	2.892	3.300	4.152	4.212	4.560	4.848	5.184
5.196	5.412	5.556	6.78	6.864	6.864	6.988	8.412
9.312	9.864	10.512	10.584	12.792	12.804	17.340	

The data visualization plots are presented in Figure 4. It was reported that there are some extreme observations and the nucleation intensity is asymmetric (bimodal-right-skewed). The dataset's exponential features are demonstrated by the null hypotheses, which are disproved. When $\hat{\Delta} = 0.0001074$, it is found to exceed the pertinent critical value in Table 2.

6.1.3. Dataset III: Leukaemia

Check out the information from Abouammoh et al. [43]. These numbers indicate a group of 43 leukemia patients from a Saudi Arabian Ministry of Health hospital, with order values in years, as follows:

0.315	0.496	0.699	1.145	1.208	1.263	1.414	2.025	2.036	2.162
2.211	2.370	2.532	2.693	2.805	2.910	2.912	3.192	3.263	3.348
3.348	3.427	3.499	3.534	3.718	3.751	3.858	3.986	4.049	4.244
4.323	4.323	4.381	4.392	4.397	4.647	4.753	4.929	4.973	5.074
5.203	5.274	5.384							

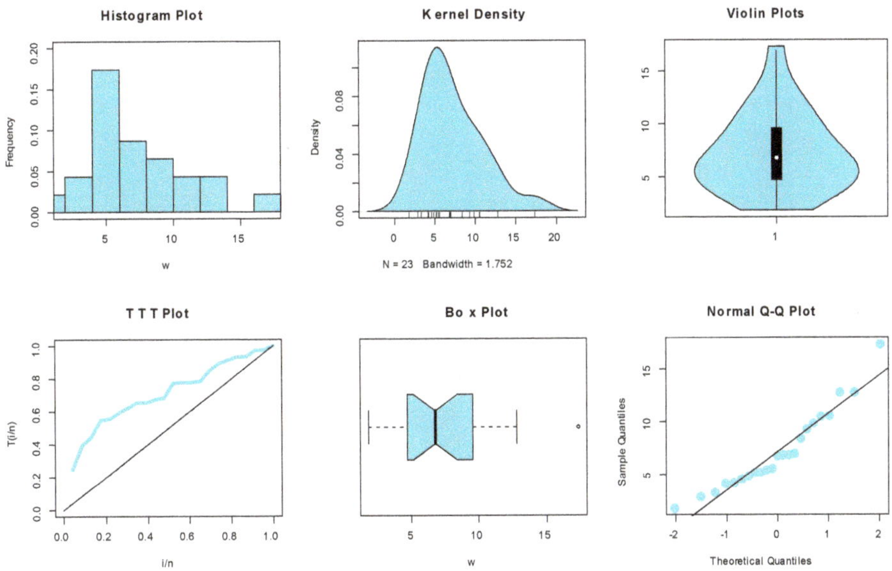

Figure 4. Non-parametric plots for dataset II.

The data representation plots are sketched in Figure 5; there are no extreme observations and the nucleation intensity is asymmetric (left-skewed). It was discovered that the critical value, which can be found in Table 2, is exceeded by $\hat{\Delta} = 0.0001222$. We then accept H_1, which states that the data collection has $NBRULC$ properties rather than exponential growth.

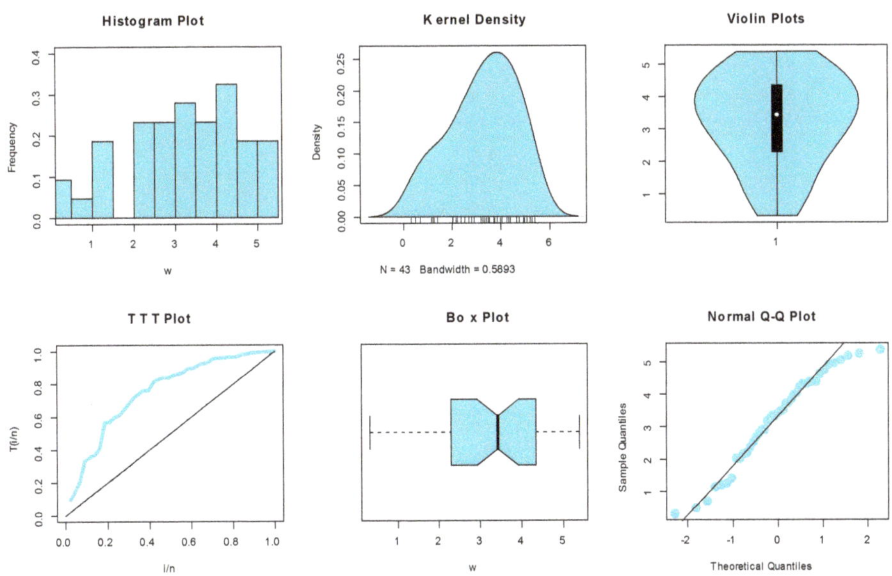

Figure 5. Non-parametric plots for dataset III.

6.1.4. Dataset IV: Leukaemia

Take a look at the data below, which show the survival periods (in years) following the diagnoses of 43 patients with specific kinds of leukemia (see Kotz and Johnson [44]). The data can be listed as follows:

0.019	0.129	0.159	0.203	0.485	0.636	0.748	0.781	0.869	1.175
1.206	1.219	1.219	1.282	1.356	1.362	1.458	1.564	1.586	1.592
1.781	1.923	1.959	2.134	2.413	2.466	2.548	2.652	2.951	3.038
3.6	3.655	3.754	4.203	4.690	4.888	5.143	5.167	5.603	5.633
6.192	6.655	6.874							

The data visualization plots are presented in Figure 6; it is clear that there are no extreme observations and the nucleation intensity is asymmetric-bimodal (right-skewed). The dataset's exponential features are demonstrated by the null hypotheses, which are disproved. When $\hat{\Delta} = 0.0001048$, is found, it exceeds the relevant critical value in Table 2.

6.1.5. Dataset V: Carbon Fibers

Two sets of data that were introduced by Badar and Priest [45] and used by Kundu and Gupta [46] are discussed in this segment. The strength of individual carbon fibers evaluated under tension at gauge lengths of 20 mm is measured in set A using GPA. For set B, individual carbon fibers were tested under stress at gauge lengths of 10 mm; the strength was evaluated in GPA. Size 63 applies to sets A and B. The data visualization plots are listed in Figures 7 and 8.

Dataset A:

1.312	1.314	1.479	1.552	1.700	1.803	1.861	1.865	1.944
1.958	1.966	1.997	2.006	2.021	2.027	2.055	2.063	2.098
2.140	2.179	2.224	2.240	2.253	2.270	2.272	2.274	2.301
2.301	2.359	2.382	2.382	2.426	2.434	2.435	2.478	2.490
2.511	2.514	2.535	2.554	2.566	2.570	2.586	2.629	2.633
2.642	2.648	2.684	2.697	2.726	2.770	2.773	2.800	2.809
2.818	2.821	2.848	2.880	2.954	3.012	3.067	3.084	3.090

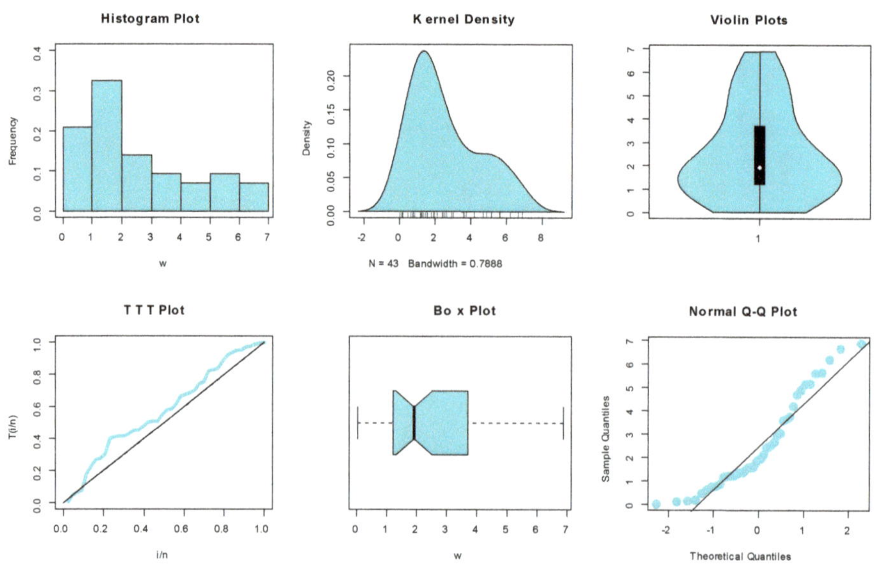

Figure 6. Non-parametric plots for dataset IV.

In such a case, the estimated value, $\hat{\Delta} = 0.0001036$, exceeds the crucial value shown in Table 2 by a significant amount. Given the $\alpha = 0.05$ significant level, it is true because these types of data satisfy the $NBRULC$ characteristic.

Dataset B:

1.901	2.132	2.203	2.228	2.257	2.350	2.361	2.396	2.397
2.445	2.454	2.474	2.518	2.522	2.525	2.532	2.575	2.614
2.616	2.618	2.624	2.659	2.675	2.738	2.740	2.856	2.917
2.928	2.937	2.937	2.977	2.996	3.030	3.125	3.139	3.145
3.220	3.223	3.235	3.243	3.264	3.272	3.294	3.332	3.346
3.377	3.408	3.435	3.493	3.501	3.537	3.554	3.562	3.628
3.852	3.871	3.886	3.971	4.024	4.027	4.225	4.395	5.020

In such a case, the estimated value, $\hat{\Delta} = 0.0001131$, exceeds the crucial value shown in Table 2 by a significant amount. Given the $\alpha = 0.05$ significant level, it is true because these types of data satisfy the $NBRULC$ characteristic.

6.1.6. Dataset VI: COVID-19

According to EL-Sagheer et al. [47], this information indicates the fatality rate for COVID-19 in the Netherlands from 31 March to 30 April 2020. The information is as follows:

14.918	10.656	12.274	10.289	10.832	7.099	5.928	13.211
7.968	7.584	5.555	6.027	4.097	3.611	4.960	7.498
6.940	5.307	5.048	2.857	2.254	5.431	4.462	3.883
3.461	3.647	1.974	1.273	1.416	4.235		

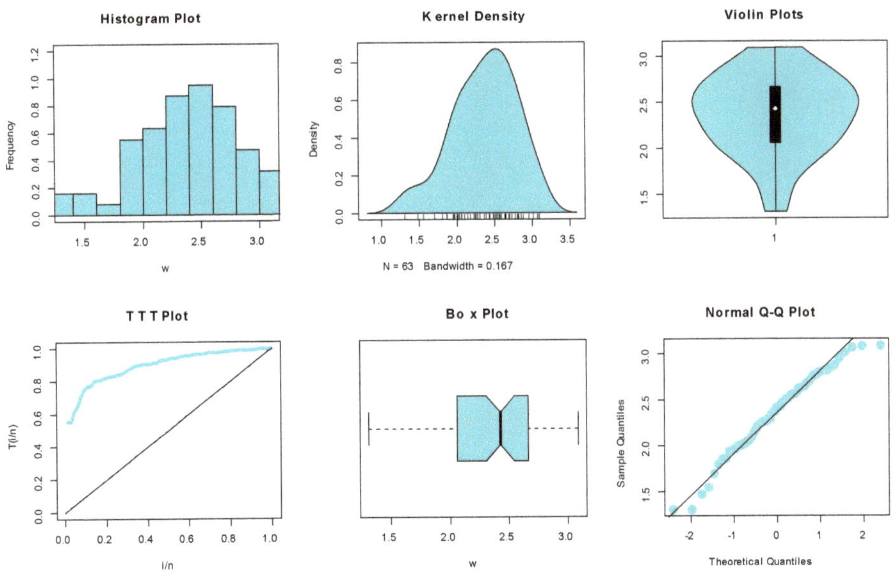

Figure 7. Non-parametric plots for set A of dataset V.

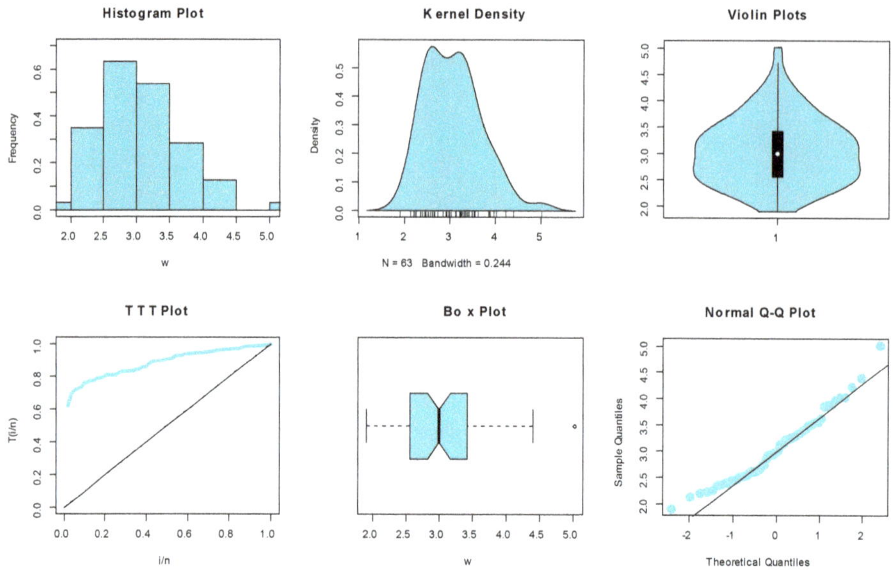

Figure 8. Non-parametric plots for set B of dataset V.

The data visualization plots are presented in Figure 9. It was discovered that the critical value, which can be found in Table 2, is exceeded by $\hat{\Delta} = 0.0001081$. We then accept H_1, which states that the data collection has $NBRULC$ properties rather than exponential growth.

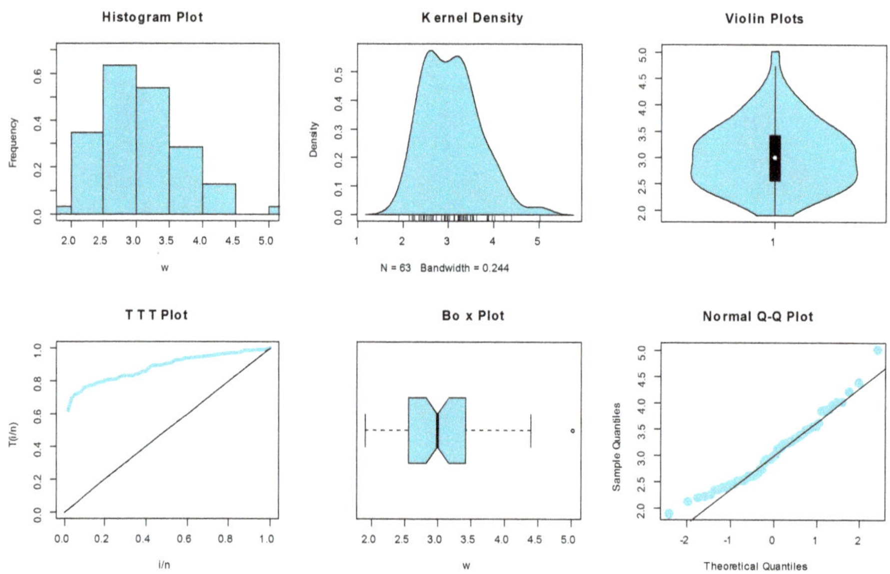

Figure 9. Non-parametric plots for dataset VI.

6.1.7. Dataset VII: COVID-19

According to Almongy et al. [48], this information indicates the fatality rate for COVID-19 in Italy from 27 February to 27 April 2020. The information is as follows:

4.571	7.201	3.606	8.479	11.410	8.961	10.919	10.908	6.503
18.474	11.010	17.337	16.561	13.226	15.137	8.697	15.787	13.333
11.822	14.242	11.273	14.330	16.046	11.950	10.282	11.775	10.138
9.037	12.396	10.644	8.646	8.905	8.906	7.407	7.445	7.214
6.194	4.640	5.452	5.073	4.416	4.859	4.408	4.639	3.148
4.040	4.253	4.011	3.564	3.827	3.134	2.780	2.881	3.341
2.686	2.814	2.508	2.450	1.518				

The data representation plots are listed in Figure 10. The dataset's exponential features are demonstrated by the null hypotheses, which are disproved. When $\hat{\Delta} = 0.0001027$, it is determined to exceed the critical value specified in Table 2.

6.1.8. Dataset VIII: Wind Speed

We used the following dataset, which was originally obtained from NCDC. These data represent the wind speed measured in knots for the first sample (set A) for 23 days and the second sample for 25 days (see, Ghazal et al. [49]).

Dataset A:

8.6	3.8	5.4	4.4	2.2	3.8	4.5	6.3
3.4	4.1	3.8	8.6	13.0	11.3	12.4	12.4
5.0	3.4	3.8	5.3	3.6	5.8	4.2	

The data visualization plots are presented in Figure 11 (set A); there are no extreme observations and the nucleation intensity is asymmetric-bimodal (right-skewed).

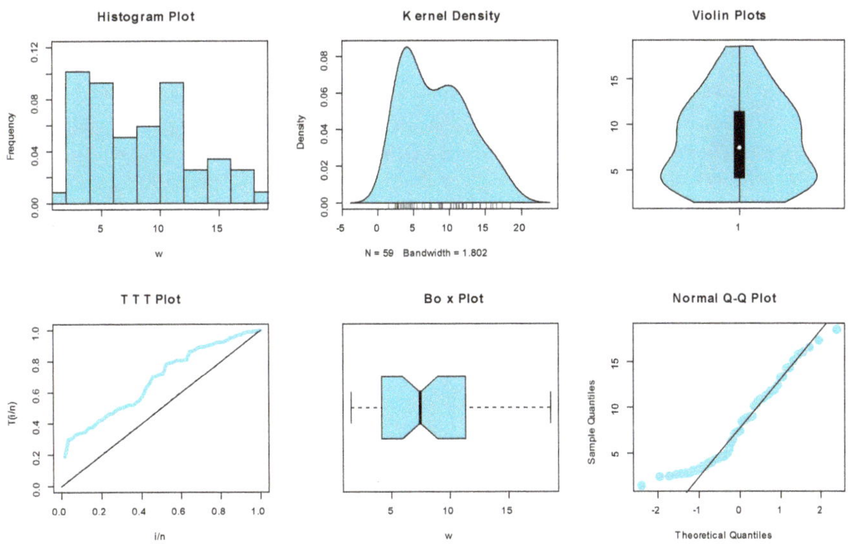

Figure 10. Non-parametric plots for dataset VII.

In such a case, the estimated value, $\hat{\Delta} = 0.0001084$, exceeds the crucial value shown in Table 2 by a significant amount. Given the $\alpha = 0.05$ significant level, it is true because these types of data satisfy the $NBRULC$ characteristic.

Dataset B:

2.4	2.9	3.3	3.4	3.5	3.7	3.8	3.9	4.0
4.1	4.2	4.5	4.6	4.8	5.1	5.3	5.5	6.0
6.2	6.5	7.8	8.2	8.4	9.4	10.9		

The data visualization plots are presented in Figure 12 (set B); there are some extreme observations and the nucleation intensity is asymmetric-multimodal (right-skewed). In such a case, the estimated value, $\hat{\Delta} = 0.0001183$, exceeds the crucial value shown in Table 2 by a significant amount. Considering the significance level of $\alpha = 0.05$, it can be concluded that these types of data satisfy the $NBRULC$ characteristic.

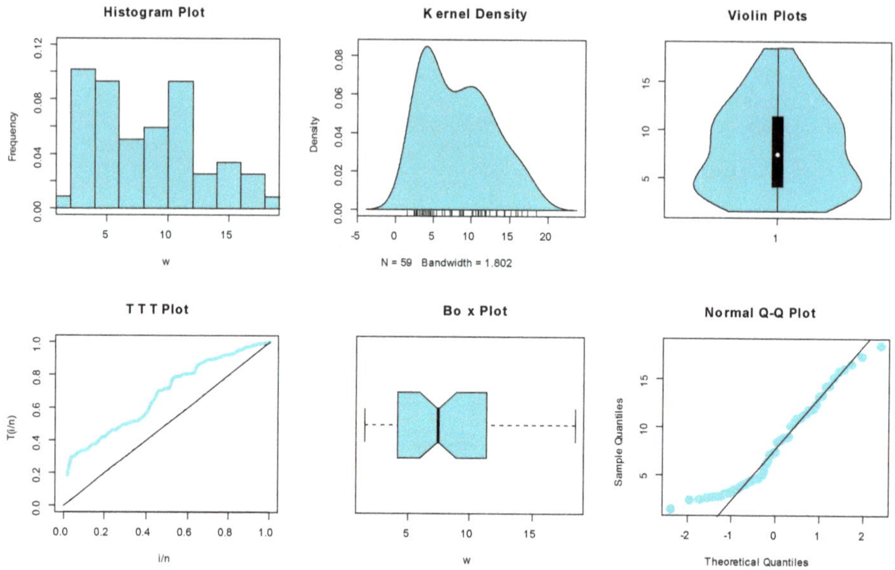

Figure 11. Non-parametric plots for set A of dataset VIII.

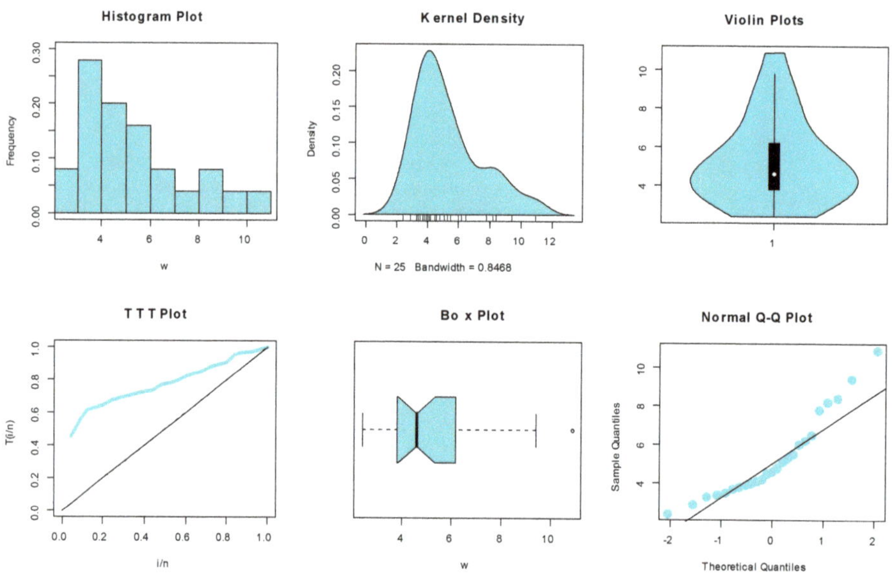

Figure 12. Non-parametric plots for set B of dataset VIII.

6.2. Censored Data

6.2.1. Dataset IX: Lung Cancer

The following data represent the number of weeks that 61 individuals, who received cyclophosphamide for incurable lung cancer, survived and were considered in the studies by Lagakos and Williams [50] and Lee and Wolfe [51]. For the patients whose treatments were stopped due to a deteriorating condition, there are 28 censored observations and 33 uncensored observations.

- Censored observations:

0.14	0.14	0.29	0.43	0.57	0.57	1.86	3.00	3.00	3.29
3.29	6.00	6.00	6.14	8.71	10.57	11.86	15.57	16.57	17.29
18.71	21.29	23.86	26.00	27.57	32.14	33.14	47.29		

- Uncensored observations:

0.43	2.86	3.14	3.14	3.43	3.43	3.71	3.86	6.14	6.86	9.00
9.43	10.71	10.86	11.14	13.00	14.43	15.71	18.43	18.57	20.71	29.14
29.71	40.57	48.57	49.43	53.86	61.86	66.57	68.71	68.96	72.86	72.86

When considering all available survival statistics, both censored and uncensored, we discover that Table 4's essential value exceeds our conclusion, which is $\Delta_c(0.9) = -0.00099279$. We can, therefore, clearly see the exponential nature of the data.

6.2.2. Dataset XI: Melanoma

Consider the information from Susarla and Van Ryzin [52]. These numbers represent the survival rates of 46 melanoma patients. Among them, 35 (non-censored material) have complete lifetime information. The following observations have been redacted, in order, as follows:

13	14	19	19	20	21	23	23	25	26
26	27	27	31	32	34	34	37	38	38
40	46	50	53	54	57	58	59	60	65
65	66	70	85	90	98	102	103	110	118
124	130	136	138	141	234				

The following is the hierarchy of the censored observations:

16	21	44	50	55	67	73	76	80	81
86	93	100	108	114	120	124	125	129	130
132	134	140	147	148	151	152	152	158	181
190	193	194	213	215					

If we take into account both censored and uncensored survival statistics, the essential value in Table 4 exceeds our outcome, which is $\Delta_c(0.9) = -2.65634 \times 10^{-23}$. The exponential properties of the data are, therefore, evident to us.

7. Conclusions

An exponential comparison of different life distributions has garnered much attention. Based on the goodness-of-fit technique, we introduced a new test statistic in this study to evaluate the exponential versus non-exponential NBRULC class of life distributions. For the uncensored and censored data, Tables 1 and 3 calculated and tabulated the critical values for this test. The efficiency of the Pitman asymptotic efficiency was discussed, and power estimates were simulated for families of the most common age distribution in reliability. The Monte Carlo critical points for the null distribution were simulated. Moreover, the power estimations of this test were computed for a few typical alternative distributions. Several key values were listed along with the power estimates for the censored and uncensored data for this test; moreover, the issue of properly suppressed data was also discussed. To illustrate the usefulness of the recommended test in the reliability analyses of censored and uncensored data, this paper covered several applications.

Author Contributions: Conceptualization, M.S.E., L.A.A.-E. and R.M.E.-S.; methodology, W.B.H.E. and M.E.-M.; software, W.B.H.E. and M.E.-M.; validation, H.N.A. and R.M.E.-S.; formal analysis, M.S.E., H.N.A. and M.E.-M.; investigation, W.B.H.E. and R.M.E.-S.; resources, M.S.E.; data curation, L.A.A.-E.; writing—original draft, H.N.A., M.E.-M. and R.M.E.-S.; writing—review and editing, M.S.E. and L.A.A.-E.; visualization, M.E.-M.; supervision, W.B.H.E.; project administration, M.S.E. and R.M.E.-S. All authors have read and agreed to the published version of the manuscript.

Funding: Princess Nourah bint Abdulrahman University Researchers Supporting Project and Prince Sattam bin Abdulaziz Universities under project numbers (PNURSP2023R443) and (PSAU/2023/R/1444), respectively.

Data Availability Statement: All datasets are reported within the article.

Acknowledgments: Princess Nourah bint Abdulrahman University Researchers Supporting Project number (PNURSP2023R443), Princess Nourah bint Abdulrahman University, Riyadh, Saudi Arabia. This study is supported via funding from Prince Sattam bin Abdulaziz University, project number (PSAU/2023/R/1444).

Conflicts of Interest: The authors declare no conflict of interest.

Sample Availability: All datasets are reported within the article.

References

1. Bryson, M.C.; Siddiqui, M.M. Some criteria for aging. *J. Am. Stat. Assoc.* **1969**, *64*, 1472–1483. [CrossRef]
2. Bhattacharyya, D.; Khan, R.A.; Mitra, M. A test of exponentiality against DMTTF alternatives via L-statistics. *Stat. Probab. Lett.* **2020**, *165*, 108853. [CrossRef]
3. Barlow, R.E.; Proschan, F. *Statistical Theory of Reliability and Life Testing*; To Begin With: Silver Spring, MD, USA, 1981.
4. Klefsjo, B. The HNBUE and HNWUE classes of life distributions. *Nav. Res. Logist.* **1982**, *29*, 331–344. [CrossRef]
5. Khan, R.A.; Bhattacharyya, D.; Mitra, M. Exact and asymptotic tests of exponentiality against nonmonotonic mean time to failure type alternatives. *Stat. Pap.* **2021**, *62*, 3015–3045. [CrossRef]
6. Kumazawa, Y. A class of tests statistics for testing whether new is better than used. *Commun. Stat. Theory Methods* **1983**, *12*, 311–321. [CrossRef]
7. Mahmoud, M.A.W.; EL-Sagheer, R.M.; Etman, W.B.H. Testing exponentiality against new better than renewal used in Laplace transform order. *J. Stat. Appl. Probab.* **2016**, *5*, 279–285. [CrossRef]
8. Mahmoud, M.A.W.; EL-Sagheer, R.M.; Etman, W.B.H. Moments inequalities for NBRUL distributions with hypotheses testing applications. *Austrian J. Stat.* **2018**, *47*, 95–104.
9. Majumder, P.; Mitra, M. A test for detecting Laplace order dominance and related Bahadur efficiency issues. *Stat. Pap.* **2019**, *60*, 1921–1937. [CrossRef]
10. Bhattacharyya, D.; Khan, R.A.; Mitra, M. Tests for Laplace order dominance with applications to insurance data. *Insur. Math. Econ.* **2021**, *99*, 163–173. [CrossRef]
11. Navarro, J. Preservation of DMRL and IMRL aging classes under the formation of order statistics and coherent systems. *Stat. Probab. Lett.* **2018**, *137*, 264–268. [CrossRef]
12. Abu-Youssef, S.E.; Hassan, E.M.A.; Gerges, S.T. A new nonparametric class of life distributions based on ordering moment generating approach. *J. Stat. Appl. Probab. Lett.* **2020**, *7*, 151–162.
13. Ghosh, S.; Mitra, M. A new test for exponentiality against HNBUE alternatives. *Commun. Stat. Theory Methods* **2020** *49*, 27–43. [CrossRef]
14. Navarro, J.; Pellerey, F. Preservation of ILR and IFR aging classes in sums of dependent random variables. *Appl. Stoch. Model. Bus. Ind.* **2022**, *38*, 240–261. [CrossRef]
15. El-Morshedy, M.; Al-Bossly, A.; EL-Sagheer, R.M.; Almohaimeed, B.; Etman, W.B.H.; Eliwa, M.S. A moment inequality for the NBRULC class: Statistical properties with applications to model asymmetric data. *Symmetry* **2022**, *14*, 2353. [CrossRef]
16. EL-Sagheer, R.M.; Abu-Youssef, S.E.; Sadek, A.; Omar, K.M.; Etman, W.B.H. Characterrization and testing NBRUL class of life distributions based on Laplace transform technique. *J. Stat. Appl. Probab.* **2022**, *11*, 1–14.
17. Gadallah, A.M.; Mohammed, B.I.; Al-Babtain, A.A.; Khosa, S.K.; Kilai, M.; Yusuf, M.; Bakr, M.E. Modeling various survival distributions using a nonparametric hypothesis testing based on Laplace transform approach with some real applications. *Comput. Math. Methods Med.* **2022**, *2022*, 5075716. [CrossRef]
18. Mansour, M.M.M. Assessing treatment methods via testing exponential property for clinical data. *J. Stat. Appl. Probab.* **2022**, *11*, 109–113.

19. Ghosh, S.; Mitra, M. A weighted integral approach to testing against HNBUE alternatives. *Stat. Probab. Lett.* **2017**, *129*, 58–64. [CrossRef]
20. Majumder, P.; Mitra, M. A test of exponentiality against alternatives. *J. Nonparametr. Stat.* **2019**, *31*, 794–812. [CrossRef]
21. Lai, C.D.; Xie, M. *Stochastic Ageing and Dependence for Reliability*; Springer: New York, NY, USA, 2006.
22. Etman, W.B.H.; EL-Sagheer, R.M.; Abu-Youssef, S.E.; Sadek, A. On some characterizations to NBRULC class with hypotheses testing application. *Appl. Math. Inf. Sci.* **2022**, *16*, 139–148.
23. Ghosh, S.; Majumder, P. A moment inequality for decreasing mean time to failure distributions with hypothesis testing application. *J. Stat. Comput. Simul.* **2022**, *92*, 2875–2890. [CrossRef]
24. Bakr, M.E.; Al-Babtain, A.A. Non-parametric hypothesis testing for unknown aged class of life distribution using real medical data. *Axioms* **2023**, *12*, 369. [CrossRef]
25. Ghosh, S.; Mitra, M. On the exact distribution of generalized Hollander-Proschan type statistics. *Commun. Stat. Simul. Comput.* **2022**, *51*, 5051–5067. [CrossRef]
26. Alqifar, H.; Eliwa, M.S.; Etman, W.B.H.; El-Morshedy, M.; Al-Essa, L.A.; EL-Sagheer, R.M. Reliability class testing and hypothesis specification: NBRULC-$t_\circ$ characterizations with applications for medical and engineering data modeling. *Axioms* **2023**, *12*, 414. [CrossRef]
27. Mahmoud, M.A.W.; Abdul Alim, N.A. A goodness of fit approach to NBURFR and NBARFR classes. *Econ. Qual. Control* **2006** *21*, 59–75. [CrossRef]
28. Kayid, M.; Diab, L.S.; Alzughaibi, A. Testing NBU (2) class of life distribution based on goodness of fit approach. *J. King Saud-Univ.-Sci.* **2010**, *22*, 241–245. [CrossRef]
29. Bera, S.; Bhattacharyya, D.; Khan, R.A.; Mitra, M. Test for harmonic mean residual life function: A goodness of fit approach. *Math. Comput. Simul.* **2023**, *203*, 58–70. [CrossRef]
30. Mahmoud, M.A.W.; Diab, L.S.; Radi, D.M. Testing exponentiality against RNBUL class of life distribution based on goodness of fit. *J. Stat. Appl. Probab.* **2019**, *8*, 57–66. [CrossRef]
31. Abu-Youssef, S.E.; Ali, N.S.A.; Bakr, M.E. Used better than aged in mgf ordering class of life distribution with application of hypothesis testing. *J. Stat. Appl. Probab. Lett.* **2020**, *7*, 23–32.
32. Bakr, M.E.; Nagy, M.; Al-Babtain, A.A. Non-parametric hypothesis testing to model some cancers based on goodness of fit. *AIMS Math.* **2022**, *7*, 13733–13745. [CrossRef]
33. Abu-Youssef, S.E.; El-Toony, A.A. A new class of life distribution based on Laplace transform and It's applications. *Inf. Sci. Lett.* **2022**, *11*, 355–362.
34. Abu-Youssef, S.E.; Gerges, S.T. Based on the goodness of fit approach, a new test statistics for testing NBUC$_{mgf}$ class of life distributions. *Pak. J. Stat.* **2022**, *38*, 129–144.
35. Etman, W.B.H.; El-Morshedy, M.; Eliwa, M.S.; Almohaimeed, A.; EL-Sagheer, R.M. A new reliability class-test statistic for life distributions under convolution, mixture and homogeneous shock model: Characterizations and applications in engineering and medical fields. *Axioms* **2023**, *12*, 331. [CrossRef]
36. Lee, A.J. U-Statistics-Theorem and Practice. In *Statistics Textbooks Monographs*; Marcel Dekker: New York, NY, USA, 1990; p. 110.
37. Mugdadi, A.R.; Ahmad, I.A. Moment inequalities derived from comparing life with its equilibrium form. *J. Stat. Plan. Inference* **2005**, *134*, 303–317. [CrossRef]
38. Kango, A.I. Testing for new is better than used. *Commun. Stat. Theory Methods* **1993**, *12*, 311–321.
39. Abdel Aziz, A.A. On testing exponentiality against RNBRUE alternatives. *Appl. Math. Sci.* **2007**, *35*, 1725–1736.
40. Kaplan, E.L.; Meier, P. Nonparametric estimation from incomplete observation. *J. Am. Stat. Assoc.* **1958**, *53*, 457–481. [CrossRef]
41. Kocha S.C. Testing exponenttality against monotone failure rate average. *Commun. Stat. Theory Methods* **1985**, *14*, 381–392. [CrossRef]
42. Pavur, R.J.; Edgeman, R.L.; Scott, R.C. Quadratic statistics for the goodness-of-fit test of the inverse Gaussian distribution. *IEEE Trans. Reliab.* **1992**, *41*, 118–123. [CrossRef]
43. Abouammoh, A.M.; Abdulghani, S.A.; Qamber, I.S. On partial orderings and testing of new better than renewal used classes. *Reliab. Eng. Syst. Saf.* **1994**, *43*, 37–41. [CrossRef]
44. Kotz, S.; Johnson, N.L. *Encyclopedia of Statistical Sciences*; Wiley: New York, NY, USA, 1983.
45. Bader, M.G.; Priest, A.M. Statistical aspects of fibre and bundle strength in hybrid composites. In *Progress in Science and Engineering of Composites*; Hayashi, T., Kawata, K., Umekawa, S., Eds.; ICCM-IV: Tokyo, Japan, 1982; pp. 1129–1136.
46. Kundu, D.; Gupta, R.D. Estimation of P[Y<X] for Weibull Distributions. *IEEE Trans. Reliab.* **2006**, *55*, 270–280.
47. EL-Sagheer, R.M.; Eliwa, M.S.; Alqahtani, K.M.; EL-Morshedy, M. Asymmetric randomly censored mortality distribution: Bayesian framework and parametric bootstrap with application to COVID-19 data. *J. Math.* **2022**, *2022*, 8300753. [CrossRef]
48. Almongy, H.M.; Almetwally, E.M.; Aljohani, H.M.; Alghamdi, A.S.; Hafez, E.H. A new extended rayleigh distribution with applications of COVID-19 data. *Results Phys.* **2021**, *23*, 104012. [CrossRef] [PubMed]
49. Ghazal, M.G.M.; EL-Sagheer, R.M.; Mahmoud, M.A.W.; Al-Babtain, A.A.; Bakr, M.E.; Hasaballah, M.M. Inference for two populations 3-Burr-XII in presence of joint progressive censoring. *Hindawi Complex.* **2022**, *2022*, 6171714. [CrossRef]
50. Lagakos, S.W.; Williams, J.S. Models for censored survival analysis: A cone class of variable-sum models. *Biometrika* **1978**, *65*, 181–189. [CrossRef]

51. Lee, S.Y.; Wolfe, R.A. A simple test for independent censoring under the proportional hazards model. *Biometrics* **1998**, *54*, 1176–1182. [CrossRef]
52. Susarla, V.; Vanryzin, J. Empirical Bayes estimations of a survival function right censored observation. *Ann. Stat.* **1978**, *6*, 710–755. [CrossRef]

Σ mathematics

MDPI

Article

The Log-Bimodal Asymmetric Generalized Gaussian Model with Application to Positive Data

Guillermo Martínez-Flórez [1,*,†], Roger Tovar-Falón [1,*,†] and Heleno Bolfarine [2]

1 Departamento de Matemáticas y Estadística, Facultad de Ciencias Básicas, Universidad de Córdoba, Montería 230002, Colombia
2 Departamento de Estatística, Instituto de Matemática e Estatística (IME), Universidade de São Paulo, São Paulo 1010, Brazil; hbolfar@ime.usp.br
* Correspondence: guillermomartinez@correo.unicordoba.edu.co (G.M.-F.); rjtovar@correo.unicordoba.edu.co (R.T.-F.)
† These authors contributed equally to this work.

Abstract: One of the most widely known probability distributions used to explain the probabilistic behavior of positive data is the log-normal (LN). Although the LN distribution is capable of adjusting data types, it is not always fully true that the model manages to adequately model the behavior of the response of interest since in some cases, the degree of skewness and/or kurtosis of the data are greater or less than those that the LN distribution can capture. Another peculiarity of the LN distribution is that it only fits unimodal positive data, which constitutes a limitation when dealing with data that present more than one mode (bimodality). On the other hand, the log-normal model only fits unimodal positive data and in reality there are multiple applications where the behavior of materials is bimodal. To fill this gap, this paper introduces a new probability distribution that is capable of fitting unimodal or bimodal positive data with a high or low degree of skewness and/or kurtosis. The new distribution is a generalization of the LN distribution. For the new proposal, its main properties are studied and the process of estimation of the parameters involved in the model is carried out from a classical perspective using the maximum likelihood method. An important feature of this distribution is the non-singularity of the Fisher information matrix, which guarantees the use of asymptotic theory to study the properties of the parameter estimators. A Monte Carlo type simulation study is carried out to evaluate the properties of the estimators and finally, an illustration is presented with a set of data related to the concentration of nickel in soil samples, allowing to show that the proposed distribution fits extremely well in certain situations.

Keywords: bimodality; generalized Gaussian model; maximum likelihood estimation; positive data

MSC: 60E05; 62E10

1. Introduction

Until a few years ago, the modeling of positive data was limited to the use of some distributions which are characterized by being of asymmetric type, such as the gamma, Weibull, exponential and log-normal (LN) models. In geochemistry, the fundamental law enunciated by Ahrens [1], "the concentration of a chemical element in a rock has a logarithm-normal distribution", converted to the LN distribution, one of the most used for modeling the concentration of chemical elements.The LN distribution denoted by $\mathrm{LN}(\mu, \sigma^2)$, is defined from the transformation of the random variable $Y = \log(X)$, where $X \sim \mathrm{N}(\mu, \sigma^2)$. The model has wide applicability in studies about survival time materials in engineering sciences and some economic studies.

Another type of asymmetric distribution, used for fitting positive data, is the log-skew-normal (LSN) model introduced by Azzalini et al. [2], which is an extension of the original skew-normal (SN) distribution proposed by Azzalini [3]. From the SN model, numerous families of asymmetric distributions have been introduced and studied in detail, for example, the symmetric-asymmetric family of distributions with probability density function (PDF) given by

$$\varphi_{\mathrm{A}}(y;\lambda) = 2f(y)G(\lambda y), \quad y \in \mathbb{R}, \tag{1}$$

where $\lambda \in \mathbb{R}$, f is a symmetric PDF around zero, G is an absolutely continuous symmetric distribution function, and λ is a parameter that controls the asymmetry. The SN model is a special case of the model in (1), which is obtained by letting $f = \phi$ and $G = \Phi$, the PDF and the cumulative distribution function (CDF) of the normal distribution. The extension of the location-scale version of the SN model follows by applying the linear transformation $Z = \xi + \eta Y$, where $\xi \in \mathbb{R}$ and $\eta > 0$. This is denoted by $\mathrm{SN}(\xi, \eta, \lambda)$, and the standard case by $\mathrm{SN}(\lambda)$. Additional works focused on the study of the SN distribution were carried out by Azzalini and Dalla Valle [4], Henze [5] and Chiogna [6], among others.

An extension of the SN model for fitting positive data denoted by $\mathrm{LSN}(\xi, \eta, \lambda)$ was introduced by Azzalini et al. [2]. This extension has PDF given by

$$f_{\mathrm{LSN}}(y;\xi,\eta,\lambda) = \frac{2}{\eta y}\phi\left(\frac{\log(y)-\xi}{\eta}\right)\Phi\left(\lambda\frac{\log(y)-\xi}{\eta}\right), \quad y \in \mathbb{R}^+, \tag{2}$$

where ϕ and Φ are the PDF and CDF of the standard normal distribution, respectively, and λ is a parameter which controls the asymmetry and kurtosis in the model. The LSN distribution is commonly used for modeling data with skewness and kurtosis coefficients greater than the LN distribution can fit. Notice that, letting $\lambda = 0$ in the Equation (2), the LSN reduces to the LN model.

As an alternative to the SN model, Durrans [7] introduced another type of asymmetric distribution, called fractional order statistics model, and in much of the statistical literature referred to as alpha-power (AP) model. Properties of the AP model were studied by Gupta and Gupta [8] and Pewsey et al. [9]. The AP has PDF given by

$$\varphi_{\mathrm{F}}(y;\alpha) = \alpha f(y)\{F(y)\}^{\alpha-1}, \quad y \in \mathbb{R}, \tag{3}$$

where $\alpha \in \mathbb{R}^+$ is a parameter that controls the skewness and kurtosis of the distribution, and F is an absolutely continuous distribution function with PDF $f = dF$. In the particular case of $F = \Phi$ in (3), we said that the random variable Y follows the generalized Gaussian (or power-normal) distribution, and is denoted by $Y \sim \mathrm{PN}(\alpha)$. The extension of the location-scale of the PN model, denoted by $\mathrm{PN}(\xi, \eta, \alpha)$, to the case of positive data was proposed by Martínez-Flórez et al. [10], who defined the log-power-normal (LPN) model whose PDF is given by

$$\varphi_{\mathrm{LPN}}(y;\xi,\eta,\alpha) = \frac{\alpha}{\eta y}\phi\left(\frac{\log(y)-\xi}{\eta}\right)\left\{\Phi\left(\frac{\log(y)-\xi}{\eta}\right)\right\}^{\alpha-1}, \quad y \in \mathbb{R}^+, \tag{4}$$

where $\xi \in \mathbb{R}$ and $\eta > 0$ are parameters of location and scale, respectively. This model is denoted by $Y \sim \mathrm{LPN}(\xi, \eta, \alpha)$. The LPN model contains, as a special case, the LN model when $\alpha = 1$.

Contrary to the LSN model in which the information matrix is singular for the case $\lambda = 0$, Martínez-Flórez et al. [10] showed that the LPN model has information matrix non-singular when $\alpha = 1$. Thus, in the LPN model, statistical inference based on the theory of large samples can be carried out. The normality of the vector of maximum likelihood estimator (MLE) for the model parameters can be tested by using the likelihood-ratio statistic. The LPN was studied also by Martínez-Flórez et al. [11].

In the statistical literature, it is well known that the SN and PN models are restricted to the case of unimodal data set; so, extensions to the bimodal situations of these two models have been considered by some authors. For example, Arnold et al. [12] defined the bimodal model known as "the extended normal-asymmetric two-pieces model" (ETN), whose PDF is given by

$$f_{\mathrm{ETN}}(y;\lambda,\beta)=2c_{\lambda}\phi(y)\Phi(\lambda|y|)\Phi(\beta y),\quad y\in\mathbb{R},\tag{5}$$

where $\lambda,\beta\in\mathbb{R}$, and c_λ is a normalizing constant. For the ETN model, Arnold et al. [12] showed that the information matrix is singular when $\lambda=\beta=0$.

Concerning bimodal positive data, Bolfarine et al. [13] introduced the log-bimodal-skew-normal model, which is denoted by $Y\sim\mathrm{LBSN}(\xi,\eta,\lambda,\beta)$. The LBSN model is an extension of the SN distribution and is adequate for modeling bimodal positive data. The PDF of the LBSN model is given by

$$\varphi_{\mathrm{LBSN}}(y;\xi,\eta,\lambda,\beta)=\frac{2}{y\eta}\frac{1+\beta x^2}{1+\beta}\phi(x)\Phi(\lambda x),\quad y\in\mathbb{R}^{+},\tag{6}$$

where $x=(\log(y)-\xi)/\eta$, with $\xi,\lambda\in\mathbb{R},\beta,\eta\in\mathbb{R}^{+}$.

Recently, Bolfarine et al. [14] extended the unimodal generalized Gaussian model of Durrans [7] to situations of bimodal asymmetric data by considering the alternative of the ETN model developed by Arnold et al. [12]. The extension of Bolfarine et al. [14], which is denoted by $\mathrm{ABPN}(\beta,\alpha)$, has density function given by

$$\varphi(y;\beta,\alpha)=2\alpha c_{\alpha}\phi(y)\{\Phi(|y|)\}^{\alpha-1}\Phi(\beta y),\quad y\in\mathbb{R},\tag{7}$$

where ϕ and Φ are the PDF and CDF of the standard normal distribution, respectively, and, $c_\alpha=(2^{\alpha-1})/(2^{\alpha}-1)$, with $\alpha\in\mathbb{R}^{+}$, and $\beta\in\mathbb{R}$. Bolfarine et al. [14] showed that the PDF in (7) is bimodal and asymmetric for values of $\alpha>1$, and certain values of β; and unimodal for $\alpha\leq 1$. Therefore, the ABPN model can be used for fitting data with a high degree of asymmetry and bimodality. For the ABPN model, the authors also showed that the information matrix is non-singular in the neighborhood of $\alpha=1$, contrary to the case of the ETN model of Arnold et al. [12], whose information matrix is singular for the case $\lambda=\beta=0$. Hence, normality of the MLE for the parameters of the ABPN model can be tested by using the large sample theory together with the likelihood-ratio statistic.

In the current literature, there are few distributions for fitting bimodal positive data, and therefore, this work is focused to propose a new distribution which is adequate to fit data with this behavior. The proposed model generalizes the fundamental law of geochemistry of [1], and in addition, is more flexible than the LN, LSN and LPN models, which are contained as special cases.

The rest of the paper is organized as follows: Section 2 introduces the log-bimodal asymmetric generalized Gaussian model, and its main properties are enunciated and studied. The moment, score function, and the observed and expected information matrix are obtained. The inference for the parameters of the model is realized by using the maximum likelihood method. The results of a simulation study and its respective discussion are presented in Section 3. In Section 4, an application to a real data set consisting of samples of concentration of nickel in soil is presented to illustrate the use of the new model. Finally, a discussion about the proposed model is presented in Section 5.

2. The Log-Uni-Bi-Modal Asymmetric Generalized Gaussian Model

In this section, we introduce a new model which generalizes some distributions already known in the statistical literature for fitting positive data. This model contains two parameters that make it more flexible than the LN, LSN and LPN models, and is obtained from considering the alternative two-pieces skew-normal model for bimodal asymmetric data of Arnold et al. [12].

Definition 1. *If random variable Y is distributed with density function given by:*

$$\varphi(y;\xi,\eta,\beta,\alpha) = \frac{k_\alpha}{y}\phi\left(\frac{\log(y)-\xi}{\eta}\right)\left\{\Phi\left(\frac{|\log(y)-\xi|}{\eta}\right)\right\}^{\alpha-1}\Phi\left(\frac{\beta(\log(y)-\xi)}{\eta}\right), \quad (8)$$

for $y \in \mathbb{R}^+$; where $\xi, \beta \in \mathbb{R}; \alpha, \eta \in \mathbb{R}^+$, and $k_\alpha = \alpha 2^\alpha/(2^\alpha - 1)$ is the normalizing constant, then Y follows a log-bimodal asymmetric generalized Gaussian distribution, also called log-bimodal asymmetric power-normal (LABPN) distribution, with parameter $\boldsymbol{\theta} = (\xi, \eta, \beta, \alpha)^\top$. We use the notation $Y \sim LABPN(\xi, \eta, \beta, \alpha)$.

In density function (8), β is an asymmetry parameter, α is a shape parameter, ξ is a location parameter and η is a scale parameter.

Although the new distribution is a little more complicated than the existing methodologies, this does not constitute a limitation in its applicability. On the one hand, the main benefit of this new proposal is the possibility of fitting positive data that present bimodality and a high degree of asymmetry and kurtosis that cannot be captured by existing models in the current literature. On the other hand, the existence of statistical packages today facilitates their implementation in practical terms.

From Definition 1, some special cases of the LABPN model are followed by letting specific values of the parameters. For example, when $\alpha = 1$ and $\beta = 0$ the LN model follows; for $\alpha = 1$, the LSN model is obtained; and, if $\beta = 0$ and $(\log(y) - \xi)/\eta > 0$ the LPN model follows. Finally, when $\alpha = 2$, then $Y \sim \text{ETN}(1, \beta)$. These results are presented in the following properties:

Property 1. *If $Y \sim LABPN(\xi, \eta, \beta, \alpha)$, then $LABPN(\xi, \eta, 0, 1) = LN(\xi, \eta^2)$, where LN denote the log-normal distribution.*

Property 2. *If $Y \sim LABPN(\xi, \eta, \beta, \alpha)$, then $LABPN(\xi, \eta, \beta, 1) = LSN(\xi, \eta, \beta)$, where LN denote the log-skew normal distribution, see Azzalini et al. [2].*

Property 3. *If $Y \sim LABPN(\xi, \eta, \beta, \alpha)$ and $\log(Y) > \xi$ for all $Y \in \mathbb{R}^+$, then $LABPN(\xi, \eta, 0, \alpha) = LPN(\xi, \eta, \alpha)$, where LN denote the log-skew normal distribution, see Martínez-Flórez et al. [10].*

Property 4. *If $Y \sim LABPN(\xi, \eta, \beta, 2)$, then $Y \sim ETN(\xi, \eta, 1)$, where LN denote the log-skew normal distribution, see Arnold et al. [12].*

Differentiating the density function regarding y, we have that the derivative of $\varphi(y; \xi, \eta, \beta, \alpha)$ is null at

$$\alpha - 1 = |z|\frac{\Phi(|z|)}{\phi(z)}\left[1 + \frac{1}{z} - \frac{\beta}{z}\frac{\phi(\beta z)}{\Phi(\beta z)}\right], \quad y > 0,$$

where $z = (\log(y) - \xi)/\eta$. Now, for $y > 0$ such that $-\infty < z < 0$, we have

$$\lim_{\beta\to\infty} \frac{\beta}{z}\frac{\phi(\beta z)}{\Phi(\beta z)} = -\infty,$$

and for $y > 0$, such that $0 < z < \infty$, we have

$$\lim_{\beta\to-\infty} \frac{\beta}{z}\frac{\phi(\beta z)}{\Phi(\beta z)} = -\infty.$$

Therefore, for $\alpha > 1$ and certain values of $-\infty < \beta < \infty$ satisfying

$$0 < \left[1 + \frac{1}{z} - \frac{\beta}{z}\frac{\phi(\beta z)}{\Phi(\beta z)}\right] < \infty,$$

we have a log-bimodal model. Figure 1 reveals how the parameters α and β control the skewness, kurtosis and shape of the LABPN model.

2.1. Moments

The moments of the random variable Y with LABPN distribution do not have explicit form; however, the rth moment for the standard case of the LABPN model, that is, $\xi = 0$ and $\eta = 1$, which is denoted by LABPN(β, α), can be obtained by using the formula:

$$\mu_r = \mathbb{E}(Z^r) = k_\alpha \int_0^\infty (\exp(-rz) + \exp(rz))\phi(z)\{\Phi(z)\}^{\alpha-1}\Phi(\beta z)dz.$$

where $z = \log(y), y > 0$. Thus, the rth moment of $Y \sim$ LABPN$(\xi, \eta, \beta, \alpha)$ can be obtained from the expression:

$$\mathbb{E}(Y^r) = \sum_{k=0}^{r} \binom{r}{k} \xi^k \eta^{r-k} \mu_{r-k}.$$

The following result is similar to that given for the LN, LSN and LPN models.

Property 5. *For all $\alpha \in \mathbb{R}^+$, the moment-generating function (MGF) of the random variable $Y \sim LABPN(\xi, \eta, \beta, \alpha)$ does not exist.*

Proof. The result is obvious for $\alpha = 1$ and $\beta = 0$, since this corresponds to the case of the LN model. For $\alpha = 1$, the LSN model follows and for $\beta = 0$ and $z > 0$ for all $y = \log(z) \in \mathbb{R}^+$, we have the case of the LPN model.

For $0 < t < a < \infty$ (without loss of generality, we took $\xi = 0$ and $\eta = 1$), we have by definition

$$\begin{aligned} M_Y(t) = \mathbb{E}(e^{tY}) &= k_\alpha \int_0^\infty \frac{e^{ty}}{y}\phi(\log(y))\Big\{\Phi(|\log(y)|)\Big\}^{\alpha-1}\Phi(\beta\log(y))dy, \quad y \in \mathbb{R}^+, \\ &= k_\alpha \int_0^1 \frac{1}{y}e^{ty}\phi(\log(y))\Big\{1 - \Phi(\log(y))\Big\}^{\alpha-1}\Phi(\beta\log(y))dy \\ &\quad + k_\alpha \int_1^\infty \frac{1}{y}e^{ty}\phi(\log(y))\Big\{\Phi(\log(y))\Big\}^{\alpha-1}\Phi(\beta\log(y))dy, \end{aligned}$$

Letting $h_\beta(y) = \frac{2}{y}e^{ty}\phi(\log(y))\Phi(\beta\log(y))dy$, it follows for $\beta > 0$ that

$$\liminf_{y\to\infty} \Phi(\beta\log(y)) \geq \frac{1}{2},$$

see Lin and Stoyanov [15]. In addition, by letting $\alpha = \alpha_0$, we get

$$0 < 2\alpha_0\{\Phi(\log(y))\}^{\alpha_0-1} < k_{\alpha_0}\{\Phi(\log(y))\}^{\alpha_0-1},$$

then, if $y \to \infty$ it follows that $h_\beta(y) \to \infty$ and $0 < k_{\alpha_0}\{\Phi(\log(x))\}^{\alpha_0-1} \longrightarrow k_{\alpha_0}$, where it is obtained that $0 < 2\alpha_0 < k_{\alpha_0}$; therefore, for

$$A(\alpha) = k_\alpha \int_1^\infty \frac{1}{y}e^{ty}\phi(\log(y))\Big\{\Phi(\log(y))\Big\}^{\alpha-1}\Phi(\beta\log(y)),$$

we conclude that $A(\alpha_0)(y) = \infty$. On the other hand, following Arnold and Lin [16],

$$\lim_{y\to\infty} \frac{-\log(\Phi(-y))}{y^2} = \frac{1}{2},$$

we have for $\beta < 0$, and $y \to \infty$, the approximation

$$\log(\Phi(\beta\log(y))) \simeq -\frac{1}{2}(\beta\log(y))^2;$$

therefore, when $y \to \infty$, we have for fixed α that

$$\begin{aligned}\log\left(\frac{1}{2}k_{\alpha_0}h_\beta(y)\{\Phi(\log(y))\}^{\alpha_0-1}\right) &\simeq -\frac{1}{2}\log(2\pi)+\log(k_{\alpha_0})-\log(2y)+ty\\ &-\frac{1}{2}(1+\beta^2)(\log(y))^2+(\alpha_0-1)\log(\Phi(\log(y))) \longrightarrow \infty\end{aligned}$$

from which we can conclude that $A(\alpha_0)(y) = \infty$. Thus, for all $\alpha \in \mathbb{R}^+$ and $\beta \in \mathbb{R}$, the variable random Y does not have MGF when $t > 0$. Therefore, $M_Y(t)$ does not exist, and the proof is completed. □

2.2. Statistical Inference

Given a random sample of size n, $\mathbf{Y}$ such that, $\mathbf{Y} = (Y_1, Y_2, \ldots, Y_n)$, with $Y_i \sim$ LABPN$(\xi, \eta, \beta, \alpha)$, the log-likelihood function for the parameter $\boldsymbol{\theta} = (\xi, \eta, \beta, \alpha)^\top$ can be written as

$$\begin{aligned}\ell(\boldsymbol{\theta}; X) &= n(\log(\alpha)+\log(c_\alpha)-\log(\eta))+\sum_{i=1}^{n}\log(\phi(z_i))\\ &+(\alpha-1)\sum_{i=1}^{n}\log(\Phi(|z_i|))+\sum_{i=1}^{n}\log(\Phi(\beta z_i)),\end{aligned}$$

where $z_i = (\log(y_i) - \xi)/\eta$, for $i = 1, \ldots, n$. The corresponding score functions, obtained by taking the first derivative of the log-likelihood function, are given by

$$U(\xi) = \frac{1}{\eta}\sum_{i=1}^{n} z_i - \frac{\alpha-1}{\eta}\sum_{i=1}^{n}\text{sgn}(z_i)\frac{\phi(|z_i|)}{\Phi(|z_i|)} - \frac{\beta}{\eta}\sum_{i=1}^{n}\frac{\phi(\beta z_i)}{\Phi(\beta z_i)} = 0$$

$$U(\eta) = -\frac{n}{\eta} + \frac{1}{\eta}\sum_{i=1}^{n} z_i^2 - \frac{\alpha-1}{\eta}\sum_{i=1}^{n}|z_i|\frac{\phi(|z_i|)}{\Phi(|z_i|)} - \frac{\beta}{\eta}\sum_{i=1}^{n} z_i\frac{\phi(\beta z_i)}{\Phi(\beta z_i)} = 0$$

$$U(\beta) = \sum_{i=1}^{n} z_i\frac{\phi(\beta z_i)}{\Phi(\beta z_i)} = 0,$$

$$U(\alpha) = \frac{n}{\alpha} - \frac{n\log 2}{1-2^{-\alpha}} + \sum_{i=1}^{n}\log(2\Phi(|z_i|)) = 0.$$

2.3. Observed Information Matrix

The elements of the observed information matrix are obtained by multiplying by -1 the second partial derivatives of the log-likelihood function regarding the parameters, by using the expression

$$k_{\theta_r,\theta_p} = -\frac{\partial^2\ell(\boldsymbol{\theta}; \boldsymbol{y})}{\partial\theta_r\partial\theta_p}, \quad r, p = 1, 2, 3, 4, \tag{9}$$

with $\theta_1 = \xi$, $\theta_2 = \eta$, $\theta_3 = \beta$ and $\theta_4 = \alpha$. These elements are presented in detail in Appendix A.

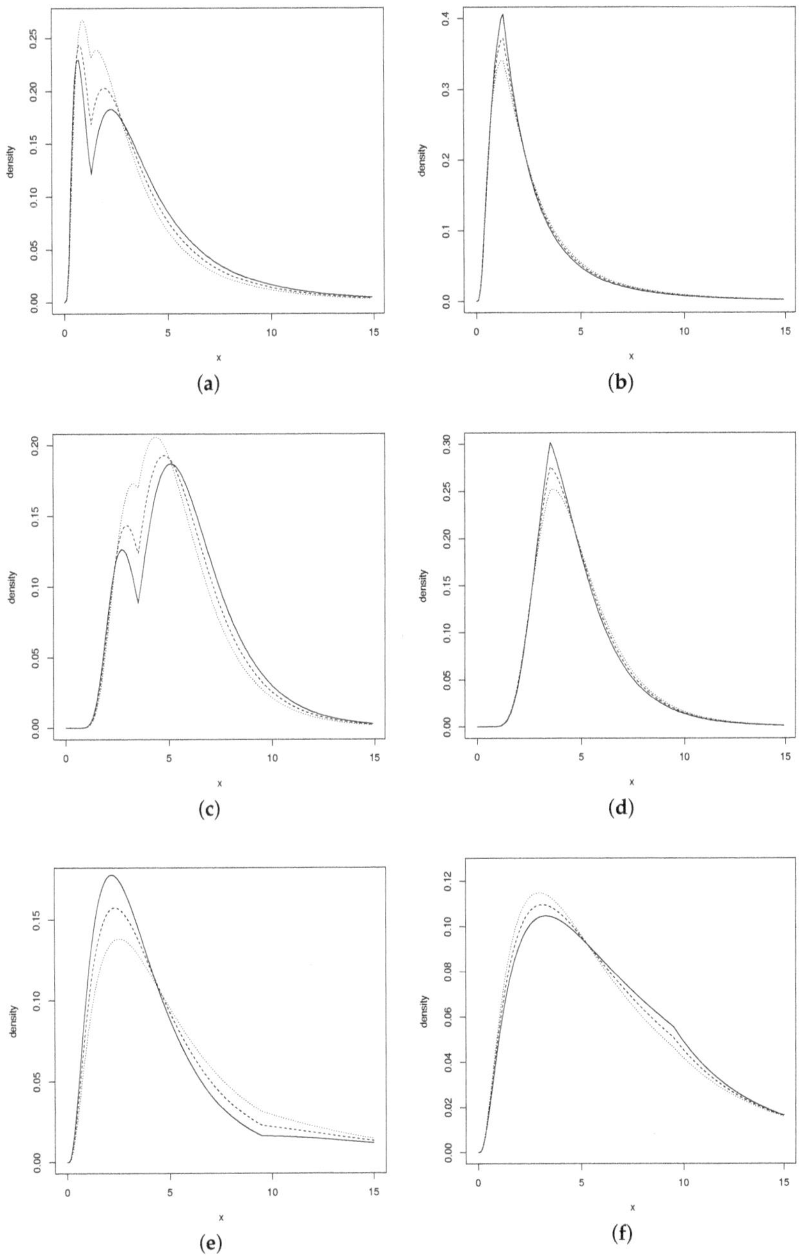

Figure 1. PDF of the LABPN model with parameter $\boldsymbol{\theta}$, for: (**a**) $\boldsymbol{\theta} = (0.25, 1.0, 1.0, \alpha)$ with $\alpha = 3.25$ (solid line), 2.5 (dashed line), 1.75 (dotted line); (**b**) $\boldsymbol{\theta} = (0.25, 1.0, 1.0, \alpha)$ with $\alpha = 0.25$ (solid line), 0.5 (dashed line), 0.75 (dotted line); (**c**) $\boldsymbol{\theta} = (1.25, 0.5, 1.0, \alpha)$ with $\alpha = 3.25$ (solid line), 2.5 (dashed line), 1.75 (dotted line); (**d**) $\boldsymbol{\theta} = (1.25, 0.5, 1.0, \alpha)$ with $\alpha = 0.25$ (solid line), 0.5 (dashed line), 0.75 (dotted line); (**e**) $\boldsymbol{\theta} = (2.25, 1.0, -1.0, \alpha)$ with $\alpha = 3.25$ (solid line), 2.5 (dashed line), 1.75 (dotted line) and (**f**) $\boldsymbol{\theta} = (2.25, 1.0, -1.0, \alpha)$ with $\alpha = 0.25$ (solid line), 0.5 (dashed line), 0.75 (dotted line).

2.4. Expected Information Matrix

Under the assumption that the regularity conditions are satisfied, the elements of the expected information matrix can be calculated by multiplying by n^{-1}, the expected value of the corresponding elements of the observed information matrix, that is,

$$I_{\theta_r\theta_p} = n^{-1}E\left\{-\frac{\partial^2 \ell(\boldsymbol{\theta};\mathbf{y})}{\partial\theta_r\partial\theta_p}\right\}, \quad r,p = 1,2,3,4,$$

In Appendix A, the explicit expressions of the elements of the expected information matrix are presented. The expectations of the expressions involved in the components of the information matrix must be calculated numerically. In the particular case where $\alpha = 1$ and $\beta = 0$, so that

$$\varphi(y;\xi,\eta,1,0) = \frac{1}{y\eta}\phi\left(\frac{\log(y)-\xi}{\eta}\right),$$

is the density function of the LN model of location-scale version, the information matrix becomes

$$\mathbf{I}(\boldsymbol{\theta}) = \begin{pmatrix} \frac{1}{\eta^2} & 0 & \frac{\mathbb{E}[\mathrm{sgn}(Z)W]}{\eta} & \frac{1}{\eta}\sqrt{\frac{2}{\pi}} \\ 0 & \frac{2}{\eta^2} & \frac{\mathbb{E}[\mathrm{sgn}(Z)ZW]}{\eta} & 0 \\ \frac{\mathbb{E}[\mathrm{sgn}(Z)W]}{\eta} & \frac{\mathbb{E}[\mathrm{sgn}(Z)ZW]}{\eta} & 1-2(\log 2)^2 & 0 \\ \frac{1}{\eta}\sqrt{\frac{2}{\pi}} & 0 & 0 & \frac{2}{\pi} \end{pmatrix},$$

whose determinant $|\mathbf{I}(\boldsymbol{\theta})| \neq 0$, then the information matrix is non-singular in the neighborhood of $\alpha = 1$ and $\beta = 0$, that is, for the LN model. This is not the case for the model of Azzalini and Dalla Valle [4] for which the Fisher information matrix is singular in the neighborhood of $\lambda = 0$. Furthermore, the upper sub-matrix of size 2×2 corresponds to the Fisher information matrix of the LN model. Therefore, for n large

$$\hat{\boldsymbol{\theta}} \xrightarrow{D} N_4(\boldsymbol{\theta}, \mathbf{I}(\boldsymbol{\theta})^{-1}),$$

$\hat{\boldsymbol{\theta}}$ is consistent and has asymptotic normal distribution with covariance matrix $\mathbf{I}(\boldsymbol{\theta})^{-1}$. Inferences based on confidence intervals and hypothesis testing for the location, scale and shape parameters can be realized by using sampling properties for large samples of the MLE.

3. Simulation Study

This section presents a Monte Carlo simulation study, which was carried out with the objective of evaluating the behavior of the maximum likelihood estimators for the LABPN distribution.

For this simulation, the maxLik function of the statistical software R Development Core Team [17], version 4.2.3 was used and data from the LABPN distribution were generated, considering the values of the parameters: $\xi = 1.0$ and $\eta = 0.5$, and different values of the parameters β and α.

For each scenario, 5000 random samples from the LABPN distribution were generated with the sample sizes $n = 40, 80, 150, 200$ and 500. As quality measures to evaluate the behavior of the MLEs; the bias and the mean square error (MSE) were used. These measurements were calculated as

$$Bias(\hat{\delta}^{(j)}) = \frac{1}{5000}\sum_{i=1}^{5000}(\hat{\delta}_i^{(j)} - \delta^{(j)}),$$

and

$$MSE(\hat{\delta}^{(j)}) = \frac{1}{5000}\sum_{i=1}^{5000}(\hat{\delta}_i^{(j)} - \delta)^2$$

where $\hat{\delta}_i^{(j)}$ is the estimate of $\delta^{(j)}$ for the ith sample. The results of the simulation study are presented in the Table 1.

Table 1. Bias and mean square error (MSE) of maximum likelihood estimates.

		$\beta = -0.5, \alpha = 2.5$		$\beta = 0.5, \alpha = 2.5$		$\beta = -1.0, \alpha = 4.0$		$\beta = 1.0, \alpha = 4.0$	
n	**Estimator**	**Bias**	**MSE**	**Bias**	**MSE**	**Bias**	**MSE**	**Bias**	**MSE**
40	$\widehat{\xi}$	−0.0204	0.0097	0.0214	0.0111	−0.0454	0.0096	0.0453	0.0105
	$\widehat{\eta}$	−0.0553	0.0055	−0.0528	0.0057	−0.0602	0.0063	−0.0607	0.0063
	$\widehat{\beta}$	0.0536	0.0771	−0.0286	0.0994	−0.0507	0.1639	0.0551	0.1720
	$\widehat{\alpha}$	0.9402	2.0237	0.9276	2.0091	0.6232	1.8534	0.6793	2.0535
80	$\widehat{\xi}$	−0.0196	0.0060	0.0207	0.0064	−0.0440	0.0065	0.0444	0.0064
	$\widehat{\eta}$	−0.0458	0.0036	−0.0453	0.0036	−0.0554	0.0044	−0.0556	0.0044
	$\widehat{\beta}$	0.0253	0.0480	−0.0278	0.0505	−0.0360	0.0710	0.0237	0.0605
	$\widehat{\alpha}$	0.5918	0.8999	0.5726	0.8761	0.3439	0.8127	0.3104	0.7778
150	$\widehat{\xi}$	−0.0189	0.0046	0.0205	0.0041	−0.0438	0.0053	0.0439	0.0051
	$\widehat{\eta}$	−0.0435	0.0029	−0.0427	0.0029	−0.0547	0.0039	−0.0533	0.0038
	$\widehat{\beta}$	0.0233	0.0338	−0.0246	0.0321	−0.0226	0.0452	0.0234	0.0469
	$\widehat{\alpha}$	0.4946	0.5760	0.4644	0.5701	0.2630	0.5238	0.2539	0.5615
200	$\widehat{\xi}$	−0.0179	0.0036	0.0203	0.0033	−0.0421	0.0042	0.0403	0.0041
	$\widehat{\eta}$	−0.0414	0.0025	−0.0418	0.0026	−0.0530	0.0035	−0.0521	0.0034
	$\widehat{\beta}$	0.0202	0.0263	−0.0224	0.0245	−0.0164	0.0339	0.0202	0.0360
	$\widehat{\alpha}$	0.4294	0.4353	0.4104	0.4471	0.2315	0.4298	0.2464	0.3938
500	$\widehat{\xi}$	−0.0176	0.0019	0.0201	0.0019	−0.0398	0.0027	0.0383	0.0024
	$\widehat{\eta}$	−0.0401	0.0019	−0.0409	0.0020	−0.0496	0.0028	−0.0492	0.0027
	$\widehat{\beta}$	0.0155	0.0126	−0.0180	0.0123	−0.0103	0.0151	0.0113	0.0137
	$\widehat{\alpha}$	0.3399	0.2192	0.3457	0.2251	0.1605	0.1672	0.1559	0.1709

From the table, it can be seen that in general, as the sample size increases, the bias and the MSE of all parameter estimators tend to decrease and they approach zero. Thus, MLEs are asymptotically consistent and large-sample theory can be used to perform interval estimation of parameters as well as hypothesis testing based on likelihood ratio statistics.

4. Application to the Nickel Content in the Soil Data

For the illustration, we use a data set which was previously analyzed by Bolfarine et al. [13], who fitted the LBSN model. The data consists of 86 samples of nickel content (in Ni(μg g^{-1})) in soil samples analyzed at the Department of Mines of the University of Atacama, Chile. The descriptive statistics for this data set are: $n = 86$, mean $= 21.337$, standard deviation $= 16.639$, skewness $= 2.440$, and kurtosis $= 12.0443$. For this same data set, the skewness and kurtosis coefficients of the logarithm of the nickel content for the 86 samples were also calculated, which were −0.4490 and 3.7344, respectively; therefore, the assumption that the logarithm of the nickel content follows an LN model is inadequate.

Bolfarine et al. [13] found that the LBSN model fitted the nickel content data better than the LN model. As an alternative to the LBSN model, we fitted the LABPN model. To compare our proposal, we also fitted the LN and LSN Azzalini et al. [2] models. The MLEs of the fitted models, which were obtained numerically using the optimal function of the statistical package [17], are presented in the Table 2 with the respective standard errors in parentheses. For obtaining the parameter estimates, we used the optim function from the [17] package.

To compare the fitted models, we computed the estimated values of the AIC Akaike [18], which is given by $AIC = -2\hat{\ell}(\cdot) + 2k$, $BIC = -2\hat{\ell}(\cdot) + \log(n)k$ Schwarz [19], and the modified AIC criterion [20], typically called the consistent AIC, namely, $CAIC = -2\hat{\ell}(\cdot) + (1 + \log(n))k$, where k is the number of parameters for the considered model. The best model is the one with the smallest AIC (or BIC or CAIC). According to the AIC, BIC and CAIC statistics, the best models are the LBSN and LABPN.

Table 2. Estimated parameters (standard error) for the LN, LSN, LBSN and LABPN models.

Parameter	LN	LSN	LBSN	LABPN
ξ	2.828 (0.078)	3.486 (0.154)	1.784 (0.163)	1.689 (0.098)
η	0.728 (0.055)	0.979 (0.128)	0.778 (0.077)	0.937 (0.071)
α			4.958 (3.471)	6.111 (1.170)
β		−1.596 (0.587)	1.253 (0.296)	1.567 (0.324)
AIC	671.6	671.0	665.6	665.6
BIC	676.4	678.3	675.3	675.3
CAIC	678.4	681.3	679.3	679.3

The bimodality hypothesis can also be formally tested from the system of hypotheses

$$H_0 : \alpha = 1 \quad \text{versus} \quad H_1 : \alpha \neq 1,$$

which is equivalent to compare the LSN and LABPN models. Since the Fisher information matrix is non-singular, we used the likelihood-ratio statistic, namely,

$$\Lambda_1 = \frac{\mathcal{L}_{\text{LSN}}(\hat{\xi}, \hat{\eta}, \hat{\beta})}{\mathcal{L}_{\text{LESPN}}(\hat{\xi}, \hat{\eta}, \hat{\beta}, \hat{\alpha})},$$

where $\mathcal{L}(\cdot)$ is the likelihood function.

After substituting the estimated values of the parameters, we have

$$-2\log(\Lambda_1) = -2(-332.5 + 328.8) = 7.4,$$

which is greater than the 5% critical value of the chi-squared distribution, $\chi^2_{1,95\%} = 3.84$. This result leads to the rejection of the null hypothesis; therefore, we conclude that the LABPN model fits best the nickel concentration data.

To compare the LN model with the LABPN model, we considered the system of hypotheses

$$H_0 : (\alpha, \beta) = (1, 0) \quad \text{versus} \quad H_1 : (\alpha, \beta) \neq (1, 0),$$

which can be tested by using the likelihood-ratio statistic given by

$$\Lambda_2 = \frac{\mathcal{L}_{\text{LN}}(\hat{\xi}, \hat{\eta})}{\mathcal{L}_{\text{LABPN}}(\hat{\xi}, \hat{\eta}, \hat{\alpha}, \hat{\beta})}.$$

Considering the estimated values, we get $-2\log(\Lambda_2) = 10$, which is greater than the critical value of the chi-square distribution with two degrees of freedom, $\chi^2_{2,95\%} = 5.99$. Again, we rejected the null hypotheses H_0, and we concluded that the LABPN model fits the nickel content data better than the LN model.

Now, to compare the LBSN and LABPN models, it is necessary to consider a test for non-nested models. Thus, we suppose that $f(y_i|\mathbf{x}_i, \theta)$ and $g(y_i|\mathbf{x}_i, \beta)$ are the corresponding non-nested densities to be compared. To test the hypothesis of no differences between these densities, that is,

$$H_0 : \mathbb{E}\left[\log \frac{f(y_i|\mathbf{x}_i, \theta)}{g(y_i|\mathbf{x}_i, \beta)}\right] = 0,$$

Vuong [21] proposed the likelihood-ratio statistic given by

$$T_{\mathrm{LR,NN}} = \frac{1}{\sqrt{n}} \frac{LR(\hat{\theta}, \hat{\beta})}{\hat{\omega}^2},$$

where

$$\hat{\omega}^2 = \frac{1}{n}\sum_{i=1}^{n}\left(\log\frac{f(y_i|\mathbf{x}_i,\hat{\theta})}{g(y_i|\mathbf{x}_i,\hat{\beta})}\right)^2 - \left(\frac{1}{n}\sum_{i=1}^{n}\left(\log\frac{f(y_i|\mathbf{x}_i,\hat{\theta})}{g(y_i|\mathbf{x}_i,\hat{\beta})}\right)\right)^2,$$

is an estimator for the variance of $\frac{1}{\sqrt{n}}LR(\hat{\theta}, \hat{\beta})$. One can show that, under H_0, if $n \to \infty$, then

$$T_{\mathrm{LR,NN}} \xrightarrow{D} N(0,1).$$

The null hypothesis of equivalence of the models is rejected at significance level δ in favor of the LABPN model, that is, better fit (or worse fit) compared to the LBSN model, if $T_{\mathrm{LR,NN}} > z_{\delta/2}$ (or $T_{\mathrm{LR,NN}} < -z_{\delta/2}$). For the nickel concentration data, we obtained $T_{LR,NN} = -0.54$, which is less than the critical value $z_{0.025} = 1.96$; therefore, there are no statistical differences between the LBSN and LABPN models. In this way, the LABPN model is a useful alternative to fit the nickel concentration data. Figure 2 shows the fitted densities and QQplot plots for the LSN and LABPN models. These plots also show evidence that the LABPN model fits better than the other considered models. The QQplot in Figure 2c also shows that the LABPN model has a good fit.

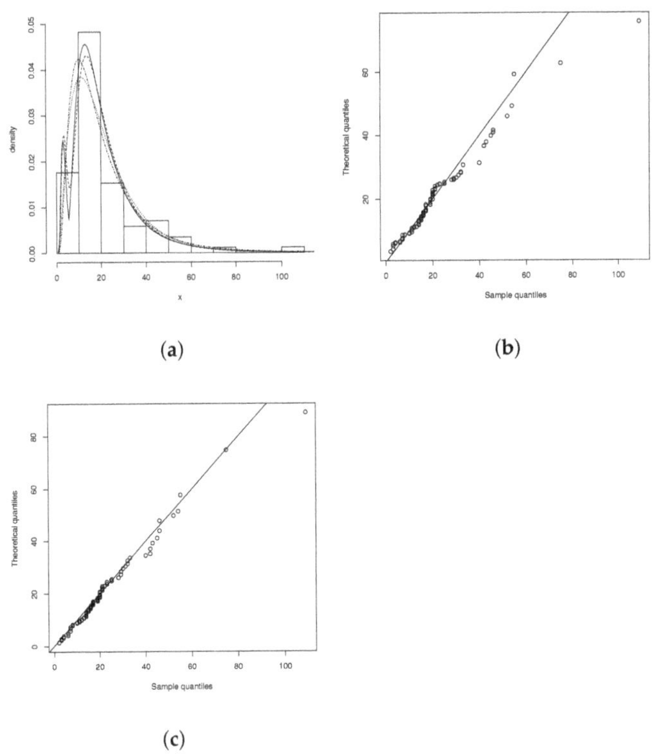

Figure 2. (**a**) Histogram for the nickel concentration variable. Densities fitted by maximum likelihood: LN (dotted-dashed line), LSN (dotted line), BLSN (dashed line) and LABPN (solid line), (**b**) QQplot LSN and (**c**) QQplot LABPN.

5. Concluding Remarks

In this work, a new family of parametric distributions capable of fitting unimodal and bimodal positive data is introduced. The main properties of the new family were studied. This new family is obtained by considering the Arnold et al. [12] and Durrans [7] models and extends some existing models in the literature, among them, the log-normal, log-skew norm, log-bimodal-skew-normal and log-bimodal-power-normal. This new distribution is also very flexible and can fit unimodal and bimodal data with high (or low) degrees of skewness and kurtosis. To obtain the estimates of the parameters in the model, a classical approach was considered by using the maximum likelihood method together with iterative Newton–Raphson algorithms for the optimization of the likelihood function. The score functions were presented and the Fisher information matrix was shown to be non-singular, which allows statistical inference to be carried out through the theory of large samples and the use of likelihood-ratio statistics. The applicability of the new family was illustrated by considering a data set corresponding to nickel content in soil samples. The results showed better fit of the proposed family compared to other existing models in the literature.

Author Contributions: Conceptualization, G.M.-F. and R.T.-F.; methodology, G.M.-F., R.T.-F. and H.B.; software, G.M.-F. and R.T.-F.; validation, G.M.-F., R.T.-F. and H.B.; formal analysis, G.M.-F. and R.T.-F.; investigation, G.M.-F. and R.T.-F.; resources, G.M.-F. and R.T.-F.; data curation, G.M.-F. and R.T.-F.; writing—original draft preparation, G.M.-F. and R.T.-F.; writing—review and editing, G.M.-F., R.T.-F. and H.B.; visualization, G.M.-F. and R.T.-F.; supervision, G.M.-F. and R.T.-F.; project administration, G.M.-F. and R.T.-F.; funding acquisition, G.M.-F. and R.T.-F. All authors have read and agreed to the published version of the manuscript.

Funding: The research of G. Martinez-Flórez and R. Tovar-Falón was supported by Fondo de Investigación de la Vicerrectoría de Investigación, Universidad de Córdoba, Colombia.

Institutional Review Board Statement: Not applicable.

Informed Consent Statement: Not applicable.

Data Availability Statement: Details about available data are given in Section 3.

Acknowledgments: G. Martínez-Flórez and R. Tovar-Falón acknowledge the support given by Universidad de Córdoba, Montería, Colombia.

Conflicts of Interest: The authors declare no conflict of interest.

Appendix A. Information Matrix Elements

If the elements of the observed information matrix are denoted by $k_{\xi\xi}, k_{\eta\xi}, \ldots, k_{\beta\beta}, \ldots, k_{\alpha\alpha}$, then you have to

$$
\begin{aligned}
k_{\xi\xi} &= \frac{n}{\eta^2} + \frac{\alpha-1}{\eta^2}\sum_{i=1}^{n} w_i(w_i + |z_i|) + \frac{\beta^2}{\eta^2}\sum_{i=1}^{n} w_{1i}(\beta z_i + w_{1i}), \\
k_{\eta\xi} &= \frac{2n}{\eta^2}\bar{z} + \frac{\alpha-1}{\eta^2}\sum_{i=1}^{n} \operatorname{sgn}(z_i) w_i(-1 + |z_i|(w_i + |z_i|)) \\
&\quad -\frac{\beta}{\eta^2}\sum_{i=1}^{n} w_{1i}(1 - \beta z_i(\beta z_i + w_{1i})), \\
k_{\beta\xi} &= \frac{1}{\eta}\sum_{i=1}^{n} w_{1i}(1 - \beta z_i(\beta z_i + w_{1i})), \\
k_{\eta\eta} &= -\frac{n}{\eta^2} + \frac{3}{\eta^2}\sum_{i=1}^{n} z_i^2 + \frac{\alpha-1}{\eta^2}\sum_{i=1}^{n} |z_i| w_i(-2 + |z_i|(w_i + |z_i|)) \\
&\quad +\frac{\beta}{\eta^2}\sum_{i=1}^{n} z_i w_{1i}(-2 + \beta z_i(\beta z_i + w_{1i})),
\end{aligned}
$$

$$
\begin{aligned}
k_{\beta\eta} &= \frac{1}{\eta}\sum_{i=1}^{n} z_i w_{1i}(1-\beta z_i(\beta z_i + w_{1i})),\\
k_{\beta\beta} &= \sum_{i=1}^{n} z_i^2 w_{1i}(\beta z_i + w_{1i}), \quad k_{\alpha\xi} = \frac{1}{\eta}\sum_{i=1}^{n}\text{sgn}(z_i)w_i,\\
k_{\alpha\eta} &= \frac{1}{\eta}\sum_{i=1}^{n}|z_i|w_i, \quad k_{\alpha\beta}=0, \quad k_{\alpha\alpha} = n\Big(\alpha^{-2} - 2^{\alpha}(2^{\alpha}-1)^{-2}(\log 2)^2\Big),
\end{aligned}
$$

where $w_{1i} = \phi(\beta z_i)/\Phi(\beta z_i)$. After making some calculations, the elements of the expected information matrix are given by

$$
\begin{aligned}
I_{\xi\xi} &= \frac{1}{\eta^2} + \frac{(\alpha-1)}{\eta^2}(\mathbb{E}(|Z|W) + \mathbb{E}(W^2)) + \frac{\beta^2}{\eta^2}(\beta\mathbb{E}(ZW_1) + \mathbb{E}(W_1^2)),\\
I_{\xi\eta} &= \frac{2}{\eta^2}\mathbb{E}(Z) + \frac{(\alpha-1)}{\eta^2}(\mathbb{E}(\text{sgn}(Z)Z^2W) + \mathbb{E}(ZW^2) - \mathbb{E}(\text{sgn}(Z)W))\\
&\quad + \frac{\beta}{\eta^2}(\beta^2\mathbb{E}(Z^2W_1) + \beta\mathbb{E}(ZW_1^2) - \mathbb{E}(W_1)),\\
I_{\xi\alpha} &= \frac{1}{\eta}\mathbb{E}(\text{sgn}(Z)W),\\
I_{\xi\beta} &= \frac{1}{\eta}(\beta^2\mathbb{E}(Z^2W_1) + \beta\mathbb{E}(ZW_1^2) - \mathbb{E}(W_1)),\\
I_{\eta\eta} &= -\frac{1}{\eta^2} + \frac{3}{\eta^2}\mathbb{E}(Z^2) + \frac{(\alpha-1)}{\eta^2}(-2\mathbb{E}(|Z|W) + \mathbb{E}(Z^3W) + \mathbb{E}(Z^2W^2))\\
&\quad + \frac{\beta}{\eta}(\beta^2\mathbb{E}(Z^3W_1) + \beta\mathbb{E}(Z^2W_1^2) - 2\mathbb{E}(ZW_1)),\\
I_{\eta\alpha} &= \frac{1}{\eta}\mathbb{E}(|Z|W),\\
I_{\eta\beta} &= \frac{1}{\eta}(\beta^2\mathbb{E}(Z^3W_1) + \beta\mathbb{E}(Z^2W_1^2) - \mathbb{E}(ZW_1)),\\
I_{\beta\beta} &= \frac{1}{\eta}(\beta\mathbb{E}(Z^3W_1) + \beta\mathbb{E}(Z^2W_1^2)),\\
I_{\beta\alpha} &= 0,\\
I_{\alpha\alpha} &= \frac{1}{\alpha^2} - \frac{2^{\alpha}(\log 2)^2}{(2^{\alpha}-1)^2},
\end{aligned}
$$

where $W = \phi(|Z|)/\Phi(|Z|)$ and $W_1 = \phi(\beta Z)/\Phi(\beta Z)$.

References

1. Ahrens, L.H. The lognormal distribution of the elements (A fundamental law of geochemistry and its subsidiary). *Geochim. Cosmochim. Acta* **1954**, *5*, 49–73. [CrossRef]
2. Azzalini, A.; Cappello, D.; Kotz, S. Log-skew-normal and log-skew-*t* distributions as models for family income data. *J. Income Distrib.* **2002**, *11*, 12–20. [CrossRef]
3. Azzalini, A. A class of distributions which includes the normal ones. *Scand. J. Stat.* **1985**, *12*, 171–178.
4. Azzalini, A.; Dalla Valle, A. The multivariate skew-normal distribution. *Biometrika* **1996**, *83*, 715–726. [CrossRef]
5. Henze, N. A probabilistic representation of the skew-normal distribution. *Scand. J. Stat.* **1986**, *13*, 271–275.
6. Chiogna, M. Some results on the scalar Skew-normal distribution. *J. Ital. Stat. Soc.* **1998**, *1*, 1–14. [CrossRef]
7. Durrans, S.R. Distributions of fractional order statistics in hydrology. *Water Resour. Res.* **1992**, *28*, 1649–1655. [CrossRef]
8. Gupta, R.C.; Gupta, R.D. Analyzing skewed data by power normal model. *Test* **2008**, *17*, 197–210. [CrossRef]
9. Pewsey, A.; Gómez, H.W.; Bolfarine, H. Likelihood-based inference for power distributions. *Test* **2012**, *21*, 775–789. [CrossRef]
10. Martínez-Flórez, G.; Bolfarine, H.; Gómez, H.W. The log-power-normal distribution with application to air pollution. *Environmetrics* **2014**, *25*, 44–56. [CrossRef]

11. Martínez-Flórez, G.; Bolfarine, H.; Gómez, H.W. Asymmetric regression models with limited responses with an application to antibody response to vaccine. *Biom. J.* **2013**, *55*, 156–172. [CrossRef]
12. Arnold, B.C.; Gómez, H.W.; Salinas, H.S. On Multiple Constraint Skewed Models. *Stat. J. Theor. Appl. Stat.* **2009**, *43*, 279–293. [CrossRef]
13. Bolfarine, H.; Gómez, H.W.; Rivas, L. The log-bimodal-skew-normal model. A geochemical application. *J. Chemom.* **2011**, *25*, 329–332. [CrossRef]
14. Bolfarine, H.; Martínez-Flórez, G.; Salinas, H.S. Bimodal symmetric-asymmetric power-normal families. *Commun. Stat. Theory Methods* **2018**, *47*, 259–276. [CrossRef]
15. Lin, G.D.; Stoyanov, J. The logarithmic Skew-Normal distributions are Moment-Indeterminate. *J. Appl. Probab. Trust.* **2009**, *46*, 909–916. [CrossRef]
16. Arnold, B.C.; Lin, G.D. Characterization of the skew-normal and generalized chi distributions. *Sankhyā* **2004**, *66*, 593–606.
17. R Development Core Team. *R: A Language and Environment for Statistical Computing*; R Foundation for Statistical Computing: Vienna, Austria, 2023. Available online: http://www.R-project.org (accessed on 31 May 2023).
18. Akaike H. A new look at statistical model identification. *IEEE Trans. Autom. Control.* **1974**, *19*, 716–722. [CrossRef]
19. Schwarz, G. Estimating the dimension of a model. *Ann. Stat.* **1978**, *61*, 461–464. [CrossRef]
20. Bozdogan, H. Model selection and Akaike's information criterion (AIC): The general theory and its analytical extensions. *Psychometrika* **1987**, *52*, 345–370. [CrossRef]
21. Vuong, Q.H. Likelihood tatio tests for model selection and non-nested hypotheses. *Econometrica* **1989**, *57*, 307–333. [CrossRef]

mathematics

MDPI

Article

Bivariate Unit-Weibull Distribution: Properties and Inference

Roger Tovar-Falón *,†, Guillermo Martínez-Flórez *,† and Luis Páez-Martínez

Departamento de Matemáticas y Estadística, Facultad de Ciencias Básicas, Universidad de Córdoba, Monteria 230002, Colombia; lpaezmartinez03@correo.unicordoba.edu.co
* Correspondence: rjtovar@correo.unicordoba.edu.co (R.T.-F.); guillermomartinez@correo.unicordoba.edu.co (G.M.-F.)
† These authors contributed equally to this work.

Abstract: In this article, we introduce a novel bivariate probability distribution that is absolutely continuous. Considering the Farlie–Gumbel–Morgenstern (FGM) copula and the unit-Weibull distribution, we can obtain a bivariate unit-Weibull distribution. We evaluate the main properties of the new proposal and use two estimation methods to estimate the parameter for the bivariate probability distribution. A brief Monte Carlo simulation study is conducted to assess the behavior of the employed estimation method and the characteristics of the estimators. Ultimately, as an illustration, a real-life application is presented, demonstrating the utility of the proposal.

Keywords: bivariate probability distribution; distribution for bounded data; proportion data; two-step estimation; copula

MSC: 60E05; 62H05

1. Introduction

The probability distribution of proportion or rate data has been extensively studied as it is a prevalent finding in research across all domains of knowledge. The beta distribution is perhaps the most widely recognized. Furthermore, many extensions have been made, such as the beta regression model proposed by Ferrari and Cribari-Neto [1], studied later by Branscum et al. [2], and the beta distribution with an excess of zeros and/or ones of Ospina and Ferrari [3], which was extended to the class of inflated beta regression models, see [4], among others. Other outstanding works are those of Paolino [5], Cribari-Neto and Vasconcellos [6], Kieschnick and Mccullough [7] and Vasconcellos and Cribari-Neto [8].

Alternatives to the beta distribution for analysis of bounded data have been considered by other authors. Martínez-Flórez et al. [9] introduced a mixture model between a Bernoulli process and the power normal distribution to model proportions or rates with inflation at zero and/or one values. Given the flexibility of the power normal distribution to fit high degrees of kurtosis and skewness, this proposal is a viable alternative to the beta model. On the other hand, from the logarithmic transformation of the type $X = \exp(-Y)$, where Y is an absolutely continuous random variable with positive support, it is possible to define new families of adequate distributions to fit data in the interval $(0, 1)$. Such obtained distributions are generically called unit-f, where f is the density to which the transformation is applied. Based on this idea, the unit-Gamma distribution, see [10], the log-Lindley distribution, see [11], and unit-Weibull, unit-Birnbaum–Saunders and unit-Lindley distributions, see work by Mazucheli et al. [12–14], have been developed. In addition, Martínez-Flórez et al. [15] introduced a class of distributions to model rates and proportions through an extension of the alpha-power extension of the skew normal distribution. The authors proposed a regression model based on this distribution for bounded responses.

An extension of the unit-Birnbaum–Saunders distribution and its associated regression model was introduced by Martínez-Flórez and Tovar-Falón [16], while another proposed method capable of fitting data between zeros and/or ones (inclusive) with inflation on the zeros/ones values was considered by Martínez-Flórez et al. [17].

Although there are many proposals developed to model proportion or rate data, there are few works that address the problem of this type of response from a multivariate perspective, that is, models capable of jointly modeling two or more responses in the interval $(0,1)$ in such a way that the possible correlations existing in the responses can be considered. In relation to this, some authors have recently made some contributions, among which the works of Lemonte and Moreno-Arenas [18] and more recently Martínez-Flórez et al. [19] stand out.

This paper aims to introduce a novel multivariate distribution to handle responses in the region $(0,1) \times (0.1)$ jointly. The new distribution, which is called the bivariate unit-Weibull distribution is obtained from an extension of the univariate unit-Weibull distribution introduced by Mazucheli et al. [12] by using the Farlie–Gumbel–Morgenstern (FGM) copula, see [20].

In all areas of knowledge, the proposed model can be used to model proportion, rate, or index data. Particularly in the field of engineering, it is common to come across this type of information as a result of investigations, for example, to model the percentage of carbon dioxide and the concentration of ozone in the atmosphere, see [21,22], among others. The proposal can also prove to be advantageous for analyzing data sets from other domains of study, such as the social sciences and civic culture. For instance, it can be utilized to analyze data on laws pertaining to drunk driving and traffic fatalities in 48 states in the United States of America, see [23], or data on the Human Development Index and illiteracy rate, see [18,24].

The main benefits of using this proposal are related to the applicability of a usual regression model, which is the prediction or estimate of the mean response, given the values of the covariates considered in the model. Studying the relationship between the dependent variables and the covariates in such a way means that that this can be used in making decisions that help solve real-life problems.

The univariate unit-Weibull distribution has the follow cumulative distribution function (cdf) and probability density function (pdf), respectively.

$$F(y;\alpha,\beta) = \exp\left(-\alpha(-\log y)^{\beta}\right); \quad 0 < y < 1, \tag{1}$$

where $\alpha, \beta > 0$, and

$$f(y;\alpha,\beta) = (1/y) \times \alpha\beta(-\log y)^{\beta-1} \exp\left(-\alpha(-\log y)^{\beta}\right); \quad 0 < y < 1, \tag{2}$$

where α, β are the scale and shape parameters, respectively. More details and properties of the univariate unit-Weibull distribution can be found in [12].

The following describes the remainder of the article. Section 2 presents the bivariate UW distribution and some of its structural properties are also derived. In Section 3, the statistical inference process is carried out considering two estimation methods. The expected and observed information matrices are also derived. The outcomes of a simulation study and its corresponding discourse are presented in Section 4. Finally, application to real data is provided in Section 5.

2. Bivariate Unit-Weibull Distribution

In this section, a bivariate extension of the unit-Weibull (UW) distribution [12] is proposed. This extension is obtained from the Farlie–Gumbel–Morgenstern (FGM) copula discussed by Gumbel [20] and is called the bivariate unit-Weibull (BVUW) distribution. This new distribution is very attractive, since it allows modeling bivariate data whose response lies on the plane $(0,1)^2$.

To introduce the BVUW distribution, we follow the idea of Almetwally et al. [25] using the FMG copula. Thus, according to the theorem of Sklar [26], Definition 1 follows.

Definition 1. *A random vector* $X = (X_1, X_2)^\top$ *is said to have a BVUW distribution, if its joint pdf is given by,*

$$f(x_1, x_2) = \frac{1}{x_1}\alpha_1\beta_1(-\ln x_1)^{\beta_1-1}e^{-\alpha_1(-\ln x_1)^{\beta_1}}\frac{1}{x_2}\alpha_2\beta_2(-\ln x_2)^{\beta_2-1}e^{-\alpha_2(-\ln x_2)^{\beta_2}}$$
$$\times\left(1+\theta\left(1-2e^{-\alpha_1(-\ln x_1)^{\beta_1}}\right)\left(1-2e^{-\alpha_2(-\ln x_2)^{\beta_2}}\right)\right), \quad 0 < x_1, x_2 < 1, \qquad (3)$$

where $-1 < \theta < 1$ *and* $\alpha_1, \alpha_2, \beta_1, \beta_2 > 0$.

For the joint pdf given in (3), the notation BVUW$(\alpha_1, \alpha_2, \beta_1, \beta_2, \theta)$ is used. The picture in Figure 1 shows how the BVUW distribution looks in three dimensions for certain values of α_1, α_2, β_1, β_2 and θ. In the figure, one can observe the different shapes that the UW density can fit, for example, symmetrical and asymmetrical shapes in the shape of a bell or a bathtub.

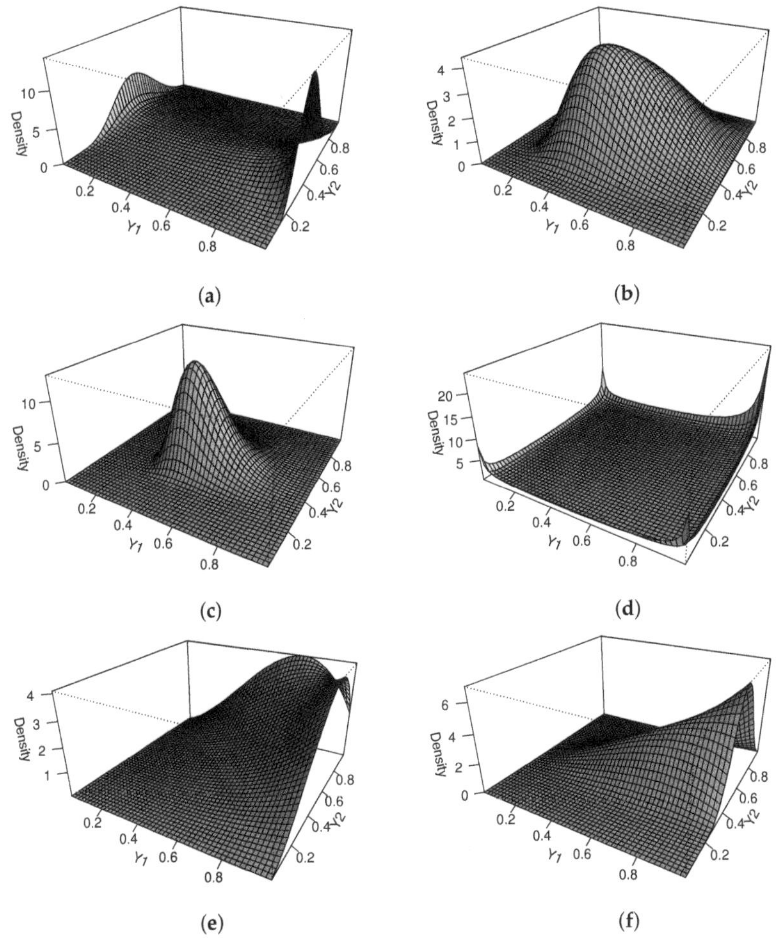

Figure 1. Joint probability density function of the BVUW distribution with parameter vector $\varphi = (\alpha_1, \alpha_2, \beta_1, \beta_2, \theta)$ for **(a)** $\varphi = (1.0, 1.5, 0.5, 2.5, -0.75)$ **(b)** $\varphi = (1.5, 1.5, 2.0, 2.0, 0.75)$, **(c)** $\varphi = (2.0, 2.0, 3.5, 3.5, 0.25)$, **(d)** $\varphi = (1.0, 1.0, 0.5, 0.5, 0.25)$, **(e)** $\varphi = (2.5, 2.5, 1.0, 1.0, -0.75)$, **(f)** $\varphi = (2.5, 2.5, 1.0, 2.5, 0.75)$.

The joint cdf of the BUW distribution can be written as

$$F(x_1,x_2) = e^{-\alpha_1(-\ln x_1)^{\beta_1}} e^{-\alpha_2(-\ln x_2)^{\beta_2}} \left[1+\theta\left(1-e^{-\alpha_1(-\ln x_1)^{\beta_1}}\right)\left(1-e^{-\alpha_2(-\ln x_2)^{\beta_2}}\right)\right] \quad (4)$$

where $-1 < \theta < 1; 0 < x_1, x_2 < 1; \alpha_1, \alpha_2, \beta_1, \beta_2 > 0$.

From Definition 1, we have the following theorem.

Theorem 1. *Let* $(X_1, X_2) \sim BVUW(\alpha_1, \alpha_2, \beta_1, \beta_2, \rho)$, *then*

1. $X_j \sim UW(\alpha_j, \beta_j)$ *for* $j = 1, 2$.
2. *The pdf of* X_1, *given* $X_2 = x_2$, *is*

$$f(x_1 \mid x_2) = \frac{1}{x_1}\alpha_1\beta_1(-\ln x_1)^{\beta_1-1}u(x_1)\left[1+\theta(1-2u(x_1))(1-2u(x_2))\right]$$

where $u(x_j) = e^{-\alpha_j(-\ln x_j)^{\beta_j}}$, *for* $j = 1, 2$,

3. *The pdf of* X_i, *given* $X_2 = x_2$, *is*

$$f(x_i \mid x_j) = \frac{1}{x_i}\alpha_i\beta_i(-\ln x_i)^{\beta_i-1}e^{-\alpha_i(-\ln x_i)^{\beta_i}}\left[1+\theta(1-2u(x_i))(1-2u(x_j))\right]$$

where $u(x_i) = e^{-\alpha_i(-\ln x_i)^{\beta_i}}$, *for* $i = 1, 2$.

4. *The cdf* X_i, *given* $X_2 = x_2$, *is*

$$F(x_i \mid x_j) = (1+\theta)u(x_i) - \theta e^{-2\alpha_i(-\ln y_i)^{\beta_i}} - 2\theta u(x_i)u(x_j) + 2\theta e^{-\alpha_j(-\ln y_j)^{\beta_j} - 2\alpha_i(-\ln y_i)^{\beta_i}}.$$

2.1. Generating Random Variables

The conditional distribution method proposed by Nelsen [27] is employed to generate a random sample from a joint unit-Weibull distribution. It is noteworthy that the joint distribution function can be formulated as follows,

$$f(x_1, x_2) = f(x_1)f(x_2 \mid x_1)$$

By utilizing the subsequent procedures, we can generate a bivariate sample by utilizing the conditional approach.

1. From a uniform $(0, 1)$ distribution, generate U_1 and U_2 independently of each other.
2. Let $X_1 = \exp\left(-(-\ln U_1/\alpha_1)^{1/\beta_1}\right)$.
3. Allow $F(x_2 \mid x_1) = U_2$ to determine X_2 through numerical simulation.
4. Repeat Steps 1 to 3 n times to get the result $(x_{1i}, x_{2i}), i = 1, 2, \ldots, n$.

2.2. Product Moments

Proposition 1. *Let* $\mathbf{X} = (X_1, X_2)^\top$ *be a random vector with a* $BVUW(\boldsymbol{\varphi})$ *distribution, with* $\boldsymbol{\varphi} = (\alpha_1, \alpha_2, \beta_1, \beta_1, \theta)$; *then, the rth and sth moments about zero can be computed in the following way*

$$\begin{aligned}\mu_{rs} &= E(X_1^r X_2^s) \\ &= \int_0^1\int_0^1 x_1^r x_2^s \frac{1}{x_1}\alpha_1\beta_1(-\ln x_1)^{\beta_1-1}e^{-\alpha_1(-\ln x_1)^{\beta_1}} \frac{1}{x_2}\alpha_2\beta_2(-\ln x_2)^{\beta_2-1}e^{-\alpha_2(-\ln x_2)^{\beta_2}} \\ &\quad \times \left(1+\theta\left(1-2e^{-\alpha_1(-\ln x_1)^{\beta_1}}\right)\left(1-2e^{-\alpha_2(-\ln x_2)^{\beta_2}}\right)\right)dx_1dx_2 \end{aligned} \quad (5)$$

2.3. Correlation Coefficient

Let $\mathbf{X} = (X_1, X_2)^\top$ be a random vector with a BVUW($\boldsymbol{\varphi}$) distribution, then the correlation coefficient between X_1 and X_2 is given by:

$$\rho = cor(Y_1, Y_2) = \frac{E(Y_1Y_2) - E(Y_1)E(Y_2)}{\sigma_1\sigma_2} \tag{6}$$

where

$$\sigma_j = \sqrt{E(Y_j - E(Y_j))^2} \quad \text{for} \quad j = 1, 2.$$

By means of a numerical simulation carried out in the R Development Core Team [28] software, it was found that the range of possible values for the correlation coefficient is:

$$-\frac{1}{3} \leq \rho \leq \frac{1}{3}$$

Table 1 shows some values of the correlation coefficient for certain parameters.

Table 1. Correlation coefficient values for some selected parameter values.

α_1	α_2	β_1	β_2	θ	ρ
3.0	2.0	1.0	1.0	−0.75	−0.235
3.0	2.0	1.0	1.0	−0.25	−0.078
3.0	2.0	1.0	1.0	0.25	0.078
3.0	2.0	1.0	1.0	0.75	0.235
1.5	2.5	1.0	1.0	−0.99	−0.317
1.5	2.5	1.0	1.0	0.50	0.160
4.5	1.5	1.0	1.0	−0.99	−0.307
4.5	1.5	1.0	1.0	0.99	0.307
7.0	2.0	1.0	1.0	−0.90	−0.269
7.0	2.0	1.0	1.0	−0.50	−0.150
7.0	2.0	1.0	1.0	−0.10	−0.030
3.5	1.8	1.0	1.0	0.90	0.281
2.0	12	1.0	2.5	−0.80	−0.258
3.5	1.8	1.8	1.5	0.99	0.325
0.9	3.0	1.0	1.0	−0.990	−0.315

2.4. Reliability Function

The joint survival function can be expressed as a copula of its marginal survival functions using the reliability function, where X_1 and X_2 are random variables with survival functions $\bar{F}(x_1)$ and $\bar{F}(x_2)$, see Almetwally et al. [25].

Proposition 2. *The reliability function of the marginal unit-Weibull distributions for the univariate case is given as follows:*

$$R(x_j) = 1 - F(x_j) = 1 - e^{-\alpha_j(-\ln x_j)^{\beta_j}}; \quad 0 < x_j < 1, \quad \alpha, \beta > 0, \quad j = 1, 2.$$

Proposition 3. *The joint survival function for the FGM copula Nelsen [27] is*

$$H(x_1, x_2) = 1 - F(x_1) - F(x_2) + C(F(x_1), F(x_2)).$$

It then follows that the reliability function of the joint FGM distribution for the bivariate UW distribution is

$$\begin{aligned} H(x_1, x_2) &= 1 - e^{-\alpha_1(-\ln x_1)^{\beta_1}} - e^{-\alpha_2(-\ln x_2)^{\beta_2}} \\ &\quad + e^{-\alpha_1(-\ln x_1)^{\beta_1}} e^{-\alpha_2(-\ln x_2)^{\beta_2}} \left[1 + \theta\left(1 - e^{-\alpha_1(-\ln x_1)^{\beta_1}}\right)\left(1 - e^{-\alpha_2(-\ln x_2)^{\beta_2}}\right)\right]. \end{aligned}$$

Proposition 4. *Basu [29] defines the hazard function for the bivariate case as*

$$h(x_1, x_2) = \frac{f(x_1, x_2)}{H(x_1, x_2)}.$$

Then, the hazard function of the FGM joint BUW distribution is,

$$h(x_1, x_2) = \frac{\frac{1}{x_1}\alpha_1\beta_1(-\ln x_1)^{\beta_1-1}e^{-\alpha_1(-\ln x_1)^{\beta_1}}\frac{1}{y_2}\alpha_2\beta_2(-\ln x_2)^{\beta_2-1}e^{-\alpha_2(-\ln x_2)^{\beta_2}}}{1-F(x_1)-F(x_2)+e^{-\alpha_1(-\ln x_1)^{\beta_1}}e^{-\alpha_2(-\ln x_2)^{\beta_2}}\left[1+\theta\left(1-e^{-\alpha_1(-\ln x_1)^{\beta_1}}\right)\left(1-e^{-\alpha_2(-\ln x_2)^{\beta_2}}\right)\right]}$$
$$\times\left(1+\theta\left(1-2e^{-\alpha_1(-\ln x_1)^{\beta_1}}\right)\left(1-2e^{-\alpha_2(-\ln x_2)^{\beta_2}}\right)\right).$$

3. Statistical Inference for the BUW Distribution

In this section, two distinct estimation techniques are presented that are employed to estimate the parameters of the BVUW distribution, namely, maximum likelihood estimation (MLE) and estimation by inference functions for margins (IFM). These methods were also considered by Almetwally et al. [25].

3.1. Maximum Likelihood Estimation (MLE)

Under this parametric method, the MLE is found to estimate the parameters of the model jointly and in a single step. The log-likelihood function is given by

$$\ln L = \sum_{i=1}^{n}[\ln(f_1(x_{1i})f_2(x_{2i})c(F_1(x_{1i}), F_2(x_{2i}); \theta))]$$

To obtain estimates for each parameter, we use the log-likelihood function. We define

$$\begin{aligned} a(x_j; \alpha_j, \beta_j) &= 1 - 2F(x_j; \alpha_j, \beta_j) \\ &= 1 - 2e^{-\alpha_j(-\ln x_j)^{\beta_j}}, \quad j = 1, 2. \end{aligned}$$

A bivariate unit-Weibull distribution has a likelihood function defined by

$$L = (\alpha_1\alpha_2\beta_1\beta_2)^n \prod_{i=1}^{n}\left(\frac{1}{x_{1i}}\frac{1}{x_{2i}}(-\ln x_{1i})^{\beta_1-1}(-\ln x_{2i})^{\beta_2-1}\right)e^{-\sum_{i=1}^{n}\alpha_1(-\ln x_1)^{\beta_1}-\sum_{i=1}^{n}\alpha_2(-\ln x_2)^{\beta_2}}$$
$$\times\prod_{i=1}^{n}(1+\theta(a(x_{1i};\alpha_1,\beta_1))(a(x_{2i};\alpha_2,\beta_2))).$$

The corresponding log-likelihood function of a BVUW distribution is subsequently provided by

$$\begin{aligned} \ln L = {} & n(\ln\alpha_1 + \ln\beta_1 + \ln\alpha_2 + \ln\beta_2) + \sum_{i=1}^{n}\ln\left(\frac{1}{x_{1i}}\right) + \sum_{i=1}^{n}\ln\left(\frac{1}{x_{2i}}\right) \\ & + (\beta_1 - 1)\sum_{i=1}^{n}\ln(-\ln x_{1i}) + (\beta_2 - 1)\sum_{i=1}^{n}\ln(-\ln x_{2i}) \\ & - \sum_{i=1}^{n}\alpha_1(-\ln x_1)^{\beta_1} - \sum_{i=1}^{n}\alpha_2(-\ln x_2)^{\beta_2} \\ & + \sum_{i=1}^{n}\ln(1+\theta(a(y_{1i};\alpha_1,\beta_1))(a(y_{2i};\alpha_2,\beta_2))) \end{aligned}$$

To obtain the estimations, we equate the derivatives of the log-likelihood function with respect to each parameter to zero. This is performed by determining the equation score in the following manner:

$$\frac{\partial \ln L}{\partial \alpha_1} = \frac{n}{\alpha_1} - \sum_{i=1}^{n}(-\ln x_{1i})^{\beta_1} + \sum_{i=1}^{n} \frac{2\theta(a(x_{2i};\alpha_2,\beta_2))(-\ln x_{1i})^{\beta_1} e^{-\alpha_1(-\ln x_{1i})^{\beta_1}}}{(1+\theta(a(x_{1i};\alpha_1,\beta_1))(a(x_{2i};\alpha_2,\beta_2)))}$$

$$\frac{\partial \ln L}{\partial \alpha_2} = \frac{n}{\alpha_2} - \sum_{i=1}^{n}(-\ln x_{2i})^{\beta_2} + \sum_{i=1}^{n} \frac{2\theta(a(x_{1i};\alpha_1,\beta_1))(-\ln x_{2i})^{\beta_2} e^{-\alpha_2(-\ln x_{2i})^{\beta_2}}}{(1+\theta(a(x_{1i};\alpha_1,\beta_1))(a(x_{2i};\alpha_2,\beta_2)))}$$

$$\begin{aligned}\frac{\partial \ln L}{\partial \beta_1} &= \frac{n}{\beta_1} + \sum_{i=1}^{n}\ln(-\ln x_{1i}) - \sum_{i=1}^{n}\alpha_1(-\ln x_{1i})^{\beta_1}\ln(-\ln x_{1i}) \\ &- \sum_{i=1}^{n} \frac{2\alpha_1\theta(a(x_{2i};\alpha_2,\beta_2))\ln(-\ln x_{1i})(-\ln x_{1i})^{\beta_1} e^{-\alpha_1(-\ln x_{1i})^{\beta_1}}}{(1+\theta(a(x_{1i};\alpha_1,\beta_1))(a(x_{2i};\alpha_2,\beta_2)))}\end{aligned}$$

$$\begin{aligned}\frac{\partial \ln L}{\partial \beta_2} &= \frac{n}{\beta_2} + \sum_{i=1}^{n}\ln(-\ln x_{2i}) - \sum_{i=1}^{n}\alpha_1(-\ln x_{2i})^{\beta_2}\ln(-\ln x_{2i}) \\ &- \sum_{i=1}^{n} \frac{2\alpha_2\theta(a(x_{1i};\alpha_1,\beta_1))\ln(-\ln x_{2i})(-\ln x_{2i})^{\beta_2} e^{-\alpha_2(-\ln x_{2i})^{\beta_2}}}{(1+\theta(a(x_{1i};\alpha_1,\beta_1))(a(x_{2i};\alpha_2,\beta_2)))}\end{aligned}$$

and

$$\frac{\partial \ln L}{\partial \theta} = \sum_{i=1}^{n} \frac{(a(x_{1i};\alpha_1,\beta_1))(a(x_{2i};\alpha_2,\beta_2))}{(1+\theta(a(x_{1i};\alpha_1,\beta_1))(a(x_{2i};\alpha_2,\beta_2)))}$$

The MLE $\widehat{\boldsymbol{\varphi}} = (\widehat{\alpha}_1, \widehat{\beta}_1, \widehat{\alpha}_2, \widehat{\beta}_2, \widehat{\theta})$ can be obtained by simultaneously solving the score equations.

It is possible to obtain the MLE $\widehat{\boldsymbol{\varphi}} = (\widehat{\alpha}_1, \widehat{\beta}_1, \widehat{\alpha}_2, \widehat{\beta}_2, \widehat{\theta})$ by solving the score equation,

$$\frac{\partial \ln L}{\partial \theta} = 0, \quad \frac{\partial \ln L}{\partial \beta_j} = 0, \quad \frac{\partial \ln L}{\partial \alpha_j} = 0, \quad j = 1,2$$

The estimates are obtained by performing iterative numerical methods such as Newton–Raphson or quasi-Newton methods.

3.2. Information Matrix

In this section, we shall explicate the components of the information matrix for the BUW distribution that have been observed and expected. According to the definition, the elements of the observed information matrix are found using the expression

$$j_{\varphi_p,\varphi_q} = -\frac{\partial^2 \ln L(\boldsymbol{\varphi})}{\partial\varphi_p \partial\varphi_q}, \quad \varphi_p, \varphi_q \in (\alpha_1, \alpha_2, \beta_1, \beta_2, \theta) \tag{7}$$

where $L(\boldsymbol{\varphi})$ is the log-likelihood function associated with the parameter vector $\boldsymbol{\varphi} = (\alpha_1, \alpha_2, \beta_1, \beta_2, \theta)$. These elements are presented in detail in Appendix A. The expected information matrix is determined by taking the expected value of the observed information matrix and using the expression.

$$i_{\varphi_p,\varphi_q} = -\frac{1}{n}E\left(\frac{\partial^2 \ln L(\boldsymbol{\varphi})}{\partial\varphi_p \partial\varphi_q}\right) \tag{8}$$

The above values are obtained numerically by using iterative methods, and therefore the information matrix can also be obtained numerically. Using the theory of large samples, the maximum likelihood estimator $\widehat{\boldsymbol{\varphi}}$ asymptotically follows a normal distribution with

$$\widehat{\boldsymbol{\varphi}} \xrightarrow{d} \mathrm{N}_5(\boldsymbol{\varphi}, \boldsymbol{\Sigma}_{\boldsymbol{\varphi}})$$

where $\boldsymbol{\Sigma}_{\boldsymbol{\varphi}} = \mathrm{Var}(\widehat{\boldsymbol{\varphi}}) = (i_{\varphi_p,\varphi_q})^{-1}$. The approximation to $\mathrm{N}_5(\boldsymbol{\varphi}, (i_{\varphi_p,\varphi_q})^{-1})$ can be used to construct confidence intervals for $\alpha_1, \alpha_2, \beta_1, \beta_2$ and θ; these are given by $\varphi_p \mp z_{1-\delta/2}\sqrt{\widehat{\sigma}_{pp}}$ for $\varphi_p \in (\alpha_1, \alpha_2, \beta_1, \beta_2, \theta)$, where $\widehat{\sigma}_{pp}$ is on the diagonal of the matrix $\boldsymbol{\Sigma}_{\boldsymbol{\varphi}}$ for each parameter and is the quantile $100(\delta/2)\%$ of the standard normal distribution.

3.3. Estimation by Inference Functions for Margins (IFM)

This two-step estimation parametric method was proposed by Joe [30]. Each marginal distribution parameter is evaluated separately in the initial stage.

$$\ln L_1 = \sum_{j=1}^{n} \ln f_1(y_{1j}, \delta_1); \qquad \ln L_2 = \sum_{j=1}^{n} \ln f_2(y_{2j}, \delta_2)$$

The subsequent step entails maximizing the log-likelihood function of the copula density by utilizing the maximum likelihood estimates of the marginals $\widehat{F}_1(x_{1j}, \delta)$ and $\widehat{F}_2(x_{2j}, \delta)$ to estimate the copula parameter. For a UW marginal distribution, the log-likelihood function is defined as follows.

$$\ln L_j = \sum_{i=1}^{n} \ln\left(\frac{1}{x_{ji}}\right) + n\left(\ln(\alpha_j) + \ln(\beta_j)\right) + (\beta_j - 1)\sum_{i=1}^{n} \ln(-\ln x_{ji}) - \alpha_j \sum_{i=1}^{n} (-\ln x_{ji})^{\beta_j}$$

The maximum likelihood estimators $(\widehat{\alpha}_1, \widehat{\beta}_1, \widehat{\alpha}_2, \widehat{\beta}_2)$ can be obtained by simultaneously solving the likelihood equations,

$$\frac{\partial \ln L}{\partial \beta_j} = 0, \quad \frac{\partial \ln L}{\partial \alpha_j} = 0, \quad j = 1, 2$$

That is,

$$\frac{\partial \ln L_j}{\partial \beta_j} = \frac{n}{\beta_j} + \sum_{i=1}^{n} (-\ln x_{ji}) - \alpha_j \sum_{i=1}^{n} (-\ln x_{ji})^{\beta_j} \ln(-\ln x_{ji}) = 0$$

$$\frac{\partial \ln L_j}{\partial \alpha_j} = \frac{n}{\alpha_j} - \sum_{i=1}^{n} (-\ln x_{ji})^{\beta_j} = 0$$

then,

$$\widehat{F}_j(x_j) = e^{-\alpha_j(-\ln x_j)^{\beta_j}}.$$

As per the preceding procedure, the IFM estimation of a bivariate unit-Weibull distribution is defined as follows,

$$\ln L_{IFM} = \sum_{i=1}^{n} \ln\Big(1 + \theta(1 - 2\widehat{F}_1(x_{1i}))(1 - 2\widehat{F}_2(x_{2i}))\Big).$$

Based on this, the differentiation of the log-likelihood function with respect to θ thus is

$$\frac{\partial \ln L_{IFM}}{\partial \theta} = \sum_{i=1}^{n} \frac{(a(x_{1i}, \widehat{\alpha}_1, \widehat{\beta}_1))(a(x_{2i}, \widehat{\alpha}_2, \widehat{\beta}_2))}{(1 + \theta(a(x_{1i}, \widehat{\alpha}_1, \widehat{\beta}_1))(a(x_{2i}, \widehat{\alpha}_2, \widehat{\beta}_2)))}.$$

The estimate of the θ parameter is computed numerically by letting

$$\frac{\partial \ln L_{IFM}}{\partial \theta} = 0$$

The closed form expression for the maximum likelihood estimator $\widehat{\theta}$ is not available, and its computation necessitates numerical execution using a nonlinear optimization algorithm such as optimize or uniroot in R Development Core Team [28].

For the IFM method, the asymptotic variance matrix does not have a closed form. Joe [30] defines the inference functions as,

$$\sum_{i=1}^{n} \boldsymbol{g}(Y;\eta)$$

where $\boldsymbol{g}^{\top} = (g_1^{\top}, \ldots, g_m^{\top}, g_d^{\top})$, $g_j = \frac{\partial l_j}{\partial \alpha_j}$ for $j = 1, \ldots, m$, corresponding to the equation,

$$g_d = \frac{\partial l}{\partial \delta}$$

Thus, the asymptotic variance matrix is given by,

$$\boldsymbol{V} = (-\boldsymbol{D}_g^{-1})\boldsymbol{M}_g(-\boldsymbol{D}_g^{-1}), \tag{9}$$

where $\boldsymbol{M}_g = \text{Cov}(\boldsymbol{g}(Y;\eta)) = E(\boldsymbol{g}\boldsymbol{g}^{\top})$ and $\boldsymbol{D}_g = E\left(\frac{\partial \boldsymbol{g}(Y;\eta)}{\partial \eta^{\top}}\right)$.

Other approaches can be used to perform the inference on the model in practical situations, for example, Bayesian methods. Nevertheless, in this work, the classical estimation of the parameters is considered using the methods described above. Based on the research conducted by Kundu and Gupta [31], Zhou et al. [32] and Peralta et al. [33], Bayesian methods can be proposed.

4. Monte Carlo Simulation Study

In this particular section, a Monte Carlo simulation study was conducted with the objective of comparing two copula-based estimation techniques, namely maximum likelihood and estimation by inference of marginal functions, in order to determine the BVUW distribution parameters.

For this simulation, the maxLik function of the statistical software [28] was used and data from the BVUW distribution were generated considering the following values of the parameters $\alpha_1, \beta_1, \alpha_2, \beta_2$ and θ:

- Scenario 1: $\alpha_1 = 1.5, \beta_1 = 3.5, \alpha_2 = 0.5, \beta_2 = 2.0, \theta = 0.25$.
- Scenario 2: $\alpha_1 = 1.5, \beta_1 = 3.5, \alpha_2 = 0.5, \beta_2 = 2.0, \theta = 0.75$.
- Scenario 3: $\alpha_1 = 1.5, \beta_1 = 3.5, \alpha_2 = 0.5, \beta_2 = 2.0, \theta = -0.25$.
- Scenario 4: $\alpha_1 = 1.5, \beta_1 = 3.5, \alpha_2 = 0.5, \beta_2 = 2.0, \theta = -0.75$.
- Scenario 5: $\alpha_1 = 2.5, \beta_1 = 1.5, \alpha_2 = 1.5, \beta_2 = 1, \theta = 0.25$.
- Scenario 6: $\alpha_1 = 2.5, \beta_1 = 1.5, \alpha_2 = 1.5, \beta_2 = 1, \theta = 0.75$.

For each scenario, 5000 random samples were generated using the algorithm presented in Section 2.1 for the sample sizes $n = 30, 50, 75, 100, 200$ and 500. As quality measures to evaluate the benefits of the MLE and IFM methods, the bias, mean square error (MSE), confidence interval length (CIL) and the interval coverage rate (ICR) were used. These measurements were calculated as

$$Bias(\hat{\delta}^{(j)}) = \frac{1}{5000}\sum_{i=1}^{5000}(\hat{\delta}_i^{(j)} - \delta^{(j)}), \quad MSE(\hat{\delta}^{(j)}) = \frac{1}{5000}\sum_{i=1}^{5000}(\hat{\delta}_i^{(j)} - \delta)^2$$

and

$$CIL(\hat{\delta}^{(j)}) = \frac{1}{5000}\sum_{i=1}^{5000} 2z_{(0.975)} \times ee(\hat{\delta}^{(j)})$$

where $\hat{\delta}_i^{(j)}$ is the estimate of $\delta^{(j)}$ for the ith sample, and $ee(\hat{\delta}^{(j)})$ is the standard error of $\hat{\delta}_i^{(j)}$. The ICR is calculated as the proportion of the confidence interval that contain the true value of the parameter below the nominal 95% level. The outcomes of the simulation study are shown in Tables A1–A3 in Appendix B.

Based on the data presented in the tables, it can be observed that, in general, as the sample size increases, the bias, MSE and CIL of all parameter estimators tend to decrease with the implementation of MLE and IFM methods. In regard to the ICR, the values obtained are very similar to the reference value of 95%. On the other hand, for large n sample sizes, the MLE and IFM methods produce very similar results in terms of bias, MSE and CIL values. Furthermore, both estimation methods have better results in terms of estimations when the copula parameter is not high, that is, for values of the parameter θ in the interval $(-0.6, 0.6)$.

The IFM method produces better results when estimating the copula parameter theta. This phenomenon can be attributed in part to the fact that the IFM methodology comprises two estimation steps: the first step involves the estimation of the marginal distribution parameters, followed by the estimation of the copula parameter by incorporating the estimates of the previous marginal distribution parameters.

5. Illustration

This application demonstrates the relevance of the WUB model in a practical context. To accomplish this goal, a collection of facts is considered, focusing on the legislation governing drunk driving and fatalities from traffic collisions in states of the United States of America during the period from 1980 to 2004, as revealed by a thorough investigation conducted by Freeman [23].

The database is accessible within the woolridge library of R Development Core Team [28] software, where it is designated as driving. It contains information related to current legislation, accident records and demographic characteristics. For this particular application, the variables unemployment rate (x_1) and the percent population aged 14 to 24 (x_2) were employed, and the BUW distribution was subsequently adjusted. Likewise, to compare with our proposal, the bivariate Johnson SB (BVSJB) distribution of Lemonte and Moreno-Arenas [18], the bivariate normal (BVN) distribution and the conditional bivariate skew normal (BVSN) distribution of Arnold et al. [34] were studied.

For the purpose of comparison, the Akaike information criterion (AIC) [35] and the Bayesian information criterion (BIC) [36] were employed. These measures are defined in the following:

$$\text{AIC} = -2\ell(\widehat{\theta}) + 2p \quad \text{and} \quad \text{BIC} = -2\ell(\widehat{\theta}) + n\log(n)$$

The parameter p represents the number of parameters and the log-likelihood function $\widehat{\ell}(\cdot)$ was evaluated at the MLEs of the parameters. It is best to choose the model with the smallest AIC or BIC. We used the maxLik function of the statistical package [28] to fit the bivariate model.

The parameters of these models were estimated using the maximum likelihood method. The standard errors are shown in parentheses in Table 2. According to the AIC and BIC criteria, the BVUW distribution provides the best fit.

The graphs in Figure 2 show the contours of the BVN, BVSN and BVUW distributions. We carried out a bivariate Kolmogorov–Smirnov test. For the special case of the BVUW model,

$$d_n(\text{WUB}) = \max\{3.1061671 \times 10^{-21}, 5.1055311 \times 10^{-20}\} = 5.105531 \times 10^{-20};$$

therefore, it is possible to conclude that the BVUW model is well suited to the present data set.

Table 2. MLE (SE) for the fitted models.

Parameters	BVSJB	BVN	BVSN	BVUW
α_1	0.1554(0.0010)	0.1532(0.0005)	0.1546(0.0005)	18.0497(0.3906)
α_2	0.0624(0.0018)	0.0595(0.0005)	0.0602(0.0005)	9.3641(0.1949)
β_1	5.0188(0.9010)			1.9351(0.0032)
β_2	2.7763(0.1020)			3.0170(0.0096)
σ_1	1.7204(0.6972)	0.0003(0.00001)	0.0188(0.0003)	
σ_2	8.0839(0.2439)	0.0004(0.00001)	0.0207(0.0004)	
λ	3.2156(0.5746)	0.0001(0.00001)	0.6973(0.0594)	0.9990(0.0038)
AIC	−10,980.07	−12,250.64	−12,245.92	−12,447.81
BIC	−10,944.44	−12,225.19	−12,220.47	−12,422.36

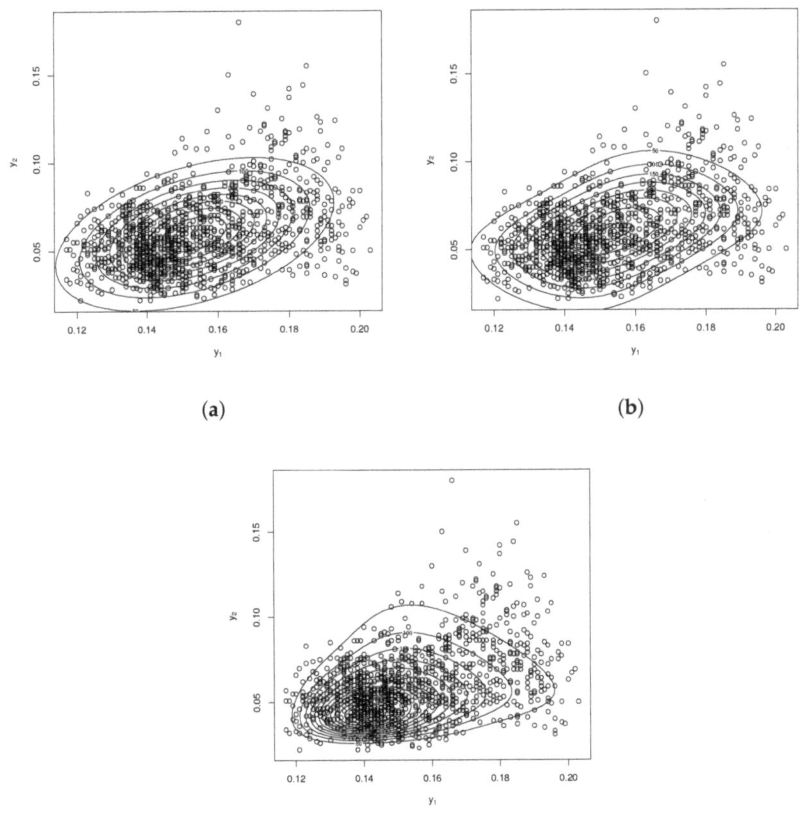

Figure 2. Contour plots for the fitted models. (**a**) BVN, (**b**) BVSN and (**c**) BVUW.

6. Concluding Remarks

Although there are several proposals for fitting proportion, rate or index data, very few focus on the problem of fitting multivariate responses, for example, in the region $(0,1) \times (0,1)$.

In this work, a new bivariate distribution was proposed to model data whose response falls within the region $(0,1) \times (0,1)$. It is possible to obtain the new distribution by extending the univariate unit-Weibull distribution introduced by Mazucheli et al. [12]. For the proposed distribution, the main properties such as the joint density function and the joint distribution function were studied. The moments were also studied and two methods of estimation of the parameters involved in the model were considered. The results of a Monte Carlo-type simulation study showed good asymptotic properties of the parameter estimators and that the two estimation methods are equally efficient. Finally, application to a real data set showed that the proposed model is a viable alternative to analyze proportion, rate or index data in a multivariate context.

Future work could use the results of this proposal to consider how to extend the case of regression models and make inferences about the models from a Bayesian perspective.

Author Contributions: Conceptualization, R.T.-F. and G.M.-F.; methodology, R.T.-F., G.M.-F. and L.P.-M.; software, R.T.-F. and G.M.-F.; validation, R.T.-F., G.M.-F. and L.P.-M.; formal analysis, R.T.-F., G.M.-F. and L.P.-M.; investigation, R.T.-F. and G.M.-F.; resources, R.T.-F. and G.M.-F.; data curation, R.T.-F. and G.M.-F.; writing—original draft preparation, R.T.-F. and G.M.-F.; writing—review and editing, R.T.-F., G.M.-F. and L.P.-M.; visualization, R.T.-F. and G.M.-F.; supervision, R.T.-F. and G.M.-F.; project administration, R.T.-F. and G.M.-F.; funding acquisition, R.T.-F. and G.M.-F. All authors have read and agreed to the published version of the manuscript.

Funding: The research of R. Tovar-Falón and G. Martinez-Flórez was supported partially by project: Resolución de Problemas de Situaciones Reales Usando Análisis Estadístico a través del Modelamiento Multidimensional de Tasas y Proporciones; Esquemas de Monitoreamiento para Datos Asimétricos no Normales y una Estrategia Didáctica para el Desarrollo del Pensamiento Lógico-Matemático. Universidad de Córdoba, Colombia, Acta de Compromiso Número FCB-05-19.

Institutional Review Board Statement: Not applicable.

Informed Consent Statement: Not applicable.

Data Availability Statement: Details about available data are given in Section 5.

Acknowledgments: G. Martínez-Flórez and R. Tovar-Falón acknowledge the support given by Universidad de Córdoba, Montería, Colombia.

Conflicts of Interest: The authors declare no conflict of interest.

Appendix A. Elements of the Observed Information Matrix

This section presents the elements of the observed information matrix presented in Section 3.

The following elements are obtained using the expression in (7) and after some algebraic simplifications:

$$j_{\alpha_1,\alpha_1} = \frac{n}{\alpha_1^2} + \sum_{i=1}^{n} \frac{2\theta(a(x_2;\alpha_2,\beta_2))(-\ln x_{1i})^{2\beta_1} e^{-\alpha_1(-\ln x_{1i})^{\beta_1}}((1+\theta(a(x_1;\alpha_1,\beta_1))(a(x_2;\alpha_2,\beta_2)))}{(1+\theta(a(x_{1i};\alpha_1,\beta_1))(a(x_{2i};\alpha_2,\beta_2)))^2}$$
$$+ \sum_{i=1}^{n} \frac{2\theta(a(x_2;\alpha_2,\beta_2))(-\ln x_{1i})^{2\beta_1} e^{-\alpha_1(-\ln x_{1i})^{\beta_1}}\left(2\theta(a(x_2;\alpha_2,\beta_2))e^{-\alpha_1(-\ln x_{1i})^{\beta_1}}\right)}{(1+\theta(a(x_{1i};\alpha_1,\beta_1))(a(x_{2i};\alpha_2,\beta_2)))^2}$$

$$j_{\alpha_1,\alpha_2} = \sum_{i=1}^{n} \frac{-4\theta(-\ln x_{1i})^{\beta_1} e^{-\alpha_1(-\ln x_{1i})^{\beta_1}}(-\ln x_{2i})^{\beta_2} e^{-\alpha_2(-\ln x_{2i})^{\beta_2}}}{(1+\theta(a(x_{1i};\alpha_1,\beta_1))(a(x_{2i};\alpha_2,\beta_2)))^2}$$

$$
\begin{aligned}
j_{\alpha_1,\beta_1} = & \frac{-2\theta(a(x_{2i};\alpha_2,\beta_2))(-\ln x_{1i})^{\beta_1}\ln(-\ln x_{1i})e^{-\alpha_1(-\ln x_{1i})^{\beta_1}}}{(1+\theta(a(x_{1i};\alpha_1,\beta_1))(a(x_{2i};\alpha_2,\beta_2)))} \\
& \times \frac{(1+\theta(a(x_{1i};\alpha_1,\beta_1))(a(x_{2i};\alpha_2,\beta_2)))\left(1-\alpha_1(-\ln x_{1i})^{\beta_1}\right)}{(1+\theta(a(x_{1i};\alpha_1,\beta_1))(a(x_{2i};\alpha_2,\beta_2)))} \\
& + \frac{2\theta(a(x_{2i};\alpha_2,\beta_2))(-\ln x_{1i})^{\beta_1}\ln(-\ln x_{1i})e^{-\alpha_1(-\ln x_{1i})^{\beta_1}}}{(1+\theta(a(x_{1i};\alpha_1,\beta_1))(a(x_{2i};\alpha_2,\beta_2)))} \\
& \times \frac{\left(2\theta\alpha_1(a(x_{2i};\alpha_2,\beta_2))(-\ln x_{1i})^{\beta_1}e^{-\alpha_1(-\ln x_{1i})^{\beta_1}}\right)}{(1+\theta(a(x_{1i};\alpha_1,\beta_1))(a(x_{2i};\alpha_2,\beta_2)))} \\
& + \sum_{i=1}^{n}(-\ln x_{1i})^{\beta_1}\ln(-\ln x_{1i})
\end{aligned}
$$

$$
j_{\alpha_1,\beta_2} = \sum_{i=1}^{n}\frac{-4\theta\alpha_2(-\ln x_{1i})^{\beta_1}e^{-\alpha_1(-\ln x_{1i})^{\beta_1}}\ln(-\ln x_{2i})(-\ln x_{2i})^{\beta_2}e^{-\alpha_2(-\ln x_{2i})^{\beta_2}}}{(1+\theta(a(x_{1i};\alpha_1,\beta_1))(a(x_{2i};\alpha_2,\beta_2)))^2}
$$

$$
j_{\alpha_1,\theta} = \sum_{i=1}^{n}\frac{-2(a(x_{2i};\alpha_2,\beta_2))(-\ln x_{1i})^{\beta_1}e^{-\alpha_1(-\ln x_{1i})^{\beta_1}}}{(1+\theta(a(x_{1i};\alpha_1,\beta_1))(a(x_{2i};\alpha_2,\beta_2)))^2}
$$

$$
\begin{aligned}
j_{\alpha_2,\alpha_2} = & \frac{n}{\alpha_2^2} + \sum_{i=1}^{n}\frac{2\theta(a(x_1;\alpha_1,\beta_1))(-\ln x_{2i})^{2\beta_2}e^{-\alpha_2(-\ln x_{2i})^{\beta_2}}((1+\theta(a(x_1;\alpha_1,\beta_1))(a(x_2;\alpha_2,\beta_2)))}{(1+\theta(a(x_{1i};\alpha_1,\beta_1))(a(x_{2i};\alpha_2,\beta_2)))^2} \\
& + \sum_{i=1}^{n}\frac{2\theta(a(x_1;\alpha_1,\beta_1))(-\ln x_{2i})^{2\beta_2}e^{-\alpha_2(-\ln x_{2i})^{\beta_2}}\left(2\theta(a(x_2;\alpha_2,\beta_2))e^{-\alpha_1(-\ln x_{1i})^{\beta_1}}\right)}{(1+\theta(a(x_{1i};\alpha_1,\beta_1))(a(x_{2i};\alpha_2,\beta_2)))^2}
\end{aligned}
$$

$$
j_{\alpha_2,\beta_1} = \sum_{i=1}^{n}\frac{-4\theta\alpha_1(-\ln x_{2i})^{\beta_2}e^{-\alpha_2(-\ln x_{2i})^{\beta_2}}\ln(-\ln x_{1i})(-\ln x_{1i})^{\beta_1}e^{-\alpha_1(-\ln x_{1i})^{\beta_1}}}{(1+\theta(a(x_{1i};\alpha_1,\beta_1))(a(x_{2i};\alpha_2,\beta_2)))^2}
$$

$$
\begin{aligned}
j_{\alpha_2,\beta_2} = & \sum_{i=1}^{n}\frac{-2\theta(a(x_{1i};\alpha_1,\beta_1))(-\ln x_{2i})^{\beta_2}\ln(-\ln x_{2i})e^{-\alpha_2(-\ln x_{2i})^{\beta_2}}}{(1+\theta(a(x_{1i};\alpha_1,\beta_1))(a(x_{2i};\alpha_2,\beta_2)))} \\
& \times \frac{(1+\theta(a(x_{1i};\alpha_1,\beta_1))(a(x_{2i};\alpha_2,\beta_2)))\left(1-\alpha_2(-\ln x_{2i})^{\beta_2}\right)}{(1+\theta(a(x_{1i};\alpha_1,\beta_1))(a(x_{2i};\alpha_2,\beta_2)))} \\
& + \sum_{i=1}^{n}\frac{2\theta(a(x_{1i};\alpha_1,\beta_1))(-\ln x_{2i})^{\beta_2}\ln(-\ln x_{2i})e^{-\alpha_2(-\ln x_{2i})^{\beta_2}}}{(1+\theta(a(x_{1i};\alpha_1,\beta_1))(a(x_{2i};\alpha_2,\beta_2)))} \\
& \times \frac{\left(2\theta\alpha_2(a(x_{1i};\alpha_1,\beta_1))(-\ln x_{2i})^{\beta_2}e^{-\alpha_2(-\ln x_{2i})^{\beta_2}}\right)}{(1+\theta(a(x_{1i};\alpha_1,\beta_1))(a(x_{2i};\alpha_2,\beta_2)))} \\
& + \sum_{i=1}^{n}(-\ln x_{2i})^{\beta_2}\ln(-\ln x_{2i})
\end{aligned}
$$

$$
j_{\alpha_2,\theta} = \sum_{i=1}^{n}\frac{-2(a(x_{1i};\alpha_1,\beta_1))(-\ln x_{2i})^{\beta_2}e^{-\alpha_2(-\ln x_{2i})^{\beta_2}}}{(1+\theta(a(x_{1i};\alpha_1,\beta_1))(a(x_{2i};\alpha_2,\beta_2)))^2}
$$

$$
\begin{aligned}
j_{\beta_1,\beta_1} &= \sum_{i=1}^{n} \frac{-2\alpha_1\theta(a(x_{2i};\alpha_2,\beta_2))\ln(-\ln x_{1i})^2(-\ln x_{1i})^{\beta_1}e^{-\alpha_1(-\ln x_{1i})^{\beta_1}}}{(1+\theta(a(x_{1i};\alpha_1,\beta_1))(a(x_{2i};\alpha_2,\beta_2)))} \\
&\times \frac{(1+\theta(a(x_{1i};\alpha_1,\beta_1))(a(x_{2i};\alpha_2,\beta_2)))\left(1-\alpha_1(-\ln x_{1i})^{\beta_1}\right)}{(1+\theta(a(x_{1i};\alpha_1,\beta_1))(a(x_{2i};\alpha_2,\beta_2)))} \\
&+ \sum_{i=1}^{n} \frac{4\alpha_1^2\theta^2(a(x_{2i};\alpha_2,\beta_2)^2)\ln(-\ln x_{1i})^2(-\ln x_{1i})^{2\beta_1}e^{-2\alpha_1(-\ln x_{1i})^{\beta_1}}}{(1+\theta(a(x_{1i};\alpha_1,\beta_1))(a(x_{2i};\alpha_2,\beta_2)))^2} \\
&+ \sum_{i=1}^{n} \alpha_1 \ln(-\ln x_{1i})^2(-\ln x_{1i})^{\beta_1} + \frac{n}{\beta_1^2}
\end{aligned}
$$

$$
j_{\beta_1,\beta_2} = \sum_{i=1}^{n} \frac{-2\alpha_1\theta\ln(-\ln x_{1i})(-\ln x_{1i})^{\beta_1}e^{-\alpha_1(-\ln x_{1i})^{\beta_1}}}{(1+\theta(a(x_{1i};\alpha_1,\beta_1))(a(x_{2i};\alpha_2,\beta_2)))^2}
$$

$$
j_{\beta_1,\theta} = \sum_{i=1}^{n} \frac{-2\alpha_1(a(x_{2i};\alpha_2,\beta_2))\ln(-\ln x_{1i})(-\ln x_{1i})^{\beta_1}e^{-\alpha_1(-\ln x_{1i})^{\beta_1}}}{(1+\theta(a(x_{1i};\alpha_1,\beta_1))(a(x_{2i};\alpha_2,\beta_2)))^2}
$$

$$
\begin{aligned}
j_{\beta_2,\beta_2} &= \sum_{i=1}^{n} \frac{-2\alpha_2\theta(a(x_{1i};\alpha_1,\beta_1))\ln(-\ln x_{2i})^2(-\ln x_{2i})^{\beta_2}e^{-\alpha_2(-\ln x_{2i})^{\beta_2}}}{(1+\theta(a(x_{1i};\alpha_1,\beta_1))(a(x_{2i};\alpha_2,\beta_2)))} \\
&\times \frac{(1+\theta(a(x_{1i};\alpha_1,\beta_1))(a(x_{2i};\alpha_2,\beta_2)))\left(1-\alpha_2(-\ln x_{2i})^{\beta_2}\right)}{(1+\theta(a(x_{1i};\alpha_1,\beta_1))(a(x_{2i};\alpha_2,\beta_2)))} \\
&+ \sum_{i=1}^{n} \frac{4\alpha_2^2\theta^2(a(x_{1i};\alpha_1,\beta_1)^2)\ln(-\ln x_{2i})^2(-\ln x_{2i})^{2\beta_2}e^{-2\alpha_2(-\ln x_{2i})^{\beta_2}}}{(1+\theta(a(x_{1i};\alpha_1,\beta_1))(a(x_{2i};\alpha_2,\beta_2)))^2} \\
&+ \sum_{i=1}^{n} \alpha_2 \ln(-\ln x_{2i})^2(-\ln x_{2i})^{\beta_2} + \frac{n}{\beta_2^2}
\end{aligned}
$$

$$
j_{\beta_2,\theta} = \sum_{i=1}^{n} \frac{-2\alpha_2(a(x_{1i};\alpha_1,\beta_1))\ln(-\ln x_{2i})(-\ln x_{2i})^{\beta_2}e^{-\alpha_2(-\ln x_{2i})^{\beta_2}}}{(1+\theta(a(x_{1i};\alpha_1,\beta_1))(a(x_{2i};\alpha_2,\beta_2)))^2}
$$

$$
j_{\theta,\theta} = \sum_{i=1}^{n} \frac{(a(x_{1i};\alpha_1,\beta_1)^2)(a(x_{2i};\alpha_2,\beta_2)^2)}{(1+\theta(a(x_{1i};\alpha_1,\beta_1))(a(x_{2i};\alpha_2,\beta_2)))^2}
$$

Appendix B. Simulation Tables

Table A1. Quality measure (QM) of the estimates obtained under the MLE and IMF methods: Scenarios 1 and 2.

Scenario 1		MLE Method					IFM Method				
n	QM	$\widehat{\alpha}_1$	$\widehat{\beta}_1$	$\widehat{\alpha}_2$	$\widehat{\beta}_2$	$\widehat{\theta}$	$\widehat{\alpha}_1$	$\widehat{\beta}_1$	$\widehat{\alpha}_2$	$\widehat{\beta}_2$	$\widehat{\theta}$
30	Bias	0.0405	0.1680	0.0048	0.0845	−0.0647	0.0408	0.1676	0.0044	0.0854	−0.0701
	MSE	0.0907	0.3265	0.0168	0.1211	0.1956	0.0910	0.3229	0.0166	0.1195	0.2005
	CIL	1.1173	2.0657	0.4760	1.1742	2.0777	1.1157	2.0645	0.4749	1.1736	2.0586
	ICR	0.9549	0.9542	0.9246	0.9386	0.9689	0.9573	0.9542	0.9245	0.9390	0.9741
50	Bias	0.0235	0.0906	0.0029	0.0543	−0.0320	0.0248	0.0926	0.0029	0.0543	−0.0342
	MSE	0.0482	0.1672	0.0097	0.0617	0.1535	0.0489	0.1682	0.0097	0.0614	0.1558
	CIL	0.8501	1.5614	0.3678	0.8916	1.6133	0.8508	1.5624	0.3678	0.8917	1.6055
	ICR	0.9550	0.9543	0.9331	0.9338	0.9451	0.9533	0.9533	0.9331	0.9393	0.9428
75	Bias	0.0189	0.0551	0.0048	0.0296	−0.0181	0.0197	0.0552	0.0048	0.0296	−0.0206
	MSE	0.0323	0.1062	0.0063	0.0375	0.1121	0.0326	0.1067	0.0062	0.0373	0.1113
	CIL	0.6904	1.2591	0.3011	0.7176	1.3245	0.6909	1.2596	0.3013	0.7177	1.3186
	ICR	0.9448	0.9550	0.9373	0.9366	0.9441	0.9455	0.9544	0.9408	0.9374	0.9415
100	Bias	0.0119	0.0405	0.0026	0.0222	−0.0154	0.0123	0.0400	0.0029	0.0219	−0.0166
	MSE	0.0239	0.0808	0.0047	0.0260	0.0869	0.0239	0.0808	0.0047	0.0259	0.0859
	CIL	0.5944	1.0851	0.2601	0.6189	1.1532	0.5948	1.0853	0.2604	0.6190	1.1485
	ICR	0.9477	0.9510	0.9403	0.9544	0.9477	0.9450	0.9490	0.9389	0.9537	0.9477
200	Bias	0.0079	0.0258	0.0008	0.0083	−0.0007	0.0080	0.0258	0.0009	0.0081	−0.0013
	MSE	0.0119	0.0383	0.0022	0.0125	0.0439	0.0119	0.0383	0.0022	0.0125	0.0437
	CIL	0.4184	0.7630	0.1836	0.4342	0.8182	0.4187	0.7633	0.1838	0.4343	0.8160
	ICR	0.9467	0.9533	0.9453	0.9540	0.9393	0.9473	0.9527	0.9467	0.9527	0.9387
500	Bias	0.0025	0.0063	−0.0008	0.0062	−0.0010	0.0025	0.0062	−0.0008	0.0061	−0.0012
	MSE	0.0044	0.0146	0.0009	0.0052	0.0172	0.0044	0.0146	0.0009	0.0052	0.0172
	CIL	0.2634	0.4794	0.1160	0.2743	0.5192	0.2636	0.4796	0.1160	0.2744	0.5183
	ICR	0.9507	0.9547	0.9467	0.9427	0.9547	0.9513	0.9527	0.9480	0.9420	0.9540
Scenario 2											
30	Bias	0.0593	0.1801	0.0029	0.0908	−0.2892	0.0625	0.1920	0.0034	0.0916	−0.2993
	MSE	0.0997	0.3186	0.0159	0.1133	0.2248	0.1049	0.3375	0.0165	0.1185	0.2341
	CIL	1.1301	2.0703	0.4740	1.1771	1.9724	1.1329	2.0781	0.4744	1.1778	2.0189
	ICR	0.9568	0.9568	0.9290	0.9424	0.9302	0.9557	0.9547	0.9241	0.9389	0.9505
50	Bias	0.0291	0.1007	0.0012	0.0637	−0.1823	0.0263	0.1021	0.0006	0.0637	−0.1826
	MSE	0.0495	0.1678	0.0093	0.0644	0.1246	0.0495	0.1703	0.0094	0.0651	0.1251
	CIL	0.8510	1.5651	0.3658	0.8948	1.5255	0.8517	1.5682	0.3669	0.8962	1.5299
	ICR	0.9545	0.9516	0.9370	0.9302	0.9486	0.9536	0.9536	0.9366	0.9290	0.9612
75	Bias	0.0229	0.0679	0.0026	0.0417	−0.1263	0.0238	0.0673	0.0030	0.0404	−0.1264
	MSE	0.0321	0.1070	0.0060	0.0378	0.0777	0.0326	0.1077	0.0061	0.0381	0.0783
	CIL	0.6900	1.2622	0.2990	0.7203	1.2294	0.6927	1.2644	0.3006	0.7215	1.2356
	ICR	0.9486	0.9593	0.9398	0.9486	0.9575	0.9477	0.9582	0.9425	0.9442	0.9747
100	Bias	0.0172	0.0522	0.0015	0.0302	−0.1007	0.0172	0.0523	0.0015	0.0297	−0.1016
	MSE	0.0240	0.0827	0.0047	0.0266	0.0576	0.0243	0.0830	0.0047	0.0266	0.0575
	CIL	0.5946	1.0875	0.2586	0.6200	1.0706	0.5967	1.0897	0.2599	0.6211	1.0661
	TCR	0.9452	0.9486	0.9351	0.9503	0.9646	0.9432	0.9491	0.9307	0.9524	0.9766
200	Bias	0.0095	0.0325	0.0004	0.0101	−0.0368	0.0102	0.0313	0.0005	0.0099	−0.0363
	MSE	0.0120	0.0391	0.0022	0.0126	0.0277	0.0122	0.0390	0.0022	0.0126	0.0278
	CIL	0.4169	0.7626	0.1823	0.4334	0.7398	0.4193	0.7647	0.1837	0.4347	0.7382
	ICR	0.9463	0.9553	0.9433	0.9530	0.9605	0.9453	0.9542	0.9424	0.9549	0.9749
500	Bias	0.0023	0.0078	−0.0009	0.0063	−0.0068	0.0026	0.0070	−0.0008	0.0061	−0.0052
	MSE	0.0044	0.0145	0.0009	0.0052	0.0125	0.0044	0.0147	0.0009	0.0052	0.0129
	CIL	0.2619	0.4782	0.1151	0.2735	0.4667	0.2636	0.4797	0.1160	0.2744	0.4621
	TCR	0.9563	0.9549	0.9494	0.9460	0.9706	0.9506	0.9526	0.9438	0.9445	0.9675

Table A2. Quality measure of the estimates obtained under the MLE and IMF methods: Scenario 3 and 4.

Scenario 3		**MLE Method**					**IFM Method**				
n	**QM**	$\widehat{\alpha}_1$	$\widehat{\beta}_1$	$\widehat{\alpha}_2$	$\widehat{\beta}_2$	$\widehat{\theta}$	$\widehat{\alpha}_1$	$\widehat{\beta}_1$	$\widehat{\alpha}_2$	$\widehat{\beta}_2$	$\widehat{\theta}$
30	Bias	0.0374	0.1699	0.0068	0.0826	0.0878	0.0429	0.1724	0.0074	0.0821	0.0927
	MSE	0.0868	0.3288	0.0167	0.1187	0.2061	0.0940	0.3299	0.0168	0.1182	0.2156
	CIL	1.1148	2.0670	0.4777	1.1732	2.0815	1.1176	2.0667	0.4767	1.1715	2.0661
	ICR	0.9527	0.9566	0.9310	0.9380	0.9744	0.9533	0.9563	0.9337	0.9352	0.9721
50	Bias	0.0225	0.0900	0.0043	0.0517	0.0400	0.0214	0.0903	0.0047	0.0511	0.0450
	MSE	0.0487	0.1688	0.0099	0.0602	0.1509	0.0486	0.1682	0.0098	0.0598	0.1514
	CIL	0.8496	1.5605	0.3685	0.8906	1.6170	0.8489	1.5606	0.3686	0.8904	1.6097
	ICR	0.9532	0.9546	0.9362	0.9376	0.9489	0.9519	0.9534	0.9385	0.9350	0.9519
75	Bias	0.0175	0.0519	0.0045	0.0300	0.0158	0.0176	0.0518	0.0044	0.0303	0.0138
	MSE	0.0328	0.1063	0.0063	0.0370	0.1133	0.0326	0.1062	0.0062	0.0370	0.1136
	CIL	0.6896	1.2578	0.3009	0.7181	1.3217	0.6899	1.2582	0.3011	0.7184	1.3177
	ICR	0.9420	0.9556	0.9413	0.9365	0.9427	0.9450	0.9552	0.9409	0.9382	0.9402
100	Bias	0.0114	0.0393	0.0031	0.0214	−0.0051	0.0113	0.0392	0.0031	0.0212	−0.0044
	MSE	0.0239	0.0807	0.0047	0.0257	0.0850	0.0238	0.0809	0.0047	0.0258	0.0844
	CIL	0.5940	1.0847	0.2603	0.6189	1.1487	0.5943	1.0851	0.2605	0.6191	1.1441
	ICR	0.9489	0.9482	0.9408	0.9509	0.9509	0.9456	0.9489	0.9415	0.9489	0.9469
200	Bias	0.0079	0.0258	0.0010	0.0082	−0.0005	0.0080	0.0258	0.0009	0.0083	0.0001
	MSE	0.0119	0.0383	0.0022	0.0124	0.0446	0.0119	0.0383	0.0022	0.0124	0.0444
	CIL	0.4184	0.7630	0.1837	0.4342	0.8182	0.4187	0.7633	0.1838	0.4344	0.8158
	ICR	0.9493	0.9513	0.9507	0.9507	0.9407	0.9473	0.9527	0.9540	0.9527	0.9400
500	Bias	0.0025	0.0062	−0.0008	0.0060	−0.0013	0.0025	0.0062	−0.0008	0.0061	−0.0011
	MSE	0.0044	0.0146	0.0009	0.0051	0.0173	0.0044	0.0146	0.0009	0.0051	0.0172
	CIL	0.2634	0.4794	0.1160	0.2743	0.5193	0.2636	0.4796	0.1160	0.2744	0.5184
	ICR	0.9513	0.9540	0.9507	0.9447	0.9573	0.9513	0.9527	0.9513	0.9447	0.9573
Scenario 4											
30	Bias	0.0402	0.1742	0.0083	0.0899	0.2911	0.0463	0.1864	0.0093	0.0926	0.2995
	MSE	0.0844	0.3241	0.0166	0.1144	0.2160	0.0988	0.3481	0.0172	0.1169	0.2258
	CIL	1.1148	2.0707	0.4777	1.1762	1.9978	1.1207	2.0754	0.4778	1.1774	2.0209
	ICR	0.9588	0.9631	0.9262	0.9360	0.9393	0.9508	0.9559	0.9231	0.9364	0.9579
50	Bias	0.0235	0.1047	0.0044	0.0544	0.1941	0.0271	0.1017	0.0049	0.0550	0.1966
	MSE	0.0496	0.1712	0.0099	0.0591	0.1292	0.0515	0.1708	0.0103	0.0603	0.1295
	CIL	0.8488	1.5659	0.3677	0.8918	1.5209	0.8523	1.5661	0.3687	0.8926	1.5376
	ICR	0.9553	0.9553	0.9329	0.9377	0.9436	0.9478	0.9573	0.9307	0.9402	0.9658
75	Bias	0.0167	0.0658	0.0027	0.0365	0.1315	0.0198	0.0598	0.0021	0.0373	0.1324
	MSE	0.0325	0.1136	0.0060	0.0379	0.0813	0.0329	0.1130	0.0061	0.0381	0.0809
	CIL	0.6872	1.2606	0.2992	0.7198	1.2148	0.6910	1.2610	0.3003	0.7215	1.2337
	ICR	0.9400	0.9472	0.9463	0.9418	0.9346	0.9435	0.9496	0.9426	0.9417	0.9664
100	Bias	0.0114	0.0495	0.0025	0.0245	0.0905	0.0104	0.0495	0.0016	0.0261	0.0895
	MSE	0.0238	0.0842	0.0045	0.0250	0.0544	0.0238	0.0850	0.0045	0.0253	0.0543
	CIL	0.5918	1.0856	0.2588	0.6192	1.0481	0.5940	1.0885	0.2601	0.6213	1.0537
	ICR	0.9503	0.9435	0.9409	0.9572	0.9563	0.9452	0.9427	0.9435	0.9536	0.9755
200	Bias	0.0084	0.0297	0.0013	0.0100	0.0387	0.0089	0.0287	0.0011	0.0100	0.0399
	MSE	0.0120	0.0386	0.0022	0.0125	0.0285	0.0120	0.0383	0.0022	0.0125	0.0285
	CIL	0.4166	0.7617	0.1825	0.4337	0.7375	0.4189	0.7638	0.1839	0.4350	0.7376
	ICR	0.9482	0.9512	0.9497	0.9474	0.9684	0.9461	0.9528	0.9506	0.9513	0.9813
500	Bias	0.0024	0.0071	−0.0008	0.0063	0.0040	0.0023	0.0069	−0.0007	0.0061	0.0036
	MSE	0.0044	0.0147	0.0009	0.0051	0.0127	0.0044	0.0148	0.0009	0.0051	0.0129
	CIL	0.2619	0.4781	0.1151	0.2735	0.4650	0.2635	0.4797	0.1161	0.2744	0.4621
	ICR	0.9526	0.9560	0.9464	0.9444	0.9547	0.9517	0.9523	0.9510	0.9462	0.9598

Table A3. Quality measure of the estimates obtained under the MLE and IMF methods: Scenario 5 and 6.

Scenario 5		MLE Method					IFM Method				
n	QM	$\widehat{\alpha}_1$	$\widehat{\beta}_1$	$\widehat{\alpha}_2$	$\widehat{\beta}_2$	$\widehat{\theta}$	$\widehat{\alpha}_1$	$\widehat{\beta}_1$	$\widehat{\alpha}_2$	$\widehat{\beta}_2$	$\widehat{\theta}$
30	Bias	0.1408	0.0687	0.0665	0.0435	−0.0683	0.1419	0.0716	0.0653	0.0424	−0.0720
	MSE	0.3577	0.0572	0.1152	0.0302	0.1945	0.3623	0.0592	0.1125	0.0299	0.1997
	CIL	2.0970	0.8835	1.1390	0.5880	2.0834	2.0962	0.8848	1.1362	0.5866	2.0627
	ICR	0.9664	0.9578	0.9445	0.9391	0.9766	0.9633	0.9541	0.9442	0.9388	0.9755
50	Bias	0.0780	0.0391	0.0420	0.0274	−0.0310	0.0804	0.0397	0.0429	0.0271	−0.0353
	MSE	0.1716	0.0309	0.0613	0.0155	0.1540	0.1740	0.0309	0.0611	0.0154	0.1553
	CIL	1.5612	0.6693	0.8616	0.4460	1.6160	1.5625	0.6696	0.8620	0.4458	1.6061
	ICR	0.9592	0.9529	0.9424	0.9339	0.9487	0.9588	0.9532	0.9455	0.9392	0.9441
75	Bias	0.0552	0.0239	0.0313	0.0149	−0.0176	0.0559	0.0237	0.0319	0.0148	−0.0206
	MSE	0.1094	0.0197	0.0370	0.0094	0.1123	0.1101	0.0196	0.0370	0.0093	0.1113
	CIL	1.2555	0.5397	0.6963	0.3588	1.3253	1.2558	0.5398	0.6967	0.3589	1.3186
	ICR	0.9632	0.9537	0.9469	0.9367	0.9442	0.9592	0.9544	0.9462	0.9374	0.9415
100	Bias	0.0367	0.0174	0.0206	0.0110	−0.0149	0.0374	0.0172	0.0212	0.0109	−0.0166
	MSE	0.0800	0.0148	0.0268	0.0065	0.0872	0.0803	0.0148	0.0267	0.0065	0.0859
	CIL	1.0753	0.4651	0.5980	0.3094	1.1532	1.0757	0.4651	0.5984	0.3095	1.1484
	ICR	0.9631	0.9510	0.9370	0.9544	0.9484	0.9624	0.9490	0.9362	0.9537	0.9477
200	Bias	0.0237	0.0111	0.0065	0.0041	−0.0012	0.0238	0.0110	0.0065	0.0041	−0.0013
	MSE	0.0393	0.0070	0.0118	0.0031	0.0436	0.0393	0.0070	0.0118	0.0031	0.0437
	CIL	0.7532	0.3270	0.4180	0.2171	0.8183	0.7535	0.3271	0.4183	0.2172	0.8160
	ICR	0.9453	0.9533	0.9460	0.9540	0.9400	0.9480	0.9527	0.9487	0.9527	0.9387
500	Bias	0.0069	0.0027	0.0015	0.0031	−0.0010	0.0069	0.0027	0.0015	0.0031	−0.0012
	MSE	0.0147	0.0027	0.0046	0.0013	0.0172	0.0147	0.0027	0.0046	0.0013	0.0172
	CIL	0.4716	0.2055	0.2633	0.1372	0.5192	0.4717	0.2055	0.2634	0.1372	0.5183
	ICR	0.9533	0.9547	0.9507	0.9427	0.9547	0.9533	0.9527	0.9493	0.9420	0.9533
Scenario 6											
30	Bias	0.1775	0.0747	0.0646	0.0428	−0.2893	0.1901	0.0834	0.0664	0.0470	−0.2994
	MSE	0.3854	0.0579	0.1121	0.0281	0.2221	0.4210	0.0615	0.1114	0.0298	0.2341
	CIL	2.1327	0.8858	1.1364	0.5872	2.0001	2.1476	0.8912	1.1369	0.5895	2.0130
	ICR	0.9701	0.9590	0.9369	0.9435	0.9391	0.9684	0.9568	0.9399	0.9389	0.9515
50	Bias	0.0854	0.0433	0.0442	0.0308	−0.1791	0.0858	0.0435	0.0437	0.0320	−0.1838
	MSE	0.1687	0.0306	0.0552	0.0157	0.1200	0.1726	0.0312	0.0559	0.0162	0.1253
	CIL	1.5643	0.6708	0.8600	0.4471	1.5351	1.5669	0.6721	0.8619	0.4482	1.5338
	ICR	0.9639	0.9513	0.9561	0.9318	0.9581	0.9630	0.9526	0.9554	0.9298	0.9649
75	Bias	0.0669	0.0297	0.0356	0.0200	−0.1269	0.0672	0.0288	0.0359	0.0202	−0.1264
	MSE	0.1082	0.0197	0.0365	0.0095	0.0776	0.1091	0.0198	0.0366	0.0095	0.0783
	CIL	1.2607	0.5412	0.6959	0.3600	1.2439	1.2628	0.5419	0.6984	0.3607	1.2354
	ICR	0.9654	0.9592	0.9504	0.9459	0.9690	0.9616	0.9582	0.9538	0.9442	0.9738
100	Bias	0.0486	0.0223	0.0244	0.0150	−0.0983	0.0500	0.0224	0.0234	0.0148	−0.1014
	MSE	0.0807	0.0153	0.0266	0.0067	0.0576	0.0823	0.0152	0.0268	0.0066	0.0575
	CIL	1.0801	0.4660	0.5972	0.3100	1.0676	1.0827	0.4670	0.5992	0.3106	1.0655
	ICR	0.9582	0.9465	0.9406	0.9498	0.9632	0.9608	0.9491	0.9391	0.9525	0.9750
200	Bias	0.0307	0.0139	0.0068	0.0049	−0.0361	0.0294	0.0134	0.0071	0.0048	−0.0359
	MSE	0.0402	0.0072	0.0118	0.0032	0.0277	0.0402	0.0072	0.0119	0.0031	0.0278
	CIL	0.7541	0.3268	0.4160	0.2167	0.7413	0.7557	0.3277	0.4184	0.2173	0.7375
	ICR	0.9480	0.9554	0.9546	0.9524	0.9673	0.9454	0.9543	0.9550	0.9550	0.9742
500	Bias	0.0070	0.0033	0.0011	0.0030	−0.0059	0.0073	0.0029	0.0014	0.0030	−0.0051
	MSE	0.0147	0.0027	0.0045	0.0013	0.0126	0.0147	0.0027	0.0046	0.0013	0.0129
	CIL	0.4702	0.2049	0.2617	0.1367	0.4666	0.4718	0.2056	0.2634	0.1372	0.4620
	ICR	0.9544	0.9558	0.9483	0.9455	0.9741	0.9527	0.9520	0.9466	0.9446	0.9655

References

1. Ferrari, S.; Cribari-Neto, F. Beta regression for modelling rates and proportions. *Appl. Stat.* **2004**, *31*, 799–815. [CrossRef]
2. Branscum, A.J.; Johnson, W.O.; Thurmond, M.C. Bayesian beta regression: Applications to household expenditure data and genetic distance between foot-and-mouth diseases viruses. *Aust. N. Z. J. Stat.* **2007**, *49*, 287–301. [CrossRef]
3. Ospina, R.; Ferrari, S.L.P. Inflated beta distribution. *Stat. Pap.* **2010**, *51*, 111–126. [CrossRef]

4. Ospina, R.; Ferrari, S.L.P. A general class of zero-or-one inflated beta regression models. *Comput. Stat. Data Anal.* **2012**, *56*, 1609–1623. [CrossRef]
5. Paolino, P. Maximum likelihood estimation of models with beta-distributed dependent variables. *Political Anal.* **2001**, *9*, 325–346. [CrossRef]
6. Cribari-Neto, F.; Vasconcellos, K.L.P. Nearly unbiased maximum likelhood estimation for the beta distribution. *J. Stat. Comput. Simul.* **2002**, *72*, 107–118. [CrossRef]
7. Kieschnick, R.; Mccullough, B.D. Regression analysis of variates observed on $(0,1)$. *Stat. Model.* **2003**, *3*, 193–213. [CrossRef]
8. Vasconcellos, K.L.P.; Cribari-Neto, F. Improved maximum likelihood estimation in a new class of beta regression models. *Braz. J. Probab. Stat.* **2005**, *19*, 13–31.
9. Martínez-Flórez, G.; Bolfarine, H.; Gómez, H.W. Power-models for proportions with zero/one excess. *Appl. Math. Inf. Sci.* **2018**, *12*, 293–303. [CrossRef]
10. Grassia, A. On a family of distributions with argument between 0 and 1 obtained by transformation of the Gamma distribution and derived compound distributions. *Aust. J. Stat.* **1977**, *19*, 108–114. [CrossRef]
11. Gómez-Déniz, E.; Sordo, M.A.; Calderín-Ojeda, E. The Log-Lindley distribution as an alternative to the Beta regression model with applications in insurance. *Insur. Math. Econ.* **2013**, *54*, 49–57. [CrossRef]
12. Mazucheli, J.; Menezes, A.F.B.; Ghitany, M.E. The unit-Weibull distribution and associated inference. *J. Appl. Probab. Stat.* **2018**, *13*, 1–22.
13. Mazucheli, J.; Menezes, A.; Dey, S. The unit-Birnbaum-Saunders distribution with applications. *Chil. J. Stat.* **2018**, *9*, 47–57.
14. Mazucheli, J.; Menezes, A.F.B.; Chakraborty, S. On the one parameter unit-Lindley distribution and its associated regression model for proportion data. *J. Appl. Stat.* **2019**, *49*, 700–714. [CrossRef]
15. Martínez-Flórez, G.; Azevedo-Farias, R.B.; Tovar-Falón, R. New Class of Unit-Power-Skew-Normal Distribution and Its Associated Regression Model for Bounded Responses. *Mathematics* **2022**, *10*, 3035. [CrossRef]
16. Martínez-Flórez, G.; Tovar-Falón, R. New Regression Models Based on the Unit-Sinh-Normal Distribution: Properties, Inference, and Applications. *Mathematics* **2021**, *9*, 1231. [CrossRef]
17. Martínez-Flórez, G.; Gómez, H.W.; Tovar-Falón, R. Modeling Proportion Data with Inflation by Using a Power-Skew-Normal/Logit Mixture Model. *Mathematics* **2021**, *9*, 1989. [CrossRef]
18. Lemonte, A.J.; Moreno-Arenas, G. On a multivariate regression model for rates and proportions. *J. Appl. Stat.* **2019**, *46*, 1084–1106. [CrossRef]
19. Martínez-Flórez, G.; Lemonte, A.J.; Moreno-Arenas, G.; Tovar-Falón, R. The Bivariate Unit-Sinh-Normal Distribution and Its Related Regression Model. *Mathematics* **2022**, *10*, 3125. [CrossRef]
20. Gumbel, E.G. Bivariate exponential distributions. *J. Am. Stat. Assoc.* **1960**, *292*, 698–707. [CrossRef]
21. Gokhale, S.; Khare, M. Vehicle wake factor for heterogeneous traffic in urban environments. *Int. J. Environ. Pollut.* **2007**, *30*, 97–105. [CrossRef]
22. Martínez-Flórez, G.; Azevedo-Farias, R.B.; Tovar-Falón, R. An Exponentiated Multivariate Extension for the Birnbaum-Saunders Log-Linear Model. *Mathematics* **2022**, *10*, 1299. [CrossRef]
23. Freeman, D.G. Drunk Driving Legislation and Traffic Fatalities: New Evidence on BAC 08 Laws. *Contemp. Econ. Policy* **2007**, *25*, 293–308. [CrossRef]
24. Martínez-Flórez, G.; Vergara-Cardozo, S.; Tovar-Falón, R.; Rodriguez-Quevedo, L. The Multivariate Skewed Log-Birnbaum–Saunders Distribution and Its Associated Regression Model. *Mathematics* **2023**, *11*, 1095. [CrossRef]
25. Almetwally, E.M.; Muhammed, H.Z.; El-Sherpieny, E.S.A. Bivariate Weibull Distribution: Properties and Different Methods of Estimation. *Ann. Data. Sci.* **2020**, *7*, 163–193. [CrossRef]
26. Sklar, A. Random variables, joint distributions, and copulas. *Kybernetica* **1973**, *9*, 449–460.
27. Nelsen, R.B. *An Introduction to Copulas*, 2nd ed.; Springer: New York, NY, USA, 2010.
28. R Development Core Team. *R: A Language and Environment for Statistical Computing*; R Foundation for Statistical Computing: Vienna, Austria, 2021. Available online: http://www.R-project.org (accessed on 31 July 2021).
29. Basu, A. Bivariate failure rate. *J. Am. Stat. Assoc.* **1971**, *66*, 103–104. [CrossRef]
30. Joe, H. Asymptotic efficiency of the two-stage estimation method for copula-based models. *J. Multivar. Anal.* **2005**, *94*, 401–419. [CrossRef]
31. Kundu, D.; Gupta, A.K. Bayes estimation for the Marshall-Olkin bivariate Weibull distribution. *Comput. Stat. Data Anal.* **2013**, *57*, 271–281. [CrossRef]
32. Zhou, S.; Xu, A.; Tang, Y.; Shen, L. Fast Bayesian Inference of Reparameterized Gamma Process With Random Effects. *IEEE Trans. Reliab.* **2023**, 1–14. [CrossRef]
33. Peralta, D.; DeOliveira, R.P.; Achcar, J.A. A hierarchical Bayesian analysis for bivariate Weibull distribution under left-censoring scheme. *J. Appl. Stat.* **2023**, 1–20. [CrossRef]
34. Arnold, B.C.; Castillo, E.; Sarabia, J.M. Conditionally specified multivariate skewed distributions. *Sankhya Indian J. Stat. Ser. A* **2002**, *64*, 206–226.

35. Akaike, H. A new look at statistical model identification. *IEEE Trans. Autom. Control* **1974**, *19*, 716–722. [CrossRef]
36. Schwarz, G. Estimating the dimension of a model. *Ann. Stat.* **1978**, *6*, 461–464. [CrossRef]

mathematics

MDPI

Article

Extropy and Some of Its More Recent Related Measures for Concomitants of K-Record Values in an Extended FGM Family

Mohamed A. Abd Elgawad [1,2,*], Haroon M. Barakat [3], Metwally A. Alawady [3], Doaa A. Abd El-Rahman [4], Islam A. Husseiny [3], Atef F. Hashem [1,5] and Naif Alotaibi [1]

1 Department of Mathematics and Statistics, Faculty of Science, Imam Mohammad Ibn Saud Islamic University (IMSIU), Riyadh 11432, Saudi Arabia; affaragalla@imamu.edu.sa (A.F.H.); nmaalotaibi@imamu.edu.sa (N.A.)
2 Department of Mathematics, Faculty of Science, Benha University, Benha 13518, Egypt
3 Department of Mathematics, Faculty of Science, Zagazig University, Zagazig 44519, Egypt; hbarakat2@hotmail.com (H.M.B.); ma_alawady@yahoo.com (M.A.A.); ishusseiny@gmail.com (I.A.H.)
4 Department of Basic Science, Faculty of Computers and Informatics, Suez Canal University, Ismailia 41522, Egypt; doaa.abdelshafi@ci.suez.edu.eg
5 Mathematics and Computer Science Department, Faculty of Science, Beni-Suef University, Beni-Suef 62511, Egypt
* Correspondence: moaasalem@imamu.edu.sa; Tel.:+966-590022352

Abstract: This study uses an effective, recently extended Farlie–Gumbel–Morgenstern (EFGM) family to derive the distribution of concomitants of K-record upper values (CKRV). For this CKRV, the negative cumulative residual extropy (NCREX), weighted NCREX (WNCREX), negative cumulative extropy (NCEX), and weighted NCEX (WNCEX) are theoretically and numerically examined. This study presents several beautiful symmetrical and asymmetric relationships that these inaccuracy measurements satisfy. Additionally, empirical estimations are provided for these measures, and their visualizations enable users to verify their accuracy.

Keywords: FGM family; concomitants; K-record values; weighted negative cumulative residual extropy; weighted negative cumulative extropy; non-parametric estimation

MSC: 60B12; 62G30

1. Introduction

One of the most fundamental techniques in stochastic multivariate analysis is the concept of a family of multivariate distributions. Families of bivariate distributions with known marginals have drawn attention for many years. The Farlie–Gumbel–Morgenstern (FGM) family is regarded as one of the world's first bivariate distribution families. When the FGM family turns into a copula (i.e., when the marginals are uniform), the correlation coefficient between the FGM family's marginals reaches its minimum value of -0.33 and highest value of 0.33. The FGM distribution is, therefore, best suited for data with low correlation coefficients. Despite this constraining restriction, the FGM family has increasingly replaced conventional multivariate normal models in various applications and is now extensively used in several different fields. In a study by Ghosh et al. [1], the FGM family was applied to model the interdependence between environmental and biological variables. In another study by Shrahili and Alotaibi [2], variants of this copula were employed to simulate real-world datasets with symmetric characteristics.

Numerous modifications to the FGM copula that have been discussed in the literature aim to improve the correlation between the inner marginals. Ebaid et al. [3] presented the symmetric generalization of the FGM copula, and Barakat et al. [4] have since considered it. They discovered that the admissible range and correlation claims made by Ebaid et al. [3] were false. Barakat et al. [4] revised the copula's allowable range. The symbol for this extension is EFGM, and it has a more straightforward function than many known generalizations of the FGM family, such as Bairamov–Kotz–Becki–FGM, Huang–Kotz FGM (see [5,6]), and iterated FGM (see Barakat and Husseiny, [7]). Recently, Abd Elgawad et al. [8] revealed and discussed some distributional traits of concomitants of order statistics (OSs) arising from the EFGM family. The work by Abd Elgawad et al. [8] is expanded upon in this research to include $K-$record values in the perspective of some recent information measures. The cumulative distribution function (CDF) and probability density function (PDF) of the EFGM family, denoted by EFGM(c,d), are given, respectively, by (cf. [4])

$$H_{T,W}(t,w) = H_T(t)H_W(w)\left[1 + c\overline{H}_T(t)\overline{H}_W(w)(1 + dH_T(t))(1 + dH_W(w))\right] \tag{1}$$

and

$$h_{T,W}(t,w) = h_T(t)h_W(w)\left\{1 + c\left[1 + 2(d-1)H_T(t) - 3dH_T^2(t)\right]\left[1 + 2(d-1)H_W(w) - 3dH_W^2(w)\right]\right\}, \tag{2}$$

where the marginals $H_T(t)$ and $H_W(w)$ are continuous, and $\overline{H}_X(.) = 1 - H_X(.)$. Barakat et al. [4] clarified that the natural parameter space Λ (the admissible set of parameters c and d that ensure $H_{T,W}(t,w)$ is a bonafide CDF) is convex. The set Λ is given by $\Lambda = \Lambda^+ \cup \Lambda^-$, where

$$\begin{aligned}
\Lambda^+ &= \left\{(c,d) : 0 \le d \le 1, -\frac{1}{(1+d)^2} \le c \le \frac{1}{(1+d)};\ \text{or } d > 1, -\frac{1}{(1+d)^2} \le c \le \frac{1}{(1+d)^2}\right\}, \\
\Lambda^- &= \left\{(c,d) : -2 \le d \le 0,\ -1 \le c \le 0;\ \text{or } d < -2, -\frac{1}{(1+d)^2} \le c \le \frac{1}{(1+d)^2}\right\}.
\end{aligned}$$

Let $\{T_i, i \ge 1\}$ be a set of independent random variables (RVs) with the same continuous CDF $H_T(.)$ and PDF $h_T(.)$. The observation T_j is called an upper record value when $T_j > T_i$ for every $i < j$. A similar definition can be given for lower record values. Due to the rarity of upper record values, which restricts their use in various applications, we can switch to a more flexible model, which is $K-$record upper values (KRVs), where we can always expect the occurrence of KRVs more frequently than upper record values. Considering the KRV model, refer to Dziubdziela and Kopociński [9]. For a fixed $K \ge 1$, the PDF of the Nth KRV is given by

$$g_{T_{N,k}}(t) = \frac{K^N}{\Gamma(N)}\left[-\ln \overline{H}_T(t)\right]^{N-1}\overline{H}_T^{K-1}(t)h_T(t), N \ge 1, \tag{3}$$

where $\Gamma(.)$ is the gamma function. For more details about this model and its applications, refer to [10–13].

Let a random bivariate sample $(T_i, W_i), i = 1, 2, \ldots$, have a common continuous CDF $H_{T,W}(t,w) = P(T \le t, W \le w)$. When the investigator is just interested in studying the sequence of $K-$records, $T_{N,K}$, of the first component T, the second component associated with the KRV of the first one is termed as the concomitant of that KRV, denoted by $W_{[N,K]}$. Several papers, including [14–17], discussed the PDF of CKRV $W_{[N,K]}$. This concomitant's PDF is provided by

$$h_{[N,K]}(w) = \int_{-\infty}^{\infty} h_{W|T}(w|t)g_{T_{N,K}}(t)dt, \tag{4}$$

where $h_{W|T}(w|t)$ is the conditional PDF of W, given T.

The extropy (EX) was proposed by Lad et al. [18]. Earlier in academic literature, EX was used to contrast with entropy. The EX refers to an organism's intelligence, functional order, vitality, energy, life, experience, and capacity for growth and improvement. The EX of an RV T with PDF $h_T(t)$ is defined as (see [18,19])

$$EX(T) = -\frac{1}{2}\int_0^\infty h_T^2(t)dt = -\frac{1}{2}\int_0^1 h_T(H_T^{-1}(u))du \leq 0. \tag{5}$$

Qiu [20] reviewed several characterizations, as well as the EX-lower bounds for OSs and record values. Qiu and Jia [21] examined residual EX using OSs. Irshad et al. [22] refined the concept of past EX for concomitants of OSs from the FGM family. In addition, they studied the cumulative past EX and dynamic cumulative past EX for the concomitant of rth OS. There have been many studies of EX measures in conjunction with generalized OSs, such as Almaspoor et al. [23], Husseiny and Syam [24], and Husseiny et al. [25]. Additionally, Jahanshahi et al. [26] proposed a measure of uncertainty for RVs, known as cumulative residual extropy, abbreviated by CREX, which is given by

$$CREX(T) = -\frac{1}{2}\int_0^\infty \overline{H}_T^2(t)dt = -\frac{1}{2}\int_0^1 \frac{(1-u)^2}{h_T(H_T^{-1}(u))}du, \tag{6}$$

which is always negative. Consequently, the negative CREX (NCREX) shall be

$$\zeta R(T) = \frac{1}{2}\int_0^\infty \overline{H}_T^2(t)dt = \frac{1}{2}\int_0^1 \frac{(1-u)^2}{h_T(H_T^{-1}(u))}du. \tag{7}$$

Recently, Hashempour et al. [27] proposed a new information measure called weighted CREX (WCREX), which assigns more importance to large values of the considered RV, as well as EX and CREX; this measure is permanently negative and is defined by

$$CREX^w(T) = -\frac{1}{2}\int_0^\infty t\overline{H}_T^2(t)dt = -\frac{1}{2}\int_0^1 \frac{H_T^{-1}(u)(1-u)^2}{h_T(H_T^{-1}(u))}du. \tag{8}$$

Thus, the positive one would be called weighted negative cumulative residual extropy (WNCREX) and is expressed as

$$\zeta R^w(T) = \frac{1}{2}\int_0^\infty t\overline{H}_T^2(t)dt = \frac{1}{2}\int_0^1 \frac{H_T^{-1}(u)(1-u)^2}{h_T(H_T^{-1}(u))}du. \tag{9}$$

Also, a negative cumulative extropy (NCEX) has been introduced, similar to (7), by Tahmasebi and Toomaj [28]; that is,

$$\zeta(T) = \frac{1}{2}\int_0^\infty (1 - H_T^2(t))dt = \frac{1}{2}\int_0^1 \frac{1-u^2}{h_T(H_T^{-1}(u))}du. \tag{10}$$

Furthermore, Chaudhary et al. [29] investigated another new information measure called weighted negative cumulative extropy (WNCEX), which is defined by

$$\zeta^w(T) = \frac{1}{2}\int_0^\infty t(1 - H_T^2(t))dt = \frac{1}{2}\int_0^1 \frac{H_T^{-1}(u)(1-u^2)}{h_T(H_T^{-1}(u))}du. \tag{11}$$

Motivations of the Work

This study builds upon the work of Abd Elgawad et al. [8] regarding the OSs model, developing a significant parallel model about record values. Numerous real-world experiments lead to the concomitants of record values. These concomitants offer a practical and effective method for organizing and analyzing bivariate record data. One of the main motivations for this work is the practicality and realism of the KRV model, especially considering the rarity of record values. Another driving factor is the application of recent uncertainty measures to our model, which have broad implications across various scientific fields.

This paper is organized as follows: In Section 2, we derive the marginal distribution of CKRV based on the EFGM family and obtain the EX, NCREX, WNCREX, NCEX, and WNCEX for CKRV. In addition, in Section 3, numerical studies based on some well-known distributions are carried out. Moreover, Section 4 introduces the issue of non-parametric estimation of the mentioned measures through simulation studies. Finally, Section 5 presents the study's conclusion.

2. CKRV Based on EFGM(c,d) and EX, with Some of Its Associated Measures

In this section, we derive the marginal distribution of CKRV based on the EFGM family. Moreover, the EX, NCREX, WNCREX, NCEX, and WNCEX for CKRV are obtained.

2.1. The Marginal Distribution of CKRV Based on EFGM(c,d)

In the next theorem, we obtain a useful representation for the PDF of $W_{[N,K]}$. We use the notation $T \sim H_T$ to signify that T is distributed as H_T.

Theorem 1. *Let $V_1 \sim H_W^2$ and $V_2 \sim H_W^3$. Then*

$$\begin{aligned} h_{[N,K]}(w) &= h_W(w)\Big\{1+\eta[1+2(d-1)H_W(w)-3dH_W^2(w)]\Big\} \\ &= (1+\eta)h_W(w)+(d-1)\eta h_{V_1}(w)-d\eta h_{V_2}(w), \end{aligned} \tag{12}$$

where

$$\eta = -c(d+1)+2c(2d+1)\left(\frac{K}{K+1}\right)^N - 3cd\left(\frac{K}{K+2}\right)^N.$$

Proof. The PDF of CKRV is derived, starting with (4) as follows:

$$\begin{aligned} h_{[N,K]}(w) &= \int_{-\infty}^{\infty} h_{W|T}(w|t)g_{T_{N,K}}(t)dt \\ &= \int_{-\infty}^{\infty} h_W(w)\Big\{1+c[1+2(d-1)H_T(t)-3dH_T^2(t)] \\ &\times \quad [1+2(d-1)H_W(w)-3dH_W^2(w)]\Big\}g_{T_{N,K}}(t)dt \\ &= h_W(w)\Big\{1+\eta[1+2(d-1)H_W(w)-3dH_W^2(w)]\Big\}, \end{aligned}$$

where

$$\eta = c\int_{-\infty}^{\infty}\Big[1+2(d-1)H_T(t)-3dH_T^2(t)\Big]g_{T_{N,K}}(t)dt.$$

Using $H_T(t) = 1-\overline{H}_T(t)$ and simple algebra, we have

$$\eta = -c(d+1)+2c(2d+1)I_1-3cdI_2, \tag{13}$$

such that, for $p = 1,2$

$$I_p = \int_{-\infty}^{\infty}\overline{H}_T^p(t)g_{T_{N,K}}(t)dt.$$

Taking the transformation $\overline{H}_T(t) = e^{-z}$, we have

$$I_p = \frac{K^N}{\Gamma(N)}\int_0^{\infty} z^{N-1}e^{-z(K+p)}dz = \left(\frac{K}{K+p}\right)^N. \tag{14}$$

Finally, by using (13) with (14). The proof is completed. □

Remark 1. *If $K = 1$ in Theorem 1, we obtain the case of upper record values.*

Remark 2. *When the value of K is large, we can use the approximation $\eta \approx c$. Moreover, when the value of N is large, we can use the approximation $\eta \approx -c(d+1)$. Finally, when both K and N are large, such that $K \sim N$, we have $\eta \approx -c(d+1) + 2c(2d+1)e^{-1} - 3cde^{-2}$.*

Corollary 1. *By using Theorem 1, the marginal CDF of CKRV and its survival function satisfy the following two elegant symmetry relationships:*

$$H_{[N,K]}(w) = (1+\eta)H_W(w) + (d-1)\eta H_{V_1}(w) - d\eta H_{V_2}(w) \tag{15}$$

and

$$\overline{H}_{[N,K]}(w) = (1+\eta)\overline{H}_W(w) + (d-1)\eta \overline{H}_{V_1}(w) - d\eta \overline{H}_{V_2}(w). \tag{16}$$

2.2. EX and Some of Its More Recent Related Measures

In this section, the measures EX, NCREX, WNCREX, NCEX, and WNCEX for CKRV $W_{[N,K]}$ based on EFGM(c,d) are derived.

2.2.1. EX of CKRV for EFGM(c,d)

Using (5) and (12), the EX of $W_{[N,K]}$ is given by

$$\begin{aligned} EX_{[N,K]}(W) &= -\frac{1}{2}\int_0^{\infty} h^2_{[N,K]}(w)dw \\ &= -\frac{1}{2}\int_0^{\infty} h^2_W(w)\Big[A_1^2 + A_2^2H_W^2(w) + A_3^2H_W^4(w) + 2A_1A_2H_W(w) \\ &+ 2A_1A_3H_W^2(w) + 2A_2A_3H_W^3(w)\Big]dw \\ &= A_1^2EX(W) - A_1A_2E[h_W(w)H_W(w)] - \left(\frac{1}{2}A_2^2 + A_1A_3\right)E[h_W(w)H_W^2(w)] \\ &- A_2A_3E[h_W(w)H_W^3(w)] - \frac{1}{2}A_3^2E[h_W(w)H_W^4(w)], \end{aligned} \tag{17}$$

where $A_1 = 1+\eta$, $A_2 = 2(d-1)\eta$, and $A_3 = -3d\eta$.

We can write $EX_{[N,K]}(W)$ in terms of the quantile function (QF). Let the QF be $Q(u) = H_W^{-1}(u)$, then the quantile density function is given by $q(u) = 1/h_W(Q(u))$, where the derivative of $Q(u)$ is respect to u and is denoted by $q(u)$ (i.e., $Q'(u) = q(u)$). Thus, $EX_{[N,K]}(W)$ is given by

$$\begin{aligned} EX_{[N,K]}(W) &= A_1^2EX(W) - A_1A_2E\left[\frac{U}{q(u)}\right] - \left(\frac{1}{2}A_2^2 + A_1A_3\right)E\left[\frac{U^2}{q(u)}\right] \\ &- A_2A_3E\left[\frac{U^3}{q(u)}\right] - \frac{1}{2}A_3^2E\left[\frac{U^4}{q(u)}\right], \end{aligned}$$

where $EX(W)$ is the EX of W, and U is a uniformly distributed RV on $(0,1)$.

Example 1. *Assume that the random vector (T,W) follows the extended Weibull family (denoted by EWF). As mentioned in [30], the EWF has its CDF and PDF described as follows*

$$\begin{aligned} H_T(t) &= 1 - e^{-\varrho G(t;\tau)}, \\ h_T(t) &= \varrho g(t;\tau)e^{-\varrho G(t;\tau)}, \end{aligned} \tag{18}$$

respectively, where $\varrho > 0$, τ is a vector of parameters, and $G(t,\tau)$ is a non-negative, continuous, monotonically increasing, differentiable function of t, dependent on the parameter vector τ, such that $G(t,\tau) \to 0^+$ as $t \to 0^+$ and $G(t,\tau) \to +\infty$ as $t \to +\infty$. $g(t;\tau)$ is the derivative of $G(t;\tau)$. Using (18) in (1), the CDF of EFGM with EWF (denoted by EFGM-EWF) is given by

$$H_{T,W}(t,w) = \left(1-e^{-\varrho_1 G(t;\tau_1)}\right)\left(1-e^{-\varrho_2 G(w;\tau_2)}\right)\left[1+ce^{(-\varrho_1 G(t;\tau_1)-\varrho_2 G(w;\tau_2))}\right.$$
$$\times \left.\left(1+d\left(1-e^{-\varrho_1 G(t;\tau_1)}\right)\right)\left(1+d\left(1-e^{-\varrho_2 G(w;\tau_2)}\right)\right)\right]. \quad (19)$$

According to (17), the EX of $W_{[N,K]}$ *is*

$$\begin{aligned} EX_{[N,K]}(W) &= A_1^2 EX(W) - A_1 A_2 E\left[\varrho_2 g(w;\tau_2)e^{-\varrho_2 G(w;\tau_2)}\left(1-e^{-\varrho_2 G(w;\tau_2)}\right)\right] \\ &- \left(\frac{1}{2}A_2^2 + A_1 A_3\right)E\left[\varrho_2 g(w;\tau_2)e^{-\varrho_2 G(w;\tau_2)}\left(1-e^{-\varrho_2 G(w;\tau_2)}\right)^2\right] \quad (20) \\ &- A_2 A_3 E\left[\varrho_2 g(w;\tau_2)e^{-\varrho_2 G(w;\tau_2)}\left(1-e^{-\varrho_2 G(w;\tau_2)}\right)^3\right] \\ &- \frac{1}{2}A_3^2 E\left[\varrho_2 g(w;\tau_2)e^{-\varrho_2 G(w;\tau_2)}\left(1-e^{-\varrho_2 G(w;\tau_2)}\right)^4\right]. \end{aligned}$$

Example 2. *Based on Example 1, by using* $\varrho_i G(x,\tau_i) = -log(1-x)$ *(i.e.,* $\varrho_i = 1$*) and* $\varrho_i g(x,\tau_i) = \frac{1}{1-x}$ *for* $x = t, w$ *and* $i = 1,2$*, respectively, with (19), we obtain the joint uniform distribution with parameters 0 and 1 as EFGM (denoted by EFGM-UD), which is given by*

$$H_{T,W}(t,w) = tw[1+c(1-t)(1-w)(1+dt)(1+dw)]. \quad (21)$$

According to (20), the EX of $W_{[N,K]}$ *is*

$$\begin{aligned} EX_{[N,K]}(W) &= -\frac{1}{2}A_1^2 - \frac{1}{6}A_2^2 - \frac{1}{10}A_3^2 - \frac{1}{2}A_1A_2 - \frac{1}{3}A_1A_3 - \frac{1}{4}A_2A_3 \\ &= -\frac{1}{2} - \left(\frac{1}{6} + \frac{1}{6}d + \frac{1}{15}d^2\right)\eta^2. \end{aligned}$$

Example 3. *Based on Example (1), by putting* $\varrho_i G(x,\tau_i) = \frac{x}{\lambda_i}$ *(i.e.,* $\varrho_i = \frac{1}{\lambda_i}$*) for* $x = t, w$ *and* $i = 1,2$*, respectively, and* $\varrho_i g(x,\tau) = \frac{1}{\lambda_i}$*, in (19), we obtain the joint exponential distribution with parameters* $\lambda_i > 0$ *as the EFGM family (denoted by EFGM-ED), which is given as*

$$H_{T,W}(t,w) = \left(1-e^{-\frac{t}{\lambda_1}}\right)\left(1-e^{-\frac{w}{\lambda_2}}\right)\left[1+ce^{-\left(\frac{t}{\lambda_1}+\frac{w}{\lambda_2}\right)}\left(1+d\left(1-e^{-\frac{t}{\lambda_1}}\right)\right)\left(1+d\left(1-e^{-\frac{w}{\lambda_2}}\right)\right)\right]. \quad (22)$$

Moreover, in view of (20), we have

$$\begin{aligned} EX_{[N,K]}(W) &= -\lambda_2\left[\frac{1}{4}A_1^2 + \frac{1}{24}A_2^2 + \frac{1}{60}A_3^2 - \frac{1}{6}A_1A_2 + \frac{1}{12}A_1A_3 + \frac{1}{20}A_2A_3\right] \\ &= -\lambda_2\left[\frac{1}{4} + \left(\frac{1}{6} + \frac{1}{12}d\right)\eta + \left(\frac{1}{12} + \frac{1}{20}d + \frac{1}{60}d^2\right)\eta^2\right]. \end{aligned}$$

2.2.2. NCREX of CKRV for EFGM(c,d)

We can obtain $\zeta R_{[N,K]}(W)$ by using (7) and (16) as

$$\begin{aligned} \zeta R_{[N,K]}(W) &= \frac{1}{2}\int_0^\infty \overline{H}^2_{[N,K]}(w)dw \\ &= \frac{1}{2}\int_0^\infty \left[(1+\eta)^2\overline{H}^2_W(w) + (d-1)^2\eta^2\overline{H}^2_{V_1}(w) + d^2\eta^2\overline{H}^2_{V_2}(w)\right. \\ &+ 2(d-1)(1+\eta)\eta\overline{H}_W(w)\overline{H}_{V_1}(w) - 2d(1+\eta)\eta\overline{H}_W(w)\overline{H}_{V_2}(w) \\ &- \left.2d(d-1)\eta^2\overline{H}_{V_1}(w)\overline{H}_{V_2}(w)\right]dw. \end{aligned}$$

Then,

$$\begin{aligned}\zeta R_{[N,K]}(W) &= (1+\eta)^2\zeta R(W)+(d-1)^2\eta^2\zeta R(V_1)+d^2\eta^2\zeta R(V_2)\\ &+ (d-1)(1+\eta)\eta E\left[\frac{\overline{H}_W(w)\overline{H}_{V_1}(w)}{h_W(w)}\right]-d(1+\eta)\eta E\left[\frac{\overline{H}_W(w)\overline{H}_{V_2}(w)}{h_W(w)}\right]\\ &- d(d-1)\eta^2 E\left[\frac{\overline{H}_{V_1}(w)\overline{H}_{V_2}(w)}{h_W(w)}\right].\end{aligned} \tag{23}$$

Also, it can be expressed in another form using QF as

$$\begin{aligned}\zeta R_{[N,K]}(W) &= \frac{1}{2}(1+\eta)^2E\left[(1-U)^2q(u)\right]+\frac{1}{2}(d-1)^2\eta^2E\left[\left(1-U^2\right)^2q(u)\right]\\ &+ \frac{1}{2}d^2\eta^2E\left[\left(1-U^3\right)^2q(u)\right]+(d-1)(1+\eta)\eta E\left[(1-U)\left(1-U^2\right)q(u)\right]\\ &- d(1+\eta)\eta E\left[(1-U)\left(1-U^3\right)q(u)\right]-d(d-1)\eta^2E\left[\left(1-U^2\right)\left(1-U^3\right)q(u)\right].\end{aligned}$$

Example 4. *Let* (T,W) *follow EFGM.*

- *According to EFGM-EWF, which is defined by (19), using (23), the NCREX of* $W_{[N,K]}$ *is given by*

$$\begin{aligned}\zeta R_{[N,K]}(W) &= \frac{1}{2}(1+\eta)^2E\left[\frac{e^{-\varrho_2G(w;\tau_2)}}{\varrho_2g(w;\tau_2)}\right]\\ &+ \frac{1}{2}(d-1)^2\eta^2E\left[\frac{e^{\varrho_2G(w;\tau_2)}}{\varrho_2g(w;\tau_2)}\left(1-\left(1-e^{-\varrho_2G(w;\tau_2)}\right)^2\right)^2\right]\\ &+ \frac{1}{2}d^2\eta^2E\left[\frac{e^{\varrho_2G(w;\tau_2)}}{\varrho_2g(w;\tau_2)}\left(1-\left(1-e^{-\varrho_2G(w;\tau_2)}\right)^3\right)^2\right]\\ &+ (d-1)(1+\eta)\eta E\left[\frac{1}{\varrho_2g(w;\tau_2)}\left(1-\left(1-e^{-\varrho_2G(w;\tau_2)}\right)^2\right)\right]\\ &- d(1+\eta)\eta E\left[\frac{1}{\varrho_2g(w;\tau_2)}\left(1-\left(1-e^{-\varrho_2G(w;\tau_2)}\right)^3\right)\right]\\ &- d(d-1)\eta^2E\left[\frac{e^{\varrho_2G(w;\tau_2)}}{\varrho_2g(w;\tau_2)}\left(1-\left(1-e^{-\varrho_2G(w;\tau_2)}\right)^2\right)\left(1-\left(1-e^{-\varrho_2G(w;\tau_2)}\right)^3\right)\right].\end{aligned} \tag{24}$$

- *For EFGM-UD, which is given by (21), using (24), NCREX of* $W_{[N,K]}$ *is given by*

$$\zeta R_{[N,K]}(W)=\frac{1}{6}-\left(\frac{1}{12}+\frac{1}{30}d\right)\eta+\left(\frac{1}{60}+\frac{1}{60}d+\frac{1}{210}d^2\right)\eta^2.$$

- *By choosing* $\varrho_iG(x,\tau_i)=-log(1-w^{\beta_i})$ *(i.e.,* $\varrho_i=1$*) in EFGM-EWF, we obtain the EFGM with power function distribution marginals (denoted by EFGM-PFD), which is given by*

$$H_{T,W}(t,w)=t^{\beta_1}w^{\beta_2}[1+c\left(1-t^{\beta_1}\right)\left(1-w^{\beta_2}\right)(1+dt^{\beta_1})(1+dw^{\beta_2})],\ \beta_i>0,\ i=1,2. \tag{25}$$

Also, by using $\varrho_iG(x,\tau_i)$ *and* $\varrho_ig(x,\tau_i)$ *into (24), we have*

$$\begin{aligned}\zeta R_{[N,K]}(W) &= \beta_2^2\Bigg\{\frac{1}{1+3\beta_2+2\beta_2^2}\\ &+ \left[\frac{-2}{1+6\beta_2+11\beta_2^2+6\beta_2^3}-\frac{2}{1+9\beta_2+26\beta_2^2+24\beta_2^3}d\right]\eta\\ &+ \left[\frac{1}{1+9\beta_2+26\beta_2^2+24\beta_2^3}+\frac{1}{1+12\beta_2+47\beta_2^2+60\beta_2^3}d\right.\\ &+ \left.\frac{1}{1+15\beta_2+74\beta_2^2+120\beta_2^3}d^2\right]\eta^2\Bigg\}.\end{aligned}$$

- *For EFGM-ED with parameters $\lambda_i, i=1,2$, whose CDF is (22), the $\zeta R_{[N,K]}(W)$ is given by*

$$\zeta R_{[N,K]}(W)=\frac{1}{\lambda_2}\left[\frac{1}{4}-\left(\frac{1}{6}+\frac{1}{12}d\right)\eta+\left(\frac{1}{24}+\frac{1}{20}d+\frac{1}{60}d^2\right)\eta^2\right].$$

2.2.3. WNCREX of CKRV for EFGM(c,d)

Using (9) and (16), the WNCREX of $W_{[N,K]}$ can be simply obtained as follows:

$$\begin{aligned}\zeta R^w_{[N,K]}(W) &= \frac{1}{2}\int_0^\infty w\overline{H}^2_{[N,K]}(w)dw\\ &= \frac{1}{2}\int_0^\infty w[(1+\eta)^2\overline{H}^2_W(w)+(d-1)^2\eta^2\overline{H}^2_{V_1}(w)+d^2\eta^2\overline{H}^2_{V_2}(w)\\ &+ 2(d-1)(1+\eta)\eta\overline{H}_W(w)\overline{H}_{V_1}(w)-2d(1+\eta)\eta\overline{H}_W(w)\overline{H}_{V_2}(w)\\ &- 2d(d-1)\eta^2\overline{H}_{V_1}(w)\overline{H}_{V_2}(w)]dw.\end{aligned}$$

Then,

$$\begin{aligned}\zeta R^w_{[N,K]}(W) &= (1+\eta)^2\zeta R^w(W)+(d-1)^2\eta^2\zeta R^w(V_1)+d^2\eta^2\zeta R^w(V_2)\\ &+ (d-1)(1+\eta)\eta E\left[\frac{W\overline{H}_W(w)\overline{H}_{V_1}(w)}{h_W(w)}\right]-d(1+\eta)\eta E\left[\frac{W\overline{H}_W(w)\overline{H}_{V_2}(w)}{h_W(w)}\right]\\ &- d(d-1)\eta^2 E\left[\frac{W\overline{H}_{V_1}(w)\overline{H}_{V_2}(w)}{h_W(w)}\right].\end{aligned} \tag{26}$$

In addition, it can be written in terms of QF. Thus, the corresponding $\zeta R^w_{[N,K]}(W)$ based on the QF is given by

$$\begin{aligned}\zeta R^w_{[N,K]}(W) &= \frac{(1+\eta)^2}{2}E\Big[(1-U)^2q(u)Q(u)\Big]+\frac{(d-1)^2\eta^2}{2}E\Big[\left(1-U^2\right)^2q(u)Q(u)\Big]\\ &+ \frac{d^2\eta^2}{2}E\Big[\left(1-U^3\right)^2q(u)Q(u)\Big]+(d-1)(1+\eta)\eta E\Big[(1-U)\left(1-U^2\right)q(u)Q(u)\Big]\\ &- d(1+\eta)\eta E\Big[(1-U)\left(1-U^3\right)q(u)Q(u)\Big]-d(d-1)\eta^2E\Big[\left(1-U^2\right)\left(1-U^3\right)q(u)Q(u)\Big].\end{aligned}$$

Example 5. *Let T and W follow EFGM.*

- *According to EFGM-EWF, which is defined by (19), and by using (26), the WNCREX of $W_{[N,K]}$ is*

$$
\begin{aligned}
\zeta R^{w}_{[N,K]}(W) &= \frac{1}{2}(1+\eta)^2 E\left[\frac{We^{-\varrho_2 G(w;\tau_2)}}{\varrho_2 g(w;\tau_2)}\right] \\
&+ \frac{1}{2}(d-1)^2\eta^2 E\left[\frac{We^{\varrho_2 G(w;\tau_2)}}{\varrho_2 g(w;\tau_2)}\left(1-\left(1-e^{-\varrho_2 G(w;\tau_2)}\right)^2\right)^2\right] \\
&+ \frac{1}{2}d^2\eta^2 E\left[\frac{We^{\varrho_2 G(w;\tau_2)}}{\varrho_2 g(w;\tau_2)}\left(1-\left(1-e^{-\varrho_2 G(w;\tau_2)}\right)^3\right)^2\right] \\
&+ (d-1)(1+\eta)\eta E\left[\frac{W}{\varrho_2 g(w;\tau_2)}\left(1-\left(1-e^{-\varrho_2 G(w;\tau_2)}\right)^2\right)\right] \\
&- d(1+\eta)\eta E\left[\frac{W}{\varrho_2 g(w;\tau_2)}\left(1-\left(1-e^{-\varrho_2 G(w;\tau_2)}\right)^3\right)\right] \\
&- d(d-1)\eta^2 E\left[\frac{We^{\varrho_2 G(w;\tau_2)}}{\varrho_2 g(w;\tau_2)}\left(1-\left(1-e^{-\varrho_2 G(w;\tau_2)}\right)^2\right)\left(1-\left(1-e^{-\varrho_2 G(w;\tau_2)}\right)^3\right)\right].
\end{aligned}
\tag{27}
$$

- *For EFGM-UD, which is defined by (21), and by using (27), the WNCREX of* $W_{[N,K]}$ *is*

$$
\zeta R^{w}_{[N,K]}(W) = \frac{1}{24} - \left(\frac{1}{30}+\frac{1}{60}d\right)\eta + \left(\frac{1}{120}+\frac{1}{105}d+\frac{1}{336}d^2\right)\eta^2.
$$

- *For EFGM-PFD, which is defined in (25), and by using (27), the WNCREX of* $W_{[N,K]}$ *would be*

$$
\begin{aligned}
\zeta R^{w}_{[N,K]}(W) &= \beta_2^2\Bigg\{\frac{1}{8+12\beta_2+4\beta_2^2} \\
&+ \left[\frac{-1}{4+12\beta_2+11\beta_2^2+3\beta_2^3} - \frac{1}{4+18\beta_2+26\beta_2^2+12\beta_2^3}d\right]\eta \\
&+ \left[\frac{1}{8+36\beta_2+52\beta_2^2+24\beta_2^3} + \frac{1}{4+24\beta_2+47\beta_2^2+30\beta_2^3}d\right. \\
&+ \left.\frac{1}{8+60\beta_2+148\beta_2^2+120\beta_2^3}d^2\right]\eta^2\Bigg\}.
\end{aligned}
$$

- *According to EFGM-ED, which is described in (22), and by using (27), the WNCREX of* $W_{[N,K]}$ *is given by*

$$
\zeta R^{w}_{[N,K]}(W) = \frac{1}{\lambda_2^2}\left[\frac{1}{8} - \left(\frac{5}{36}+\frac{13}{144}d\right)\eta + \left(\frac{13}{288}+\frac{77}{1200}d+\frac{29}{1200}d^2\right)\eta^2\right].
$$

- *Putting* $\varrho_i G(x,\tau_i) = \frac{x^2}{2\lambda_i}$ *(i.e.,* $\varrho_i = \frac{1}{2\lambda_i}$*) in EFGM-EWF, we obtain EFGM with Rayleigh distribution marginals (denoted by EFGM-RD), which is given by*

$$
H_{T,W}(t,w) = \left(1-e^{-\frac{t^2}{2\lambda_1}}\right)\left(1-e^{-\frac{w^2}{2\lambda_2}}\right)\left[1+ce^{-\left(\frac{t^2}{2\lambda_1}+\frac{w^2}{2\lambda_2}\right)}\left(1+d\left(1-e^{-\frac{t^2}{2\lambda_1}}\right)\right)\left(1+d\left(1-e^{-\frac{w^2}{2\lambda_2}}\right)\right)\right].
$$

Therefore, the WNCREX of $W_{[N,K]}$ *would be*

$$
\zeta R^{w}_{[N,K]}(W) = \lambda_2^2\left[\frac{1}{4} + \left(\frac{-1}{6}-\frac{1}{12}d\right)\eta + \left(\frac{1}{24}+\frac{1}{20}d+\frac{1}{60}d^2\right)\eta^2\right].
$$

- *Choosing $\varrho_i G(x,\tau_i) = -\alpha_i log(\frac{\sigma_i}{x})$ (i.e., $\varrho_i = -\alpha_i$), in EFGM- EWF, we obtain EFGM with Pareto type-I distribution marginals (denoted by EFGM-PID), as follows*

$$H_{T,W}(t,w) = \left(1-\left(\frac{\sigma_1}{t}\right)^{\alpha_1}\right)\left(1-\left(\frac{\sigma_2}{w}\right)^{\alpha_2}\right)\left[1+c\frac{\sigma_1^{\alpha_1}\sigma_2^{\alpha_2}}{t^{\alpha_1}w^{\alpha_2}}\left(1+d\left(1-\left(\frac{\sigma_1}{t}\right)^{\alpha_1}\right)\right)\left(1+d\left(1-\left(\frac{\sigma_2}{w}\right)^{\alpha_2}\right)\right)\right], \quad (28)$$

Further, by using (27), we have

$$\begin{aligned}\zeta R^{w}_{[N,K]}(W) &= \sigma_2^2\Bigg\{\frac{1}{-4+4\alpha_2}+\left[\frac{-4\alpha_2}{4-10\alpha_2+6\alpha_2^2}-\frac{\alpha_2^2}{-4+18\alpha_2-26\alpha_2^2+12\alpha^3}d\right]\eta \\ &+ \left[\frac{\alpha_2^2}{-8+36\alpha_2-52\alpha_2^2+24\alpha^3}+\frac{3\alpha_2^3}{8-56\alpha_2+142\alpha_2^2-154\alpha^3+60\alpha_2^4}d\right. \\ &+ \left.\frac{3\alpha_2^4}{-8+80\alpha_2-310\alpha_2^2+580\alpha^3-522\alpha_2^4+180\alpha_2^5}d^2\right]\eta^2\Bigg\}.\end{aligned}$$

Figure 1a,b depicts the WNCREX of $W_{[N,K]}$ from EFGM-PFD for various values of N and K at $d=-3$. The following properties can be extracted from Figure 1.

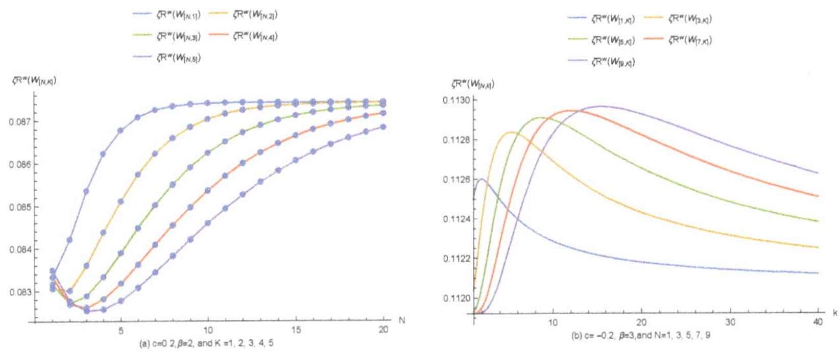

Figure 1. WNCREX of $W_{[N,K]}$ from EFGM-PFD.

1. With fixed N, c, and β, the value of $\zeta R^{w}_{[N,K]}(W)$ increases as K decreases (see Figure 1a) and stability occurs for large N.
2. For the fixed large K, the value of $\zeta R^{w}_{[N,K]}(W)$ increases with the increasing N; see Figure 1b.

Figure 2a,b depicts the WNCREX of $W_{[N,K]}$ from EFGM-RD for various values of N and K at $d=2$. The following properties can be extracted from Figure 2.

1. Stability occurs for large N and K, see Figure 2a,b.
2. With fixed c and σ, the values of $\zeta R^{w}_{[N,K]}(W)$ are very near to each other as N and K rise.

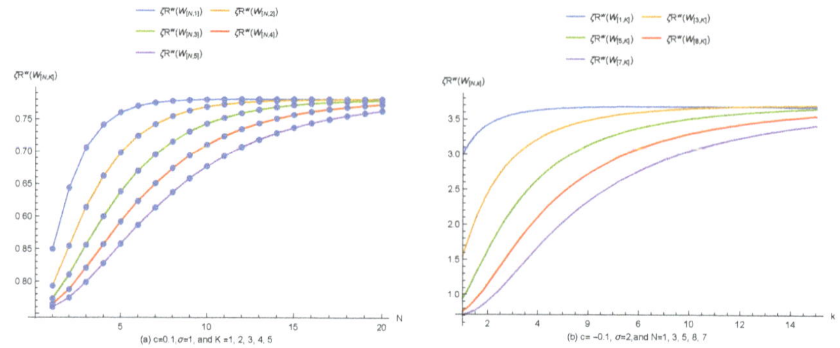

Figure 2. WNCREX of $W_{[N,K]}$ from EFGM-RD.

2.2.4. NCEX of CKRV for EFGM(c,d)

We can calculate the NCEX of CKRV $W_{[N,K]}$ as follows:

$$\begin{aligned}\zeta_{[N,K]}(W) &= \frac{1}{2}\int_0^\infty \left[1 - H^2_{[N,K]}(w)\right]dt \\ &= \int_0^\infty \overline{H}_{[N,K]}(w)dw - \zeta R_{[N,K]}(W) \\ &= \int_0^\infty [(1+\eta)\overline{H}_W(w) + (d-1)\eta\overline{H}_{V_1}(w) - d\eta\overline{H}_{V_2}(w)]dw - \zeta R_{[N,K]}(W).\end{aligned}$$

Using (23) and simple algebra, we have

$$\begin{aligned}\zeta_{[N,K]}(W) &= (1+\eta)E\left[\frac{\overline{H}_W(w)}{h_W(w)}\right] + (d-1)\eta E\left[\frac{\overline{H}_{V_1}(w)}{h_W(w)}\right] - d\eta E\left[\frac{\overline{H}_{V_2}(w)}{h_W(w)}\right] \\ &- (1+\eta)^2\zeta R(W) - (d-1)^2\eta^2\zeta R(V_1) - d^2\eta^2\zeta R(V_2) \\ &- (d-1)(1+\eta)\eta E\left[\frac{\overline{H}_W(w)\overline{H}_{V_1}(w)}{h_W(w)}\right] + d(1+\eta)\eta E\left[\frac{\overline{H}_W(w)\overline{H}_{V_2}(w)}{h_W(w)}\right] \\ &+ d(d-1)\eta^2 E\left[\frac{\overline{H}_{V_1}(w)\overline{H}_{V_2}(w)}{h_W(w)}\right].\end{aligned}$$

According to QF, $\zeta_{[N,K]}(W)$ is given by

$$\begin{aligned}\zeta_{[N,K]}(W) &= (1+\eta)E[(1-U)q(u)] + (d-1)\eta E\left[\left(1-U^2\right)q(u)\right] - d\eta E\left[\left(1-U^3\right)q(u)\right] \\ &- \frac{1}{2}(1+\eta)^2 E\left[(1-U)^2 q(u)\right] - \frac{1}{2}(d-1)^2\eta^2 E\left[\left(1-U^2\right)^2 q(u)\right] \\ &- \frac{1}{2}d^2\eta^2 E\left[\left(1-U^3\right)^2 q(u)\right] - (d-1)(1+\eta)\eta E\left[(1-U)\left(1-U^2\right)q(u)\right] \\ &+ d(1+\eta)\eta E\left[(1-U)\left(1-U^3\right)q(u)\right] + d(d-1)\eta^2 E\left[\left(1-U^2\right)\left(1-U^3\right)q(u)\right]. \quad (29)\end{aligned}$$

Example 6. *Let T and W follow the EFGM family*

- *For EFGM-EWF, which is defined by (19), and by using (29), the NCEX of* $W_{[N,K]}$ *is*

$$
\begin{aligned}
\zeta_{[N,K]}(W) &= (1+\eta)E\left[\frac{1}{\varrho_2 g(w;\tau_2)}\right] \\
&+ (d-1)\eta E\left[\frac{e^{\varrho_2 G(w;\tau_2)}}{\varrho_2 g(w;\tau_2)}\left(1-\left(1-e^{-\varrho_2 G(w;\tau_2)}\right)^2\right)\right] \\
&- d\eta E\left[\frac{e^{\varrho_2 G(w;\tau_2)}}{\varrho_2 g(w;\tau_2)}\left(1-\left(1-e^{-\varrho_2 G(w;\tau_2)}\right)^3\right)\right] - \frac{1}{2}(1+\eta)^2 E\left[\frac{e^{-\varrho_2 G(w;\tau_2)}}{\varrho_2 g(w;\tau_2)}\right] \\
&- \frac{1}{2}(d-1)^2\eta^2 E\left[\frac{e^{\varrho_2 G(w;\tau_2)}}{\varrho_2 g(w;\tau_2)}\left(1-\left(1-e^{-\varrho_2 G(w;\tau_2)}\right)^2\right)^2\right] \\
&- \frac{1}{2}d^2\eta^2 E\left[\frac{e^{\varrho_2 G(w;\tau_2)}}{\varrho_2 g(w;\tau_2)}\left(1-\left(1-e^{-\varrho_2 G(w;\tau_2)}\right)^3\right)^2\right] \qquad (30) \\
&- (d-1)(1+\eta)\eta E\left[\frac{1}{\varrho_2 g(w;\tau_2)}\left(1-\left(1-e^{-\varrho_2 G(w;\tau_2)}\right)^2\right)\right] \\
&+ d(1+\eta)\eta E\left[\frac{1}{\varrho_2 g(w;\tau_2)}\left(1-\left(1-e^{-\varrho_2 G(w;\tau_2)}\right)^3\right)\right] \\
&+ d(d-1)\eta^2 E\left[\frac{e^{\varrho_2 G(w;\tau_2)}}{\varrho_2 g(w;\tau_2)}\left(1-\left(1-e^{-\varrho_2 G(w;\tau_2)}\right)^2\right)\left(1-\left(1-e^{-\varrho_2 G(w;\tau_2)}\right)^3\right)\right].
\end{aligned}
$$

- *For EFGM-UD, as clarified in (21), the following equation is derived using (30):*

$$
\zeta_{[N,K]}(W) = \frac{1}{3} - \left(\frac{1}{12} + \frac{1}{20}d\right)\eta - \left(\frac{1}{60} + \frac{1}{60}d + \frac{1}{210}d^2\right)\eta^2.
$$

- *For EFGM-ED, with parameters as defined in (22), the equation using (30) is given by*

$$
\zeta_{[N,K]}(W) = \frac{1}{\lambda_2}\left[\frac{3}{4} - \left(\frac{1}{3} + \frac{1}{4}d\right)\eta - \left(\frac{1}{24} + \frac{1}{20}d + \frac{1}{60}d^2\right)\eta^2\right].
$$

- *For EFGM-PID, with parameters as mentioned in (28), by using (30), then*

$$
\begin{aligned}
\zeta_{[N,K]}(W) &= \sigma_2\left\{\frac{-1+3\alpha_2}{2-6\alpha_2+4\alpha_2^2}\left[\frac{2\alpha_2^2}{-1+6\alpha_2-11\alpha_2^2+6\alpha_2^3} + \frac{6\alpha_2^3}{1-10\alpha_2+35\alpha_2^2-50\alpha^3+24\alpha_2^4}d\right]\eta\right. \\
&- \left[\frac{\alpha_2^2}{-1+9\alpha_2-26\alpha_2^2+24\alpha^3} + \frac{6\alpha_2^3}{1-14\alpha_2+71\alpha_2^2-154\alpha^3+120\alpha_2^4}d\right. \\
&+ \left.\left.\frac{3\alpha_2^4}{-1+20\alpha_2-155\alpha_2^2+580\alpha^3-1044\alpha_2^4+720\alpha_2^5}d^2\right]\eta^2\right\}.
\end{aligned}
$$

2.2.5. WNCEX of CKRV for EFGM(c,d)

Similar to ζ, we can obtain ζ^w of $W_{[N,K]}$ as

$$\begin{aligned}
\zeta^{w}_{[N,K]}(W) &= (1+\eta)E[(1-U)q(u)Q(u)] + (d-1)\eta E\left[\left(1-U^2\right)q(u)Q(u)\right] \\
&- d\eta E\left[\left(1-U^3\right)q(u)Q(u)\right] - \frac{1}{2}(1+\eta)^2 E\left[(1-U)^2 q(u)Q(u)\right] \\
&- \frac{1}{2}(d-1)^2\eta^2 E\left[\left(1-U^2\right)^2 q(u)Q(u)\right] - \frac{1}{2}d^2\eta^2 E\left[\left(1-U^3\right)^2 q(u)Q(u)\right] \\
&- (d-1)(1+\eta)\eta E\left[(1-U)\left(1-U^2\right)q(u)Q(u)\right] \\
&+ d(1+\eta)\eta E\left[(1-U)\left(1-U^3\right)q(u)Q(u)\right] \\
&+ d(d-1)\eta^2 E\left[\left(1-U^2\right)\left(1-U^3\right)q(u)Q(u)\right].
\end{aligned} \tag{31}$$

Example 7. *Suppose that T and W follow the EFGM family*

- *For EFGM-EWF, which is defined by (19), by using (31), the WNCEX of* $W_{[N,K]}$ *is*

$$\begin{aligned}
\zeta^{w}_{[N,K]}(W) &= (1+\eta)E\left[\frac{W}{\varrho_2 g(w;\tau_2)}\right] \\
&+ (d-1)\eta E\left[\frac{We^{\varrho_2 G(w;\tau_2)}}{\varrho_2 g(w;\tau_2)}\left(1-\left(1-e^{-\varrho_2 G(w;\tau_2)}\right)^2\right)\right] \\
&- d\eta E\left[\frac{We^{\varrho_2 G(w;\tau_2)}}{\varrho_2 g(w;\tau_2)}\left(1-\left(1-e^{-\varrho_2 G(w;\tau_2)}\right)^3\right)\right] - \frac{1}{2}(1+\eta)^2 E\left[\frac{We^{-\varrho_2 G(w;\tau_2)}}{\varrho_2 g(w;\tau_2)}\right] \\
&- \frac{1}{2}(d-1)^2\eta^2 E\left[\frac{We^{\varrho_2 G(w;\tau_2)}}{\varrho_2 g(w;\tau_2)}\left(1-\left(1-e^{-\varrho_2 G(w;\tau_2)}\right)^2\right)^2\right] \\
&- \frac{1}{2}d^2\eta^2 E\left[\frac{We^{\varrho_2 G(w;\tau_2)}}{\varrho_2 g(w;\tau_2)}\left(1-\left(1-e^{-\varrho_2 G(w;\tau_2)}\right)^3\right)^2\right] \\
&- (d-1)(1+\eta)\eta E\left[\frac{W}{\varrho_2 g(w;\tau_2)}\left(1-\left(1-e^{-\varrho_2 G(w;\tau_2)}\right)^2\right)\right] \\
&+ d(1+\eta)\eta E\left[\frac{W}{\varrho_2 g(w;\tau_2)}\left(1-\left(1-e^{-\varrho_2 G(w;\tau_2)}\right)^3\right)\right] \\
&+ d(d-1)\eta^2 E\left[\frac{We^{\varrho_2 G(w;\tau_2)}}{\varrho_2 g(w;\tau_2)}\left(1-\left(1-e^{-\varrho_2 G(w;\tau_2)}\right)^2\right)\left(1-\left(1-e^{-\varrho_2 G(w;\tau_2)}\right)^3\right)\right].
\end{aligned} \tag{32}$$

- *For EFGM-UD, we have*

$$\zeta^{w}_{[N,K]}(W) = \frac{1}{8} - \left(\frac{1}{20} + \frac{1}{30}d\right)\eta - \left(\frac{1}{120} + \frac{1}{105}d + \frac{1}{336}d^2\right)\eta^2.$$

- *For EFGM-ED, we have*

$$\zeta^{w}_{[N,K]}(W) = \frac{1}{\lambda_2^2}\left[\frac{7}{8} - \left(\frac{11}{18} + \frac{25}{48}d\right)\eta - \left(\frac{13}{288} + \frac{77}{1200}d + \frac{29}{1200}d^2\right)\eta^2\right].$$

- *For EFGM-RD, we have*

$$\zeta R^{w}_{[N,K]}(W) = \lambda_2^2\left[\frac{3}{4} - \left(\frac{1}{3} + \frac{1}{4}d\right)\eta - \left(\frac{1}{24} + \frac{1}{20}d + \frac{1}{60}d^2\right)\eta^2\right].$$

3. Numerical Study for the EX, NCREX, WNCREX, NCEX, and WNCEX

Tables 1–6 display the EX, NCREX, and WNCREX of $W_{[N,K]}$ from EFGM. The following properties can be extracted:

Table 1 displays the EX of $W_{[N,K]}$ from the EFGM copula.

- The value of $EX(W_{[N,K]};c) = EX(W_{[N,K]};-c)$, at $d = -3, 0.9, 2$.
- For $N > 1$, large K ($K \geq 40$), and $d = -3, -1, 0.9$, the value of $EX(W_{[N,K]};|c|)$ increases as the value of N increases.
- For $N > 1$, large K ($K \geq 40$), and $d = 2$, the value of $EX(W_{[N,K]};|c|)$ decreases as the value of N increases.

Table 2 displays the EX of $W_{[N,K]}$ based on EFGM-UD.

- For $N > 1$ and large K ($K \geq 40$), the value of $EX(W_{[N,K]};c)$ increases as the value of N increases along with the values of parameters (c,d) as $(-0.2,-3)$, $(0.2,0.9)$, and $(-0.1,2)$.
- For $N > 1$ and large K ($K \geq 40$), the value of $EX(W_{[N,K]};c)$ decreases as the value of N increases along with the values of parameters (c,d) as $(0.2,-3)$, $(-0.75,-1)$, $(-0.25,-1)$, $(0.9,-0.2)$, and $(0.1,2)$.

NCREX in $W_{[N,K]}$ based on EFGM copula, NCREX in $W_{[N,K]}$ based on EFGM-ED, WNCREX in $W_{[N,K]}$ based on EFGM copula, and WNCREX in $W_{[N,K]}$ based on EFGM-ED all satisfy the same asymmetry properties extracted for EX in $W_{[N,K]}$ from EFGM-ED (Table 2).

Moreover, in the earlier version of this paper, we presented an extra four tables for NCEX in $W_{[N,K]}$ based on EFGM copula, NCEX in $W_{[N,K]}$ based on EFGM-ED, WNCEX in $W_{[N,K]}$ based on EFGM copula, and WNCEX in $W_{[N,K]}$ based on EFGM-ED. Responding to the reviewers' comments about the excessive number of tables, we removed these extra tables, knowing that the same asymmetry properties, as extracted for EX in $W_{[N,K]}$ from EFGM-ED, also hold for these removed tables.

Table 1. EX in $W_{[N,K]}$ from the EFGM copula.

		$d=-3$		$d=-1$		$d=0.9$		$d=2$	
K	N	$c=-0.2$	$c=0.2$	$c=-0.75$	$c=-0.25$	$c=-0.2$	$c=0.2$	$c=-0.1$	$c=0.1$
2	1	−0.500296	−0.500296	−0.501042	−0.500116	−0.503464	−0.503464	−0.503407	−0.503407
2	3	−0.500280	−0.500280	−0.501775	−0.500197	−0.504957	−0.504957	−0.504749	−0.504749
2	5	−0.509920	−0.509920	−0.501079	−0.500120	−0.523053	−0.523053	−0.526828	−0.526828
2	7	−0.523524	−0.523524	−0.500329	−0.500037	−0.537641	−0.537641	−0.546456	−0.546456
6	1	−0.500340	−0.500340	−0.510762	−0.501196	−0.511352	−0.511352	−0.508801	−0.508801
6	3	−0.502672	−0.502672	−0.500001	−0.500000	−0.503523	−0.503523	−0.504500	−0.504500
6	5	−0.502570	−0.502570	−0.501708	−0.500190	−0.500037	−0.500037	−0.500315	−0.500315
6	7	−0.500417	−0.500417	−0.502927	−0.500325	−0.501888	−0.501888	−0.501237	−0.501237
40	1	−0.507091	−0.507091	−0.530776	−0.503420	−0.514590	−0.514590	−0.508321	−0.508321
40	3	−0.502546	−0.502546	−0.520221	−0.502247	−0.513887	−0.513887	−0.509327	−0.509327
40	5	−0.500485	−0.500485	−0.512740	−0.501416	−0.512936	−0.512936	−0.509918	−0.509918
40	7	−0.500003	−0.500003	−0.507577	−0.500842	−0.511804	−0.511804	−0.510114	−0.510114
100	1	−0.509078	−0.509078	−0.534630	−0.503848	−0.514752	−0.514752	−0.507955	−0.507955
100	3	−0.506407	−0.506407	−0.529423	−0.503269	−0.514562	−0.514562	−0.508484	−0.508484
100	5	−0.504327	−0.504327	−0.524863	−0.502763	−0.514319	−0.514319	−0.508947	−0.508947
100	7	−0.502751	−0.502751	−0.520883	−0.502320	−0.514028	−0.514028	−0.509341	−0.509341

Table 2. EX in $W_{[N,K]}$ from EFGM-ED at $\lambda_2 = 0.5$.

		$d=-3$		$d=-1$		$d=0.9$		$d=2$	
K	N	$c=-0.2$	$c=0.2$	$c=-0.75$	$c=-0.25$	$c=-0.2$	$c=0.2$	$c=-0.1$	$c=0.1$
2	1	−0.123657	−0.126435	−0.120182	−0.123307	−0.113982	−0.137343	−0.114444	−0.136667
2	3	−0.126394	−0.123693	−0.132466	−0.127341	−0.139923	−0.111974	−0.138892	−0.112657
2	5	−0.134587	−0.118514	−0.130705	−0.126812	−0.159545	−0.099277	−0.160551	−0.098197
2	7	−0.141051	−0.116300	−0.128049	−0.125989	−0.170707	−0.093696	−0.173601	−0.091548
6	1	−0.126541	−0.123565	−0.112295	−0.119868	−0.106026	−0.148318	−0.108578	−0.144292
6	3	−0.121247	−0.129588	−0.124808	−0.124936	−0.113894	−0.137455	−0.112965	−0.138502
6	5	−0.121311	−0.129492	−0.132310	−0.127294	−0.123794	−0.126220	−0.121671	−0.128432
6	7	−0.123417	−0.126714	−0.134828	−0.128032	−0.133986	−0.116737	−0.131897	−0.118506
40	1	−0.132902	−0.119314	−0.108231	−0.116846	−0.103818	−0.151764	−0.108993	−0.143720
40	3	−0.129469	−0.121327	−0.109635	−0.118193	−0.104269	−0.151045	−0.108138	−0.144903
40	5	−0.126852	−0.123299	−0.111563	−0.119459	−0.104902	−0.150048	−0.107661	−0.145573
40	7	−0.124863	−0.125138	−0.113794	−0.120633	−0.105696	−0.148821	−0.107506	−0.145792
100	1	−0.134106	−0.118731	−0.107956	−0.116433	−0.103716	−0.151929	−0.109320	−0.143274
100	3	−0.132459	−0.119543	−0.108353	−0.116999	−0.103836	−0.151736	−0.108851	−0.143916
100	5	−0.130984	−0.120368	−0.108878	−0.117554	−0.103990	−0.151489	−0.108454	−0.144463
100	7	−0.129662	−0.121198	−0.109511	−0.118097	−0.104177	−0.151191	−0.108126	−0.144920

Table 3. NCREX in $W_{[N,K]}$ based on EFGM copula.

		$d=-3$		$d=-1$		$d=0.9$		$d=2$	
K	N	$c=-0.2$	$c=0.2$	$c=-0.75$	$c=-0.25$	$c=-0.2$	$c=0.2$	$c=-0.1$	$c=0.1$
2	1	0.167233	0.166122	0.172991	0.168758	0.177954	0.156043	0.176974	0.156974
2	3	0.166137	0.167217	0.158634	0.163961	0.154035	0.180249	0.155289	0.178900
2	5	0.163806	0.170236	0.160383	0.164555	0.140612	0.197140	0.141023	0.197142
2	7	0.162557	0.172457	0.163179	0.165499	0.134158	0.206390	0.133927	0.207775
6	1	0.166084	0.167274	0.187525	0.173449	0.187588	0.147921	0.183531	0.151388
6	3	0.168430	0.165094	0.166897	0.166744	0.178054	0.155955	0.178564	0.155580
6	5	0.168395	0.165122	0.158786	0.164013	0.167808	0.165532	0.169737	0.163653
6	7	0.167341	0.166022	0.156399	0.163198	0.158759	0.174937	0.160752	0.172804
40	1	0.164202	0.169638	0.202837	0.178235	0.190550	0.145580	0.183043	0.151789
40	3	0.165129	0.168386	0.195648	0.176006	0.189934	0.146061	0.184051	0.150962
40	5	0.165973	0.167395	0.189434	0.174054	0.189079	0.146734	0.184621	0.150499
40	7	0.166722	0.166612	0.184065	0.172346	0.188022	0.147574	0.184806	0.150349
100	1	0.163916	0.170066	0.205177	0.178954	0.190690	0.145471	0.182663	0.152104
100	3	0.164312	0.169479	0.201985	0.177973	0.190526	0.145599	0.183210	0.151651
100	5	0.164698	0.168944	0.198977	0.177042	0.190314	0.145764	0.183677	0.151268
100	7	0.165072	0.168458	0.196142	0.176160	0.190059	0.145963	0.184065	0.150951

Table 4. NCREX in $W_{[N,K]}$ based on EFGM-ED at $\lambda_2 = 0.5$.

		$d=-3$		$d=-1$		$d=0.9$		$d=2$	
K	N	$c=-0.2$	$c=0.2$	$c=-0.75$	$c=-0.25$	$c=-0.2$	$c=0.2$	$c=-0.1$	$c=0.1$
2	1	0.505648	0.494537	0.521094	0.506973	0.548594	0.455150	0.546296	0.457407
2	3	0.494686	0.505489	0.473245	0.490983	0.446783	0.558576	0.450112	0.555050
2	5	0.470954	0.535246	0.479067	0.492962	0.391923	0.632996	0.389872	0.639289
2	7	0.457850	0.556852	0.488380	0.496108	0.366321	0.674366	0.361141	0.689354
6	1	0.494154	0.506059	0.569655	0.522620	0.590719	0.421552	0.576212	0.433355
6	3	0.517518	0.484152	0.500769	0.500256	0.549026	0.454782	0.553521	0.451371
6	5	0.517167	0.484440	0.473750	0.491155	0.504873	0.495168	0.513692	0.486650
6	7	0.506724	0.493537	0.465809	0.488440	0.466523	0.535518	0.473890	0.527455
40	1	0.475038	0.529394	0.620934	0.538602	0.603777	0.411993	0.573977	0.435068
40	3	0.484511	0.517080	0.596844	0.531158	0.601059	0.413952	0.578600	0.431538
40	5	0.493045	0.507258	0.576044	0.524640	0.597284	0.416699	0.581216	0.429564

Table 4. *Cont.*

		$d=-3$		$d=-1$		$d=0.9$		$d=2$	
K	N	$c=-0.2$	$c=0.2$	$c=-0.75$	$c=-0.25$	$c=-0.2$	$c=0.2$	$c=-0.1$	$c=0.1$
40	7	0.500552	0.499450	0.558084	0.518940	0.592630	0.420129	0.582068	0.428926
100	1	0.472086	0.533588	0.628780	0.541003	0.604398	0.411549	0.572233	0.436414
100	3	0.476169	0.527835	0.618079	0.537725	0.603670	0.412070	0.574742	0.434480
100	5	0.480122	0.522583	0.607998	0.534618	0.602737	0.412741	0.576881	0.432844
100	7	0.483931	0.517788	0.598501	0.531674	0.601610	0.413553	0.578665	0.431489

Table 5. WNCREX in $W_{[N,K]}$ based on EFGM copula.

		$d=-3$		$d=-1$		$d=0.9$		$d=2$	
K	N	$c=-0.2$	$c=0.2$	$c=-0.75$	$c=-0.25$	$c=-0.2$	$c=0.2$	$c=-0.1$	$c=0.1$
2	1	0.042230	0.041118	0.043778	0.042364	0.046519	0.037175	0.046286	0.037397
2	3	0.041133	0.042214	0.038994	0.040765	0.036335	0.047515	0.036663	0.047157
2	5	0.038696	0.045125	0.039575	0.040963	0.030814	0.054922	0.030571	0.055512
2	7	0.037294	0.047194	0.040505	0.041278	0.028226	0.059030	0.027637	0.060458
6	1	0.041080	0.042270	0.048651	0.043931	0.050717	0.033800	0.049261	0.034975
6	3	0.043401	0.040064	0.041744	0.041692	0.046563	0.037138	0.047005	0.036790
6	5	0.043366	0.040093	0.039045	0.040783	0.042154	0.041183	0.043035	0.040331
6	7	0.042336	0.041018	0.038253	0.040511	0.038315	0.045215	0.039052	0.044408
40	1	0.039123	0.044559	0.053815	0.045533	0.052016	0.032838	0.049039	0.035148
40	3	0.040101	0.043358	0.051387	0.044787	0.051746	0.033035	0.049498	0.034792
40	5	0.040968	0.042389	0.049294	0.044133	0.051370	0.033312	0.049758	0.034592
40	7	0.041722	0.041612	0.047489	0.043562	0.050907	0.033657	0.049842	0.034528
100	1	0.038814	0.044965	0.054607	0.045774	0.052078	0.032793	0.048865	0.035283
100	3	0.039241	0.044407	0.053527	0.045445	0.052006	0.032846	0.049115	0.035088
100	5	0.039650	0.043896	0.052511	0.045133	0.051913	0.032913	0.049327	0.034923
100	7	0.040041	0.043427	0.051554	0.044838	0.051801	0.032995	0.049504	0.034787

Table 6. WNCREX in $W_{[N,K]}$ based on EFGM-ED at $\lambda_2 = 0.5$.

		$d=-3$		$d=-1$		$d=0.9$		$d=2$	
K	N	$c=-0.2$	$c=0.2$	$c=-0.75$	$c=-0.25$	$c=-0.2$	$c=0.2$	$c=-0.1$	$c=0.1$
2	1	0.517904	0.482719	0.524627	0.508138	0.589698	0.419457	0.589988	0.419617
2	3	0.483191	0.517399	0.468815	0.489483	0.404717	0.608386	0.406127	0.607259
2	5	0.408642	0.612232	0.475596	0.491791	0.310868	0.750063	0.298787	0.776836
2	7	0.367995	0.681503	0.486449	0.495460	0.269140	0.830349	0.250938	0.880013
6	1	0.481509	0.519207	0.581443	0.526410	0.669099	0.360905	0.649309	0.375500
6	3	0.555642	0.449981	0.500897	0.500299	0.590505	0.418808	0.604236	0.408448
6	5	0.554522	0.450887	0.469404	0.489684	0.508890	0.491209	0.526360	0.474529
6	7	0.521319	0.479559	0.460159	0.486519	0.439646	0.565345	0.450411	0.553077
40	1	0.421397	0.593523	0.641603	0.545092	0.693981	0.344582	0.644848	0.378608
40	3	0.451110	0.554247	0.613322	0.536389	0.688792	0.347913	0.654080	0.372211
40	5	0.478006	0.523014	0.588930	0.528770	0.681594	0.352597	0.659311	0.368646
40	7	0.501747	0.498259	0.567890	0.522111	0.672733	0.358465	0.661016	0.367494
100	1	0.412172	0.606930	0.650820	0.547901	0.695166	0.343826	0.641371	0.381053
100	3	0.424935	0.588546	0.638249	0.544067	0.693777	0.344712	0.646376	0.377540
100	5	0.437322	0.571783	0.626413	0.540434	0.691994	0.345853	0.650645	0.374575
100	7	0.449287	0.556502	0.615266	0.536991	0.689844	0.347235	0.654209	0.372122

4. Non-Parametric Estimation of NCREX, WNCREX, NCEX, and WNCEX

In this section, we study the non-parametric estimators of NCREX, WNCREX, NCEX, and WNCEX of the CKRV, $W_{[N,K]}$. Furthermore, the mean and variance of the empirical measures (EMs) of the CKRV, $W_{[N,K]}$, are deduced. Let W_i, $i = 1,2,\ldots,n$, be a random sample from an absolutely continuous CDF H_W and $W_{1:n} \leq W_{2:n} \leq \ldots \leq W_{n:n}$ display the OSs of $W_1, W_2, \ldots, W_n$. Then the EM of $H_W(w)$ is given by

$$\widehat{H}_W(w) = \begin{cases} 0, & w < W_{1:n}, \\ \frac{i}{n}, & W_{i:n} \leq w \leq W_{i+1:n}, \\ 1, & w > W_{n:n}. \end{cases} \tag{33}$$

From (33) into (15), we have the EM of $H_{[N,K]}(w)$ as

$$\begin{aligned} \widehat{H}_{[N,K]}(w) &= (1+\eta)\widehat{H}_W(w) + (d-1)\eta\widehat{H}^2_W(w) - d\eta\widehat{H}^3_W(w) \\ &= (1+\eta)\left(\frac{i}{n}\right) + (d-1)\eta\left(\frac{i}{n}\right)^2 - d\eta\left(\frac{i}{n}\right)^3. \end{aligned} \tag{34}$$

4.1. EM of NCREX in CKRV Based on EFGM(c,d)

According to (33), the EM of $\zeta R_{[N,K]}(W)$ is given by

$$\begin{aligned} \widehat{\zeta R}_{[N,K]}(W) &= \frac{1}{2}\int_0^\infty \left[1 - \widehat{H}_{[N,K]}(w)\right]^2 dw \\ &= \frac{1}{2}\int_0^\infty \left[1 - \left((1+\eta)\left(\frac{i}{n}\right) + (d-1)\eta\left(\frac{i}{n}\right)^2 - d\eta\left(\frac{i}{n}\right)^3\right)\right]^2 dw \\ &= \frac{1}{2}\sum_{i=1}^{n-1}\int_{W_{i:n}}^{W_{i+1:n}} \left[1 - (1+\eta)\left(\frac{i}{n}\right) - (d-1)\eta\left(\frac{i}{n}\right)^2 + d\eta\left(\frac{i}{n}\right)^3\right]^2 dw \\ &= \frac{1}{2}\sum_{i=1}^{n-1} U_i\left[1 - (1+\eta)\left(\frac{i}{n}\right) - (d-1)\eta\left(\frac{i}{n}\right)^2 + d\eta\left(\frac{i}{n}\right)^3\right]^2, \end{aligned}$$

where $U_i = W_{i+1:n} - W_{i:n}$, $i = 1,2,\ldots,n-1$, are sample spacings. Thus, the expectation and variance of the empirical NCREX are given by

$$E\left[\widehat{\zeta R}_{[N,K]}(W)\right] = \frac{1}{2}\sum_{i=1}^{n-1} E[U_i]\left[1 - (1+\eta)\left(\frac{i}{n}\right) - (d-1)\eta\left(\frac{i}{n}\right)^2 + d\eta\left(\frac{i}{n}\right)^3\right]^2 \tag{35}$$

and

$$Var\left[\widehat{\zeta R}_{[N,K]}(W)\right] = \frac{1}{4}\sum_{i=1}^{n-1} Var[U_i]\left[1 - (1+\eta)\left(\frac{i}{n}\right) - (d-1)\eta\left(\frac{i}{n}\right)^2 + d\eta\left(\frac{i}{n}\right)^3\right]^4. \tag{36}$$

Example 8. *Assume that* (T_i, W_i), $i = 1,2,\ldots,n$, *is a random sample from EFGM-UD with parameters 0 and 1 for each* T_i *and* W_i. *By using (35) and (36), we have*

$$E\left[\widehat{\zeta R}_{[N,K]}(W)\right] = \frac{1}{2(n+1)}\sum_{i=1}^{n-1}\left[1 - (1+\eta)\left(\frac{i}{n}\right) - (d-1)\eta\left(\frac{i}{n}\right)^2 + d\eta\left(\frac{i}{n}\right)^3\right]^2$$

and

$$Var\left[\widehat{\zeta R}_{[N,K]}(W)\right] = \frac{n}{4(n+1)^2(n+2)}\sum_{i=1}^{n-1}\left[1 - (1+\eta)\left(\frac{i}{n}\right) - (d-1)\eta\left(\frac{i}{n}\right)^2 + d\eta\left(\frac{i}{n}\right)^3\right]^4.$$

Example 9. *Let (T_i, W_i), $i = 1, 2, \ldots, n$, be a random sample from EFGM-ED with parameters λ_1 and λ_2, respectively. Then, we have*

$$E\left[\widehat{\zeta R}_{[N,K]}(W)\right] = \frac{1}{2\lambda_2}\sum_{i=1}^{n-1}\frac{1}{n-i}\left[1-(1+\eta)\left(\frac{i}{n}\right)-(d-1)\eta\left(\frac{i}{n}\right)^2+d\eta\left(\frac{i}{n}\right)^3\right]^2$$

and

$$Var\left[\widehat{\zeta R}_{[N,K]}(W)\right] = \frac{1}{4\lambda_2^2}\sum_{i=1}^{n-1}\frac{1}{(n-i)^2}\left[1-(1+\eta)\left(\frac{i}{n}\right)-(d-1)\eta\left(\frac{i}{n}\right)^2+d\eta\left(\frac{i}{n}\right)^3\right]^4.$$

Figure 3 shows the relation between NCREX and the empirical NCREX in $W_{[N,K]}$ from EFGM-UD, at $n = 100$. It can be extracted that, at any value of N, the values of NCREX are very close to the values of the empirical NCREX, as long as n is large.

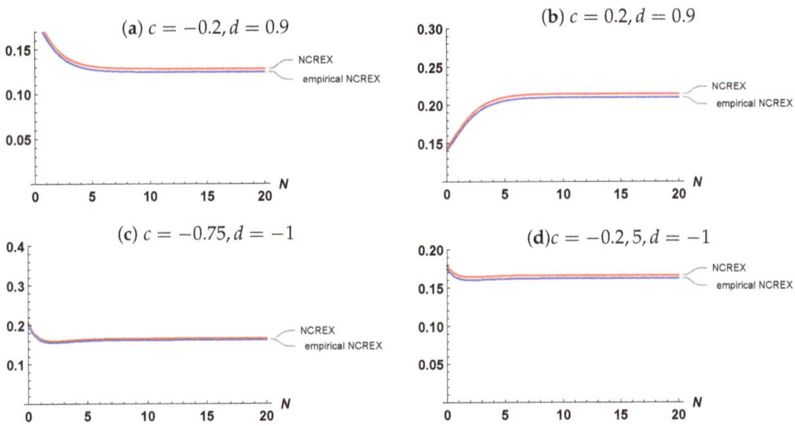

Figure 3. Representation of NCREX and empirical NCREX based on $W_{[N,K=1]}$ from EFGM-UD.

Table 7 displays the values of $E\left[\widehat{\zeta R}_{[N,K]}(W)\right]$ and $Var\left[\widehat{\zeta R}_{[N,K]}(W)\right]$ for the EFGM-ED model at $K = 2$, $n = 10$, and $d = 0.5$. The following features can be extracted:

1. With fixed N and λ_2, $E\left[\widehat{\zeta R}_{[N,K]}(W)\right]$ and $Var\left[\widehat{\zeta R}_{[N,K]}(W)\right]$ increase as c increases.
2. With fixed N and c, $E\left[\widehat{\zeta R}_{[N,K]}(W)\right]$ and $Var\left[\widehat{\zeta R}_{[N,K]}(W)\right]$ increase as λ_2 increases.

Table 7. $E\left[\widehat{\zeta R}_{[N,K]}(W)\right]$ and $Var\left[\widehat{\zeta R}_{[N,K]}(W)\right]$ for EFGM-ED at $K = 2$, $n = 10$, and $d = 0.5$.

		$E\left[\widehat{\zeta R}_{[N,K]}(W)\right]$				$Var\left[\widehat{\zeta R}_{[N,K]}(W)\right]$			
N	λ_2	$c = -0.2$	$c = -0.1$	$c = 0.1$	$c = 0.2$	$c = -0.2$	$c = -0.1$	$c = 0.1$	$c = 0.2$
3	0.5	0.102492	0.107408	0.117768	0.123213	0.001551	0.001662	0.001911	0.002051
3	1	0.204985	0.214816	0.235537	0.246426	0.006204	0.006646	0.007643	0.008204
3	2	0.409970	0.429632	0.471073	0.492852	0.024818	0.026585	0.030574	0.032817
5	0.5	0.092915	0.102344	0.123384	0.134995	0.001350	0.001548	0.002056	0.002377
5	1	0.185829	0.204687	0.246767	0.269990	0.005400	0.006191	0.008222	0.009507
5	2	0.371659	0.409375	0.493535	0.539980	0.021598	0.024766	0.032889	0.038028
8	0.5	0.087208	0.099217	0.127056	0.142886	0.001238	0.001480	0.002154	0.002612
8	1	0.174415	0.198434	0.254113	0.285773	0.004954	0.005921	0.008616	0.010449
8	2	0.348831	0.396868	0.508226	0.571545	0.019815	0.023684	0.034463	0.041796
10	0.5	0.085830	0.098448	0.127985	0.144904	0.001212	0.001464	0.002179	0.002675
10	1	0.171660	0.196897	0.255971	0.289808	0.004850	0.005856	0.008717	0.010699
10	2	0.343320	0.393793	0.511941	0.579617	0.019399	0.023423	0.034869	0.042796

4.2. EM of WNCREX in CKRV Based on EFGM(c,d)

Using (9) and (34), the EM of $\zeta R^{w}_{[N,K]}(W)$ is given by

$$\begin{aligned}\widehat{\zeta R^{w}}_{[N,K]}(W) &= \frac{1}{2}\int_{0}^{\infty} w\left[1-\widehat{H}_{[N,K]}(w)\right]^{2}dw \\ &= \frac{1}{2}\sum_{i=1}^{n-1} Z_i\left[1-(1+\eta)\left(\frac{i}{n}\right)-(d-1)\eta\left(\frac{i}{n}\right)^{2}+d\eta\left(\frac{i}{n}\right)^{3}\right]^{2},\end{aligned}$$

where $Z_i = \frac{W^2_{i+1:n}-W^2_{i:n}}{2}$, $i = 1,2,\ldots,n-1$.

Example 10. *Let (T_i, W_i), $i = 1,2,\ldots,n$, be a random sample from the EFGM family. Furthermore, let W_i have a distribution with PDF $h_W(w) = 2w$, $0 < w < 1$. According to Chakraborty et al. [31], W_i^2 has a standard UD. Furthermore, the RVs $Z_i = \frac{W^2_{i+1:n}-W^2_{i:n}}{2}$, $i = 1,2,\ldots,n-1$, follow beta distribution with a mean $\frac{1}{2(n+1)}$ and variance $\frac{n}{4(n+1)^2(n+2)}$. Thus,*

$$E\left[\widehat{\zeta R^{w}}_{[N,K]}(W)\right] = \frac{1}{4(n+1)}\sum_{i=1}^{n-1}\left[1-(1+\eta)\left(\frac{i}{n}\right)-(d-1)\eta\left(\frac{i}{n}\right)^{2}+d\eta\left(\frac{i}{n}\right)^{3}\right]^{2}$$

and

$$Var\left[\widehat{\zeta R^{w}}_{[N,K]}(W)\right] = \frac{n}{16(n+1)^2(n+2)}\sum_{i=1}^{n-1}\left[1-(1+\eta)\left(\frac{i}{n}\right)-(d-1)\eta\left(\frac{i}{n}\right)^{2}+d\eta\left(\frac{i}{n}\right)^{3}\right]^{4}.$$

Example 11. *Suppose (T_i, W_i), $i = 1,2,\ldots,n$, is a random sample from the EFGM family. If W_i has RD with PDF $h_W(w) = 2\lambda w e^{-\lambda w^2}$; $w, \lambda > 0$. Then, the RVs $Z_i = \frac{W^2_{i+1:n}-W^2_{i:n}}{2}$, $i = 1,2,\ldots,n-1$, follow the exponential distribution with a mean $\frac{1}{2\lambda(n-i)}$ and variance $\frac{1}{4\lambda^2(n-i)^2}$. Moreover, the mean and variance of $\widehat{\zeta R^{w}}_{[N,K]}(W)$ are, respectively, given by*

$$E\left[\widehat{\zeta R^{w}}_{[N,K]}(W)\right] = \frac{1}{4\lambda}\sum_{i=1}^{n-i}\frac{1}{n-i}\left[1-(1+\eta)\left(\frac{i}{n}\right)-(d-1)\eta\left(\frac{i}{n}\right)^{2}+d\eta\left(\frac{i}{n}\right)^{3}\right]^{2}$$

and

$$Var\left[\widehat{\zeta R^{w}}_{[N,K]}(W)\right] = \frac{1}{16\lambda^2}\sum_{i=1}^{n-1}\frac{1}{(n-i)^2}\left[1-(1+\eta)\left(\frac{i}{n}\right)-(d-1)\eta\left(\frac{i}{n}\right)^{2}+d\eta\left(\frac{i}{n}\right)^{3}\right]^{4}.$$

Table 8 presents $E\left[\widehat{\zeta R^{w}}_{[N,K]}(W)\right]$ and $Var\left[\widehat{\zeta R^{w}}_{[N,K]}(W)\right]$ for EFGM-ED at $K = 2$, $n = 10$, and $d = 0.5$. Table 8 shows the following features:

1. Generally, with fixed N and λ_2, $E\left[\widehat{\zeta R^{w}}_{[N,K]}(W)\right]$ and $Var\left[\widehat{\zeta R^{w}}_{[N,K]}(W)\right]$ increase with increasing c.
2. Generally, with fixed N and c, $E\left[\widehat{\zeta R^{w}}_{[N,K]}(W)\right]$ and $Var\left[\widehat{\zeta R^{w}}_{[N,K]}(W)\right]$ increase with increasing λ_2.

Table 8. $E\left[\widehat{\zeta R^w}_{[N,K]}(W)\right]$ and $Var\left[\widehat{\zeta R^w}_{[N,K]}(W)\right]$ for EFGM-ED at $K=2$, $n=10$, and $d=0.5$.

		$E\left[\widehat{\zeta R^w}_{[N,K]}(W)\right]$				$Var\left[\widehat{\zeta R^w}_{[N,K]}(W)\right]$			
N	λ_2	$c=-0.2$	$c=-0.1$	$c=0.1$	$c=0.2$	$c=-0.2$	$c=-0.1$	$c=0.1$	$c=0.2$
3	0.5	0.051246	0.053704	0.058884	0.061607	0.000388	0.000415	0.000478	0.000513
3	1	0.102492	0.107408	0.117768	0.123213	0.001551	0.001662	0.001911	0.002051
3	2	0.204985	0.214816	0.235537	0.246426	0.006204	0.006646	0.007643	0.008204
5	0.5	0.046457	0.051172	0.061692	0.067497	0.000337	0.000387	0.000514	0.000594
5	1	0.092915	0.102344	0.123384	0.134995	0.001350	0.001548	0.002056	0.002377
5	2	0.185829	0.204687	0.246767	0.269990	0.005400	0.006191	0.008222	0.009507
8	0.5	0.043604	0.049609	0.063528	0.071443	0.000310	0.000370	0.000538	0.000653
8	1	0.087208	0.099217	0.127056	0.142886	0.001238	0.001480	0.002154	0.002612
8	2	0.174415	0.198434	0.254113	0.285773	0.004954	0.005921	0.008616	0.010449
10	0.5	0.042915	0.049224	0.063993	0.072452	0.000303	0.000366	0.000545	0.000669
10	1	0.085830	0.098448	0.127985	0.144904	0.001212	0.001464	0.002179	0.002675
10	2	0.171660	0.196897	0.255971	0.289808	0.004850	0.005856	0.008717	0.010699

4.3. EM of NCEX in CKRV Based on EFGM(c,d)

From (34) and (10), we obtain the EM of $\zeta_{[N,K]}$ as

$$\begin{aligned}\widehat{\zeta}_{[N,K]}(W) &= \frac{1}{2}\int_0^\infty \left[1-\widehat{H}^2_{[N,K]}(w)\right]dw \\ &= \frac{1}{2}\sum_{i=1}^{n-1} U_i\left[1-\left((1+\eta)\left(\frac{i}{n}\right)+(d-1)\eta\left(\frac{i}{n}\right)^2-d\eta\left(\frac{i}{n}\right)^3\right)^2\right].\end{aligned}$$

Example 12. *Suppose that* (T_i, W_i), $i=1,2,\ldots,n$, *is a random sample from EFGM-UD with parameters 0 and 1. Thus,*

$$E\left[\widehat{\zeta}_{[N,K]}(W)\right] = \frac{1}{2(n+1)}\sum_{i=1}^{n-1}\left[1-\left((1+\eta)\left(\frac{i}{n}\right)+(d-1)\eta\left(\frac{i}{n}\right)^2-d\eta\left(\frac{i}{n}\right)^3\right)^2\right]$$

and

$$Var\left[\widehat{\zeta}_{[N,K]}(W)\right] = \frac{n}{4(n+1)^2(n+2)}\sum_{i=1}^{n-1}\left[1-\left((1+\eta)\left(\frac{i}{n}\right)+(d-1)\eta\left(\frac{i}{n}\right)^2-d\eta\left(\frac{i}{n}\right)^3\right)^2\right]^2.$$

Example 13. *Let* (T_i, W_i), $i=1,2,\ldots,n$, *be a random sample from EFGM-ED. Then, we have*

$$E\left[\widehat{\zeta}_{[N,K]}(W)\right] = \frac{1}{2\lambda_2}\sum_{i=1}^{n-1}\frac{1}{n-i}\left[1-\left((1+\eta)\left(\frac{i}{n}\right)+(d-1)\eta\left(\frac{i}{n}\right)^2-d\eta\left(\frac{i}{n}\right)^3\right)^2\right]$$

and

$$Var\left[\widehat{\zeta}_{[N,K]}(W)\right] = \frac{1}{4\lambda_2^2}\sum_{i=1}^{n-1}\frac{1}{(n-i)^2}\left[1-\left((1+\eta)\left(\frac{i}{n}\right)+(d-1)\eta\left(\frac{i}{n}\right)^2-d\eta\left(\frac{i}{n}\right)^3\right)^2\right]^2.$$

Figure 4 shows the relation between NCREX and the empirical NCEX in $W_{[N,K]}$ from EFGM-UD, at $n=100$. It can be concluded that NCREX and empirical NCREX have very similar values.

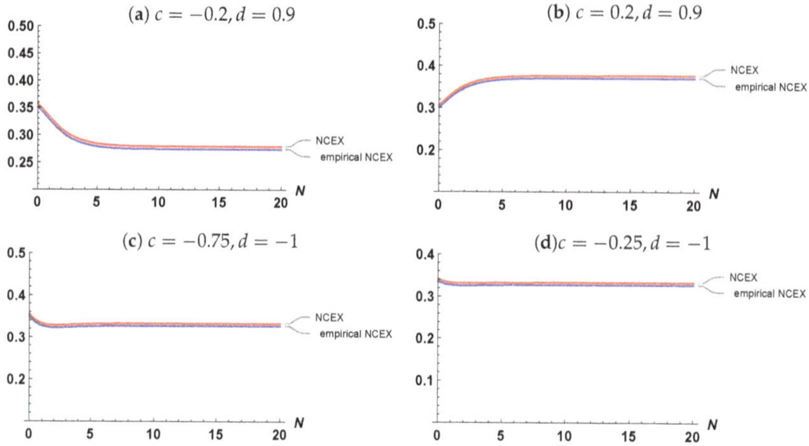

Figure 4. Representation of NCEX and empirical NCEX based on $W_{[N,K=1]}$ from EFGM-UD.

Table 9 shows $E\left[\widehat{\zeta}_{[N,K]}(W)\right]$ and $Var\left[\widehat{\zeta}_{[N,K]}(W)\right]$ for EFGM-ED at $K = 2$, $n = 10$, and $d = 0.5$. It is observed that:

1. At fixed N and λ_2, $E\left[\widehat{\zeta}_{[N,K]}(W)\right]$ and $Var\left[\widehat{\zeta}_{[N,K]}(W)\right]$ increase as the value of c increases.
2. At fixed N and c, $E\left[\widehat{\zeta}_{[N,K]}(W)\right]$ and $Var\left[\widehat{\zeta}_{[N,K]}(W)\right]$ increase as the value of λ_2 increases.

Table 9. $E\left[\widehat{\zeta}_{[N,K]}(W)\right]$ and $Var\left[\widehat{\zeta}_{[N,K]}(W)\right]$ for EFGM-ED at $K = 2$, $n = 10$, and $d = 0.5$.

		$E\left[\widehat{\zeta}_{[N,K]}(W)\right]$				$Var\left[\widehat{\zeta}_{[N,K]}(W)\right]$			
N	λ_2	$c = -0.2$	$c = -0.1$	$c = 0.1$	$c = 0.2$	$c = -0.2$	$c = -0.1$	$c = 0.1$	$c = 0.2$
3	0.5	0.317745	0.327711	0.347113	0.356549	0.011409	0.012208	0.013878	0.014747
3	1	0.635491	0.655422	0.694226	0.713098	0.045635	0.048830	0.055513	0.058989
3	2	1.270980	1.310840	1.388450	1.426200	0.182540	0.195321	0.222053	0.235954
5	0.5	0.296643	0.317435	0.356837	0.375448	0.009847	0.011385	0.014774	0.016601
5	1	0.593286	0.634870	0.713675	0.750895	0.039389	0.045538	0.059097	0.066403
5	2	1.186570	1.269740	1.427350	1.501790	0.157557	0.182153	0.236388	0.265614
8	0.5	0.282818	0.310796	0.362931	0.387088	0.008918	0.010875	0.015356	0.017820
8	1	0.565635	0.621591	0.725862	0.774177	0.035674	0.043501	0.061424	0.071280
8	2	1.131270	1.243180	1.451720	1.548350	0.142696	0.174003	0.245696	0.285121
10	0.5	0.279318	0.309126	0.364441	0.389948	0.008695	0.010750	0.015503	0.018129
10	1	0.558636	0.618252	0.728881	0.779895	0.034780	0.042999	0.062010	0.072515
10	2	1.117270	1.236500	1.457760	1.559790	0.139120	0.171997	0.248041	0.290061

4.4. EM of WNCEX in CKRV Based on EFGM(c,d)

Based on (11), the EM of $\zeta^{w}_{[N,K]}(W)$ is given by

$$\widehat{\zeta^{w}}_{[N,K]}(W) = \frac{1}{2}\int_{0}^{\infty} w\left[1 - \widehat{H}^{2}_{[N,K]}(w)\right]dw. \tag{37}$$

Using the CDF representation of CKRV that is established in (15) and substituting into (37), the empirical measure of $\zeta^{w}_{[N,K]}(W)$ can be calculated as

$$\begin{aligned}\widehat{\zeta^{w}}_{[N,K]}(W) &= \frac{1}{2}\int_{0}^{\infty} w\left[1-\left((1+\eta)\left(\frac{i}{n}\right)+(d-1)\eta\left(\frac{i}{n}\right)^{2}-d\eta\left(\frac{i}{n}\right)^{3}\right)^{2}\right]dw \\ &= \frac{1}{2}\sum_{i=1}^{n-1} Z_i\left[1-\left((1+\eta)\left(\frac{i}{n}\right)+(d-1)\eta\left(\frac{i}{n}\right)^{2}-d\eta\left(\frac{i}{n}\right)^{3}\right)^{2}\right].\end{aligned}$$

Example 14. *Assume* (T_i, W_i), $i = 1,2,\ldots,n$, *is a random sample from the EFGM family and the RV* W_i *follows a distribution with the PDF* $h_W(w) = 2w, \quad 0 < w < 1$. *Therefore, we obtain*

$$E\left[\widehat{\zeta^{w}}_{[N,K]}(W)\right] = \frac{1}{4(n+1)}\sum_{i=1}^{n-1}\left[1-\left((1+\eta)\left(\frac{i}{n}\right)+(d-1)\eta\left(\frac{i}{n}\right)^{2}-d\eta\left(\frac{i}{n}\right)^{3}\right)^{2}\right]$$

and

$$Var\left[\widehat{\zeta^{w}}_{[N,K]}(W)\right] = \frac{n}{16(n+1)^{2}(n+2)}\sum_{i=1}^{n-1}\left[1-\left((1+\eta)\left(\frac{i}{n}\right)+(d-1)\eta\left(\frac{i}{n}\right)^{2}-d\eta\left(\frac{i}{n}\right)^{3}\right)^{2}\right]^{2}.$$

Example 15. *Suppose* (T_i, W_i), $i = 1,2,\ldots,n$, *is a random sample from the EFGM family. If the RV* W_i *follows the Rayleigh distribution with the PDF* $h_W(w) = 2\lambda w e^{-\lambda w^2}$; $w, \lambda > 0$, *then, we have*

$$E\left[\widehat{\zeta^{w}}_{[N,K]}(W)\right] = \frac{1}{4\lambda}\sum_{i=1}^{n-i}\frac{1}{n-i}\left[1-\left((1+\eta)\left(\frac{i}{n}\right)+(d-1)\eta\left(\frac{i}{n}\right)^{2}-d\eta\left(\frac{i}{n}\right)^{3}\right)^{2}\right]$$

and

$$Var\left[\widehat{\zeta^{w}}_{[N,K]}(W)\right] = \frac{1}{16\lambda^{2}}\sum_{i=1}^{n-1}\frac{1}{(n-i)^{2}}\left[1-\left((1+\eta)\left(\frac{i}{n}\right)+(d-1)\eta\left(\frac{i}{n}\right)^{2}-d\eta\left(\frac{i}{n}\right)^{3}\right)^{2}\right]^{2}.$$

Table 10 clarifies a numerical application of Example 15 at $K = 2$, $n = 10$, and $d = 0.5$ and some distinct values of the parameters c, λ_2, and N. It is apparent that

1. For fixed N and λ_2, $E\left[\widehat{\zeta^{w}}_{[N,K]}(W)\right]$ and $Var\left[\widehat{\zeta^{w}}_{[N,K]}(W)\right]$ increase as c increases.
2. For fixed N and c, $E\left[\widehat{\zeta^{w}}_{[N,K]}(W)\right]$ and $Var\left[\widehat{\zeta^{w}}_{[N,K]}(W)\right]$ increase as λ_2 increases.

Table 10. $E\left[\widehat{\zeta^{w}}_{[N,K]}(W)\right]$ and $Var\left[\widehat{\zeta^{w}}_{[N,K]}(W)\right]$ for EFGM-ED at $K = 2$, $n = 10$, and $d = 0.5$.

		$E\left[\widehat{\zeta^{w}}_{[N,K]}(W)\right]$				$Var\left[\widehat{\zeta^{w}}_{[N,K]}(W)\right]$			
N	λ_2	$c=-0.2$	$c=-0.1$	$c=0.1$	$c=0.2$	$c=-0.2$	$c=-0.1$	$c=0.1$	$c=0.2$
3	0.5	0.158873	0.163855	0.173556	0.178275	0.002852	0.003052	0.003470	0.003687
3	1	0.317745	0.327711	0.347113	0.356549	0.011409	0.012208	0.013878	0.014747
3	2	0.635491	0.655422	0.694226	0.713098	0.045635	0.048830	0.055513	0.058989
5	0.5	0.148321	0.158718	0.178419	0.187724	0.002462	0.002846	0.003694	0.004150
5	1	0.296643	0.317435	0.356837	0.375448	0.009847	0.011385	0.014774	0.016601
5	2	0.593286	0.634870	0.713675	0.750895	0.039389	0.045538	0.059097	0.066403
8	0.5	0.141409	0.155398	0.181465	0.193544	0.002230	0.002719	0.003839	0.004455

Table 10. *Cont.*

N	λ_2	$E\left[\widehat{\zeta^{w}}_{[N,K]}(W)\right]$ $c=-0.2$	$c=-0.1$	$c=0.1$	$c=0.2$	$Var\left[\widehat{\zeta^{w}}_{[N,K]}(W)\right]$ $c=-0.2$	$c=-0.1$	$c=0.1$	$c=0.2$
8	1	0.282818	0.310796	0.362931	0.387088	0.008918	0.010875	0.015356	0.017820
8	2	0.565635	0.621591	0.725862	0.774177	0.035674	0.043501	0.061424	0.071280
10	0.5	0.139659	0.154563	0.182220	0.194974	0.002174	0.002687	0.003876	0.004532
10	1	0.279318	0.309126	0.364441	0.389948	0.008695	0.010750	0.015503	0.018129
10	2	0.558636	0.618252	0.728881	0.779895	0.034780	0.042999	0.062010	0.072515

5. Conclusions

Despite the fact that the EFGM family is as efficient as many other generalizations of the FGM family in terms of correlation level, its flexibility, and usability render it superior to many of these generalizations. Owing to this advantage, most PDFs in this paper are linear functions of other simpler distributions. This study has yielded useful representations of the PDF, CDF, and survival function of CKRV, along with some elegant symmetry relationships between them.

EX and its more recent related measures for CKRV were derived from the EFGM family, where a numerical study was carried out to reveal some features of these measures. Also, the QF based on these measures was derived. In addition, we derived non-parametric estimators of NCREX, WNCREX, NCEX, and WNCEX. An empirical analysis of the NCREX and NCEX has produced distinct results.

Author Contributions: Conceptualization, M.A.A.E., H.M.B., M.A.A., I.A.H., A.F.H. and N.A.; Methodology, M.A.A.E., H.M.B., M.A.A., D.A.A.E.-R., I.A.H., A.F.H. and N.A.; Software, M.A.A.E., D.A.A.E.-R., I.A.H., A.F.H. and N.A.; Validation, M.A.A.E., H.M.B., M.A.A., D.A.A.E.-R., I.A.H., A.F.H. and N.A.; Formal analysis, H.M.B., M.A.A., D.A.A.E.-R., I.A.H., A.F.H. and N.A.; Investigation, M.A.A.E., H.M.B., M.A.A., I.A.H., A.F.H. and N.A.; Resources, M.A.A.E., H.M.B., M.A.A., D.A.A.E.-R., I.A.H., A.F.H. and N.A.; Data curation, M.A.A.E., H.M.B., M.A.A., I.A.H., A.F.H. and N.A.; Writing—original draft, M.A.A.E., D.A.A.E.-R. and A.F.H.; Writing—review & editing, M.A.A.E., M.A.A., D.A.A.E.-R., I.A.H. and N.A.; Visualization, H.M.B. All authors have read and agreed to the published version of this manuscript.

Funding: This work was supported and funded by the Deanship of Scientific Research at Imam Mohammad Ibn Saud Islamic University (IMSIU) (grant number IMSIU-RG23114).

Data Availability Statement: The data used to support the findings of this study are available within the article.

Acknowledgments: The authors would like to express their sincere gratitude to the anonymous reviewers for their insightful comments and recommendations that raised the caliber of this paper.

Conflicts of Interest: The authors declare that they have no competing interests.

Abbreviations

RVs	random variables
CDF	cumulative distribution function
PDF	probability density function
QF	quantile function
FGM	Farlie–Gumbel–Morgenstern
EFGM	extended Farlie–Gumbel–Morgenstern
OSs	order statistics
KRVs	*K*-record upper values
EX	extropy
CREX	cumulative residual extropy

CKRV	*K*-record upper values
NCREX	negative cumulative residual extropy
WNCREX	weighted negative cumulative residual extropy
NCEX	negative cumulative extropy
WNCEX	weighted negative cumulative extropy
EFGM-UD	EFGM family with uniform marginals
EFGM-ED	EFGM family with exponential marginals
EFGM-PFD	EFGM family with power function distribution marginals
EFGM-PID	EFGM family with Pareto type-I distribution marginals

References

1. Ghosh, S.; Sheppard, L.W.; Holder, M.T.; Loecke, T.D.; Reid, P.C.; Bever, J.D.; Reuman, D.C. Copulas and their potential for ecology. *Adv. Ecol. Res.* **2020**, *62*, 409–468.
2. Shrahili, M.; Alotaibi, N. A new parametric life family of distributions: Properties, copula and modeling failure and service times. *Symmetry* **2020**, *12*, 1462. [CrossRef]
3. Ebaid, R.; Elbadawy, W.; Ahmed, E.; Abdelghaly, A. A new extension of the FGM copula with an application in reliability. *Comm. Statist. Theory Meth.* **2022**, *51*, 2953–2961. [CrossRef]
4. Barakat, H.M.; Alawady, M.A.; Husseiny, I.A.; Abd Elgawad, M.A. A more flexible counterpart of a Huang-Kotz's copula-type. *Comptes Rendus Acad. Bulg. Sci.* **2022**, *75*, 952–958. [CrossRef]
5. Bairamov, I. New generalized Farlie-Gumbel-Morgenstern distributions and concomitants of order statistics. *J. Appl. Statist.* **2001**, *28*, 521–536. [CrossRef]
6. Mohamed, M.S. On concomitants of ordered random variables under general forms of Morgenstern family. *Filomat* **2019**, *33*, 2771–2780. [CrossRef]
7. Barakat, H.M.; Husseiny, I.A. Some information measures in concomitants of generalized order statistics under iterated Farlie-Gumbel-Morgenstern bivariate type. *Quaest. Math.* **2021**, *44*, 581–598. [CrossRef]
8. Abd Elgawad, M.A.; Barakat, H.M.; Abd El-Rahman, D.A.; Alyami, S.A. Scrutiny of a more flexible counterpart of Huang-Kotz-FGM-distributions in the perspective of some information measures. *Symmetry* **2023**, *15*, 1257. [CrossRef]
9. Dziubdziela, W.; Kopociński, B. Limiting properties of the k-th record values. *Appl. Math.* **1976**, *2*, 187–190. [CrossRef]
10. Aly, A.E. Prediction of the exponential fractional upper record-values. *Math. Slovaca* **2022**, *72*, 491–506. [CrossRef]
11. Alawady, M.A.; Barakat, H.M.; Mansour, G.M.; Husseiny, I.A. Information measures and concomitants of k-record values based on Sarmanov family of bivariate distributions. *Bull. Malays. Math. Sci. Soc.* **2023**, *46*, 9. [CrossRef]
12. Berred, M. *K*-record values and the extreme-value index. *J. Stat. Plann. Inf.* **1995**, *45*, 49–63. [CrossRef]
13. Fashandi, M.; Ahmadi, J. Characterizations of symmetric distributions based on Renyi entropy. *Statist. Probab. Lett.* **2012**, *82*, 798–804. [CrossRef]
14. Bdair, O.M.; Raqab, M.Z. Mean residual life of kth records under double monitoring. *Bull. Malays. Math. Sci. Soc.* **2014**, *37*, 457–464.
15. Chacko, M.; Shy Mary, M. Concomitants of k-record values arising from Morgenstern family of distributions and their applications in parameter estimation. *Stat. Papers* **2013**, *54*, 21–46. [CrossRef]
16. Chacko, M.; Muraleedharan, L. Inference based on k-record values from generalized exponential distribution. *Statistica* **2018**, *78*, 37–56.
17. Thomas, P.Y.; Anne, P.; Veena, T.G. Characterization of bivariate distributions using concomitants of generalized (k) record values. *Statistica* **2014**, *74*, 431–446.
18. Lad, F.; Sanfilippo, G.; Agro, G. Extropy: Complementary dual of entropy. *Stat. Sci.* **2015**, *30*, 40–58. [CrossRef]
19. Husseiny, I.A.; Barakat, H.M.; Mansour, G.M.; Alawady, M.A. Information measures in records and their concomitants arising from Sarmanov family of bivariate distributions. *J. Comp. Appl. Math.* **2022**, *408*, 114120. [CrossRef]
20. Qiu, G. The extropy of order statistics and record values. *Stat. Probab. Lett.* **2017**, *120*, 52–60. [CrossRef]
21. Qiu, G.; Jia, K. The residual extropy of order statistics. *Stat. Probab. Lett.* **2018**, *133*, 15–22. [CrossRef]
22. Irshad, M.R.; Archana, K.; Al-Omari, A.I.; Maya, R.; Alomani, G. Extropy based on concomitants of order statistics in Farlie-Gumbel-Morgenstern Family for random variables representing past life. *Axioms* **2023**, *12*, 792. [CrossRef]
23. Almaspoor, Z.; Tahmasebi, S.; Jafari, A.A. Measures of extropy for concomitants of generalized order statistics in Morgenstern family. *J. Stat. Theory Appl.* **2021**, *21*, 1–20. [CrossRef]
24. Husseiny, I.A.; Syam, A.H. The extropy of concomitants of generalized order statistics from Huang-Kotz-Morgenstern bivariate distribution. *J. Math.* **2022**, *6385998*. [CrossRef]
25. Husseiny, I.A.; Alawady, M.A.; Alyami, S.A.; Abd Elgawad, M.A. Measures of extropy based on concomitants of generalized order statistics under a general framework from iterated morgenstern family. *Mathematics* **2023**, *11*, 1377. [CrossRef]
26. Jahanshahi, S.; Zarei, H.; Khammar, A. On cumulative residual extropy. *Probab. Eng. Inf. Sci.* **2020**, *34*, 605–625. [CrossRef]
27. Hashempour, M.; Kazemi, M.R.; Tahmasebi, S. On weighted cumulative residual extropy: Characterization, estimation and testing. *Statistics* **2022**, *56*, 681–698. [CrossRef]

28. Tahmasebi, S.; Toomaj, A. On negative cumulative extropy with applications. *Commun. Stat. Theory Methods* **2021**, *51*, 5025–5047. [CrossRef]
29. Chaudhary, K.S.; Gupta, N.; Kumar Sahu, P. On general weighted cumulative residual extropy and general weighted negative cumulative extropy. *Statistics* **2023**, *57*, 1117–1141. [CrossRef]
30. Jafari, A.A.; Almaspoor, Z.; Tahmasebi, S. General results on bivariate extended Weibull Morgenstern family and concomitants of its generalized order statistics. *Ric. Mat.* **2021**, 1–22. [CrossRef]
31. Chakraborty, S.; Das, O.; Pradhan, B. Weighted negative cumulative extropy with application in testing uniformity. *Phys. A Stat. Mech. Appl.* **2023**, *624*, 128957. [CrossRef]

mathematics

MDPI

Review

An In-Depth Review of the Weibull Model with a Focus on Various Parameterizations

Yolanda M. Gómez [1,†], Diego I. Gallardo [1,*,†], Carolina Marchant [2,†], Luis Sánchez [3,†] and Marcelo Bourguignon [4,†]

1 Departamento de Estadística, Facultad de Ciencias, Universidad del Bío-Bío, Concepción 4081112, Chile; ygomez@ubiobio.cl
2 Faculty of Basic Sciences, Universidad Católica del Maule, Talca 3480112, Chile; cmarchant@ucm.cl
3 Institute of Statistics, Universidad Austral de Chile, Valdivia 5110566, Chile; luis.sanchez@uach.cl
4 Statistics Department, Federal University of Rio Grande do Norte, Natal 59078-970, RN, Brazil; marcelo.bourguignon@ufrn.br
* Correspondence: dgallardo@ubiobio.cl
† These authors contributed equally to this work.

Abstract: The Weibull distribution is a versatile probability distribution widely applied in modeling the failure times of objects or systems. Its behavior is shaped by two essential parameters: the shape parameter and the scale parameter. By manipulating these parameters, the Weibull distribution adeptly captures diverse failure patterns observed in real-world scenarios. This flexibility and broad applicability make it an indispensable tool in reliability analysis and survival modeling. This manuscript explores five parameterizations of the Weibull distribution, each based on different moments, like mean, quantile, and mode. It meticulously characterizes each parameterization, introducing a novel one based on the model's mode, along with its hazard and survival functions, shedding light on their unique properties. Additionally, it delves into the interpretation of regression coefficients when incorporating regression structures into these parameterizations. It is analytically established that all five parameterizations define the same log-likelihood function, underlining their equivalence. Through Monte Carlo simulation studies, the performances of these parameterizations are evaluated in terms of parameter estimations and residuals. The models are further applied to real-world data, illustrating their effectiveness in analyzing material fatigue life and survival data. In summary, this manuscript provides a comprehensive exploration of the Weibull distribution and its various parameterizations. It offers valuable insights into their applications and implications in modeling failure times, with potential contributions to diverse fields requiring reliability and survival analysis.

Keywords: regression models; reparameterization; survival modeling; Weibull distribution

MSC: 62N02; 62J99

1. Background

The Weibull distribution is a popular continuous probability distribution that is commonly utilized to model the lifetimes or failure times of objects or systems. It was initially introduced by Waloddi Weibull in 1951 [1] and has since found applications in various fields. For instance, in reliability engineering, Keshevan et al. [2] employed the Weibull distribution to model the Hertzian fracture of Pyrex glass. In another study, Queeshi and Sheikh [3] used the Weibull distribution to analyze adhesive wear in metals. Similarly, Durham and Padgett [4] applied the distribution to carbon fibers and small composite specimens. Almeida [5] investigated the failure of coating using the Weibull distribution, while Fok et al. [6] focused on its use for brittle material. Additionally, Newell et al. [7]

employed the distribution to study compressive failure in high-performance polymers and Li et al. [8] analyzed concrete components using the Weibull distribution.

The distribution mentioned above has been widely applied as a flexible modeling tool in various fields, addressing a diverse range of issues. It has been successfully utilized in disciplines such as quality control, weather forecasting, industrial engineering, electric systems engineering, communications systems engineering, hydrology, and more. For instance, Bebbington and Lai [9] utilized it for volcanic eruptions, while Durrans [10] and Heo et al. [11] applied it to regional flood frequency analysis. Fleming [12] used it to describe the dynamics of foliage biomass on Scots pine. In the field of Economics, Roed and Zhang [13] employed it to analyze unemployment duration data. In the context of wireless communications, the Weibull distribution is very flexible. Ikki and Ahmed [14] analyzed the performance of multi-hop relaying systems over Weibull fading channels in terms of bit error rate and outage probability. A similar analysis of the bit error rate and outage probability over multi-hop Weibull fading channels was also conducted by Wang et al. [15].

The Weibull distribution is defined by two parameters: the shape parameter (ν) and the scale parameter (λ). The shape parameter determines the shape of the distribution curve, while the scale parameter determines the characteristic magnitude or scale of the failure times. Depending on the value of the shape parameter ν, the Weibull distribution can exhibit different shapes. When $\nu > 1$, the distribution is positively skewed, indicating a decreasing failure rate over time. This shape is commonly known as the bathtub curve and is often observed in reliability analysis. In this curve, failures are more likely to occur either early on, due to manufacturing defects or initial wear, or in the later stages, due to aging or wear-out effects. When $\nu = 1$, the distribution simplifies to the exponential distribution, which is the only continuous distribution with a constant hazard function on the positive axis. For $\nu < 1$, the distribution is negatively skewed, indicating an increasing failure rate over time (Rinne [16]).

The versatility and importance of this distribution can be seen in its close relationship with several well-known distributions in statistics. It includes other distributions as special cases, such as the exponential distribution (when the shape parameter ν is equal to 1) and the Rayleigh distribution (when ν is equal to 2). Furthermore, if T follows a Weibull distribution, then $Y = \lambda(1 - \nu \log(T/\nu))$ follows an extreme-value distribution. By applying a simple log transformation, the Weibull distribution can also be converted into the Gumbel distribution. Additionally, it acts as a limit distribution for the Burr distribution, establishing a significant connection between these distributions (Lai and Xie [17]). These relationships further emphasize the importance and wide-ranging applicability of the Weibull distribution in statistical modeling and analysis.

The Weibull distribution is widely used in modeling lifetimes because it can effectively represent different failure patterns observed in real-life situations. Failure data can be classified into two types: complete data and incomplete (censored) data. Complete data refer to cases where the actual observed values are known for every observation in the dataset. On the other hand, censored data occur when the actual observed values are unknown for some or all of the observations. It is worth noting that there are various types of censoring; more information can be found in the work by Lawless [18]. Several studies have examined the application of the Weibull distribution in analyzing censored data. For example, Ghitany et al. (2005) [19] and Klakattawi (2022) [20] extended the Weibull model and applied it to bladder cancer data, Joarder (2011) [21] and Jia et al. (2016) [22] studied leukemia data, and Lee et al. (2007) [23] focused on the head-and-neck-cancer trial. The Weibull distribution has an intriguing application in models involving a fraction of cure. This distribution is particularly well-suited for estimating the time it takes for cancer cells to produce detectable cancer. As a result, it has gained significant popularity in this field. Several studies, including those by Chen et al. [24], Yin and Ibrahim [25], Rodrigues et al. [26], Gallardo et al. [27], and Azimi et al. [28], have extensively explored this topic.

There are numerous extensions, generalizations, and modifications to the Weibull distribution. These developments have emerged to address the requirements of empirical datasets that exhibit characteristics beyond what can be effectively captured by a standard two-parameter Weibull model (Lai and Xie [17]). These extended models can be broadly classified into three groups: univariate, multivariate, and stochastic process models. Univariate models focus on enhancing the flexibility of the Weibull distribution for single variable analysis. Multivariate models extend the Weibull framework to handle multiple variables and their dependencies. Stochastic process models delve into time-dependent and dynamic variations of the Weibull distribution. Noteworthy references, such as Murthy et al. [29,30], provide insights into these diverse extensions and shed light on the advancements made in modeling techniques beyond the traditional Weibull framework. Silva et al. [31] derived the power-series extended Weibull class of distributions. Santos-Neto et al. [32] and Nascimento et al. [33] introduced a family of distributions encompassing well over forty variants. For more details about the generalizations and modifications of the Weibull distribution, see Murthy [30], Nadarajah and Kotz [34], Pham and Lai [35], and Almalki and Nadarajah [36], as well as the references therein. The analysis of the truncated Weibull distribution has been explored in many papers. For example, Wingo [37] proposed the left-truncated Weibull distribution. The right-truncated Weibull distribution has been analyzed by Zhang and Xie [38]. The doubly-truncated Weibull distribution has been studied in work by McEwen and Parresol [39].

In summary, the Weibull distribution is a versatile probability distribution that finds widespread application in modeling the failure times of objects or systems. The distribution's characteristics and behaviors are determined by two key parameters: the shape parameter and the scale parameter. The shape parameter governs the shape of the distribution, allowing it to range from exponential to highly skewed distributions. On the other hand, the scale parameter influences the location and spread of the distribution. By manipulating these parameters, the Weibull distribution can effectively capture various failure patterns observed in real-world scenarios. Its flexibility and wide range of applications make it a valuable tool in reliability analysis and survival modeling.

The main objectives of this manuscript are as follows:

1. We perform a review of the different parameterizations of the Weibull distribution documented in the literature, including the interpretation of the regression coefficients, when incorporating regression structures into these parameterizations.
2. We introduce a novel parameterization of the Weibull model based on the mode of this distribution.
3. We theoretically explore the equivalence of the five parameterizations of the Weibull distribution in the context of regression models, since there is no discussion connecting all the mentioned parameterizations.

The manuscript is organized as follows. In Section 2, five parameterizations of the Weibull distribution are introduced. Three of these parameterizations are mean-based, one is quantile-based, and the last one is mode-based. Each parameterization is characterized by examining the respective hazard and survival functions. Section 3 delves into the interpretation of regression coefficients when regression structures are incorporated into the parameters of the five Weibull model parameterizations. In Section 5, we analytically demonstrate that the five parameterizations of the Weibull model discussed in the previous section define the same log-likelihood function. Section 6 presents Monte Carlo (MC) simulation studies for parameter estimation and residuals. In Section 6, the analyzed models are applied to real data. Specifically, two illustrations are provided to exemplify their applicability and use in material fatigue life and survival data. should be noted that all models have been implemented using the R-project code (https://www.r-project.org/, accessed on 5 December 2023). Finally, Section 7 summarizes the main conclusions of the manuscript and discusses possible avenues for future work.

2. Weibull Parameterizations

As discussed in Section 1, the Weibull distribution is one of the most used models in reliability analysis because it is a parsimonious model with a simple expression for the density, survival, and hazard functions, and with some interesting properties. For instance, it can assume a decreasing, increasing, or constant hazard rate, depending only on the shape parameter ν (<1, >1, or =1, respectively). However, the Weibull distribution has many parameterizations in the literature, depending on the study.

The accelerated failure time (AFT) model, which is employed as the base parameterization, is used for the Weibull model; it has hazard and survival functions given by

$$h(t;\lambda,\nu) = \frac{\nu}{\lambda}\left[\frac{t}{\lambda}\right]^{\nu-1}, \quad t,\nu,\lambda > 0.$$

and

$$S(t;\lambda,\nu) = \exp\left(-\left[\frac{t}{\lambda}\right]^{\nu}\right), \quad t,\nu,\lambda > 0,$$

respectively, with λ and ν parameters of scale and shape, respectively. This parameterization is referred to as WEI(λ,ν). An alternative parameterization of the Weibull model is associated with the proportional hazards model, in which the hazard and survival functions are given by

$$h(t;\lambda,\nu) = \nu\lambda t^{\nu-1}, \quad t,\nu,\lambda > 0$$

and

$$S(t;\lambda,\nu) = \exp(-\lambda t^{\nu}), \quad t,\nu,\lambda > 0,$$

respectively. This parameterization is referred to as WEI2(λ,ν), where λ and ν act as the scale and shape parameters, respectively. A third alternative parameterization of the Weibull model is related to its mean. Fernandes et al. [40] propose a reparameterization that expresses the Weibull distribution in terms of the process mean, enabling straightforward monitoring of the Weibull mean. In this parameterization, the hazard and survival functions are given by

$$h(t;\lambda,\nu) = \frac{\nu}{\gamma}\left[\frac{t}{\gamma}\right]^{\nu-1}, \quad t,\nu,\lambda > 0$$

where $\gamma = \lambda/\Gamma(1+1/\nu)$ and

$$S(t;\lambda,\nu) = \exp\left(-\left[\frac{t}{\gamma}\right]^{\nu}\right), \quad t,\nu,\lambda > 0,$$

respectively. This parameterization is referred to as WEI3(λ,ν). In this case, $\mathbb{E}(T) = \lambda$.

Recently, a fourth parameterization for the Weibull distribution was introduced by Sánchez et al. [41]. In this parameterization, the hazard and survival functions are given by

$$h(t;\lambda,\nu) = -\log(1-q)\frac{\nu}{\lambda}\left[\frac{t}{\lambda}\right]^{\nu-1}, \quad t,\nu,\lambda > 0.$$

where $q \in (0,1)$ and

$$S(t;\lambda,\nu) = \exp\left(\log(1-q)\left[\frac{t}{\lambda}\right]^{\nu}\right), \quad t,\nu,\lambda > 0,$$

respectively. This parameterization is referred to as WEI4(λ,ν). In this case, λ represents the q-quantile of the distribution.

Alternatively, a fifth parameterization of the Weibull is proposed, based on its mode. The main motivation for re-parameterizing the model in terms of this measure is associated with the robustness of the mode (above the mean, for example) and the fact that it is a measure that has been used more frequently in the literature in recent years. For instance, see Yao and Li [42], Chen [43], and Bourguignon et al. [44]. In this parameterization, the hazard and survival functions are given by

$$h(t;\lambda,\nu) = \frac{[\nu-1]}{\lambda}\left[\frac{t}{\lambda}\right]^{\nu-1}, \quad t,\nu,\lambda > 0.$$

and

$$S(t;\lambda,\nu) = \exp\left(-\left[1-\frac{1}{\nu}\right]\left[\frac{t}{\lambda}\right]^{\nu}\right), \quad t,\lambda > 0, \nu > 1.$$

This parameterization is referred to as WEI5(λ,ν). In this case, λ represents the mode of the distribution. Table 1 presents the mean, mode, q-quantile, and variance for the five parameterizations of the Weibull distribution explored in this study.

Table 1. Different measures for the five parameterization of the Weibull distribution. In all parameterizations, the parameter space for (λ,ν) is $\mathbb{R}^2_+$, except for the WEI5 model, where the parameter space is $\mathbb{R}_+ \times (1,\infty)$.

Model	Mean	Mode	q-Quantile	Variance
WEI	$\lambda\Gamma\left(1+\frac{1}{\nu}\right)$	$\begin{cases} \lambda\left[\frac{(\nu-1)}{\nu}\right]^{1/\nu} & \text{, if } \nu > 1 \\ 0 & \text{, if } \nu \leq 1 \end{cases}$	$\lambda[-\log(1-q)]^{1/\nu}$	$\lambda^2\omega(\nu)$
WEI2	$\lambda^{-1/\nu}\Gamma\left(1+\frac{1}{\nu}\right)$	$\begin{cases} \left[\frac{(\nu-1)}{\lambda\nu}\right]^{1/\nu} & \text{, if } \nu > 1 \\ 0 & \text{, if } \nu \leq 1 \end{cases}$	$\left[\frac{-\log(1-q)}{\lambda}\right]^{1/\nu}$	$\lambda^{-2/\nu}\omega(\nu)$
WEI3	λ	$\begin{cases} \frac{\lambda}{\Gamma(1+\frac{1}{\nu})}\left[\frac{(\nu-1)}{\nu}\right]^{1/\nu} & \text{, if } \nu > 1 \\ 0 & \text{, if } \nu \leq 1 \end{cases}$	$\frac{\lambda}{\Gamma(1+\frac{1}{\nu})}[-\log(1-q)]^{1/\nu}$	$\lambda^2\frac{\omega(\nu)}{\Gamma^2(1+\frac{1}{\nu})}$
WEI4	$\frac{\lambda\Gamma(1+\frac{1}{\nu})}{[-\log(1-q)]^{1/\nu}}$	$\begin{cases} \lambda\left[\frac{(\nu-1)}{\nu[-\log(1-q)]}\right]^{1/\nu} & \text{, if } \nu > 1 \\ 0 & \text{, if } \nu \leq 1 \end{cases}$	λ	$\lambda^2\left[\log^2(1-q)\right]^{-2/\nu}\omega(\nu)$
WEI5	$\lambda\left[1-\frac{1}{\nu}\right]^{-1/\nu}\Gamma\left(1+\frac{1}{\nu}\right)$	λ	$\lambda\left[\frac{-\nu\log(1-q)}{(\nu-1)}\right]^{1/\nu}$	$\lambda^2\left[1-\frac{1}{\nu}\right]^{-1/\nu}\omega(\nu)$

NOTE: $\omega(\nu) = \Gamma(1+\frac{2}{\nu}) - \Gamma^2\left(1+\frac{1}{\nu}\right)$.

For a set of p covariates observed for each individual and the intercept term, say $\mathbf{x}_i^\top = (1, x_{1i}, x_{2i}, \ldots, x_{pi})$, and for the four parameterizations, it is typical to include a regression structure in λ, as follows

$$\lambda_i = g(\mathbf{x}_i^\top\boldsymbol{\beta}), \quad i = 1,\ldots,n, \tag{1}$$

where $\boldsymbol{\beta} = (\beta_0, \beta_1, \beta_2, \ldots, \beta_p)$, and $g(\cdot)$ is a twice differentiable function, such as $g: \mathbb{R} \to \mathbb{R}^+$. The most common choice is $g(u) = \exp(u)$, which also facilitates the interpretation of the regression coefficients. In each model, such interpretation depends on its specific parameterization (WEI, WEI2, WEI3, WEI4, and WEI5). However, it will be demonstrated that when a regression structure is incorporated solely into λ, as in Equation (1), without affecting the shape parameter ν, then all five models share the same probability density function (PDF) and, consequently, the same log-likelihood function. Furthermore, it will also be demonstrated that introducing a dual regression structure for both λ and ν in the WEI, WEI2, WEI3, and WEI4 models results in different PDFs among the models.

3. Interpretation of the Coefficients

In this section, we explore the varying interpretations of regression coefficients in the Weibull model across different parameterizations. Let us consider two individuals with associated covariates, $\mathbf{x}_i = (1, x_{i1}, \ldots, x_{ij}, \ldots, x_{ip})$ and $\mathbf{x}_i^* = (1, x_{i1}, \ldots, x_{ij}+1, \ldots, x_{ip})$, which is that $\mathbf{x}_i$ and $\mathbf{x}_i^*$ are identical, except for an increase of one unit in the j-th covariate. The scenario where the j-th covariate is quantitative will be focused on. However, in all cases, a similar interpretation can be applied to x_{ij}, assuming two categories (labeled as 0 and 1). Note that $\mathbf{x}_i^{*\top}\boldsymbol{\beta} = \mathbf{x}_i^\top\boldsymbol{\beta} + \beta_j$.

3.1. WEI Model

For the AFT parameterization, we obtain

$$S(t; \lambda_i, \nu) = \exp\left(-\left[\frac{t}{\lambda_i}\right]^\nu\right) = S_0(\lambda_i^{-1} t; \nu), \quad t > 0,$$

where $S_0(t) = \exp(-t^\nu)$. In this context, λ_i^{-1} is known as the accelerator factor. More precisely, as mentioned by Kleinbaum and Klein [45], "the accelerator factor is a ratio of survival times corresponding to any fixed value of $S(t)$". In this case, to facilitate the interpretation of the coefficients, it is set $g(u) = \exp(u)$. Consequently, the interpretations of covariates are as follows: If $\exp(\beta_j) = 2$, then the median survival time doubles when the j-th covariate is increased by one unit, compared to the median survival time when the j-th covariate remains unchanged.

Remark 1. *For WEI2, WEI3, and WEI4 parameterizations, the traditional link function is* $g(u) = \exp(u)$.

3.2. WEI2 Model

In this case, the quotient between the hazard function related to $\mathbf{x}_i$ and $\mathbf{x}_i^*$ is

$$\frac{h(t; \mathbf{x}_i, \nu)}{h(t; \mathbf{x}_i^*, \nu)} = \frac{\exp(\mathbf{x}_i^{*\top}\boldsymbol{\beta})\nu t^{\nu-1}}{\exp(\mathbf{x}_i^\top\boldsymbol{\beta})\nu t^{\nu-1}} = \exp(\beta_j).$$

This does not depend on t (hence, the name 'proportional hazard models'). Therefore, $\exp(\beta_j)$ should be interpreted as the increase (or decrease) in the hazard function when the j-th covariate increases by one unit.

3.3. WEI3 Model

In this case, the expected value of the distribution is $\mathbb{E}(T_i; \mathbf{x}_i) = \lambda_i$. Therefore, the quotient between the mean related to $\mathbf{x}_i$ and $\mathbf{x}_i^*$ is

$$\frac{\mathbb{E}(T_i; \mathbf{x}_i^*)}{\mathbb{E}(T_i; \mathbf{x}_i)} = \frac{\exp(\mathbf{x}_i^{*\top}\boldsymbol{\beta})}{\exp(\mathbf{x}_i^\top\boldsymbol{\beta})} = \exp(\beta_j).$$

Therefore, $\exp(\beta_j)$ should be interpreted as the percentage increase (or decrease) in the mean when the j-th covariate is increased by one unit.

3.4. WEI4 Model

In this case, the $100 \times q$-th quantile of the distribution is $\tau_q(\mathbf{x}_i) = \lambda_i$. Therefore, the quotient between the $100 \times q$-th quantile related to $\mathbf{x}_i$ and $\mathbf{x}_i^*$ is given by

$$\frac{\tau_q(\mathbf{x}_i^*)}{\tau_q(\mathbf{x}_i)} = \frac{\exp(\mathbf{x}_i^{*\top}\boldsymbol{\beta})}{\exp(\mathbf{x}_i^\top\boldsymbol{\beta})} = \exp(\beta_j).$$

Then, $\exp(\beta_j)$ represents the percentage increase (or decrease) in the $100 \times q$-th quantile when the j-th covariate is increased by one unit.

3.5. WEI5 Model

For this model, the mode of the distribution is $\mathrm{Mo}(T_i;\mathbf{x}_i) = \lambda_i$. Therefore, the model related to $\mathbf{x}_i$ and $\mathbf{x}_i^*$ is

$$\frac{\mathrm{Mo}(T_i;\mathbf{x}_i^*)}{\mathrm{Mo}(T_i;\mathbf{x}_i^*)} = \frac{\exp(\mathbf{x}_i^{*\top}\boldsymbol{\beta})}{\exp(\mathbf{x}_i^{\top}\boldsymbol{\beta})} = \exp(\beta_j).$$

In this case, $\exp(\beta_j)$ represents the percentage increase (or decrease) in the mode when the j-th covariate is increased by one unit.

3.6. The Bi-Univocity among the Four Parameterizations When Modeling Only λ

To date, there is no discussion in the literature about the connection between the different parameterizations of the Weibull distribution when incorporating regression structures into these parameterizations. The following theorem establishes the biunivocal relationship between the WEI, WEI2, WEI3, WEI4, and WEI5 models when modeling only λ.

Theorem 1. *Let $Y_1,\ldots,Y_n$ be independent random variables, such as $Y_i \sim WEI(\lambda_i,\nu)$, where $\lambda_i = \exp(-\mathbf{x}_i^\top\boldsymbol{\beta})$, $i = 1,\ldots,n$ and a constant shape parameter ν. Consider alternative parameterizations for the Weibull model, such as $Y_i \sim WEI2(\lambda_i^\star,\tau)$, $Y_i \sim WEI3(\lambda_i^\star,\tau)$, $Y_i \sim WEI4(\lambda_i^\star,\tau)$ or $Y_i \sim WEI5(\lambda_i^\star,\tau)$, with $\lambda_i^\star = \exp(\mathbf{x}_i^\top\boldsymbol{\delta})$ and a non-modeled τ. If intercept terms are considered in $\mathbf{x}_i$, then the elements of $(\boldsymbol{\delta}^\top,\tau)$ can be obtained uniquely from $(\boldsymbol{\beta}^\top,\nu)$.*

Proof. Equating the hazard functions for the WEI2, WEI3, WEI4, and WEI5 models with those associated with the WEI model, we obtain $\lambda_i = k(\lambda_i^\star,\tau)$ and $\nu = \tau$, where $k(\lambda_i^\star,\tau) = \left[\lambda_i^\star\right]^{-1/\tau}$, for the WEI2 model, $k(\lambda_i^\star,\tau) = \lambda_i^\star \times \left[\tau\{\Gamma(1+1/\tau)\}^\tau\right]^{-1}$, for the WEI3 model, $k(\lambda_i^\star,\tau) = \lambda_i^\star \times -\log(1-q)$, for the WEI4 model and $k(\lambda_i^\star,\tau) = \lambda_i^\star \times \left[1-\frac{1}{\tau}\right]^{1/\tau}$, for the WEI5 model. Considering the partitions $\mathbf{x}_i^\top = (1,\mathbf{x}_i^{\triangle\top})$, $\boldsymbol{\beta}^\top = (\beta_0,\boldsymbol{\beta}^{\triangle\top})$ and $\boldsymbol{\delta}^\top = (\delta_0,\boldsymbol{\delta}^{\triangle\top})$, i.e., $\mathbf{x}_i^{\triangle\top}$, $\boldsymbol{\beta}^{\triangle\top}$ and $\boldsymbol{\delta}^{\triangle\top}$ are related to the non-intercept terms of $\mathbf{x}_i^\top$, $\boldsymbol{\beta}^\top$ and $\boldsymbol{\delta}^\top$, respectively. With this, the equation $\lambda_i = k(\lambda_i^\star,\tau)$ assumes the following forms for each case:

- WEI2 model:

$$\exp\left(-\beta_0 - \mathbf{x}_i^{\triangle\top}\boldsymbol{\beta}^\triangle\right) = \exp\left(\frac{\delta_0}{\tau} + \frac{\mathbf{x}_i^{\triangle\top}\boldsymbol{\delta}^\triangle}{\tau}\right).$$

  In this case, we conclude that $\delta_0 = -\tau\beta_0$ and $\boldsymbol{\beta}^\triangle = -\boldsymbol{\delta}^\triangle/\tau$.

- WEI3 model:

$$\exp\left(-\beta_0 - \mathbf{x}_i^{\triangle\top}\boldsymbol{\beta}^\triangle\right) = \exp\left(\delta_0 - \log\tau - \tau\log\Gamma(1+1/\tau) + \mathbf{x}_i^{\triangle\top}\boldsymbol{\delta}^\triangle\right).$$

  Here, it can be concluded that $\delta_0 = -\beta_0 + \log\tau + \tau\log\Gamma(1+1/\tau)$ and $\boldsymbol{\beta}^\triangle = \boldsymbol{\delta}^\triangle$.

- WEI4 model:

$$\exp\left(-\beta_0 - \mathbf{x}_i^{\triangle\top}\boldsymbol{\beta}^\triangle\right) = \exp\left(\delta_0 + \log(-\log(1-q)) + \mathbf{x}_i^{\triangle\top}\boldsymbol{\delta}^\triangle\right),$$

  where we conclude that $\delta_0 = -\beta_0 - \log(-\log(1-q))$ and $\boldsymbol{\beta}^\triangle = \boldsymbol{\delta}^\triangle$.

- WEI5 model:

$$\exp\left(-\beta_0 - \mathbf{x}_i^{\triangle\top}\boldsymbol{\beta}^\triangle\right) = \exp\left(\delta_0 + \frac{1}{\tau}\log\left(1-\frac{1}{\tau}\right) + \mathbf{x}_i^{\triangle\top}\boldsymbol{\delta}^\triangle\right).$$

In this case, we conclude that $\delta_0 = -\beta_0 - \frac{1}{\tau}\log\left(1 - \frac{1}{\tau}\right)$ and $\beta^{\triangle} = \delta^{\triangle}$.

Note that in all cases, $(\delta^\top, \tau)$ can be obtained uniquely from $(\beta^\top, \nu)$. $\square$

Remark 2. *Theorem 1 implies that when only λ is modeled in the WEI, WEI2, WEI3, WEI4, and WEI5 models, all the distributions produce the same PDF. Consequently, model selection criteria, such as the Akaike Information criterion (AIC) and Bayesian information criterion (BIC), yield identical values.*

Remark 3. *When an additional set of covariates, denoted as $\mathbf{z}_i$ (not necessarily identical to $\mathbf{x}_i$), is considered to model the shape parameter as $\nu_i = h(\mathbf{z}_i^\top \zeta)$, where $h : \mathbb{R} \to \mathbb{R}^+$, the five parameterizations of the Weibull model define different PDFs. This distinction arises because the relationship $\lambda_i = k(\lambda_i^\star, \tau_i)$ incorporates only the covariates $\mathbf{x}_i$ on the left side of the equation, while both sets of covariates are involved on the right side.*

4. Inference

In this section, we discuss the estimation procedure in a unified way for the WEI, WEI2, WEI3, WEI4, and WEI5 models from a classical approach. The asymptotic distribution of the estimators is also presented.

Parameter Estimation

Let $Y_1, \ldots, Y_n$ be n independent random variables, where each Y_i, $i = 1, \ldots, n$, follows a WEI, WEI2, WEI3, WEI4, or WEI5 model. The log-likelihood function for $\boldsymbol{\theta}^\top = (\boldsymbol{\beta}^\top, \boldsymbol{\delta}^\top)$ has the form

$$\ell(\boldsymbol{\theta}) = \sum_{i=1}^{n} \ell_i(\lambda_i, \nu_i; y_i),$$

where

$$\ell_i(\lambda_i, \nu_i; y_i) \quad = \quad \log \nu_i - \log \lambda_i + (\nu_i - 1)[\log t_i - \log \lambda_i] - \left[\frac{t_i}{\lambda_i}\right]^{\nu_i},$$

with $\lambda_i = k(\lambda_i^\star, \nu_i)$, $\lambda_i^\star = g(\mathbf{x}_i^\top \boldsymbol{\beta})$ and $\nu_i = h(\mathbf{z}_i^\top \boldsymbol{\delta})$. The function $k(\cdot,\cdot)$ is defined in Table 2 for the different parameterizations of the WEI model.

Table 2. Function $k(\lambda, \nu)$ for the different parameterizations of the WEI model.

Model	WEI	WEI2	WEI3	WEI4	WEI5
$k(\lambda,\nu)$	λ	$\lambda^{-1/\nu}$	$\lambda[\nu\{\Gamma(1+1/\nu)\}^\nu]^{-1}$	$-\lambda\log(1-q)$	$\lambda\left[1-\frac{1}{\nu}\right]^{1/\nu}$

The maximum likelihood (ML) estimates of $\boldsymbol{\beta}$ and $\boldsymbol{\delta}$ are computed as the solution of the non-linear system $\boldsymbol{U}(\boldsymbol{\theta}) = \mathbf{0}_{q+r}$, where $\mathbf{0}_{q+r}$ denotes a $(q+r) \times 1$ vector of zeros and $\boldsymbol{U}(\boldsymbol{\theta})$ is given by

$$\boldsymbol{U}(\boldsymbol{\theta}) = \begin{bmatrix} \partial\ell(\boldsymbol{\theta})/\partial\boldsymbol{\beta} \\ \partial\ell(\boldsymbol{\theta})/\partial\boldsymbol{\delta} \end{bmatrix} = \begin{bmatrix} \mathbf{X}^\top \mathbf{A}_\lambda \mathbf{C}_\lambda \mathbf{D}_\lambda \\ \mathbf{Z}^\top \mathbf{A}_\nu \mathbf{D}_\nu \end{bmatrix},$$

where $\mathbf{A}_u = \mathrm{diag}(a_u^{(1)}, \ldots, a_u^{(n)})$, $\mathbf{C}_\lambda = \mathrm{diag}(c_\lambda^{(1)}, \ldots, c_\lambda^{(n)})$, $\mathbf{D}_u = \mathrm{diag}(d_u^{(1)}, \ldots, d_u^{(n)})$, for $u \in \{\lambda, \nu\}$, $a_\lambda^{(i)} = g'(\mathbf{x}_i^\top \boldsymbol{\beta})$, $a_\nu^{(i)} = h'(\mathbf{z}_i^\top \boldsymbol{\delta})$ and

$$c_\lambda^{(i)} = \begin{cases} 1 & \text{, for the WEI model} \\ -\frac{1}{\nu}\lambda^{-1/\nu-1} & \text{, for the WEI2 model} \\ [\nu\{\Gamma(1+1/\nu)\}]^{-1} & \text{, for the WEI3 model} \\ -\log(1-q) & \text{, for the WEI4 model} \\ [1-1\nu]^{1/\nu} & \text{, for the WEI5 model} \end{cases}$$

$$d_\lambda^{(i)} = -\frac{\nu_i}{\lambda_i} + \frac{\nu_i}{\lambda_i}\left[\frac{t_i}{\lambda_i}\right]^{\nu_i},$$

$$d_\nu^{(i)} = \frac{1}{\nu_i} + \log t_i - \log\lambda_i - \left[\frac{t_i}{\lambda_i}\right]^{\nu_i}[\log t_i - \log\lambda_i].$$

The Fisher information matrix for models can be written as

$$\mathbf{I}(\boldsymbol{\theta}) = \mathbb{E}\left[\begin{array}{cc} -\partial^2\ell(\boldsymbol{\theta})/\partial\boldsymbol{\beta}\partial\boldsymbol{\beta}^\top & -\partial^2\ell(\boldsymbol{\theta})/\partial\boldsymbol{\beta}\partial\boldsymbol{\delta}^\top \\ \cdot & -\partial^2\ell(\boldsymbol{\theta})/\partial\boldsymbol{\delta}\partial\boldsymbol{\delta}^\top \end{array}\right] = \widetilde{\mathbf{X}}^\top\mathbf{W}(\boldsymbol{\theta})\widetilde{\mathbf{X}},$$

where

$$\widetilde{\mathbf{X}} = \begin{pmatrix} \mathbf{X} & \mathbf{0}_{p\times 1} \\ \mathbf{0}_{q\times 1} & \mathbf{Z} \end{pmatrix} \quad \text{and}$$

$$\mathbf{W}(\boldsymbol{\theta}) = \left[\begin{array}{cc} \mathbf{A}_\lambda\mathbf{C}_\lambda\mathbf{V}_{\lambda\lambda}\mathbf{C}_\lambda\mathbf{A}_\lambda & \mathbf{A}_\lambda\mathbf{V}_{\lambda\nu}\mathbf{C}_\lambda\mathbf{A}_\nu \\ \mathbf{A}_\nu\mathbf{V}_{\lambda\nu}\mathbf{C}_\lambda\mathbf{A}_\lambda & \mathbf{A}_\nu\mathbf{V}_{\nu\nu}\mathbf{A}_\nu \end{array}\right],$$

with $\mathbf{V}_{uv} = \mathrm{diag}(V_{uv}^{(1)}, \ldots, V_{uv}^{(n)})$, for $u, v \in \{\lambda, \nu\}$, where

$$V_{\lambda\lambda}^{(i)} = -\mathrm{E}\left(\frac{\partial^2\ell_i(\boldsymbol{\theta})}{\partial\lambda_i^2}\right) = -\mathrm{E}\left(\frac{\nu_i}{\lambda_i^2} - \frac{\nu_i(\nu_i+1)}{\lambda_i^2}\left[\frac{t_i}{\lambda_i}\right]^{\nu_i}\right) = \frac{\nu_i^2}{\lambda_i^2},$$

$$\begin{aligned} V_{\nu\nu}^{(i)} &= -\mathrm{E}\left(\frac{\partial^2\ell_i(\boldsymbol{\theta})}{\partial\nu_i^2}\right) = -\mathrm{E}\left(-\frac{1}{\nu_i^2} - \left[\frac{t_i}{\lambda_i}\right]^{\nu_i}[\log t_i - \log\lambda_i]\right) \\ &= \frac{1}{\nu_i^2} + \frac{1}{\nu_i}\left[\psi'(1) + \psi^2(1) + 2\nu_i\log\lambda_i\psi(1) + \nu_i^2\log^2\lambda_i - \psi(2) - \nu_i\log\lambda_i + \nu_i\log^2\lambda_i\right], \end{aligned}$$

$$V_{\lambda\nu}^{(i)} = -\mathrm{E}\left(\frac{\partial^2\ell_i(\boldsymbol{\theta})}{\partial\lambda_i\partial\nu_i}\right) = -\mathrm{E}\left(-\frac{1}{\lambda_i^2} + \frac{1}{\lambda_i}\left[\frac{t_i}{\lambda_i}\right]^{\nu_i} + \frac{\nu_i}{\lambda_i}\left[\frac{t_i}{\lambda_i}\right]^{\nu_i}[\log t_i - \log\lambda_i]\right) = -\frac{\psi(2)}{\lambda_i}.$$

An alternative way to obtain the ML estimates of $\boldsymbol{\theta}$ is by using the Fisher scoring iterative procedure, providing the following estimation algorithm:

$$\begin{aligned} \widehat{\boldsymbol{\theta}}^{(k+1)} &= \widehat{\boldsymbol{\theta}}^{(k)} + \left[\mathbf{I}\left(\widehat{\boldsymbol{\theta}}^{(k)}\right)\right]^{-1} \times \mathbf{U}\left(\widehat{\boldsymbol{\theta}}^{(k)}\right) \\ &= \widehat{\boldsymbol{\theta}}^{(k)} + \left[\widetilde{\mathbf{X}}^\top\mathbf{W}\left(\widehat{\boldsymbol{\theta}}^{(k)}\right)\widetilde{\mathbf{X}}\right]^{-1}\widetilde{\mathbf{X}}^\top\mathbf{W}_1\left(\widehat{\boldsymbol{\theta}}^{(k)}\right), \quad k = 0, 1, 2, \ldots, \end{aligned}$$

where $\mathbf{W}_1(\boldsymbol{\theta}) = (\mathbf{A}_\lambda\mathbf{C}_\lambda\mathbf{D}_\lambda, \mathbf{A}_\nu\mathbf{D}_\nu)^\top$. We recommend initializing the algorithm by using, as an initial guess for $\boldsymbol{\beta}$, the ordinary least squares estimates obtained from the linear regression of the transformed responses: $g(y_1), \ldots, g(y_n)$ on $\mathbf{X}$, i.e., $(\mathbf{X}^\top\mathbf{X})^{-1}\mathbf{X}^\top\mathbf{Z}$, where $\mathbf{Z} = (g(y_1), \ldots, g(y_n))^\top$.

In order to approach the interval estimation and hypothesis testing on the model parameters $\boldsymbol{\beta}$ and $\boldsymbol{\delta}$, normal approximation for the ML estimators can be applied. Note that under certain conditions for the parameters, the asymptotic distribution of $\sqrt{n}(\widehat{\boldsymbol{\theta}} - \boldsymbol{\theta})$ is multivariate normal $N_{q+r}(\mathbf{0}_{q+r}, \mathbf{I}^{-1}(\boldsymbol{\theta}))$.

Let the θ_j be the jth component of $\boldsymbol{\theta}$. The asymptotic $100(1-\gamma)\%$ confidence interval for θ_j is given by

$$\widehat{\theta}_j \pm z_{1-\gamma/2}\,\mathrm{se}(\widehat{\theta}_j), \qquad j = 1, \ldots, q+r,$$

where $\mathrm{se}(\widehat{\theta}_r)$ is the asymptotic standard error of $\widehat{\theta}_j$, which is the square root of the jth diagonal element of the inverse of $\mathbf{I}(\widehat{\boldsymbol{\theta}})$.

5. Monte Carlo Simulation Studies

In this section, we assess the performances of the ML estimators through MC simulations, compare their empirical biases and mean squared error (MSE), and evaluate the residuals for WEI models. The WEI4 and WEI5 models are implemented in R software (version 4.2, accessed on 5 December 2023). www.r-project.org and a routine has been developed for the aforementioned simulations. The R-code can be obtained from https://github.com/lsanchez2020/Weibull_reparameterized.git.

5.1. MC Simulation Study I: Behavior of the ML Estimators

For WEI4 (with $q = 0.5$) and WEI5 models, the following regression structure is considered:

$$\lambda_i = \exp\left(\mathbf{x}_i^\top \boldsymbol{\beta}\right), \quad \text{and} \quad \nu_i = \exp(\mathbf{z}_i^\top \boldsymbol{\zeta}), \quad i = 1, \ldots, n.$$

To assess the performance of the ML estimators for the WEI4 and WEI5 models, both the bias and the MSE are reported. The bias and MSE are calculated as follows:

$$\widehat{\mathrm{Bias}}(\widehat{\varphi}) = \frac{1}{B}\sum_{j=1}^{B}(\widehat{\varphi}_j - \varphi), \qquad \widehat{\mathrm{MSE}}(\widehat{\varphi}) = \frac{1}{B}\sum_{j=1}^{B}(\widehat{\varphi}_j - \varphi)^2,$$

where $\widehat{\varphi}_j$ is the estimate in the jth replicate, φ is the true value of the parameter, and B is the number of MC replicates; 5000 MC replicates are conducted, where the explanatory variables are simulated from a Uniform (0, 1) distribution. Four scenarios for the true values of the parameters are considered: (i) true values of β_1, β_2, ζ_1, and ζ_2 are 0.2, 1.0, 0.2, and 1.0; (ii) true values of β_1, β_2, ζ_1, and ζ_2 are 0.2, 0.5, 0.2, and 1.0; (iii) true values of β_1, β_2, ζ_1, and ζ_2 are 0.5, 1.0, 0.2, and 1.0; and (iv) true values of β_1, β_2, ζ_1, and ζ_2 are 0.5, 1.5, 0.2, and 1.0.

Tables 3 and 4 report the ML estimation results for the bias and the MSE of the WEI4 and WEI5 model estimators, respectively. A general trend observed in these tables is that—as the sample size increases—both bias and MSE decrease, as expected in a Monte Carlo study. Therefore, the results confirm the consistence and un-biasing of the ML estimators.

Table 3. Bias and MSE for the WEI4 model parameters, with the indicated sample size and true values of the parameters.

	$\beta_1 = 0.2$; $\beta_2 = 1.0$; $\zeta_1 = 0.2$; $\zeta_2 = 1.0$							
	Bias				MSE			
n	β_1	β_2	ζ_1	ζ_2	β_1	β_2	ζ_1	ζ_2
30	−0.0028	0.0013	0.0761	0.0232	0.0808	0.2592	0.2330	0.6466
50	−0.0039	0.0035	0.0371	0.0296	0.0502	0.1470	0.0972	0.3091
100	−0.0005	0.0007	0.0152	0.0179	0.0206	0.0661	0.0411	0.1357
500	−0.0001	0.0000	0.0048	−0.0005	0.0043	0.0134	0.0080	0.0253

Table 3. *Cont.*

	$\beta_1 = 0.2$; $\beta_2 = 0.5$; $\zeta_1 = 0.2$; $\zeta_2 = 1.0$							
	Bias				MSE			
n	β_1	β_2	ζ_1	ζ_2	β_1	β_2	ζ_1	ζ_2
30	−0.0153	0.0185	0.0533	0.0503	0.0843	0.2499	0.1846	0.5915
50	0.0021	−0.0036	0.0368	0.0318	0.0430	0.1333	0.0937	0.3019
100	0.0013	−0.0010	0.0144	0.0223	0.0206	0.0619	0.0470	0.1478
500	−0.0004	0.0001	0.0037	0.0029	0.0041	0.0134	0.0075	0.0238
	$\beta_1 = 0.5$; $\beta_2 = 1.0$; $\zeta_1 = 0.2$; $\zeta_2 = 1.0$							
	Bias				MSE			
n	β_1	β_2	ζ_1	ζ_2	β_1	β_2	ζ_1	ζ_2
30	0.0024	−0.0136	0.0596	0.0539	0.0867	0.2542	0.1826	0.5722
50	−0.0047	0.0017	0.0326	0.0285	0.0515	0.1707	0.0911	0.3315
100	−0.0004	−0.0012	0.0184	0.0132	0.0238	0.0713	0.0403	0.1326
500	−0.0016	0.0023	0.0020	0.0038	0.0045	0.0137	0.0078	0.0248
	$\beta_1 = 0.5$; $\beta_2 = 1.5$; $\zeta_1 = 0.2$; $\zeta_2 = 1.0$							
	Bias				MSE			
n	β_1	β_2	ζ_1	ζ_2	β_1	β_2	ζ_1	ζ_2
30	0.0007	−0.0067	0.0533	0.0574	0.0802	0.2363	0.1851	0.6371
50	−0.0052	0.0021	0.0315	0.0368	0.0487	0.1529	0.0943	0.3092
100	−0.0012	0.0016	0.0194	0.0071	0.0251	0.0714	0.0422	0.1316
500	0.0006	−0.0020	0.0040	0.0022	0.0045	0.0134	0.0076	0.0243

Table 4. Bias and MSE for the WEI5 model parameters, with the indicated sample size and true values of the parameters.

	$\beta_1 = 0.2$; $\beta_2 = 1.0$; $\zeta_1 = 0.2$; $\zeta_2 = 1.0$							
	Bias				MSE			
n	β_1	β_2	ζ_1	ζ_2	β_1	β_2	ζ_1	ζ_2
30	−0.0019	0.0099	0.0192	0.1226	0.1699	0.4900	0.0889	0.3378
50	0.0082	−0.0045	0.0149	0.0620	0.0877	0.2437	0.0454	0.1648
100	0.0075	−0.0051	0.0050	0.0333	0.0659	0.1702	0.0158	0.0642
500	0.0003	0.0001	0.0031	0.0022	0.0067	0.0177	0.0025	0.0110
	$\beta_1 = 0.2$; $\beta_2 = 0.5$; $\zeta_1 = 0.2$; $\zeta_2 = 1.0$							
	Bias				MSE			
n	β_1	β_2	ζ_1	ζ_2	β_1	β_2	ζ_1	ζ_2
30	0.0043	−0.0059	0.0211	0.1135	0.2746	0.5124	0.0865	0.3565
50	0.0021	0.0046	0.0164	0.0617	0.1146	0.2692	0.0366	0.1447
100	0.0012	0.0027	0.0035	0.0396	0.0454	0.1138	0.0178	0.0673
500	0.0015	−0.0020	0.0018	0.0058	0.0067	0.0181	0.0027	0.0108
	$\beta_1 = 0.5$; $\beta_2 = 1.0$; $\zeta_1 = 0.2$; $\zeta_2 = 1.0$							
	Bias				MSE			
n	β_1	β_2	ζ_1	ζ_2	β_1	β_2	ζ_1	ζ_2
30	0.0074	−0.0023	0.0188	0.1126	0.1963	0.5392	0.0832	0.3169
50	−0.0019	0.0055	0.0123	0.0638	0.1380	0.3698	0.0434	0.1694
100	0.0006	−0.0019	0.0035	0.0338	0.0360	0.1027	0.0158	0.0626
500	0.0015	−0.0020	0.0009	0.0076	0.0066	0.0175	0.0026	0.0107

Table 4. *Cont.*

	$\beta_1 = 0.5$; $\beta_2 = 1.5$; $\zeta_1 = 0.2$; $\zeta_2 = 1.0$							
	Bias				MSE			
n	β_1	β_2	ζ_1	ζ_2	β_1	β_2	ζ_1	ζ_2
30	−0.0136	0.0217	0.0205	0.1142	0.4725	1.5218	0.0842	0.3431
50	0.0013	0.0040	0.0104	0.0720	0.0886	0.2640	0.0414	0.1756
100	−0.0034	0.0078	0.0056	0.0324	0.0485	0.1301	0.0226	0.0738
500	0.0004	−0.0003	0.0010	0.0063	0.0062	0.0169	0.0027	0.0108

5.2. MC Simulation Study II: Residuals Analysis

We delve into the analysis of the Cox–Snell (CS) and randomized quantile (RQ) residuals for the WEI4 and WEI5 models. The computation of the CS residual is as follows:

$$\widehat{r}_i^{\mathrm{CS}} = -\log(\widehat{S}(y_i; \boldsymbol{x}_i)), \quad i = 1, \ldots, n,$$

where $\widehat{S}(y_i|\boldsymbol{x}_i)$ is the estimated survival function obtained from the fitted model with values $\boldsymbol{x}_i$ for the explanatory variables. The survival functions of the models under consideration are presented in Section 2. The RQ residual is defined as

$$\widehat{r}_i^{\mathrm{RQ}} = \Phi^{-1}(\widehat{S}(y_i|\boldsymbol{x}_i)), \quad i = 1, \ldots, n,$$

where Φ^{-1} is the quantile function of the standard normal distribution.

For this investigation, we maintain the same simulation scenario as in the MC simulation study I, as outlined above. Tables 5 and 6 display the empirical mean, standard deviation (SD), and coefficient of skewness (CSk) of the CS and RQ residuals. Theoretical expectations for these statistics are 1, 1, and 2, respectively, for the CS residuals, and 0, 1, and 0, respectively, for the RQ residuals, due to their respective theoretical distributions being exponential and standard normal. The results in Tables 5 and 6 demonstrate that, in general, both types of residuals provide good approximations for the WEI4 and WEI5 models.

Table 5. Mean, SD, and CSk of the CS and randomized quantile residuals for the WEI4 model, with the indicated sample size and true values of the parameters.

	$\beta_1 = 0.2$; $\beta_2 = 1.0$; $\zeta_1 = 0.2$; $\zeta_2 = 1.0$					
	Randomized Quantile			Cox–Snell		
n	Mean	SD	CSk	Mean	SD	CSk
30	−0.0176	1.0197	0.0225	0.9879	0.9686	1.2599
50	−0.0064	1.0067	0.0761	0.9936	1.0119	1.8385
100	0.0057	0.9918	0.1559	1.0024	1.0380	1.9373
500	0.0085	0.9903	0.1282	1.0057	1.0256	1.9420
	$\beta_1 = 0.2$; $\beta_2 = 0.5$; $\zeta_1 = 0.2$; $\zeta_2 = 1.0$					
	randomized quantile			Cox–Snell		
n	mean	SD	CSk	mean	SD	CSk
30	−0.0124	0.9931	0.3132	0.9862	1.0388	1.4458
50	−0.0045	1.0443	−0.3680	1.0011	0.9207	1.3308
100	−0.0268	1.0082	−0.0545	0.9732	1.0482	2.7658
500	−0.0038	0.9844	0.2264	0.9942	1.0366	2.0337

Table 5. *Cont.*

	$\beta_1 = 0.5$; $\beta_2 = 1.0$; $\zeta_1 = 0.2$; $\zeta_2 = 1.0$					
	randomized quantile			Cox–Snell		
n	mean	SD	CSk	mean	SD	CSk
30	−0.0190	1.0429	−0.2383	0.9903	0.9126	1.0349
50	−0.0207	1.0441	−0.4426	0.9851	0.9050	1.1128
100	−0.0300	1.0318	−0.2247	0.9815	0.9164	1.8438
500	−0.0064	1.0036	−0.0312	0.9937	1.0155	2.4167
	$\beta_1 = 0.5$; $\beta_2 = 1.5$; $\zeta_1 = 0.2$; $\zeta_2 = 1.0$					
	randomized quantile			Cox–Snell		
n	mean	SD	CSk	mean	SD	CSk
30	0.0280	0.9916	0.3017	1.0226	1.0364	1.2727
50	0.0098	1.0222	−0.1606	1.0113	0.9557	1.2558
100	−0.0207	1.0208	−0.1657	0.9843	0.9607	1.6202
500	−0.0116	0.9978	0.0671	0.9904	0.9961	1.9101

Table 6. Mean, SD, and CSk of the Cox–Snell and randomized quantile residuals for the WEI5 model, with the indicated sample size and true values of the parameters.

	$\beta_1 = 0.2$; $\beta_2 = 1.0$; $\zeta_1 = 0.2$; $\zeta_2 = 1.0$					
	Randomized Quantile			Cox–Snell		
n	Mean	SD	CSk	Mean	SD	CSk
30	0.0319	0.9772	0.0273	1.0073	0.9587	1.3523
50	−0.0288	1.0180	0.1452	0.9868	0.9880	1.1914
100	0.0152	1.0165	−0.3226	1.0084	0.9403	1.4739
500	−0.0029	1.0066	−0.0848	0.9978	0.9802	1.7448
	$\beta_1 = 0.2$; $\beta_2 = 0.5$; $\zeta_1 = 0.2$; $\zeta_2 = 1.0$					
	randomized quantile			Cox–Snell		
n	mean	SD	CSk	mean	SD	CSk
30	0.0726	0.9760	−0.0228	1.0433	0.9477	1.2336
50	0.0131	1.0012	−0.0942	1.0043	0.9477	1.5201
100	−0.0237	0.9867	0.3180	0.9791	1.0466	2.1566
500	0.0099	0.9854	0.1456	1.0048	1.0183	2.0615
	$\beta_1 = 0.5$; $\beta_2 = 1.0$; $\zeta_1 = 0.2$; $\zeta_2 = 1.0$					
	randomized quantile			Cox–Snell		
n	mean	SD	CSk	mean	SD	CSk
30	−0.0715	1.0858	−0.1631	0.9710	0.9773	1.7365
50	−0.0193	1.0235	−0.0200	0.9914	0.9712	1.6429
100	−0.0115	1.0165	−0.0516	0.9960	0.9590	1.4681
500	−0.0127	1.0102	−0.0333	0.9930	0.9906	1.8522
	$\beta_1 = 0.5$; $\beta_2 = 1.5$; $\zeta_1 = 0.2$; $\zeta_2 = 1.0$					
	randomized quantile			Cox–Snell		
n	mean	SD	CSk	mean	SD	CSk
30	0.0197	1.0379	−0.4223	1.0133	0.9251	1.3285
50	0.0156	1.0119	0.0220	1.0156	1.0344	2.2866
100	0.0032	1.0122	−0.1720	1.0023	0.9195	1.1461
500	0.0031	1.0092	−0.1179	1.0044	0.9577	1.5290

6. Real Data Illustrations

In this section, the analyzed parametrizations to real data are applied to demonstrate their effectiveness and applicability. In Illustrations 1 and 2, models WEI4 and WEI5, as well as WEI1, WEI2, and WEI3, respectively, showcase their applicability in real-life scenarios.

6.1. Illustration 1: Concrete Fatigue Life Dataset

The dataset under analysis represents the fatigue life of concrete specimens, measured in cycles (multiplied by 10^{-3}). The dataset is defined by the applied stress-causing failure, with ratios of 0.95, 0.90, and 0.825. A lower ratio is expected to correspond to a longer number of cycles until failure. Each ratio is accompanied by 15 observations, as outlined in ([46], p. 88). The `concrete fatigue life` is designated as the response variable, and the `ratio` is identified as the covariate.

Initially, we provide an exploratory analysis of the response variable. Table 7 presents some descriptive statistics, including SD, CSk, the coefficient of variation (CV), and coefficient of kurtosis (CK). Additionally, Figure 1 displays the corresponding histogram and boxplot. From Table 7 and Figure 1, it is evident that the dataset exhibits considerable variability (CV = 131.401%), positive skewness (CSk = 1.414), heavy tails (CK = 0.771), and the presence of outliers (case nos. 40, 41, 42, 43, 44, and 45).

Table 7. Descriptive statistics of the concrete fatigue life dataset.

n	min	Max	Mean	Median	SD	CSk	CV	CK
45	37	5598	1216.58	342	1598.60	1.41	131.40	0.77

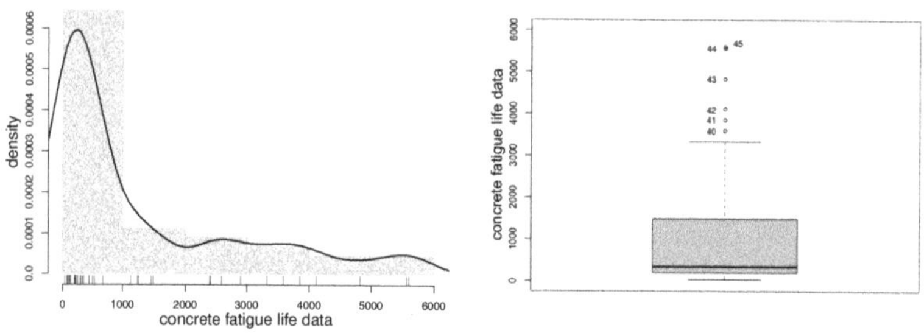

(**a**) (**b**)

Figure 1. Histogram with the density kernel estimation (**a**) and boxplot (**b**) for the concrete fatigue life dataset.

In this study, a regression structure is incorporated into the WEI4 (with $q = 0.5$) and WEI5 models for both λ and ν, as follows:

$$\lambda_i = \exp\left(\mathbf{x}_i^\top \boldsymbol{\beta}\right), \quad \nu_i = \exp(\mathbf{x}_i^\top \boldsymbol{\zeta}), \quad i = 1, \ldots, 45,$$

where $\boldsymbol{\beta} = (\beta_0, \beta_1)^\top$, and $\boldsymbol{\zeta} = (\zeta_0, \zeta_1)^\top$ represent the regression coefficients, and $\mathbf{x}_i^\top = (1, x_{1i})$ denotes the respective design matrix, with x_{1i} being the i-th observation of the covariate `ratio`.

Table 8 presents the fitting of these models, including parameter estimation using the ML method, the respective standard errors, the associated Z-test p-value, the AIC, and the p-value from the Kolmogorov–Smirnov (KS), Anderson–Darling (AD), and Cramer von Mises (CVM) goodness-of-fit tests for the CS and RQ residuals. It is important to note that the theoretical distributions for CS and RQ residuals are exponential and standard normal, respectively. In this table, it can be observed that for modeling λ, both regression coefficients (intercept and slope) are significant. However, this situation is not observed in the modeling of ν, where none of the regression coefficients are significant.

Additionally, Figures 2 and 3 provide quantile–quantile (QQ) goodness-of-fit plots with simulated envelopes for the CS and RQ residuals. Consistent with the goodness-of-fit test results, both residuals are well-fitted to the exponential and standard normal distributions, respectively.

Table 8. ML estimates, SEs, p-values, AIC, and KS p-value of the indicated model.

		WEI4			WEI5		
	Parameter	**Estimate**	**SE**	**p-Value**	**Estimate**	**SE**	**p-Value**
λ	β_1	29.2805	1.4737	<0.0001	29.5963	1.8853	<0.0001
	β_2	−25.8166	1.6582	<0.0001	−26.3132	2.1276	<0.0001
ν	ζ_1	1.4702	2.2139	0.5066	1.5362	1.8117	0.3965
	ζ_2	−0.7999	2.4753	0.7466	−0.8740	2.0218	0.6655
AIC		635.03			635.02		
KS p-value		0.8729 (CS)	0.4339 (RQ)		0.8753 (CS)	0.4102 (RQ)	
AD p-value		—	0.1082 (RQ)		—	0.1117 (RQ)	
CVM p-value		—	0.1203 (RQ)		—	0.1234 (RQ)	

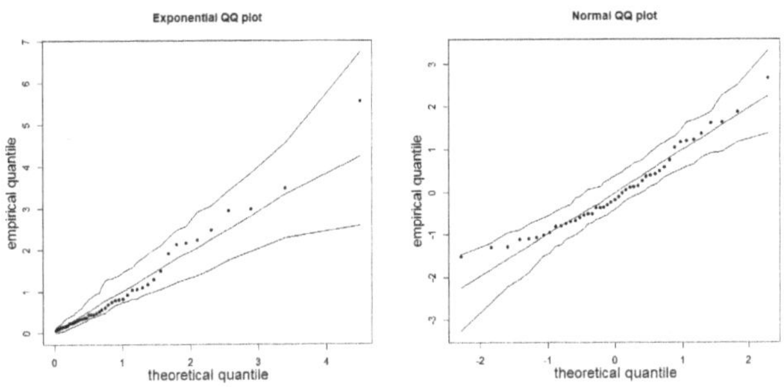

(a) (b)

Figure 2. QQ plot with the envelope of CS (**a**) and RQ (**b**) residuals for the WEI4 model.

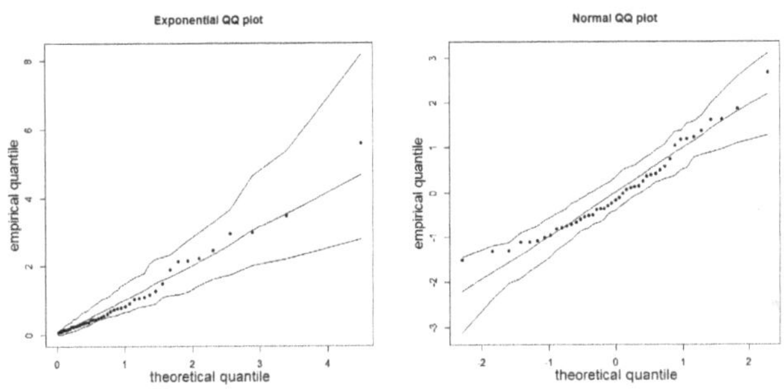

(a) (b)

Figure 3. QQ plot with the envelope of CS (**a**) and RQ (**b**) residuals for the WEI5 model.

6.2. Illustration 2: Ovarian Dataset

The ovarian cancer data (ovarian) are also considered, which are included in the `survival` package, R version 3.5-7 [47]. This dataset contains censored observations and will be used to illustrate the reparameterized Weibull model in the context of censored data. It comprises information on 26 patients with stage III and IV ovarian carcinoma who were treated with radical surgery and postoperative chemotherapy. The covariates used are the minimal residual disease (`residual`), which indicates a tumor mass of less than 2 cm in diameter, and the patient's `age` in years. Figure 4 displays the Kaplan–Meier (K-M) estimator for both `residual` and `age`. Descriptively, it is evident that both covariates have an impact on patient survival. In addition, and similar to the last application, in Figure 5, the QQ plot and simulated envelope for the RQ residuals are provided, suggesting that this kind of residual is reasonably fitted to the standard normal distribution.

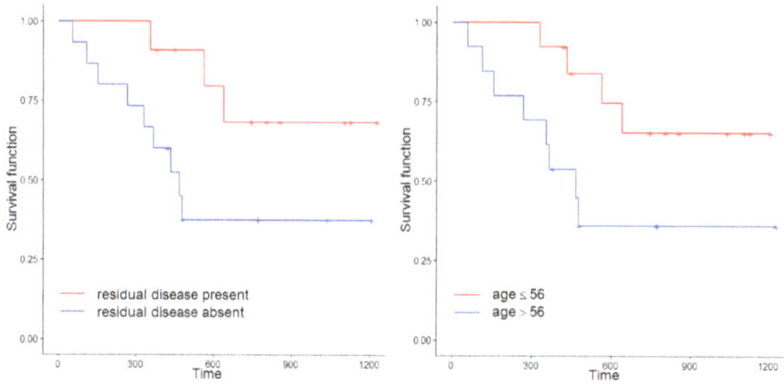

Figure 4. K-M estimator for ovarian dataset separated by the `residual` (**left panel**) and `age` (**right panel**).

Table 9 shows the AIC for the WEI, WEI2, and WEI3 models in the ovarian dataset with different combinations of covariates in λ and ν. As discussed previously, the AIC is the same for the three models if covariates are not included in ν and differ if ν is modeled. The results also suggest that the best combination is to include the covariates `residual` plus `age` in λ, but not in ν. Table 10 shows the estimate, the corresponding SE for the WEI2 model (it could have been any of them), and the p-value from the KS, AD, and CVM goodness-of-fit tests for RQ residuals.

Table 9. The AIC for the fitted model ovarian dataset.

Covariates		Model		
λ	ν	WEI	WEI2	WEI3
Only intercept	Only intercept		199.91	
`Residual` plus `age`	Only intercept		186.04	
`Residual` plus `age`	`Residual` plus `age`	189.56	190.04	189.53

Finally, Figure 6 shows the mean, median, and mode of the WEI, WEI2, and WEI3 models. As proved in Theorem 1, such measures are identical for the three models because no covariates are included in the dispersion parameter.

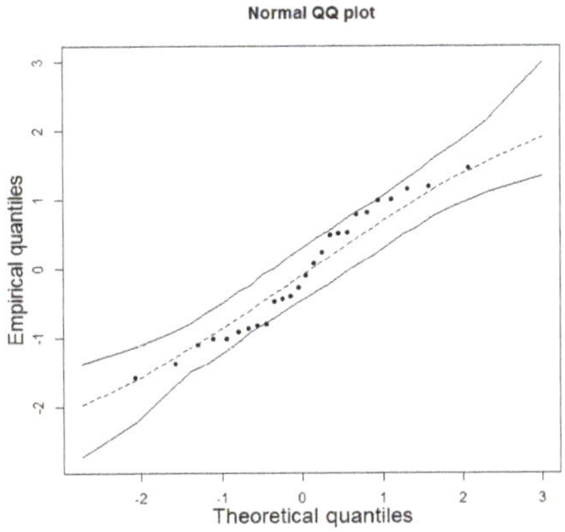

Figure 5. QQ plot with the envelope of RQ residuals for the ovarian dataset. Note that the plot is identical for WEI, WEI2, and WEI3 models.

Table 10. ML estimate, standard error (SE) for WEI2, considering the `residual` plus `age` covariates for the ovarian dataset.

		WEI2	
	Parameters	**Estimate**	**SE**
λ	`Intercept`	−20.5374	1.1339
	`residual`	0.9720	0.4152
	`age`	0.1401	0.0207
ν	`Intercept`	0.5559	0.0155
AIC		186.04	
KS p-value		0.6703	
AD p-value		0.1916	
CVM p-value		0.1895	

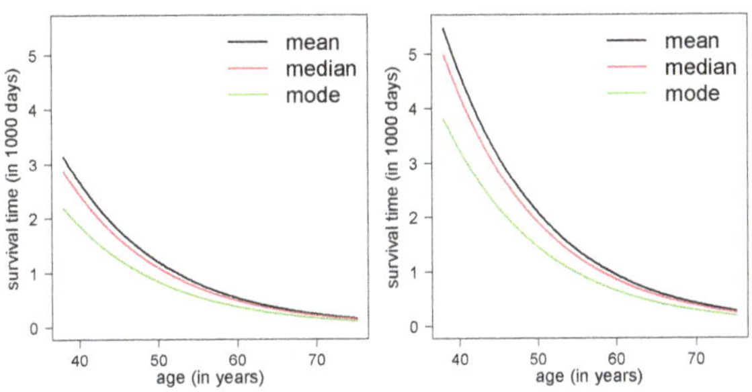

Figure 6. Different measures of central tendency for the survival time in the ovarian problem in terms of `age`: `residual = 1` (**left panel**) and `residual = 2` (**right panel**). The plots are identical for WEI, WEI2, and WEI3 models.

7. Conclusions and Future Work

In this paper, a general parameterization for Weibull regression models was introduced, based on central tendency measures and shape parameters. A comprehensive review of Weibull regression models was provided, specifically focusing on different parameterizations of the Weibull distribution that utilize central tendency measures. The interpretation of regression coefficients when incorporating regression structures into these parameterizations was also explored. Furthermore, closed-form expressions for the expected Fisher information matrix have been derived for this general parameterization of Weibull regression models. Two types of residuals were explored, and maximum likelihood inference was implemented for estimating model parameters. The performance of this inference method was assessed through Monte Carlo simulations.

A significant result, as established in Theorem 1, is that when modeling only λ in the WEI, WEI2, WEI3, WEI4, and WEI5 models, the same probability density function is yielded by all these parameterizations. Therefore, in these cases, it does not matter which model is used, as the conclusions for any measure of interest must be the same for any of the five models.

To illustrate the practical relevance of the approach, two real-world applications using authentic datasets were presented. These applications underscored the adequacy of the introduced Weibull models when data present an asymmetric distribution. Depending on which parameter is of interest in the study, one model will be more convenient to use than the other.

As part of future research, the plan is to develop an R package that facilitates inference in WEI4 and WEI5 regression models.

Author Contributions: Conceptualization, D.I.G., Y.M.G. and M.B.; methodology, D.I.G., Y.M.G. and M.B.; software, D.I.G., Y.M.G., C.M., L.S. and M.B.; validation, formal analysis, D.I.G., Y.M.G., C.M., L.S. and M.B.; investigation, D.I.G., Y.M.G., C.M., L.S. and M.B.; resources; data curation, Y.M.G. and C.M.; writing—original draft preparation, D.I.G., Y.M.G., C.M., L.S. and M.B.; writing—review and editing, D.I.G., Y.M.G., C.M., L.S. and M.B.; visualization, D.I.G., Y.M.G., C.M. and L.S. All authors have read and agreed to the published version of the manuscript.

Funding: This research received no external funding

Data Availability Statement: Data and computational codes are available upon request from the authors.

Conflicts of Interest: The authors declare no conflicts of interest.

References

1. Weibull, W. A statistical distribution function of wide applicability. *J. Appl. Mech.* **1951**, *18*, 293–296 [CrossRef]
2. Keshevan, K.; Sargent, G.; Conrad H. Statistical analysis of the Hertzian fracture of pyrex glass using the Weibull distribution function. *J. Mater. Sci.* **1980**, *15*, 839–844. [CrossRef]
3. Queeshi, F.S.; Sheikh, A.K. Probabilistic characterization of adhesive wear in metals. *IEEE Trans. Reliab.* **1997**, *46*, 38–44.
4. Durham, S.D.; Padgett, W.J. Cumulative damage model for system failure with application to carbon fibers and composites. *Technometrics* **1997**, *39*, 34–44. [CrossRef]
5. Almeida, J.B. Application of Weilbull statistics to the failure of coatings. *J. Mater. Process. Technol.* **1999**, *93*, 257–263. [CrossRef]
6. Fok, S.L.; Mitchell, B.C.; Smart, J.; Marsden, B.J. A numerical study on the application of the Weibull theory to brittle materials. *Eng. Fract. Mech.* **2001**, *68*, 1171–1179. [CrossRef]
7. Newell, J.A.; Kurzeja, T.; Spence, M.; Lynch, M. Analysis of recoil compressive failure in high performance polymers using two-, four-parameter Weibull models. *High Perform. Polym.* **2002**, *14*, 425–434. [CrossRef]
8. Li, Q.S.; Fang, J.Q.; Liu, D.K.; Tang, J. Failure probability prediction of concrete components. *Cem. Concr. Res.* **2003**, *33*, 1631–1636. [CrossRef]
9. Bebbington, M.S.; Lai, C.D. On nonhomogeneous models for volcanic eruptions. *Math. Geol.* **1996**, *28*, 585–599. [CrossRef]
10. Durrans, S.R. Low-flow analysis with a conditional Weibull tail model. *Water Resour. Res.* **1996**, *32*, 1749–1760. [CrossRef]
11. Heo, J.H.; Boes, D.C.; Salas, J.D. Regional flood frequency analysis based on a Weibull model: Part 1. Estimation, asymptotic variances. *J. Hydrol.* **2001**, *242*, 157–170. [CrossRef]
12. Fleming, R.A. The Weibull model and an ecological application: Describing the dynamics of foliage biomass on Scots pine. *Ecol. Model.* **2001**, *138*, 309–319. [CrossRef]
13. Roed, K., Zhang, T. A note on the Weibull distribution and time aggregation bias. *Appl. Econ. Lett.* **2002**, *9*, 469–472. [CrossRef]
14. Ikki, S.S.; Ahmed, M.H. Performance of multi-hop relaying systems over Weibull fading channels. In *New Technologies, Mobility and Security*; Springer: Amsterdam, The Netherlands, 2007; pp. 31–38.
15. Wang, P.; Zhang, J.; Guo, L.; Shang, T.; Cao, T.; Wang, R.; Yang, T. Performance analysis for relay-aided multihop BPPM FSO communication system over exponentiated Weibull fading channels with pointing error impairments. *IEEE Photon. J.* **2015**, *7*, 1–20. [CrossRef]
16. Rinne, H. *The Weibull Distribution: A Handbook*; Chapman and Hall/CRC: New York, NY, USA, 2008.

17. Lai, C.; Xie, M. Weibull Distributions and Their Applications. In *Springer Handbook of Engineering Statistics;* Pham, H., Ed.; Springer: New York, NY, USA, 2006; pp. 63–78.
18. Lawless, J.F. *Statistical Models and Methods for Lifetime Data;* Wiley: New York, NY, USA, 1982.
19. Ghitany, M.E.; Al-Hussaini, E.K.; Al-Jarallah, R.A. Marshall–Olkin extended weibull distribution and its application to censored data. *J. Appl. Stat.* **2005**, *32*, 1025–1034. . [CrossRef]
20. Klakattawi, H.S. Survival analysis of cancer patients using a new extended Weibull distribution. *PLoS ONE* **2022**, *17*, e0264229. [CrossRef]
21. Joarder, A.; Krishna, H.; Kundu, D. Inferences on Weibull parameters with conventional type-I censoring. *Comput. Stat. Data Anal.* **2011**, *55*, 1–11. . [CrossRef]
22. Jia, X.; Wang, D.; Jiang, P.; Guo, B. Inference on the reliability of Weibull distribution with multiply Type-I censored data. *Reliab. Eng. Syst. Saf.* **2016**, *150*, 171–181.. [CrossRef]
23. Lee, C.; Famoye, F.; Olumolade, O. Beta-Weibull Distribution: Some Properties and Applications to Censored Data. *J. Mod. Appl. Stat. Methods* **2007**, *6*, 173–186. [CrossRef]
24. Chen, M.H.; Ibrahim, J.G.; Sinha, D. A new Bayesian model for survival data with a surviving fraction. *J. Am. Stat. Assoc.* **1999**, *94*, 909–919. [CrossRef]
25. Yin, G.; Ibrahim, J.G. Cure rate models: A unified approach. *Can. J. Stat.* **2005**, *33*, 559–570. [CrossRef]
26. Rodrigues, J.; Cordeiro, G.M.; Cancho, V.; Balakrishnan, N. Relaxed Poisson cure rate models. *Biom. J.* **2016**, *58*, 397–415. [CrossRef] [PubMed]
27. Gallardo, D.I.; Gómez, Y.M.; Gómez, H.W.; De Castro, M. On the use of the modified power series family of distributions in a cure rate model context. *Stat. Methods Med. Res.* **2020**, *29*, 1831–1845. [CrossRef] [PubMed]
28. Azimi, R.; Esmailian, M.; Gallardo, D.I.; Gómez, H.J. A New Cure Rate Model Based on Flory–Schulz Distribution: Application to the Cancer Data. *Mathematics* **2022**, *10*, 4643. [CrossRef]
29. Murthy, D.N.P.; Baik, J.; Bulmer, M.; Wilson, R.J. Two-dimensional modelling of failures. In *Springer Handbook of Engineering Statistics;* Pham, H., Ed.; Springer: Heidelberg/Berlin, Germany, 2004.
30. Murthy, D.N.P.; Xie, M.; Jiang, R. *Weibull Models;* Wiley: New York, NY, USA, 2003.
31. Silva, R.B.; Bourguignon, M.; Dias, C.R.B.; Cordeiro, G.M. The compound class of extended Weibull power series distributions. *Comput. Stat. Data Anal.* **2013**, *58*, 352–367. [CrossRef]
32. Santos-Neto, M.; Bourguignon, M.; Zea, L.M.; Nascimento, A.D.C.; Cordeiro, G.M. The Marshall-Olkin extended Weibull family of distributions. *J. Stat. Distrib. Appl.* **2014**, *1*, 1–24. [CrossRef]
33. Nascimento, A.D.C.; Bourguignon, M.; Zea, L.M.; Santos-Neto, M.; Silva, R.B.; Cordeiro, G.M. The gamma extended Weibull family of distributions. *J. Stat. Theory Appl.* **2014**, *13*, 1–16. [CrossRef]
34. Nadarajah, S.; Kotz, S. On some recent modifications of Weibull distribution. *IEEE Trans. Reliab.* **2005**, *54*, 561–562. [CrossRef]
35. Pham, H.; Lai, C-D. On recent generalizations of the Weibull distribution. *IEEE Trans. Reliab.* **2007**, *56*, 454–458. [CrossRef]
36. Almalki, S.J.; Nadarajah, S. Modifications of the Weibull distribution: A review. *Reliab. Eng. Syst. Saf.* **2014**, *124*, 32–55. [CrossRef]
37. Wingo, D.R. The left-truncated Weibull distribution: Theory and computation. *Stat. Pap.* **1989**, *30*, 39–48. [CrossRef]
38. Zhang, T.; Xie, M. On the upper truncated Weibull distribution and its reliability implications Reliability. *Eng. Syst. Saf.* **2011**, *96*, 194–200. [CrossRef]
39. McEwen, R.P.; Parresol, B.R. Moment expressions and summary statistics for the complete and truncated Weibull distribution. *Commun. Stat. Theory Methods* **1991**, *20*, 1361–1372. [CrossRef]
40. Fernandes, F.H.; Lee, H.L.; Bourguignon, M. About Shewhart control charts to monitor the Weibull mean. *Qual. Reliab. Eng. Int.* **2019**, *35*, 2343–2357. [CrossRef]
41. Sánchez, L.; Leiva, V.; Saulo, H.; Marchant, C.; Sarabia, J. A new quantile regression model and its diagnostic analytics for a weibull distributed response with applications. *Mathematics* **2021**, *9*, 2768. [CrossRef]
42. Yao, W.; Li, L. A New Regression Model: Modal Linear Regression. *Scand. J. Stat.* **2013**, *41*, 656–671. [CrossRef]
43. Chen, Y.C. Modal regression using kernel density estimation: A review. *WIREs Comput. Stat.* **2018**, *10*, e1431. [CrossRef]
44. Bourguignon, M.; Leao, J.; Gallardo, D.I. Parametric modal regression with varying precision. *Biom. J.* **2020,** *62*, 202–220. [CrossRef]
45. Kleinbaum, D.G.; Klein, M. Survival analysis : A self-learning text. In *Statistics for Biology and Health*, 3rd ed.; Kleinbaum, D.G., Klein, M., Eds.; Springer: New York, NY, USA, 2012.
46. Leiva, V. *The Birnbaun-Saunders Distribution;* Elsevier: Amsterdam, The Netherlands , 2016.
47. Therneau, T.M. A Package for Survival Analysis in R. R Package Version 3.5-7, CRAN. 2023. Available online: https://CRAN.R-project.org/package=survival (accessed on 5 December 2023).

mathematics

MDPI

Article

A Bivariate Power Lindley Survival Distribution

Guillermo Martínez-Flórez [1], Barry C. Arnold [2] and Héctor W. Gómez [3,*]

1. Departamento de Matemáticas y Estadística, Facultad de Ciencias, Universidad de Córdoba, Córdoba 2300, Colombia; guillermomartinez@correo.unicordoba.edu.co
2. Statistics Department, University of California Riverside, Riverside, CA 92521, USA; barnold@ucr.edu
3. Departamento de Estadística y Ciencias de Datos, Facultad de Ciencias Básicas, Universidad de Antofagasta, Antofagasta 1240000, Chile

* Correspondence: hector.gomez@uantof.cl

Abstract: We introduce and investigate the properties of new families of univariate and bivariate distributions based on the survival function of the Lindley distribution. The univariate distribution, to reflect the nature of its construction, is called a power Lindley survival distribution. The basic distributional properties of this model are described. Maximum likelihood estimates of the parameters of the distribution are studied and the corresponding information matrix is identified. A bivariate power Lindley survival distribution is introduced using the technique of conditional specification. The corresponding joint density and marginal and conditional densities are derived. The product moments of the distribution are obtained, together with bounds on the range of correlations that can be exhibited by the model. Estimation of the parameters of the model is implemented by maximizing the corresponding pseudo-likelihood function. The asymptotic variance–covariance matrix of these estimates is investigated. A simulation study is performed to illustrate the performance of these parameter estimates. Finally some examples of model fitting using real-world data sets are described.

Keywords: survival distribution; Lindley survival distribution; maximum likelihood; conditional specification

MSC: 62E10; 62F10

1. Introduction

The Lindley (L) distribution, which was first introduced by Lindley [1], has been found to be useful in many research areas. In particular, it has been applied in survival analysis in many scientific arenas, including engineering, health, economics, etc. Ghitany et al. [2] studied the statistical properties of this distribution and showed that it was preferred to the exponential distribution in several applications. Several generalizations of the L model have been proposed by a variety of authors who have studied the properties of the extended models and have investigated their suitability in various application areas. Ghitany et al. [3] proposed a class of weighted L distributions. Ramos and Louzada [4] introduced a generalized weighted L model. Ristic and Balakrishnan [5] investigated the gamma–Lindley model. MirMostafaee et al. [6] studied the beta L distribution. Bakouch et al. [7] introduced an extended L distribution. Ghitany et al. [3] developed a two-parameter weighted L distribution. Nadarajah et al. [8] described a generalized L (GL) distribution. Ghitany et al. [9] introduced the power L distribution, Ashour and Eltehiwy [10] proposed the exponentiated power L distribution, Asgharzadeh et al. [11] introduced a Weibull Lindley distribution, Khokhar et al. [12] studied the Zografos Balakrishnan Power Lindley Distribution, Algarni [13] introduced a new generalized Lindley distribution, and Chhetri et al. [14] in the Cubic Rank Transmuted Lindley Distribution, among others.

This is a representative listing of variations on the Lindley theme, but it is not intended to be a complete list. The density function of the L distribution is of the form

$$f_L(x) = \frac{\theta^2}{\theta+1}(1+x)e^{-\theta x}, x > 0, \tag{1}$$

where the parameter θ is positive. If a random variable X has density (1) we write $X \sim L(\theta)$. The corresponding distribution function is

$$F_L(x) = 1 - \frac{\theta+1+\theta x}{\theta+1}e^{-\theta x}, x > 0, \tag{2}$$

The survival function ($S_L(x)$) and hazard or failure rate function ($r_L(x)$) of this distribution are, respectively,

$$S_L(x) = \frac{\theta+1+\theta x}{\theta+1}e^{-\theta x} \quad \text{and} \quad r_L(x) = \frac{\theta^2(x+1)}{\theta+1+\theta x}.$$

Lindley noted that $r_L(0) = \frac{\theta^2}{\theta+1}$ and that $r_L(x)$ is an increasing function of x and of θ. Moreover, $\frac{\theta^2}{\theta+1} < r(x) < \theta$. Since the failure function increases in X, the distribution is IFR and the validity of the following chain of implication is well established. $IFR \Rightarrow IFRA \Rightarrow NBU \Rightarrow NBUE$ where IFR, IFRA, NBU, NBUE denote an increasing failure rate, an increasing failure rate average, new being better than used, and new being better than used in expectation, respectively (see Barlow and Proschan, [15]).

The first objective of this research project is to provide a flexible extension of the univariate L distribution that can adapt to a range of asymmetry and kurtosis features of data. The flexible model is based on the power of the survival function of the classical L model. The second objective is to extend discussion to the bivariate case, because there are few bivariate extensions of even the basic L model. The distributional properties of the proposed bivariate power L model are investigated and a method is proposed for estimation of its parameters.

The paper evolves as follows: In Section 2, we deliver the power Lindley survival model. In Section 3, we perform inference in the power Lindley model. In Section 4, we deliver the bivariate power Lindley survival model. In Section 5, estimation of the parameters is accomplished using pseudo-likelihood. In Section 6, a simulation study is carried out. In Section 7 two applications are made to real data sets.

2. The Power Lindley Survival Model

In this paper, we will introduce a new extension of the L model called the power L survival (PLS) distribution. The distribution function of this model is of the form

$$F_{PLS}(x) = 1 - \left(\frac{\theta+1+\theta x}{\theta+1}\right)^{\alpha} e^{-\alpha\theta x}, \quad x > 0, \tag{3}$$

in which both θ and α are positive parameters. The corresponding density function is

$$f_{PLS}(x) = \frac{\alpha\theta^2}{(\theta+1)^{\alpha}}(1+x)(\theta+1+\theta x)^{\alpha-1}e^{-\alpha\theta x}, \quad x > 0. \tag{4}$$

If a random variable X has this density, we will write $X \sim PLS(\theta, \alpha)$. Figure 1 shows the form of the PLS density for various values of the parameters, varying the value of the parameter θ for the cases (a) $\alpha = 0.5$ and (b) $\alpha = 2.0$.

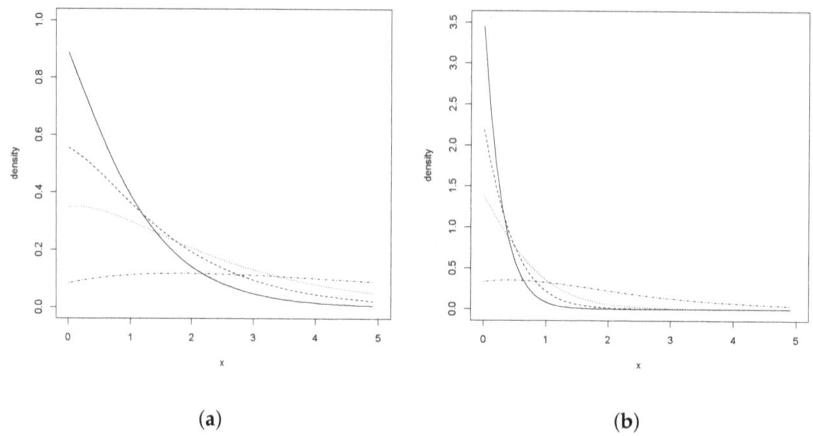

Figure 1. Graphs of the PLS density for θ =0.5 (line of points and dashes), 1.25, 1.75 (broken line), 2.5 (continuous line) with (**a**) $\alpha = 0.5$ and (**b**) $\alpha = 2.0$.

Observe that $PLS(\theta, 1) = L(\theta)$, and that the PLS distribution is more flexible than the L distribution and, as a consequence of observations of Lindley [1], the PLS distribution can be expected to outperform the exponential model in certain applications. The PLS distribution is thus a flexible alternative to the exponential and L models because of the introduction of the shape parameter α.

The survival function and the hazard function of the PLS distribution are, respectively,

$$S_{PLS}(x) = \left(\frac{\theta + 1 + \theta x}{\theta + 1}\right)^{\alpha} e^{-\alpha\theta x} = S_L^{\alpha}(x) \quad \text{and} \quad r_{PLS}(x) = \frac{\alpha\theta^2(x+1)}{\theta + 1 + \theta x} = \alpha r_L(x).$$

The fact that the survival function of the PLS distribution is the α power of the Lindley survival function is the reason for the name selected for the PLS distribution. Note that, as a consequence of the relationship beteen the L and PLS survival functions, the corresponding hazard rates are proportional.

One may verify that

- $r_{PLS}(x)$ is an increasing function in x and of θ, for each α.
- $r_{PLS}(0) = \frac{\alpha\theta^2}{\theta+1}$ and $\lim_{x\to\infty} r_{PLS}(x) = \alpha\theta$, so that $\frac{\alpha\theta^2}{\theta+1} < r_{PLS}(x) < \alpha\theta$.
- For $\alpha > 1$, $r_{PLS}(x) > r_L(x)$ and for $\alpha < 1$, $r_{PLS}(x) < r_L(x)$.
- Since the PLS distribution has an increasing failure rate, the following chain of implications hold for it: $IFR \Rightarrow IFRA \Rightarrow NBU \Rightarrow NBUE$

A situation in which a PLS distribution will be encountered is one in which we are dealing with the lifetime of a system consisting of n independent L distributed (i.e., $L(\theta)$) components connected in series. The system lifetime is, therefore, a random variable with a $PLS(\theta, n)$ distribution. Allowing the parameter n in this model to be a positive real number instead of an integer, we are led to the full PLS model.

The PLS distribution has finite moments of all orders. The expressions for its moments involve the incomplete gamma function denoted by $F_G(x : \alpha, \beta)$ and defined by

$$F_G(x; \alpha, \beta) = \int_0^x \frac{u^{\alpha-1} e^{-(u/\beta)}}{\Gamma(\alpha)\beta^{\alpha}}\, du.$$

Thus, we have

$$\mu = E(X) = \int_0^\infty [1 - F_{PLS}(x)]dx = \frac{e^{\alpha(\theta+1)}\Gamma(\alpha)[1 - F_G(\theta+1;\alpha+1,\alpha)]}{\alpha^\alpha \theta(\theta+1)^\alpha}. \tag{5}$$

For $r = 2, 3, \ldots$ the r'th moment is expressible as

$$\begin{aligned} E(X^r) &= \tfrac{\alpha e^{\alpha(\theta+1)}}{(\theta+1)^\alpha} \sum_{j=0}^{r} \sum_{k=0}^{r-j} \binom{r}{j}\binom{r-j}{k} \tfrac{\theta^{k+1-r}\Gamma(\alpha+j)[1-F_G(\theta+1;\alpha+j,\alpha)]}{\alpha^{\alpha+j}} + \\ & \tfrac{\alpha e^{\alpha(\theta+1)}}{(\theta+1)^\alpha} \sum_{j=0}^{r+1} \sum_{k=0}^{r+1-j.} \binom{r+1}{j}\binom{r-j+1}{k} \tfrac{\theta^{k-r}\Gamma(\alpha+j)[1-F_G(\theta+1;\alpha+j,\alpha)]}{\alpha^{\alpha+j}} \end{aligned} \tag{6}$$

From these formulas, expressions can be obtained for the variance, skewness and kutosis of the distribution.

A small-scale simulation study has been conducted to evaluate the range of possible values for the coefficients of asymmetry and kurtosis for $\alpha \in (0.05, 1500]$. Calculations were performed using the function `integrate` in R software [16]. The values of θ considered were between 0.05 and 300. The results indicated that the range of values for the coefficients of asymmetry and kurtosis for the model were given by $\sqrt{\beta_1} \in [0.4710, 2.8813]$ and $\beta_2 \in [2.0236, 11.4217]$. These intervals include the corresponding ranges for the Lindley model which were, respectively, $(\sqrt{2}, 2)$ and $(6, 9)$. This confirms the observation that has already been made that the PLS model is more flexible than the L model.

An expression is available for the moment-generating function of the PLS distribution; thus,

$$M_X(t) = \frac{e^{\frac{\alpha\theta - t}{\theta}(\theta+1)}\Gamma(\alpha)}{\alpha^{\alpha-1}(\theta+1)^\alpha}\left[F_G\left(\theta+1;\alpha+1,\frac{\alpha\theta-t}{\theta}\right) - F_G\left(\theta+1;\alpha,\frac{\alpha\theta-t}{\theta}\right)\right] \tag{7}$$

for $t < \alpha\theta$.

Quantile Function

The p'th quantile $(0 < p < 1)$ of the PLS distribution can be expressed as

$$Z_p = F_L^{-1}(1 - (1-p)^{\frac{1}{\alpha}}),$$

where $F_L^{-1}(\cdot)$ is the Lindley quantile function. We can thus use the same technique as that used by Jodrá [17] to generate variables with L distributions to instead generate PLS variables. An alternative expression for the PLS quantiles involving a special function is available in the form

$$Z_p = -1 - \frac{1}{\theta} - \frac{1}{\theta}W_{-1}(-(\theta+1)e^{-(\theta+1)}(1-p)^{1/\alpha}),$$

where $W_{-1}(\cdot)$ is the Lambert function with branch -1.

Thus, to generate a random variable, X, with a $PLS(\theta, \alpha)$ distribution, we can generate U, a $uniform(0,1)$ variable, and set

$$X = -1 - \frac{1}{\theta} - \frac{1}{\theta}W_{-1}(-(\theta+1)e^{-(\theta+1)}(1-U)^{1/\alpha}).$$

3. Inference

For a random sample of size n from the $PLS(\theta, \alpha)$ distribution, the log-likelihood function of the parameter vector (θ, α), omitting the constant term, is given by

$$\ell(\theta, \alpha) = n \ln\left(\frac{\alpha\theta^2}{(\theta+1)^\alpha}\right) + (\alpha - 1)\sum_{i=1}^n \ln(\theta + 1 + \theta x_i) - \alpha\theta \sum_{i=1}^n x_i \tag{8}$$

The score functions, defined as the derivatives of the log-likelihood function with respect to the parameters, are

$$U(\alpha) = \frac{n}{\alpha} - n\ln(\theta+1) + \sum_{i=1}^{n} \ln(\theta+1+\theta x_i) - \theta \sum_{i=1}^{n} x_i \tag{9}$$

$$U(\theta) = \frac{2n}{\theta} - \frac{n\alpha}{\theta+1} + (\alpha-1)\sum_{i=1}^{n} \frac{x_i+1}{\theta+1+\theta x_i} - \alpha \sum_{i=1}^{n} x_i \tag{10}$$

Equating these expressions to zero, we have the likelihood equations whose solutions provide us with the maximum likelihood estimates of θ and α.

The observed information matrix, which is minus the matrix of the second derivatives of the log-likelihood with respect to the parameters, has elements of the form

$$j_{\theta\theta} = \frac{2n}{\theta^2} - \frac{n\alpha}{(\theta+1)^2} + (\alpha-1)\sum_{i=1}^{n} \frac{(x_i+1)^2}{(\theta+1+\theta x_i)^2}, \tag{11}$$

$$j_{\theta\alpha} = \frac{n}{\theta+1} - \sum_{i=1}^{n} \frac{x_i+1}{\theta+1+\theta x_i} + \sum_{i=1}^{n} x_i \tag{12}$$

$$j_{\alpha\alpha} = \frac{n}{\alpha^2}. \tag{13}$$

The elements of the expected information matrix (or Fisher information), defined as the expected values of the elements of the observed information matrix, are given by

$$i_{\theta\theta} = \frac{2}{\theta^2} - \frac{\alpha}{(\theta+1)^2} + \frac{\alpha(\alpha-1)e^{\alpha\theta}}{\theta^2(\theta+1)^{\alpha}} \sum_{j=0}^{\infty} \binom{\alpha-3}{j} \frac{\Gamma(j+4)[1-F_G(1;j+4,\alpha\theta)]}{\alpha^{j+4}} \tag{14}$$

$$i_{\alpha\theta} = \mu + \frac{1}{\theta+1} - \frac{\alpha e^{\alpha\theta}}{\theta(\theta+1)^{\alpha}} \sum_{j=0}^{\infty} \binom{\alpha-2}{j} \frac{\Gamma(j+3)[1-F_G(1;j+3,\alpha\theta)]}{\alpha^{j+3}} \tag{15}$$

$$i_{\alpha\alpha} = \frac{1}{\alpha^2}. \tag{16}$$

A bivariate normal approximation for the joint distribution of the maximum likelihood estimates, $\hat{\theta}$ and $\hat{\alpha}$, can then be used to construct confidence intervals for θ and α.

4. A Bivariate Model

For the construction of a bivariate PLS (BPLS) model, we will make use of the approach discussed by Arnold at al. [18] based on conditional distributions.

According to Arnold et al. [18], a two-dimensional random vector (X_1, X_2) has a distribution that is conditionally specified, if the conditional distribution of X_1 given that $X_2 = x_2$ for each x_2 is a member of a specified parametric family of distributions and also that the conditional distribution of X_2 given that $X_1 = x_1$ for each x_1 is a member of a possibly different specified parametric family of distributions.

Suppose now that the joint BPLS distribution function $F_{BPLS}(x_1, x_2)$ of the random vector (X_1, X_2) is such that the conditional distributions of X_1 given $X_2 = x_2$ and the conditional distributions of X_2 given $X_1 = x_1$ are all members of the PLS family of distributions which are absolutely continuous with respect to the Lebesgue measure. We denote this by writing

$$X_1 | X_2 = x_2 \sim PLS_1(\theta_1, \omega(x_2)) \tag{17}$$

and

$$X_2 | X_1 = x_1 \sim PLS_2(\theta_2, \tau(x_1)), \tag{18}$$

where ω and τ are positive dependence functions which are to be determined.

In such a case, we can recognize that, for fixed choices of θ_1 and θ_2, we have conditionals in given one-parameter exponential families and we can identify the corresponding joint density using a result from Arnold and Strauss [19]. We can make the following argument. If $f_{X_1}(x_1)$ and $f_{X_2}(x_2)$ are marginal densities for a joint PLS density $f_{BPLS}(x_1, x_2)$ with conditional densities given by (17) and (18), then it follows that

$$\begin{aligned} f_{BPLS}(x_1, x_2) &= \tau(x_1) f_{X_1}(x_1) f_L(x_2; \theta_2)\{1 - F_L(x_2; \theta_2)\}^{\tau(x_1)-1} \\ &= \omega(x_2) f_{X_2}(x_2) f_L(x_1; \theta_1)\{1 - F_L(x_1; \theta_1)\}^{\omega(x_2)-1}, \end{aligned} \tag{19}$$

since both expressions are representations of the joint density. For this equality to hold, it must be the case that (see Arnold et al. [20] or Arnold and Strauss [21])

$$\omega(x_2) = \alpha_1 - \alpha_{12} \ln[1 - F_L(x_2; \theta_2)] \tag{20}$$

and

$$\tau(x_1) = \alpha_2 - \alpha_{12} \ln[1 - F_L(x_1; \theta_1)], \tag{21}$$

with α_1, α_2, positive real constants and $\alpha_{12} \geq 0$.

Then, using the theorems that appear in the work of Arnold and Strauss [22] and Arnold et al. ([18], chapter 4), we obtain

$$\begin{aligned} f_{BPLS}(x_1, x_2) = k(\underline{\alpha}) \prod_{j=1}^{2} \left[\frac{\theta_j^2 (\theta_j + 1 + \theta_j x_j)^{\alpha_j - 1}(1 + x_j)}{(\theta_j + 1)^{\alpha_j}} \right] e^{-\sum\limits_{j=1}^{2} \alpha_j \theta_j x_j} \\ \times e^{-\alpha_{12} \left[\prod\limits_{j=1}^{2} \left\{ \ln\left(\frac{\theta_j + 1 + \theta_j x_j}{\theta_j + 1} \right) - \theta_j x_j) \right\} \right]} \end{aligned} \tag{22}$$

where the parameter vector $\underline{\alpha} = (\theta_1, \theta_2, \alpha_1, \alpha_2, \alpha_{12})'$ and $k(\underline{\alpha})$ is a normalizing constant.

The corresponding conditional densities are

$$f_{X_1|X_2}(x_1|x_2) = \frac{\theta_1^2 \omega(x_2)(\theta_1 + 1 + \theta_1 x_1)^{\omega(x_2)-1}(1 + x_1)}{(\theta_1 + 1)^{\omega(x_2)}} e^{-\theta_1 \omega(x_2) x_1} \tag{23}$$

where

$$\omega(x_2) = \alpha_1 - \alpha_{12} \ln\left(\frac{\theta_2 + 1 + \theta_2 x_2}{\theta_2 + 1} \right) + \alpha_{12} \theta_2 x_2$$

and

$$f_{X_2|X_1}(x_2|x_1) = \frac{\theta_2^2 \tau(x_1)(\theta_2 + 1 + \theta_2 x_2)^{\tau(x_1)-1}(1 + x_2)}{(\theta_2 + 1)^{\tau(x_1)}} e^{-\theta_2 \tau(x_1) x_2} \tag{24}$$

where

$$\tau(x_1) = \alpha_2 - \alpha_{12} \ln\left(\frac{\theta_1 + 1 + \theta_1 x_1}{\theta_1 + 1} \right) + \alpha_{12} \theta_1 x_1$$

The marginal densities are given by

$$f_{X_1}(x_1) = k(\underline{\alpha}) \frac{\theta_1^2 (\theta_1 + 1 + \theta_1 x_1)^{\alpha_1 - 1}(1 + x_1) e^{-\alpha_1 \theta_1 x_1}}{(\theta_1 + 1)^{\alpha_1} [\alpha_2 - \alpha_{12}(\ln(\theta_1 + 1 + \theta_1 x_1) - \ln(\theta_1 + 1)) + \alpha_{12} \theta_1 x_1]} \tag{25}$$

and

$$f_{X_2}(x_2) = k(\underline{\alpha}) \frac{\theta_2^2 (\theta_2 + 1 + \theta_2 x_2)^{\alpha_2 - 1}(1 + x_2) e^{-\alpha_2 \theta_2 x_2}}{(\theta_2 + 1)^{\alpha_2} [\alpha_1 - \alpha_{12}(\ln(\theta_2 + 1 + \theta_2 x_2) - \ln(\theta_2 + 1)) + \alpha_{12} \theta_2 x_2]} \tag{26}$$

The case of independence corresponds to setting $\alpha_{12} = 0$.

The conditional distributions corresponding to the conditional densities in (23) and (24) are of the forms

$$F_{X_1|X_2}(x_1|x_2) = 1 - \left(\frac{\theta_1 + 1 + \theta_1 x_1}{\theta_1 + 1}\right)^{\omega(x_2)} e^{-\theta_1 \omega(x_2) x_1} \tag{27}$$

and

$$F_{X_2|X_1}(x_2|x_1) = 1 - \left(\frac{\theta_2 + 1 + \theta_2 x_2}{\theta_2 + 1}\right)^{\tau(x_1)} e^{-\theta_2 \tau(x_1) x_2}. \tag{28}$$

Contour graphs of the BPLS density are displayed in Figure 2 for two representative parameter vectors. In both cases, it is concluded that the distribution is unimodal.

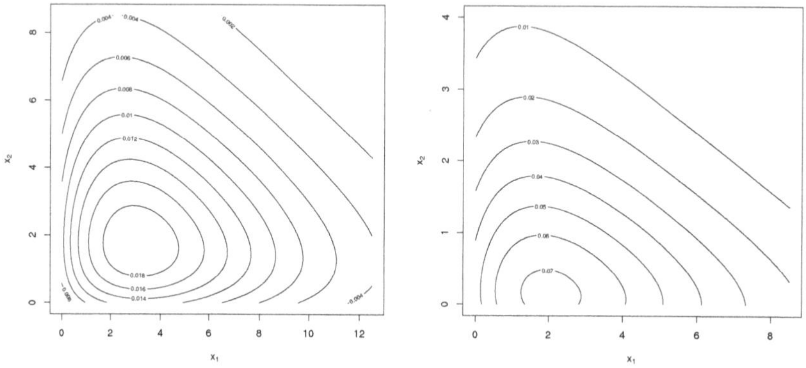

Figure 2. Contours for the BPLS model (**a**) BPLS (0.15, 0.25, 2.5, 2.0, 1.50) and (**b**) BPLS (0.25, 0.75, 1.75, 1.25, 0.75).

Expressions for the (non-linear) regression functions can be written involving the Lambert function. Thus,

$$E(X_1|X_2 = x_2) = -\frac{\theta_1 + 1}{\theta_1} - \frac{1}{\theta_1}\int_0^1 W_{-1}\left(\frac{\theta_1 + 1}{e^{\theta_1 + 1}}(y - 1)\right) y^{\omega(x_2) - 1} dy \tag{29}$$

and

$$E(X_2|X_1 = x_1) = -\frac{\theta_2 + 1}{\theta_2} - \frac{1}{\theta_2}\int_0^1 W_{-1}\left(\frac{\theta_2 + 1}{e^{\theta_2 + 1}}(y - 1)\right) y^{\tau(x_1) - 1} dy \tag{30}$$

The variances (σ_1^2 and σ_2^2), the covariance (σ_{12}) and the correlation (ρ_{12}) can be written in terms of the Lambert function and the exponential integral function (defined below).

$$\sigma_j^2 = \frac{(\theta_j + 1)^2}{\alpha_{12}\theta_j^2} e^{\frac{\alpha_1\alpha_2}{\alpha_{12}}}\left[-Ei(0) + \frac{2}{\theta_j + 1} h_1(y) + \frac{1}{(\theta_j + 1)^2} h_2(y)\right] \frac{e^{\frac{2\alpha_1\alpha_2}{\alpha_{12}}}}{\alpha_{12}^2\theta_j^2}\left[(\theta_j + 1)(-Ei(0)) + h_1(y)\right]^2$$

where

$$-Ei(x) = \int_x^\infty \frac{e^{-z}}{z} dz, \quad h_1(y) = \int_0^\infty \frac{W_{-1}\left(\frac{\theta_j + 1}{e^{\theta_j + 1}}\left(e^{(\alpha_{12}y - \alpha_1\alpha_2)/(\alpha_j\alpha_{12})} - 1\right)\right) e^{-y}}{y} dy$$

and

$$h_2(y) = \int_0^{\infty} \frac{W_{-1}^2\left(\frac{\theta_j+1}{e^{\theta_j+1}}\left(e^{(\alpha_{12}y-\alpha_1\alpha_2)/(\alpha_j\alpha_{12})}-1\right)\right)e^{-y}}{y}dy.$$

$$\begin{aligned}\sigma_{12} &= \tfrac{1}{\theta_1\theta_2}\int_0^1\int_0^1 g(y_1,y_2)\left[\prod_{j=1}^{2}(\theta_j+1)+\prod_{j=1}^{2}W_{-1}\left(\frac{\theta_j+1}{e^{\theta_j+1}}(y_j-1)\right)\right]\prod_{j=1}^{2}y_j^{\alpha_j-1}dy_j + \\ &\tfrac{1}{\theta_1\theta_2}\int_0^1\int_0^1 g(y_1,y_2)\left[\sum_{j=1}^{2}\prod_{j'=1,\, j'\neq j}^{2}(\theta_j+1)W_{-1}\left(\frac{\theta_{j'}+1}{e^{\theta_{j'}+1}}(y_{j'}-1)\right)\right]\prod_{j=1}^{2}y_j^{\alpha_j-1}dy_j \qquad (31)\end{aligned}$$

and $\rho_{12} = \frac{\sigma_{12}}{\sigma_1\sigma_2}$, where

$$g(y_1,y_2) = y_1^{-\alpha_{12}\ln(y_2)} - \frac{1}{(\alpha_1-\alpha_{12}\ln(y_2))(\alpha_2-\alpha_{12}\ln(y_1))}.$$

The values of the correlation coefficient were calculated for a variety of parametric configurations and are displayed in Tables 1 and 2. The range of correlations encountered was [−0.8667, 0.9814], which is broader than the range of correlations in many well-known bivariate survival models.

Table 1. Correlation coefficients for the BPLS model.

		$\theta_1 = 0.50$ and $\theta_2 = 0.75$			$\theta_1 = 0.75$ and $\theta_2 = 1.50$			$\theta_1 = 1.30$ and $\theta_2 = 1.70$		
α_2	α_1	$\alpha_{12} = 0.25$	$\alpha_{12} = 1.0$	$\alpha_{12} = 1.75$	$\alpha_{12} = 0.25$	$\alpha_{12} = 1.0$	$\alpha_{12} = 1.75$	$\alpha_{12} = 0.25$	$\alpha_{12} = 1.0$	$\alpha_{12} = 1.75$
	0.25	−0.0453	−0.0279	−0.0215	−0.1542	−0.0958	−0.0743	−0.3329	−0.2079	−0.1622
0.1	0.75	−0.0429	−0.0263	−0.0190	−0.1633	−0.1008	−0.0737	−0.3871	−0.2401	−0.1773
	1.25	−0.0389	−0.0233	−0.0157	−0.1722	−0.1036	−0.0709	−0.5090	−0.3039	−0.2112
	0.25	−0.0457	−0.0275	−0.0200	−0.1564	−0.0950	−0.0701	−0.3423	−0.2099	−0.1562
0.25	0.75	−0.0375	−0.0207	−0.0124	−0.1433	−0.0803	−0.0494	−0.3443	−0.1952	−0.1225
	1.25	−0.0290	−0.0135	−0.0050	−0.1283	−0.0611	−0.0245	−0.3791	−0.1825	−0.0775
	0.25	−0.0419	−0.0243	−0.0163	−0.1442	−0.0848	−0.0577	−0.3246	−0.1930	−0.1331
0.50	0.75	−0.0261	−0.0104	−0.0017	−0.1003	−0.0417	−0.0091	−0.2471	−0.1056	−0.0264
	1.25	−0.0118	0.0025	0.0113	−0.0526	0.0086	0.0469	−0.1577	0.0211	0.1349
	0.25	−0.0374	−0.0206	−0.0124	−0.1293	−0.0727	−0.0448	−0.2998	−0.1705	−0.1068
0.75	0.75	−0.0153	−0.0007	0.0081	−0.0593	−0.0047	0.0285	−0.1505	−0.0151	0.0685
	1.25	0.0039	0.0171	0.0259	0.0161	0.0727	0.1114	0.0467	0.2164	0.3369
	0.25	−0.0248	−0.0100	−0.0016	−0.0871	−0.0366	−0.0077	−0.2246	−0.0962	−0.0227
1.5	0.75	0.0125	0.0251	0.0338	0.0473	0.0952	0.1290	0.1302	0.2625	0.3587
	1.25	0.0437	0.0550	0.0637	0.1924	0.2426	0.2822	0.6350	0.8083	0.9552

Table 2. Correlation coefficients for the BPLS model.

		$\theta_1 = 3.50$ and $\theta_2 = 5.75$			$\theta_1 = 2.75$ and $\theta_2 = 6.50$			$\theta_1 = 5.0$ and $\theta_2 = 2.75$		
α_2	α_1	$\alpha_{12} = 2.0$	$\alpha_{12} = 2.75$	$\alpha_{12} = 3.50$	$\alpha_{12} = 2.0$	$\alpha_{12} = 2.75$	$\alpha_{12} = 3.50$	$\alpha_{12} = 2.0$	$\alpha_{12} = 2.75$	$\alpha_{12} = 3.50$
	2.25	0.2874	0.3062	0.3220	0.3485	0.3700	0.3878	0.3646	0.3887	0.4088
1.0	3.0	0.3265	0.3423	0.3557	0.3948	0.4125	0.4274	0.4063	0.4263	0.4433
	3.75	0.3547	0.3684	0.3802	0.4274	0.4426	0.4555	0.4367	0.4540	0.4689
	4.5	0.3763	0.3885	0.3991	0.4520	0.4653	0.4767	0.4603	0.4757	0.4890
	2.25	0.3796	0.3919	0.4027	0.4291	0.4427	0.4546	0.4946	0.5104	0.5241
2.0	3.0	0.4175	0.4278	0.4369	0.4714	0.4827	0.4926	0.5334	0.5465	0.5580
	3.75	0.4453	0.4542	0.4621	0.5021	0.5118	0.5204	0.5627	0.5739	0.5839
	4.5	0.4670	0.4748	0.4819	0.5258	0.5344	0.5420	0.5860	0.5959	0.6048

Table 2. *Cont.*

α_2	α_1	$\theta_1 = 3.50$ and $\theta_2 = 5.75$			$\theta_1 = 2.75$ and $\theta_2 = 6.50$			$\theta_1 = 5.0$ and $\theta_2 = 2.75$		
		$\alpha_{12} = 2.0$	$\alpha_{12} = 2.75$	$\alpha_{12} = 3.50$	$\alpha_{12} = 2.0$	$\alpha_{12} = 2.75$	$\alpha_{12} = 3.50$	$\alpha_{12} = 2.0$	$\alpha_{12} = 2.75$	$\alpha_{12} = 3.50$
	2.25	0.4480	0.4566	0.4643	0.4939	0.5033	0.5117	0.5878	0.5987	0.6083
3.5	3.0	0.4865	0.4936	0.5000	0.5361	0.5438	0.5507	0.6263	0.6352	0.6432
	3.75	0.5151	0.5211	0.5267	0.5671	0.5737	0.5796	0.6559	0.6635	0.6704
	4.5	0.5376	0.5429	0.5478	0.5914	0.5971	0.6024	0.6798	0.6864	0.6925
	2.25	0.4988	0.5051	0.5108	0.5438	0.5506	0.5569	0.6540	0.6618	0.6689
5.5	3.0	0.5384	0.5435	0.5483	0.5868	0.5924	0.5975	0.6934	0.6998	0.7057
	3.75	0.5680	0.5724	0.5764	0.6188	0.6235	0.6278	0.7241	0.7295	0.7345
	4.5	0.5915	0.5953	0.5989	0.6440	0.6481	0.6519	0.7492	0.7539	0.7583

The transformation $Y_1 = -\ln(1 - F_L(X_1))$ and $Y_2 = -\ln(1 - F_L(X_2))$ yields the bivariate exponential conditionals model discussed in detail by Arnold et al. [18].

$$f_{Y_1Y_2}(y_1, y_2) = \mathbf{k}(\alpha_1, \alpha_2, \alpha_{12}) \exp(-\alpha_1 y_1 - \alpha_2 y_2 - \alpha_{12} y_1 y_2) \tag{32}$$

Note that the exponential conditionals distribution exhibits only a very limited range of negative correlations.

Consistent asymptotically normal moment-based estimates of α_1, α_2 and α_{12} as functions of the y_is are available.

$$\widetilde{\alpha}_1 = \frac{\widetilde{\gamma}}{\overline{y}_1(\widetilde{\gamma} + I(\widetilde{\gamma} - 1))}, \quad \widetilde{\alpha}_2 = \frac{\widetilde{\gamma}}{\overline{y}_2(\widetilde{\gamma} + I(\widetilde{\gamma} - 1))} \quad \text{and} \quad \widetilde{\alpha}_{12} = \frac{\widetilde{\gamma}(\widetilde{\gamma} - 1)}{\overline{y}_1\overline{y}_2(\widetilde{\gamma} + I(\widetilde{\gamma} - 1))},$$

where $\widetilde{\gamma} = \frac{I}{1+\rho_{Y_1Y_2}I}$ with $\rho_{Y_1Y_2} = cor(y_1, y_2)$ and $I = cv(y_1)cv(y_2)$, where cor is the usual Pearson correlation between Y_1 and Y_2 and $cv(y) = \sqrt{S_y^2}/\overline{y}$. If we, in addition, have available consistent estimates of θ_1 and θ_2, we can make use of these exponential conditionals estimates in conjunction with an estimated inverse transformation to develop estimates for the parameters of the BPLS distribution.

A Bivariate Lindley Conditionals Model

If we wish to identify a bivariate Lindley survival model with Lindley conditionals (BLCs), it is tempting to merely set $\alpha_1 = \alpha_2 = 1$ in the BPLS model. This will indeed result in a valid bivariate survival model, but it will still have power Lindley conditional distributions. To identify the model with Lindley conditionals, we must return to definition of the Lindley distribution and recognize that it corresponds to a one-parameter exponential family of distributions with parameter θ. Applying the result obtained by Arnold and Strauss [22], we can identify the BLC model as one with conditionals

$$X_1|X_2 = x_2 \sim L(\theta_1 + \theta_{12}x_2), \quad X_2|X_1 = x_1 \sim L(\theta_2 + \theta_{12}x_1)$$

and joint density given by

$$f(x_1, x_2; \underline{\theta}) \propto (1 + x_1)(1 + x_2) exp\{-\theta_1 x_1 - \theta_2 x_2 - \theta_{12} x_1 x_2\}, \quad x_1, x_2 > 0. \tag{33}$$

The marginal and conditional densities for this model are given as follows:

$$f(x_1) = k(\theta)\frac{(x_1 + 1)(1 + \theta_2 + \theta_{12}x_1)}{(\theta_2 + \theta_{12}x_1)^2} \exp(-\theta_1 x_1), \quad x_1 > 0,$$

$$f(x_2) = k(\theta)\frac{(x_2 + 1)(1 + \theta_1 + \theta_{12}x_2)}{(\theta_1 + \theta_{12}x_2)^2} \exp(-\theta_2 x_2), \quad x_2 > 0.$$

$$f(x_1|x_2) = \frac{(x_1+1)(\theta_1+\theta_{12}x_2)^2}{(1+\theta_1+\theta_{12}x_2)}\exp(-(\theta_1+\theta_{12}x_2)x_1), \ x_1 > 0,$$

$$f(x_2|x_1) = \frac{(x_2+1)(\theta_2+\theta_{12}x_1)^2}{(1+\theta_2+\theta_{12}x_1)}\exp(-(\theta_2+\theta_{12}x_1)x_2), \ x_2 > 0.$$

Note that the BLC density can be written in the form

$$f(x_1,x_2;\underline{\theta}) \propto p(x_1,x_2)exp\{-\theta_1x_1-\theta_2x_2-\theta_{12}x_1x_2\}, \ x_1,x_2 > 0. \tag{34}$$

Thus, it can recognized as a weighted bivariate exponential conditionals density with weight function $p(x_1,x_2)$. If we wish to decide whether a given data set will be best fitted by a BPLS or by a BLC model, we cannot simply test the hypothesis $H_0: \ \alpha_1 = \alpha_2 = 1$. The models are not nested and the decision regarding which will best fit the data will likely involve comparing the maximized pseudo-likelihoods of the two models.

5. Estimation

In order to estimate the parameters of a BPLS model based on a sample from that distribution, we will employ the method of pseudo-likelihood which utilizes the conditional likelihoods. The reason for this is that the nature of the normalizing constant in the BPLS density makes use of the usual maximum likelihood (ML) approach somewhat difficult. The pseudo-likelihood approach involve maximization of the logarithm of the product of the conditional densities, which avoids the necessity of dealing with the normalizing constant, $k(\underline{\alpha})$. In this case, although $k(\underline{\alpha})$ is troublesome, ML estimation could be accomplished by a computer-intensive search involving repeated evaluation of the expression for the normalizing constant which, though available, involves the exponential integral function. Thus,

$$k(\underline{\alpha}) = \frac{ce^{-1/c}}{-Ei(1/c)},$$

where

$$c = \frac{\alpha_{12}}{\alpha_1\alpha_2}.$$

In this situation, pseudo-likelihood is an attractive alternative.

Pseudo-Likelihood Estimation for the BPLS Distribution

An early reference for the technique known as pseudo-likelihood estimation is Besag [23]. In the bivariate case, the method involves replacing the log-likelihood function by the product of the two conditional likelihood functions and seeking parameter values that will maximize this conditional objective function. A convenient reference for discussion of pseudo-likelihood estimates and their properties is Arnold and Strauss [22]. Such estimates are typically consistent and asymptotically normal, though somewhat less efficient than the more elusive ML estimates.

The pseudo likelihood corresponding to a single observation (X_1, X_2) from a BPLS distribution is defined to be

$$L_p(\underline{\beta}) = f_{X_1|X_2}(x_1|x_2)f_{X_2|X_1}(x_2|x_1). \tag{35}$$

The pseudo-likelihood function corresponding to sample of size n from the BPLS distribution is then given by

$$L_p^{(n)}(\underline{\beta}) = \prod_{i=1}^{n} f_{X_1|X_2}(x_{i1}|x_{i2})f_{X_2|X_1}(x_{i2}|x_{i1}).$$

The pseudo-likelihood estimate of the parameter vector $\underline{\beta}$ is that value of $\underline{\beta}$ which maximizes $L_p^{(n)}(\underline{\beta})$. Equivalently, it is the value that maximizes the log-pseudo-likelihood, denoted by $\ell_p^{(n)}(\underline{\beta})$. For a sample from the BPLS distribution, we have

$$\begin{aligned}\ell_p(\underline{\beta}) &= 2n\log(\theta_1\theta_2) + \textstyle\sum_{i=1}^n(\ln(b_2(x_{i1})) + \ln(b_1(x_{i2}))) + \sum_{i=1}^n \ln((1+x_{i1})(1+x_{i2})) \\ &+ \textstyle\sum_{i=1}^n((b_1(x_{i2})-1)\ln(\theta_1+1+\theta_1x_{i1}) + (b_2(x_{i1})-1)\ln(\theta_2+1+\theta_2x_{i2})) \\ &- \textstyle\sum_{i=1}^n(b_1(x_{i2})\ln(\theta_1+1) + b_2(x_{i1})\ln(\theta_2+1)) - \sum_{i=1}^n(\theta_2x_{i2}b_2(x_{i1}) + \theta_1x_{i1}b_1(x_{i2})).\end{aligned} \tag{36}$$

where $b_1(x_2) = \omega(x_2)$ and $b_2(x_1) = \tau(x_1)$.

The pseudo-score functions are defined to be the partial derivatives of the log-pseudo-likelihood with respect to each of the parameters in the model, denoted by $U_p(\underline{\beta}) = (U_p(\theta_1), U_p(\theta_2), U_p(\alpha_1), U_p(\alpha_2), U_p(\alpha_{12}))'$.

In the case of the BPLS model, the elements of the pseudo-score vector are given as follows:

$$\begin{aligned}U_p(\theta_j) &= \tfrac{2n}{\theta_j} - \textstyle\sum_{i=1}^n \frac{x_{ij}+1}{\theta_j+1+\theta_jx_{ij}} + \sum_{i=1}^n \frac{x_{ij}b_j(x_{ij'})\left(1-(\theta_j+1)^2-\theta_j(\theta_j+1)x_{ij}\right)}{(\theta_j+1)(\theta_j+1+\theta_jx_{ij})} - \\ &\tfrac{\alpha_{12}}{\theta_j+1}\textstyle\sum_{i=1}^n x_{ij}\frac{1-(\theta_j+1)^2-\theta_j(\theta_j+1)x_{ij}}{\theta_j+1+\theta_jx_{ij}}\left[\frac{1}{b_{j'}(x_{ij})} + \ln\left(\frac{\theta_{j'}+1+\theta_{j'}x_{ij'}}{\theta_{j'}+1}\right) - \theta_{j'}x_{ij'}\right]\end{aligned}$$

for $j = 1,2$ and $j' = 1,2$ with $j' \neq j$,

$$U_p(\alpha_j) = \sum_{i=1}^n\left[\frac{1}{b_j(x_{ij'})} + \ln\left(\frac{\theta_j+1+\theta_jx_{ij}}{\theta_j+1}\right) - \theta_jx_{ij}\right]$$

for $j = 1,2$ and $j' = 1,2$ with $j' \neq j$ and

$$\begin{aligned}U_p(\alpha_{12}) &= -\textstyle\sum_{i=1}^n\left[\frac{1}{b_2(x_{i1})} + \ln\left(\frac{\theta_2+1+\theta_2x_{i2}}{\theta_2+1}\right) - \theta_2x_{i2}\right]\left[\ln\left(\frac{\theta_1+1+\theta_1x_{i1}}{\theta_1+1}\right) - \theta_1x_{i1}\right] \\ &- \textstyle\sum_{i=1}^n\left[\frac{1}{b_1(x_{i2})} + \ln\left(\frac{\theta_1+1+\theta_1x_{i1}}{\theta_1+1}\right) - \theta_1x_{i1}\right]\left[\ln\left(\frac{\theta_2+1+\theta_2x_{i2}}{\theta_2+1}\right) - \theta_2x_{i2}\right].\end{aligned}$$

The estimating equations consist of the elements of the pseudo-score vector set equal to zero. The solution to these equations is the vector of maximum pseudo-likelihood (MPL) estimates. The solutions are typically obtained by iterative numerical means, such as Newton–Raphson or quasi-Newton.

The asymptotic distribution MPL estimates for the BPLS model can be identified using the results of Arnold and Strauss [21].

Thus, the pseudo-likelihood estimators $\hat{\underline{\beta}}$ of $\underline{\beta}$ are consistent and asymptotically normally distributed with an asymptotic covariance matrix given by

$$\Sigma_p = J^{-1}(\underline{\beta})K(\underline{\beta})J^{-1}(\underline{\beta})$$

(see Arnold and Strauss, 1991 [19]), where for $l, m = 1,2$

$$K_{lm}(\underline{\beta}) = \mathbb{E}\left[\left\{\frac{\partial\ell_p(\underline{\beta})}{\partial\beta_l}\right\}\left\{\frac{\partial\ell_p(\underline{\beta})}{\partial\beta_m}\right\}'\right] \text{ and } J_{lm}(\underline{\beta}) = -\mathbb{E}\left[\frac{\partial^2\ell_p(\underline{\beta})}{\partial\beta_l\partial\beta_m}\right].$$

Typically MPL estimates are less efficient than ML estimates (see Tibaldi et al., [24]), but the relative ease of computation offsets the loss of efficiency.

As a consistent estimator of the asymptotic covariance matrix of the MPL estimates, we can use the sandwich estimator proposed by Cheng and Riu [25]. This estimator can be obtained as follows.

Let $U_{pi}(\underline{\beta}) = \frac{\partial \ell_{pi}(\underline{\beta})}{\partial \underline{\beta}}$, be the vector of pseudo-scores for the ith observation, and then define

$\hat{J}_n(\underline{\beta}) = -\frac{1}{n}\sum_{i=1}^{n} \frac{\partial U_{pi}(\underline{\beta})}{\partial \underline{\beta}'}|_{\widetilde{\underline{\beta}}}$, which is the sum over all of the observations of the matrix of second derivatives of

$\ell_p(\underline{\beta})$ evaluated at the pseudo-estimator $\widetilde{\underline{\beta}}$.

Define

$\hat{K}_n(\underline{\beta}) = \frac{1}{n}\sum_{i=1}^{n} U_{pi}(\underline{\beta})U_{pi}(\underline{\beta})'|_{\widetilde{\underline{\beta}}}$, then a consistent estimator of the asymptotic covariance matrix is given as follows:

$$\hat{\Sigma}(\widetilde{\underline{\beta}}) = \frac{1}{n}\hat{J}_n^{-1}(\widetilde{\underline{\beta}})\hat{K}_n(\widetilde{\underline{\beta}})\hat{J}_n^{-1'}(\widetilde{\underline{\beta}}).$$

Setting $w_{ij} = \frac{\theta_j+1+\theta_j x_{ij}}{\theta_j+1}$, $q_{ij} = x_{ij}\frac{1-(\theta_j+1)^2-\theta_j(\theta_j+1)x_{ij}}{(\theta_j+1)(\theta_j+1+\theta_j x_{ij})}$ and $z_{ij} = \frac{(1+2\theta_j)x_{ij}^2+2(\theta_j+1)x_{ij}}{(\theta_j+1)^2(\theta_j+1+\theta_j x_{ij})^2}$, the elements of the matrix of second derivatives of the log-pseudo-likelihood function with respect to the parameters

$H(\underline{\beta}) = \{h_{\beta_j\beta_{j'}}\}$ of the BPLS distribution are given as follows:

$$\begin{aligned} h_{\theta_j\theta_j} &= -\frac{2n}{\theta_j^2} + \alpha_{12}\sum_{i=1}^{n}\frac{b_{j'}(x_{ij})z_{ij}-\alpha_{12}q_{ij}^2}{b_{j'}^2(x_{ij})} + \sum_{i=1}^{n}\frac{(1+x_{ij})^2}{(\theta_j+1+\theta_j x_{ij})^2} - \sum_{i=1}^{n} b_j(x_{ij'})z_{ij} \\ &\quad + \alpha_{12}\sum_{i=1}^{n} z_{ij}\left[\ln(w_{ij'}) - \theta_{j'}x_{ij'}\right] \end{aligned}$$

$$h_{\theta_j\theta_{j'}} = -\alpha_{12}\sum_{i=1}^{n} x_{ij'}q_{ij'}q_{ij} - \alpha_{12}\sum_{i=1}^{n} x_{ij}q_{ij}q_{ij'},$$

$$h_{\alpha_j\theta_j} = \sum_{i=1}^{n} x_{ij}q_{ij}, \qquad h_{\alpha_{j'}\theta_j} = -\alpha_{12}\sum_{i=1}^{n}\frac{x_{ij}q_{ij}}{b_{j'}^2(x_{ij})},$$

$$h_{\alpha_{12}\theta_j} = -\sum_{i=1}^{n} x_{ij}q_{ij}\left[2(\ln(w_{ij'}) - \theta_{j'}x_{ij'}) + \frac{b_{j'}(x_{ij}) + \alpha_{12}(\ln(w_{ij}) - \theta_j x_{ij})}{b_{j'}^2(x_{ij})}\right],$$

$$h_{\alpha_j\alpha_j} = -\sum_{i=1}^{n}\frac{1}{b_j^2(x_{ij'})}, \qquad h_{\alpha_{j'}\alpha_j} = 0, \qquad h_{\alpha_{12}\alpha_j} = \sum_{i=1}^{n}\frac{\ln(w_{ij'}) - \theta_{j'}x_{ij'}}{b_j^2(x_{ij'})}$$

and

$$h_{\alpha_{12}\alpha_{12}} = -\sum_{i=1}^{n}\sum_{j=1}^{2}\left[\frac{\ln(w_{ij}) - \theta_j x_{ij}}{b_{j'}(x_{ij})}\right]^2.$$

We then have

$$\hat{J}_n(\underline{\beta}) = -\frac{1}{n}H(\underline{\beta})|_{\widetilde{\underline{\beta}}}$$

from which we may obtain the estimated covariance matrix of Cheng and Riu [25] for the BPLS model.

6. Numerical Results

6.1. Univariate Simulation

A simulation study was carried out to investigate the behavior of the ML estimate of the parameters θ and α in the PLS distribution. A set of 5000 samples from the PLS distribution were simulated for each combination of parameter values $\theta = 0.5, 2.5, 7.5$ and $\alpha = 0.5, 2.5, 4.5$ with sample sizes $n = 30, 50, 150$ and 300 respectively. For fixed values of the parameters θ and α, and utilizing a sample of n $U(0,1)$ variables, we generate X's of the following form

$$X = -1 - \frac{1}{\theta_0} - \frac{1}{\theta_0} W_{-1}(-(\theta_0+1)e^{-(\theta_0+1)}(1-U)^{1/\alpha_0}),$$

which have the $PLS(\theta_0, \alpha_0)$ distribution. For this random sample we construct the corresponding log-likelihood function $\ell(\theta_0, \alpha_0; X)$ which is used to obtain the ML estimates of the parameters using the optim function in R. This procedure was repeated $m = 5000$ times and using the estimates obtained, we computed values of the bias ($|Bias|$) and root of the mean square error ($\sqrt{MSE}$) of the estimates in the forms

$$|\text{Bias}(\theta_j)| = \frac{1}{m}\left|\sum_{k=1}^{m}\left(\frac{\hat{\theta}_j^{(k)} - \theta_j}{\theta_j}\right)\right|; \quad \text{RMSE}(\theta_j) = \sqrt{\frac{1}{m}\sum_{k=1}^{m}\left(\hat{\theta}_j^{(k)} - \theta_j\right)^2},$$

respectively, where $\hat{\theta}_j^{(k)}$ is the estimator of θ_j for the jth sample and m the iterations number.

The average relative bias and average root mean squared error of the ML estimates of the parameters are presented in Tables 3 and 4.

As is to be expected, since the estimates are consistent, the relative bias and the root mean squared errors of the estimates decrease in almost all cases as the sample size increases. The results in the Tables confirm the expected good performance of ML estimation for this model.

Table 3. Simulations for $\hat{\theta}$ for the PLS model with 5000 iterations for θ = 0.5, 2.5, 7.5 and α = 0.5, 2.5, 4.5 with sample sizes n = 30, 50, 100 and 300, respectively.

		$n=30$		$n=50$		$n=100$		$n=300$	
θ	α	$\lvert Bias\rvert$	$\sqrt{MSE}$	$\lvert Bias\rvert$	$\sqrt{MSE}$	$\lvert Bias\rvert$	$\sqrt{MSE}$	$\lvert Bias\rvert$	$\sqrt{MSE}$
	0.5	0.0634	0.3384	0.0632	0.3019	0.0594	0.3463	0.0246	0.1677
0.5	2.5	0.0207	0.1659	0.0116	0.1124	0.0209	0.1359	0.0005	0.0349
	4.5	0.0076	0.0768	0.0040	0.0618	0.0018	0.0404	0.0014	0.0290
	0.5	0.2408	0.7052	0.1018	0.4233	0.0413	0.3438	0.0114	0.1619
2.5	2.5	0.0266	0.7298	0.0110	0.6882	0.0052	0.3668	0.0045	0.4449
	4.5	0.0072	0.3723	0.0071	0.3507	0.0006	0.2592	0.0002	0.1827
	0.5	0.0245	0.1888	0.0161	0.1902	0.0052	0.1445	0.0003	0.0407
7.5	2.5	0.0230	0.2440	0.0118	0.2012	0.0106	0.2336	0.0021	0.1091
	4.5	0.0254	0.4401	0.0093	0.3756	0.0013	0.2473	0.0061	0.2347

Table 4. Simulations for $\hat{\alpha}$ for the PLS model with 5000 iterations for θ = 0.5, 2.5, 7.5 and α = 0.5, 2.5, 4.5 with sample sizes n = 30, 50, 150, and 300, respectively.

		$n=30$		$n=50$		$n=100$		$n=300$	
θ	α	$\lvert Bias\rvert$	$\sqrt{MSE}$	$\lvert Bias\rvert$	$\sqrt{MSE}$	$\lvert Bias\rvert$	$\sqrt{MSE}$	$\lvert Bias\rvert$	$\sqrt{MSE}$
	0.5	0.1646	0.4287	0.1086	0.3726	0.0651	0.2775	0.0333	0.1945
0.5	2.5	0.0222	0.3653	0.0292	0.3712	0.0237	0.3727	0.0170	0.2220
	4.5	0.0322	0.3272	0.0305	0.3103	0.0124	0.4404	0.0100	0.2139
	0.5	0.2217	0.5397	0.0873	0.3250	0.0298	0.1284	0.0079	0.0594
2.5	2.5	0.3146	0.8976	0.2523	0.8676	0.0868	0.4347	0.0513	0.5333
	4.5	0.1305	0.5626	0.0935	0.6519	0.0323	0.5542	0.0194	0.3495
	0.5	0.0200	0.1006	0.0109	0.0774	0.0037	0.0524	0.0014	0.0291
7.5	2.5	0.0889	0.4399	0.0494	0.3323	0.0267	0.2325	0.0083	0.1319
	4.5	0.1174	0.5963	0.0799	0.4741	0.0346	0.3322	0.0210	0.2233

6.2. Simulation Study for the BPLS Distribution

A simulation study, similar to that discussed in the previous subsection, was carried out for the BPLS distribution, but in this case employing MPL estimates of the model parameters, $\underline{\beta} = (\theta_1, \theta_2, \alpha_1, \alpha_2, \alpha_{12})$, That is to say, realizations of the bivariate exponential conditionals distribution (discussed in detail by Arnold et al. [18], in particular; see equation 32), were simulated, and using the following inverse transformation $Y_1 = -\ln(1 - F_L(X_1; \theta_1))$ and $Y_2 = -\ln(1 - F_L(X_2; \theta_2))$, we obtained a sample from the $BPLS(\theta_1, \theta_2, \alpha_1, \alpha_2, \alpha_{12})$. The corresponding pseudo-likelihood function was then maximized numerically using the optim function provided in the R-project.

The relative bias and root mean squared errors of the estimates were investigated in a small study involving 1000 simulated random samples of each of the sizes $n = 30, 60, 90$ and 200 for three different parametric scenarios: scenario 1 with $\underline{\beta} = (0.50, 0.75, 1.25, 2.75, 1.0)$, scenario 2 with $\underline{\beta} = (1.50, 0.25, 0.75, 1.50, 0.50)$, and scenario 3 with $\underline{\beta} = (0.25, 0.50, 2.50, 2.0, 1.50)$. The results of this simulation study are presented in Table 5.

Table 5. Simulations for the $BPLS(\underline{\beta})$ model with 1000 iterations and with sample sizes n = 30, 60, 90 and 200, respectively.

n	$\|Bias\|$	$\sqrt{MSE}$	$\|Bias\|$	$\sqrt{MSE}$	$\|Bias\|$	$\sqrt{MSE}$	$\|Bias\|$	$\sqrt{MSE}$	$\|Bias\|$	$\sqrt{MSE}$
Scenario 1										
30	0.1236	0.6551	0.3269	1.0653	1.0899	2.1701	0.6024	2.6989	1.6199	2.5336
60	0.0862	0.5256	0.251	0.8143	0.8629	1.8099	0.5326	2.3808	1.2446	2.1412
90	0.0622	0.4936	0.1920	0.6754	0.6280	1.4775	0.4337	2.0347	0.9237	1.8002
200	0.0498	0.3112	0.1328	0.5381	0.3910	1.1129	0.3562	1.7097	0.5017	1.3194
Scenario 2										
30	1.0233	0.7638	0.1750	0.4802	1.0195	1.6341	0.4081	1.7194	2.1485	2.2890
60	0.9859	0.5943	0.1240	0.3482	0.9494	1.3375	0.2200	1.3114	2.0599	1.8930
90	0.9111	0.4675	0.1092	0.2816	0.9412	1.1967	0.0978	1.1076	2.0110	1.6285
200	0.8156	0.4537	0.0769	0.1576	0.8658	0.9036	0.0213	0.8472	1.8631	1.2091
Scenario 3										
30	0.2784	0.5608	0.1469	0.6254	0.4837	2.0776	0.7651	2.2199	0.7959	2.1892
60	0.2730	0.5033	0.1065	0.5472	0.1677	1.7553	0.6526	1.8444	0.3805	1.7982
90	0.2350	0.4009	0.0843	0.4638	0.1510	1.6180	0.6017	1.6769	0.3212	1.5325
200	0.2342	0.2880	0.0536	0.3308	0.0525	1.2179	0.3898	1.2856	0.1142	1.0140

The results in the table confirm that the absolute value of the bias and the root mean squared error of the MPL estimators of the model parameters decrease as the sample sizes increase, and that the estimators are approximately unbiased. The performance of the MPL estimators for moderate sample sizes is deemed to be satisfactory, and the performance for larger sample sizes is more than satisfactory, as is to be expected because of the consistent asymptotic normality of such estimates, as discussed in Section 5.

7. Applications of the Models

7.1. Application 1

To illustrate the utility of the PLS model, we analyze a real data set dealing with the active repair times (X) for an airborne communication transceiver. The data are taken from Jorgensen [26].

Descriptive statistics for the data set are presented in Table 6. The quantities $\sqrt{b_1}$ and b_2 indicate the sample asymmetry and kurtosis coefficients, respectively.

Table 6. Descriptive statistics for the active repair times (X).

n	mean	variance	$\sqrt{b_1}$	b_2
40	4.0125	26.6801	2.6158	10.0226

Table 6 reveals a positively skewed distribution for the variable (X) denoting active repair times. Moreover, the asymmetry and kurtosis coefficients for X are quite far from what would be expected with the L distribution.

To model the active repair times, we use the L, GL and PLS models. To compare the quality of the fit of each of the models, we use the AIC (Akaike, [27])) criterion, namely AIC$= -2\hat{\ell}(\cdot) + 2p$, where p denotes the number of parameters in the model. We also consider the BIC (Schwarz, [28])) criterion, namely BIC$= -2\hat{\ell}(\cdot) + \ln(n)p$, and the modified AIC criterion, typically called the consistent AIC (CAIC, see Bozdogan, [29])), namely CAIC$=-2\hat{\ell}(\cdot) + (1 + \ln(n))p$, where again, p is the number of parameters for the model being considered. The best model is considered to be the one with the smallest AIC (or BIC, or CAIC).

Maximum likelihood estimators and estimated standard errors (in parenthesis) for the L, GL and PLS models were computed by maximizing likelihood using the function optim in R. The results are presented in Table 7, together with the values of the AIC, BIC and CAIC criteria for each of the models. To obtain initial values for θ and α, the LindleyR and fitdisrplus libraries of R-project were used, with which an estimate for the θ parameter of the L distribution could be obtained. With this value, we use Equation (9), the score of the α parameter of the PL equal to zero (score equation for α of the PLS), and from this equation we obtain an initial value for the α parameter. From the table, we determine that model PLS exhibits the best fit to the data set, according to the AIC, BIC or CAIC criteria. The graphs in Figure 3a–c reveal that the PLS model's fit is quite good.

Table 7. Parameter estimates and estimated standard errors for L, GL and PLS distributions.

Parameter	L	GL	PLS
θ	0.4241(0.0306)	0.3588(0.0588)	67.9071(5.4333)
α	–	0.7459(0.1676)	0.0036(0.0006)
AIC	199.582	199.821	195.161
BIC	201.271	203.199	198.545
CAIC	202.271	205.199	200.545

Figure 3a–c show, respectively, the empirical cdf for the active repair times (solid line), the qq-plot for the PLS model, and the qq-plot with envelopes for the PLS model. In (a), the dotted line corresponds to the cdf for the PLS model, calculated with the estimates of the parameters of the PLS model.

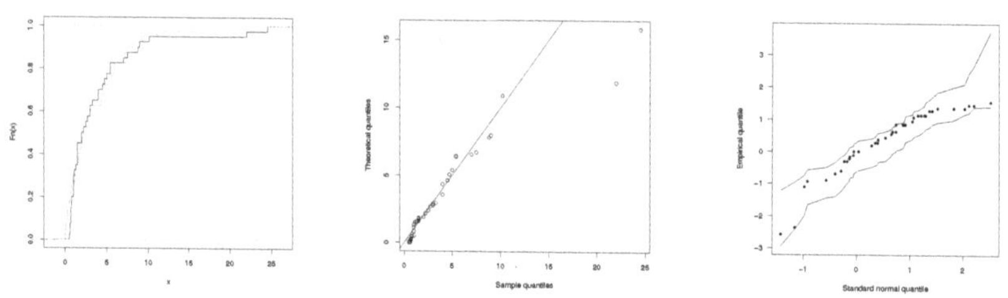

(a) (b) (c)

Figure 3. Graphs for the PLS model (**a**) cdf (**b**) qq-plot and (**c**) envelope.

Additionally, the Kolmogorov–Smirnov test statistic (KS) for the fit to the PLS model yields the value $KS = 0.150$, with a corresponding p-value $= 0.759$, giving support to the hypothesis that the active repair time variable has a PLS distribution.

Figure 4a,b shows the qq-plot for the L and GL distributions, calculated with the estimates of the parameters in each model; it can be observed that both models do not fit well with the data set studied.

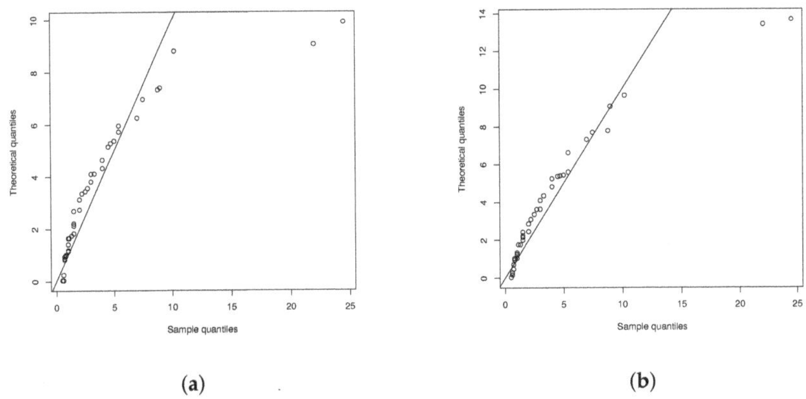

Figure 4. q-q plot for (**a**) L model and (**b**) GL Model.

Finally, we consider testing the hypothesis of no difference between the PLS and the L distributions for the data set under study, which corresponds to testing the hypotheses

$$H_0 : \alpha = 1 \text{ versus } H_1 : \alpha \neq 1,$$

using the statistic

$$\Lambda = \frac{\ell_L(\hat{\boldsymbol{\theta}})}{\ell_{PLS}(\hat{\boldsymbol{\theta}})}.$$

For the available data, we find

$$-2\log(\Lambda) = 6.416$$

which is greater than the 5% chi square critical value, $\chi^2_{1,95\%} = 3.8414$. Hence, the PLS model seems to be a useful alternative to be used for modeling active repair time data.

7.2. Application 2

In this example, a bivariate data set will be considered. The suitability of the BPLS model will be assessed by comparing its comportment with that of three competing bivariate models. The data set contains 51 data points corresponding to the 51 largest cities in the United States. For each city measurements are provided for the average precipitation per day in millimeters (X_1) and the average daily maximum temperature in Celcius degrees (X_2). The data are available from the US National Center for Climatalogical Data (NCDC) at https://www.ncdc.noaa.gov (accessed on 25 August 2022).

To analyse this data set, we consider three models: The Morgenstern type bivariate Lindley (BLM) distribution (see Vaidyanathan et al. [30]); the bivariate exponential of Gumbel (BEG) distribution (see Gumbel [31]); and the BPLS distribution. To compare the fits of the models, we use the AIC, BIC and CAIC criteria ML estimators and estimated standard errors (in parenthesis), as three of the bivariate models were computed using the function optim in R. For estimation of the parameters, we first fitted the marginal densities for each coordinate and combined these parametric estimates using the method explained in Section 4 to obtain the values used as initial values in the iterative process of estimation using the full bivariate data set.

For the BPLS model, estimates were obtained by maximizing the pseudo-likelihood.

Parameter estimates for model parameters are presented in Table 8, together with the AIC and BIC criteria. Contours for the BLM, BEG and the BPLS models are presented in Figure 5, which clearly indicates a better fit for the BPLS model.

Table 8. Parameter estimates and estimated standard errors for BLM, BEG and BPLS distributions.

Parameter	BLM	BEG	BPLS
θ_1	0.0266(0.0026)		0.0082(0.0003)
θ_2	0.1880(0.0196)		0.0752(0.0010)
α_1		0.0120(0.0017)	5.0075(1.5483)
α_2		0.0807(0.0150)	3.0053(1.2481)
α_{12}	0.9756(0.4637)	0.9936(0.4999)	4.8559(2.6724)
AIC	854.5633	887.3073	843.1525
BIC	860.3583	893.1028	852.8116
CAIC	863.3583	896.1028	857.8116

For the BPLS model, we may consider

$$H_0 : (\alpha_1, \alpha_2, \alpha_3) = (1,1,0) \quad \text{versus} \quad H_1 : (\alpha_1, \alpha_2, \alpha_3) \neq (1,1,0)$$

Note that, under H_0, we have a bivariate L distribution model with independent marginals for (X_1, X_2).

An appropriate test involves use of a Wald-type statistic whose distribution follows from the asymptotic normality of the pseudo-maximum likelihood estimator $\underline{\hat{\beta}}$. This statistic can be defined as

$$W_n = (C\underline{\hat{\beta}} - b)'(\hat{G}(\underline{\hat{\beta}}))^{-1}(C\underline{\hat{\beta}} - b),$$

where $\hat{G}(\underline{\hat{\beta}})$ is a submatrix of $\hat{\Sigma}(\underline{\tilde{\beta}})$ corresponding to the vector $(\alpha_1, \alpha_2, \alpha_3)$, $C = (\mathbf{0}_{3\times 2}\ \mathbf{I}_3)$ and $b = (1,1,0)$, which, under the null hypothesis, follows the chi square distribution with three degrees of freedom.

With the given data, we obtain $W_n = 110.9424$ with a $p_{value} << 0.05$, indicating that the BPLS model is significantly better at the 5% level.

To evaluate the goodness-of-fit of the BPLS model to the given data set, we use the multivariate Kolmogorov–Smirnov test of goodness-of-fit proposed by Justel et al. [32]). For the case of a bivariate distribution, the bivariate Kolmogorov–Smirnov (BKS) statistic is of the form

$$d_n = \sup_{(x_1,x_2)\in\mathbb{R}^2} |F_n(x_1, x_2) - F(x_1, x_2)|,$$

where F_n is the empirical distribution function of the sample and F is some specified distribution function. When F, is not known, the bivariate Kolmogorov–Smirnov statistic is defined by

$$dn(F) = \max\{D^1, D^2\},$$

where

$$D^1 = \sup_{(x_1,x_2)\in\mathbb{R}^2} |G_n(y_1, y_2) - y_1 \times y_2|$$

using the transformation $y_1 = F_{X_1}(x_1)$ and $y_2 = F_{X_1|X_2}(x_1|x_2)$ and

$$D^2 = \sup_{(x_1,x_2)\in\mathbb{R}^2} |G_n(y_2, y_1) - y_2 \times y_1|$$

using the transformation $y_2 = F_{X_2}(x_2)$ and $y_1 = F_{X_2|X_1}(x_2|x_1)$, where G_n is the empirical distribution function of the sample.

In our case involving the BPLS model, we find

$$d_n(BPHL) = \max\{0.1322, 0.1787\} = 0.1787,$$

which is less than the 5% critical value provided in Table 1 of Justel et al. [32] (the critical value is not provided for $n = 51$, but by referring to the given values for $n = 50$ and $n = 60$ we can justify our claim). We may conclude that the fit of the data to the BPLS model is acceptable.

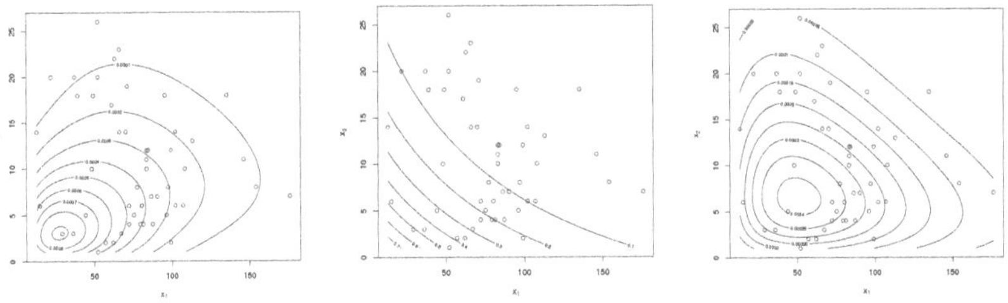

(a) (b) (c)

Figure 5. Contours for (**a**) BLM distribution, (**b**) BEG distribution and (**c**) BPLS distribution.

Author Contributions: Conceptualization, G.M.-F., B.C.A. and H.W.G.; software, G.M.-F.; methodology, G.M.-F., B.C.A. and H.W.G.; formal analysis, G.M.-F. and B.C.A.; investigation, G.M.-F., B.C.A. and H.W.G.; writing—original draft preparation, G.M.-F., B.C.A. and H.W.G.; writing—review and editing, G.M.-F., B.C.A. and H.W.G.; validation, G.M.-F., B.C.A. and H.W.G.; resources, H.W.G. All authors have read and agreed to the published version of the manuscript.

Funding: The research of G. Martínez-Flórez was supported by the project: "Aplicación de Metodologías Estadísticas a Datos de Vigilancia en Salud Pública en Colombia", FCB-03-23. Universidad de Córdoba, Colombia. The research of H.W. Gómez was supported by SEMILLERO UA-2024 and PUENTE UA projects, Chile.

Data Availability Statement: The original contributions presented in the study are included in the article, further inquiries can be directed to the corresponding author.

Acknowledgments: The authors are very grateful to the anonymous referees for their efforts in improving the manuscript. G. Martínez-Flórez-G acknowledge the support given by Universidad de Córdoba, Montería, Colombia

Conflicts of Interest: The authors declare no conflicts of interest.

References

1. Lindley, D.V. Fiducial Distributions and Bayes' Theorem. *J. R. Stat. Soc. Ser. B* **1958**, *20*, 102–107. [CrossRef]
2. Ghitany, M.E.; Atieh, B.; Nadarajah, S. Lindley distribution and its application. *Math. Comput. Simulat.* **2008**, *78*, 493–506. [CrossRef]
3. Ghitany, M.E.; Al-qallaf, F.; Al-Mutairi, D.K.; Hussain, H.A. A two parameter weighted Lindley distribution and its applications to survival data. *Math. Comput. Simulat.* **2011**, *81*, 1190–1201. [CrossRef]
4. Ramos, P.L.; Louzada, F. The generalized weighted Lindley distribution: Properties, estimation, and applications. *Cogent. Math.* **2016**, *3*, 1256022. [CrossRef]
5. Ristić, M.M.; Balakrishnan, N. The gamma exponentiated exponential distribution. *J. Stat. Comput. Simul.* **2012**, *82*, 1191–1206. [CrossRef]
6. MirMostafaee, S.M.T.K.; Mahdizadeh, M.; Nadarajah, S. The beta Lindley distribution. *J. Data Sci.* **2015**, *13*, 603–626. [CrossRef]
7. Bakouch, H.S.; Al-Zahrani, B.M.; Al-Shomrani, A.A.; Marchi, V.A.A.; Louzada, F. An extended Lindley distribution. *J. Korean Stat. Soc.* **2012**, *41*, 75–85. [CrossRef]
8. Nadarajah, S.; Bakouch, H.S.; Tahmasbi, R.A. Generalized Lindley distribution. *Sankhya B* **2011**, *73*, 331–359. [CrossRef]
9. Ghitany, M.E.; Al-Mutairi, D.K.; Balakrishnan, N.; Al-Enezi, L.J. Power Lindley distribution and associated inference. *Comput. Stat. Data Anal.* **2013**, *64*, 20–33. [CrossRef]
10. Ashour, S.K.; Eltehiwy, M.A. Exponentiated power Lindley distribution. *J. Adv. Res.* **2015**, *6*, 895–905.

[CrossRef]
11. Asgharzadeh, A.; Nadarajah, S.; Sharafi, F. Weibull Lindley distribution. *REVSTAT* **2018**, *16*, 87–113.
12. Khokhar, J.; Khalil, R.; Shahid, N. Zografos Balakrishnan Power Lindley Distriution. *J. Data Sci.* **2020**, *18*, 279–298.
13. Algarni, A. On a new generalized lindley distribution: Properties, estimation and applications. *PLoS ONE* **2021**, *16*, e0244328. [CrossRef] [PubMed]
14. Chhetri, S.; Mdziniso, N.; Ball, C. Cubic Rank Transmuted Lindley Distribution with Applications. *Rev. Colomb. Estadística-Appl. Stat.* **2022**, *45*, 65–83. [CrossRef]
15. Barlow, R.E.; Proschan, F. *Statistical Theory of Reliability and Life Testing. Probability Models*; To Begin With: Silver Springs, MD, USA; New York, NY, USA, 1981.
16. R Core Team. *R: A Language and Environment for Statistical Computing*; R Foundation for Statistical Computing: Vienna, Austria, 2021. Available online: https://www.R-project.org/ (accessed on 15 January 2024).
17. Jodrá, P. Computer generation of random variables with Lindley or Poisson–Lindley distribution via the Lambert W function. *Math. Comput. Simulat.* **2010**, *81*, 851–859. [CrossRef]
18. Arnold, B.C.; Castillo, E.; Sarabia, J.M. *Conditional Specification of Statistical Models*; Springer Series in Statistics; Springer: Berlin/Heidelberg, Germany, 1999.
19. Arnold, B.C.; Strauss, D.J. Bivariate distributions with conditionals in prescribed exponential families. *J. R. Stat. Soc. Ser. B.* **1991**, *53*, 365–375. [CrossRef]
20. Arnold, B.C.; Martínez-Flórez, G.; Gómez, H.W. Bivariate Proportional Hazard Models: Structure and Inference. *Symmetry* **2022**, *14*, 2073. [CrossRef]
21. Arnold, B.C.; Strauss, D.J. Bivariate distributions with exponential conditionals. *J. Am. Statist. Assoc.* **1988**, *83*, 522–527. [CrossRef]
22. Arnold, B.C.; Strauss, D.J. Pseudolikelihood estimation: Some examples. *Sankhya Ser. B* **1991**, *53*, 233–243.
23. Besag, J. Statistical Analysis of Non-Lattice Data. *J. R. Stat. Soc. Ser. D* **1975**, *24*, 179–195. [CrossRef]
24. Tibaldi, F.; Molenberghs, G.; Burzykowsky, T.; Geys, H. Pseudolikelohood estimation for a marginal multivariate survival model. *Stat. Med.* **2004** *23*, 947–963. [CrossRef]
25. Cheng, C.; Riu, J. On estimating linear relationships when both variables are subject to heteroscedastic measurement errors. *Technometrics* **2006**, *48*, 511–519. [CrossRef]
26. Jorgensen, B. *Statistical Properties of the Generalized Inverse Gaussian Distribution*; Springer: New York, NY, USA, 1982.
27. Akaike, H. A new look at the statistical model identification. *IEEE Trans. Autom. Control.* **1974**, *19*, 716–723. [CrossRef]
28. Schwarz, G. Estimating the dimension of a model. *Ann. Stat.* **1978**, *6*, 461–464. [CrossRef]
29. Bozdogan, H. Model selection and Akaike's information criterion (AIC): The general theory and its analytical extensions. *Psychometrika* **1987**, *52*, 345–370. [CrossRef]
30. Vaidyanathan, V.S.; Varghese, A.S. Morgenstern type bivariate Lindley distribution. *Stat. Optim. Inf. Comput.* **2016**, *4*, 132–146. [CrossRef]
31. Gumbel, E.J. Bivariate Exponential Distributions. *J. Am. Statist. Assoc.* **1960**, *55*, 698–707. [CrossRef]
32. Justel, A.; Peña, D.; Zamar, Z. A multivariate Kolmogorov-Smirnov test of goodness of fit. *Stat. Probab. Lett.* **1997**, *35*, 251–259. [CrossRef]

MDPI AG
Grosspeteranlage 5
4052 Basel
Switzerland
Tel.: +41 61 683 77 34

Mathematics Editorial Office
E-mail: mathematics@mdpi.com
www.mdpi.com/journal/mathematics

www.ingramcontent.com/pod-product-compliance
Lightning Source LLC
Chambersburg PA
CBHW040811250926
51850CB00007BA/1139
* 9 7 8 3 7 2 5 8 7 9 5 3 3 *